Beyond Legal Minds

Value Inquiry Book Series

VOLUME 326

Studies in Jurisprudence

The titles published in this series are listed at *brill.com/vibs* and *brill.com/sj*

Beyond Legal Minds

Sex, Social Violence, Systems, Methods, Possibilities

By

William Allen Brant

TUTA SUB AEGIDE PALLAS · 1683 ·

BRILL
RODOPI

LEIDEN | BOSTON

Cover illustration: created by tuncelsafa06. Retrieved from Pixabay. Illustration falls under the CC0 creative commons license.

The Library of Congress Cataloging-in-Publication Data is available online at http://catalog.loc.gov

Typeface for the Latin, Greek, and Cyrillic scripts: "Brill". See and download: brill.com/brill-typeface.

ISSN 0929-8436
ISBN 978-90-04-38531-3 (paperback)
ISBN 978-90-04-38595-5 (e-book)

Contents

Acknowledgements

I am grateful to the following people for their thoughtful contributions to *Beyond Legal Minds*. I am indebted to Bram Oudenampsen for his editorial support with Brill. I thank my former colleagues, Prof. Dimitar Elchinov, who edited this work, and my mentor, Judge Vincent Luizzi.

I am appreciative of the friendly receptiveness of the Philosophy and Philology Faculty at the Johannes Gutenberg University in Mainz, Germany since 2004. I am very appreciative of the teachings of Professors Thomas Metzinger in Mainz and Stephan Grotz, currently at the Catholic Private University of Linz, for their courses on neuroethics and the concept of possibility. I am appreciative of the suggestion to incorporate the concept of *lex imperfecta* by apl-Professor Gerhard Horsmann in Mainz. I thank Ulli Haus for his suggestions on readability. I thank Jan Kohlstrung for his insights on biology. I thank Dr. Marcus Nabielek for moral support and insights on twentieth century German philosophy. I am thankful for my conversations with Charlie Jacobs in Kunming, China on the issue of slavery. I thank Phil Post in Foshan, China for his insights on the concept of theft in the closing chapter. I am thankful for interpretations, translations, primary and secondary research of Yawen Cheng in the Sichuan province of China. I thank James Baraldi for his insights. I give a special thanks to Rex Kozak for his interview with me about the famous class sessions in 1968 he experienced under the innovative teachings of Jane Elliot, inspired by the assassination of Dr. Martin Luther King Jr.

I thank Prof. Rebecca Raphael for her encouragement and invitation to the naturalization ceremony of Rwandan hero, Paul Rusesabagina. I thank the former United States Ambassador to Burundi, Robert Krueger, who served during the genocide, for his insightful presentations at Texas State University and in New Braunfels. I appreciate former Justice David M. Medina for his insights on privileges in the legal institution and his role as a guest lecturer for a course I taught at Texas State University. I thank Professors Paul Hart, Cyrus Cassells and Dwight Watson at Texas State University. I am grateful for the support from the Department of Philosophy at Texas State University-San Marcos, especially from Professors Craig Hanks, Gilbert Fulmer and Dean Geuras. I thank Prof. Daniel Baker, Christopher "Twister" Marquis, and Jay Koltermann for their support in San Marcos. I thank Associate Provost Timothy Hulsey at the University of Tennessee.

I am grateful for the ideas in sociology and philosophy shared by Prof. Alexander Gungov and ideas in epistemology and theory of mind shared by Prof. Aneta Karageorgieva at Sofia University St. Kliment Ohridski in Bulgaria. I am thankful for the opportunity to exchange ideas on scientific methodology with Prof. Sergey Gerdzhikov during hikes in the Rila Mountains. I thank Sensei Carlos Duarte Romero and Pablo Muñoz at the University of Antioquia in Medellín, Colombia. I give thanks to Director Quetzalcóatl Oregal Leja of the High-Performance Unit in the Department of Physical Culture of the University of Guadalajara.

Special thanks are necessary for my brother-in-law, Sam Feagins, my sister, our parents, step-parents, and grandmothers in Texas who I visited periodically between my years of living in Germany, China, Colombia, Bulgaria and Mexico, the places I wrote this book. All these people have had deep impacts on the creation of this book. Thank you all.

William A. Brant
Guadalajara, México
October 2018

Figures

Introduction

Some human beings commit violent acts against others. Some of them are also not penalized for their wrongdoings. Some human groups also act violently, whether it is against a government, a business, a gender, racial or religious group etc. We might say that there is nothing more important than reducing violence for humans during the 21st century, and reducing violence also involves increasing fairness.

Violence seemingly ruins peoples' lives across the planet every moment and shatters others' expectations for future endeavors. For these reasons, I wrote *Beyond Legal Minds* to offer a better understanding of the societal causes of violence and the methods that enable us to study the systems most directly concerned with violence. I wrote this book as a set of innovative proposals, new scientifically testable hypotheses and new expansions of theories, especially social dominance theory.

Understanding violence within any society requires an understanding of the systems that both reduce and increase violence, dominance, and subordination. One such system is a legal system and its subsystem called the "penal system" or "criminal justice system." There are efforts to stop violence and to prevent and deter violence, which are efforts made by the law. However, the law also uses violence and threatens violence against others. Presumably, the law is sometimes terribly unfair and ruins peoples' lives every moment somewhere across the planet, and the law sometimes shatters others' expectations for completing their goals and even unfairly prevents groups from reaching their objectives. So, how can we best begin to study violence? How can we find ways to reduce violence and increase fairness? In what ways can we improve human cultures via increasing the proportions of peaceful activities? Can we attain these goals by focusing on the law and its many relations within society? *Beyond Legal Minds* provides an interdisciplinary set of answers to the latter questions and argues for approaches and solutions, concerning the rise in violence as a type of social phenomenon. It aims to transcend the bureaucratic divisions of any single field of study.

Undoubtedly, it is important that we understand the law to certain extents in the legal systems in which we live. One way of focusing on the law concerns the roles of violence and the factors and conditions that instigate violent acts. The law can be quite violent with its implementations of killings, shootings, solitary confinements, incarcerations of people under terrible conditions, arrests, searches, transfers of properties and financial penalties. The law also

 | DOI:10.1163/9789004385955_002

threatens violence toward people at multiple hierarchical levels with policing, judging, and lawmaking in the political realm.

However, another leading role that the law plays is reducing violence, especially when the legal procedures are perceived as being fair and just. Law enforcement agents deter, prevent and diminish criminality and violence. Lawmakers pass bills that positively affect the people or that have direct impacts on the reduction of violence. Judges and juries make legal decisions to imprison those with tendencies toward violence.

The dual roles that the law is responsible for are implementations, threats, and the controlling of violence as well as reductions of violence and violent threats. These dual roles that the law plays are conflictive and thereby often results in fierce conflicts between social groups and the institution of law. Naturally, ideologies arise that are counter-opposed to other legal ideologies about what the law is, what it should be, and with which side the support comes, either with the status quo or for alternatives. The law's control of violence and violent threats from the law often appear to be a way in which the law grants privileges to certain groups and imposes disadvantages upon other social groups.

The control of violence and violent threats by the law is certainly most recognizable with the noticeable privileges of paradigmatic groups, such as sons and daughters of sheriffs, lawmakers and judges, especially their sons between the ages of late adolescence and early and middle adulthood. When these latter sorts of groups with exercisable privileges, concerning the law, threaten and act out violently, they tend to be confronted quite differently than the poverty-stricken and other low-status group members. We may also understand nepotism as a naturally arising favoritism within the political, economic and legal systems, which is exercised beyond the recognitions of many legal minds; for this reason and the inclusion of the theoretic chapter on possibility theories, I have titled the book *Beyond Legal Minds*. Humans are unaware of the social reality about the overall amount, and the numerous, specific locations and times during which nepotism, favoritism, snitching, and deceptions are involved in any legal system.

Parental positions of power for privileged groups probably clandestinely tend to allow youths' evasiveness from legal consequences of criminality, which promotes criminality and nepotism. Parents with power in the legal and political realms certainly have wielded this influence and set of relations to allow their offspring to escape legal penalties. This happens in all legal systems, presumably. Indeed, evidence for the wrongdoings of sons of law enforcement agents, sons and daughters of lawmakers, and the progeny of judges has even been covered up, destroyed, and disregarded. This places the privileged groups in situations in which they are beyond the decision-making capabilities of some legal minds for several reasons, such as convictions and plea bargains in favor of the members of these groups.

Realistically, any research of such groups would be hard-pressed to find funding from any institution. Institutions answer to lawmakers who would be placing themselves and their families or colleagues at risk if they offered funding for the investigative production of such evidence of wrongdoings. Moreover, political figures would likely be pressured by law enforcement agents and judges (i.e., who would otherwise place their family members at the danger of the harsh penalties of the law) after any investigations and publications about the inherent privileges of their families or instances of unfair advantages are publicized, which would thereby disallow cover-ups, prevent the destruction of evidence, and prevent unfair plea-bargaining.

Most research in the field of jurisprudence begins by means of providing what a peculiar group of people think about the law. This peculiar group consists of philosophers, members of the legal institution, and other people from high-status socio-economic groups. Specifically, the peculiar group are those who have free time for leisurely thinking about aspects of the law involving positive and negative critiques (Bourdieu, 2000, p. 2). Largely, the peculiarity of the latter groups is that they have sufficient amounts of free time to research and produce works for legal studies, and they thereby compose a minute portion of populaces.

The peculiar group of thinkers about jurisprudence is generally unburdened by the daily stresses that most of humanity continuously faces because most humans strive to support their families with arduous work under conditions that developed countries would label as being below their own poverty lines. Consequently, jurisprudence tends to refrain from offering accounts of what certain others think about the law, such as low-status group members who treat it extremely disrespectfully.

For example, the latter groups sometimes refer to police as "pigs" and to lawmakers as "war pigs," "warmongers" and other derogatory names. See the example in Ch. 1.3 of the song lyrics that treat legal professionals relatively more disrespectfully by the music group, N.W.A. Disrespectfulness directed toward legal professionals is arguably more intense and arguably more frequently implemented by the groups of thinkers who are generally uninvolved in the academic debates involving jurisprudence.

Jurisprudence tends to abstain from describing how the privileged groups are in situations beyond the investigative scopes and penalties of the law. *Beyond Legal Minds* provides accounts about how others think about the law, especially those who are violently opposed to the law, terrified by it, and who are even in comedic disagreement with certain aspects of the law. Jurisprudential studies often lack the latter sorts of perspectives on the law when these alternative perspectives fail to treat the law respectfully, honorably, seriously, positively and peacefully.

One presumption of *Beyond Legal Minds* is that studying the logic of thought that provokes violent opposition to the law is worthwhile. So, hostile, disrespectful, cynical and violence-provoking legal ideologies are better suited as research focal points from which to understand the law. Brant argues that the rational lines of argumentation of jurisprudential accounts are very often ideological and less favorable for providing academically honest, especially brutally honest, investigative analyses of the law. These abovementioned legal ideologies are more closely associated with the problems of violent and destructive outbursts and thereby offer better ways to investigate the ever-important role of law as both an instigating and reducing factor of crime and as hierarchy enhancing and hierarchy attenuating systems within society.

The aim of this investigation of *Beyond Legal Minds* is to form a theoretical framework via interdisciplinary accounts of legal science, other sciences, and philosophy of law. Presumably, combining these various perspectives contributes to the development of potential means of reducing violence. These contributions are partially met via understanding peoples' interrelations and roles within the legal system and subsequent ideologies and mental states that arise before violent outbursts of individuals.

This book is an investigation that confronts a set of contrasts between considerations of the law as a necessary system concerning political economies and as a system containing a necessary subsystem, namely, the criminal justice system. The criminal justice system functions to implement controlled threats and violence. These threats and violence tend to subordinate lower status groups, thereby granting certain advantages to dominant groups of the populace.

Beyond Legal Minds began as a research project focusing upon the law and violence, the law's impact upon social groups' interrelations, and the emergence of ideology. The focus is on legal ideology in relation to how people think about the law with special attention paid to jurisprudence. As such, this book has demanded research in the fields of philosophy of law, psychology and sociology of law. It has since developed with a much more eclectic set of academic resources within the disciplines of library science, biology, neuroscience, policing science, anthropology, modal analysis, ontology, logic, population studies, history, and communication studies.

The first two chapters provide analyses of the various relations of law. They include the importance of understanding legal systems and the irrational ways in which people perceive, assume and conceive of actions as being merely legal and illegal. Such irrational conceiving contributes to legal ideologies and requires the conception of alegality. The addition of the concept of alegality is necessary for an understanding and the comprehensiveness of the concept of legal systems.

The social importance of legal systems is argued to permeate many aspects of daily life within societies. Their importance greatly contributes to and facilitates the pre-established social hierarchies. These hierarchies are continually enhanced or attenuated by legal systems. The preestablished social hierarchies, which legal systems significantly impact, are in the forms of socio-economic classes, races, sexes or combinations of them.

The percentage of members of some distinct group in prison and the population of that same group within the society at large is a signifying, factorable determination of the presence of the social hierarchy. Some groups are often disproportionately penalized more intensely and more frequently via legal authorities in that society's prison system. For example, such groups are overrepresented in the prison system, like the aborigines of Australia.

Legal systems retain the statuses of being necessary subsystems for societies with diversified economies. People who feel unsafe within their environments are unable to stably produce goods and services because they concern themselves with protecting themselves, friends, family, and at least their own belongings. Therefore, a societal subsystem must initially arise that stabilizes their expectations. One expectation that is stabilized involves wrongdoers being deterred from their future maladaptive and destructive behaviors.

Expectations of people within a society are stabilized. Thereby an increased probability of receiving compensations from others arises. The others are sometimes apprehended and judged fairly for societal and criminal justice. Such stabilized expectations are well-founded and practical for the functions of societal subsystems (e.g., transportation, education and economic subsystems).

The outright presumptions, beliefs in, and expectations about the current existence of societal stabilization disallow certain analyses. Certain analyses are prevented from proceeding beyond legal minds since a form of legal ideology is already implemented. These so-called mental states result from people's perceptions of the apparent stabilization of societal subsystems, word-of-mouth, and mass media systems about them. Via coming to an understanding of processes within societies, resulting in perceived stabilizations of peoples' beliefs, *Beyond Legal Minds* provides a critique of the underpinnings of legal-mindedness and legal ideology.

Practically speaking, penal systems of criminal justice stabilize expectations for members of society. They can destabilize expectations for subordinate groups. Penal systems enable many people to feel secure enough to create their own human environmental niches in some society. The systems are integral in the development of the primary, secondary, tertiary, quaternary sectors of economies, and divisions of labor that arise rapidly via private enterprises.

The stabilization of expectations initiates the possibility for social groups to work and specialize in businesses. Stabilizations of expectations require pre-established political, economic, defensive and legal systems. These systems allow for members of society to predict how their procedures shall affect them, inducing feelings of security within the populace when they are just. The systems thereby create opportunities for constructive societal advancements through procedural justice and societal justice (Tyler, 2006).

Understanding legal systems requires "sociological imaginations" (Mills, 1959). Charles Wright Mills (1916–62) was an influential American sociologist. He argued that sociological imaginations are ways of thinking that allow individuals to overlook and think beyond their own circumstances and minds. Instead, people tend to think sociologically unimaginatively via attributing uniqueness (in unrealistic ways) to their own circumstances.

One who thinks sociologically and imaginatively realizes that any given individual is one of many similarly situated people. However, struggles with individualistic circumstances (e.g., joblessness and marital divorce) very likely result in personal and destructive emotional states that cause the individual to focus inward. For example, focusing inward sometimes involves one thinking of one's own feelings of worthlessness and loneliness, lack of a sense of belongingness, and low self-esteem.

The lack of a sociological imagination coincides with thinking about oneself personally and emotionally. This can facilitate developments of inferiority complexes. Feelings of inferiority greatly hinder the individual's ability to think in socio-historical ways about the real situations of social groups (See Ch. 3.3). Lacking the sociological imagination obstructs one's thinking about all the similarly situated people. The lack thereby promotes social ideologies when the individual and such people have frequent interactions.

Sociological imaginations allow for the larger picture of social movements to be recognized. They characterize imaginations of the learned and facilitate rational predictions about changing conditions for classes of people in society.

The sociological imagination is crucial for the individual to at least temporarily suppress his or her own thoughts about him or herself. Simultaneously, it suppresses his or her thoughts of others with whom he or she has come into direct contact. The suppression of thoughts about oneself and about those whom one meets or observes are sometimes necessary conditions for the reduction of self-destructive thoughts. These tend to lower the self-confidence of the individual. The lowering of self-confidence and increase in self-destructiveness often result from perceptions of worsening conditions with which the person lives.

Suppressing the autobiographically and biographically directed thoughts allows one to consider the social and historical determinants and economic factors. These determinants and factors tend to affect the individual as a member of a social group or class in quite common ways at that time in the society. The sociological imagination thereby contributes to the constructive and realistic understanding of the individual's worsening conditions. The individual becomes enlightened of the fact that the circumstances do not result from his or her own incompetences. The person becomes aware of many others who undergo the same sort of situations during those relevant times of the society.

Understanding relations of law and legal systems requires sociological imaginations. Reaching our understandings requires systematically organized sources of information with external and internal consistency. The information needs to be publicized and to have on-going financial resources that allow for stable distributions of purchasable information. The information comes in the forms of images and words.

Mass media systems often hastily produce daily articles providing much of the information that is distributed to people. They offer the means by which any populace within a legal system attains knowledge of important events. Such events include business practices, social movements, weather, art, protests, religious acts, and violence in the forms of isolated and non-isolated attacks, wars and genocides.

Mass media outlets distribute annually, monthly, daily and sometimes hourly. They produce purchasable and organized information. The mass media outlets are crucial means through which substantial portions of our understandings of legal systems develop.

Mass media systems are used frequently by lawmakers, police, lawyers and potential politicians to deceptively portray events. Deceptions are wrought via overrepresenting and underrepresenting events and promoting their own services via advertisements. The latter social processes greatly contribute to the emergence of legal ideologies.

Legal ideologies subsist because of failures of people to critically analyze the systems from which they attain information. The ideologies thereby hinder the abilities of people to think critically in historically and sociologically motivated ways via the sociological imagination. The Rodopi Publishing House is one of many exemplary producers of purchasable and well-organized information that is mass produced but which, alternatively, involves scholarly critical thinking processes that expand much lengthier time periods before their publications. Rodopi products demand the sociological imagination for any given social research.

The sociological imagination is often challenging to exercise. Underrepresentations of events by means of mass media systems can lead multitudes of people to consider a type of event to be quite rare, despite that type's frequent recurrence. The frequency of police brutality tends to be ignored and underestimated when police brutality reports are withheld, when they are placed late enough within the records, or when they are publicized less frequently than they occur on average.

Understandings of legal systems are intermediated by mass media systems. Mass media systems facilitate ideologies via the over- and underrepresentation of information and disinformation. Not all the mass media workers are deliberately involved in distributing disinformation, though. Some are fooled by the ideology.

When the public underestimates the amount of recurrence of events that reflect poorly on the status quo (e.g., police brutality), reports accurately describing the frequency of these sorts of events are more likely to be mistaken. They are mistaken as exaggerations, overestimations, political attacks against lawmakers, law enforcement officials etc. The sporadic, journalistic reporting of police brutality and violence from other groups can lead to the public deniability of facts.

Also, facts about violence and police brutality are naturally suppressed via system justificatory behaviors, beliefs in a just world, and faith in the fairness or efficiency of our own societal subsystems. Legal systems function to suppress facts about brutality, threats, and violence to stabilize societal expectations. The public often tends to deny maleficent performances of their own lawmakers, judges, and law enforcement officials (i.e., people exhibit system justificatory behaviors). The public promotes ideologies. Ideologies are attained from the over- and underrepresentation of information from sources they trust.

Legal ideology often forms from superimposing a false dichotomy as a binary code on people's behaviors within society. The binary code is what one considers to be "a legal or an illegal act" without exception. The jurisprudential conception of alegality is absent regarding the latter legal ideology.

A legal system is required for the determination of the legality and illegality of any type of action, though. That is the decision-making of the legitimate authority in society. The initial developments of each legal system must involve acts that are neither legal nor illegal. No legal system can decide what is legal and illegal during its own initial stages of advancement. It must first become the legitimate authority.

Applying the false dichotomy to the presentation of information about products and behaviors (i.e., the legal/illegal dichotomy) facilitates reproductions of legal ideologies. It also exacerbates the societal problems with ideologies via intensifying them when the gradations of legality and illegality lack consideration. Multifarious gradations of legality and illegality offer lawmakers overwhelming numbers of options for creations of carefully constructed laws.

In Chapter 2, the logical analysis of the gradations of legality illustrates there are measurable degrees of legality concerning services and products. Gradations of the legality of a good or service allow the legal sales but illegal purchases of the same product. They dub the illegal sales but legal purchases of the same service, legal possessions but illegal sales of some product, legal possessions but illegal purchases of something, legal possessions but both illegal sales and illegal purchases of a product, and, of course, the legal purchases, legal sales, and legal possessions of the same product.

Some jurisdictions legally permit the possession of a product (e.g., alcohol) for some within specified areas but prohibit the sale and purchase at certain times. Gradations of legality are ever-changing for various products and services. These gradations permit social experimentation regarding changing the intensity of the legalization or illegalization of something. They permit the observations and some control of the reduction of some maladaptive types of behaviors of citizens, customers, sellers and consumers via the application of the concept of "concomitant variation" regarding those people and some product or service (Mill, 1843, pp. 470–479).

Behaviors of citizenry, foreigners and social groups can be classified to allow differing amounts of legality for each group. This enhances societal hierarchies and involves implementing restrictions on legal behaviors of some groups. Intensifying and perpetuating legal ideology occurs when lawmakers and potential politicians (and others) recognize the interests and preferences of certain groups toward the legality or illegality of some behavior or product.

Political candidates synchronize their agreements with potential voters and strategically modulate their disagreements to maximize voter support. For elections, political candidates focus on the specific restrictions or permissions of the utilizations, purchases, or sales of commodities and focus on the action, with which the group of potential constituents agrees when the political figure also agrees.

The third chapter is presented to demonstrate how great the ranges of levels of analyses and levels of observations are regarding the law, interconnected social factors, and legal systems. The vastness of the ranges of levels of both analyses and observations demands various methods of observations and measurements within and without laboratory settings.

Research is still disorganized for interdisciplinary analyses that strongly incorporate philosophic investigations of the material, which is a methodological problem for law. Various scholars are directly confronted with bureaucratic categorizations of academic disciplines. Disciplines are based on political financing for public universities. Departmentalization and bureaucratic standards hinder the study of objects or real phenomena crucial to the study of law insofar as arbitrary divisions are superimposed.

One methodological approach in the field of library science is the theory of integrative levels. It aims to facilitate research by integrating fields of study, creating multiple interdisciplinary ways of defining and classifying concepts. It can better explain diverse types of real phenomena. The theory does this via systems that classify in very similar organizational ways to taxonomic classifications in biology. The integrative levels theory is based within the ontology of Nicolai Hartmann and biological research in the subfield of phylogenetic systematics or cladistics.

Chapter 3 presents an example of an ontology of law by means of the Integrative Levels Classification System. This system classifies distinct forms of law and types of laws as subclasses in similar manners to ways that biological species are classified within specific genera, and genera are classified within families, orders, classes, phyla and kingdoms.

The third chapter also presents a set of methodological problems burdening legal researchers. Poorer scholars have disadvantages because of the readily accessible but illegal access to information and the digital divide. Poorer scholars lack finances to regularly purchase research for augmentation, improvement, and submission. Wealthier scholars have the financial means to purchase custom-designed research.

Some scholars submit custom-designed writings with false authorship for publication. The latter malpractice still results in major political figures' career-changing falls from the political realm. Plagiarism is being discovered in their theses and dissertations. Probably, others' works are being strategically copied via ghost authors in the files of politicians getting caught for plagiarism.

During biographic thinking, one thinks of another's dealings with the law. Socio-historic thinking occurs less frequently. It happens when one thinks about historical events, social movements, and social facts to understand the object of thought. The object of thought is part of the process of the individual's discovery of real phenomena.

The latter ways of thinking coincide with certain academic disciplines, their methods, their ranges of levels of analyses and ranges of levels of observations.

Psychology and neuroscience often involve the autobiographical and biographical ways of thinking. They have methodologies that often situate individuals under laboratory conditions. That is, metaphorically observing individual trees but not the whole forest.

Sociology coincides with the socio-historic way of thinking. In sociology, the individual is overlooked during the process of focusing on more than one individual. Observations happen outside of laboratory settings. The process metaphorically involves observing multiple trees or the entire forest but not just a focus on a single tree.

The psychological and sociological levels of analyses of law are briefly presented. The chemical and neurobiological, historical and comedic levels of analysis of the law are presented with specialized sets of problems for their own levels of analysis of the law.

The repeated insistence to continue the departmentalizations of the academic disciplines continue to be problematic for the treatment of each level of analysis. Researching the real phenomena via multiple levels of analyses and multiple levels of observations often fails.

Rigid depictions of the objects of study arise consequently. Certain ways of thinking are superimposed. There is a refraining from allowing other ways of thinking to permeate the analytic processes coinciding with bureaucratic divisions in universities.

Chapter 4 combines the efforts of social psychologists, philosophers, and sociologists. It is an analysis of the psychology of mass deception and ideology involved after societies have been violently attacked and before wars begin.

Leaders of attacked nations often mischaracterize the attackers as being "cowardly" before they enter war. The leaders also falsely describe certain aspects of violence against their people. Inadvertent mischaracterizations of "enemies" are given.

False descriptions of the attackers and the alleged attackers serve several roles. The mass media broadcasts of such false descriptions receive controversial responses. Some citizens express their disagreement with the leadership.

Controversy subsists between the leadership of the society under attack and those who espouse alternative explanations and descriptions of the violence. Alternative explanations of violence involve denouncing the leadership's given reasons for foreign attacks. Alternative explanations for violence and attacks lead people to become outraged at disagreements with leadership. Such situations frequently bring forth radical, emotionally driven decisions. Leaders thereby increasingly change their leadership styles toward more autocratic ones.

Domestic conflict ensues between those supporting the leadership, especially corporate media, and citizenry dissatisfied with the digression of political decisions toward violence by leadership. Meanwhile, citizens justify, support, and many even believe they are defending the systems in which they live. These are system justificatory behaviors.

Frequently, leadership deceives followers into attacking a group or another nation. The other nation is held blameworthy, although it is neither responsible for an initial attack nor preparations for an attack against their nation.

The so-called opponents of the leadership are denounced by individuals who appear to side with leaders through mass media outlets. This happens via mass media broadcasts. The alleged opponents of the leadership often provide veridical descriptions of mischaracterizations and disinformation presented by the leadership.

Bickering and insults against people's characters are broadcast. It is presented as if it is the relevant controversy regarding the violence. Resulting emotions and other mental states (e.g., beliefs, desires, and expectations) contribute to the formation of ideology.

With legal ideology, some lawmakers are granted stronger approval ratings and have increased perceptions of legitimacy. Politicians are thereby enabled to pass various violent and threatening laws. Political opponents often acquiesce out of fear of public denouncement during perceived states of emergencies.

The leadership labels people via ideological sets of binary codes. Masses are indoctrinated. The first stage of the creation of one type of ideology involves encoding many supposed opponents or attackers as "villains." People who greatly risked or relinquished their lives while acting on behalf of the defense of their own society are encoded as "heroes." Derogatory connotations are given to words that are used to describe villains.

For instance, villains were called "communists" during Red Scares in the US and "terrorists" in the 21st century. The process of labeling villains involves leadership that is more reckless. Recklessly labeling villains enables fear to spread more rapidly.

Societal uncertainties arise about whom the enemies are. One type of uncertainty involves the deceptive way in which languages are used to refer to villains as "them or they." That is the outgroup.

Heroes are referred to as "us or we." That is the in group. Heroes are called "patriots," and images of them are used for advancing violent causes. The heroes and heroines are selected very cautiously via politicians. Many more people are labeled "villains" than there would be without the emergence of such ideology. Hence, many more people are mistakenly identified as "villains." The process happens domestically with criminals as "villains," too.

The first stage of forming massive public, legal and political ideologies involves increased amounts of deportations, violations of privacy rights, and torture. Many other infringements of human rights happen. Infringements of rights of the unborn occur. Corporations get legal permissions to produce and dump excessive waste. The latter violations of human rights occur when laws change, are overlooked, or emergency laws come into effect.

Plenary laws become effective during situations of emergency. Emergencies or perceived ones rapidly change legal ideologies. They allow autocratic leadership styles to arise. Autocracies suppress political dissents and two-way communications.

A second dichotomy forms with the massive public ideology. Villains are encoded as "cowards." Heroes and heroines are encoded as "courageous." Unhesitant defenders of the leadership are also labeled as "brave," regardless of misguided political decisions. The latter individuals are rather reckless. Leadership argues that they have the highest degrees of "courage, valor, loyalty and honor." This is broadcasted by the mass media to the citizenry.

The vice of "recklessness" transforms via the intensification of the public ideology. The mistaken role of "reckless behaviors" becomes the "virtue of courage." The transformation is crucial to the ideology. Often, the reckless actions protect those who are perceived as defending the society or their ways of life.

During crises, acts of "patience and hesitation" and requests for them are considered "vices" via the emerging legal ideology. Destabilizing expectations of the populace increases societal impatience. Ever increasing societal impatience culminates in a war-ready society of reactionaries. Reactionaries agree with their leaders' resultantly violent political decisions. They react aggressively against outspoken and oppositional citizens.

People living in a society under attack are desperate. They feel motivated to decrease insecurities. People thinking ideologically and systematically form false beliefs in predictable ways. The latter errors in judgments account for part of the structure of ideology. The mixed emotional and ideological attitudes create an atmosphere and zeitgeist of grave insecurity.

Self-imposed legitimization is reinforced by mass media broadcasts. Controversy and disinformation are wrought from the ordinary channels of information providers. From people's increased perceptions of the legitimacy of their leaders and the increasing roles of controversy and disinformation, frustrations and impatience arise in society. Rising frustrations and impatience increase the frequencies and intensities of violence and war.

Through legal ideology, attacking and eradicating those labeled by leaders as "villains and cowards" becomes legitimized. The legitimization is then perceived as part of the process of restoring the status of security in society. Perceiving worldly events through the lens of the legal ideology brings leaders' self-imposed legitimizations.

States of insecurity and conditions of emergency thusly promote the onslaught of war via increasing public approval and attributing legitimacy to leadership. Leadership is then increasingly involved in the process of blaming and labeling so-called "villains." The processes distract populaces from the atrocities they fund and underrepresent in the frequency of mass media broadcasts in relation to frequencies of other events. Preventing the latter processes and creations of legal ideologies requires greater understandings of the processes.

As explained in Chapter 4, social groups utilize hard and soft power against other groups to undermine them and to change their ideologies. Hard power is the use of physical coercion or force. It sometimes involves real threats without the actual occurrence of violence or oppression. Soft power involves seductions, desecrations of revered objects, especially holy books in the 21st century. The ownership of the objects is less important. Soft power is used to replace values, beliefs and desires. It is used to replace other ways of thinking about other values, beliefs, and desires. Soft power is significant when implemented between societies with different religions and different treatments of the sexes, age groups and races.

Film production and Hollywood's use of soft power include ways in which ideologies can form, be replaced, or even be dispelled. The impact and influence of soft power often appear to evade the understandings of leaders. Leaders may express utter surprise at the reactions of a social group to the single loss of a sacred object of theirs. Leaders may expect stronger reactions from the use of hard power. Instead, people sometimes react much more violently toward the implementations and demonstrations of soft power and more peacefully in response to the use of hard power against them, and vice versa can also be the case.

Chapter 4 also presents a brief critique of a popular 21st century theoretic model called "social intuitionism" within the newly arising field of moral psychology. This field is misguided. The field undermines the importance of certain aspects of ethical decision-making, especially deontological theories. Deontologists often maintain that individuals only deserve praise for what they are not inclined to do already and for what they simultaneously perform against their own inclinations. For praise, they should instead perform acts out of a sense of moral duty.

Experimental conditions for situations that involve truly ethical acts and decision-making for duty ethicists are shown to be too complex to establish under laboratory settings. They also require too much preparation for field observations, which is evident from the current literature and methodologies.

Aspects of moral decision-making are argued to be crucial in the field of law. Some moral psychologists are shown to espouse legal and political ideologies within their works. In their publications, they support the moral sanctity of politicians who advocate certain legal and political decisions.

Within this book, I offer descriptions of paradigmatic groups utilized to provide such analyses of ideologies of the law and measurable social groups which are more likely to oppose the law in numerous ways. The paradigmatic groups include the sons of small town sheriffs, sons of lawmakers, and sons of judges who are either adolescents or young adults (i.e., the privileged groups). Additionally, this book offers more extensive analyses on some of the following groups, such as Jews who live in the Arab world, Islamic Arabs living within the Israeli legal system, African Americans, teenagers, foreigners in Europe and Asia, 21st century slaves, populations of prisoners and their racial and socioeconomic statuses in relation to their populations at large.

Such groups bring profound changes within society. So, it is less significant whether the latter groups are social groups with coordinated efforts or not, whether their distances, sizes, and intimacy are great or not, and whether they have formal organizations and endurance among their members, which are factors attributed to social groups (Oliver & Gerald, 1988).

The fifth chapter provides theoretic contributions of *Beyond Legal Minds*, applying possibility theory to several different legal issues and legal theory. Chapter 5 establishes a theoretic framework that facilitates methods of problem-solving for legal problems in various realms.

Chapter 5 presents an analysis of three comprehensive conceptions of possibility. Via the three conceptions, the category and mode of possibility is illustrated to be: (1) greater than reality with regard to the size of the content included with reality (i.e., inclusive disjunctive possibility); (2) equal to reality in respect to the size of their content (i.e., real possibility); or (3) less than reality in relation to the sizes of their contents (i.e., what I call "recollected possibility"). Legal maxims concerning necessity, possibility, and impossibility are applied in ways that are interpreted differently via each of the three conceptions of possibility. Examples of law and legal systems illustrate the application of the theoretical concepts to the formation of testable hypotheses for legal sciences.

The fifth chapter presents arguments that recollected possibility is a functional and viable conception for further investigations. The concept of recollected possibility treats the concept of possibility as a mere but important aspect of the cognitive process of realization. The events, locations, and time spans of things as well as processes are recognized as real and unreal during the realizations. Recollected possibility utilizes both inclusive disjunctive possibility and real possibility for classifications. Recollected possibility incorporates possibility theory for artificial intelligence, regarding information's meaning rather than transmission.

All three concepts are demonstrated to be important in relation to how anyone thinks about the law. Altogether, the three conceptions provide a comprehensive framework for philosophic and methodological investigations. Investigations will be in relation to decision-making and general problem-solving. Decision-making is analyzed in relation to courts of law, law enforcement agents, lawmakers and legal systems. It regards those who make choices within legal systems and criminal justice systems, in general.

Chapter 5 argues that all legal theory begins with the presumption that the theoretic negation of reality is completely irrelevant. Legal theory thereby begins with the assumption of the givenness of reality. Much of legal discourse concerns what is real, fake and unreal, what actually happened, and what had not or did not occur. Experience places the theoretic negation of reality in a realm apart from legal theory because reality is given in experience.

The theoretic and foundational strategies for defense attorneys are laid out with examples. These strategies are applicable to prosecutors and provide bases for criticisms of the legal process for verdicts. The strategies are based on interpretations of two modalities, to wit, necessity and coincidence.

Many of the legal judgments in courts of law concern the descriptions of events as "necessary ones." Considerations of necessitation lead juries and judges to refrain from placing moral blameworthiness and guilt upon the defendants. Similarly, various legal judgments often involve the descriptions of events as "coincidental ones." Considerations of coincidences also lead juries and judges to refrain from placing moral blameworthiness and guilt on the defendants. The resulting judgments are demonstrated to hinder ethical decision-making in courts of law.

The last chapter, The F-Problem, is a necessary portion of *Beyond Legal Minds.* The closing chapter concerns the most fundamental cause of the existence of humankind, to wit, sexual reproduction. Sexual reproduction coincides with intensifying competitions for resources and sex partners, which leads to escalations of aggression, famines, diseases, and poverty. The F-Problem is a balance problem between the birthrate and the death rate for any species that sexually reproduces.

The human F-Problem has changed its requirements for balance over the last 12,000 years. The global population has increased dramatically regarding human birthrates and decreased death rates, especially since the early 20th century. The F-Problem is also the problem of sexual intercourse-motivated and fertilization-related behaviors. These behaviors have impacts on sexual reproduction, nepotism, and population growth.

Crises and dangers result from these behaviors directly or indirectly. The dangers include the roles of sexual intercourse-motivated and fertilization-related behaviors with environmental problems resulting from fluctuating birth rates that exceed the fluctuating human death rates, exponential human population growth, inbreeding, and overpopulation.

The solution to the F-problem is the creation of a sustainable practice of balancing the birthrate and the death rate in the most humane ways for sexually reproducing species. The F-problem demands an analysis of competitiveness, domination, subordination, and the process of victimization. The latter phenomena are to be analyzed in relation to competition concerning sex partners and impacts on sexual selection in societies.

The ultimate chapter reconceptualizes the use of the term "human generation." The concept is reconceptualized for implementations of measurements. The measurements account for the 20th and 21st centuries' inclusions of people with increased life spans and fluctuating numbers of births from young adolescent mothers.

Ten to fourteen-year-old adolescent girls, during some decades in developed countries, give birth more frequently than forty-five to forty-nine-year-old women. These facts entail changing intergenerational relations from generation to generation, which shape the culture and education levels of youths born to adolescent parents. Their offspring are more prone to depression and delinquency. So, the F-problem is also conceived as intensifying or becoming less intense regarding the conditions and ages of the parents for some generations as opposed to others.

Overpopulation is argued to involve the vast increase in competitiveness for finite resources. Such increases in competitiveness increase frequencies and intensities of victimizations. Victimization is conceptualized as a process through which two or more individuals assume the roles of victim and victimizer. Victimization is presented as a basic form of theft or stealing. Victimizers take away the time, energy, money, property, or the abilities to make decisions of someone else (i.e., against the autonomies of victims).

As shown in the final chapter, processes of victimizations impact the human population growth rate. Victims face disadvantages. Victims are confronted with different types of opportunities regarding their sexual selections of mates than victimizers.

Victimization is an important set of dual processes of the criminal justice system. The law partially functions to impact the victimization process within society. The criminal justice system sometimes reverses the roles of the victim and the victimizer, who are both presented with the chances of assuming the opposite roles. So, victimizers become victims via criminal justice. Victims frequently become crucial to the process of victimizing their victimizers, whether the victims are now plaintiffs, jurors, judges, police, lawyers etc.

The last chapter shows two ways the legal system functions. The legal system is a set of processes that impacts the frequency and intensity of the victimizations within society. Such systems thereby create victims out of victimizers and victimizers out of victims. The legal system (i.e., via its subsystem of penalization for criminal justice) provides chances for victims to reverse the roles for domination and subordination.

The latter set of reversals (i.e., after the verdicts) increases the probability for victimizers to become subordinated via the legal procedures of the law enforcement system and the judiciary system of courts of law. Records are publicized. The latter actions all contribute to the stabilization of expectations of the society.

Victimizers assume the roles of victims to some extent when victimizers are accused, indicted, and/or given the verdict of "guilty" within a court of law. The freedoms of the individual are partially rescinded after the summoning of the defendant. So, the victimization process is often reversed or controlled via the legal system regarding the initial victimization. That is, the victimizer is first faced with the risk of being penalized and thus victimized. False accusations are made by victimizers.

The legal system also contributes to the frequencies and intensities of victimizations in society. Members of the legal institutions implement controlled threats and violence against lower status groups to greater extents (i.e., in proportion to their population sizes) than higher status groups. Members of the legal institution, who work under bureaucratic rule sets, tend to provide lower status groups with systematic disadvantages. Legal penalties and other disadvantages, which are imposed on individuals, impact the sexual selection process.

The law searches, confiscates, arrests, convicts, gives maximum penalties and even executes lower status group members more frequently and more intensely or brutally. In human societies, lower status groups are identified by race, sex and socio-economic class. The tendencies toward treating people differently impact dissimilar groups differently concerning their sexual selections.

The injustices in legal systems have many impacts on natural processes of sexual selection. So, the F-problem within societies is viewable foundationally as incorporating injustices in legal systems.

One major flaw concerning directions of legal systems and their legislation is their tendency to support ideological forms of eugenics. A set of misconceptions (i.e., about members of the same race being the best matches for sexual reproduction with each other) contributes to legal systems often promoting some degrees of inbreeding. However, legal systems also demote incest partly by implementing laws that forbid siblings, first cousins, and children to marry their own relatives and parents.

One systematic approach to solutions to the F-problem (i.e., regarding less ideological forms of eugenics) involves greater extents of intergroup and interracial sexual reproduction. This could yield healthier offspring. The offspring would likely be more biologically diverse. The offspring could also provide sexually and genetically related reasons for legal systems to refrain from victimizing lower status racial groups, hypothetically. There are still concerns that arise with diversity in the latter respect, too.

The final chapter illustrates that legal institutions have passed laws and enforced them in ways that have led societies to more frequently sterilize lower status group members. Such people include some people referred to derogatorily as "gypsies" or Romani people in Europe, blacks in America, aborigines in Australia, and non-whites in Germany and Brazil. The increased frequency of incarceration of lower status groups within societies also has noteworthy impacts on processes of sexual selection and sexual reproduction.

A function of incarceration is to separate the sexes and reduce the sexual reproduction of targeted, low-status groups in societies. Arguably, societies are implementing a form of artificial selection with the officiality of legal systems. The members of lower status groups, who are imprisoned, would engage more often in sexual intercourse than if they were not incarcerated. This is due to their ages and thereby greater potentials for sexual reproductive success, and able-bodied men compose a sizable proportion of prison and jail populations.

Legal systems contribute to the enhancements and continuations of human social hierarchies of societies via favoring dominant groups over subordinate ones. Favoring dominant groups impacts the society's sexual reproductions. The support involves an artificial selection of societal human generations.

Favoring dominant groups leads directly to preventions of sexual reproductions. There are preventions of sex performed by males of lower status groups and who have higher sexual potencies (e.g., 20 to 30-year-old black males in the USA) than other low-status group members (e.g., the elderly of a subordinate group).

The last chapter contributes to social dominance theory by suggesting that legal imprisonment necessarily involves the separation of the sexes to reduce the likelihoods of the society's sexual reproductions, especially reductions for subordinate group members. There are a few exceptions, such as sexual intercourse during conjugal visitations in prison.

Sometimes systematic disadvantages are given by criminal justice systems to lower status groups. These types of disadvantages show favoritism toward the sexual reproductions of higher status groups. They demonstrate a tendency to oppose the sexual reproductions of lower status groups in the society.

Two functions of legal systems include hindering the breeding of the society's subordinate social groups and providing the legal status of human intergroup breeding. The systematic ways that criminal justice systems mistreat lower status groups tend to be eugenically and ideologically opposed to intergroup breeding. Such facts are underrepresented within social dominance theory and system justification theory. We need greater emphases on the roles of societal systems and institutions providing favors that also favor the breeding of dominant human social groups. That is, criminal justice systems constantly impact "who is able and who is unable to be born from whom." The systems impact human generations.

The political and legal ideologies concerning eugenics involve methods for improvements of the reproduction of offspring in ill-founded and "idealistic ways." Methods have been politically and legally implemented in ways that homogenize human populations. Decreases in genetic diversity and inbreeding humans to greater degrees have been officially legislated. Legal systems, lawmakers, law enforcement agents and judges within courts of law have exacerbated the F-problem.

A serious and ongoing F-problem is that the earth's environments have upper limitations for the sizes of human populations with tendencies toward destructiveness. The finiteness of resources is an aspect of the "economic problem" coupled with human desires to mate, sexually reproduce, and to elect lawmakers who politically support their way of life.

Politicians tend to support legal permissiveness of most people to impregnate or to give birth. Lawmakers have historically granted or presumed that there is a legal right to impregnate and to give birth within societies. Legally-minded people tend to ideologically presume they should have rights to procreate. It is questionable whether the latter legal-mindedness can be surpassed (i.e., going beyond legal minds and legal ideologies).

The roles of natural human urges, desires, legal and political ideologies contribute to F-problems. This includes the overpopulation of humans and other species. Consider species that tend to reproduce in greater numbers coinciding with human populations. This gives rise to processes of degradation of environments, human poverty, famines, diseases, and violent conflicts. Violent conflicts, victimizations, dominance, subordination and sociological reasons for their continuation are the focal points of *Beyond Legal Minds*.

It remains disputable whether humans can develop abilities to effectively surpass their own legal and ideological ways of thinking. Can we effectively alter the current unplanned course for politically and legally-guided future human generations? It is questionable whether humans can think and act in significant ways that go beyond legal minds.

The first steps toward solutions require the clarifications of the associated F-problems for legal systems in a globalizing world. *Beyond Legal Minds* begins this journey toward a solution by focusing on the goal of "reducing violence." This book offers methods and points out misconceptions and dangerous ideologies. *Beyond Legal Minds* concludes that the most fundamental and known reasons for our existence, sex and reproduction, are necessary to investigate as reasons for what threatens our existence.

Sex and sexual reproduction are intricately intertwined with legal systems, mental states, and their sociological interrelations. So, proceeding beyond legal minds requires better understandings of sex, reproduction, and their secretive natures in human beings. With this comes some largely unknown processes, including intersexual and intrasexual selection.

Lastly, as research is a continuous process, there is no ultimately conclusive fact or set of arguments to be granted. The last chapter presents a conclusive section. It reiterates causes of social violence.

The ranges of potential avenues of research have been opened for wider access by *Beyond Legal Minds*. Hypotheses generated in the following chapters will serve us in knowledge-acquisition when social scientists confirm and disconfirm theories guiding their own works. The author's approach in this book is derived from the goal of focusing on and improving methodologies for attaining knowledge, especially regarding solutions to lessen violence.

CHAPTER 1

Relations of Law

There are many different relations of law. Law has relations to political systems and economic systems of societies. Law is involved in most people's daily lives when they drive to work or legally buy produce from the markets. Law also has relations with various societal hierarchies. For instance, the law has different relations with privileged groups and dominant societal groups than law does with subordinate or low-status groups.

The different relations that law has with different groups are important to understand. Understanding the latter relations allow us to better understand the role of law regarding causing violence. For these reasons, it behooves us to focus on analyses of the law that come from various fields of study.

Many different fields involve the study of violence. These fields often combine with legal studies. It befits us to include these relations of other fields with the study of law and violence, especially for the goal of reducing violence, since the law serves both to increase and reduce the frequency and intensity of violence and of threats of violence in each society at times.

The 21st century has witnessed an amazing surplus of various specialties presenting fundamentally distinct levels of observation and analysis of the law. Various specialties range from the cognitive neuropsychology of law, computer science, public administration, biology, and anthropology of law to the sociology and history of jurisprudence and law. Some may await new specializations, combining the latter disciplines into increasingly specified themes with capabilities of forming multiple subfields of study and arising as new fields, e.g., the history of the computer science of biological determinants of legislation and criminal behaviors.

Whether the departmentalizations or bureaucratic divisions of the latter academic disciplines and practices can continue to undergo such ways of dividing social groups of academics who produce valuable information in societies is, at least, dubious. These departmentalizations appear to conflict with the overall purpose of knowledge management and the study of real phenomena because the divisions of departments disallow the knowledge about real phenomena to be easily accessible to all departments. These issues will be addressed in detail in the coming chapters.

Law is a peculiar field of study that incorporates both theory and practice in ways that other disciplines usually do not. Traditionally, experts in the field of medicine presume that they already know what medicine is while the study

 | DOI:10.1163/9789004385955_003

of law continuously questions what the essence of law is. Medical students, for example, might be less inclined to inquire to such a degree what "medicine" is, yet law students often inquire what "law" is because the discipline of law also involves much philosophic inquiry. Moreover, when we consider the disagreements between lawyers and judges about what individual laws are, we must also consider frequent disagreements about the law in practice (Dworkin, 1986, pp. 3–6).

Presumably, no academic discipline is more essential than the other for the task of explaining what law is, though. Thinking is requisite for the law to exist as well as for an understanding of what the law is to arise (i.e., what cognitive psychology investigates). Behaviors, hormones, and brain activity are necessary elements, too, which are what biology, endocrinology, and neuroscience investigate. The performances of multicultural groups and their comparisons with one another at different times or eras (i.e., that which sociology, cultural anthropology, and history study), and the rational investigation of logical arguments about the science and philosophy of law each add pertinent levels of analysis and observation, providing fundamental insights about what "law" is in accordance with all individual worldviews concerning the law.

Each field of study is worthwhile and necessary for any comprehensive and consistent theory of the law and criminal justice to form, yet many of the divisions of departments are arbitrary. They are political divisions that prevent knowledgeable social psychologists and anthropologists from teaching in sociology departments or vice versa. Some fields of study are combined in diverse ways into single departments, such as the fields of linguistics and philosophy at the Massachusetts Institute of Technology, the fields of sociology and social anthropology at the Central European University, and the study of law is combined with various disciplines.

Different studies provide differing vantage points and ways of thinking that focus upon specialized aspects of the law. Brief accounts of multiple fields of study of the law are incorporated in this book to reconcile many seemingly contradictory ideologies of the law. Ideologies, opinions, and views of the law that involve mental states, which are associated most closely with violence, revolution, terrorism, and war, are given greater credence within the following investigation provided here. The latter types of relevant mental states include contempt, anger, hatred, disgust, sadness, schadenfreude, and fear. However, analyses of the reduced amounts of the mental state of happiness and the mental state of surprise are relevant, too, although they may play more limited roles regarding investigations that aim to understand and ultimately reduce violence.

Respect and honor are often given to those who hold positions directly affiliated with the law, while any vices attributed to the law are still typically presented in the most respectful manners by scholars (Kerruish, 1991). However, many ideologies, mental states, and vocal expressions about the law are counter-opposed, peacefully or violently, to the law. In the latter sense, the law is observed and analyzed by some scholars as a terroristic system that implements threats in organized manners, provocations, and violence, which are imposed systematically more often against certain groups with lower social standings, according to social dominance theorists, such as Sidanius and Pratto (1993, 1999 & 1999b). Many groups, therefore, offer ideological support for disagreements and resistance movements against the law in stark contrast to types of obedience and conformity that are espoused by many others.

Investigating or even merely forming hypotheses about the latter groups (i.e., via combining various fields of study for insights about multiple ideological views of the law) involves the need for a critical analysis of social uprisings and the effects of law and subsequently arising ideologies as the "causes of social conflict." As a cause of social conflict, ideologies may be contributing factors to violence, potential or partial causes, or causes that allow law to be analyzed as an effect and counter-effect of potential civil unrest.

The deterrence of crime involves preparations and plans implemented via the legal system, which is, in part, derived from deterrence theory. Deterrence theory was popularized by Cesare Beccaria and Jeremy Bentham who worked to combine rational choice theory with strategies of deterrence, which became a prolific way of viewing the deterrence of crimes during the latter half of the 18th century until other psychological and biological theories overshadowed the incorporation of rational choice-based theories with deterrence theory (Paternoster, 2010).

From a sociological standpoint, the deterrence of crime (e.g., deterrence of burglary, organized crime, traffic violations etc.) can be quantitatively and qualitatively differentiated from social uprisings, civil rights movements, protests that escalate with violence, and revolutions. Deterrence theory does not appear to encapsulate the breadth of violence that often results from conflicts between those with vehemently opposing ideologies, distinct positions of power in society, and changing relations of power. Walter Benjamin (2007, p. 281) even argues that lawmaking is immediately a "manifestation of violence" insofar as legislating is power-making. Such considerations profoundly complicate the goal of reducing violence via the legal system and are also worthwhile.

Lawmaking can result in changes of power relations in several ways. Some of these ways are subtle. In some legal systems, violations for exceeding the maximum speed limit result in two types of penalties (i.e., a fine that requires the accused individuals to pay a certain amount that each person is penalized for that crime in addition to a negative mark against the person's driving record). In other legal systems, an individual is legally required to pay a graduated fee and penalty in accordance with a sliding scale in relation to his or her financial income so that those who have higher incomes are more harshly, and arguably more fairly, penalized with financial penalties in comparison to the former penalizations within the former legal systems, and, additionally, individuals receive negative scores on their driving records.

The differences between the two types of systems based on wealth (i.e., in the form of legal considerations of income) may lead one to inquire about fairness and justice within both types of penal systems of criminal justice. The former types of systems appear unfair to the extent that indigent people are penalized more harshly than affluent people, giving the lower classes greater disadvantages via financial penalties that reduce greater percentages of their incomes. The latter types of systems focus on income to implement penalties at higher monetary rates, even though those with higher incomes may also have financial burdens and debts. Moreover, affluence in many cases is not best characterized as income, but rather affluence is better characterized regarding one's assets when they are far greater than all of one's debts as well as greater than the assets of most others.

The latter example of comparisons involves the functions of legal systems within some current state of affairs. Yet if we propose changes to any of these systems so that one system's treatment of such penalties becomes like the other type of system, then we might very well be confronted with protests that escalate into violence, social uprisings and changes within the social order and power relations. The prominent German sociologist Heinrich Popitz (1992, p. 63) ascertains that violence can only be contained if and only if social order is maintained since such containment and maintenance are necessary conditions for one another.

Changes in either penal system regarding traffic fines would certainly change the social order. Whether violence could be contained would likely involve the maintenance of the social order, the application of the concept of fairness, and possibly explaining the emergence of graduated penalty fees and explaining that, arguably, the poverty-stricken have been treated unfairly for their crimes or unfairly for their meagre wages or salaries. For instance, the penalty of twenty-five percent of a person's monthly income who works 40 hours per week for minimum wage is presumably unfairer in comparison to another who commits the same offense and who receives a penalty of only one percent of his or her monthly income when he or she also works 40 hours per week. A fairer system of penalization thusly appears possible.

On the other hand, "old wealth" (i.e., especially those with many assets but relatively low incomes amongst the affluent) have continued to receive privileges that the rest of society lacks in relation to law, such as the Rothschild family. More details on the Rothschilds from 1798 to 1999 can be discovered in Niall Ferguson's two volume series, *The House of the Rothschilds*.

Alternatively, the change in the traffic fine policies from graduated penalty fees to flat fees, which would be the same for each citizen, could involve ways of maintaining the social order. Consider arguing for fairness, despite the contradictory nature of such a conclusion with the conclusions of arguments for the opposite type of change. The existing state of affairs appears to be justifiable via arguments arising from the legal ideology in place, regardless of the imposition.

The espousal of legal ideology lacks a sound argument from which it can maintain rational and fair reasons for maintaining the status quo via the way in which the legal system penalizes people. A multitude of reasons may be presented instead of any single sufficient reason. For instance, the death penalty has been argued for by many who espouse a legal ideology in the state of Texas in the United States. Short arguments have been presented on flyers within some courthouses, such as the Boerne Court House, which presented multiple arguments in support of capital punishment (i.e., arguing for the recompense of punishment for the wrongdoing, deterring crime etc.) rather than presenting any argument in profound depth that would thusly serve to provide a sufficient reason.

The focus of the legal ideology is upon the so-called culprit rather than the system and process of the execution itself, which requires executioners, selection committees for executioners, and legal rights to kill convicts. Further issues are the impacts of acts of killing and decision-making on all the involved and their family members, and how these employees of the legal system are people who maintain clandestine identities as "unknown executioners," in the 21st century.

The arguers who support the death penalty typically fail to consider the executions of the past that resulted in the killings of people who were innocent of the crimes for which they were accused. Executing the rightly convicted murderers also disallows any continuation of observations of the murderers' legal ideologies and psychological states. The executions also reduce the likelihood that we can further understand the origins of violence by means of analyzing the culprits' motivations and living conditions from what the culprits choose to share with investigators.

We may very well distinguish arguments in favor of the death penalty, in general, from arguments in favor of the death penalty within large political economies and civil societies. Practicality needs to be considered in relation to the death penalty, too. For instance, if there is a man who kills two people on an island with a total of fifty inhabitants, and the other islanders' have reasons to believe that the killer will kill again (e.g., he may say that he is going to murder someone else), killing the killer is extremely likely to be a morally sufficient and sustainable practice to at least temporarily reduce the island's human violence and create better conditions for social harmony. Failing to implement the death penalty in the latter situation may lead to social unrest, increased amounts and intensities of violence and threats of violence. Building a cage for the culprit, guarding, and nourishing him are probably not pragmatic options.

Contrarily, the implementation of the death penalty within a civil society, such as England during the middle of the 20th century or the United States during the 21st century, may very well lead to social unrest and societal disharmony. On the other hand, it may not, despite whether innocent people are executed, and despite whether executioners tend to commit suicide more frequently or not or whether their family members do. These aspects of the law and their relations within society to violence and social unrest are closely intertwined with different legal ideologies that tend to differ from region to region. Some regions have inhabitants who are better able to think critically and who espouse ideologies that less frequently result in implementations of violence and threats of violence.

Understanding the differences between regions and attaining knowledge as to why certain regions are less likely to utilize critical thinking skills concerning legal and social issues is crucial for forming general conceptions of legal ideologies to aid in ways of changing ideology to reduce societal violence. People tend to discount or underestimate future events regarding consequences and the reactions of members of criminal justice systems, which play significant roles within the formations of dangerous ideologies that breed violence (Cook, 1980). For example, ten-year prison sentences are rated far less than twice as severe as five-year prison sentences on average, according to those who have experienced the penalties of the penal system (McClelland & Alpert, 1985, p. 311; Pasternoster, 2010, p. 822).

Obviously, the various forms of punishment each have the effect of deterring crime to some extent, especially when law enforcement agents are present and when we compare the forms of punishment to the utter lack of penalization. However, the impulsive criminal and spontaneous acts of violence and other crimes involve wrongdoers overlooking the increase of the harshness of legal penalties based on the types of crimes. Moreover, people who write books about the law are generally not impulsive people who spontaneously lash out violently.

Additionally, the law functions as a system which people tend to support, justify, and defend, especially during states of emergency, which promote the status quo, protect, and advance interconnected systems within which the society's populace live. The latter interconnected systems include the political, economic, and legal systems, even if such systems work against the best interests of some of the supporters' own social groups with which they identify themselves. People often justify and thereby encourage and support the law to maintain and thereby promote the continual formation of beliefs, which may very well function effectively to stabilize our own expectations and reinforce others' expectations about the enforcement of law (Luhmann, 1987; Di Viggiano, 2011, pp. 110–112). The latter actions in favor of the law are system justificatory behaviors and are insightful regarding explaining how and why certain slaves supported the institution of slavery even against their own interests and how and why 21st century institutions are supported against the interests of their supporters (e.g., private prisons).

One important supportive belief related to law is the belief that we live in a just world in which people tend to get what they deserve. When certain social groups strongly believe that we live within an unjust world, many of those individuals tend to behave in disorderly, and in apparently irrational, aggressive, and violent ways. For instance, Dalbert et al. (2001) demonstrated that prisoners endorse stronger beliefs that the world is unjust and that the belief in a just world correlates with preferences for a major political party, religiousness, and wellbeing in respect to life satisfaction, emotions, and mood levels.

"The law" is elaborately, but only partially, defined as an intricate system and institution because the law institutionalizes and is institutionalized by other systems and so are its own members who also institutionalize the coming generations who work directly with the law. The law makes demands for various systems within society to obey and enforces penalties against many for exhibiting disobedience.

The law systematically incorporates new generations, innovative ideas, and changing ways of doing things within a legal institution, consisting of judges, lawmakers, lawyers, clerks, police etc., which are necessary for statehood and nationhood to subsist. The latter incorporations, the legal institution, and nationhood are important aspects concerning the stability of a public's expectations. Most importantly the law is systematic as a stabilizing force for the production and reproduction of expectations, which is a massive set of mental states of the populace of the society, and they range greatly from expectations about violence and destruction being reduced by the law to expectations about violence and destruction being increased by the law, depending on who and from what group the expectations in the society come. The analysis of the law as a stabilizing force for public expectations entails that judges, police, and lawmakers' decisions tend to be perceived as "consistent and non-arbitrary" to certain extents, even though individual judges, law enforcers, and politicians sometimes make unfair and unjust decisions and mistakes or may even do that systematically against lower status groups.

Presumably, even people who are strongly motivated to commit crimes more often, arguably, tend to refrain from crime when they expect that a law enforcement agent is nearby the places where such crimes would be committed by them. Rarely does one ever commit a crime with the motivation to face the penalization procedures of the criminal justice system. So, penalties for criminals are typically perceived as forms of punishment by the criminals. There may very well be ways of approaching the comparative study of legal systems to demonstrate a difference between those legal systems and others within which citizens and non-citizens are strongly discouraged from undergoing the penal procedures of the criminal justice system.

Refraining from committing certain types of crimes, if one is compelled to commit them, further stabilizes expectations about the order within the society to which the legal system contributes. The latter order and stability are repeatedly reproduced within the other societal subsystems by the legal system. Moreover, the view of law as a stabilizing force of expectations relates to observations and analyses that demonstrate that if one perceives the procedures of law as being fair, one is far more likely to obey the law (Luhmann, 1987; Tyler, 2006a).

Our ways of understanding the law as a societal system and institution involve emotions and mental states, such as beliefs, expectations, and desires, which color and shape our understandings to the highest degrees. So, descriptions of the law as a system and institution are perhaps best expressed via illustrations of the feelings of individuals within situations that arise out of human environments interconnected with the law. With the emotions that arise along with the functions and nature of the law, the opinions, communications, ideologies, and teachings come as well–a process which sometimes involves social groups and significant movements for social change.

There are psychological reasons to believe that the law does not act in favor of any particular group, that we are all equal according to the measures of the law, that law is fair, and that law serves to protect and promote peace. The latter psychological reasons contribute to purely positive outlooks and philosophies of law, which will be greatly undermined within the content of this book. Yet still, the law is treated as a necessity for humanity.

1 Understanding the Social Importance of Legal Systems

Multiple ways of thinking allow us to understand legal systems. One may consider the legal system, within which one lives, to contain an environmental niche through which one may find opportunities of employment via policing, policy making, protecting the legal rights of clients etc. Another may express resentment for unfair treatment against one or one's own family for false accusations or indictments that are wrought by members of the legal institution. However, the latter way of understanding legal systems is psychological or individualistic rather than sociological or statistical; it provides mere anecdotal evidence rather than statistically significant conclusions and substantial evidence, which may greatly hinder one in such situations from drawing probabilistic inferences about the law or functions of the legal system.

The latter types of understandings and attitudes may alter the ways that individuals evaluate and understand the societal importance of their legal systems as well as how they impact the individual as just one of many representatives of various social groups based upon age, gender, race, and socio-economic class, and the understanding of the individual likely undergoes changes over time with maturation (Mills, 1959; Kerruish, 1991).

2 Legal Systems as Crucial Parts of Real Statehood and Theoretic Minimal States

Many countries, such as small island nations, have relatively small legal systems. Other nations have enormous legal systems. There is no clearly established minimum or maximum size of a legal system based upon population. We do not know how many people are required to form a legal system or how much communication is involved. Small island developing states, which include approximately fifty-one nations and fifty-nine million people altogether, provide good examples of societies that show the bare necessities for statehood (Bodley, 2011, p. 529). Each small island developing state, apart from Cuba, has a population of under ten million people, according to the CIA *World Factbook* (2016) and Bodley (2011).

Small island nations are often unable to afford many types of diagnostic tools within their hospitals or for the maintenance of a military. Such nations may lack central banking and borrow currencies from other nations (Bodley, ibid). Importations, storage, distributions, telecommunications, and the production and allocation of electricity may be handled by means of the governments of the smaller nations instead of the private sector. Departmental tasks or ministries of the government (e.g., the department of education, the department of transportation etc.) may combine several functions within single departments.

Yet even with the various functions of the governments of small island nations, which are typically performed by corporate entities in larger nations, small island nations are still likely to have at least small police forces and "limited legal systems" (ibid., p. 529). The existence of the limited legal systems and police forces of small island nations provide us with an example of what human societies probably need for the formation of minimal statehood with the essentials for a functioning government. Robert Nozick (1974, pp. 24–25) asserts that:

> [U]nder the usual conception of a state, each person living within (or even sometimes traveling outside) its geographical boundaries gets (or at least, is entitled to get) its protection. Unless some private party donated sufficient funds to cover the costs of such protection (to pay for detectives, police to bring criminals into custody, courts, and prisons), or unless the state found some service it could charge that would cover these costs, one would expect that a state which offered protection so broadly would be redistributive.

A redistributive state, as conceived by Nozick, is one with which some people pay more for others to attain the services of protection by the state. The businesses within the private sector are not well-equipped and would unlikely be motivated by profit to charge some people for providing protection services to them as well as to others. So, the public sector remains the likeliest set of organizations to provide the service of protection to the people who do not or cannot even financially contribute. Nozick and like-minded theorists, however, face the problem of explaining why other public-sector business activities (e.g., water, electricity, mass transportation, health, and education), with which we are familiar, are not necessary for the state to provide as public goods and public services. However, we may conclude that there is often a type of consensus that legal systems (or at least important aspects of them, such as policing) are both essential for real statehood as well as theoretic minimal states.

The examples of small island developing states provide confirming evidence for the fact that legal and criminal justice systems are bare necessities for statehood or necessary conditions for a theoretically minimal state, which involves implementing tax laws for the state's policing, lawmaking, and judicial processes. Comparative analyses between states with limited legal systems and those that offer greater capabilities for protective services are suitable along with examples of nations that contain legal systems but have corporations that offer extensive amounts of certain types of protective services with the state (e.g., the SST security corporation in Bulgaria in the 21st century). Nozick argues that each individual has the legal and moral right to defend oneself, and in a complex society it would be extremely difficult to maintain a job along with other responsibilities while protecting oneself. So, we may conceive or expect that within societies, which lack statehood and legal systems, an individual might hire a person or a group for protection. Moreover, others would do the same and may even purchase greater amounts of protection (ibid., p. 24).

People may hire the same group to protect their freedoms. The job of the protector is not only protection. Protectors defend people, punish those who violated the rights of the protected, and take compensations from violators. They reduce violence directly and indirectly by allowing those who have been harmed to await the procedures of the protection agency to attain compensation. Furthermore, those individuals who are hired for defensive purposes provide judging services, especially amongst their own clients. However, clients may attempt to take advantage of other clients or may attempt to take advantage of their own protection agency itself insofar as the agency's clients falsely report being wronged by nonclients when the clients believe that the nonclients possess assets. Thus, protection agencies in the same geographic regions are tested and evaluated based on their practical applications of fairness within their judgments of people, property, and injuries and, of course, their decisions to acquire assets, provide services, or to punish those who they rightly or mistakenly deem to be "wrongdoers."

Protection agencies must compete with one another in respect to profit, control of the market, and various virtues, such as fairness and punctuality. Competition is heightened when clients from opposing agencies enter conflicts over property, damages etc. Nozick (ibid., pp. 15–16) maintains that there are three basic possibilities worthy of consideration in respect to the competitiveness and conflicts between two or more protection agencies. Firstly, the protection agencies may enter battles, and one wins, protects its clients' interests, and likely increases its clientele. Secondly, each protection agency may win their conflicts but only near the apexes of their protective forces, and borders thereby would likely arise, regarding which clients would likely either move closer to the center of their protective agency's forces or join another agency instead. Violence is hereby reduced in several respects via the movement toward the protective services of the clients, and many nonclients can benefit from the role of the protective agency's power to deter theft, fraud, and violations of rights, especially when nonclients are not strictly identified as "nonclients" by potential violators.

Thirdly, protective agencies may realize that the continual conflicts between themselves (i.e., on behalf of supporting their clients) require "preventive measures" to maximize profits, which may result in peaceful resolutions via seeking neutrality and impartiality within the judgments of a third party that judges and determines the consequences for the clients, in which case there is an emergence of "a system of appeals courts and agreed upon rules about jurisdiction and the conflict of laws" (ibid., p. 16). If the latter set of possibilities becomes actualized, the society develops the unification of a judicial system, which affects the future decisions of the protection agencies.

The latter development from the state of anarchy begins to transform into something that resembles a minimal state or several of them with different geographical legal-like jurisdictions. Violence is thereby diminished regarding clients violating clients of alternative protection agencies because the agencies relinquish the power, responsibility, and burdens to determine such judicial verdicts. However, it is disputable exactly when and how such judicial systems would handle nonclients who are independent from any protection agency. Conflicts would certainly arise for these people, whether they are migrants, tourists, drifters, or too poor to purchase protective services.

As time elapses, the group of protectors begin acquiring ever more customers. Individuals have contracts with some protection group, and they can terminate the contracts at any time. Presumably, the services would simply cease to exist for those who violated or terminated the contract. When the group of protectors becomes so large that the vast majority of the population is defended by one agency, the agency becomes a "dominant protection agency" (Nozick, 1974). A series of conflicts of interests is likely to happen in this situation and also before the dominant protection agency even arises.

Some clients of the dominant protection agency will probably violate independent individuals who are not part of the contract. Some independent will likely seek compensation because the individual has nothing to lose by doing this. At this point, during which the freelancer seeks the protection agency's services for the wrongdoing, the protection agency is still obligated to protect the client. So, the nonclient theoretically cannot gain any compensation from the client that violated him or her. This is a tremendous disadvantage for any nonclient, which could result in the more extensive exploitation of nonclients by protected clients. Similar situations arise for illegal migrants who are exploited by citizens of the nation who may extort illegal aliens via threatening to turn them into the authorities, e.g., many illegal migrants from Central American are violated in Mexico during the 21st century, which are depicted in films, such as *Sin Nombre* (i.e., Without Name) in 2009.

The failures of the protection agency can create controversy when the individuals who are violated are clients who are merely tardy with their payments to the dominant protection agency. There is greater controversy when the individuals who violate others are the clients of the protection agency itself because those clients may also need additional protection since they are avoiding revengeful retaliations from those who they have violated. The philosophical problems arise for the dominant protection agency since the agency either protects the interests of its own clients in the latter sort of situations, albeit maintaining loyalty as a virtue, which is one philosophy, or instead the agency upholds the ever-developing principles of justice and fairness against the loyalty toward certain clients, which is another philosophy.

Upholding the developing principles of justice and fairness, i.e., instead of maintaining loyalty to its own clients, is a stance derived from the decision-making processes, fair assessments, and judicial compromises. The principles of justice and fairness are exceedingly difficult to uphold in cases that involve favoritism and nepotism and friends and family, and in well-developed systems, the systematic searches, exposures, and eradications of favoritism and nepotism allow for justice and fairness to be better upheld via investigators, journalists, lawyers, judges etc. Judicial compromises are given by the agency in support of some of its clients and against some of its other clients' misbehaviors, especially against those who have violated the former ones, and then via the transfer of these principles of justice and fairness by the protection agency to nonclients who have been violated by its clients, which would demonstrate a type of fundamental overcoming of favoritism by means of justice and fairness.

It may also be a rational stance for the dominant protection agency to maintain fair judgments in support of nonclients to discourage both clients' wrongdoings against nonclients and to suppress potential retaliations against clients subsequently. So, a direct reason for upholding justice and fairness also involves mutual benefit because siding with nonclients in certain situations, in which they have been evidently violated, would likely decrease violent retaliations that would require extra time, effort, and resources from the protective agency. Protection agencies that have been continuously confronted with such problems probably have tended to assess the risks of retaliation in accordance with an analysis of the expenses of the overall services of the agency.

Exploitation is likely to arise when there is an allowance of those protected by a dominant protection agency's services to severely violate those who fail to pay for protection services. In certain cases, the damages or potential damages instilled by a client of the protection agency and against a nonclient, who has severely been wronged, may not be worth the risks of his or her continued protection by the agency, unless the client and wrongdoer is authoritatively commanded to provide a judicially-determined and fair compensation to the nonclient. It is an aspect of human nature for stories to arise with great popularity after tremendous injustices, which are wrought by one party under the protection of a dominant authority against another. The popularity of such stories and general dislike of injustice play major influential roles on authorities to maintain fairness.

During the early 16th century, a merchant from the area near present-day Berlin named Hans Kohlhase was attacked on his way to the fair in Leipzig. Several of Hans's horses were presumably stolen by servants of Günter von Zaschwitz. Kohlhase was unable to attain compensation for his losses after he paid for the return of his horses. So, Hans Kohlhase gathered many men to rob, burn, and plunder villages all around Saxony after the courts of law failed to grant him compensation (Chisolm, 1911, p. 887).

A partially fictional version of Kohlhase's story was published as a novella in 1810 by Heinrich von Kleist called *Michael Kohlhaas*, which has been produced as films in 1969 and 2013. Kohlhase's motivations for destroying many portions of Saxony and undermining the status quo and legal system with violence are naturally arising motivations of an individual who has been harshly violated without being compensated. Although the vengeance of Kohlhase was extreme, the case at least illustrates reasons to uphold procedural justice and provide fair judgments and to seriously consider and demonstrate the serious considerations of compensations for those who have been wronged because the violation of one's rights is well-known to stir the negative emotions of anger, disgust, and contempt, which may lead to dangerous ideologies. Dangerous ideologies can spread, and they involve destruction, violence, and motivations to even overthrow legitimate authorities or, at least established authorities, with vengeance.

If the dominant protection agency protects the client who violated some nonclient, which likely happened to Kohlhase, and does not allow the nonclient compensation, then the agency supports the infringement of the nonclient's freedoms by its own clients and therefore perpetuates the situational variables that promote unfairness. Of course, promoting unfairness, in general, creates social disorder, despite continual attempts of the protective association to promote social order and fairness. "Unfairness" may not describe the situation or potential circumstance of each nonclient, though, since family members of clients, their friends, or those from the same racial group as the majority of clients, for instance, might allow for the protection agency to discriminate against nonclients in an organized fashion that results in the least conflict and least protest amongst its own members and overall, at least temporarily.

The law often functions in a manner such that those who are trusted with the tasks of protecting the rights of others (i.e., lawyers) tend to construct argumentation that benefits their own best interests, especially insofar as their interests are aligned with their clients' interests. Rather than producing the best arguments that would facilitate juridical judgments of the truth of the matter, the best arguments for the pair (i.e., the attorney/s and client/s) are created instead. The stance of the attorney and client is further supported by any experts they hire, and experts are also inclined to make statements and responses that place the client-attorney position as the priority over any position that may benefit the opposition, despite whether the response that benefits the opposition would be true, honest, open, and fair.

The philosophical problem involves a complex set of variables for the consideration of theory and praxis in respect to the ethical issue and the principle of fairness. Can the advocate of the client and legal professional afford to continuously uphold the principle of fairness via relinquishing the best arguments for his or her clients (i.e., when in conflict with truth, justice, or fairness) and instead uphold the most enlightening arguments that are open and honest? In short, the answer is negative when the system in which one works does not contain intensely negative consequences for the ones who deceptively present arguments with misleading facts, half-truths, and outright lies to support their causes.

Likewise, the questionable nature of the limitations of the privileges and services to the client lies with whether the agency (or lawyer) can afford to uphold the principle of fairness for nonclients, which requires time, effort, and money. However, it also remains disputable whether the agency (or lawyer) can know whether the support of fairness for compensations of nonclients is affordable. For instance, some lawyers purposefully ask their clients to only answer specific questions that they ask, for instance, and the lawyers show no interest in whether their clients are guilty of the crime for which they have been indicted. Clients may be asked to answer questions in ways that falsely suggest that they fail to remember certain details of events or that they are less certain than they actually are.

The stance of many advocates of clients is that "evidence takes precedence over truthfulness, especially when what is accepted as evidence would allow for the clients' wrongdoings to be overlooked." When evidence suggesting the wrongdoing of the client does not exist, the client is instructed to deny or to plead ignorance to the wrongdoing, which may involve outright lying. The truth of the matter is less important to the practical sciences insofar as only what is interpreted as evidence is utilized by those who judge, say, for the protection agency.

For the protection agency and its clients, the consideration of the limitations of the privileges and services to clients is also disputable because any services supporting nonclients must not provide moral or practical reasons for its clients to terminate their contracts for the agency's protection services. Negligence and the unjust, unethical, and unfair treatment of nonclients,[1] which can become rampant, coincides with knowingly presenting misinformation or presenting facts in misleading ways, especially for supporting clients at the expense of the disadvantages of nonclients, and especially when the cases originally arose because of the mistreatment of nonclients and when there is a lack of evidence for the wrongdoing that was performed by the accused. On the other hand, it is somewhat relieving and fairer to have a system that allows for one who is accused more than once of wrongdoings to be under greater suspicion and for multiple accusations to serve as a form of evidence of some type of wrongdoings.

To abolish the disadvantages that the nonclients have, the dominant protection agency provides its services for nonclients free of charge. The dominant protection agency becomes a state when all the individuals within the society are protected (Nozick, 1974, pp. 113–118). It may be worthy to mention that individuals who travel to other states are in the same situation as the people who were nonclients and received free services. The people who were not covered ought to be covered so that the nonclients would not be prohibited from gaining compensation and protecting themselves; this is the principle of compensation. This is the minimal state, according to Nozick. Nozick (1974, pp. 113–114) ascertains that:

> A protective agency dominant in a territory does satisfy the two crucial necessary conditions for being a state. It is the only generally effective enforcer of a prohibition on others' using unreliable enforcement procedures (calling them as it sees them), and it oversees these procedures. And the agency protects those nonclients in its territory whom it prohibits from using self-help enforcement procedures on its clients, in their dealings with its clients, even if such protection must be financed (in apparent redistributive fashion) by its clients.

The ideal libertarian state only requires people to pay the absolute minimum payment that it would take to provide three paramount functions: (1) the local protection industry or police; (2) a system of judges so that a third and neutral party can make decisions regarding criminals; and (3) the military is the last aspect of this political and economic system for which people must pay taxes.

1 Of course, many people who are not clients may deceive others into believing that they are indeed clients of the protection agency or some lawyer, too.

The libertarian holds the right to own property very highly; and therefore, taxes are kept at as low a percentage as possible because taxes are property (i.e., the private property of individuals transferred and transformed into public property) in accordance with the legal system.

For similar reasons, Nozick's ideal government is a laissez-faire capitalistic economic system, which means that the government does not have the right to interfere with the trading, distribution of goods, or transactions of capitalists, unless they are violating the rights of citizens. The black market or underground economy would exist only with regard to the sale of products and services that involve violence (e.g., hired murderers and selling internal organs without consent), the infringements of people's rights, fraud, and theft. We may assert the following testable hypothesis, against which only one example is necessary to refute it: In the history of political economic systems there are not any examples of states where the minimalist form of government has existed for any significant amount of time.

There are probably many reasons why the Nozick-type of minimalist state is unrealistic regarding its priority of protecting property, especially money. First, privileged groups tend to be given advantages in all societies, and low-status groups tend to be given disadvantages, and the problem of the failure to account and compensate for these societal tendencies would exacerbate the problem. Furthermore, a society consists of mostly women, children, and elderly people rather than of men who can sexually reproduce, and men of reproductive age often impregnate women and fail to uphold their fatherly duties and moral responsibilities to their partners and their children.

To discourage the latter type of misbehaviors (i.e., fathering children without accepting any responsibility for their support) and to promote the support of mothers and children, it appears that social programs need to be created via taxes for facilitating public services for children and mothers, such as education, transportation, child support, or other social programs that compensate for fatherlessness or motherlessness. The latter type of societal problems is a fundamental one that precedes the economic problem and is called the "F-problem" (See Ch. 6).

One outcome of the societal failures to instill family values, support the institutions of marriage and the family, and to instill the ideology of the responsible and supportive father may be anarchy itself. Anarchy may very well be conceived as a form of questioning, criticisms, and skepticisms against the major institutions and systems of the society, including slavery, types of servitude, and corporate systems with limited legal liability and their abilities to file lawsuits, which is like Noam Chomsky's characterizations of anarchy in his 2005, *On Anarchism*. Powerful individuals or groups are assumed by anarchists to have the burden of proof to demonstrate why they deserve their positions of power and authority.

For Nozick, the formation of the state from the condition of anarchy and development or placement of protective forces largely involve reasonable reactions and rational decisions that are made either because of violence, theft or fraud. They may naturally provide victims with reasons to behave violently in retaliation. The development of fair and just judicial decision-making tends to arise from a set of decisions that alleviated the initial emotional responses from victimization to some extent because victims are expected by judicial authorities to await verdicts for compensations and penalizations. Also, some victims are awarded compensations for their victimizations, some victimizers are penalized, and people realize this, especially when they live within a society that is efficient enough to allow just decisions to be regularly publicized. Apparently, even before the existence of a minimal state there are intricate processes already in place that involve both the enforcement of rules and judicial decisions against violence and against the factors that increase the likelihood of violent outbursts.

Within developed, developing, and underdeveloped nations, the legal systems and legal ideologies may also be analyzable in accordance with Nozick's conception of state formation. The conditions of underdeveloped nations can sometimes and in some places also resemble the Hobbesian "state of nature" and may lead to greater frequencies of analytic discourse concerning both the risk of life in the society and the search for security. Developed, developing and underdeveloped nations' legal systems range in order from greater complexity regarding social and societal relations to less complexity in that regard. In virtue of potentiality, more complex societal systems tend to be more capable of producing superior technologies and societal systems for transport, communication, law, trade etc. This, however, does not mean that the cultures of developed countries are more complex.

Even less complex systems exist, such as ones without statehood and with either dominant protection agencies, multiple, competitive protection agencies, or anarchy (e.g., consider tribal cultures in the Amazon). Tribal cultures are probably more challenging to analyze, regarding Nozick's conception of the minimalist state, until they have trouble attaining necessary resources. This results in conflicts. With Nozick's conception of the minimalist state, it is challenging to analyze tribes until they engage in conflict with other tribes. The conceptions of protection services, judging, and military services involve concepts of institutions based on extant ones. They do not easily allow for reconciliations of the roles that tribesmen and women assume regarding protection and decision-making. Small portions or vast portions of their populaces may serve these roles that many societal subsystems play in civil national economies.

The roles of violence and dangerous legal ideologies vary regarding each type of societal system of developed, developing, and underdeveloped countries. The methods are also questionable concerning investigations of the ways in which violence can be reduced by means of understanding the conditions that both lead to fairer decisions, procedural justice, and more stable expectations for compensations and penalizations. One important sociological inquiry asks: How can violence be reduced via directly changing dangerous legal ideologies by means of transforming expectations in society?

Expectations are certainly different within developed, developing, and underdeveloped nations, and play fundamental roles regarding the cultures of these three types of countries. We may discover that worsening socio-economic conditions almost invariably lead to dangerous legal ideologies, i.e., when the conditions are perceived as worsening in respect to certain social relations. Social dominance theory and system justification theory are worthwhile for the analysis of the associations between dangerous legal ideologies (e.g., advocating the destruction of parts of societal systems, murders, crippling boycotts, assassinations etc.) and socio-economic conditions that worsen for people. The latter people may form social groups or discover certain factors with which they can commonly identify themselves and sometimes become members of social groups. The dominance and subordination histories of people sharing common characteristics or circumstances during the same epoch are important to understand as coinciding factors with such people promoting, supporting, and defending the systems in which they live, especially despite the disadvantages the systems may impose upon them.

3 Sociological Imaginations and Dangerous Legal Ideologies

An individual may think about herself quite often. She may think of another person instead. Sometimes she might think of many people who form a crowd or a social group. All the latter thoughts about people are important regarding shaping the way she thinks about members of the legal institution, such as police, judges, lawyers, lawmakers etc. When events occur that demand legal experts, political action, police, soldiers etc., her experiences and thoughts are likely to play ever more important roles in shaping the range of her ideas, her horizon, and her concept of law. Moreover, the media also plays crucial roles in providing her with information about people, natural and human-caused occurrences, and about the law.

In essence, she forms a legal ideology, which can promote peace, indifference, or destruction. Her emotions, experiences and reactions to important incidents all play special roles in the formation of her legal ideology. The problem and question at hand is whether we can begin to philosophically or conceptually and scientifically or measurably understand and predict the future formation of the individual or group's legal ideology to the extent that it is either peaceful, neutral, or dangerous for the prosperity of the society.

Any solution to the problem of forming understandings of people's legal ideologies must involve initial conceptual analyses of sociological imaginations, other ways of thinking, the objects of thought, as well as of peaceful, neutral, and dangerous legal ideologies. It may appear obvious that certain types of experiences of events associated with certain types of reactions by the legal system will tend to lead to specific types of ideologies. Some people tend to be more prone to accepting certain types of legal ideologies based on their relations with the law.

When a class of people becomes wealthier during a monetary crisis, e.g., billionaires, unemployment for other economic classes rises. When wars occur, certain groups of people are sent to the frontlines, and others find safer means of serving the nations. When a president and civil rights leaders are assassinated, the political experiences hallmark and remain the primary political memories of perhaps most of one national generation. When a leader must testify that he behaved in a manner that he knows is distasteful for many of his fellow countrymen and women, the shame, excitement, and embarrassment are used by one group against another for some sort of gain and recognition. Following the violent attacks in and around New York City on September 11th, 2001, for instance, many nations had new realizations of false senses of security. Security was amplified in multiple nations' airports, especially in developed countries in Western Europe.

With each of the abovementioned social events what is ever-challenging is to separate oneself from personal and familial problems, feelings of lower self-confidence and insecurity that come with joblessness, the fears and uncertainties that coincide with the outbreak of war, the sorrows and directionlessness that mark the loss of leaders, the malicious joy or schadenfreude of one group and shame of another that signify the realizations of lying or sexual misconduct of leaders, and the panic, hatred, and vengefulness that resides after a fierce and premeditated set of attacks.

For you and me, the task of individuals understanding the social importance of others within a legal system involves distancing ourselves from these states of mind (i.e., low self-esteem, insecurity, directionlessness, shame, hatred etc.) to recognize the social movements that inevitably sweep all of us with these events that powerfully cause the experiences we undergo. These mental states assuredly play a major part in the emotional susceptibility to, and creation of, ideologies inasmuch as the verifiable social events do as well as their representations by media outlets.

With mental states[2] or emotions, consider the feelings of, say, worthlessness and inner dialogs (i.e., language usage) where people claim to themselves that they are "no good" simply because of joblessness, for instance. Those emotional mental states arise naturally and are not easily prevented by an understanding of a high unemployment rate, for example. Our resultant mental states are at issue, and they impact and are impacted by our "sociological imaginations." Charles Wright Mills (1959, p. 5) maintains:

> The sociological imagination enables its possessor to understand the larger historical scene in terms of its meaning for the inner life and the external career of a variety of individuals. It enables him to take into account how individuals, in the welter of their daily experience, often become falsely conscious of their social positions. Within that welter, the framework of the psychologies of a variety of men and women are formulated.

With the sociological imagination, one begins to understand that he or she is one of many people who are similarly situated in the same types of circumstances and who undergo the same sorts of experiences. The latter understanding, however, requires that the individual relinquish the imposing idea that his or her circumstances are unique. Mills (ibid.) continues:

> By such means the personal uneasiness of individuals is focused upon explicit troubles and the indifference of publics is transformed into involvement with public issues. The first fruit of this imagination—and the first lesson of the social science that embodies it—is the idea that the individual can understand his own experience and gauge his own fate only by locating himself within his period, that he can know his own chances in life only by becoming aware of those of all individuals in his circumstances.

2 By "mental states," there is no need to assume any distinction between the physical aspects and the mental aspects of life or humanity, except insofar as the mental states refer to a realm of real phenomena that is only analyzable from certain levels of analysis, which are associated with certain levels of observation (See Ch. 2). The types of observations involved can include facial expressions of contempt, fear, sadness etc. and the usage of language that is self-deprecating, which impede sociological imaginations, for example.

Every sociological and psychological imagination offers some level of analysis from some perspective—from one's own personal model of atoms, biological cells, and networks of neurons to the modeling of entire groups of people, humanity as a whole, and different environments, whether it be one's own thoughts about oneself concerning the law, the thoughts about another person's beliefs regarding sports and politics, or the motivations behind the abovementioned events of maldistributions of wealth, warring, assassinating, deceiving or betraying, and terrorizing. Each conception of one's own experiences from his or her autobiography or of biographies of others who one experienced, and of the social history one conceptualizes—presents its author and theorist with models from which hypotheses are formed, and the testable ones can really spark the fires of science that shed new knowledge and enlighten.

Not only the American legal system is challenged by each of the events briefly described on the previous pages—for instance, by inflexible tax laws (i.e., allowing billionaires to gain more wealth via accruing interest while simultaneously intensifying debt crises), from the increase of crime by the newly unemployed, from the illegal deserters of war, from the riots following Dr. Martin Luther King Junior's assassination, from the resignation of US President Nixon, from the impeachment of President Clinton, and from the racist beatings of Arab and Muslim Americans and multinational declarations of war or "military operations" against Arab and Islamic nations during the 21st century.

Nevertheless, the members of the legal institution undergo the very same political experiences that lead others to deviate from their normal actions. Should we not assume that some of the most important decisions of lawmakers, judges, clandestine government agents, and police are made during and after the impacts these events have on each law member's long-lasting conscious experiences concerning these events and their representations via media outlets? How can such an assumption contribute to our understandings of the social, philosophical, and scientific importance of legal systems?

That which is mentioned so far concerns merely pieces of the contemporary American story with certain parallels to others. Many histories remain to be told. Likewise, they involve the identical emotions, the same mental states, and events of loss and gain, jubilation and shamefulness, and hatred and fear driven by other social events in addition to the beliefs, desires, and expectations about another populace, which are directed, in part, by mass communication, educations, legal, political, and other societal subsystems.

That which is revealed so far comprises a glimpse of memorable social events, human emotions, and tendencies of behaviors associated with them, which all greatly contribute to the formations of ideologies.

The view of law as a social institution within a society and within an international community involves a hierarchical and well-structured system of individuals and their communications, which serve to perpetuate their own social institution. The perpetuation and protection of law by the members of its institution involves arguments on its behalf, for instance, and these members include lawyers, judges, legal clerks, sheriffs, deputies, etc. Insofar that these are arguments presented by the members of this social institution who are supporting its social status, there are ideologues and ideologies.

The legal ideology espoused by members of a legal institution in the form of arguments, and the same arguments put forth by nonmembers of this institution, are different to the extent that the latter group is more likely to include members who are negatively impacted by laws that they served to protect only after they have been successfully deceived by the former group's legal ideology. However, some of these individuals form a group supporting the legal institution and benefit indirectly, although the group lacks the responsibilities that being a member of the legal institution requires. Some examples of the latter types of groups include the "sons of small town sheriffs, politicians, and judges" who have ideologies reflecting their unique situations with the law.

For instance, the idea of the "law's favored groups" is analyzable regarding sons of small town sheriffs, who possess exercisable power based on a combination of others' rational fears of the legal institution, including peoples' rational fears of legal bureaucracy and the disproportionate threats instilled by the criminal justice system, which benefits dominant group members and is detrimental to subordinate groups (Sidanius & Pratto, 1999b; See Ch. 2.8).

Ideology has an intuitively obvious connection to law if it is assumed that the legal system is legislated by some political system and law is, in part, a body of enforceable rules that govern socioeconomic relations (Sypnowich, 2010). Politics, law, and economics appear to be relationally inseparable from the standpoint of ideology critique because ideology is roughly a system of political and economic ideas. For instance, ideologies can be fascist, socialist, communist, capitalist, and liberal, and economic, political, and legal systems can be described as possessing these characteristics as well. Moreover, a single law can be viewed as the expression of a political or economic ideology. To this extent, a theory of law must incorporate political, economic, and especially legal ideology within it for the sake of comprehensiveness.

Ideologies are those systems of thought utilized by groups, social classes, or individuals concerning ideals about how and why to act and which are largely based on political, legal, and economic ideas (Brant, 2012a, p. 182; Kearney, 2003). No ideology is ever accepted as a set of beliefs by one who possesses any understandings of its historical underpinnings or a sociological imagination of the group who holds the ideology. There is never a realization of the circumstances that led to the formation of the ideals or ideas of the ideology by the ideology holder. So, those accepting ideologies fail to recognize where they are historically situated and often how they are socioeconomically situated.

Ideology impacts many people and can play a leading role in the behaviors that cause terrible atrocities, such as war and genocide (Shelton, 2005). Donald Dutton (2007, p. 108) describes the role of ideology amongst the organizers of genocide:

> In Staub's model the frustration of basic needs (e.g., material deprivation, political chaos, realistic conflict) and the identification of a scapegoat constitute the instigating conditions for the destructive process. In Rwanda, long term deprivation, political chaos, and a long-standing belief that the Tutsi were dangerous interlopers coalesced into a perfect storm of violence. The deprivation produces heightened in-group identification, particularly amongst authoritarian people who seek a strong leader, perception of out-group threat, and a destructive ideology. The latter presents an exclusionary world vision and is called, *in extremis*, an ideology of antagonism.

All societies undergo frustrations of basic needs, time periods where needs for security increase, and where political conflicts occur. In each society, there are also tendencies to blame groups for societal problems, especially blaming lower status groups or minority groups. Dutton (ibid.) continues:

> When subordinate groups demand more, they threaten the basic need satisfaction of the dominant group whose "legitimizing ideology" is threatened and who then react with increasingly harsh acts of repression and aggression. In Rwanda, the push by the RPF and the death of the president served as such precipitating threats. Although not genocide, the lynchings in the Southern United States can also be viewed from this perspective. The loss of the Civil War and the continuing presence of the "free negro" threatened the legitimizing ideology of the South.

The Rwandan Patriotic Front (RPF), which is the leading political party during the early 21st century, invaded Rwanda on October 1, 1990, beginning the Rwandan Civil War from 1990 to 1994. On April 6, 1994, the event that greatly influenced genocidal violence during the following 100 days was the assassination of Rwandan President Juvenal Habyarimana, the leader of the Hutu people. Between April 7th and mid-July of 1994 somewhere between 500,000 and 1,000,000 people were killed in Rwanda, and a clear majority of them were Tutsis. The Tutsis were viewed as scapegoats through the ideology of antagonism. Dutton (ibid.) continues:

> Staub argued that two types of out-group stereotyping exist. The lesser is devaluation of the out-group, while the more intense form specifically sees the out-group as having achieved gains through prior injustice. Hitler saw the Jews this way, and the Hutu extremists portrayed the Tutsi in this way. Once initiated, violence generates an evolution in perpetrators; the personality of individuals, social norms, institutions, and culture all change incrementally in ways that make greater violence easier and more likely (Staub, 1999, p. 182; Waller, 2002, p. 134).

The German East African colony integrated Rwanda in 1899 when the Tutsi people were in administrative power of the country. The Tutsi lords continued to control local regions while the Germans were in power of the colony. After Germany's defeat in the First World War, the League of Nations (1920–1946) gave the responsibility to Belgium to control both Rwanda and Burundi in 1916. The Tutsis remained in political power over the local affairs. The Hutus were given greater access to some arable land and were encouraged by the Belgians to grow coffee trees (Middleton, 2002, p. 216).

Land shortages, increasing human population in the region, the rise in power of the Hutus from the coffee cash crop, and growing ethnic tensions resulted in a massacre, which largely consisted of genocidally murdering tens of thousands of people in 1959. As a result, the Belgians allowed elections to occur in 1961 and granted independence to Rwanda in 1962. The Hutu people elected their candidate, Grégoire Kayibanda, and the Hutus came into power over the Tutsi people who had been the leading and dominant group in the Rwandan society until the administrative and economic changes in hierarchical powers during the middle of the 20th century.

In 1994, Rwanda was one of the most densely populated regions in Africa and had a shortage of arable land, which increased competition for the farming land and increased social tensions (Uvin, 1998; Middleton, 2002). Moreover, the relations of dominance had rapidly changed from the Tutsis to the Germans to the Belgians, and finally the previously subordinated Hutus became the dominant group in the Rwandan society. Dutton (ibid.) continues:

> The usual moral principles that prohibit violence and protect people are replaced by "higher" values protecting purity, goodness, and well-being

> of the in-group, and creating a better society by destroying the victims. A utopian vision is offered that excludes some people and justifies their exclusion in the service of the vision. A progressive restructuring of group norms occurs in line with this ideological shift. Albert Bandura (1979 & 1988) describes the process of moral disengagement that allows "reprehensible conduct" to occur and recur.

Staub's model is tested with every program, especially governmental programs which involve reparations or advantages for groups that have been historically placed at disadvantages. For instance, in the USA, the affirmative action program facilitates the hiring of individuals of minority and racial groups. Staub's model maintains that the more intense type of stereotyping involves the perception of any outgroup attaining achievements by means of prior injustices. The model is presented with disconfirming evidence when programs, such as "affirmative action" in the US, are tolerated or accepted.

However, it is possible that such sorts of programs are neither wholly accepted nor completely tolerated by the dominant group that is expected to make reparations. Affirmative action programs have various names in various societies, such as "positive discrimination" in India and Britain and "sons of the soil" in Indonesia and Malaysia. In support of Staub's model, most of the programs that offer underprivileged groups certain advantages are described as "temporary," despite their continued growth (Sowell, 2004, p. 2).

Dutton (2007) maintains that the generation of violence, given certain social conditions, brings an even greater likelihood that more intense violence will be wrought. The latter social conditions are political chaos, deprivations regarding material goods or resources that satisfy basic human needs (e.g., healthy food, clean water, fresh air, which can lead to serious problems in many cities), and violent conflicts involving weaponry. Additionally, identifications of recognizable scapegoats may facilitate the escalation of violence.

From the standpoints of researchers, what can and should cast doubt upon the latter facilitating factors for escalations of violence are violent outbreaks that may lack some of these social conditions of the escalations of violence for other reasons. These other reasons can include ideologies of domination that may come from natural tendencies of males, for example, to engage in sex and sexual reproduction with certain persons or to prevent others from having sex with those persons but that are frustrated and prevented by the circumstances in that society (See Ch. 6).

Consider the creations of "rape factories" or "rape camps" during the Yugoslavian conflict (Askin, 1997, p. 275). The rape facilities of all sides, forced impregnations, forced maternities (i.e., when women are held hostage after rapes and released only after they are late in the stages of pregnancy to prevent or discourage abortions), castrations and killings of soldiers who refused to rape, sterilizations, and sexual mutilations all certainly must be considered in terms of prolonged violence with the thousands of pregnancies and systematic rapes that occurred in former Yugoslavia (ibid., pp. 273–275). Some isolated incidents of violence may involve combinations of the social conditions that are hypothesized to lead to prolonged violent outbursts, but they may only last short spans.

Dutton (2007) ascertains that moral principles are responsible for the prohibition of violence and the protection of others. Contrarily, many ethicists have argued for the implementation of violence from different ethical perspectives. Immanuel Kant's deontology (i.e., duty-based ethics) also incorporated justifications for implementations of the death penalty. They ideologically justified Prussia's executions. They were for crimes that "deserved" the harshness of such penalizations, according to Kant's (1797) *Grounding of the Metaphysics of Morals*.

Likewise, the moral principles of consequentialism and utilitarianism could be utilized for justifying violence, especially if such violence leads to the best consequences or the greatest amount of good or utility for the largest number of individuals, for instance. Even arguments for prolonged violence are considered by many to be justifiable in accordance with some of the principles of just war theory. That is, there is no consensus by ethicists when it comes to moral justifications for or against violence, in general.

Social dominance theorists provide alternative explanations for the legitimizations of prolonged violence as opposed to just impulsive, emotional, or short outbursts of violence. Harry Eckstein (2004, pp. 574–596) categorizes the escalations of prolonged violence into two distinct types of theories. The two types of theories of prolonged violence are the contingency theories and inherency theories.

Contingency theories are those that presume that both groups and individuals typically engage in peaceful activities but resort to violent political acts after the frustrations of basic needs, such as in Staub's model. Alternatively, contingency theories presume that groups of people and individuals are typically motivated to alter their situations and surroundings to become more privileged and to increase the amounts of their power when they (i.e., as power-seekers) predict that the attainable advantages resulting from violence outweigh all the expenditures and risks. Eckstein (ibid.) maintains within his metatheoretical analysis that the contingency theories are classified similarly with the culturist theories, which foundationally presume that violence is based upon learning the orientation to act.

The inherency theories are classified with the theories of the rationalists, which assume that violence stems from emotionless calculations to the extent that actions are based upon decision-makers' vicious determinations after reasonable cost-benefit analyses are considered. We may consider, for instance, the calculations of many corporations in developing countries during their periods of industrialization, in which cases thousands of unskilled workers move into cities with manufacturing, construction, packaging, and factories for wage-workers but under unsafe and terrible working conditions (e.g., working extremely long hours with dangerous equipment in mills and factories, child labor, etc.). Anti-union violence was used against workers on strike, against union leaders, and involved goon squads (i.e., a group of mercenaries or people prone to acting criminally) who implemented controlled threats, violence, and espionage against unions when companies' workers went on strike.[3] Of course, powerful unions also hired goon squads against companies.

Although Eckstein (ibid., p. 595) leans toward a simplified version of a contingency theory after his analysis, what may be very worthwhile is to consider such theories as possible ways of thinking and behaving for different demographical groups, individuals with different personality-types, and for those with violent tendencies who have different situational variables and different ideologies. Consider the fact that theorists are not always excluded from the participation in prolonged violence. Theorists who advocate the rationalist approach, which maintains that the cost-effectiveness and rational calculations of issues play major roles before violence occurs, may believe that they are individuals who would be more likely to become violent after they have calculated the expenditures and risks. Theorists may tend to be those sorts of people who act less often on impulsivities or random violence as a result of the calculations of risks.

Theorists probably tend to be far removed from the conditions that instigate prolonged violence because theorists require free time and thereby live under conditions that are different from manual laborers and those who undergo massive exploitation of their labor. Some theorists may very well have reasons to uphold particular systems of thought, such as the inherency theories of calculating risks and benefits of violence before it is used, but they may also be personal, anecdotal, or psychological reasons rather than statistical

3 Labor violence occurred, for instance, in France, Wales, and the United States in the early 20th century, and the causes of labor violence range from cultural, racial, and hereditary clashes to biological or instinctive factors, as protests against environmental conditions or even acts that are influenced by ideology as at least partial causes, according to Jeffreys-Jones (1979, p. 246).

and sociological ones. Prolonged violence generally is not typically associated with impulsive behaviors, though.

Since the outlooks of the contingency and inherency theories include supporting evidence for them, another theoretical approach is an eclectic one that allows for scientific evidence to offer both confirming and disconfirming evidence for each so-called theoretic approach in a way that is akin to treating them both as hypotheses. The hypotheses can be further specified to the extent that the inherency hypothesis may presume that a certain amount of institutional or non-institutional education or some sufficient amount of experience is required for individuals to undergo the decision-making process in such ways that involve rational but violent behaviors being performed by them. On the other hand, the contingency hypothesis may involve certain assumptions about individuals' educational backgrounds but also presume that certain factors, such as old age and fear of the loss of financial stability, are contributing factors to the outbursts of violence for certain types of people (i.e., either from a demographic perspective or because of alternative situational factors, etc.).

Dutton (2007) also maintains that a notion of utopia arises within the ideologies or minds of the individuals who resort to prolonged violence to the extent that the utopian vision emerges for the individuals' ingroups insofar as the people begin to view the violence as promoting the wellbeing of their own group. The utopian vision is argued by Dutton to involve both the exclusion of certain people as well as the justification for their exclusion.

The ideology of the utopian exclusion of another group within society is a dangerous ideology which can even be promoted by the legal system and supported by other forms of legal ideology. For these reasons, it is important to analyze the interconnections between ideology and utopia, especially while paying close attention to the exclusions of people and lack of recognition, such as the lack of recognition of people of African descent in the USA as citizens in the 19th century and lack of recognition of aborigines in Australia as citizens in the 20th century, including exclusions from voting, the census, etc.

Karl Mannheim's (1929) *Ideology and Utopia* contributes to the subject of sociology of knowledge with an investigation of how humans think in respect to their everyday lives and how it functions within politics as an instrument of collective actions, i.e., as opposed to more utopian ways of thinking that are described within logic and philosophical books about how one is best able to think rationally. Rational, logical, and valid argumentative ways of thinking are perhaps atypical ways of thinking for most humans most of the time since there are indeed pitfalls in human reason that are known as fallaciously and irrationally derived statements and invalid arguments. Mannheim dispels the idea that a group or crowd has a way of thinking that is, in some sense, more important than the ways of thinking of the individuals who compose it. The importance of the latter notion may tend to be overlooked insofar as people often categorize groups of people together and refer to them as thinking as one unit altogether.

For instance, we may dispel the idea that a nation can think or that a nation has motivations to perform certain actions since a nation lacks an apparatus through which it could think. So, believing or arguing that "Russia thinks such and such about China, and the USA is angry with India about so and so" is greatly misguided and contributes to many overgeneralizations in important ways that obstruct social understandings of the latter national legal systems, for instance. Despite the latter overgeneralizations, people may very well view nations like they view individuals and pass policies based on misperceptions about an entire populace. Mannheim maintains:

> It is the main thesis of the sociology of knowledge that there are ways of thinking that cannot become adequately understood since their societal origins remain obscure. However, it is true that only the individual is capable of thinking. There is no such metaphysical being, like the mind of the group, which thinks above and beyond the heads of the individuals and whose ideas the individual solely reproduces. (Mannheim, 1995, p. 4) [Es ist die Hauptthese der Wissensoziologie, dass es Denkweisen gibt, die solange nicht adaequat verstanden werden können, als ihr gesellschaftlicher Ursprung im Dunkeln bleibt. Es ist allerdings wahr, dass nur das Individuum des Denkens fähig ist. Es gibt kein solches metaphysisches Wesen wie den Gruppengeist, der über den Köpfen der Individuen und über sie hinweg denkt und dessen Ideen das Individuum bloss reproduziert.]

Motivations for action or predictions of behaviors are based upon individual beliefs and desires (Bennet, 1991; Harman, 1978; Premack & Woodruff, 1978; Stich, 1978; Ziv & Frye, 2003). Sometimes others' desires influence changes in one's own intentions, for example, from an individual's indifference to certain objects to her longings to them. So, an individual may not care for something until he or she believes that another individual wants it. Likewise, one nation may not be inclined to invest time, effort, or money in a specific location until another nation expends their resources on its behalf.

The purpose of Mannheim's *Ideology and Utopia* directly concerns a focus on the social origins of knowledge. It is concerned with knowledge about the political system and politics and the loss of obstacles impeding knowledge-acquisition, such as its ideological status and utopian visions. The goal is to become increasingly scientific for the sociology of knowledge's endeavors to progress via productions of diagnoses and prognoses for disorders and injustices in society (Tamdgidi, 2002, p. 123; Berger & Luckmann, 1991). To begin the intellectual development that is involved in the replacement of ideology and utopia with science, the following question must be answered affirmatively: Is it possible to overcome or transcend our biases so that we understand society upon scientific grounds and change accordingly the human social environments in which we live?

Many of us conclude that such an overcoming is possible, including those who undertake research concerning the procedural justice of the law, such as Tyler et al. (1997). Additionally, system justification theory suggests that such optimistic hope and expectation, concerning human generations' abilities to control and repeatedly recreate our social environments, is important for multiple people to make decisions on behalf of societal improvements. Understanding the social importance of the law requires recognition of the need for legal systems to incorporate relevant information from sciences to greater extents than they have done historically for improvements to be made via reductions of the unjust victimizations of groups and of general unfairness in society.

It is important to note that the sociology of law has a very insignificant impact upon any society's law itself, especially in virtue of sociologists' abilities to identify and describe social injustices that continue, despite sociologists' efforts to reduce and prevent them. Questions remain whether political decisions made with scientific outcomes for diminishing the frequency of social injustices could largely substitute corruption in politics for corruption in science.

That is, if the results of a few studies concerning injustice (e.g., sociological methods, observations, and statistics demonstrating that African American drivers tend to be pulled over by police more frequently than other social groups) can determine legal policy, would corruption in the law enforcement system be substituted with corruption in the academic system? This could very well happen if departments of sociology became institutions of social power with the abilities to influence the processes of the penal system because institutions would attract those who seek power and may institutionalize its members to be power-seekers. Perhaps the distribution of power and influence over the criminal justice system would improve the conditions of it, though, especially from those who engage in academic research that requires rigorous investigations for several years over social groups, justice, and legal systems.

Understanding the social importance of legal systems involves taking the latter sort of inquiry seriously. Such inquiry is especially important in relation to law makers' tendencies to pass legislation, which is advantageous for certain social groups. The inquiry is also significant in relation to judges and law enforcement agents' tendencies to uphold procedural justice by treating people equally regarding legislation (DeCremer & Tyler, 2004; Tyler, 2006a & 2006b). The advantages gained by social groups based on new legislation is questionable regarding whether such laws are detrimental for other groups, especially those groups that lack recognition or lack an established social identity (e.g., minorities, low-status groups, homeless people, foreigners, homosexuals, etc.).

The practicality of focusing upon memorable events resides in the use of our abilities to predict and prepare for coming social events which concern the clear majority of society. Of course, memorable events often require the role of the mass media representing the events with images and words. In China, for instance, the Tiananmen Square Massacre in 1989 in Beijing later involved the censorship of the press as well as the people who witnessed the massacre of hundreds or possibly thousands of students and others protesting against the government. The publications of newspaper articles and history books within mainland China, apart from Hong Kong and Macau, do not refer to it as a massacre.

More accurate predictions of social events occur when the prediction is based upon greater understandings of susceptibilities of social groups. The understandings of the susceptibilities of social groups are easily influenced via combinations of their own roles within the social events and redirection of individuals' wills of other groups toward common causes, including support or encouragement of wars, political leaders' resignations or assassinations, social dominance over subordinate groups, etc.

For example, the musical group of rappers, N.W.A. (i.e., Niggaz Wit Attitude) wrote and produced a hit song in August of 1988 called "Fuck Tha Police," which are the lyrics of the chorus of the song. The song is briefly analyzed and compared to other songs, and the lyrics are partially written by Samuels (2004, pp. 147 & 151). It is noteworthy to keep in mind that the song has been listened to by tens of millions of people multiple times, and a movie "Straight Outta Compton" was inspired by the events surrounding the production of N.W.A.'s album with the same title. The songwriters, O'Shea Jackson, Andre Romell Young, Lorenzo Jerald Patterson, and Harry Lamar Iii Whitaker with the copyright through (Sony, 1988) wrote:

> N.W.A. Right about now,
> N.W.A. court is in full effect
> Judge Dre presiding
> In the case of N.W.A. vs. the Police Department
> Prosecuting attorneys are MC Ren, Ice Cube

And Eazy-motherfucking-E
Order, order, order
Ice Cube, take the motherfucking stand
Do you swear to tell the truth, the whole truth
And nothing but the truth so help your black ass?
You goddamn right!
Well won't you tell everybody what the fuck you gotta say?

The first part of the song and abovementioned lyrics establish the musical group's performers as the judges, witnesses as well as the prosecutors, prosecuting the members of the police department in California. Jackson et al. (Sony, 1988) write:

Fuck the police coming straight from the underground
A young nigga got it bad cause I'm brown
And not the other color so police think
They have the authority to kill a minority
Fuck that shit, cause I ain't the one
For a punk motherfucker with a badge and a gun
To be beating on, and thrown in jail
We can go toe to toe in the middle of a cell
Fucking with me cause I'm a teenager
With a little bit of gold and a pager
Searching my car, looking for the product
Thinking every nigga is selling narcotics

The performer, Ice Cube or O'Shea Jackson, as a songwriter wrote about many of his experiences with the criminal justice system in the United States. The other songwriters on the album, Young, Patterson, and Whitaker, did as well. N.W.A. and many others in the music genre of gansta rap, political rap, or hip-hop frequently maintained that violence, threats, racism, sexism, and ageism are implemented angrily by the police, especially within certain jurisdictions. N.W.A sang and rapped about their intense anger and desires to retaliate against the police, which can be heard in their lyrics when Jackson et al. (ibid) continue:

You'd rather see, me in the pen
Than me and Lorenzo rolling in a Benz-o
Beat a police out of shape
And when I'm finished, bring the yellow tape

To tape off the scene of the slaughter
Still getting swoll off bread and water
I don't know if they fags or what
Search a nigga down, and grabbing his nuts
And on the other hand, without a gun they can't get none
But don't let it be a black and a white one
Cause they'll slam ya down to the street top
Black police showing out for the white cop

The abovementioned lyrics may illustrate the mere desires of Jackson et al. (ibid.) to fight in a (prison or jail) cell with a police officer, the songwriters' thoughts about the police preferring black men to be in jail or in prison rather than as successful men, and their desires to "slaughter" the police. The lyricists portray the police as sexually molesting men by grabbing a black male's testicles during the police search. They question the sexual orientation of the police and provocatively claim that police need a gun to have sex.

Lastly, the songwriters maintain that it is more intense brutality when a black police officer is with a white police officer because the black officer displays greater dominance like an Uncle Tom-type figure against his or her own racial group, or it is perhaps a way to identify with the racially motivated brutalities of white police against young black males. Jackson et al. (Sony, 1988) write:

Ice Cube will swarm
On any motherfucker in a blue uniform
Just cause I'm from the CPT
Punk police are afraid of me, huh A young nigga on the warpath
And when I'm finished, it's gonna be a bloodbath
Of cops, dying in L.A
Yo Dre, I got something to say

After the chorus repeats "Fuck the police!," Jackson et al. (ibid.) continue:

Pull your god damn ass over right now
Aww shit, now what the fuck you pullin me over for?
Cause I feel like it!
Just sit your ass on the curb and shut the fuck up
Man, fuck this shit
Aight, smartass, I'm taking your black ass to jail!
MC Ren, will you please give your testimony

To the jury about this fucked up incident?
Fuck the police and Ren said it with authority
Because the niggas on the street is a majority
A gang is with whoever I'm stepping
And the motherfucking weapon is kept in

The songwriters portray an incident where the police offensively request for a man to pull his car over to the side of the road, and then the man rudely asks why he was pulled over. The police officer gives him a completely arbitrary reason. Jackson et al. (Sony, 1988) write:

A stash box, for the so-called law
Wishing Ren was a nigga that they never saw
Lights start flashing behind me
But they're scared of a nigga so they mace me to blind me
But that shit don't work, I just laugh
Because it gives them a hint not to step in my path
For police, I'm saying, "Fuck you punk!"
Reading my rights and shit, it's all junk
Pulling out a silly club, so you stand
With a fake-ass badge and a gun in your hand

The latter lines demonstrate that the arbitrariness of violence, threats, and jailing lead the songwriters to strongly doubt that the police are a "legitimate" authority, and they maintain that the establishment of rights or the United States Miranda Rights are totally ineffective for the latter reasons, presumably. Jackson et al. (Sony, 1988) write:

But take off the gun so you can see what's up
And we'll go at it punk, and I'ma fuck you up!
Make you think I'mma kick your ass
But drop your gat, and Ren's gonna blast
I'm sneaky as fuck when it comes to crime
But I'ma smoke them now and not next time
Smoke any motherfucker that sweats me
Or any asshole that threatens me
I'm a sniper with a hell of a scope
Taking out a cop or two, they can't cope with me
The motherfucking villain that's mad
With potential, to get bad as fuck

The songwriters write about a character who threatens violence against the police and claims to do it in a way that would lead the police to believe that the man, Ren, who is one of the songwriters and performers, wants a fight without weapons, and then he would deviously murder the police with a rifle. Importantly, the anger and desire to retaliate against the law enforcement agents are interpreted to be at elevated levels that could still worsen, which can be heard in the last two lines by the songwriters.

Some authors analyze this song and others as well as use them within their pedagogies for teaching learners about the race-relations in certain regions and about leadership (Martinez, 1998). In the following section of this chapter, there is an analysis of the Rodney King beating and racially charged riots that followed, and it is noteworthy that the popularity of this song and others increased greatly and became a major success in the music industry, especially during 1991 in California, when the broadcast of Mr. King's beating and the riots occurred. The song, "Fuck Tha Police," reached the Rolling Stones chart that listed the song as one of the top 500 songs in history.

The entire song is much easier to understand during the performance of it. One may focus on the anger and violence directed from the police. Anger and violence is directed at young, black men. The song expresses the desires for retaliation and anger directed toward the police from the songwriters and their audiences. Their audiences include millions of people from around the world. The song was banned from broadcasts in many countries (e.g., Australia) after being aired over the radio for a few months. Only about half of the song is written above.

Perhaps an obvious hypothesis that we may construct from the depictions of the legal system and criminal justice system within any society is this: The greater the amount and popularity of music that suggests or directly accuses law enforcers (or lawmakers) of being violent and threatening violence in arbitrary ways, the greater is the possibility that the region or society includes jurisdictions (or creates them elsewhere) with unnecessary violence that is, at least, partially escalated unnecessarily by the law enforcers (or lawmakers). The arbitrary reasons for violence and threats of violence typically involve the factors or conditions that characterize low-status groups, such as race and poverty, but also include other "isms," like ageism and sexism.

Ideologies are certainly communicated. They can be communicated through music, other arts, and messages, but they need to be communicated. Moreover, some ideologies, especially those closely associated with violence and retaliation, can be dangerous because they are involved in the process of becoming violent and influencing others to partake in violence, which can even be inadvertent for multiple social groups.

Sometimes dangerous ideologies are expressed in the forms of popular culture, and when the ideologies are prevented from being expressed by law enforcers, the ideologies can be reconfirmed, legitimized, or have increases in the frequencies or intensities of their potentially dangerous messages in societies. The censorship of N.W.A.'s music, attempted preventions of their performances by policing, and discouragements by the United States Federal Bureau of Investigation (FBI) led to riots, protests, and greater publicity for the artists.

What appeared to be unaddressed by the legal system was the extremely passionate set of communicative responses toward members of the legal institution who responded, in turn, with attempts to restrict and suppress the music. The anger, frustrations, hatred, grievances about injustices, contempt, and disgusts, which were all clearly voiced by the band members, were not ignored. However, the expressive communications of the band were responded to in the uncouth and unintelligent ways of reactionaries, which, presumably, demonstrated some predictable truth-telling by the songwriters about some law enforcers and led to even greater conflicts with the police and increased investigations performed by the FBI.

Regardless of whether certain ideologies lead crowds of people to form social movements, whether the conflicts between opposing ideologies drive the crowds against other social groups, or whether the interrelated events or causes of the social movements bring about the particular ideologies, the investigations of ideologies for predicting and preventing violence is still worthwhile. Understanding the social importance of legal systems requires investigations into the impact of memorable events, their impacts on social groups, and ideologies that are largely formed based on such events' impacts on the social groups, with which the mass media systems play enormous roles.

Ideologies are dangerous. Utopian ideologies are even more dangerous because they can exclude groups of people from society and be utilized for the justifications of prolonged violence. Sociological imagination functions to dispel ideology but requires one to focus away from the ego of the individual and even away from the firsthand experiences with others to, instead, uphold the statistical data attained from and interpreted by social theorists, social workers, sociologists etc. Many people, however, tend to trust the information that is mass produced on a daily or weekly basis and refrain from reading detailed analyses by academics who have more profound insights about societies.

4 Mass Media Broadcasts of Social Events: Security with Systems

Opinions are largely formed by means of the broadcasts of mass media systems. Information and misinformation are spread widely by such systems.

Some of the images and words of the broadcasts lead to major decisions by societal systems, such as the legal system. News broadcasts, for instance, can enable a single event to attain a heightened status of importance. The event with the heightened status of significance can also lead a society into a state of crisis or emergency, such as the broadcast of the burning of a religious relic or national flag that is held sacred by others.

Security generally assumes completely different forms within societies under states of emergency. Nations, during states of emergency, isolate themselves more frequently away from intercultural exchanges, especially with cultures of an outgroup of people who are suspected of having involvements in the causes of the state of emergency. During these states of emergency, constituents of politicians can support or allow for laws to form and be implemented that are authoritarian, dominating, and lead to residual violence, especially against other societies, minorities, low-status groups, and foreigners. What results thereafter can very well be the legal permission to engage in prolonged violence. The question is whether humans can progress beyond these legal minds with ideologies in ways that reduce violence.

Understanding relations of law, social groups, and legal systems requires sociological imaginations, which are largely dependent upon mass media broadcasts and purchasable information. The sources of information required for the sociological imagination are systematically organized, publicized, and have financial resources that allow for the stable distribution of purchasable images and words describing at least some amount of real social phenomena. Yet there are the exceptions of fictitious, sarcastic, and cynical news sources (Brant, 2012a, pp. 175–216). The 21st century witnesses mass media systems invoking the hasty production of daily and even hourly articles, images, and sound bites that provide much information that is distributed to people. Media broadcasts offer the means by which any populace within a legal system attains knowledge of major events (e.g., disseminating information about business practices, weather, disasters, art, religion, and violence in the forms of isolated and unisolated attacks, wars, and genocides).

The daily production of journalistic information (e.g., within daily newspapers) creates a system of researchers and editors who generally demand fewer references before the publications of their information than scientific information does since science requires more support from citations, for instance. Scientists also attempt to repeat their observations to describe real phenomena more accurately.

The production and consumption of daily journalistic information influences consumers who become familiar with the product and its organizational structure. A system of expectations about the presentation of information develops through which the consumers, who are the readers or audience members of the mass media programs, become comfortable with the presentation methods and may even oppose certain types of improvements or changes. The system of expectations about the presentations of information involves the functions of fictional entertainment as well as newsworthy journalistic information and misinformation about the occurrences of real and unreal events.

The news is presented oftentimes with an overabundance of advertisements that can also exceed the amount of news that is presented. The ads in many market economies often do not teach consumers and customers about the products the merchants attempt to sell, but rather use deception to lead customers to buy inferior products, to make purchases based on packaging and the placements of the products at eye-level, for instance. Mass media broadcasts also typically do not teach people about the quality of products that are for ordinary consumption. Mass media systems therefore have much room for improvement.

The lower levels of integrity of journalists who publish their works with haste, with misinformation, and even with false authorship, which includes plagiarism as well as buying custom-designed articles from other authors, evidently decrease even more with the increasing speeds of transmissions of communications. The descriptive presentations of the levels of good, mediocre, and poor journalism are typically absent, and yet they could very well be presented briefly with each of the new works from both experienced and inexperienced journalists based on their published and unpublished works that are evaluated by selected and educated evaluators inside and outside of the industry. The social consequences of violence and threats of violence that result from the portrayals of real and unreal events via mass broadcasts also tend to lack the proper methods of attributing blameworthiness and responsibility to the appropriate parties involved in the mass broadcasts of the information and misinformation.

One type of possible improvement or change in the presentation of information for media outlets could involve the inclusion of multiple references to increase the rational acceptance of arguments and statements. The presentations of relevant scientific articles and excerpts from scientific books in relevant journalistic articles could be placed within newspaper articles to present a contrast between the journalistic information that is produced with less time, less effort, and with more secrecy regarding information sources, for instance, and the relevant scientific information that is produced with greater time and effort as well as with more transparency. The latter could include the contrast between the fast output of mass-distributed information (i.e., daily and weekly journalistic information) and the slower output of mass-distributed information (i.e., monthly and yearly analyses involving theoretic frameworks and unfamiliar conceptions), and presentations of information that have been thoughtfully developed and revised many more times than the ordinary types of pieces the consumers use to regularly inform themselves.

To reduce the frequency and intensity of ideological thinking, the continuous process of creation of social media systems contributes to the revision of broadcast language and misinformation, greater relevancy and consistency of the couplings of images and words, greater emphasis on underrepresentations of types of information broadcast to the public, greater clarity and warnings against overrepresentations of types of information (e.g., overrepresenting a nation's people as being overly violent and overrepresenting their population of men), greater emphasis or access to the positive and negative evaluations of journalists and parties involved with the broadcasts of information and misinformation, which may include negative evaluations of journalists and editors who produce invalid arguments, and who even assert conclusions that are true but unreasonably express such conclusions based on falsehoods and irrelevancies.

The common sources of news lack evaluative forms of presentation regarding the changing quality of the professionals, the methods, the arguments and citations, and worthy support of the information. Common news sources have contributed to the lack of familiarity with well-cited and reasoned research because news is generally published for the layman and also lacks the pedagogical strategies for developing the skills of its readers. The news typically lacks the presentation of information that would require highly educated readers for it to be adequately interpreted and generally lacks the presentations of the means of acquiring skills for attaining knowledge about the type of information broadcasted. Advertisements and commercials are included with the presentations of information broadcasted via mass media outlets oftentimes instead.

Within mass media systems there are checks in place that aim to reduce the overall amount of indecency, offensive expressions, and socially unacceptable acts, yet what needs to be addressed are those images, words and soundbites that are communicated to the public within a society which result in greater amounts of unwanted social reactions and violence. It is questionable whether the actions taken against the parties involved with the media are the best actions for this purpose. The United States Federal Communication Commission, for instance, maintains and enforces policies quite strongly against the expression of offensive language, profanities and events that are sexual in nature, yet the public and cultural ideas about what is indecent, offensive, and profane are quite diverse (Lipschultz, 2008).

Television programs during the late 20th and early 21st centuries in America are allowed to depict extremely violent events that include killings, murders, tortures etc. within the news and entertainment shows, whilst the depictions of young girls and women's' nipples, areolas, vaginas and buttocks as well as males' buttocks and penises, and generally the exposures of humans' internal anatomies are disallowed by the Federal Communication Commission. In the United States, violence is often overrepresented in its depictions upon television, especially concerning entertainment. In the United States, sex, nudity, and sexually associated images and soundbites are comparatively underrepresented. The result of the latter facts is an underemphasis upon the social consequences that result from the latter infrequently depicted materials.

Sociologically speaking, we may seriously inquire whether the depictions of violence and destruction, to which American children have been exposed for many decades now, have inadvertently led to the callous decisions to wage war by at least greater numbers of the public who have suffered from the harmful effects of this excessive violence portrayed by the media or, perhaps, whether the willingness to go to war or to frequently finance violent and destructive military operations creates a culture of legally-minded people who prefer overrepresentations of violence and threats of violence. According to the United States Federal Communication Commissioner, Michael J. Copps (ibid., p. 242):

> It is time for us to step up to the plate and tackle the issue of violence in the media. The U.S. Surgeon General, the American Academy of Pediatrics, the American Psychological Association, the American Medical Association, and countless other medical and scientific organizations that have studied this issue have reached the same conclusion: exposure to graphic and excessive media violence has harmful effects on the physical and mental health of our children.

Mass media outlets are crucial means through which substantial portions of people's understandings of legal systems and society develop. Mass media systems are also used frequently by lawmakers, lawyers and potential politicians to deceptively portray events via overrepresentations and underrepresentations as well as to promote their services via advertisements. Each type of social event's overrepresentation or underrepresentation distracts people from recognizing other types of events of greater or lesser importance.

Distractions, interpretations of conspiracies, and misinformation are facilitated via spreading images and words through mass media outlets, which shape minds or ideologies, social consciousness, the zeitgeist or mood of the people considerably in the 20th and 21st centuries. Some violent events should be followed by evaluative systems of communication of information about the misinformation that is output by the mass media system to expose the underlying ideologies. When the legally-minded people have attempted to legitimize violence through media outlets, and violence occurs, the experiences of the mass media broadcasts likely become deep-rooted memories of entire generations' very first, or most memorable political experiences.

We are now confronted with news organizations able to escape the penalization, blame or the tarnishing of their reputations after they have broadcast misinformation intentionally for higher ratings. By using misinformation, they can reduce the costs for journalists to enter areas of conflict at least with certain groups in societies since they neither need to enter them nor remain within the conflict areas until they uncover stories. For instance, how best can an Arab Muslim in Germany interpret German news media misrepresenting revolts in Syria via the German media showing video footage of Iraq but labeling it as "Syrian video footage," if the person actually recognizes the misrepresentation? Once such a blatant misrepresentation and misinformation are displayed by a corporation or another organization that expects the public to accept the news footage as "accurate," certain groups may even begin to presume that the organizations attempt to persuade the public via deception. People may very well seek alternative news sources, especially those of a radically distinctive character.

During this era, and more than ever before, social events and broadcasts of them are instantaneously and significantly impacting the entire planet. There are many examples of broadcasted events concerning the law. Often the broadcasts of the events make greater impacts upon societies than the same events being broadcasted.

Sometimes the broadcast of an event (e.g., a brutality) is anecdotal or coincidental insofar as the broadcast depicts merely an infrequently occurring event. Some broadcasts of infrequently occurring events even depict a set of relations that are extraordinary, shocking, or enraging because they involve inciting the prejudicial ways of reacting to some type of injustice, although the purpose of the representation may largely be for entertainment and increasing viewership. Some instances of the type of injustice that is falsely assumed to be one out of relatively many instances of that type of injustice lead potentially to systemic problems. The presumed identity of the victimized person and the presumed identity of the culprit bring reasons for strong concerns because the mass broadcast of the identities and the incident can lead to social unrest, protests, riots or worse. The mistreatment of workers who earn hourly wages and racist mishandlings are two types of examples with which many societies have intense historic concerns, which can facilitate protests, riots, and uprisings when they are broadcasted.

The depictions of such injustices, which result in the latter triggers of social movements, may give audiences misrepresentative impressions of the societal system. Such depictions of injustices give misrepresentations via their overrepresentations. In virtue of people attributing many of such instances of brutality to the society as systemic problems within the society, which the legal system fails to reconcile, the problems still may not escalate or incite violence, despite the readiness of the crowds and despite the provocations for social reactions that stem from inferior quality or dangerously expressive journalism.

Misrepresentations by the media, especially overrepresentations of the social injustices of a social group with a history of injustices against them (e.g., blacks in England after the abolition of slavery and again after the attainment of voting rights of these people with African descent) are often tolerated by the social group undergoing the misfortunes and domination. The types of toleration that the disadvantaged social groups have are of special interest for system justification theorists who focus on the support and justifications given to systems by the individuals who are members of these lower status social groups. The systems supported by the less fortunate people (i.e., especially during societal states of crisis), even during periods where they are unfairly and unjustly enduring massive disadvantages, comparatively, while they coexist with other social groups, are those systems in which they live (i.e., the societal system, and economic, political and legal subsystems). What are the conditions under which the members of the disadvantaged social groups tend to defend the societal systems that are detrimental to them? What role does the media system play regarding disadvantaged groups' subordinations?

Misrepresentations of events' frequencies by the mass media system are dangerous insofar as they facilitate the emergence of ideologies and impulsive behaviors of social groups, especially violent ones. Misrepresentations by means of the mass media system may also be intentional or thoughtfully planned to dissuade the outburst of violence and decrease dangers. Governments do play active roles in misleading their populaces via mass media systems. Reading declassified government documents allows one to understand that the domestic population, rather than the international community, is generally the population from which top secrets are kept to prevent the society's populace from understanding the intentions, plans, and strategies for the attempts at attaining more power.

Misrepresentations of infrequently occurring events (i.e., falsely representing the events as frequently occurring events instead) via media outlets may lead to the untrustworthiness of the sources and people responsible. The latter types of misrepresentations may lead certain groups to doubt the representations of frequently occurring events that are only very rarely captured in the forms of images and audio recordings, such as police brutality in certain regions.

The event of the African American driver, Rodney King, being pulled over in Los Angeles on March 3, 1991 for exceeding the speed limit, involved a brief car chase and resulted in twenty-one police officers of the Los Angeles Police Department and California Highway Patrol allowing Mr. King to be severely beaten by three white officers (Jacobs, 2004, p. 81). The brutality against Rodney King was captured on film by George Holliday, an observer and amateur cameraman who was filming the incident unbeknownst to the police. Mr. Holliday sold the video to a Los Angeles TV station (ibid.):

> [T]he Rodney King case has become the defining instance of police brutality in Los Angeles, despite the fact that the city paid more than $20 million between 1986- 1990 in judgments, settlements, and jury verdicts against Los Angeles police officers in over 300 lawsuits dealing with the excessive use of force. Despite the frequency with which the Rodney King videotape was broadcast, the build-up to crisis was more gradual than during the uprisings of 1965 or 1992. This can be seen by examining news coverage during the first week after the precipitating events for the three crises.

The heightened importance of an event by means of its overrepresentation within the media is observable and sometimes signified by the sheer number of redundant news articles, television broadcasts etc. However, just the overall amount of coverage of an event does not necessarily determine the social impact or movements that follow the event and its coverage. Jacobs (ibid., pp. 81–82) continues:

> For the six newspapers of the study, the first week's news coverage totaled 203 articles for the 1965 Watts uprisings and 375 articles for the 1992 uprisings, but only forty-one articles during the first week of the 1991 Rodney King crisis. Indeed, it is quite possible that any of the other excessive force cases could have yielded social dramas of the magnitude of Rodney King, just as the impact of the Rodney King beating might not have exceeded that of the cases preceding it.

The video broadcasts perhaps provided the conditions under which the need for excessive newspaper articles was lessened. The recording of the beating allowed Rodney King's victimization to be widely observed by the public. The images of the videotape showed proof of the brutal domination and excessive flailing of a black man by white police officers, and the latter images are and were, in 1991, very relatable and easily associated with the brutal domination of whites over blacks throughout the early history of the American society as well as the during the Civil Rights Movement during the 1960s.

Jacobs (ibid., p. 82) also points out that "there existed a history of conflict between Police Chief Daryl Gates and minority groups in Los Angeles." Moreover, in 1991 the likelihood that amateur cameraperson was both walking around and filming was quite low. The sizes of video cameras were much larger in 1991 than during the 21st century, and many citizens with African descent could immediately form opinions about whether the police officers and police force would have escaped responsibility and justice for committing such violence if they had not been filmed.

The idea that a random and coincidental event of a person at a medium distance (i.e., not too short so that the police fail to notice the camera and not too far away so that the images are viewable and analyzable) who is standing with a video camera is "necessary" for police officers, committing brutalities against black citizens, to be tried in a court of law in ways that demonstrate procedural justice and lengthy investigations of the accused is relevant. The latter idea of "a random cameraperson being needed for justice" is relevant because it does infuriate those who are directly and negatively affected as well as their friends or families.

The idea of the requirement of a random cameraperson for justice for some is one that signifies there are irrational requirements for the fulfillment of justice for some peoples. Such irrational requirements are still relevant today, even though the chances that an amateur cameraperson recording a violent event are much higher than in 1991. Dangerous ideologies can develop from such ideas of unfairness and injustice within the penal system—ideologies of frustration and retaliation, for instance. Many minorities and low-status groups are confronted with their people being shot by police officers, even though they were unarmed. The idea that audio and video recordings are necessary for indictments could very well develop with the increase in the distribution and the ease of access to technologies and may affect multiple groups in the future. On the other hand, other technologies might allow for audio and video recordings to be covered up, allowing for low-status groups to be victimized continuously in the future, too.

The incident with Rodney King may not have involved mostly racist and sadistic motives on part of those three police officers. Yet, the attack was likely perceived by much of the public as an act of racism and sadism, and especially by those who have endured acts that are easily interpreted as racist or sadistic and that were performed by a law enforcement member. For instance, the greater intensity of fear that African Americans experience with police officers is suggestive of the fact that their group endures greater amounts of racist and sadistic acts.

The overabundance of officers who permitted the continuation of the beating or encouraged it but did not participate in walloping Mr. King may have been perceived by the public as being negligent or amused by schadenfreude, to which those, who socially identify themselves with Mr. King, would likely incite outrage. This again can lead to the formation of dangerous legal ideologies about the penal system's inherent unfairness and injustice. The lack of video footage in similar cases leaves much open to public interpretation and allows rumors and hearsay to spread and to color the interpretations.

There is symbolism present within the real story: The conflict between one man who is beaten down repeatedly by his captors and is, ironically, the "King," and, ironically, King was beaten with a "rod," for which his given name, Rodney, is the short form, to wit, Rod. King both, arguably, represents the grandest one as well as one with whom many can also sympathize, identify, and understand in virtue of his confrontation against a greater force, an authority, being outnumbered and being dominated. The irony is that the police failed to spare the rod for Rod, especially in relation to the racial history of referring to black men as "boys" or never attaining adulthood or manhood, despite maturation and the folk saying, "spare the rod and spoil the child." If the symbolism here is disregarded as failing to meaningfully invoke an outnumbered and black King in the face of adversity of violent white power, beating him with rods bearing his own name, then perhaps, at least, for some people the name of the beaten man named "Rodney King" by a rod is more memorable.

Perhaps what we may also acquire from an understanding of Jacobs' analysis is that the overrepresentation of some event by the media, the public broadcast of which is likely to provoke public protests, riots, or violent outbursts, need not involve overrepresentation when certain elements are present that strongly emphasize the role of conflict within the society. The role of the public perception of the event based on the media broadcasts is perhaps greatly influenced by the intensity of how striking and memorable the representations of the event are, especially as an event of conflict involving characters who jeopardize the life or quality of life of another character, with whom identifiable social groups can sympathize in several ways.

Appropriately analyzing the events, such as the Rodney King event, involves triple roles and heightened importance for the mass media systems (e.g., the police beating of Rodney King, the set of news broadcasts of images and words of the beating of Rodney King, and the riots that followed the former two events). That is, what forms the triple roles of events is, first, the event itself, then second, the broadcasts of images and words regarding that event, and third, the events that arise contiguously and perhaps resultantly from the event and broadcasts of them.

What is also necessary to understand to appropriately analyze the events with triple roles and heightened importance for the mass media systems is that issues, such as the weather, as well as the demographics of the population, played important and necessary roles to the extent that if the weather had been well below the freezing temperature the weeks before, during and after the riot, or if the weather had exceeded about 38° C or 100° F during those weeks, or if the population consisted of far fewer males between the ages of fifteen and forty and more elderly people, then the riots following the mass media's broadcasts of the beating of Rodney King on video would almost certainly not have occurred. Preparing for violence and preventing it require considering the ages of the populaces of cities.

Moreover, the facts about whether the rioters had job opportunities, hopes of graduating from some school or university, classes to attend, or work to finish are important ones and crucial for the prediction of riots as well as for any understanding of them before the conditions that facilitate them can be altered via the legal system. For instance, many scholars conclude that young African American males are more likely to go to jail than to attend a college course (Weitzer, 1996; Wordes & Bynum, 1995). On the other hand, what would have occurred during the week of the Rodney King Riots, if the hundreds of people who were perceived by police as being the most likely candidates to riot had been sent letters explaining that they had won significant amounts of money in a lottery, or, better yet, if they had been sent letters that described jobs, studies and training opportunities for them? It would at least appear that the potential for a riot allows us to weigh the costs of violence and destruction of the city against the costs of multiple preventive measures, and the occurrences of riots and their costs justify expenditures for reducing violence and destruction.

Of course, there are other events that also have three-way roles and heightened importance with their occurrences, coverages via media, and social impacts that occur as results of them. These events may also involve the increased susceptibility of a society to undergo destruction and violence that is wrought by the citizens themselves, even if the society has been influenced by foreign agents. In many of these situations, the peoples' perceptions of their leadership become increasingly important.

An example of a social event and its representations directly affecting the entire planet is the destruction of the World Trade Center buildings, which was immediately—and has been constantly—broadcast worldwide. The September 11th events' statuses as tragedy and terror facilitated a moratorium to allowing foreigners, i.e., without official permission, to enter the vast number of US military bases around the world, which had contributed to significant cultural exchanges before September 2001.

The emotions of fear, sadness, dismay and vengeance have been expressed in quite obvious ways concerning the experiences of so many people impacted by the occurrences on September 11th. As a result, many voluntarily joined or supported the military and other security forces, which have wrought stricter policies, more manpower, and technology available at airports, borders, etc., and which may be well-defined as reactions to insecurities formed because of the September attacks. Massive amounts of depictions via the mass media system and globally broadcast representations of conspiracy theories have been put forth by individuals who reuse the images and soundbites from the attacks to reformulate many possible interpretations of the events.

The obviousness of the latter emotions of fear, sadness, confusion, and dismay, which are associated with tragedies, may well detract from the emotions experienced and expressed by those who are members of opposing ideologies since the latter people likely underwent feelings of schadenfreude and zeal that come with successfully met goals of strategic and destructive plans (Chiao & Mathur, 2010; Cikara et al., 2011; Cikara & Fiske, 2012). The experiences of malicious joy have not been obvious, but it can well be argued that they are more useful to understand the origins of these experiences (i.e., amongst the social settings making them more probable to arise within each person) and for preventing similar happenings. For instance, the malicious glee that is felt by an individual is stronger when he judges that the competence of others is ranked highly, and the warmth, kindness or generosity is ranked lowly (Cikara et al., 2010; Cikara & Fiske, 2012).

Some events involving schadenfreude are relatively unimportant, but when the events become broadcasted, they receive a heightened importance for some people, and can thereby lead to violent and destructive behaviors. The Florida pastor burning a Koran on September 11, 2010, was a very significant social event, according to many religious people who uphold the sanctity of the holy book. Yet the burning of any single book that goes unnoticed by the masses is insignificant on its own.

The world broadcast of the burning of the holy book sparked a series of social movements with murderous consequences largely caused by the global mass media system via the spread of images and words and perhaps a lack of understanding concerning the role of soft power involved in the attempt to undermine the religion of Islam (See Ch. 4.4). Presumably, the global mass media system functions largely to attain profit because it is corporate-driven, and it attempts to represent shocking, violent, destructive, and terrifying events, amongst others, to maximize audiences' attention spans upon the media long enough to increase the frequency of people buying mass media products and services.

The media system's managers utilize their power and influence to prevent members of the media from acquiring the responsibility and answerability for their combined efforts that support the system controlled by corporations. Media coverage is filtered through the emotions of those who manage it.

Consider the media coverage of a country that is about to go to war with another one, that is already at war with another country, or that just finished the last battle with another country. Since the country's populace is composed of mostly women and children, presumably, an accurate representation of the other country would consist of enormous amounts of coverage of women and children, and yet we are hard-pressed to find such coverage since the coverage is almost entirely of men who are at their sexual reproductive peaks and of military age, instead.

The abovementioned pastor's wishes and thoughtlessness, the killings of soldiers within Islamic countries (i.e., directly resulting from the broadcasts of the burning holy book), and the roles of the people attempting to honor, respect, and defend the sanctity of their sacred book all happened in the latter order, namely, the burning, the broadcasting and then the reactionary responses of killers who were offended by the offensive action of the pastor. Yet the mass media systems' roles in the social outcome are greatly underemphasized, even though if the mass media system had displayed a caricature of the burning Koran instead, the impact of that image being broadcast to the same masses would have likely resulted in violence and destruction, too.

The latter sorts of examples raise the questions about how exactly the mass media organizations can be held accountable for their contributions to dangerous ideologies, violence, and destruction that are triggered by offensive images and words. Obviously, radio, television, newspaper, magazine and satellite broadcasting cannot successfully escape being held directly responsible for broadcasting misinformation that their own nation is under attack by a neighboring country, that a natural disaster will happen in the very near future etc. Such broadcasts would likely cause massive panics with people fleeing cities, for instance.

However, other events, which the mass media system broadcasts, involve all sorts of mistakes or inaccuracies, some of which sometimes increase the news ratings for organizations. The broadcasts also often lead to panics, protests, riots, destruction, violence, killings etc. Consider the image in 1990 of Vlade Divac that was taken after he and the Yugoslavian national team won the gold medal in the World Games for basketball. The image shows that Mr. Divac (i.e., a Serbian man and 21st century NBA Hall of Famer) took and dropped a Croatian flag on the ground, and the image may have been used as propaganda by the Croatian media to attain support for gaining independence from Yugoslavia, which occurred very violently in the Yugoslavian Wars for independence from 1991 to 2001.

Another problem that we face as analysts of the events, their broadcasts, their societal impacts, consequences, and interpretations is that there is no separation of the events from the broadcasts because they are inevitably intertwined to the extent that we cannot know exactly what would happen if the broadcasts would have been handled much differently, except for some. For instance, we know that if the pastor would have privately burned a book, then at least some of the destruction, violence, and killings of American troops in Afghanistan would not have occurred (i.e., as far as we can, presumably, know counterfactual conditionals).

For the latter sorts of reasons, it behooves us to consider placing editorial teams and journalists in positions of responsibility as professionals (i.e., where they understand their responsibilities), to promote journalists and mass media broadcasters as those who honorably give us knowledge and provide information, and to demote them for negligence and misinformation. In some sense, there is nothing more damaging to societies, regarding violence and destruction, that coincides with the dissemination of misinformation than creative writers or novelists who works as a journalist without scruples. Journalists have profound impact on legislation, too.

Indisputably, the experiences of tragedy and terror and repeated broadcasts of them contributed to motivating policy changes that brought about the ever more secretive nature of the US military since September 2001. Certain types of heightenings of security were made. The heightened security was instantiated at the expense of dramatic reductions of intimately friendly relations with natives living near US military bases and losses of their access to parts of US military bases abroad in their nations' own borders.

"Security," which is *Sicherheit* in German, is an idea that incorporates notions of knowledge or certainty (i.e., "*sicher*" in German means "certain") as well as safety (Bauman, 1998; Freedman, 2003). If something is unsustainable, it lacks security, regardless of whether it is an organism, culture, information system, societal system, or subsystem, such as the legal system. The idea of security is not best conceived as an end-state of a goal but rather as a dynamic attempt to coordinate cost-effectiveness of legal, cultural, and information technologies with the formation of more stable production and reproduction of efficient services.

Undoubtedly, there are also psychological conceptions of motivations to overcome insecurities that play interrelated roles with the idea of security, concerning the mental or physical health of the individual as well as the individual's necessities and motivations, e.g., the need to feel safe (Maslow, 1943). The psychological motivations to overcome insecurities are typically inextricably tied to the insecurities of the family and more abstractly related to the social groups with which one identifies oneself.

Perhaps a misconception about security, which involves the latter relation of the social group to the psychological conception of insecurities, is that security includes the idea of the secure force making the first attack or being the aggressor. Preemptive attacks may be principally orchestrated by a leader (e.g., one with the legal authority to wage war, which some presidents and prime ministers lack) to attack before another social group is expected to attack one's ingroup. Of course, executing a first attack ensures a conflict, multiple uncertainties, and the lack of control of the outcome of the conflict for the dominating force. Wars and violent conflicts often result in grave losses to the security of both the attacker and attacked for the latter reasons.

Generally, decisions to engage in wars and violent conflicts are decided by lawmakers who are susceptible to following tenets of their own ideologies' arguments and further susceptible to their own insecurities, which are exacerbated by certain perceived states of emergency (Augustine-Adams, 2005). Impatience of legislators concerning diplomacy couples dangerously and consistently with soldiers' "happy trigger fingers" via what we may hypothesize as being positively correlated with the early onsets of wars. The role of waiting periods of time and providing suggestions for postponements of attacks are crucial factors to consider for increasing security, especially during perceived states of emergency or crisis. Waiting and producing suggestions for postponing conflict involve reducing violent reactions at least during some time span.

The September 2001 attacks affected ideological conceptions of the interrelations between knowledge, security, secrecy, and a welcoming openness of cultural exchanges in respect to changing the American military ideology (Zedner, 2009; Ackerman 2004; Tribe & Gudridge 2004; Agamben 2004). The attacks created a prolonged state of crisis and emergency and wrought the power of the plenary laws (Augustine-Adams, 2005). Friendly invitations and cultural exchanges with non-US citizens living near US military bases were dramatically reduced during the aftermath of the September 2001 attacks. It is questionable whether changing perceptions, ideologies, and varying amounts of anti-Americanism will actually contribute to increasing the danger of US citizens working in foreign countries and on US military bases, despite intensified security authorization procedures.

For instance, even part-time faculty members employed by universities with teaching contracts on the military bases were not permitted to enter without preauthorized and official invitations in certain countries, such as Germany. The author of this book, you now read, serves as one example of such a university faculty member and American citizen who was denied entrance to the American military base in Wiesbaden, Germany in 2012 during the office hours of his own university colleagues at the University of Maryland University College on the US military base. I held my passport and was not permitted to enter without an invitation letter.

Fewer invitations for experiencing US culture abroad have resulted in an undesirable set of changes, if not damaging alterations, in communications. The legal actions abroad have not been nearly as serious as the domestic situation in the United States of America. For instance, Freedman (2003, p. 752) maintained that "censorship can be imposed, political rights suspended, young men conscripted, and aliens deported all in the name of security." Moreover, these sorts of changes are legal in nature and concern the procedures for governmental employees' actions that were made during emotional moments caused by a perceived emergency. This emergency status of the USA is something about which citizens of every nation have been reminded ever since the mass media began repeatedly broadcasting the September attacks. Kif Augustine-Adams (2005, pp. 702–703) writes:

> Prior to September 11, 2001, it seemed improbable that Congress would again exercise its plenary power over immigration to exclude immigrants based on race, as it did in the nineteenth century Chinese Exclusion Acts. The Exclusion Acts and Supreme Court case law upholding them spawned the plenary power doctrine, a doctrine which, as its name implies, articulates Congress' unfettered power over immigration. As the Supreme Court stated in *Mathews v. Diaz*, "in the exercise of its broad power over naturalization and immigration, Congress regularly makes rules that would be unacceptable if applied to citizens."

Plenary power is power, especially for legal decisions, that involves absolute control and no review of checks and balances by other systems. Without having limitations, the federal government can quickly make decisions and implement policies that would normally require slower processes of approval. The United States Constitution and laws allow for the implementation of plenary power, although in the USA they are used infrequently. Kif Augustine-Adams (2005, p. 703) continues:

> It is no longer a remote possibility that Congress would consider discrimination in immigration legislation, discrimination based on race, religion, or other criteria that would be unconstitutional if applied to citizens, but which the plenary power doctrine allows when noncitizens and immigration are at issue. For example, as a matter of administrative law though not congressional mandate, the United States Department of Justice instituted, in mid-2002, an immigration registration system that required nationals of certain Arab and Muslim countries to be fingerprinted and photographed at the U.S. border prior to entry.

The discriminatory practices are not restricted to just those from Arab and Islamic countries because others who appear to be or to dress like Muslims or Arabs have also been more frequently questioned, interrogated etc. after September 2001. We may hypothesize that people with lighter and whiter skin are given advantages insofar as their time and efforts are not wasted as frequently, especially at US border crossings and in airports. Kif Augustine-Adams (ibid.)

> When responding to criticism of its proposed registration requirement, the Department of Justice invoked the plenary power doctrine to "strongly disagree that the rule is invidiously discriminatory." Relying on numerous Supreme Court cases, the Department stated bluntly, "The political branches of the government have plenary authority in the immigration area."

Consider societies in states of emergency. Augstine-Adams' (2005) analysis of the use of plenary powers concerns the full power given to the United States Congress concerning some aspect of law. States of crises require greater investments of time and energy to reach an understanding of social conditions and changes in directions of leaderships. Investigations of the conditions and changes in directions of leadership during times of crisis can be dangerous because descriptions of what the leaders are doing (i.e., as opposed to what leaders want the public to know about their decisions) can place the leaders in opposition with the investigators.

When leaders terminate directors of investigatory agencies, there is room for much concern. Instead people invest their time reading mass-produced information that involves fast circulations, less attention to methods for attaining knowledge, less revision, less reliance upon court cases and their critiques, less focus on prior ways that leaders have managed crises, and such investments of time and efforts for investigative analyses are, of course, not only less sophisticated but able to misdirect and reproduce ideologies.

The efficiency with which communications have been occurring have diminished the delay time to an almost instantaneous time interval, during which people across the planet communicate via the internetworking of the World Wide Web and relatively private intranets. The entire world now has a virtual connection that even stretches into outer space for astronauts residing in the international space station and two land rovers and three satellites orbiting Mars in 2012. Space law is a newly emerging field that incorporates all the technology, data and images collected in outer space from satellites, for example, as well as the events that occur on Earth that are related to outer space, such as objects that fall on the Earth's surface and the liabilities for those objects (Tronchetti, 2013, p. viii).

Communications are not only incredibly fast but are becoming well-organized by the sheer number of people they aim to affect. National security agencies reserve the rights to remain secretive, intercept, overhear, and oversee communications. Thereby legal, practical, and philosophical sets of problems arise: What are the legal limitations of privacy once security (e.g., at the national, border crossing, city level etc.) has become compromised? What are the legal limits of security when realizations of the lack of privacy occur and threaten security via serious demands and intentions to maintain or come to greater conditions of privacy?

Edward Snowden discovered that the intelligence community is continuously accessing images and words exchanged, saved, and thought to be private between citizens. In many cases, the Central Intelligence Agency and the National Security Agency activate computers, cellular phones, and other devices to access the audio and video functions for surveillance. The agencies recorded images and sounds unbeknownst to owners of the devices. Recordings facilitate extortions, stalking, and other rampant violations of privacy. Intelligence industry workers can utilize nude images of people who merely undress in front of their computers that they had recently deactivated. They can discover sexual relations thought to be secretly held between citizens, find out information about insider business deals, and many other secretive and legal actions. They can use images to exploit, extort, and gain competitive advantages over governments.

Another issue that concerns the latter covert actions by the intelligence industry is that when intelligence workers activate people's devices, especially with cameras and microphones, the devices require more energy. So, by activating the people's devices without permission, the governmental agencies require these people to use extra electricity, pay for extra electricity, as well as to pay for any other services that allow them access to the internet, which the people may have intended not to use or to just use them sparingly. These agencies are basically stealing electricity and stealing access to internet services of the people who undergo surveillance, which is direct exploitation and theft that falls into the category of alegal actions that are socially tolerated because of security-related ideologies (See Ch. 2).

If precise enough measurements can be taken about the consumption of energy for the devices' software programs, especially cameras, microphones, and global positioning systems, individuals who constantly use the devices could determine that extra energy for certain programs had been used. What this type of surveillance promotes are forms of paranoia at the level of the individual and societal paranoia where multitudes begin to act as if they live under the conditions of a panopticon[4] in Foucault's philosophy. These abovementioned issues, which were largely voiced by Edward Snowden, directly concern legal systems and their roles in the ideological attempts to increase security with compromises in respect to human privacy, as well as human social and civil behaviors.

Another issue of concern is that a creation of a dominance and subordination relationship along the lines of information technology begins to develop, although it is different from other relations of dominance and subordination. People who generally have access to the information of others and who can more readily observe them are generally higher within some sort of hierarchical system and institution. However, intelligence workers observe all sorts of people from rich to poor, with or without political power, and it is questionable what happens because of this form of dominance. Some of the intelligence workers spying on foreign leaders or accessing the social media profiles of adolescents may be observed by their superiors, but at some level of the hierarchy

4 Within a panopticon the individual is in a situation where the individual can be easily observed without being able to observe the observers of him or her. Prisons, corporate work stations and schools are often constructed or rearranged in ways that allow authority figures at the top of the hierarchy to watch and listen without being noticed and to have certain areas of access (e.g., teachers' lounges, guard towers, and offices) that are off limits to subordinates. Managers sometimes have work stations that are behind lower level employees so that managers more frequently observe what their subordinates do and so that subordinate workers' behaviors are altered because of their work environment.

of the intelligence workers, the institution ends, and there is an absolute failure to observe the highest levels of intelligence workers or their superiors who may understand very little about the actions of their subordinates. Of course, the superiors can be placed under investigation as well, though.

The developments of human societies over the last five hundred years took place from the least developed national economies, the "underdeveloped countries" with large primary sectors of agriculture, mining, forestry, and fishing, which required many thousands of years to develop from the first civilizations with farming. The next stage of the development became the "developing countries," undergoing the processes of industrialization with the creations of factories and much larger construction and manufacturing sectors in comparison to the primary sectors of these economies transitioning from agrarian societies to industrializing ones. During the 20th century, many countries de-industrialized via having their manufacturing, packaging and other secondary sector jobs and industries placed within other economies that mass-produce consumer goods, and these de-industrialized economies have become service economies with vast numbers of jobs within the tertiary sectors.

In the future, we may even witness such a growth of the range of intelligence services and other industries in the quaternary sectors that entire economies become based upon these sorts of industries (i.e., research and development, intelligence, information and communication technology, and media) so that the knowledge sector of the economy of some nation becomes the main sector for economic activity and employment. The functions of such an economy based on an enlarged quaternary sector on the world stage are mysterious, but would be, presumably, less mysterious to economists of the hyperdeveloped economy.

The likelihood of the development of such a knowledge-based economy is greater with the development of artificial intelligence, robotics, and other means by which many types of employment positions in the service industries could be replaced (e.g., financial, banking, legal services, cashiers, military, education, distribution etc.) with artificial intelligence and robots. Yet the replacement of the service-based economy with a knowledge-based economy would appear to be one that may exclude humans entirely from many of the positions of employment. For these reasons, we are in greater need of professional ethics, which demands fairness, respect, and justice for workers, despite changes in systems that can make employees redundant and therefore unnecessary or inefficient for the continuation of businesses. Legal systems are the systems in place that are necessary for the legal and contractual agreements of employees and businesses to be respected and to satisfy the requirement of fairness.

Why should we care about legal systems in virtue of our own personal feelings of security? The recognition of the way nations (dis)respect their neighbors at their borders, the manner in which societies allow their wealthiest to accumulate riches after tax laws and their poorest to benefit from social programs or not, and the ways that nations (man)handle their low-status groups, as well as the environments in which they live, such as minorities and the poverty-stricken people in ghettos or cheap housing, depend fundamentally upon nations' legal systems, and their subsystems, to wit, legislatures, law enforcement systems, court systems, penal and civil law systems. These subsystems of law make law, enforce law, interpret law, and enforce law again, respectively. At each stage of each legal process, there are groups of people who are affected in virtue of the reductions of their overall amounts of security, whether they are legitimate business owners and employees or drug dealers in cities that employ increased efforts to enforce laws prohibiting illicit drugs.

Interpretations of law occur at each stage of the legal process. The legislators and law enforcement agents must interpret law as being new or outdated, as being fair or unfair, as being relevant or irrelevant, as being moral or immoral, if enforced, for instance, because, otherwise, they begin to lose their humanity, their abilities to sympathize, their capabilities of judging fairly and begin, instead, to function robotically for a flawed system. One might maintain that interpretations of law by law enforcement agents undergo a stabilization process with innovative technologies for observation and review, such as enhanced video and audio recording devices. Lawyers often either reinforce old interpretations or attempt to make others accept new ones.

In many instances legislators, law enforcement agents, or lawyers even side with career criminals who engage in illegal underground economic or black market trade, defending them, having mutually beneficial relations with them, ignoring their illegal activities, partnering with them, participating with them in their illegal activities, and plea-bargaining with them. Yet the law or the legal system is not ordinarily recognized by most scholars as necessarily involving the regular engagement in these activities. Members of the legal institution who behave in such ways sometimes place their legal careers in jeopardy when they perform these actions.

Plea-bargaining, as a means by which career criminals are protected by law enforcement, is often made to acquire criminal informants (i.e., snitches). The United States legal system contains an abundance of snitches. According to Natapoff (2009, p. 3):

> The idea behind snitching is simple—a suspect provides incriminating information about someone else in exchange for a deal, maybe the

> chance to walk away, or a lesser charge or sentence. In practice, however, informant deals are as varied as the crimes they involve. Some are quick, informal, and routine. In the so-called buy, bust, flip technique, a police officer might release a drug addict or dealer in exchange for a tip. Other informant deals are complex, high-profile, and span many years.

Within multiple Hollywood films and television series, the snitches are often portrayed as being outsmarted by police officers. In multiple films and series, one officer plays the "good cop" who pretends to be on the side of the snitch and to protect his or her best interests, whereas the other officer plays the "bad cop" who pretends to merely be stopped from extorting or torturing the potential snitch by the good cop. Natapoff (ibid.) continues:

> In 2006, corrupt lobbyist Jack Abramoff avoided decades in prison by agreeing to snitch on the politicians he bribed. Fifteen years before that, hit man "Sammy the Bull" Gravano testified against mafia boss John Gotti in exchange for drastically reduced punishment and witness protection. The power and flexibility of the informant deal has made it a ubiquitous weapon in the law enforcement arsenal … The most dangerous versions of snitching tend to occur when law enforcement deploys criminals to generate new cases.

Much like some of the intelligence community's practices for the public, the practice of having criminal informants provide information in exchange for reduced sentences, freedom or for their protection to go into hiding (e.g., witness protection programs) is unregulated, kept secret from the public, and therefore it allows for more frequent occurrence of crimes, such as extortion, corruption, and inaccuracies regarding informants providing misinformation or law enforcement agents intentionally or inadvertently providing informants with misinformation that the informants merely confirm because, for instance, they often realize that, in certain cases, a confirmation of their own beliefs is what the police want to hear.

It is questionable and problematic how this system of (mis)information exchanges with criminal informants functions in respect to its utilization of less educated people, the poverty-stricken, racial minorities, drug addicts and those without proper legal advocates. Although this system of snitches is often the decisive factor regarding the results of tens of millions of legal cases and law enforcement investigations, the governmental systems with checks and balances performed via the judicial system, the mass media system, the public, and the legislative system are typically evaded. Moreover, the system of criminal informants has tendencies to expand rapidly (ibid.).

A conception of the legal system and a theory of legal systems require focus on the study of the nature of law within societal systems. The developing concept of the legal system also requires investigations of conclusive implications and assumptions that underlie the fact that any law must be a part of a legal system (Raz, 1980, p. 1). Joseph Raz (ibid., p. 2) also argues that legal systems do not necessarily share any particular structure, any universal relations between laws, or any type of content in common amongst all legal systems.

However, it is arguable that every legal system (i.e., ancient or modern, African, American, Asian, Australian or European) includes means by which crime is facilitated with combinations of several types of roles coupled with certain situations within legal systems, such as successful defense attorneys or legal advocates who serve career criminals and deal-makers for criminal informants. Crime is also facilitated via some of the roles that undercover agents play. The reasons for a legal system's facilitation of situations that allow crime (i.e., to have reduced chances of penalizations regarding their frequencies and intensities) may also be based on the notion of security,[5] which coincides relevantly with the need to stabilize expectations about the procedures of law. The clandestine career criminals will never lack experienced defense attorneys since identifications of criminals and non-criminals present practical challenges.

One system of thought supports the current system of criminal justice that works with snitches and maintains that if each criminal informant's plea bargain was nonexistent within some legal system, larger criminal operations would more frequently go unnoticed. Many innocent people would likely be penalized more harshly, and crime would increase under such circumstances because the valuable information would less likely be provided without external incentives or motivations (e.g., witness protection or reduced sentences). Accused or convicted people of crimes who hold valuable information would be less likely to provide the information, especially insofar as the information could bring them into further conflict with high-level criminals. However, the latter assertions and argument do not entail that the US justice system functions efficiently as an institution that reduces crime and violence with its current system of snitches and underhanded tactics in using them. The current

5 Importantly, associations with the notion of security are also subject to being an aspect of a legal ideology, which imposes certain ideas and ideals on the notion of security via false consciousness.

practices with criminal informants are very likely to be detrimental to the USA legal system.

According to Joseph Raz (1980), any comprehensive and consistent theory of legal system invokes methodologies for coming to understand and problem-solve issues concerning content, existence, identity, and structure of legal systems. Comparative analyses are implemented that involve comparing the similarities and differences between various legal systems and searching for commonalities that belong to each legal system.

If we temporarily refrain from the consideration of causation[6] in relation to legal systems, and thereby we avoid placing greater importance upon the origins of disorderly or destructive acts and the laws that follow and prohibit these acts, then we may consider that many of the features held in common by all legal systems allow us to form a theory of legal systems that involves any legal system functioning with semi-destructive processes that alter the system via promoting the disorder that the system generally functions to eradicate.

There are many types of examples of destructive acts that are systematically performed by the members of the legal institution, such as criminal informants being released with minimized penalties or without any penalty for their known wrongdoings and crimes, especially those who are expected to commit future crimes, criminal defense attorneys who defend wrongdoers, especially those who the lawyers knew were guilty, and undercover police officers who purposefully engage in crimes to retain their statuses of being undercover.

Scholars have argued that societal subsystems, such as legal systems, are autopoietic systems (Teubner, Nobles & Schiff, 2003; Teubner, 1993; Luhmann, 1986; Luhmann, 1981). Legal systems are autopoietic systems. Autopoietic systems (i.e., the systems that can reproduce and maintain themselves), such as organisms, often place themselves within conditions during which they undergo increased amounts of stress (Maturana & Varela, 1980). That is, autopoietic systems oftentimes test themselves and their capabilities and arrive at realizations through processes involving trials and errors. That is, autopoietic systems make attempts and mistakes from which systematic learning processes are placed at considerable advantages when the systems realize errors after having controlled the variables that resulted in these errors.

Gunther Teubner (1993) argued that law can reproduce itself as a system of communication networks and that law comes to realize itself as a system of interference with different autonomous networks of communication within

6 "Causation" always includes a cause and an effect and involves the necessary or sufficient conditions for events to occur in successive orders invariably and contiguously in space and time.

society. One such notable type of interference with networks of communication in society are those that arise from organized crime. It is obvious, for instance, that legal systems produce profound effects upon the type of language (e.g., jargon, slang etc.), amount, and frequency of communications used to describe illegal products and illegal services from black market business activity.[7]

The theory of legal autopoiesis maintains that society is notably a communication system with several different subsystems within it, such as the economic, legal, and political subsystems of the societal system. The latter three subsystems of society contain their own distinct communication subsystems, which each have their own code to make systematic determinations (Teubner, Nobles & Schiff, 2003).

The economic system has the code that leads to perceptions of the world in virtue of losses and profits or payment and non-payment. The profit-loss or payment-non-payment codes are the divisions by which the world is observed, economically speaking. From an economic perspective, everything becomes interpretable regarding some payment or its exclusion insofar as whether the agent at hand can produce future payments or not or profits or losses. Prebble (2008) argues that even income tax law has an autopoietic nature that involves a direct detachment from the profits of businesses. The detachment allows for the independence of each system (i.e., they remain separate and distinct from each other), although they have legally necessary interactions at regular intervals.

The medical system encodes things as healthy and unhealthy. The political system encodes events as winning or losing votes. The legal system encodes events as legal and illegal either implicitly or explicitly, which also places this binary scheme (i.e., legal/illegal) as a code that differentiates between distinct types of facts and that serves as a structure for the operations of the legal system (Luhmann, 2004, pp. 173–196).

The code of the legal system works insofar as a positive value, legality, is granted once the fact of the matter conforms to the system's norms. Alternatively, the violations of the norms of the system involve the applications of the negative value, illegality. For instance, in Columbia during the 1980s the farmers of coca plants or field hands who picked coca leaves might very well have been engaging in legal activities and so may have the distributors of the

7 By "business activity" what is meant is that the factors of production, namely, natural resources (e.g., coca leaves, oil etc.), human resources (e.g., distributors, chemists, managers, security etc.), human-made resources (e.g., trucks, tables, buildings, phones, mixers etc.) are all combined by optimistic and risk-taking entrepreneurs who have knowledge of the ways to combine the latter types of resources to produce goods and services (e.g., cocaine).

coca leaves, although the chemists who prepared cocaine with the coca leaves and the entrepreneurs who owned the business of cocaine production were performing actions encoded as "illegal" ones by the Colombian legal system.

The latter code is simple and allows for the facilitation of institutionalization processes (ibid., p. 180). Even though some politicians are lawmakers, political communications and legal communications require acts of interpretation, evaluation, and translation into the codes of each of the other systems for messages derived from one system to be communicated effectively within the other system. Teubner, Nobles, and Schiff (2003, p. 898) maintain that:

> To speak in a courtroom, one has to speak law. Whatever political cause one wishes to advance has to be pleaded, as a cause of action. A claim for resources for doctors has to become an action for breach of contract, or a judicial review, or an action for damages. To turn politics into law, one has to stop speaking politics and start speaking law. One cannot advance a claim in law by arguing about the interest groups affected, or the votes that can be gained, as one might in politics.

Within the latter theorists' framework, the systems are distinguished greatly via their encodings and communications. Teubner, Nobles and Schiff (ibid.) continue:

> To make a political dispute into a legal one, one has to reconstitute it within existing legal communications, in order for the law to recognise the political claim. And of course it works the other way. Those politicians who are dissatisfied with legal decisions, don't have to speak about case reports, pleadings, orders, etc. They can talk about a legal decision in political terms—public interest, votes lost, economic losses, etc.

All the latter causes, decisions, actions, damages, disputes, cases, pleas, verdicts, votes, and interest groups are subject to broadcasting via the mass media system, which also plays extremely important roles regarding security. The mass media system is crucial for national security and security at the international, communal, corporate, and city levels. If we apply the legal theory of autopoiesis to explain certain facets of entertainment portrayed by the media system, which is diverse in its range, because many types of events can entertain people, we are confronted with one intriguing set of events often displayed as the secretive workings of legal systems.

What the mass media broadcasts and what serves a certain role regarding security is questionable and problematic since many instances of legislators, law enforcement agents, and lawyers siding with criminals who engage in illegal underground economic or black market trade, defending them, entering mutually beneficial relations with them, ignoring illegal activities, partnering with criminals, participating with them in their illegal activities, and plea-bargaining with them are all displayed as events of entertainment. The latter forms of entertainment are not only presented within films and TV series but also newspapers as images and words about events that occurred in the society and thusly impacts it.

Moreover, the encoding of the economic system becomes very relevant insofar as incorporated and unincorporated businesses that compose much of the mass media system present the events as news stories after they have undergone the encoding of the economic system. That is, the stories can be analyzed before publication in virtue of their expected potentials to generate profit or loss. Obviously, those stories expected to generate more profit will have increased chances of being published within certain confines typically (e.g., retaining journalistic integrity and as frontpage articles). Many of the mass media giants have had billions of dollars of assets since the 1980s and act in ways to protect their wealth.

Of course, if the latter description aptly describes much of the mass media system, then those in positions of privilege or power (e.g., people who regularly and willingly share information with the media), say, over certain editors, and those with greater financial resources can have stories shortened, altered, or prevented from publication. For some of the latter reasons, Herman and Chomsky (1988, p. xlix) conclude that nonprofit organizations and networks and stations that are community-based are crucial for democracy as well as for a politically and socially successful society.

During times of relative peace and prosperity, the legal system itself will support, defend, and engage in some of the behaviors that nonetheless contribute to the set of conditions that the criminal justice system aims to eradicate. This latter aspect of the legal system is one of the most entertaining aspects displayed in movies (e.g., the American films, The Departed (2006) and Reservoir Dogs (1992), Deep Cover (1992) and the Hong Kong film, City On Fire (1987)). As portrayed, the law implements controlled threats against itself. It breaks down the legal system to rebuild itself with revised and improved structural components.

The Departed (2006) is an excellent portrayal of fictitious but believable events occurring in and around the Massachusetts State Police in Boston. After realizing that organized crime had already infiltrated the police department in Boston with loyal recruits to the criminal organizations, the police department recruits top secret police officers who are only identified as police by the pair of policemen who recruited them. One of the secret officers frequently engages in illegal activity to prevent the discovery of his identity. The police infiltrate the criminal organizations and temporarily join them, partaking in their illegal activities, too. Police also aim to prevent major crimes from occurring and plan to deliver evidence for convictions against criminal masterminds and bosses. These criminals are ordinarily undetectable or are resilient to incriminating evidence surrounding major crimes, in which they are involved and from which they profit.

Police officers sometimes place themselves in situations where they witness and allow murders as well as commit assault, fraud, and other illegal activities when they serve as undercover operatives planning to capture the major criminal players and have them convicted within courts of law. In the latter cases, society undergoes instances of alegality insofar as the police may perform illegal actions that become legitimized by the criminal justice system itself, and obviously some of these acts challenge the distinction between what is legal and illegal because the small group of officers is the one that makes the determinations about the severity of the crime that is temporarily permitted (i.e., police at least lengthen the waiting period before taking criminals who are part of a larger scheme into custody) or even outright performed by the undercover police. Undercover police officers may stage fake murders to foil criminal organizations.

The entertainment industry and mass media systems portray the aspect of law enforcement in cases where the agents are especially conflicted and undecided about whether to continue with such undercover operations. Law enforcement agents are presented by the media as fearing the wrath of the criminals, performing acts against their own wishes, and begrudgingly permitting known criminals to perform them as well. Sometimes the undercover police are also portrayed as gaining respect and loyalty for at least one criminal against whom they work. Sometimes the police are portrayed as having overwhelming desires to confide in some of those criminals who can lead to their demises (e.g., the end of the film Reservoir Dogs). The police even sympathize with a few of the criminals and sometimes help them escape the penalties of the criminal justice system.

Films, such as Catch Me If You Can (2002), portray convicted criminals who serve very small portions of their prison sentences, especially for fraud and theft via identity deceptions, and who are subsequently chosen to work with law enforcement to capture those who similarly commit such crimes. The film, Catch Me If You Can, is based on the life of a successful businessman born in the late 1940s named Frank Abagnale Jr. who impersonated a lawyer, pilot, medical doctor, and professor and who committed multiple accounts of check fraud for millions of dollars and other currencies, and later became an investigator of fraud (Salinger, 2004, p. 418).

Legal systems test themselves in many of the latter respects. They temporarily allow crimes to happen to attain access to more clandestine communications with less interference. They gain access to more information and increase kinds of misconduct they generally aim to eradicate, albeit in somewhat controlled manners. Legal systems, presumably, aim to eradicate or at least diminish wrongdoings, fraud, theft, and violence. This can come from a threat-making and violent authority but with some amount of legitimacy, too.

Autopoietic systems often test themselves in numerous ways, such as organisms that refrain from eating during periods in which food resources are plentiful. This may allow for more efficient adaptations to occur during periods with less resources. Bodybuilders train their muscles that undergo processes during which the muscles are broken down with soreness and lactic acid. This allows for increases in muscle mass. Martial artists also train so that their bodies can withstand high velocity blows with high impacts against the shins and other body parts. These are all examples of breaking down and testing systems in ways that may increase the defenses of the autopoietic systems in measurable ways.

In the previous examples, the type of events described in the American films are social systems breaking themselves down and testing themselves to strengthen their defenses and attain useful information about communications from other social systems. Whether the forms of testing and feedback can or do extend to all the aspects of the legal system is questionable. Consider whether the feedback attained from testing some part of the legal system would allow for the facilitations of improvements of the system.

Consider whether the legal system could test itself via the introduction of bogus laws brought into the bill and lawmaking processes. Such a proposal for a bill was made by congresswoman Jessica Farrar in the US state of Texas in the 21st century. It aimed to outlaw males masturbating, including in their homes. It was read in the Texas House of Representatives. It served as a form of protest against congressmen passing bills over women's reproductive rights.

Like the undercover police officer[8] who reveals herself at some point to some people, members of the party who pass the bogus bill could reveal the

8 An analogous example could be an undercover police officer joining a group of violent illegal drug distributors or illicit weapons dealers and committing crimes to acquaint the policing system and criminal justice system with more elaborate and important communications. The officer will interfere and finally will make arrests for perhaps more substantial reasons. Bogus proposals for laws test these legal subsystems, analogously.

bill as a fraudulent one that was used to test whether support for the bill is likely to involve favoritism on part of members of the party who introduce it. It could test the legislative system's process of lawmaking and introduce the flaw in the system thereafter. Lawmakers could be persuaded or required to promote and allow for fake bills to be presented intermittently to bolster support for them, despite their sketchy or maleficent content. Assessments of such cases could be valuable for understanding, improving, and preventing unfairness and injustices in the legislative branch of government.

Likewise, the judicial system could be presented infrequently and sporadically with unreal cases involving actors who test judges and juries on their abilities to make decisions with fairness and justice. Even fake judges, fake lawyers, or fake defendants as actors could legitimately test the courts, especially in certain areas that undergo social problems concerning procedural justice. The potential benefits of applying the principle of the test[9] to all areas of law appears to fit within the legal theory of autopoiesis. Moreover, the public broadcast of such investigative procedures and their results would be thoroughly informative if properly undertaken.

These ideas are commonly applied by systems to themselves because diverse types of autonomous systems in society (i.e., as well as organisms) test themselves. Autopoietic systems test themselves via breaking down parts of themselves that these systems aim, in general, to strengthen. The education system is an example of an autopoietic type of system as well. The system does offer examples of these tests.

Jane Elliot's 1968 famous social experiment, which was inspired by the mass media's broadcasts after the assassination of Martin Luther King Jr. and some racially discriminatory comments and presumptions within the questions of reporters, provides an example of a teaching method that tests the strength of part of the education system. Elliot utilized the lesson plan for this experiment to educate hundreds of students.

The teaching methodology of Elliot within her "Blue Eyes Brown Eyes" lesson plan illustrates that maladaptive behaviors that involve social dominance can take place quite frequently when arbitrary differences between people allow them to form groups (Peters, 1987). The continuous recognition of different social groups and continual identifications of flaws and mistakes of the members of another group increase the likelihood that those who perceive the flaws of the other group members will discriminate against any members of

9 The testing provides the set of conditions allowing the system to attain new avenues or points of access from which information about itself and what it aims to decrease, neutralize, and increase are met more probabilistically.

the other group, which thereby systematically disadvantages the other group in many respects. In Elliot's method, many of the students were discriminated against by the teacher who allowed other students to discriminate against them based on the color of their eyes, which they arbitrarily associated with stupidity, inferiority, inattentiveness, etc. for one group and elevated levels of intelligence and superiority for the other group, which was also based on the colors of their eyes.

When a teacher, as part of a set of lessons, provides reasons for distinguishing between groups based on privileges or superiority, the teacher assumes the role of an educator who breaks down both the institutionalization and socialization processes that the education system generally functions to support. However, simultaneously, the educator reserves the ability to rebuild and reestablish the institutionalization and socialization of the learners but with additional improvements. The additional improvements occur because of the information attained (i.e., feedback). Feedback about the process of education is attained during the controlled testing process of some aspect of the education system. During the testing certain structural components of the education system are dismantled temporarily.

What becomes obvious is that an important part of the education process for some people involves overcoming adversity, social pressures from peers and others, and discrimination, which temporarily hinders education for some, and which is implemented by key members of the education institution itself (e.g., teachers). Jane Elliot's ideas for her thoughtful lesson plan came directly and responsively after the assassination of Dr. Martin Luther King Jr. in 1968 to allow the children in her classroom to temporarily experience discrimination, privileges, and loss of privileges within a controlled learning environment.

Within an interview, which the author conducted for this book, one of the original participants and students of Jane Elliot's classroom experiment, an Iowa school principal, Rex Kozak, was asked whether he agreed with the abovementioned assessment of Jane Elliot's lesson from the perspective of a participant. Mr. Kozak maintained on February 8, 2015 via email that:

> I would have to agree very much with your assessment. If the educator is trusted and believed by the students, the educator is then given the power or authority to change the social norms and reestablish the socialization of the learners. Which through the process makes a major impact on the participant.
>
> As a participant in the exercise, I would have to say the most important element that one takes away is their own self-worth and own self-value.

> The exercise teaches one to become their own person and not to be limited by others and their limited thinking process. One has their own ability to overcome whatever is put before them, if they have the confidence and fortitude to move beyond the imposed limitations by others.
>
> I keep in mind that one has to take away the security to open the doors to opportunity. Yes, it will make everyone uncomfortable, but in the long run, it will correct the passive compliance we have now interred into within society. What the exercise teaches is needed now more than ever.

The mass media system has been responsible for publicly broadcasting several types of portrayals of Elliot's teaching methodology. Journalists have often depicted the pedagogical method as a controversial one with advantages and disadvantages. As producers of entertainment, many businesses of the mass media system promote the presentation of the teaching method as disputable, which lead to opposite-ended opinions, praise, and disdain for the methods provided by the lesson plan.

The media can overemphasize the fact that the teaching method has a temporarily negative impact on the students who are undergoing the negative discrimination and that they are having privileges taken away from them. Consequently, the students undergoing the arbitrary discriminations have lower scores and learn more slowly during the initial phase, whereas the students who contribute to discriminating against the other students and who also have more privileges have positive impacts on their scores and decrease the amount of time needed for reaching the ends of their learning activities.

The teacher is the authority figure who then switches the focus of discrimination from the blue-eyed to the brown-eyed students or vice versa for the group with the improved scores and privileges to undergo the experiences of blatant discrimination, which as Mr. Kozak attests, increases one's feelings of self-worth and values. It also creates bonds that are long-lasting. Elliot's research with hundreds of students suggests that, again, the scores of those undergoing the implementation of the lesson plan with discrimination decrease, but the scores of all the students increase on average after the set of class lessons are completed.

Much like the education system, the mass media system also tests itself in numerous ways that also temporarily undermine structural parts of the system in controlled ways. The mass media system reports its own mistakes, plagiarism scandals, use of ghost authorship and other types of false authorship, exaggerations, and lies. Distinct types of informative communications are provided in response to ways in which the media system breaks down its own parts, albeit also with control.

While political events and events that take place because of the legal system or its subsystems can lead to the public broadcasts that could cause people to protest, riot, and act violently, we are very hard-pressed to find a public broadcast about public broadcasting that leads to such protesting, riots, and violence. The scandals within the mass media system are controlled, or they are directed toward a few individuals who are responsible rather than toward a large part of the system, which would lead to structural changes being imposed upon the system from external forces, other social systems, or public demand.

The mass media systems play a vital role in the formation of security and security systems within society. They may at times undermine undercover operations of other systems, such as the operations of homicide detectives, criminal informants, and undercover police in units investigating major crimes. The public broadcast of murders and other violent crimes increase awareness and willingness to reduce them. However, the public broadcast of suicides tends to increase the frequency of suicides thereafter, especially within the first seven to ten days after the publication of a suicide event of a very popular public figure (Phillips, 1974). Suicides of teenagers also tend to increase after the media's broadcast of teenage suicides (Phillips, Lesyna & Paight, 1991; Borgatta & Montgomery, 2000, p. 3080). The public messages that mass media systems display with images and words vastly affect the society in multifarious ways that are challenging to measure.

The infrequency of reporting about violent acts can either be a sign that the acts do not frequently occur within the region the journalists are concerned with, or the infrequency can signify that the violence is so immense that journalists feel too threatened to publish about murders and destruction, in which case journalists may refrain from reporting many incidents. The latter sorts of situations occur when organized crime groups (e.g., with drug lords in Mexico) murder journalists for publishing informative pieces that may contribute to revealing the identities of murderers and connections with corrupt legal officials and political figures who are involved in the trafficking of narcotics or other illegal activities. Grayson (2009, pp. 43) writes:

> Three senior journalists at the Tijuana weekly *Zeta* also paid a heavy price for prophesying about the regime's iniquities, including its contamination by drug traffickers. Assassins executed the paper's co-founder Héctor Félix Miranda (April 20, 1988) and a chief editor Francisco Ortiz Franco (June 22, 2004), while severely wounding its editor and publisher J. Jesús Blancornelas (November 27, 1997).

Many of the newspapers and multiple businesses experienced the detrimental impact of controlled threats and violence. Grayson (ibid., p. 97) continues:

> In the past, TV, radio, and newspaper stories about the brazenness of cartels and their chieftains pressured law enforcement agencies to pursue the culprits. In recent years, fear of the assassination of journalists and bombings of printing plants has prompted *El Mañana* chain, which publishes editions in the border cities of Reynosa, Matamoros, and Nuevo Laredo, and other newspapers, to tone down and in most cases eliminate coverage of narco-crimes. A drug gang reportedly added at least one American journalist to its hit list (Simon & Lauria, 2007).

Violence against journalists can also develop to levels that are challenging to assess. Sometimes the levels of violence require international support from news agencies to begin to understand the scale at which journalists in some areas are terrorized. Grayson (ibid, p. 98) maintains:

> The Paris-based Reporters without Frontiers cited ninety-five attacks on journalists during the first half of 2008, while a World Journalists' Report on Press Freedom castigated Mexico as "one of the most dangerous countries for journalists in the world"—with twenty-eight reporters killed, eight missing, and dozens threatened, intimidated or harassed for practicing their profession during the last eight years.

The violence that escalates and involves highly organized efforts often also involves attempts to control the media outputs with scare tactics that lead to hesitations, postponements of publications of topical articles, or the destruction of the information. The latter strategies of criminal organizations to instill fear need not occur for some amount of influence or control of the media to be attained. The media system itself may also deceive the public after receiving payments from interested parties.

Organized crime members may fund and insert reporters with whom they conspire to both entertain the public, fulfill some of the journalists' contractual obligations, and to provide scapegoats as well as cover up the illegal activities of the criminal organizations. Drug traffickers in Mexico even fund entire bands to perform *narco musica*. *Narco musica* often justifies the illegal business activities of drug deals, describing drug lords and their employees as "just workers." Entire bands have been murdered for performing outside of the areas of their supporters since competition between opposing drug lords is so fierce.

Sometimes the violence is purposely reported to display fantastical representations of grotesque viciousness with torture, decapitations, and other missing body parts. While the mass media broadcasts of the intentional displays of violence and torture are frequently accurate, they serve the interests of the bosses of the violent torturers to instill ideologies of fear in the masses, and they rarely provide accurately useful information that can be utilized by law enforcement.

The mass media system often has many diverse financial resources in certain countries, in which case those who have invested or who own newspapers, TV, radio, satellite stations and other sources, such as interconnected websites, may be criticized for wrongdoings or may face more obstacles when they are involved in corruption. Contrarily, media systems with significantly less diversity, concerning their funding for broadcasting, may tend to refrain from muckraking or publicizing negative information about those who significantly finance the mass media system, such as the governments.

Journalistic contestations are necessary elements in relation to producing controversial situations with regards to politicians' expressions of their own interests. Expressions of political interests are produced by means of mass media outlets for public broadcast. If there is a lack of journalistic contestations of political ideas or there is bribery, then some of those ideas that are misleading, and thereby should be contested, can quite easily become presumptions within the society and provide support for those politicians who ideologically agree with them. Uncontested ideas can simultaneously hinder other politicians who form disagreements with the ideas.

To some degree, mass media broadcasts provide transparency of the inner workings, corruptions, and preconditions for corruption within the political and legal systems. The publications serve to expose wrongdoings, to change public perceptions toward the wrongdoers, to promote indictments of offenders as well as to gain public support against criminals. The mass media system thereby plays a crucial role regarding the security of the societal system.

It is necessary to analyze the mass media system during the process of understanding the legal system with which the media system functions. The importance of the mass media system in relation to its role of reducing violence likely has a correlation and possibly even a causal role regarding the media systems' reports and often accurate representations of violence and destruction in societies, tending to lead to less violence and destruction. There is, hypothetically, a tendency that when the media portrays the actual occurrences of violence and destruction about as frequently as they occur, the media tends to serve to reduce the overall amount of societal violence and destruction. Of course, there are a plethora of reasons for this, which include the media's access to law enforcers for interviews, advice, and suggestions, for instance.

Niklas Luhmann (2004, p. 119) argues that the law cannot be changed by any media campaign or any social movement since change only occurs by means of the legal system itself since the legal system is the determiner of the multiple forms for which it accounts. For example, the legal system determines the order of the communications and the subsystems' members to which it communicates about broadcasts, including the chiefs of police and other police in the penal system, and media campaigns can have no impact on this aspect of the system. Moreover, the legal system reconciles with public approval, disapproval, and other opinions.

Alterations of information transmissions have happened frequently within the 20th and 21st centuries, such as the distribution of mass media information via TV, radio, the internet, and print, which have increased the speeds of transmissions. Increases in the speeds of transmission can lead to greater numbers of irregularities concerning the changes of law as well as increased chances of hasty reviews. The transformations of public opinions are thereby more plausibly viewed as causally related to legal change and well described in terms of a causal relation (Brant, 2012a, pp. 176–179). Certain aspects of the communicative processes of legal systems have dramatically increased their speeds, which accounts for some of the changes in legal systems.

System theorists argue that the system of science involves encoding the world with the true/false binary distinction for generating knowledge. The mass media system is concerned with the social construction of reality. The mass media system utilizes a very different binary code, namely, with the positive and negative values that encode "information and non-information," respectively. Luhmann (2000, p. 17) writes:

> The code of the system of the mass media is the distinction of information and non-information. The system can work with information. Information, then, is the positive value, the designatory value, with which the system describes the possibilities of its own operating. But in order to have the freedom of seeing something as information or not, there must also be a possibility of thinking that something is non-informative.

According to Luhmann, the system requires both values for encodings, especially the encoding of certain things as non-information so that it is not overloaded and so that it is able to differentiate itself from the environment. The system organizes, reduces certain complexities, and does so too with its own selections. Luhmann (ibid.) continues:

> Of course, even the information that something is not information is also informative. As is typical for the reflexive values of the codings (so, for example, injustice must be able to be treated as injustice in a lawful way), the system goes into an infinite regress here. It makes its operations

> dependent upon conditions which it cannot, and then can after all, determine. But the problem of infinite regress is only posed when there is a search for ultimate explanations, and the media system has no time for this anyway.

Legal systems place requirements on what texts are accessible at public schools, what positive information about each legal system's national economy is presented to pupils in addition to what negative information about other nations is presented to students at schools, who is legally allowed to teach, how much money is allocated to particular school districts, how much tax millionaires and billionaires pay, what practices with edible plants involving pesticides and animal abuse are legally permissible for the food industry, what chemicals are legally allowed to substitute for healthy foods, the legal limits of propaganda, deception, and images in advertisements and in mass media, who can marry (e.g., there are nations that allow convicted murderers to marry members of the opposite sex but disallow homosexual marriage in 2015), as well as who is legally allowed to have sex and how they are legally allowed to have sex, how many foreign nationals are legally allowed to enter the nation and how many are deported, and what age groups should be imprisoned for not responding to governments' calls for them to serve in the military and fight wars.

Mass media systems publish much on legal systems' requirements. Knowledge of a legal system largely comes from reading, listening, and watching images and words of what the mass media system has encoded as information. As Luhmann clarifies, the mass media system, however, does not invest the time for detailed explanations since it works with short, rapid bursts of information. The latter processes can lead to problematic situations, especially in areas and times of crisis where the ordinary conditions for encoding types of events as "informative" and "non-informative" are different.

For instance, consider wartime reporters who write an article based on two or three sources in Iraq shortly after the US invasion in 2003. The sources could be consistent with each other, but to some degree the reporters may lack an understanding of what they are asked to do, and they may serve the same interests, especially since US reporters are more likely to interview Iraqis who tend to work more closely with American soldiers. Reporters may have their articles published, potential policies in the invaded country can be created and passed at least partially because of these publications' impact, and thus reporters become even more likely to continue with their unprofessional investigations, which leads to a negative feedback loop and which can lead to prolonging wars.

Is "war" a "legal condition" during which two or more groups are permitted by legal systems to engage in violence with weaponry within specific jurisdictions? International conflicts increasingly involve multinational efforts, which means that there are growing needs to make the legal conditions for wars explicit for publics. Making legal conditions for wars more transparent requires international media outlets, which must make their members become increasingly responsible, i.e., facing penalization wherever they reside, and which would affect all levels of media companies' hierarchies, especially those with executive privileges. If the members of the press are first held legally responsible on an international platform and so are their superiors, then this responsibility should foremost regard their broadcasts concerning violence and destruction. There are growing needs to plan for the expansions of legal systems' jurisdictions and roles in the 21st century.

Do billionaires subsist for any reason other than that large political economies' legal systems permit them to exist after relatively small percentages of their wealth are taxed via laws (i.e., small in proportion to the annual interest they accumulate)? Societies will likely be faced with the following legal and moral question concerning social dominance in the 21st century: Shall we legally permit a single human being to become a trillionaire and transfer such vast wealth to whatever ideological causes, social groups, or individuals he or she chooses during the 21st century? The latter questions are not questions posed by the mass media systems because many of the owners of the media are billionaires, and the certain practices, institutions, and systems within societies (e.g., the banking and financial systems) beneficially serve the owners of the means of mass media production.

Financial and economic powers of billionaires surely impact political and legal systems. Financial systems allow one individual to decide whether to create or dismantle banks, make drastic changes in the employment statuses of entire cities, and create new types of marketing goods and services. The latter types of niche marketing goods and services range from excessively expensive clothing accessories for their pets, which cost more than the average American or UK household earns annually or sometimes in a decade, to embarking on multi-million-dollar shuttle trips into outer space.

Another reason why we should care for and about legal systems is because the systems persistently affect all of us and place each of us within certain social and hierarchical relations between nations, societies, local governments, communities, families, and friends amid a globalizing world with globalizing rules of law. Mass media systems inform us of these relations to some degrees but are insufficient regarding providing in-depth explanations, and the mass media systems thereby facilitate the formations of ideologies. Thus, analyses of greater depths are required to initiate understanding of legal systems, which in turn is crucial for understanding, prevention and reduction of violence and destruction within societies.

Realization of social movements require a complex understanding of the relationship between groups that cause the movements and actions of people who compose the legal institutions, which include: police officers, judges, legal clerks, jurors, federal investigative agents, lawyers, military police, international police through Interpol, mediators, lawmakers, etc. Social movements are the sort of events about which we are interested, especially in relation to the rises and falls of households or communities, socio-economically speaking. Such events are crucial because they can shift in ways that begin to create the conditions for violence and destruction against opposing groups.

Understanding or accurately predicting how social groups will act within societies is worthwhile since such knowledge is necessary and practical to non-violently prevent escalating protest movements, revolts, violent revolutions, civil wars, and international conflicts. Means of coming to understanding must couple together the facts that: (a) contrastive distinctions that separate one society from another, in a non-geographical sense of boundaries, are based upon how people of each society think in relation to people of another society rather than merely how societies as systems buy and sell, for instance, because people buy and sell closely associated with desires, beliefs, ideologies and deceptive tactics in, for example, advertising; and (b) each legal system's written laws and enforcements of policies give us the capacity not only to imagine but also to measure how different societies think differently within their respective geographic locations.

Measurements of how different cultures and societies think in the latter types of examples may, for instance, objectively describe the amount of written language concerning policies from the time period of laws of slavery (e.g., laws supported by England under Queen Elisabeth during the late 16th century, legally allowing the shipment of slaves), the runaway slave laws, the abolition of slavery[10] in the late 19th century in the USA, the legal orders for the segregation of races, laws concerning restrictions on employment, voting, housing, buying and selling in respect to race, and civil rights laws that overcome portions of the latter racist laws in the 1960s in the USA, which required

10 Slavery, of course, still exists within societies, including the USA and Western Europe, in the 21st century. One of the institutions of slavery was the institution that involved slavers and slaves based upon race as well as a system that included overseers, plantations, and the massive exploitation of labor, especially on fields for agriculture, by slave owners.

new ways of thinking and behaving to be adopted. However, US laws in the late 1970s led to dramatically increased incarcerations, especially of young black male adults who still provide prison labor (Umseen & Piehl, 2008; Philpot & White, 2010).

Measurements of merely the written laws would involve the number of years before new developments of laws brought improvements and developments of the rights of people based upon race, and the amount of language used to describe the newly granted rights or vice versa. The latter measurements are objectively comparable to the corresponding laws of other societies, especially when the societies are also compared in virtue of the proportions of their populaces including their populations of low-status and high-status groups compared to each other and with the calculation of these populations undergoing varying intensities of penalizations via their criminal justice systems.

Numbers can be assigned to certain types of freedoms or rights, in which case the ability for a vote within a political election to count for three-fifths of the vote of another citizen, who is a member of the majority group of the society, would be assigned a lesser value than a vote that fully counts for the representation of a single citizen, for instance. So, measurements can be relational regarding comparative analyses of legal systems. The lack of language-usage within the courts and legislation to describe the freedoms or rights of people who are either minorities or members of subordinate groups in the society oftentimes signifies that the group of people is considered to have either the status of foreigners (i.e., as non-citizens have fewer rights) or property (e.g., real estate or private property).

Realizing how legal institutions' members think is generally more fruitful than knowledge of the written laws themselves because such realization entails knowing what laws police will enforce and will not enforce, what laws may be violated in the form of citations but will be dismissed in court, and what laws will proceed through the judicial system and become overthrown by the creations of new ones. Policy makers, enforcers, and interpreters of law think differently in different regions and differently at separate times.

Some fundamental problems concerning law involve either interpreting law when the laws should be enforced or enforcing the law when it ought to be interpreted. Both judges within courts of law and law enforcement agents must decide on the latter actions. The notion of a judicial branch of government is to some extent a misnomer because judgments with legal content are almost ubiquitous in law but differ regarding the time they are allotted for decision-making. Additionally, either making laws when preexisting laws should be reinterpreted or reinterpreting laws when new ones ought to be legislated present legislators and judges with complications.

Within societies that are not controlled via the autocratic leadership of dictators, the systems of checks and balances are generally implemented. Systems of checks and balances prevent almost any individual from simultaneously acting as a lawmaker, judge, jury, and law enforcement agent. Changing societal conditions (e.g., when high-status groups of people lose dominance in relation to other groups in the society or when the dominance of high-status groups is threatened) determine whether individuals can arise as, for example, democratically elected lawmakers who invoke power and influence to assume all the roles of the law (i.e., one thereby takes law into one's own hands even on a mass scale), such as Adolf Hitler during the 1930s and 1940s. The use of a scapegoat, worsening economic conditions, and heightening in-group identities, especially for dominant groups and people who may be aptly described as authoritarians, facilitate the rise of the democratically elected autocratic leaders who tend to increase the frequency and intensity of social dominance.

The rise of Hitler to power is an event upon which scholars of any society should deeply reflect. During the 1920s Germany was an extremely advanced and developed nation and society with an internationally admired political system, economic system, and legal system (Schulz, 1982). Germany was very productive in the arts, sciences and in education, in general (Guerin, 2005). However, the society underwent a series of unethical and deplorable policies, such as domestic policies that racially and culturally discriminated against peoples, international policies of violence and destruction against neighboring nations in addition to policies overseeing the takeovers of neighboring and distant nations alike.

Any nation's constitutional writings have various human interpretations, and some interpretations are more influential than others during certain times, e.g., times of emergency, war, peace, gang violence, etc. Even national anthems can be utilized for social control, such as the banned German song by allied powers (*i.e., Das Lied der Deutschen*) in 1945 in Germany. Certain interpretations of the US Constitution are advocated by some authors and rejected by others, for instance. We may hypothesize that there is probably a positive correlation between the overall education levels of individuals (i.e., specifically concerning social issues historically, conceptually, and sociologically), their sophistication levels concerning knowledge of their nation's constitutions, and the consistency of their opinions and interpretations of those constitutions.

We may also hypothesize that people with lower levels of education and less sophisticated knowledge of the contents of constitutions, less knowledge of the social sciences (e.g., anthropology, psychology, sociology etc.), and less knowledge of theories of justice tend to be easily swayed in respect to their viewpoints, interpretations, and opinions of the constitutions, especially during highly emotional times of emergency, rampant unemployment, decreasing wages, and inflation, which the German people confronted during the Great Depression of the 1930s, before they wrought a world war.

Clinton Rossiter (1948, p. 314) argued within *Constitutional Dictatorship* that absolutely any possible sacrifice is permissible in any democracy, even if democracy itself is sacrificed, because a dictatorship responds to some emergency out of necessitation, which is easily interpreted as constitutional (Dyzenhaus, 2006, p. 35). A constitutional dictatorship may arise within a democratic political economy with an advanced legal system, such as the United States, because such systems are constitutionally designed to function during times of peace and relative prosperity. That is, they function in the absence of the conditions of urgency presented in critical periods, during which constitutional precedents and principles are in grave danger, or when there are perceived dangers by a sizable portion of the populace.

In contrast to the abovementioned hypothesis that the educated in those different aspects are able to hold more consistent opinions (e.g., let us assume a politician is very knowledgeable and stable with her consistency to uphold her political stance), we observe the following: The periods of constitutional crisis involve the alterations of the governmental system at least temporarily to the degree that is required to prevail over the dangers and threats and to re-establish conditions of normality. If overcoming the dangers and threats demands the instantiation of an outright dictatorship, then the changes within the government serve the purpose foremost to maintain the condition of independence of the state and then to preserve the continuation of order in line with the constitution in support of people's social and political rights and liberties (Rossiter, 1948, pp. 5–7).

President Abraham Lincoln serves as Rossiter's (ibid., p. 229) example of an American constitutional dictator who dealt with the constitutional crisis of the Civil War. Herman and Chomsky (1988, p. 98) ascertain that Nicaragua underwent a period of state terrorism during the 1980s, during which the government terrorized journalists and placed major constraints upon the media, especially during temporary states of emergency (i.e., the emergency included US supported economic sabotage of Nicaragua for its ties to communism) when the freedom of the press in Nicaragua was vastly restricted by the state and US military decisions, which partially came from the US Espionage Act of 1917 to ban publications and incarcerate Nicaraguans (Frederick, 1987; Nichols, 1985).

Fundamental principles by which a nation organizes and governs itself, i.e., the state's constitution, are stable during times of peace, prosperity, and amongst those with sufficient knowledge. The latter principles are less stable in another respect that depends to some extent on the circumstances in which the state's citizens find themselves. The hypothetical status of the stability of opinions on the constitution involves the fact that a written or codified constitution is only effective if people have read, remember, and understand the content.

People must form interpretations and agreements about the content of a constitution for it to make any social impact. Many would prefer additional amendments. Many want to preserve the content as it is. Others would appreciate vast deletions of their constitutions and rewrites because perhaps they view the document as a package of lies or hypocrisy. Those who view the constitution as hypocritical or with cynicism hold ideologies that are worthy of further analysis in relation to the other legal ideologies as to assess their roles regarding violence and justification for war.

Mass media plays a crucial role regarding the repeatedly evaluated, fundamental principles and precedents presented as content of a state's constitution. Media propagandizes, regardless of whether it is a state of emergency or not, to serve both those who control it (e.g., members of the legal institution and others who provide the media with regular communications and information). Financers of media have much control. Chomsky and Herman (1988, p. xi) give the reason for this propagandizing:

> The representatives of these interests have important agendas and principles that they want to advance, and they are well positioned to shape and constrain media policy.

Notable events that the media covers up are relations of power between people, especially high and low-status groups, the illegal actions or immoral actions of those who control and finance the media. They include internal problems with the media itself that may lead its audience to lose trust in the organization etc. Although the latter sorts of events are given much less attention, people (i.e., citizens and non-citizens) repeatedly evaluate whether the actions within the society are consistent with the constitution, especially as it is portrayed as legitimate in the USA.

Constitutional law and similarly focused legal studies often center upon the maintenance of legitimacy in society, which involves defining the relations between the executive, judiciary, and legislative functions of government and upholding peace. The fundamental questions within political philosophy during modern times inquire what are the functions and the structures that give a political system the ability to attain legitimacy as well as the question about what exactly legitimacy is as a set of characteristics (Luhmann, 1970, p. 159; Thornhill, 2008, p. 162). Thornhill (2008, p. 163) writes:

> Normative theories of the state are typified by the argument that to obtain and preserve legitimacy, states must enshrine in law generalized principles, in which citizens recognize the conditions of their own rational freedoms. Where this is the case, citizens impute to the state the right to command and to expect obedience, and it is probable that they will be peacefully integrated under laws issued by states.

In the United States, there is an argument that every citizen deserves or should be granted the right to life, liberty, and the pursuit of happiness. Another set of laws and principles is the "right to keep and bear arms," which allows many people to own guns, although some states, cities, or provinces within the political and economic system do reserve the right to ban or require firearm licenses from gun owners. The latter right may be placed under the principle and right to life by means of self-defense of the individual via a weapon. Thornhill (ibid.) continues:

> Normative theories of state usually argue that legitimate states must order themselves in a regular legal framework; they must recognize their addressees as bearers of rights and allow these rights to dictate or precondition the content of laws; and they must assume a rationally acceded constitutional structure. In these respects, normative concepts of legitimacy and rights-based constitutionalism are very closely connected (Finn, 1991, p. 36), and constitutional rights are seen to act as the "political face" of the generalized principles required to legitimize and authorize public power (Ingram, 1994, pp. 184–185).

Thornhill argues that as the decades pass and generations of newcomers become established within the societal system's workforce, especially within the legal, political, and economic subsystems, the legitimate state must perpetuate a constitutional structure that involves giving consent or approval, or it must directly involve the rational succession of events that occur with promotions or the attainment of offices or titles, according to normative theories of statehood. Within each society under analysis, it may be observed that there are many communications of the media that support the societal subsystems as well as the principles and directions of the society. It is both questionable whether the support for the societal subsystems by the mass media involves excessive overrepresentation and also what exactly "excessive overrepresentation of communications about a system of the state" is, how to measure it, and how to define it for further measurements, which may emphasize the amount of patriotism, nationalism or anti-nationalistic oppositions.

The emphasis of the mass media system within a society having inclinations to offer communicative support, time, effort, and money to certain subsystems of the society may be quite great. Lending the latter types of supports via overrepresentations could, hypothetically, tend to lead to further inclinations to attack foreign nations that communicatively oppose the legitimacy of the political system. Opposing a nation's legitimacy regarding the market and economic system is facilitated via tariffs, embargos, and quotas, placing limits on the maximum and minimum amounts of some good or goods that can be exported by the other society. The greater the tendency of the mass media to offer overrepresentations of criticisms (e.g., blaming a race of people or group of people, high or low-status groups regarding the hierarchy of dominance of some groups over others, descriptions of inefficiencies of the societal system, of which the media is a subsystem), the more likely, hypothetically speaking, the society is to have greater inclinations to attack and to attempt to become independent from another group within the same society.

Certain other types of facts can be overrepresented and serve as propaganda for motivating a populace to support the legal wage of war against other nations. Before the US led military operation in Iraq in 2003 and after many US mass media outlets displayed images and wordings about the violence, betrayal, weaponry, torture, etc. within Iraq and against its own people, especially during the 1980s during the war between Iraq and Iran, the overrepresentations of images and descriptions of violence became major components of the propaganda supporting the invasion. What becomes apparent to the anti-propagandist is that when the first things that come to mind about a people or nation are the men who are able-bodied (e.g., fit for military service) rather than women, adolescents, children, and babies, and what comes to mind is the history of destructiveness and violent acts of the people rather than their contributions to science, art, culture, music, history, food etc., another populace has undergone systematic propagandizing via the reception of the overrepresentations of its destructive and violent acts and underrepresentations of its constructive acts.

The media facilitates the wage of war via the asymmetrical portrayal of the destructiveness of those with whom the war will be waged and the depiction of the victimization, constructiveness, and the humanity of the in-group that is opposed to the so-called destructive group. The response of the public is the want of balance, even via brute force in some cases, through the legally-granted control of the so-called destructive group (i.e., destructive, according to the propaganda) that is perceived as causing the problem. The impact of the propaganda coincides with war-ready lawmakers and increased support of aggressive politicians. The journalistic depictions thereby fuel the war machine with reactionary ideology at times. Lawmakers who promote compromises and peace treaties can be disavowed as pacifistic hesitators rather than constructive providers of mutual benefits.

In each of the latter cases, we are dealing with legal minds and people interacting within legal systems. Understanding the importance of legal systems requires knowing about a wide range of worldviews that are both possible and real, and why real worldviews are not merely possible but why they motivate actions and change the world in which we all live.

CHAPTER 2

Incomprehensiveness of Just Legality and Illegality

Most human behaviors are insignificant for the legal system to label, such as one walking through one's own home, buying food at the market, eating, sleeping, etc. These behaviors are obviously not illegal. Are these behaviors legal ones, though? Have they been legalized? There are, indeed, many types of behaviors that will later become illegal. Are these latter types of behaviors legal in the first place? This chapter demonstrates that these behaviors are not legal ones, and to do so a relatively new concept within academic literature called "alegality" is utilized to explain what happens within this important aspect of a civil society. The significance of the conception of alegality involves so many of our behaviors, goods, and services.

Sometimes new products enter certain nation, and many people advocate legalizing or criminalizing people's possessions of the products. Sometimes people from a single nation enter another nation in large numbers. Against the latter people's wills, many may argue at certain times and places that the laws need to change to slow down or to stop the amount of immigration. At first glance, it may appear that illegalizing some action or product may provide a solution. However, there are many ways to illegalize things. We can illegalize actions at certain times, in certain places, by certain types of people etc. We can illegalize products so that they are illegal to buy or sell or possess at certain times or places, too.

The actions and situations, which are encoded as either "legal" or "illegal," are often conceived of quite differently within various cultures and nations. During the early 21st century, a pack of chewing gum is an illegal product in Singapore. The activity of chewing gum in Singapore is also illegal but not in most other nations.[1]

The attributions of legality and illegality to things and human actions are human ways that legal minds categorize as activities, products, and services via legal systems. The activities of individuals are often encoded alternatively in relation to the statuses of the people (i.e., when they are foreigners, different races of people, different social classes etc.). The different codes attributed to the behaviors of different peoples and to the behaviors of distinct statuses of

1 The illegalization in Singapore probably occurred from the overuse of gum for malicious purposes, such as placing gum in electronic devices, like telephones and on elevator buttons used for public services.

 | DOI:10.1163/9789004385955_004

people impact the process of categorizing the actions of some as "being legal" and for others "being illegal," depending on whether they are members of the high or low-status groups in the society.

Social dominance is one impact that the latter types of statuses have during the decision-making processes of attributing legality and illegality to things, peoples, and their actions (e.g., attributing legal permissibility and impermissibility). For the latter reason, high-status groups are systematically given advantages in terms of reduced penalties, and there are more frequent occurrences of ignoring high-status group members' prior illegal actions via the relinquishments of charges. Simultaneously, low-status groups are given systematic disadvantages.[2] The latter factors are studied by social dominance theorists and are relevant to multiple societies and their legal systems (Sidanius et al., 2004). These factors are probably ubiquitously relevant and work systematically in similar ways within all societies with legal systems.

The processes of the Chinese criminal justice system differ quite drastically regarding low-profile and high-profile rape cases, especially when witnesses or victims tend to be foreigners of a different race, the victimizers tend to be Chinese, or the victims tend to be females from the lower socio-economic class. Given the latter social factors, the legal communications and processes of labeling such incidents as sexual misconduct as "legally permissible" can be astonishingly racist, xenophobic, domineering, and sexist. For instance, Chinese husbands are legally permitted to rape their wives in the early 21st century, and the first indictment by a male rape victim occurred in China first and only during the 21st century.

Many people are surprised at what appears to be a lack of the rule of law in China. Even witnesses who merely make police reports can be labeled as "troublemakers," which a colleague of mine experienced after he witnessed a rape, prevented the rape from continuing, and reported the rape at a university to the Chinese police. In many legal cases within various nations, the victims of rape are further victimized, especially if they report the incidents to the legal authorities or confide in their families. Others, such as witnesses, who report the "alleged" crimes can also face legal consequences, such as jail time.[3]

2 There are several ways of identifying high and low-status groups, such as determining that one group of people (e.g., by race) is overrepresented in the society's prison system, comparatively with other groups, and in comparison with the size of that particular racial group at large in the society. This indicates the group has a lower status.

3 An understanding of the culture as well as the culture's typical responses and treatments of victims of rape are often just as important as understanding the legal consequences and legally permissible actions. For instance, within many cities in China, the evidence of the use of a condom signifies to the police that the act was not rape, which is, in praxis, a judgment

Attributions of legality and illegality can thus be different in various cultures and legal systems, even regarding extremely unfair wrongdoings. Moreover, the attributions of what is legal and what is illegal are also different within the same nation for diverse types and statuses of people, which provides privileged groups with advantages and other groups with limitations. A rape victim from a high-status group in China is an entirely different legal situation than a rape victim from a small town or village.

Is it common knowledge that some of the privileged groups are the family members and friends of higher ranking police, politicians, and judges? Sometimes it is less clear who the people of high-status and low-status groups are and how, when, why, and where they are, respectively, given advantages and disadvantages by the legal system as well as what these advantages are.

The attributions of legality and illegality to certain actions are challenging. It is challenging for one to predict how a legal system at a time and place will interpret actions in virtue of the illegality or whether group members of the legal institution will deem the actions as permissible and legal under the circumstances. It is more challenging to understand the laws within different legal systems than the one or ones within which an analyst lives and experiences legal acts and communications. There is an aspect of the process of attributing legality and illegality that is logical, though, which is the same within all legal systems.

Some human activities are mundane. Other activities are legal but cross a threshold and give reasons for people to discuss whether they should undergo the processes of illegalization and criminalization. And still, there are activities that are illegal, but which also pass a dividing line and provide reasons for people to place them under the process of legalization and decriminalization. The latter processes are evaluated within this chapter.

The latter activities undergo decision-making processes that involve the conditions under which there are challenges of the distinctions between what is legal and what is illegal. These activities involve indecisions and are argued to be "alegal activities." Alegality describes aspects of the acts, politico-legal decisions, and situations that begin to alter the distinctions that are made by what are dubbed as being "legal" and "illegal." In this chapter, the concern is not merely about unfair and unjust treatment of human social groups regarding

made frequently by police, but also it is consistent with the wishes of the victim who would prefer not to be at all affiliated with the process of victimization. Additionally, it is a frequent practice for some Chinese families to refrain from washing their clothes with a family member who is a rape victim.

the law, but rather about the alternative activities and situations that are neither legal nor illegal and how exactly to conceptualize them.

1 Ideological Confusion about Legal Systems Disregarding Alegality and Fraud

In any society's education system, there are changes in teachings, facts, and ways of thinking that coincide with the emergence of new generations of people who are ready to undergo diverse types of studies, including legal studies. Resultantly, laws change, legal systems change their communications, and sometimes new legal systems emerge, say, coinciding with the arisings of new nations. It is obvious that the emergence of a new legal system involves many actions, and, conceptually speaking, it is also obvious that those actions cannot be rationally and decidedly known as "legal acts" or "illegal acts" since there needs to be a legal system already established to attribute those codes to the acts. The legal theory of autopoiesis critically analyzes the dichotomous way of thinking about encoding events as exclusively "legal" or exclusively "illegal." Teubner, Nobles, and Schiff (2003, p. 899) write:

> What makes the meaning of a fine 'legal' is the system which generates the notice of the fine. Now, and this may be difficult to understand, the notice of a fine is still 'legal' even if it has been issued under some mistake, or if the judgment was wrong, or the arrest was *ultra vires*. A fine is a legal communication because it is part of the legal system of communication – it is not only legal when that system operates in some manner which is regarded as 'correct.'

What is being defined here is the very concept of being "legal." The idea is that the concept generally ranges from what would ordinarily be interpreted as being normal, legal, and permissible and to what is interpreted as being illegal and impermissible but is legally allowed. The acts of the legitimate authority, the legal and criminal justice systems, are legal acts, despite whether they are mistakes, immoral, unethical, intolerable, and horrifying. Teubner et al. (ibid.) continue:

> To use the biological metaphor – a cancerous cell is still a cell, and a cell that has been made from its own elements – the fact that those elements have combined in unusual ways does not make it cease to be a cell. To return to the fine – a valid fine is as legal as an invalid fine – a valid communication by an official is as legal as an invalid communication. Any

> communication generated by a legal system is legal. In that case, you might ask, what is legal about a legal system's communications?

Since the 1980s, there has been a growing number of publications about the similarities of systems that demonstrate autopoiesis, which continues to contribute to legal studies via the usage of biological metaphors. Accordingly, a cancerous cell is still a cell, but a stem cell that splits and reproduces may become multiple cells that reproduce via the processes of autopoiesis (Varela, Maturana & Uribe, 1974).

Teubner et al. (ibid.) argue that the aspect that is legal about a legal system's communications is the code to which the laws apply. Communications of the legal system provide the application of the code legal/illegal, which is an opposition that is either tacit or explicit regarding each legal communication. Any letter that presents the notice of a penalty, such as a traffic violation, is the coding of the events as an illegal one. Moreover, according to Teubner et al. (ibid.), even the statements that, "this is legal," or that, "this is illegal," are legal communications.

Of course, the notice of a fine or penalization is not necessarily legal, unless it has been issued by some authority of the legal system, which does not mean that just any member of the legal institution can issue the notice for it to be legal though. Additionally, a member of the legal institution (e.g., an officer) could issue what appears to be a fine to someone but which is separate and distinct from the legal records of all the relevant legal fines.

Other organizations may systemically attempt to establish some of their practices so that they appear to function as the legal system within a society. For instance, there have been attempts, especially from debt collection agencies, to deceive people into believing that their employees are police officers, judges, and officials of the legal court system (Wilkinson, 2010; Roth; 2010). Däna Wilkinson (2010, p. 1) writes:

> It seems that Erie, Pennsylvania debt collection agency Unicredit not only set up a fake courtroom, complete with phony judge, with which to bamboozle and intimidate, but it dressed up employees like sheriff's deputies to "serve" faked court papers on consumers.

In a *Business Week* article (Associated Press, 2010) it was stated that:

> "This is an unconscionable attempt to use fake court proceedings to deceive, mislead or frighten consumers into making payments or surrendering valuables to Unicredit without following lawful procedures for debt collection," Attorney General Tom Corbett said in a statement.

The enormity of Unicredit regarding its tens of thousands of employees worldwide, thousands of branches, and hundreds of billions of dollars of assets in the early 21st century makes massive political impacts within numerous nations. It is questionable whether just the people at individual branches are largely responsible for legal violations. Regarding the Unicredit corporation's branch in Pennsylvania, it became dubious for some, psychologically speaking, whether the documents, proceedings, uniforms etc. are, in reality, aspects of the legal system at all,[4] even if these things are virtually identical to those issued from within the legal system of their jurisdiction.

One may inquire whether particular subsystems of society are, in fact, legal, such as the transportation system and the education system. Are the latter systems legal ones? Accordingly, one set of questions concerns whether the financial transactions for transport and whether the payments and accreditation system for educational certificates are largely legal regarding their methods and in accordance with the legal system with which the latter systems function in jurisdictions. These latter questions merely ask how much illegal activity transpires within the transportation and education systems, though.

The latter questions fail to inquire how much unfairness, dominance, and privileges for some groups there are within each system. From our theoretic standpoint in this chapter, transportation systems and education systems are best viewed as "alegal systems containing both legal and illegal activities" within them. Perhaps the uncommon change of a transportation system from being alegal to being illegal would cause most the lines or methods of transportation, including black market transactions, being converted into public services or the services of legitimately incorporated and unincorporated businesses (i.e., where the services had been ordinarily against the law and thereby the law penalized enough people for the illegal business activities to really demand a shift into greater frequencies of legal business transactions in that system).

For instance, in China during the 21st century, it is a widespread practice for people to hire the seat behind a motorcyclist, to pay the motorcyclist on an agreed or haggled price, and large numbers of these motorcyclists have no registered unincorporated or incorporated business. They subsist on black market transportation activity. The police sometimes regulate the motorcyclists heavily, pulling over many of them and issuing legal citations against them, but the legal fines are typically for unrelated issues, such as expired registrations.[5]

---

4 Uniforms of law enforcers and judges are commonly used by actors in movies, theaters, and television series. They are used in pornography as well as by male and female strippers for role playing.

5 Much of the legal activity or law enforcement that transpires in transportation systems is largely different in three types of nations, namely, underdeveloped, developing, and

Inquiries about alegalities concern the questions about those activities that either challenge the demarcations between what is legal and illegal or concern the questions about the activities that result in ever more frequent unfairness and injustice. The alegal activities in the latter cases may later undergo a set of complex processes of illegalization or legalization.

Various societal subsystems have corruption within them. Fraud within the education systems of Europe (e.g., plagiarizing theses and doctoral dissertations and ghost and false authorships) has largely been ignored by the European Union's legal systems in the 21st century insofar as no criminal charges and no indictments have been brought against the EU members of parliament, president, prime minister, or ministers of defense and education who have been rightly accused and convincingly investigated (Vogel, 2012; Pidd, 2011; Dillon, 2013). Fraud in the field of education can lead to the harshest examples of unfairness, despite the lack of a process of illegalization to significantly reduce fraudulent activities. Academic fraud, of course, is worldwide and has grown during the 21st century.

Some resignations have resulted, and many doctorates have been rescinded, yet legal systems remain almost entirely unconcerned with injustice, fraud, and unfairness within education systems, although academic fraud can lead to extremely unprofessional people attaining careers as the highest statuses of professionals in almost any industry. Academic fraud, cheating, and profiting from cheating, like online essay mills do, often result in other types of fraud since academic fraud is involved within the attainment of credentials required for certain positions of employment, which determine wages, including various positions of employment within any legal system. The businesses involved in buying and selling university diplomas have become a billion-dollar, global, black market industry, exceeding the economic impact of book piracy, counterfeit IDs, counterfeit passports, and counterfeit money combined, according to Havacscope Global Black Market Information (Havacscope, 2017).

Criminal prosecutions involving indictments of individuals who have attained positions of employment under such false pretenses as having fake diplomas are rare. Online essay mills that sell custom designed homework to students, which facilitate false authorship and academic fraud, are developing rapidly in ways that are interconnected with telecommunication systems and twenty-four-hour customer service representation (Brant, 2012b). If Clement Fatovic (2009) is correct, then many of these industries, especially ghost authorship industries that facilitate academic fraud and contribute to the possibility for less competent people to attain academic qualifications and

developed ones, although some nations might best be categorized as being developed regarding transport and as being developing regarding their economies overall, or vice versa.

positions of employment that require educational qualification, oppose the very basic and essential idea of law. Fatovic (ibid., p. 1) writes:

> Order is essential to the very idea of law. The aim of law is to create order where it does not exist and to stabilize it where it does exist.

Since fraudulent academic activities result in ever more frequent unfairness and injustices, we can predict that academic fraud shall undergo processes of illegalization. Many members of the legal institution have requirements for credentials that demand legitimate certifications and degrees and currently risk more fraud than in previous decades. Fraudulent practices in academia impact the legal system itself in unknown ways still. Transitions of future legal systems, classifying academic fraud as "illegal," require systems themselves to undergo several different institutional changes to assess activities (of some of their own personnel) as illegal ones.

2 Comparative Legal Studies: Western Influences on Islamic Systems

We may continue to inquire whether education systems are legal systems, illegal systems, or alegal systems. If education systems were legal systems, we might expect that they would be entirely replaced within societies that undergo colonization from other societies with their own legal systems and education systems. During or after colonization, we might expect to observe the illegalization of certain teachings and vast numbers of replacements of educational staff, if education systems were considered "legal," according to the legitimate authority, and then considered "illegal," according to the new legitimate authority.

Islamic societies, their legal systems, and their education systems present us with interesting examples of societies that are not typically considered to be greatly impacted by Western cultures, in several regards. Indeed, many people consider the drastic differences in the legal rights and education afforded to women from these cultures and vast differences regarding marriage insofar as polygyny is often morally and legally permitted. However, Islamic societies have been greatly influenced and systematically changed because of the Western world.

Consider nations and their education systems after they were colonized by other nations, such as Morocco during its protectorate status from 1912 to 1956 when the French occupation occurred. Ferro (1997, p. 121) maintains that only eleven of 706 doctors were from Morocco in 1952 while there was only one Moroccan architect, but there were over 200 European architects in Morocco.

After earning a diploma and having successes in academics in French schools, Arabs in Tunisia, Algeria, and Morocco typically faced rejection regarding employment applications, unless they pursued teaching professions. Education systems undergoing colonization were not legalized systems that provided advantages to those who proved to be successful in them. Education systems appeared to function as alegal, cultural systems emphasizing many of the colonizers' ideas and teachings and allowing for continuations of such functions.

Despite probably being the oldest university in the world, the University of al-Qarawiyyin or al-Karaouine (founded in Fes, Morocco in 859 (Meri, 2006)), it underwent decline as the elite found alternative Western education institutions in Morocco (Lulat, 2005). The presence of the French colonists in Morocco came with the construction of safe and efficient roads, bridges, more motorized vehicles, hospitals, universities, and buildings, despite riots against the French and Jews. Perhaps the educational institutions and hospitals were the most acceptable forms of change implemented by the French colonialists.

Presumably, the teachings of the French also put forth affirmations of France as the new fatherland of the Moroccan children (Ferro, 1997, p. 117). There has been perhaps a cultural domination regarding the teachings within what was a newly emerging education system of the colonists in Morocco. However, subordination of teachings within the older and established educational institutions of the Moroccans typically did not occur. Thus, we are not confronted with the illegalization of education systems but with rather what appears to be supplementations and overshadowings of them.

By merely overshadowing the education systems of the colonized people, there were many temporary allowances of the Moroccans to gain access to the French districts in burgeoning cities, such as Casablanca during the early 20th century. A set of changes around the Arab and Muslim world that involved changes in their legal systems that largely came from their education systems and from the great influences from Europe coincided with the changes in the infrastructure of Morocco, changes in the education system, and better technology for transportation and healthcare.

Wael Hallaq (1997, pp. 209–210) maintains that the preservation of the societal systems of control was facilitated via the structure of the Islamic legal systems, which were strong for over a millennium but confronted many new challenges with the presence of Western European nations during the 20th century. The highly authoritative legal doctrines of Islamic states were functional and came with the insistence by and for the people that they were morally, religiously and legally sound. They underwent a process of modernization during the 20th century insofar as many of the institutions were redefined by the Islamic legal systems, such as marriage in respect to monogamy and polygyny, divorce and child custody, family and inheritance, and the law, such as the first reform to be put into full effect by the state called the "Ottoman Law of Family Right" in 1917 (Tucker, 1996, p. 4; Hallaq, 1997, p. 210). Education systems undoubtedly had strong impact upon the acceptance, toleration, disapproval, and denial of redefining these institutions and thereby contributed to changes within the workings of the legal systems. Hallaq (ibid.) writes:

> When it became apparent that the traditional law could no longer serve Muslim society in the modern world, there were several attempts at introducing European codes lock, stock and barrel. These codes were variably French, German and Swiss. However, it was soon discovered that such codes were largely inadequate for a society that was fundamentally different from those western societies for which these codes were originally drafted. The modern Muslim states then turned to other devices that were inspired by the traditional Islamic doctrines.

The jurist Muhammad 'Abduh (1848–1905) from Egypt was an innovator and educator regarding religious and legal reforms. 'Abduh ascertained that when human reason is sound, reason can lead us to know what is just and unjust, right and wrong, and fair and unfair. The latter stance of 'Abduh was controversial and perhaps opposed to the majority's opinions in many regions populated by Islamic nations, though. In the late 19th century, religious faith and revelation appeared to many Islamic people to involve strict contradictions and disagreements with decisions based upon human reason as opposed to the supernatural.

Contradictions and disagreement generally could not be reconciled in any other way, apart from upholding revelation and the Islamic faith, according to Muslim legal traditions before the 20th century. However, many of the legal ideas that had been discarded by thinkers adhering to strict traditions were revived after the teachings of 'Abduh. 'Abduh's major line of arguments maintained that there is a consistency that is not transparent between revelation and sound reason, which never allows for any emerging contradiction because any apparent conflict between sound argumentation and revelation is either a misunderstanding of one or the other (Hallaq, 1997, p. 212).

The variables regarding the relations of Islamic law are multifarious and involve diverse cultural ways of approaching education and religion as institutional pillars of societies. Examples of external influences on cultures, such as the European impact on Islamic legal and education systems, illustrate atypical comparative approaches for analyzing and building preconceptions about scientific observations on legal systems and other systems on which there are relations of dependency.

Some maintain that the academic field of comparative law arose during the 19th and 20th centuries with a set of assumptions that comparative law differs from the law itself, that it requires justifications that law need not have, and that comparative law is best viewed as a subsidiary subdiscipline (Glenn, 2006, p. 57). Developments of comparative law have led to integrations within legal studies and the law itself. For the latter reason, some argue for the autonomy of the discipline of comparative law to be alternatively viewed as a crucial aspect of legal studies, lawmaking, and other legal processes, such as legalization, illegalization etc. (Glenn, 2006; Reimann, 1996).

If the discipline of comparative law is an integral part of the law and legal studies, then the sociology of law is likewise important for such investigations because the sociological facts are often the basis for legal changes and legislation from the outset.[6] Colonialism presents many interesting situational variables from which social scientists become capable of measuring impacts of the legal cultures upon each other. Educational institutions are crucial with regard to sociological measurements of the changes within legal systems and legal cultures, especially concerning the demographics at the schools and universities regarding the identities of administrative staff, educators, students, the types of studies that the different peoples choose, the graduates, and their positions of employment thereafter.[7]

Education systems are neither legal nor illegal systems insofar as they consist of both legal activities (e.g., teaching legitimate curriculum) and illegal activities (e.g., bribery and fraud). Legal systems refrain from holding their societies' education systems responsible for the corruption within the education systems' legitimized procedural functions. Other systems that use deceptions, which undermine education systems and profit, may also very well be established as "illegal" ones via legal systems in the future, such as companies that facilitate academic fraud.

Yet if we inquire whether the legal system is legal, we are confronted with an entirely distinct set of questions. Any legal system, however corrupt or just it is,

---

6 Despite the advantages of coming to better understandings of the law by means of comparative legal studies and the sociology of law, there are more fundamental methods for attaining knowledge through library science that typically disregard the bureaucratic, political, or departmentalized subdivisions of academic disciplines and thereby focus on their accumulations of data concerning the real phenomena under analysis (See Ch. 3.1).

7 For these reasons, it behooves us to understand the priority in eradicating academic fraud by means of undermining the profit-schemes of semi-legitimate businesses that complete homework, theses, dissertations, online classes etc. for students in multiple nations, and such fraud via false authorship causes deteriorations of the education systems in our globalizing world.

has still established and developed itself as the legal and legitimate authority presiding over territories, jurisdictions, and peoples. The legal system is also a measure with which other systems are observed and analyzed regarding the amount of legality and illegality in jurisdictions. Many systems may tend to be ignored, or sometimes systems begin to challenge the distinctions between what is legal and illegal since they are, essentially, alegal. Education systems in most nations, if not all, are becoming ever more opposingly confronted with online businesses with anonymous owners and anonymous employees in the early 21st century who custom design works from all disciplines, except for the disciplines involving live performances (e.g., dance, music and athletic performances), to sell to students who have been assigned the work as tasks for marks within an education system or for acceptance into an institution (Brant, 2016).

3 The Concept of Alegality for Comparative Legal Studies and Rights

The Germanic adjective "*egal*" has been used ever since the early 17th century (Berckenmeyer, 1712 & Köbler, 1995). "Egal" means "equal, apathetic, indifferent, unconcerned or neutral." "Egal" was probably derived from the Latin word "*aequalis*," and the French loanword is "*égal*." When something is "egal," then either it does not matter, it is unimportant, or the person or people do not care about it perhaps because it is "equal" whether the thing at issue is the case or not, according to the person or some group, for instance.

The clear majority of our behaviors within some national economy are "egal," i.e., the behaviors are neither encoded as being "legal" nor "illegal" within any written or official manner since legalizing and illegalizing all human behaviors in the diverse types of situations under which they are permissible or impermissible would be terribly impractical if not utterly impossible. The founding acts of creating legislation are impossible to categorize as "legal or illegal" since they present a situation without a legitimate authority that is established, and which can dub what is legal and illegal (Lindahl, 2008, p. 125; Roermund, 1997).

One instance of the impracticality of establishing the ubiquity of legal acts, i.e., to signify every single act that is not illegal as being "legal," may involve such mundane instances as "walking to the market to buy some spicy chili peppers with one's own earned wages". Such a behavior as walking to the market may very well be perceived to be "legal" because, ideologically speaking, many people tend to think of each behavior that is not illegal as a legal one. However, there is generally no law that establishes the legality of such necessary behaviors (e.g., visiting a market to purchase food). Lawmakers are typically unconcerned (i.e., they practice egality) with the various numbers of necessary human behaviors that are required for the survival of families, such as buying groceries.

One might contest that a general constitution or a Declaration of Independence suggests that such a behavior as "walking to the market" is within the rights of the individual who has the "unalienable right to life, liberty, and the pursuit of happiness," whereas property, on the other hand, is an alienable right. Property can be transferred and relinquished. Life, liberty, and pursuits of happiness are never able to be lost or transmitted from one to another, according to the Declaration of Independence of the USA. Thus, one may rationally argue that the content and the broad language of certain fundamental legal documents account for the mundane or everyday behaviors, which may suffice to conclude that "walking to the market" is legal, even if the founding acts for creating the legislation are not best described as "legal" or "illegal." So, for instance, the act of walking to the grocery store to buy food might fall under the more general idea of the pursuit of happiness, which may suffice for it to be legal (i.e., as legality is broadly conceived in this way).

However, if we use the example of certain lines of the US constitution or the Declaration of Independence as reasons for justifying why a black man or a black woman "walking to the market" in, say, 1963 in the South of the USA is a so-called legal behavior, it would only be fair to consider the privileges or rights for grocers to legally deny the sale of any products to black people based on their races or skin colors until the establishment of the 1964 Civil Rights Act (Bruhns, 1972, p. 241). Similar privileges of high-status groups, denials, and the lack of recognition of human rights for lower status groups have existed within nations upon all the populated continents (e.g., Australia, England, and Brazil) and within nations with histories of slavery (Bergad, 2007; Campbell, 2004). Therefore, what is evident is that, despite justice systems, there are systematically unjust dominations of some human social group over others in each of the societies.

Perchance some of the earliest citizens of the USA maintained an ideology that blacks were either "illegal aliens" or "legal property, which is alienable." Black people had legal statuses of "real estate" and "private property" (Morris, 1996, pp. 61–80). Therefore, according to this inhumane way of thinking, blacks would reasonably be prevented from attaining "inalienable rights." The latter way of thinking is a form of dehumanizing logic. It may have strengthened social domination, several types of objectification, and subordination (Mühlen, 1964).

The rights of blacks in America were probably considered by most individuals with power to be unnecessary to explicitly deny via written law until the 1857 *Dred Scott vs. Sanford*, 60 U.S. 393 Supreme Court case. The Dred Scott decision maintained that no black person was a citizen of the USA. It maintained that slavery was legally permissible anywhere in the nation (Allen, 2006, p. 1).

Black people in America strove to thoroughly challenge the distinctions made that allowed the refusals of sales of goods and services to any people based on race, beliefs, and other factors, which had been "alegal or egal" refusals and thereby permitted by law but not officially legalized. The refusal of certain practices (e.g., the sale of services and goods) because of race, for instance, was obviously unfair and outright unjust to serious intellectuals. The refusals were sometimes thoughtlessly ignored and even supported or encouraged by the members of the legal institution. Members of the legal institution defended individuals who placed blacks at disadvantages in some cases. By the latter means the US criminal justice system at least inadvertently subordinated blacks as a minority group during the 20th century by allowing asymmetrical acts of unfairness, despite whether the victims were Africans, African-English, or African-American.

The racially prejudiced distinctions that were challenged by revolutionaries involved the transformations of people's beliefs and expectations that it was legal to refuse sales based upon race (i.e., a legal ideology greatly facilitating racism) to the beliefs and expectations that such refusals were illegal and unjust (i.e., a non-racist legal ideology that is more consistent with a moral and just worldview based on a principle of fairness). Mühlen describes the mid-20th century struggles of African-Americans and others who strove to attain rights via undermining the very legitimacy of the US legal system:

> In today's mass society [revolutions] had to be, like every other undertaking, carefully planned, and the requirement was to spark their attacks in their advances becoming systematically manipulated. Occupational revolutionaries led and organized the minority of activists to begin and create crises to bring the masses to their side, establish the injustice of the opponent, and weaken their power structure. (Mühlen, 1964, p. 134) [In der heutigen Massengesellschaft müßten sie [Revolutionen] wie jedes andere Unternehmen sorgfältig geplant, das Bedürfnis nach ihnen geweckt, in ihren Vorstößen systematisch manipuliert werden. Die von Berufsrevolutionären geleitete und organisierte Minderheit der Aktivisten begann Krisen zu schaffen, um die Massen auf ihre Seite zu bringen, den Gegner ins Unrecht zu setzen und seine Machtstruktur zu schwächen.]

Occupational revolutionaries were infiltrated by governmental agencies, which utilized African-American clandestine agents and others who sought to slow down the momentum of the civil rights movement (Wendt, 2006, p. 162). However, the increasing employment of African Americans within governmental agencies placed more minorities in positions of power. Activists for the civil cause consisted of diverse groups of people who were necessary to provide credible confirmations of mistreatments of blacks in America and thereby establish the injustices and unfairness within the legal system. The mistreatments, despite being unjust, had been neither criminalized nor illegalized and required the illegalization process brought by US President Lyndon Johnson with the 1964 and 1968 Civil Rights Acts (Hasday, 2007).

Mühlen (ibid.) presumes opponents acted unjustly and assumes revolutionaries refused to tolerate the injustices. Moreover, Mühlen tacitly assumes some revolutionaries act in accordance with justice or act in morally superior ways to their opponents. The role of the virtue of fairness in revolutionary movements is questionable. Is it ethical for activists to sometimes treat others unfairly? In what ways can we maintain that activists are treating their targets (e.g., business owners, customers and other stakeholders) in fair ways when the activism focuses on boycotts, sit-ins, and other non-violent forms, for instance?

The activists cannot always act in fair ways to their opposition. Activists identify and focus on certain groups of people, against whom they swing their attacks violently and/or non-violently. Activists targets are usually not ones who are committing the most morally egregious violations against others. Some of their opposition consists of extremists who malevolently interfere with people's abilities to make decisions. They maliciously reduce their opportunities in life by raping, killing, torturing, maiming, and stealing. For practical reasons, activists focus on specific types of violators who are selected because it is less risky than extremist groups, such as the Ku Klux Klan in the United States.

For the activists, acting in a fair manner is perhaps an irrelevant issue since a system with rampant injustices needs to be changed in ways that reduce risks to the activists during the revolution. Risk reduction is accomplished when certain individuals, organizations, and businesses are targeted as part of the revolution. The targeting of the activists' opponents is based on locations, business hours, and types of businesses opposed to their movement. It is also based on their strategic plans with considerations of moral characters of owners, their customers, and other stakeholders.

Activists undermine an aspect of the culture of their opposition and struggle to bring public perceptions against their opposition. For revolutionaries, fairness is irrelevant because it is idealistic and unrealistic. They see the range of intensity of violations that the opposition has made or is predicted to make. The opposition of extremists, who would be predicted by revolutionaries to have strategic locations, stubbornness, and moral depravity to retaliate violently against the activists, is left alone at some stages of the revolution, especially when businesses are targeted for acts like sit-ins. Instead, plans for the revolution have chosen groups of their opposition who are morally depraved enough to display their moral inferiority with overreactions.

Unjust acts are those that occur in situations with unfairness that is also preventable. The refusals to sell products and services to black people during the 1960s in the South of the United States is an example of a type of unjust act with preventable unfairness. Regarding people who are becoming activists, once unfairness is recognized by those who are treated unfairly, a whole range of emotions and mental states can arise. Anger, sadness, contempt, homicidal or suicidal tendencies, feelings of overwhelming desires of vengeance may arise or fear and subservience. The directions of activists are questionable.

Overall, revolutions for civil rights appear to make significant social changes with combinations of violent and non-violent activism. The violence of activists is countered with insurgents who are clandestinely placed in the groups of activists. By placing secret agents amongst the activists with more violent tendencies, agents attain positions of power in the organization (e.g., like African American FBI agents working undercover amongst and against the Black Panther Party in the 1970s).

The founding acts of a legal system are revolutionary much like civil rights movements. Lindahl (2008) proposes that the so-called "founding acts" of a legal order are "alegal" because illegality and legality always have already some pre-established legal order as preconditions from which they are understood. Both founding acts of legal systems and civil rights movements are coordinated struggles for fairness and equal rights or vice versa, unfairness and attempted domination for some social group or groups for those who are recognized and authorized by the legal system. Some groups that seek and demand rights can also be viewed as attempting to gain competitive advantages over other groups and dominating them regarding certain aspects, such as media coverage.

The revolutionary acts and movements for human rights greatly involve alegalities since they challenge the distinctions between what is legal and illegal. The alegalities (i.e., acts that are alegal) can very well involve injustices just like illegalities can. Lindahl (2008, p. 125) writes:

> Indeed, the founding acts of legal order are themselves neither legal nor illegal because both terms of this binary distinction already presuppose a legal order as the condition for their intelligibility. Instead, foundational acts are alegal because they institute the distinction itself between legality and illegality. Only retrospectively, if they catch on, can they come to manifest themselves, albeit precariously and incompletely, as legal acts.

Since the creation of new legislation cannot yet be part of any existing legal order (Roermund, 1997), there are several types of behaviors that are alegal but become legal or illegal based upon changing wants and needs and conceptions of security within the political economy. Consequently, the very first laws that come into effect for a legal system are alegal, unstable, and have an indeterminate status in respect to whether they will endure.

For indigenous Australians, the *Constitution Alteration (Aboriginals) 1967 Act No. 55 of 1967* was created. The Attorney-General's Department in Canberra prepared the description of these changes as an Act on March 19, 2004 within the Office of Legislative Drafting, which possesses the following long title: "An Act to alter the Constitution so as to omit certain words relating to the People of the Aboriginal Race in any State and so that Aboriginals are to be counted in reckoning the Population." Before 1967, Section 127 of the Australian Constitution maintained that the indigenous people would neither be counted nor be officially recognized as human beings for purposes of the commonwealth, stating that: "In reckoning the numbers of the people of the Commonwealth, or of a State or other part of the Commonwealth, aboriginal natives shall not be counted" (ibid.). Gifford (1997, p. 2) maintains:

> Unless Parliament has prohibited it in respect of the relevant criminal offence, there is still a right in a private person to bring a prosecution for a breach of the criminal law. In a society such as that of the Australian aborigines enforcement was sometimes left to the private individual and was sometimes carried out by the hunters of the tribe or by a vengeance party.

Gifford's analysis of the Australian legal system does not include the sociological impact of the legal system as an organization that implements controlled threats and violence disproportionately against low-status groups, especially against the aborigines, whilst tending to give high-status groups advantages. Gifford (ibid., pp. 130–131) viewed the aborigines as only being a few generations removed from the culture of the Stone Age and as a people who are required to adapt to the modern Australian legal system and to give up tribal laws.

Fitzgerald (2009, p. 1) demonstrates that the indigenous people of Australia are imprisoned at a rate that is thirteen times higher than non-indigenous Australians. Well over half of the indigenous people of Australia live in the cities, they comprise about three percent of the population of Australia, but they make up over 25% of the Australian prison population, according to a June 30, 2016, estimate (Australian Bureau of Statistics, 2013; Fitzgerald, ibid.; Australian Bureau of Statistics, 2016).

What is evident regarding these statistics and a rudimentary understanding of the history of low and high-status groups in Australia is that there are vast numbers of injustices within the legal system of Australia during the 20th and 21st centuries that allow easily observable forms and cases of domination implemented by the criminal justice system itself. Gifford (ibid.), however, cannot begin to analyze the essence of the law with a definition that restricts itself to defining "law" as "an officially recognised, enforceable system of rules" because the system of rules are applied in systematically different manner to different people based upon their socio-economic class, race, age, and other factors that lead, abitrarily, to social domination in societies.

The sudden increases in the numbers of indigenous people who were denied bail, the increases in the amounts of time indigenous people spent on remand without being convicted, and the increases in the prison sentences of indigenous people, all of which occurred between 2001 and 2008 (Fitzgerald, ibid.), demonstrate an incredibly powerful aspect of the 21st century Australian legal system that is altogether ignored by analyses. Such analyses frequently attempt to describe the legal system while perpetuating the agenda to respect, defend, and support it in the process of ignoring many of the social consequences of social domination that the legal system directly contributes to in often arbitrary ways (e.g., based on race).

Legal systems often undergo societal changes that emerge from social movements that aim to overturn legislation that tolerates injustices or that aim to create legislation that prevents injustices from occurring. However, societal changes from social movements sometimes also involve changes in legal systems with the creation of legislation that increases societal and procedural injustices.

Frequently within the histories of nations, the addition to a piece of legislation that calls for a culture, race, religious group, color of people, nationality of people, ethnic group, social group, language, or heritage of a people to be respected is a legal imperative that calls for the reduction of disrespect toward some groups of people. Such an addition to legislation suggests that disrespect that has previously existed and thereby demonstrates signs of actual injustices and unfairness within the society at large and within the legal and criminal justice systems.

Legislation can also legalize mistreatments of some officially categorized group of human beings. The lack of the appropriate legislation may legally permit a social group to undergo mistreatments to higher degrees than other social groups. For black people in America, the transformation from alegality to some official legal status of recognition of them as a people (i.e., as opposed to real estate or a different type of property) involved demonstrating the need for the American political economy to illegalize slavery in the latter half of the 19th century. In 1857, the US Supreme Court ascertained that blacks were not citizens of the US within the Dred Scott v. Sanford case.

A superficial analysis of the Dred Scott case may lead one to hastily conclude that the United States judiciary system digressed from a path toward fairness and justice. However, the presence of such law does entail that the US government was at least recognizing that an individual from a race of people requested citizenship. Furthermore, the denial of citizenship to blacks in America or any people is at least, arguably, better than completely ignoring each request and failing to make any judicial decision on the matter. For implementation, the denial of citizenship requires at least the tacit recognition of the people as non-citizens who have submitted a formal request for citizenship and eligibility.

In 1865, the Thirteenth Amendment to the United States Constitution illegalized slavery within the US and all its territories. In 1868, the Fourteenth Amendment to the United States Constitution allowed for an individual to become a US citizen, despite the person's race. The Fourteenth Amendment established it to be impermissible to deny any person protection that is equal in accordance with the law of the state. However, the Fourteenth Amendment also paved the way for small incorporated businesses and large stock corporations to attain the status of persons, in which case corporations were free to file lawsuits, their owners attained limited liability, and so the amendment facilitated the creation of hierarchies that still benefited the high-status groups, which were still based upon race (Bakan, 2005).

A century after the Dred Scott case, the United States Civil Rights Movement aimed to illegalize the preventions of buying and selling products and dwelling within certain areas in hotels, apartments, houses etc., which involved denials based on race and religion until during the latter half of the 20th century changes were made (i.e., with President Lyndon Johnson's 1964 and 1968 Civil Rights Acts). Moreover, ensuring social transformations via brute force with organized agendas that aimed to eradicate social injustices via numerous means, including violence, became effective in combination with the mass broadcasts of blatant social injustices against black people, which undermined the legitimacy of the justice system, morally speaking. The awareness of unjust and immoral laws led to diminishing social tolerance and to social unacceptability.

Certain social situations require the fulfillment of certain conditions for civil rights movements to be taken seriously by the legal system. One relevant social situation is where a social group makes it more difficult for the legal order to ignore that social group. Another relevant social situation is where people make it more challenging for the stabilization of societal expectations to arise from the legal system.

For civil rights movements to be taken seriously by the legal systems, the people must also render it more difficult for there to be a continuation of the old set of beliefs that involve justifications of systems in which citizens of the society live. Destabilizing the established set of beliefs of much of the populace is the goal for changing the system. The political, judiciary, and criminal justice systems, and other governmental systems combine to compose the society's legitimate authority. However, the civil rights movements facilitate the replacement of the latter set of beliefs and the replacement of system justificatory behaviors from the opposition with system-changing tendencies of the activists.

If the social situational factors, which are detrimental to some lower status group, are not undergoing reconciliation in ways that alter the legal system's toleration of injustices, which are typically wrought against the lower status groups at higher rates, then the society may become a society where unfairness and injustice are internationally broadcast. For instance, in 1951 the Civil Rights Congress secretary, William L. Patterson, presented a historic document to the United Nations in Paris, and Paul Robeson and several other people handed the same document to a United Nations official in New York, which was called "We Charge Genocide: The Historic Petition to the United Nations for Relief from a Crime of the United States Government against the Negro People."

The United Nations approved of the Genocide Convention in 1948, and in 1951 the convention came into effect (Simon, 2007, p. 51). The indictment brought to the United Nations against the United States by the African American people probably had more of an international impact in virtue of changing global public perceptions about the ways blacks were mistreated. It exposed some lynchings and disenfranchisements of black people, especially in the South. Yet when the Civil Rights Congress was associated with the movement of communism by the US government and media, the "Red Scare" of communism largely led public opinion to lean against the charges (Martin, 1997). Charles Martin (1997, p. 35) writes:

> The rise of the Cold War added a new ideological dimension which greatly complicated the debate over these issues. As the Soviet-American rivalry heated up, the Russians regularly denounced American racial practices and attempted to exploit such mistreatment in their efforts to win the allegiance of Third World peoples.

Changes were underway that involved the exposure of alegal hangings of black people by mostly white men (i.e., often ignored or allowed by law enforcement). The unjust killings then became observable via broadcasts on the world stage. They undermined the moral integrity of the US legal system. They showed the indifference toward injustices, which depended on the social status of the groups involved. During the first week of 1923 in Rosewood, Florida USA, a massacre occurred. It involved the murders of many blacks and the destruction of Rosewood, a small town inhabited predominately by blacks. Thirty years later organizations of black people allowed such genocidal tendencies to be broadcast.

Transformations were accomplished via creating greater insecurities for the US political economy. In the United States, people had presumed that it was legal for US citizens or entrepreneurs to deny certain peoples' abilities or rights to make exchanges. They presumed it was legal to deny a people entrance in certain residential, commercial and industrial areas.

However, the refusals to permit some people to make exchanges were neither legal nor illegal, but rather they were alegal. Denials of exchanges and entrances, based on race, were challenged regarding their legality when the lower status group (being denied) became organized and populated more of America. The practices of denying access to products and places promoted rampant racism. Perhaps the denials of access arose from the attempts of groups to assert social dominance. Ideologies of dominance were reinforced via system justificatory behaviors.

Transformations were also accomplished by black leaders for the cause of civil rights by means of undermining the moral character of the governmental institutions. The moral integrity was tested in the police forces in Alabama, Mississippi, Arkansas, and several other states in which police employees were captured on film during the use of excessive force against people of color and broadcast via the mass media system during the mid-twentieth century.

The alegal denial of human rights to black people was illegalized in the political economy only after the growth of the social group and after multiple generations of people planned and struggled vehemently for fairer treatment. Great activists of the 19th century in the USA, such as Frederick Douglass, asserted that for progress to occur, life is insufficient to live without struggle because power will be wielded against those who acquiesce. Rights are, indeed, continually rescinded as such individuals comply obediently and conform to unfair and unjust standards of some existing state of affairs.

Several disadvantages for African Americans diminished, especially during the late 1950s and 1960s, which included some diminishment of the attitude of indifference about racially based injustices held by the legal system and which was expressed in the form of communications, at least, toward the most obvious injustices, allowing for the shift of many types of injustices wrought against blacks to progress from alegal to illegal, a transformation that occurred via the legal system itself. The recognition of the power and ever-developing moral stature of the social group (i.e., African American people) challenged the distinction between what was legal and illegal in accordance with the legal system. However, the disruptions within the legal system came from within and also from external sources.

The ideas of Lindahl (2008) largely concern cases when and where immigration disrupts the normal legal order that is already in place because there are significant numbers of foreigners who cross the borders. After fluctuations of migrants occur, there are also sets of border crossings that lead the political economy to change the way in which it contradistinguishes between what, how many, and where exactly it is legal and illegal in respect to border crossings of selected migrants. The reason for the new contradistinctions involves outdated notions and usages of "legality" and "illegality" in official procedures to handle influxes of migration patterns securely. Thus, the latter sets of immigration cases provide a reason why Lindahl (2008, p. 117) further develops the concept called "alegality" and why he poses fundamental questions about immigration, legal systems, and border crossings:

> What happens to the concept of security if legal disorder manifests itself not only as illegal behavior but also as alegal behavior—acts that challenge the very distinction between legality and illegality, as drawn by a political community?

What appears to happen when alegal acts wreak disorder within societies are increases in the awareness of injustices, discussions, and legislations of some solutions, which include human rights, animal rights and environmental protection. Some 21st century research has led many to further research a growing problem of injustice that has manifested within education systems. Recently developing problems, concerning alegality and the growing risks to legal order, are the sales, purchases, advertisements, and uses of ghost-authored writings for multitudes to receive credits for university courses and even for university professors to publish more works to fraudulently meet their academic publication requirements (Mahmood, 2009; Page, 2004; Brant, 2012b & 2016). A massive development of this alegal and dishonest set of business practices has allowed many global web-based companies to thrive and has allowed many students to receive degrees based on submitting homework, theses, and dissertations that were written and completed by ghostwriters, which undermines education systems and negatively impacts each industry of business.

The students pay through legitimate business websites with credit or debit cards. The businesses sometimes own many different essay mill websites with different advertising strategies (Brant, 2012b). The websites are intricately interconnected with banking systems and telecommunication systems, the latter of which facilitate the services and payments via offers of unlimited customer service through instant messaging and telephoning. In many cases, the phone and message services function every day for twenty-four hours. These online essay mills have probably also caused many politicians to lose their positions of employment and academic degrees either because of plagiarism, for which they are caught, or cyber pseudepigraphy (i.e., the use of a web-based service to hire a ghostwriter, and the use of the ghostwriter's work without giving the ghostwriter any acknowledgement (Page, 2004, 429)), including a former president of Hungary, a former German minister of defense, and European Union members of parliament so far during the 21st century (Brant, 2012b & 2016).

Some ideas about alegality and thoughts about alegal practices can be analyzed in relation to common sayings that coincide with ordinary speech about legality and illegality. German speakers, for instance, have a common saying that refers directly to legal systems, which is "*legal, illegal, oder scheißegal*," (i.e., legal, illegal, or could not care less). The latter term *scheißegal* is widely considered vulgar by German speakers. As a vulgarity, the term expresses dire concerns some folks have with decisions made (by the legal system) that do not meet their expectations (of its role) in eradicating injustices and promoting justice. Perhaps at the heart of the concepts of legality, illegality, what is *scheißegal* in German, or alegality and egalitarianism, is this notion of being "egal."

The word "egalitarian" was likely influenced by the French and German word "egal" and probably developed an early 20th century change from the usage of "equalitarian," which had been used in English at least in the late 18th century, toward the modern notion. "Egalitarianism" is either the advancement of beliefs in or believing in the equality of all people from at least some perspective or perspectives, including social, economic, legal rights, or within political life.

Without the conception of "egal" that is partially recognized via an understanding of "egalitarianism," there are sets of confusions and deceptions that arise concerning legality and illegality. I shall attempt to clarify three of these confusions that result from a lack of understanding that all behaviors in a society are not merely able to be neatly organized into the systematic binary code we call "legal" and "illegal" behaviors. Any clarification of these issues generally involves descriptions of social groups' opposite-ended interests. The importance of this is that a leading role is played by conflicts where there are shifts in political and social power, in the uses of hard power and soft power, and violence or threats of violence (See Ch. 4.4).

There is a difference between the "binary code of the legal subsystem as a whole" and the "code that is established via a legal sub-subsystem of the societal system" (e.g., the criminal justice sub-subsystem's courts of judging and law). The latter difference is that the legal subsystem is usually required to presume the given status of an action provided by legislation, which defines the "act" as being "legal or illegal, but not both simultaneously" before another legal sub-subsystem is underway with the process of providing the verdict and typical binary code of "guilty or not guilty, but not both simultaneously," for instance.

Any legal system is ever-changing based on what things and actions of people are encoded as legal and illegal as well as the frequent encodings of guilty and not guilty of the court system with judicial decisions, which change over time, despite the precedential authority of the common law system.[8] The broad interpretations of the written descriptions of illegality and the description of any person (i.e., also including contradictions from, say, defense and prosecuting attorneys and perhaps even massive amounts of misinformation), who is alleged to have illegally performed some act or to have performed an illegal act, is often given the opportunity for a defense from the accusations within the court system. After a formal or official set of legal procedures occur, the typical binary code is established: guilty EXOR not guilty, i.e., guilty or not guilty but not both.

In some systems, a ternary code may be established, such as the Scottish justice system, which establishes the following designations: *guilty*, *not guilty*, and *not proven* (Duff, 1999; Willock, 1966). Comparative analyses of legal systems often suggest that fundamental differences, such as the distinction between a binary and ternary legal code to be established by a jury, between legal subsystems in respect to procedures probably result in wide-ranging differences concerning each legal system. In respect to Scotland's justice system, few trials are permitted to involve juries in comparison to other court systems, such as the American court system (Duff, 1999, pp. 175–176).

4 Ideologies without Concepts of Alegality May Fail to Conceive of Indifference

Sometimes legal systems communicate what is legal and illegal to the populace, even if the communications of these codes are less efficient for some

8 Some scholars credit the enlightenment and positivism for the incorporation of the concept of legality into criminal law as well as key legal documents that served political purposes, such as several constitutions, including the United States Constitution of 1787 (Gallant, 2009, pp. 47–48). The Austrian Penal Code of 1787 and the French Declaration of the Rights of Man of 1789 at the beginning of the French Revolution also serve as examples of such legal documents (ibid.).

social groups within the society as opposed to others. Tourists and other foreigners tend to be less aware of the laws of the land in which they only temporarily reside. Legal systems provide society with distinctions between actions. Actions are encoded as "legal and illegal" via lawmakers. Legal systems' preestablished positions as legitimate authorities allow them to preside over some finite jurisdictions temporarily.

As with communications from figures with authority, legal systems function to stabilize expectations of each populace. Yet legal systems are generally not expected to educate an entire populace regarding the workings, established norms, and applications of the concepts of legality and illegality to actions that are categorized as such.

Sometimes the illegalization of something is not well-publicized. So, for instance, one may very well believe that some act is both legal and socially acceptable, despite the act being illegal in accordance with the legal system within which that individual lives or visits. According to Garner (2004, p. 5306), there are several ancient legal maxims that pertain to the lack of knowledge of the law that are presented in Latin with their English translations:

> *Ignorantia legis neminem excusat.* Ignorance of law excuses no one. *Ignorantia praesumitur ubi scientia non probatur.* Ignorance is presumed where knowledge is not proved. *Ignorare legis est lata culpa.* To be ignorant of the law is gross neglect of it.

The legality or illegality of some type of behavior is very often situational or circumstantial insofar as the legality or illegality of the behavior may depend upon something else, say, whether it is performed in public rather than in private. Many human behaviors performed in sports are illegal outside of the sport arenas or wrestling rings, such as pins and takedowns. The attire of divers, strippers, and swimmers is legally permitted within certain areas but may result in legal fines or very strict penalizations in other areas.

For these reasons and many more, situational variables are required for individuals to judge whether certain acts are either legal or illegal, but not all the situational variables are explicitly defined or explained. The latter judgments may contradict what has been established by the legal system as, in fact, legal and illegal, which thereby behooves us to largely consider social understandings of legality and illegality as ideological stances and opinions. Moreover, the fact that there are misunderstandings about what exactly is legal and illegal can well lead analysts to investigate the concepts of legality and illegality in relation to beliefs and desires about what is legal, beliefs and desires

	L=Legal	I=Illegal	A=Alegal
S=Socially Acceptable	$((\forall x)(Lx \,\&\, Sx)) \rightarrow {\sim}((\exists x)(Ix))$	$((\forall x)(Ix)) \rightarrow ((\exists x)(Ux))$	$((\forall x)(Ax \,\&\, Sx)) \rightarrow ((\exists x)({\sim}Px \vee Ux))$
U=Socially Unacceptable	$((\forall x)(Lx)) \rightarrow ((\exists x)(Sx))$	$((\forall x)(Ix \,\&\, Ux)) \rightarrow {\sim}((\exists x)(Lx))$	$((\forall x)(Ax \,\&\, Ux)) \rightarrow ((\exists x)(Px \vee Sx))$
P=Permissible			

FIGURE 1 Logical analysis of legal codes, alegality and acceptability

about what is illegal, and beliefs and desires about what is neither legal nor illegal in relation to what the social and legal fact of the matter is.

Ideology involves a distorted way of thinking about reality, especially social reality. Ideology often arises with the failure to account for new facts that apply to situations that emerge. Ideology also arises during attempts to conceal social facts and situational variables via unfittingly thinking about them within superimposed arbitrary categories. For the holder of the ideology, the extent to which his or her way of thinking is distorted is unbeknownst to him or her. The potentiality of the advocate of the ideology is limited in certain respects, especially insofar as there are arrested developments regarding the systematic production of knowledge and knowledge-claims since such a practitioner misunderstands his or her own involvement within the social context and surroundings during some time span (Mannheim, 1929; Wardell & Fuhrman, 1981, p. 482).

Figure 1 functions as a method that facilitates the categorizations of descriptions of the differences amongst political, social and (sub)cultural ideologies and actions. They are presented in relation to legality, social acceptance, and social unacceptability. The following logical descriptions fail to include the relevant and important concept of indifference or ambivalence, though.

People typically ignore indifference and alegality regarding such issues: (1) “Legal and socially acceptable,” (LA), means that if all the relevant actions within the confines of a society, culture, or community are both legal and socially acceptable, there is no instance in which those actions are illegal; (2) “Illegal but socially acceptable,” (IS), entails that if all the acts are illegal within this category, there is at least some case of one type of act being socially unacceptable (e.g., for some subculture or social group) at some temporal and geographic location; (3) “Legal but socially unacceptable,” (LU), means that if all acts are legal, then there is some instance where some act is socially acceptable within some temporal and geographic region; and (4) the “illegal and socially unacceptable," (IU), entails that if every act is illegal and socially unacceptable, then there is no instance in which one of the acts is legal from the perspective of the ideology at hand (Brant, 2012a).

(5) "Alegal but socially acceptable," (AS), means that in every case if the actions are both alegal and socially acceptable, then there is an instance where at least one of those acts is not permissible or is socially unacceptable for at least some social group. (6) Lastly, "alegal and socially unacceptable" acts, (AU), include types of acts that are either permissible or are socially acceptable in accordance with at least some social group within the confines of the society.

Benefits of this legal and political ideological graph are relevant when key differences between any two cultures, societies or communities are presented explicitly. Consider this in relation to the most important and interesting differences in law and what is socially acceptable and socially unacceptable. It is from this standpoint that some major differences in ideology are readily observable.

Figure 1 describes tendencies or general ways of thinking about the law, legality, and illegality in relation to acceptance and their opposing conceptions. The major criticism of these typical ways of thinking concerns a lack of attention to the role of indifference as well as to alegality. Alegality functions as a concept that allows us to better explain the drastic changes that societies and legal systems, political systems, and other social systems make in relation to what becomes socially acceptable, socially indifferent, socially unacceptable, as well as what becomes legal and illegal, enforced and unenforced by police, etc.

Two out of six of the abovementioned categories allow a distinction to be made between the general ideology of the public and the hegemonic power's ideology, namely, the legal but socially unacceptable aspects of society and the illegal but socially acceptable categories of societies, which are mostly tolerated without violent conflict by those under hegemonic rule. One challenging task is for historians, sociologists, and anthropologists to fill in the six abovementioned categories with the most historically important and interesting facts.

Once the latter facts are clearly known, the ability to determine whether a society is ruled by a hegemony as opposed to dominating powers is possible, and the demarcation criteria between the dominating powers and hegemonic powers is more easily clarified. As in much of the of the scientific literature of communication studies, hegemonic powers are conceptualized as those that provide the societal system with "noncoercive relations of domination" where the low-status groups consent actively to systems of beliefs and to hierarchical power relations in society (Mumby, 1997; Burawoy, 1979; Deetz & Mumby, 1985, 1990; Mumby, 1987, 1988; Rosen, 1985, 1988). The subordinated groups also support these systems and power relations, which often go against these groups' best interests. The concept of the dominating powers, however, includes coercive relations of power, too, which is present in the research of Antonio Gramsci (1891–1937).

Moreover, the account of a single ideology can be analyzed in relation to the numerous ways in which actions are categorized by each particular social group. Some social groups that are poverty-stricken and unaffiliated with legal institutions (e.g., people who do no work for the legal system) do not categorize some behaviors as "illegal," although the behaviors are categorized by most of the society as "illegal." For instance, the elderly in homes for assisted living believe that sharing prescription medicines is legal, although it is illegal. As a result, the group has inherent disadvantages. They may begin to depend on the exchanges, or they may be fined for their illegal use.

For them, the categories, "legal" and "illegal," are misattributed to their own action in society, like a someone who is speeding but does not realize it. Understanding the societal relations thus involves attending to what one or more social groups perceive as being legal and what they perceive as illegal. The latter groups limit their possibilities for actions, too, when they perceive of actions as being illegal that are, in fact, legal or alegal. The members of the social group may tend to refrain from performing those actions because of their legal ideology. This social group enters a state of confusion because the group forms disagreements that contribute to members of the social group actually voicing, voting, and acting out in ways that demote their own best interests.

Figure 1 thereby can represent the ideologies of various social groups or wide-ranging ideologies within a single social group. Otherwise, figure 1 can be understood differently as what involves strictly social facts about what is really legal and really illegal to do within some particular jurisdiction, and thereby the figure can be used to facilitate an understanding of these real social relations that are enforced by law with their relationship to what people at large within society find acceptable and unacceptable to perform (e.g., what is acceptable or unacceptable for them or others to buy, sell, possess, and do, despite whether it is legal or illegal, and despite whether they believe it is legal or illegal).

Figure 1 establishes the logical limitations in these latter respects upon the roles of desires and beliefs of people about legality, illegality, and even alegality, and does this with consideration to the formations of ideologies. Thus, the formations of many scientific hypotheses may generate from the assertions within figure 1, including the hypotheses from the legal and socially acceptable category that: (1) we may find important instances of illegality regarding acts that individuals incorrectly believe are legal to perform when the acts are also socially acceptable within the society; (2) there are deviations between social facts, beliefs, and expectations of people such that certain individuals falsely believe that specific acts and relations are illegal and socially unacceptable when they are instead legal but socially unacceptable.[9] The latter sorts of deviations may explain several types of deviant behaviors and allow legal theorists and practitioners to understand many types of unlawfulness to originate from legal ideologies rather than disobedience.

For instance, a twenty-five or thirty year old man or woman who has intimate or sexual relations with a seventeen year old adolescent may believe that what they do is socially acceptable as a relationship and legal, too, even though within their jurisdiction it is illegal (e.g., statutory rape), and outside of their community the relationship and intimate relations are socially unacceptable. The second set of hypotheses involves unethical business practices, say, involving deceptions. Entrepreneurs and employees who seek to gain competitive advantages may search for these sorts of tendencies of thinking described in (2) so that it becomes ever-easier to take advantage of their competition.

With each of the six abovementioned categories in figure 1 there are four considerations, regarding any particular behavior and its relations, that involve the individual either correctly or incorrectly believing the legality, illegality, or alegality of the matter and involve one either correctly or incorrectly believing the social acceptability (or unacceptability) of the matter. The latter considerations, however, assume that the analyst already knows the correct status of the social fact regarding the legal system to make any useful assessment.

To give an idea about just how complicated the role of assessment for the researcher really is, the false beliefs are also measurably divided into two other categories each. For example, the false belief about the illegality of something (e.g., purchasing a master's thesis in 2017 in the United States of America, which is alegal) is measurably comparable with the true belief that it is alegal as well as the false belief that it is legal or that it has been legalized or illegalized. Individuals may be placed into groups regarding whether they believe it

9 One may question what the significance or limitations are for socially acceptable behaviors. Cannibalism is, for instance, socially acceptable for the cannibals, especially if they have a cannibalistic tribe. However, for most people, especially non-cannibals who live in civil societies, cannibalism is socially unacceptable. Socially acceptable behaviors are those actions that are, therefore, acceptable for some social group. To realize what social groups find acceptable, observations are necessary. Observations are necessary for realizing what social groups believe is legal or illegal or unacceptable, too.

is socially acceptable or socially unacceptable. Some social groups may even be discovered to be generally indifferent about it.

The hegemony indoctrinates the society partially via imposing sets of descriptions of behaviors that are officially categorized by the society's legal system as being legal, although they are socially unacceptable for, possibly, many parts of the populace, and officially categorized as being illegal, although they are socially acceptable actions to perform for most of some parts of the populace. These latter legalizations, illegalizations, and laws are enforced without any debilitating social unrest (i.e., there is only the risk of civil unrest) by means of the hegemony's control of the major ideologies of the classes and social groups that have opposing interests.

In part, the hegemony accomplishes control over the major ideologies of the populace via the mass media system and its approach as an adversarial, antagonistic, and tetchy presenter of information and misinformation in combination with language that masks the realpolitik motivations of a policy to attain more constituents who vote against their own best interests and also in combination with multiple institutions within society that superimpose their ways of thinking upon the populace via selections of certain types of thinkers in schools and politically-motivated, handpicked textbooks and other forms of institutionalization.

As opposed to the hegemony, the dominating power reins via the implementation of fear, corruption, and physical coercion to force portions of the society to comply with an authoritarian ideology imposed upon the masses at the expense of actual civil unrest. The societies ruled by dominating powers, as opposed to hegemonies, may also greatly indoctrinate their people, such as North Korea in 2017 with its emphasis on the extent of military power its government has. With the dominating powers, there is no freedom of the press, and journalists and human rights activists may be assassinated, imprisoned, and tortured in large numbers, even if the society has greatly reduced its violence and murders overall. Perhaps industrial societies, as opposed to agrarian and developed service-oriented societies, are the likeliest candidates to be ruled by dominating powers. China, for instance, can be viewed as being ruled by dominating powers insofar it has had approximately hundreds human rights activists disappear, or they have been interrogated or indicted with the crime of "subversion of state powers." The victims include predominantly human rights lawyers, according to Amnesty International (2016) and the Human Rights in China organization (2017).

Methodologies, techniques for observations, and measurements of many factors, concerning the social structuring of public perceptions, attention spans of audiences, and opinions, have quite greatly changed their focuses from miscommunications, accidental distributions of misinformation, and low quality educational levels of the public toward focuses upon the successful communications of the instillment of controversy, confusions, and misinformation in the public, which facilitate ideologies. David Cheal (1979, pp. 109–110) writes:

> The dominant explanation for the distribution of systemic thought in mass publics has been a theory of communication deficiencies. In discussing the social structuring of political consciousness Converse (1964: 211–212) gave most attention to the diffusion of "packages" of ideas from creative sources to the masses. Diffusion, of course, depends on successful communication.

Cheal (ibid.) continues:

> Weaknesses in ideological thought were therefore explained as the result of imperfections in the transmission of information. Later studies have sought to locate these imperfections in low levels of formal education (Bishop, 1976; Stimson, 1975), or in certain types of electoral campaigns (Bennett, 1973; Field and Andersen, 1969; Nie & Anderson, 1974; Pierce, 1970; Stimson, 1975).

The latter explanations, however, are lacking, according to many scholars, including Herman and Chomksy (1988). Cheal (ibid) writes:

> Mann (1970) and Sallach (1974) … argue that the weakness of ideological thought in the masses is not attributable to deficiencies in the communication of ideas from the elites downwards. Rather the weakness is due to the success of that communication. In a class society the values of the ruling class are effectively disseminated by agencies such as the schools and the mass media. These dominant values contradict those shaped by the experiences of everyday life in the lower classes. The result is a high level of confusion and inconsistency in the political opinions of subordinate groups.

Cheal (ibid.) and Sallach (1974) both identify the latter type of dominations of the masses via thought-control to be the "hegemony," which follows the line of the thinking from Antonio Gramsci's notes from prison. Herman and Chomsky (1988) also maintain that the latter institutions are significant in the indoctrination. However, universities are also responsible for selecting academics who are indoctrinated, tolerating and even largely supporting the systems within which they live (i.e., system justificatory behaviors), according to Chomsky.

A significant difference resides between those who are members of low-status and high-status groups (i.e., subordinate and dominant social groups) in respect to what is illegal yet socially acceptable and legal yet socially unacceptable. The categories of human behaviors of the illegal yet socially acceptable and legal yet socially unacceptable acts are also aspects of the ideological structure of the types of communications of the legal system. The criminal justice system subsists within the legal system and enhances or attempts to enhance the pre-existing hierarchies of social groups in the society in support of the systematic tendency to slightly benefit dominant groups while slightly disadvantaging subordinate groups. The latter idea finds support from social dominance theorists.

It is often dogmatically presumed that what is both legal and socially acceptable encompasses most of the behaviors within any society or culture. However, alegal but socially acceptable behaviors might be considered to have the highest frequency of behaviors. "Legal and socially acceptable" for a certain group means that there is no possibility within the ideology of these individuals to allow for there to be examples of such actions that are illegal within the confines of said group, such as a society or tribe, and this becomes problematic when individuals believe wrongly in the legality of the act, producing conflict. Such relations of law are extremely important.

The fact that marijuana being smoked in certain areas is both legal and acceptable within the "Dutch sub-cultures and the Dutch society" does not serve as a counter-example of the aforementioned definition of the legal and socially acceptable category, i.e., even when we are given the fact that marijuana is illegal in most regions of the world or illegal within certain areas of Amsterdam in the 21st century, because figure 1 can be used to graph the ideology of a common culture or social groups.

The portion of the Dutch culture which dubs marijuana "legal and socially acceptable" correctly and non-ideologically (i.e., since it is legal and social groups accept it and its consumption) maintains that there is no instance in which marijuana is illegal within the particular confines of the group, namely, the geographic and temporal period, unless there is an enforcement of racist, sexist, or ageist laws since, for instance, placing legal limitations upon age demands that some aspect of the product and its relations within society are, in fact, illegal. There are gradations of legality, which are partially illustrated within figures 2 and 3 (see below). Figure 1 is a framework that accounts for the social acceptance of a group within the confines of the legal system to which they are subjected, and the figure functions to illustrate misconceptions that individuals have in relation to what is legal, illegal, and alegal as well as to provide an overview of what actually is legal, alegal, and illegal within society and what the overall views of the people are regarding the social acceptability and social unacceptability of the same acts.

Illegal and socially unacceptable acts lead to the opposite conclusions. There is no instance of illegality for what is legal and socially acceptable, in this framework. People may still be led to believe that something legal and socially acceptable is illegal. Also, there is no instance of legality for what is actually illegal and socially unacceptable, such as rape, theft, deceptive trade practices, arson, and murder. The legal facts thusly appear to be independent of individual opinions of people regarding legality and illegality (i.e., if intersubjectivity plays no role). The social conditions under which illegal acts are performed are multifarious.

A defendant may have performed an illegal act that the defendant also believes is socially unacceptable. The jury members may very well consider the act to be socially acceptable. Moreover, the defense attorney may convince the defendant to respond in ways that lead the court to believe that the defendant thought his actions were lawful and socially acceptable. This can be a strategy for reducing penalties but is risky.

Illegal but socially acceptable acts are categorized here as generally unacceptable for the hegemonic powers and therefore (because of their control and ability to rein influence via their media outlets that disperse their ideologies) these actions are illegal. The latter acts are unacceptable for the dominating powers, such as some examples of acts of human rights lawyers in the 21st century in China that have been dubbed by the government as "subversive acts to state power" (Amnesty International, 2016). The illegalization of the socially acceptable acts, such as runaway slave laws, continually benefits individuals in power. If some type of acts was acceptable for hegemonic or dominating powers and their constituents, it would be almost immediately relabeled "legal and socially acceptable."

Likewise, dominating powers categorize a set of actions as "illegal" that is socially acceptable for a substantial portion of the society. Part of the distinction that can be made between a hegemony in some society and a dominating power in another society is the sheer amount of behaviors recognized as "illegal" in the society but that are also largely socially acceptable (i.e., considering the time period, population size, and contiguous societies), which leads to greater conflicts between the populace and the society's members of the legal institution or military in the society ruled by dominating powers instead of a hegemony.

Legal but socially unacceptable acts, on the contrary, involve something being socially acceptable for the hegemonic powers or dominating powers yet unacceptable for the masses. During the 20th and 21st centuries developed countries have expanded the scope of corporate economies in developing and underdeveloped nations, facilitating increases in poor working conditions, child labor, and sweatshops in the textile industry. Some conditions resemble slave labor. An overabundance of corporate acts falls in the category of the legal but socially unacceptable.

In the society ruled via dominating powers, there is an undeveloped and poorly-supported ideology of the masses. It naturally leads more frequently to violent conflicts between the members of the legal institution or military and the populace. When more people realize that their best interests are opposed by the dominating powers (i.e., the realization involves knowing this in instances of what is legal but socially unacceptable and illegal but socially acceptable to make, do, buy, sell, or possess), then they oppose the elites in varying degrees. However, in underdeveloped nations and many developing nations, people are concerned foremost with motivations to satisfy their basic physiological needs and needs for security for themselves, their families, and friends (Maslow, 1943).

The hegemonic powers allow such acts (i.e., legal but unacceptable and illegal but acceptable ones) to remain with their statuses of legality or illegality at the potential expense of civil unrest (i.e., civil unrest will occur if the masses realize that their interests are being compromised to allow the hegemonic powers to support their own opposing interests and ideology). Hegemonic powers confuse and instill the public with ideology. The confusion comes from many different directions and diverse types of media.

Even advertising, which oftentimes comes from hegemonic powers and to subordinate societies, is used to confuse the public about the nature of corporate powers, which have immeasurable influence over governments. The advertising confuses the masses via offering miniscule amounts of information and teachings about the products the corporations sell. Customers are seduced into buying products (e.g., brands of fragrances, jewelry, or clothes) by advertisements showing the pretend attraction of sexy women and men. The figures of the men and women in advertising are shown to be wearing, driving, or using the products, for instance, which gives the association of youth, beauty, sophistication etc. with the products.

A tendency has developed for showmanship to substitute for research and usefulness so that advertising firms hire showmen and women who deceive people into buying the products rather than research scientists who teach and inform people of the products and new developments. The latter tendency allows for companies to offer lower quality products with greater attention to packaging and to the mass psychology of deception against the customers as well as groups of consumers, such as children and adolescents, who the firms use like tools via their advertisements to have the youths press and persuade their older family members to buy products for them. This is a model of confusion of customers.

The latter points about the products, deception, and confusion with advertising are applicable to services, too, and this includes some public services. For example, there are many politicians (i.e., public servants) who support the best interests of corporations and their shareholders and thereby advertise themselves in very similar ways to those described in the model of confusion of customers, and they do so for both votes and money. Politicians confuse the public, deceive many into voting and supporting them financially, refrain from teaching the public about their services, and they lie about their services as well, in which case they may say they will perform something a certain way during their campaigns, refrain from doing that once they are elected, and, again, they may lie about why they refrained from performing certain services during their campaigns for reelections. This is a model of confusion of voters (and customers of services). The model is tied closely with large stock corporations that have limited liability since they find ways to increase profits via playing crucial roles in electing political figures who are likely to provide mutual benefits.

The hegemony creates an ideology for itself that can even become popular to support, and there are classes of people or social groups that support it, even though their support for the hegemonic ideology is in opposition to their own social groups' best interests and their own interests as well in many cases. The latter support for the hegemony comes in two very different forms, namely, either through the deception of the supporters or via providing benefits for other supporters who facilitate the deception of the former supporters,[10] even

10 The benefits which lead certain people to support the hegemonic powers just benefit that individual and, presumably, his or her family but negatively impact the class to which the individual belonged, for instance, because the hegemony finds it useful to select people who appear to be from groups that are fundamentally opposed to the hegemonic ideology. Therefore, there are mass broadcasts of low-status group members in society who support massive tax cuts (i.e., even for the wealthy) and the withdrawals of finances from governmentally funded programs etc. One who confronts such individuals during

though the ideological stance negatively affects both types of supporters in either form.

The hegemony becomes a dominating force and authoritarian government when it postpones legal changes that disregard interests and powers of social groups who demand those legal changes (i.e., legalization or illegalization processes for what is, respectively, socially acceptable and socially unacceptable) and instead the hegemony begins acting like a dominating power insofar as it forcefully suppresses public uprisings, imprisons dissenters, and continues to risk further violent dissent. The hegemony is therefore not far removed from becoming a dominating power. The new election cycle may lead to fundamental changes in way a society is ruled, although power ultimately resides in the people once they become enlightened.

The masses are placed in an unfortunate position of ignorance after being indoctrinated by ideology. The most prolific ideology is the hegemony's ideology because these powerful individuals control the outlets through which their ideology can be publicized. Outlets include mass media systems and education systems. So, members of other interest groups are convinced well enough to allow their groups' interests to be jeopardized for the sake of the interests of the hegemonic powers. Of course, this does not include interest groups that are directly affected and who are explicitly opposing the hegemonic powers.

The importance of the logical conceptions in figure 1 as an explanatory device involves the representation of the structures of: (1) all categorizations of behaviors within some geographical region or society; and (2) the structure of the cultural, societal, communal, economic, political, and legal ways of thinking, with which any or all behaviors within the society are categorized correctly and ideologically.

The difference between (1) and (2) is based upon the conception that all individuals desire and believe something specific about sets of behaviors, but there are social facts about the legal status of behaviors, keeping in mind that the circumstances matter, and there are social facts about the amount of social acceptability, social indifference, and social unacceptability (i.e., (1)). Moreover, certain groups categorize peoples' behaviors similarly (i.e., some groups have ideologies (i.e., where (2) has structure). (1) is measurable via large

a broadcast (i.e., who serve a very similar role to the Uncle Tom-figure in Harriet Beecher Stowe's writings) may ask the individuals to describe what he or she thinks about a topic of political controversy, such as tax cuts for each class, and presume that there is a tendency for the low-status group representatives who support the hegemonic ideology to have no evidence of supporting such stances before having received the wages or salaries from the (corporate) organization and media through which they voice the hegemonic ideology.

enough random samples of the populace, whereas (2) requires cleverer methods of discovering the patterns of the ideologies within socially identifiable social groups, low-status, mid-status, and high-status groups, for instance.

Individuals are often deceived into advocating that which deviates from (1), in which case they have formed inaccurate beliefs about the legal status of acts and fail in many cases to recognize what acts have the standing of social acceptability or unacceptability. They may tend to vote for representatives who advocate a different stance than their own stances. Many are deceived into supporting an ideology against their own interests within a representative democracy, for example.

Some individuals are paid to support ideologies that are different from their own interests. Others support their own interests or their families' interests, for instance. In some cases, people from different social conditions are financially compensated for voicing ideological views that misrepresent the classes or low-status social groups from which they come, except to the extent that they are compensated enough to raise the level of their social statuses.

Alegal but socially acceptable and alegal but socially unacceptable actions often demonstrate the lack of consistency and lack of organization of the legal system regarding its communications or show the lack of development in relation to certain issues. When something is socially acceptable or unacceptable, the relevant question is: For whom is it socially acceptable or unacceptable? It must be acceptable or unacceptable for a social group to fit this criterion.

Consider the fact that Alabama became the thirty-seventh state to legalize the marriages of couples of the same sexes and same genders, according to the United States Supreme Court ruling in 2015, yet within approximately fifty of the sixty-seven counties in Alabama, same-sex couples were disallowed the attainments of marriage licenses either because the marriage license services were shut down entirely, or the services refrained from granting licenses to same-sex couples (Muskal, Phelps & Teague, 2015; Blinder, 2015; Stewart, 2015).

Although the highest legal court system of the nation ordered that licenses be granted to same-sex couples who meet the ordinary age requirements, the chief justice of the Supreme Court of Alabama, Roy Moore, may have defied the latter order when he warned probate judges in a letter not to issue marriage licenses to couples of the same sex, and probate judges may have defied the legal order. Roy Moore also refused to issue any licenses in Alabama where the vast majority of voters voted for marriage to exclusively involve a man and a woman with each union (Muskal, Phelps & Teague, 2015).

The latter complex set of issues, especially concerning the roles of probate judges to answer to the United States Supreme Court as opposed to the

Alabama State Supreme Court, and the apparent denial of a federal legal order may rightfully allow same-sex couples who were denied marriage licenses to file lawsuits against any of the accountable judges who acted with their legal authority and undermined the legal status of the United States Supreme Court's ruling because the judges violated the couples' legal and civil rights. Such abuses of authority have been noted by researchers who argue that prejudices of heterosexual males against non-heterosexuals and specifically against homosexual people are strongly predicted by the presence of their right-wing authoritarianism even more than the amount of their social dominance orientation and social identification of being heterosexuals (Stones, 2006). The legal issues involved in the complex set of relations concerning same-sex marriages are overcomplicated by the drastic differences between regions regarding the social acceptability and social unacceptability of marriages of those who are the same sex and gender or who have an ambiguous sex, for instance.

There is a plethora of ideologies concerning the issues of sex, sexuality, and gender. One sexual ideology maintains that there are only two sexes, male and female, which does not account for hermaphrodites and others who hold ambiguous statuses regarding their sexes. Hermaphrodites and others who are gender-neutral or who are difficult to place in the categories of male and female are often either legally and exclusively labeled at birth as "males" or "females." In these cases, one who is legally labeled a "female" is only legally permitted in certain jurisdictions to marry another person who is legally labeled as a "male."

The latter ideologies about biological sex and matrimony may even temporarily grant that each of the latter facts are true and recognize that the law acts unreasonably and arbitrarily. However, one who thinks in accordance with such ideologies would still likely and immediately conceal these facts and exclude them from further discussion after dubbing such facts to be "rare exceptions." The reason given for excluding them could be the infrequent occurrence of births of hermaphrodites and the presumption that only the majority, the males and females, matter in virtue of the formation of the concept of biological sex.

The refusal to incorporate the subconception of hermaphrodite into the concept of biological sex and then to fail to apply it to relevant issues, such as marriage, is inhumane because it irrationally disrespects people's choices and involves the treatments of human beings as means to ends rather than treating them with the richness of purpose, personhood, and humanity that they deserve. Instead, the people, especially hermaphrodites and others who are not neatly classified as male or female, are irrationally given a classification of male or female, which may contradict the classification that they have for themselves. Humans are treated as means to ends in these cases, which may temporarily facilitate lawmakers' makings of legal codes as opposed to allowing the freedom of the rational decision-making capabilities of people, such as hermaphrodites.

Basically, there are not just two sexes, male and female. An inherent unfairness arises especially for those who cannot be identified definitively as male or female. Since concept of biological sex retains a legal importance, specifically regarding access to public bathrooms, marriage etc., the misconception or ideological stance that there are only two sexes results in unfairness regarding access to types of bathrooms and access to certain types of partners for marriage. Moreover, the unfairness is grounded in the legislation that contributes to the creation of certain aspects of the societal system. Some aspects, regarding what bathroom to enter and who to marry, are of much greater importance to people who are neither males nor females.

These so-called exceptions include she-males or hermaphrodites and many other people who experience an arbitrary aspect of the system. Such exceptions suffice to illustrate the inbuilt unfairness and injustices within the legal system that forbids same-sex marriage by law because, as exceptions, they are arbitrarily identified legally as male or female, and then they are only allowed to marry the opposite sex from their legal sex. The ideology that is espoused by some who partially recognize its shortcomings is thoroughly flawed as a view about an important aspect of human nature, to wit, the aspect that involves our means of procreation for the continuation of our species.

Procreation and surviving extinction are fundamentally important to our species. The categorization of the third biological sex would be one that is infertile or lacks the self-identification of the type of sexual fertility the person can have (i.e., as a potential impregnator (male) or one who can be impregnated (female)) when the person socializes. For example, a person may be called by a male's name and socialize like a male but also be pregnant. Consider an example of limitations of the concept of biological sex applied in legal sciences to include: The type of human who both becomes pregnant and impregnates another human being at some points during that individual's lifespan.

The rise of social groups supporting gay rights explicitly allows the distinctions to be challenged between what is legal and illegal in manners that undermine the moral integrity of the legal system. The spokespeople show the unethical behaviors of members of the legal institution toward other people based on misconceptions about biological sex. They demonstrate the power, organization, and influence of the social group. The spokespeople provide the group's demands for just and fair treatment.

The spokespeople, such as those from the lesbian, gay, bisexual and transsexual groups, point out the matters of alegality and demands for changes to occur regarding the treatments of people by the legal system and members of the legal institution. The issue of homosexual marriage involves large numbers of people who support it and vast numbers of people who do not tolerate it in the 21st century in many societies. The marriages are legally recognized in some regions but not others in the United States and in other countries. The example suffices to cover both categorizations of what is alegal but socially acceptable and what is alegal but socially unacceptable. This depends on groups being analyzed and how the graph from figure 1 is utilized.

The goal, of course, for the social group supporting same-sex marriages is to secure some gradation of legality regarding equal marriage rights of same-sex couples and all other couples who are legally permitted to attain marriage licenses since the gay rights social groups do not support the legalization of just any marriage between same-sex couples. Children and young adolescents of the same sex are not being offered support by these social groups for legalizing the marriages of same-sex youths, but rather what is sought is a gradation of legality that is equally fair and just for the people of the society.

5 The Logical Structure of Legalization: Gradations of Legality

The logical structure of legalization regards the partial or total legal allowances of sales or purchases of products or services and legal allowances of certain behaviors. Such behaviors are uninhibited or in the confines of particular times (e.g., midnight till 8am) or places. Legalization sometimes proceeds via reducing the total illegalization of a product that is illegal to purchase, to sell, and to possess in the following manners: (1) Legalizing the possession of the product to some extent (i.e., regarding time and place) or the amount of the product while any purchase and sale of the product remains illegal; (2) Legalizing the sale of the product but neither the purchase nor the possession of it; (3) Legalizing the possession and the purchase of the product in some respect but not the sale of the product; (4) Legalizing the possession and the sale of the product in some respect but not the purchase of it; and (5) Legalizing the purchase, possession, and sale of the product, which more fully approaches a concept of total legalization, conceptually speaking.

Moreover, legalization may begin with the decriminalization of possessions of smaller amounts of the product, for instance, which lessens the severity of the penalization for the possession of the product, which thereby contributes to the legalization process. The first process of legalization could, for instance, move quite easily from (1) to (2) where the product is first legal to possess, and then the legal system allows for the product to be sold to particular members of the legal institution or medical community, for instance, in which cases (1) disallows the sale or purchase of the product, and (2) disallows the possession and purchase of the product. On the other hand, (3) is the way that societies allow people to buy and possess prescription drugs, which are illegal to sell to others without the prescriptions, for instance.

With only the latter five sorts of instances in mind one may be tempted to define "legalization" as a process through which legal prohibitions are removed against some product, service, or behavior that is illegal because the latter forms of legalization may appear to involve the increasing of the overall amount of legality regarding the product. However, there remains the possibility of the legalization being shifted back and forth from (1) to (2) and (2) and (3) to (4) and (5) as well as other combinations by lawmakers. In any case, it could be an ideal situation for lawmakers to be required to answer why they support one form of restricted legalization as opposed to another form that is less restricted. As we shall see, even (5), which is conceptually closer to complete legalization, can still be greatly restricted by additional laws.

The realization of the possibilities for legalization overcomplicates the decision-making process for lawmakers because they are confronted with the task of deciding upon the best fitting amount of overall legalization of a product. Legalization may involve prohibitions against certain behaviors being removed, such as lifting a legal ban against homosexual behaviors. However, the latter definition of "legalization" must also incorporate the concept of alegality in which case the products, services, or behaviors, with which the legal system is momentarily unconcerned, undergo the appropriate channeling through legitimate societal subsystems that are recognized by the legal system.

Global drug liberalization often involves the processes of relegalization, legalization, and decriminalization in different societies. Importantly, some products, such as new pharmaceutical drugs, may undergo legalization processes, even though the drugs were never illegal to use from the outset. Newly created drugs are alegal (i.e., neither legal nor illegal) in some sense (e.g., regarding possessions or even the selling and purchasing of their patents) since the legal system is, at first, unconcerned with them and does not know about their potential impacts upon society, public health, or crime.

Lawmakers often retain the ability to propose or pass bills that become laws and make certain products and services legal in a few distinct ways, which are shown within figure 2 via the various gradations of the legal status of possessions, sales, and purchases. Figure 2 represents dissimilar categories utilized to illegalize the purchase, sale, or possession of some product or to legalize the

	Illegal Purchases	Illegal Sales	Illegal Purchases and Sales
Legal Purchases		Citizens may buy the product but not sell it. Governmental institutions may sell the product to them (e.g., personal ID cards and pharmaceuticals)	
Legal Sales	Citizens may be required to sell these products and are not permitted to buy them. The government or some organization then legally buys the products, instead.		
Legal Possessions	Citizens may legally possess the product and sell it to the government, for example, but the people are not legally permitted to buy it (e.g., possession of raw ivory and alcohol after hours)	Citizens may legally keep the product. They may not sell it. Citizens are permitted to buy the product with government permission (e.g., exotic animals purchased with the gov't's permission)	An amount of the product is legally permitted, but the act of buying or selling results in legal penalties (e.g., marijuana in Mexico in Sept. 2009 as well as international ivory trade)

FIGURE 2 Gradations of legality and illegality (Brant & Brant, 2012)

purchase, sale, or possession of some product that is already illegal, depending on the initial legal status of the product. The figure can be applied to services in addition to the use of commodities and pertains directly to criminalization and decriminalization.

Conceptually speaking, criminalization and decriminalization are distinguished from illegalization and legalization insofar as some product, service, or behavior can be decriminalized but remain illegal and therefore subject to penalization, such as some illegal non-prescription drugs in Portugal during the 21st century (Hughes & Stevens, 2007, p. 1). The criminalization of some product, service, or behavior does indeed require the illegalization of it. Moreover, the decriminalization of something also logically requires the initial criminalization of it, whereas the legalization of something need not undergo the process of illegalization, and the decriminalization of something often does not amount to the legalization of it. Rainer Prätorius (2008) maintains that:

> Decriminalization logically presumes criminalization; the latter also consequently finds more interest with some justification ... There are therefore two ways of understanding decriminalization: firstly, in the narrow sense, as a legislative eradication of statutory offenses, but then also in a broader sense as complex political institutions under the inclusion of the

> legislative, executive, and judicial powers, but also of societal instances. Such decriminalization takes back the state penalties in distinguishable gradations – something which will no longer be enforced within the still existing penological norms or in which the punishment remains but replaces the old arsenal with qualitatively "milder" sanctions. (Prätorius, 2008, pp. 325–326) [Entkriminalisierung setzt logischerweise Kriminalisierung voraus; letztere findet somit auch mit einigem Recht mehr Interesse … Entkriminalisierung ist demnach zweifach zu verstehen: einmal im engeren Sinne als legislative Tilgung von Straftatbeständen, dann aber auch im weiteren Sinne als komplexe Institutionenpolitik unter Einbezug von Legislative, Exekutive und Judikative, aber auch von gesellschaftlichen Instanzen. Solche Entkriminalisierung nimmt das staatliche Strafen in unterschiedlichen Graden zurück – etwa, indem fortbestehende Strafrechtnormen nicht mehr durchgesetzt werden oder indem die Ahndung bleibt, aber qualitativ "mildere" Sanktionen das alte Arsenal ersetzen.]

Within various societies, the following behaviors and situational factors have been criminalized and decriminalized and sometimes criminalized again: abortion, drug possession and recreational drug usage, gambling, prostitution, and the use of performance enhancing drugs, such as steroids, in sports.

Figure 2 excludes several sets of categories concerning the gradations of legality. It excludes the uninhibited accessibility of some product that is legal to possess, buy, and sell, which has also been channeled through the appropriate pathways interconnected with the legal system at hand, such as sugar, which can still be embargoed, like Cuban sugar on freight ships to the USA (Crooker & Pavlovic, 2010; Haas; 1998). The latter figure also excludes the regions and time frames during which the products may be bought, possessed, and sold. Quotas and tariffs are also not considered.

Consider a hypothetical example within which a late 21st century chemist may create a new chemical compound that is used by drug addicts and others for recreational purposes. Although the new chemical compound is at least momentarily unknown to the members of the legal institution, the drug may later undergo the process of illegalization. The process of illegalization may take place abruptly insofar as the new product becomes illegal to possess, buy, and sell. The sudden change in the legal status of the drug may lead to an at least temporary but vast increase in the demand for the drug as a product, a great increase in the price, and more frequent usages.

Although the initial impacts of the illegalization or criminalization process may only be temporary, it behooves lawmakers to consider making gradual changes instead, such as illegalizing the possession of the product in certain places (e.g., motor vehicles and public transport). Lawmakers, theoretically and perhaps practically speaking, could also very well illegalize the sale of the product while refraining from illegalizing the purchase of it at least temporarily. We may hypothesize that this is a less abrupt way of policing and policymaking, depending upon the situational variables. Solely illegalizing the sale of the product while temporarily refraining from the total illegalization of the product allows for observations to be made about the societal consequences of policing solely against merchants.

From certain public policy perspectives and journalistic perspectives, the latter type of illegalization likely makes a lawmaker or many of them susceptible to the criticism that the politicians have legalized the drug or hold ideologies that support the legalization of the product, despite their creation of new laws that illegalize the drug to some extent. Moreover, journalists and editors of news sources, especially those who tend to promote shocking and provocative titles and stances within articles, would certainly, at first, bring forth both skepticism of the idea of preventing the immediate and total illegalization of the product and make some outright offensive criticisms. Such media supported attacks may indeed reveal their own political and legal opinions, even at great expenses to the public, policing, and public policy.

The latter forms of legalization are uncommon, but what is more common is the decriminalization of drugs that remain illegal, although they may assume a similar illegal status as a traffic violation or some other misdemeanor, concerning the possession and usage of lesser amounts. Portugal began the process of decriminalizing several types of drugs, despite their continued illegalization, after an increase of drug-use and drug-related health problems (e.g., HIV and AIDS) (Moreira et al., 2011; Greenwald, 2009). One manner of decriminalizing commodities and services is via a process of gradual and graded legalization, in which case either temporal or spatial restrictions are lifted, which we may consider regarding the possession and consumption of alcohol within certain jurisdictions.

Figure 3 illustrates gradations of the legality of behaviors in a particular timeframe and set of restricted locations for consuming alcohol. In several counties in Texas in the United States, the sale and purchase of alcohol are banned in non-medicinal forms. However, in these so-called "dry counties" many people legally possess alcohol purchased from neighboring counties. Although these people are not legally permitted to consume alcohol in public spaces, they are legally allowed to consume alcohol at their homes at any time. Additionally, the legal purchase of alcohol also comes with restrictions so that there are certain hours during which it is illegal to buy alcoholic beverages.

Legality of alcohol	7 days per week	Less than 7 days per week	24 hours per day	Greater than 0 hours per day
Inside and outside the city limits	no	yes	no	no
Only inside the city limits	no	yes	no	no
Only outside the city limits	no	yes	no	no
Only in public	no	yes	no	no
Only at home	yes	no	yes	yes
At home and in public	no	yes	no	no
Only in certain buildings rooms or places outdoors	yes	no	yes	yes

FIGURE 3 Gradations of legal behaviors with alcohol

The importance cannot be overstated that there should be realizations that lawmakers can select amongst an amazingly complex set of legal alternatives. The chosen set of legal alternatives facilitate the rise and fall of businesses, emergence of new criminal organizations, changes in culture, support and criticisms by journalists, different constituencies for politicians, and fluctuations of various adaptations, incarcerations, and migrations. Niklas Luhmann (2004, p. 119) writes:

> [T]he oscillations of legal change can be more erratic and more quickly prone to a review which, in turn, makes the causal relation between change of opinion and legal change appear more plausible. Without doubt this situation can be described as a causal relation. However, this still requires that a transformation of themes take place, and it does not exclude the case that adjustments in the legal system are too difficult (for instance, the filing of a general, populist suit concerning environment law) to be made as a concession to suggestions from outside.

Luhmann (ibid.) then provides his audience with a partial definition of the what the law is: "Law itself is the organ of society that is used for turning a change in public opinion into a legal form." With the complexity of the gradations of legality, lawmakers can speak to crowds and their constituencies quite differently via placing a focus upon the legalization or illegalization of the good or service about which they speak and in accordance with what their audiences prefer.

The following example shows the political strategy of the politician to the extent that he or she can strategically attain more votes based on speaking differently to two distinctly different sets of potential constituents and rely on the complexity of the gradations of legalization and illegalization to demonstrate agreements with both groups who have opposite-ended views on the same issue, such as alcohol consumption. When the politician speaks to a group of elderly people who have lived without consuming alcohol and who hold religious beliefs that lead them to disapprove of the consumption of alcohol, the politician will likely focus mostly upon both the facts that she or he supports the illegalization of the consumption of alcohol in public places. He can argue that he also supports the illegalization of the purchase and sale of alcohol.

However, when the politician confronts university students who attend a university within a county that forbids the purchase and sale of alcohol, the politician may very well claim that he or she supports the legal permission for those who are old enough to possess alcohol and to consume it at their homes. The politician may inform the university students that he also drinks alcohol occasionally at home away from the campus, or, better yet, he may tell a comedic story about his own overconsumption of alcohol, attaining a more personal connection with the students. Telling the truth, but not the whole relevant truth, becomes the key factor for the politician to retain votes and to expand the constituency via confusing and misleading the people into believing that they mostly agree with the politician. The messages for the elderly people raised and cultured within the dry county and the messages for the university students are quite different in virtue of their focuses.

Ideology critique, critical assessments of leadership and coinciding political messages are very often better to judge via the differences between their messages communicated to different social groups and crowds with different sets of interests and upbringings. For the latter reason, there are often many political parties that sponsor private and secured gatherings specifically for their own constituents. The abovementioned example, concerning the legal status of alcohol and two different social groups within a country, illustrates one important relation of lawmakers to the logical structure of the gradations of legality in virtue of their political strategies to develop their constituencies via instilling legal ideologies, especially within eligible voters. What inevitably and resultantly arises are beliefs, desires, and expectations from the public about the political figures as lawmakers in which case the expectations the people have of the elected officials can become shattered, and the people may respond in a variety of ways – through protests, for instance, but in more violent manners as well.

6 The Significance of Mental States and Ideology

Mental states include beliefs, indecisiveness, disbeliefs, desires, indifference, disgusts, shamefulness, fear, hate, expectations, hopes, and wishes, for instance. Mental states are characterized as being directed at something from some vantage points or perspectives, in accordance with phenomenology. The attribution of importance is also placed upon mental states. The instillment of political, economic, and legal ideology requires the manipulation of mental states. Our interpretations of data require mental states, namely, beliefs, disbeliefs, and indecisiveness, which are states during which other mental states are attached, such as desires, indifference, and disgusts. The idea – that if one realizes both what another person believes and what he or she wants, then one can predict the other person's behaviors – is an obviously practical and important idea when applied (Bennett, 1991; Ziv & Frye, 2003). Attributions of mental states may be applied to two or more people to predict the actions of groups and social movements.

Significant social movements occur with the actions of members of the legal institution and involve all the latter factors, including the interpretations of data, realizations of others' mental states,[11] predictions of behaviors of individuals and groups, and attributions of importance to these interpretations, realizations, and predictions. Predicting behaviors is further complicated by the fact that people believe in things and events that are unreal and disbelieve in what is real (e.g., one thinks something did not happen when, in fact, it happened). People also desire what is unattainable and unreal. The social conditions determine whether what people desire or strive for is realistically attainable during that time period and place.

In William Clifford's famous essay, "The Ethics of Belief," Clifford describes a ship owner who, despite his original concerns about the seaworthiness of his vessel, decides to allow his ship to voyage to the new world without undergoing

11 For example, most healthy four-year-olds can attribute false beliefs to Sally, a person who places a marble in a basket, but when Sally leaves the room another person, Anne, moves the marble from the basket to a box. When Sally returns, her false belief that the marble is in the basket is easily recognizable. This type of mental state is also measurable in social cognitive psychology (Baron-Cohen, Leslie & Frith, 1985; Wimmer & Perner, 1983).

any major repairs. Clifford provides two different versions of the story with identical beginnings but alternative endings. The first story involves the ship owner suppressing his doubts and suspicions about the seaworthiness of the ship, allowing the ship to sail, and finally the ship arrives at the new world, despite its need for repairs. The second version of the story commences like the first does, however, at one point the ship drifts into a strong storm, and all the people on board die.

Clifford focuses on the fact that the ship owner is just as guilty in the first case as he is in the second case where the people die because the ship owner has behaved in the exact same ways for the exact same reasons. The case becomes a legal one when we consider the moral obligations of the ship owner, risk assessment, the insurance that the ship owner would likely have, the ship owner's collection of the insurance sum based upon the policy, and the friends and family members of the deceased who would likely inquire whether the ship was seaworthy or not before the voyage. Moreover, the insurance company may demand to see the last bill for repairing the ship before paying the ship owner for his losses.

A comparison of the two cases allows one to reflectively recognize that legal systems, or the communications with which such systems operate, are generally focused on consequences and measurable losses to some party involved rather than ways of thinking, situational variables, and actions that increase the chances of losses (i.e., until the losses occur). Of course, it is also worthy to consider alternative cases during which the ships are destroyed, the ship owners spend large sums of money on repairs, lose or dispose of the receipts, have meager finances to hire the services of competent lawyers, and lose their court cases, despite their best intentions and best efforts to keep their passengers safe.

Figure 4 displays the beliefs and their correspondence with reality. The ship owner has a belief that fits within the top left category, which is a true belief about reality, within figure 4 during the first case because he believes that the ship will arrive at the new world, and it does. In the second case, the ship owner holds a belief that is false, and the ship's adequate safety-level is unreal, which is represented within the bottom left category in figure 4.

The logical relations of the mental states of belief and disbelief and the modes of reality and unreality complicate the matter and are important to understand when one analyzes any ideology. The logical relations are partially shown within figure 6. However, if one analyzes each of the logical possibilities concerning the ship owner simply regarding the reality of the matter (i.e., he owns a ship) and one's possible beliefs about that matter, then one is confronted with four straightforward and simple possibilities: either one believes

	Belief	Disbelief
Reality	These are beliefs that are true with or without justification.	These are beliefs that are false with or without justification.
Unreality	These are beliefs that are false with or without justification (i.e., they do not represent reality).	These are beliefs that are true with or without justification.

FIGURE 4 Truth-values of beliefs

he owns it, disbelieves he owns it, is undecided about whether he owns it, or has no belief about the matter whatsoever (i.e., one does not even consider the person or the ownership).

The fact of the matter about what is real or unreal is important, especially within a court of law. The figure above is best interpreted as containing four meaningful categories rather than two redundant categories. One may attempt to reformulate the ship owner's belief in the seaworthiness of the ship and the unreality of the matter instead as amounting to the ship owner disbelieving that the ship needs serious repairs, which, contrary to the disbelief, is the reality of the matter. However, the latter attempt is counterproductive because the latter formulation mistakes a different mental state as a logical relation instead.

The different mental states include belief and disbelief. An example of a mistaken logical relation is when one believes x and another person assumes that the individual disbelieves not-x. If one believes her keys are in her pocket, for instance, then she does not necessarily disbelieve that her keys are on the table instead, unless she is actively thinking about the placement of her keys and thinking of the table without them.

Perhaps the idea is most relevant to sport psychology during which an athlete is informed that she should discontinue thinking about not botching performance because thinking of not messing up does not amount to thinking about a flawless performance. The logical constructs apply here still, of course, but perhaps have more unexpected relations because mental states are often erroneously viewed as having other logically opposing mental states that are contradictory. As concepts, their oppositions and contradictory natures are not easily identifiable.

For example, oppositions of the expected/unexpected, belief/disbelief, desire/disgust do involve forms of contradictions. Something that is expected to happen and that really happens is not the same as something that is unexpected to happen that does not happen because the attitude is quite different, and the direction of the attention is totally different. The logically opposing contradiction of the expectation is no expectation rather than surprise, which concerns what is unexpected.

The logically opposing contradiction of what is unexpected is likewise a lack of the mental state altogether (e.g., a lack of surprise). The fact that one is disgusted with the behaviors of a police officer does not necessarily mean that one also has a fervent desire for that police officer to refrain from behaving in such ways because desires require thought and the directions of thought toward what is desired.

One regularly occurring mistake, concerning attributions of people's own mental states, happens when a person states that he or she "does not like something" but where the person actually dislikes the thing. The person also means that he or she dislikes it. However, the logical implication is that the person is either neutral about the thing (i.e., neither liking nor disliking it) or dislikes it, and the implicature is that the person dislikes it. So, the indifference of the individual about the object in question cannot be expressed by the negation of the concept of this mental state, liking the object, because of the implicature.

William Clifford argues that there are certain methods by which we form beliefs and disbeliefs about objects and events. These methods involve being skeptical and suspicious about each of our beliefs, especially if they affect others in some way. So, when somebody tells another person what she believes, she should first examine her belief with some degree of skepticism and doubt. In the case of the ship owner, we are confronted with a person who forms a set of beliefs about what is in his best interest, even though risks are very high for many passengers. It is worthy to consider the various instances in which people are inclined to believe something or they believe something that they also want to be real because there are many instances in which people appear to believe what they want to believe, which is a phenomenon that deserves much further investigation, especially regarding legal ideologies, pessimism, and optimism.

Figure 5 illustrates a complex correspondence of beliefs with the other mental states of desire and dislike, although the figure lacks the relations of indifference and indecisiveness and lacks the mental states' relations to the absences of any belief, disbelief, desire, disgust, indifference, and indecisiveness.

Obviously, Clifford recognizes the significance of certain types of beliefs. The beliefs that matter the most in the stories concern what we really desire to be true. The ship owner either desires for the ship to successfully sail to the new world, or he is indifferent about it because he will earn the same amount

	Belief	Disbelief
Desire	These are beliefs that are true or false, and the person wants what he believes to be real or true.	The person wants what she disbelieves is true or real. She wants her disbelief to be false.
Dislike	These are beliefs that are true or false, and the person wants what she believes to be incorrect or false.	The person wants what he disbelieves to be unreal or untrue. So, he wants his disbelief about something to be true.

FIGURE 5 Aesthetic values of beliefs

of money since he will collect the insurance money if the ship is destroyed in a storm in addition to the fares from the passengers. Assuming the ship owner is indifferent or that he wants the ship to make it safely abroad, Clifford presents us with two hypothetical situations and does not intend for readers to think that the ship owner is absolutely deplorable as the ship owner would be if he had disliked the people and thereby did not want the ship to sail safely.

Figure 5 presents some confusion in this depiction of the concepts of belief, disbelief, and the attached aesthetic values of desire and dislike. The reason for the confusion is that without reference to any real phenomenon or fact of the matter, the direction of the attention of the subject's desire or dislike is seemingly toward the belief itself rather than the object that presumably exists independent from the perceptions of it, about which the subject is aware. Although there may be a way of maintaining that the individual desires for his or her belief or disbelief to be false, there is perhaps also a general tendency for adults and adolescents to desire that their beliefs and disbeliefs about real phenomena are accurate.

The complexity of relations of frequently occurring mental states to the world and to what is unreal, which is shown in figure 6, assumes that one either believes, disbelieves, or is undecided about some event taking place. Presumably, the belief, indecision, or disbelief forms because of the individual thinking about the event. Thinking about the event requires directed thoughts toward the event in ways that are better described by one as a belief, an undecided status, or a disbelief in the occurrence of the event. The figure also assumes that one either desires, dislikes or is indifferent about some event transpiring.

The legal, economic, or political ideology of an individual is comprised of the relation of mental states shown in figure 6 as four, five, six, thirteen, fourteen, and fifteen, but the ideology may also be represented within a weaker

1	Belief	Desire	Real
2	Belief	Indifference	Real
3	Belief	Dislike	Real
4	Belief	Desire	Unreal
5	Belief	Indifference	Unreal
6	Belief	Dislike	Unreal

7	Undecided	Desire	Real
8	Undecided	Indifference	Real
9	Undecided	Dislike	Real
10	Undecided	Desire	Unreal
11	Undecided	Indifference	Unreal
12	Undecided	Dislike	Unreal

13	Disbelief	Desire	Real
14	Disbelief	Indifference	Real
15	Disbelief	Dislike	Real
16	Disbelief	Desire	Unreal
17	Disbelief	Indifference	Unreal
18	Disbelief	Dislike	Unreal

FIGURE 6 Logical possibilities of combined truth-values and aesthetic values of beliefs

form via the relations of the mental states of seven, eight, nine, ten, eleven and twelve. In accordance with Clifford's example of the ship owner, presumably, wanting the passengers to safely voyage and arrive at their destinations, also desiring to hold on to his money instead of using it for repairs, and believing (i.e., after the suppression of doubts) that the ship will make the journey successfully, we may likewise hypothesize that the ideologies of individuals tend to arise more often from the combinations of mental states of belief and desire and disbelief and dislike.

Thus, the theory of ideologies put forth here maintains that legal, economic, and political ideologies most often arise from the relations of mental states shown in four (i.e., what a person believes and wants to be true but is, in fact, unreal and false) and fifteen (i.e., what a person disbelieves and dislikes but is, in fact, real and true) within figure 6 (Brant, 2012a, pp. 93–108). We may consider any number of examples for the relations shown in number fifteen that allow for the generation of multiple hypotheses. Consider the disbeliefs that have been held by thousands of American citizens, namely, that President Barack Obama (2009–2017) lacks an American citizenship as well as their dislike of the fact or idea that President Obama is an American citizen (Louis, 2009; Spillius, 2009; Franke-Ruta, 2009; Oliphant, 2011; Tomasky, 2011).

An interesting hypothesis can be formulated from the theory of ideology and the sources for the news reports of Americans' disbeliefs. The hypothesis is at least partially testable insofar as most of those holding the ideology and conspiracy theory about the birth of President Obama, will, if correct, also tend to dislike the fact or idea that President Obama was born an American citizen. The latter reason can be used at least partially to demonstrate why there is confusion regarding the difference between believing something that is false (e.g., believing the President has no legitimate citizenship (i.e., 4, 5, & 6 from Figure 6)) and disbelieving something that is true (e.g., disbelieving the president has a legitimate citizenship (i.e., 13, 14, & 15 from Figure 6)). Consider that if the disbelief is attached to a desire about the fact of the matter (i.e., a desire for him to have a legitimate citizenship, which is 13), then it will probably be much easier to convince the person that the president has a legitimate citizenship.[12]

A social scientist may attempt to find random samples of people who disbelieve that President Obama is an American citizen or believe that he is a Muslim. The people could be either indifferent about him being an American or a Muslim or want him to be an American citizen and Christian, for example. This is how the theory of ideology presented here enables the generation of hypotheses that are testable.[13] The adage that is often applied well to people is that "they believe what they want to be true," but I argue for the instantiation of a new adage that is different (i.e., it does not amount to what the previous adage maintains), to wit, that "they disbelieve what they dislike." Yet both adages are best treated as tendencies for those who already hold ideologies and relate to the false beliefs and false disbeliefs.

We may find that ideologies are difficult to measure because they tend to be expressed during certain situations rather than others. For example, they may tend to be expressed with friends and family at the dinner table far more often than with social psychologists at a luncheon. We may do well to consider random sampling for social psychology, anthropology, political science, sociology etc. to incorporate people with right-wing or left-wing legal or political ideologies such that their families or a circle of their friends become the major part of the human environment to which this theory is applied. The accessibility to the human environments is problematic regarding internal review boards and ethics, though.

---

12 One presumption here is that the desire, indifference, or disliking involves a directedness toward the real phenomenon or fact as opposed to a directedness toward the belief or disbelief about the fact or phenomenon.

13 Baron-Cohen, Leslie and Frith (1985) illustrate the ability to measure the attributions of false beliefs in children, for instance, in their flagship essay.

Again, it is important to reassert that "if one believes and desires something S, then one does not necessarily disbelieve and dislike not-S." The role of logic and negation, concerning a belief and desire for something, cannot be logically and reasonably replaced with a disbelief and dislike for the lack of that thing (See Ch. 3.7). For example, if you believe that a policeman will protect you from gang violence and you want this protection, the latter belief and desire do not entail that you disbelieve that the policeman will not protect you and that you dislike the lack of protection. The reason for this is that your focus is on what you believe and want rather than what you disbelieve and dislike. The latter fact has certainly been needed and has been lacking within many critiques of ideologies (Brant, ibid.).

Methodologies aside, the importance of mental states and their relations to legal, economic, and political ideologies fundamentally involves the behavior of communication. Any successful communication involves the successful attributions of relevant and important mental states. Miscommunications and deceptive communications involve misattributions of mental states to others that differ from one's own mental states.

For instance, assuming another person wants to help you find the right direction to your destination might be a false assumption. In the political realm, there have been countless instances of voters who have waited until the last day to vote and who have been intentionally misdirected to locations where they were not allowed to vote at all. Unless the communicative and deceptive role of misdirecting large groups of people is systematic and negatively affects the outcome of the election, such as with computer systems calling and misdirecting potential voters in areas where they are suspected to be voting for the opposition, tactics and implementations of strategies are just normal parts of the political game for attaining political advantages. Vast amounts of money expended on gaining the political position and the latter deceptive communications facilitate the emergence of cynical ideologies and realpolitik (i.e., political pragmatism).

Mental states are obviously factors of our social positions in human group-based social hierarchies. So, mental states of a young man who is the son of a small town sheriff or Director of Police, presumably, tend to differ from mental states of the son of a sanitation worker residing in that same small town, despite their ages and genders being the same, their enrollments at the same schools, etc. Perhaps one difference between these two types of people is that the sheriff's son commits more traffic violations than the garbage man's son but tends not to be penalized as often as the sanitation worker's son is, which typically and realistically results from the closer ties of the sheriff's son with the local police. So, for such reasons one's relation to the law tends to give one inherent privileges, even if the relation is merely a familial one. Some people are even motivated and do lie about their family relations to law enforcement members or judges, for instance, to increase their chances of escaping some penalty for a traffic violation.

It is not very uncommon when a man has a friend who knows a police officer, and he is issued a speeding ticket by another policeman, from the same precinct. The man, say Daniel, tells his friend, the police officer, about what happened, and his friend informs the other officer who issued the ticket. As a result, Daniel is advised to contest the traffic violation in the relevant court of law. The officer who issued the ticket is likely to be absent from court. Thereby the penalty is dismissed. So, even friendly relations with members of the legal institution can provide privileges in cases.

Arguably, the principle task of the legal system and law is to "stabilize expectations" (Luhmann, 1987, p. 27). Often the legal system does not consider the social conditions' influences on mental states of those who benefit from friends and family who are members of the legal institution. There are also immeasurable amounts of nepotism and favoritism in legal systems.

Friends and family of the legal institution's members frequently have certain privileges. Perhaps the best-known archetype or paradigmatic social group is the group of sons of small town sheriffs or sons of military colonels and generals, especially between the ages of 15 and 35 years. The relationship to the law that sons of small town sheriffs have is definitely expected to be privileged by most of us who live within the boundaries of some legal system (i.e., rather than living within a tribe without a legal system). The latter relation of those sons is expected by people who are accustomed to observe or hear secondhand about privileges of social groups closely tied to members of the legal institution. Such a relation with the local law enforcement and such a privileged status may indeed allow certain individuals to believe with good reason that they are "above and beyond the law" within a certain jurisdiction. It therefore behooves us to clarify the roles of ideology, real privileges based upon relationships or lack thereof, and to focus on methods for further clarifications.

Even the circles of friends of privileged status family members provide extra incentive, peer pressure, and motivation for such people with a privileged status to realize and exercise their powers. The privilege of their relation comes with powers that exist with a reduced role of responsibility. Sons of sheriffs are generally isolated from one another and perhaps lack an organized social group that would provide systematic mutual benefits. In some cases, however, the sons of sheriffs of neighboring towns may benefit from the relations of their fathers and threaten or act violently against others as well as violate the law in ways that allow the local law enforcement departments in the towns to work together to conceal their delinquent behaviors.

Whether the perhaps infrequent behaviors in the latter sort of cases can really be considered deviant is questionable. Deviant behaviors may best be conceptualized in accordance with the social conditions of them. Nepotism and favoritism ordinarily allow less restricted behaviors and lesser chances for legal penalizations. Social dominance theorists may find that the social dominance orientation of many of these men and adolescents are higher (i.e., they may tend to agree more frequently with claims, such as, "To get ahead in life other groups sometimes need to be trampled.").

The variety of privileges attained because of people's relations with members of the legal institution is crucial to understand the legal system's roles. It is involved in social movements. One fascinating aspect is that mental states of the privileged and unprivileged social groups, say, regarding social dominance orientations, play major roles in the legal system as stabilizing forces of societal expectations.

The instantiation of any important social movement in a nation coincides with a legal system's actions, which support or suppress, assuage, or increase the tempo of the movement with its own authority. The legal system is responsible for providing legitimacy for that which the members of the legal institution choose through the system's procedures and communications. The role of the people's perceptions of legitimacy is crucial regarding the peace and prosperity of the society (DeCremer & Tyler, 2005; Tyler, 2006a; Tyler, 2006b; Tyler, 2010; Van der Toorn et al., 2014).

The legal institutions' choices include the continuation of privileges for some social groups and detriments for others, and the legal system organizes, commands, and even threatens with weaponry and violent force. The legal institution controls violence that is implemented by itself and that others cause. The legal institution's control of violence is sometimes misdirected in such a manner that the legal institution's members concerned with criminal justice and penalization enforce, allow, and encourage violence to be implemented disproportionately against certain groups (Sidanius, Levin & Pratto, 1996; Sidanius et al., 2004; Pratto, Sidanius & Levin, 2006).

Social dominance theory hypothesizes that these latter groups undergoing violent acts are usually subordinate groups with, practically, fewer civil rights honored by the criminal justice and judicial systems (Sidanius & Pratto, 1999). Social dominance theory maintains and statistically illustrates that low-status groups express much more fear and anxiety toward the police as well as a desire to attenuate social hierarchies (Sidanius & Pratto, 1993 & 1999). Low-status groups include the lower socio-economic class as well as many racial minorities (e.g., foreigners in Mexico, especially the ones from Central America, aborigines in Australia, Arabs in Israel and blacks in the US during the 21st century).

Contrarily, police tend to have higher "social dominance orientations" (i.e., a proposed measure for a person's differences related to domination and discrimination), which means that they believe or more "strongly agree" with the following sorts of claims more often: (1) it is sometimes necessary to use force to get what one wants; (2) to "get ahead in life" stepping on other groups is sometimes needed; and (3) it is fine if other groups have better chances in life. Low-status group members tend not to agree with (1), (2), or (3) as often (Rabinowitz, 1999). Questionnaires have been designed with the many statements, including similar statements to (1), (2), and (3). The social psychology of dominance and subordination have then been tested and applied to social dominance theory in sociology.

The public's awareness that members of the law enforcement systematically perform "socially unacceptable actions" does indeed play a significant role in respect to altering the communications of the legal system and changing the future actions of law enforcement. The blatantly, socially unacceptable actions of law enforcement agents performed in Birmingham, Alabama in 1963 and 1964 and the United States citizenry's strong contempt held for the observed behaviors as well as the beliefs and desires attributed to the Birmingham law enforcement, fire fighters hosing black children with high-pressured water, and politicians supporting the segregation of black people and white people may well be hypothesized as involving mental states and ideologies that demonstrate the preconditions for change and improvements regarding the implementation of law against peoples.

What remains unknown is exactly how and why the citizens' astonishments, beliefs, and revulsions with the implementations of the written law in certain regions contributed to changes in legal systems or legal institutions. How do the mental states, which provide the necessary elements for social cohesion and the formations of social groups and ideologies, contribute to the changes within legal systems and institutions? How can dynamic changes occur in the legal system without including such violent outbursts that inevitably result in the unethical enforcement of morally atrocious laws? Creations and continuations of intersubjective agreements provide one answer.

7 Intersubjectivity: Nationhood, Law, Politics, and Economics

Max Weber's (1904/1991) insight shows a demand for explicit recognition of the subjective and intersubjective elements that are always components of the analysis of cultural life as well as of legal culture that also changes from generation to generation. Scientific experimentation and funding is directed toward subjective and personal interests. Science is never free or totally independent from values (Goddard, 1973). Scientific research is also largely based on interests within the culture of the society.

The desires of politicians, businessmen, and scientists fixate on certain points of interest for research, much like the desires of nations are concentrated on certain projects, whether they be space exploration, environmental protection, or research and development of weaponry for war or alternate sources of energy. The study of cultural life lacks a certain amount of objectivity because of these latter desires and fixations. One type of cultural life is the life of the law as a social institution and system of culturally laden communications. In 1904, Max Weber wrote:

> There is no per se "objective" scientific analysis of cultural life or the "social appearances" independent from specific and "single-sided" viewpoints, after which they – explicitly or implicitly, consciously or unconsciously – become selected as objects of research, analyzed, and representatively divided. The reason lies in the characteristic of the aim of knowledge of any social scientific work over which a purely formal examination of the norms – legal or conventional – wants to go beyond the socially contiguous beings. (Weber, 1991, p. 499) [Es gibt keine schlechthin »objektive« wissenschaftliche Analyse des Kulturlebens oder – was vielleicht etwas Engeres, für unsern Zweck aber sicher nichts wesentlich anderes bedeutet – der »sozialen Erscheinungen« unabhängig von speziellen und »einseitigen« Gesichtspunkten, nach denen sie – ausdrücklich oder stillschweigend, bewußt oder unbewußt – als Forschungsobjekt ausgewählt, analysiert und darstellend gegliedert werden. Der Grund liegt in der Eigenart des Erkenntnisziels einer jeden sozialwissenschaftlichen Arbeit, die über eine rein formale Betrachtung der Normen – rechtlichen oder konventionellen – des sozialen Beieinanderseins hinausgehen will.]

What, however, can we claim about the "extent of subjectivity" in respect to law, politics, economics, and nations? When (or if) everybody no longer desires for a nation to exist, or when they are no longer willing to put forth the effort for the continuation of the nation, what remains? What would be the status of a border between two nations if nobody continued to believe that there was a line or barrier separating them to separate people?

How much would a currency be worth if all people believed it was a greater (or lesser) value than it is currently rated? If two laws were believed to be socially acceptable to violate by enough people, could we all then violate those laws without fear of legal penalties? If US citizens were not disgusted with the racist and partially publicized actions of the criminal justice system in Alabama in the 1960s and continued not to be disgusted (See Ch. 2.6), would there not still be grave inequalities and injustices supported by dominant groups with the authority and perceptions of legitimacy and approval of the legal, criminal justice, and judicial systems? The latter questions are only answerable insofar as we can consider intersubjectivity and apply it as a concept to real social phenomena.

The fact of the matter is that no nation, no border, no money, and no law or legal system could exist without the beliefs, desires, and expectations for them. People must continue to expect that nations, borders, currencies, and rules of law will exist tomorrow for them to continually subsist. The perpetuation of these expectations is performed via various interconnected social systems of communication, such as the legal system.

The actuality or realness of nationhood, monies, currencies, and laws is based upon certain intersubjectivities. The intersubjectivities are the interconnected social status of mental states of multiple people via the behaviors of communications, which form common assumptions in multitudes of people. The continuous existence of nations, money, and law is based on well-reasoned predictions about the future of nations, prices of currencies, and revocations, continuations, and/or alterations of laws. Subjective and intersubjective foundations for these important concepts change dynamically.

The intersubjective combinations of both mental states and ideologies form the foundational structure of the conceptions of nationhood, money, leadership, and law. Furthermore, the relations of nations, money, leaders, and law also change as the relations of peoples' properties change regarding the societal relations of production. Generations within a society also amass different presentations of their intersubjectivities with varied ideologies because they hold mental states that are directed more or less frequently toward the various social systems' communications both within and outside of their society.

All concepts of nationhood, money, and law demand and require sophisticated attributions of sets of beliefs, desires, and expectations of large social groups, and the attribution of these mental states involves beliefs about beliefs and desires that most people agree are true about the abovementioned concepts. The concept of nationhood also requires more fundamental concepts of borders, laws, traditions, leadership, common social group identities, etc. As people who think about social groups and practice sociological imagination, we realize in many cases what social groups' beliefs and desires about each of these concepts are, while in other cases the beliefs and desires of groups are incredibly deceptive.

Can the realization of beliefs and desires of a group allow us to predict the group's behaviors, though? The room for error in respect to any uncertainty, regarding a prediction of an individual's behavior, despite the knowledge of that individual's beliefs and desires, is obviously multiplied, in some sense, by the number of individuals in the social group, if we predict the social group's behaviors, unless the type of behavior is describable similarly to the patterns of the behaviors of herds. The prediction of group behavior is at times more challenging than predicting a single person's behavior, especially when the task of a predictor involves grouping the individuals under analysis, since there might not be a sufficient reason to label certain people as members of a certain social group, or members of a social group may temporarily identify themselves more or less and spend more or less time with the communications and activities of two distinctly different social groups to which they belong. For example, a police officer may tend to identify herself more with her sports team players during their season of play than she does with her co-workers at her police precinct, especially after she has been reprimanded.

People do not always identify themselves as being members of social groups within which they reside. Perhaps most members of groups would also suggest altering their own behaviors if they sense that another group observes them. Misunderstood social events are often later described by analysts, i.e., analysts that have vested interests in publicly explaining social events, in respect to an arbitrary group they have created for themselves or mass media communications.

Individuals rarely belong to one social group. So, some white police officer might be a lawyer, a crook, a family man, and a politician about to be elected. Another man might be a black convicted murderer on death row for many years and a family man who is about to be released from a Texas prison because of the recognition of a false testimony and unethical actions of a prosecutor against him (e.g., Anthony Graves in Texas in 2011). The prediction of a social group's actions becomes extremely problematic if we are required to explain the diversity of all the social groups to which each of its members belongs. This may include grouping according to members' races, sexes, ages, geographic locations, incomes and employment statuses within various industries (e.g., food, education, entertainment, medical, engineering, or military industries) and unemployment, as well with their student and non-student statuses.

The utilization of online social networking and advertising strategies, however, allow for many of these social groups to be revealed, despite deceptive messages, images, and profiles. Social groups' communications and individuals' communications, experiences, and identifications within them, especially as they are experienced hierarchically, lead to the types of intersubjectivity found in the advocacy of conceptions, such as nationhood. Each human experience involves a subject and subjective conscious experience, and intersubjectivity forms because of agreements and disagreements concerning subjective experiences.

Intersubjectivity is a concept, and the realization of intersubjectivity coincides with the recognition of certain aspects of social thinking and demands respect for others' viewpoints, and additionally, a rejection of solipsism. The rejection of solipsism and other narcissistic ideologies arises first and foremost perhaps with realizations of intersubjectivity understood via the communicative relations of people's expressions of their mental states and other messages within a social system. Intersubjectivity is required for the advancement of science itself via the continual communications of scientific social groups.

Intersubjective verifiability is indeed an important concept concerning the functionality of sciences, law and rational human interactions. "Intersubjective verifiability" is the ability for some conception to be communicated in a practical (e.g., measurably, consistently, readily, precisely and comprehensively within some context) manner between at least two individuals (Kim, 2005). According to Jordan Zlatev, Timothy Racine, Chris Sinha and Esa Itkonen (Zlatev, 2008, p. 1),

> [A]lthough other species may vary in degrees of awareness, they do not seem to be fully aware of the subjectivity of others. And whereas human beings go on to engage in discursive practices and rely on material and symbolic culture, both of which have powerful formative effects on the human mind, something more ontogenetically and phylogenetically basic seems required to be able to benefit from these central aspects of human social life. This foundation seems to be provided by a uniquely human capacity for *intersubjectivity*.

The authors (ibid.) continue:

> In the simplest terms, intersubjectivity is understood … as *the sharing of experiential content* (*e.g., feelings, perceptions, thoughts, and linguistic meanings*) *among a plurality of subjects*.

8 Ideologies: Legality, Alegality, and Illegality, Despite Social Acceptability

Two sorts of fundamental influences from social groups greatly contribute to the formations of legal, economic, and political ideology as well as other ideologies. The first influence includes the daily experiences from which individuals attain their ideas as they make their attempts to successfully perform in accordance with their plans in life, which is the primary source of the social influences that allow ideology to form (Giddens, 1971). For most people on the planet, work is the major requirement for the successful completion of our goals in life.

The employment of the individual as a worker is important herein since work provides the means through which the individual can subsist within the environmental niche that the individual has (i.e., presuming we are not analyzing people, such as multi-millionaires and billionaires, who have enough for their families to subsist without any work) and therefore greatly contributes to the ideas that the person has within a human environment. Humans have subjective reactions toward the activities that occur during daily life, especially labor.

The labor of individuals working as members of the legal institution thus has a different primary source from which they form their ideas of law. The latter ideas are shaped by means of communications between the individuals, from which innovative ideas and interchanges with other ideas can form. The shaping of the ideas from the communications between individuals is a secondary source of social influences that allow the formations of ideologies (Cheal, 1979, p. 110).

Ideology has an intuitively obvious connection to law, if it is assumed that the legal system is legislated by some political system, and at least some aspect of law is a body of enforceable rules that govern socio-economic relations (Sypnowich, 2010). Politics, law, and economics appear to be relationally inseparable from the standpoint of ideology critique because ideology is roughly a system of legal, political, and economic ideas. Ideologies can be fascist, socialist, communist, capitalist, and liberal. Legal, political, and economic systems can be described as possessing these latter characteristics as well. Moreover, a single law can be viewed as the expression of a political or economic ideology (Sypnowich, 2010). To this extent, a theory of law must incorporate political, economic, and especially legal ideology within it for the sake of comprehensiveness.

The view of law as a social institution in a society and international community involves a hierarchical and well-structured system with individuals who serve to perpetuate their own social institution. They perform their duties of judging, enforcing, mediating, advising, organizing, and creating laws whilst integrating members of the legal institution. This had already partially occurred during their schoolings. The perpetuation and protection of law by members of its institution, in a society, argue on its behalf, as lawyers, judges, legal clerks, judicial conduct board members, sheriffs, etc. Sons, daughters, other family members, and friends of lawyers, judges, sheriffs, and of other members of the legal institution argue on behalf of the legal institution as well, presenting an ideology for those who tend to have privileges because of their relations with the legal system. Importantly, they lack responsibilities of members of the legal institution.

Ideology is espoused by members of a legal institution in the form of arguments. The same arguments put forth by non-members of this institution, are categorically different to the extent that the latter group inevitably includes members who are negatively affected by laws that they serve to protect after they have been successfully deceived by the former group's legal ideology. Those who live and think with ideologies have a "false consciousness." In the Marxist sense, having a false consciousness is lacking a historical awareness of the conditions that allow the laws to arise and allow members of the legal institution to earn wages and gain social privileges, which are dependent upon their placements within the legal system's employee-based hierarchies.

Insofar as there are arguments presented by the members of the social institution of law, who continually support its social status, there are ideologues and ideologies. There are ideologues and ideologies insofar as the social institution of law provides goods and services or beneficial relations for family members that others in society lack and who thereby hold different views about the law.

Mental states are intimately connected with ideologies, and ideologies are very often political and economic in nature. Since ideologies are authoritarian, democratic, capitalistic, socialistic and communistic, they very much involve desires for types of leaderships and ways to distribute the nation's money after taxation, which is a function of the legal system and legal institution. Political, economic, and legal systems contain each of these ideologies connected with desires, indifferences, and dislikes concerning the direction of the money flow and leadership.

In each legal system, there is immense value for multiple interest groups when members of the legal institution possess the abilities to choose their own members. Choices of members or filtering of potential members is, in part, accomplished by means of requiring great expenses for accredited law schools and university studies regarding time, effort, money, and opportunity costs of becoming a paralegal, lawyer, judge, etc.

Certain types of individuals are chosen by police departments and schools for cadets based on their perceived mental states (i.e., their beliefs, desires, and hopes) to become law enforcers. The same types of people tend to choose to apply and serve as police officers. Other individuals with different mental states tend not to desire to become law enforcement agents, or they tend to be selected out of the law enforcement profession during the training and institutionalization period (e.g., 18 months for some police officer training programs), if people are not perceived to have the law enforcement institutions' desirable mental states for future law enforcers. They tend to be filtered out if they appear to lack a higher social dominance orientation.

Having higher social dominance orientations basically means that people have stronger negative attitudes and opinions about members of low-status groups (Sidanius & Pratto, 1999). Social dominance orientation is best described as an orientation of general attitudes toward social groups and intergroup relations. The score for social dominance orientation is reflective of whether the individual likes group and intergroup relations to be hierarchical or equal instead. The score also reflects the degree one desires for his or her own in-group to gain or maintain superiority in relation to out-groups (Pratto et al, 1994, p. 72).

The latter ideas are illustrated by Kugler, Cooper, and Nosek (2010) who argue that there are specific psychological motivations that correspond to individuals' oppositions to equality and their advocacy of group-based dominance. Higher or lower social dominance orientation is often variable and largely depends upon situational conditions, like emotions and mental states are, insofar as one can change from sad to angry to happy or gain or lose the desire for something (Kugler, Cooper & Nosek, 2010, pp. 118–119).

Pratto et al. (2006) maintain that group members who have high levels of social dominance orientation actually lower their levels when their groups' statuses are lower or when the group members are required to compare the status of their group to groups that have higher statuses. Levin (1996) demonstrates the latter tendency with a sample of Israeli people from a high-status group (i.e., the Askenazi people) and a low-status group (the Mizrachi people). Both groups are socially recognized Jewish people.

When the group members had been thinking about the armed conflict between Israel and Arabs (i.e., Arabs are members of an even lower status group in Israel), both Askenazi and Mizrachi people reportedly showed no significant difference in their social dominance orientations. However, there was a significant difference in their social dominance orientations when the Askenazi and Mizrachi people were requested to consider their social divisions regarding each other, in which case the high-status group members demonstrated higher social dominance orientations (Levin, 1996; Kugler, Cooper & Nosek, 2010, p. 119). Likewise, Levin (2004) demonstrates within the American culture that those who perceive a relatively significant difference in the status of ethnic groups tend to have higher social dominance orientations, if they are in the high-status group (e.g., wealthy white people), and tend to have lower social dominance orientations, if they are in the lower status group (e.g., poorer black people). Regarding social dominance and the high and low-status groups, Sidanius and Pratto (1999b, p. 202) write:

> If, on their first visit to Earth, extraterrestrial beings wanted some quick and easy way to determine which human social groups were dominant and subordinate, they would merely need to determine which groups were over- and underrepresented in societies' jails, prison cells, dungeons, and chambers of execution. As we look around the world and across human history, we consistently see that subordinates are prosecuted and imprisoned at substantially higher rates than dominants.

Researchers have investigated the sociology of imprisonment of high-status groups in comparison to low-status groups for decades. They inform us of some legal systems on which they have focused their statistical analyses. Sidanius and Pratto (ibid.) continue:

> The disproportionate imprisonment of subordinates can be seen across a wide variety of cultures and nations, including the Maori of New Zealand, the Aborigines of Australia, Native Americans in the United States and Canada, native Algerians under the French occupation, Caribbean immigrants in England, foreign immigrants in the Netherlands and Sweden, the Lapps of Finland, the Burakumin and Koreans of Japan, the Tutsi of Rwanda and Zaire, and the Arabs of Israel, just to name a few.

Practically speaking, each geographical region is under some jurisdiction of a legal system and codes of law. However, certain geographical regions make law enforcement and observations of crimes exceedingly difficult. In Afghanistan's mountainous areas, traveling one mile can require hours of hiking.

The idea of dominant groups benefitting at the expense of low-status groups is an ancient one. The idea has been revived through sociological analyses of social dominance theorists since the 1990s. Social dominance theory has been criticized, altered and improved via investigations in social psychology, anthropology, and sociological theories, such as social identity theory and system justification theory. System justification theory attempts to explain why subordinate groups sometimes outright defend or approve of legal, political, and economic systems in which they live, despite perceived and real disadvantages of doing so (Jost, 2001; Jost, Banaji & Nosek, 2004).

The social dominance conception of legal system maintains that the criminal justice and law enforcement systems function similarly to terroristic organizations. Criminal justice systems do this to serve the conservative and preservative interests of dominant groups, according to the theory. The effect of the latter tendencies are systems of domination and systems of subordination in each society with legal systems. All such societies involve the formations of social group-based hierarchical systems.

Another aspect of legal systems certainly does attenuate arbitrary hierarchies (e.g., good public defenders and civil rights lawyers). The idea of the support of pre-established social hierarchies by the legal system and privileges given to certain classes of people has roots in Marxism, critical theory, critical legal studies, and innovative approaches in sociology and social psychology.

Another conception that can be well-supported would maintain that the law is, more or less, that which we think the law is. Experientially, law functions differently for each individual based on his or her circumstances, emotional and physical responses to law enforcement, luck, location etc. "Being in the wrong place at the wrong time" is sufficient for the legal system to jail or kill an individual legitimately. People of lower socio-economic classes and certain minority group members, presumably, tend to be in those places at those times proportionately more often than higher status group members.

On the other hand, efficient policing that finds burglars who stole electronics and jewelry from a family's house legitimately serves that family. The police return their property, reestablish the family's trust in the legal system, and promote more positive attitudes of procedural justice of the legal system. To some extent, they alleviate their fears that may have temporarily taken away their beliefs in a just and good world. Expectations are further stabilized.

Obviously, there are contradictory statements about the law that people from divergent backgrounds and different theoretical viewpoints write, speak, and yell. The person who was at the "wrong place at the wrong time" may very well speak out loudly against the law in a much different manner than the family who praises the law (e.g., the ones who had their property returned to them by the law). When the law is considered a social institution, the law can be observed as protecting and serving, suppressing, and killing systematically. So, in some sense, the so-called "contradictions" that arise amongst people, talking about what the "law" is, in a social sense, are expressions of groups that describe their corresponding feelings about an institution and system that greatly aids in maintaining the power structure of the nation.

The group of sons of small town sheriffs between fifteen and thirty-five years of age probably has a very different set of conceptions of the law than the daughters of NAACP (National Association for the Advancement of Colored People) members in the United States. Nevertheless, their conceptions about what the "law" is play important roles in relation to what the law is, especially if they are active in the community. The law functions to stabilize expectations within society (Di Viggiano, 2011; Luhmann, 1987), yet the relations of people to the law with and without social privileges (e.g., privileges that friends and family of members of the legal institution have) involve a wide range of opposite-ended beliefs regarding their desires, indifference, and disgusts directed toward the law that end in drastically different expectations for some who expect law to provide peacefulness, maintain order, and to serve and protect, whereas others expect to be terrorized by the law and law enforcement: threatened, incarcerated, brutally beaten, maimed, or killed.

Understanding mental states to predict individuals and groups' behaviors provides us at least with a fast, efficient, and effective means by which we may apply preventive measures or attempt compromises before acts of violence occur. The realization that some sons of small town sheriffs believe that a certain group or socio-economic class of people feels weak and afraid combined with the recognition of their sadistic desires to take advantage of those people can allow for preventions of racist, sexist, and ageist-driven violence. So, the prevention of violence is partially realized via an understanding of the privileges and responsibilities as well as the lack of responsibilities and privileges that certain groups have because of their relations to the members of the legal institution as friends, family, strangers, or even being more vehemently opposed to members of the legal institution.

While open for debate in respect to methodology, one means of understanding important behaviors and future actions of groups concerns first recognizing significant psychological characteristics of individuals, then characterizing how the person thinks and acts within separate groups in various places, and finally describing social groups' behaviors in relation to one another. Such methods require different levels of analyses because they require different levels of observation since the units of measurement differ.

CHAPTER 3

Levels of Analyses of Law and Methods

People are naturally very secretive. We often refrain from telling others how much money we earn or who our sexual partners are. We tend not to describe ourselves as violent beings, and we usually cover much of our skin when we are in public. However, people can observe others in ways that could very well change our views about humanity.

Humans, for instance, have the physical capabilities of producing video and audio footage of a naked human being for one minute of each year of that individual's life, starting with the final minute of the birth of the person and the first minute that the individual turns one year of age. Compiling such a documentary film would require the coordinated efforts of several people who have come to a mutual understanding and agreement, especially if the individual's lifespan lasts about eighty years. Such documentary footage of a person captured by cameras would last much less than two hours.

The superficial anatomy and physical development would be easily observed. Audiences would be confronted with observations of a particular human that allow for ordered levels of analysis regarding time, measurements, and technologies. The evolution of technology would play a role within the production of the documentary, especially if innovative technology for film production is constantly utilized and older footage is remastered.

Audiences that later watch the documentary may find the footage shocking, repulsive, intriguing, attractive, sad, uplifting, boring, etc. Many members of the audience may like the person when the person is a certain age or within a certain age range (e.g., from 25 to 65 years old) but may dislike the person at other ages. Psychologists and sociologists may investigate the initial reactions of the audiences and uncover people's opinions about a single person and his or her birth, development, and death represented by audio and video footage for one minute of each year of the person's life.

We can only guess what sorts of analyses would be derived from such an undertaking, yet the level of the analysis of the person who is filmed, which merely comes from the film itself (i.e., as opposed to interviews with people who know the person, and his or her banking, driving, and educational records, etc.), is unchanging. The level of analysis of the video footage is unchanging insofar as it merely includes audio and visual material that is of a specific length and which only allows observations that involve enhancements of the material to a certain extent (e.g., increasing the volume, reducing background noises,

 | DOI:10.1163/9789004385955_005

sharpening the images etc. to attain more observational information for the analysis).

Levels of analyses are based upon levels of observations, which range from microscopic observations of things to what we observe with our unaided sense perceptions (e.g., our naked eyes) to macroscopic observations of things. The descriptions of various observations we make with tools and machines (e.g., microscopes, telescopes, and stethoscopes) require different levels of analyses to be consistent. A sociological analysis of law enforcement agents and their views on anti-child pornography legislation requires different observational information than observations of blood pressures, heart rates, sweat levels, and hormonal levels that a police officer can have or can give, even regarding his or her reactions toward child pornography and the legislation about it.

What should be obvious here is that the sheer amount of information is or can be irrelevant for the analysis, but the level of observation, from which the internally and externally consistent analysis can arise, is crucial for the analyst (Brant, 2013b). However, in many cases it can be exceedingly easy to mistake the levels of observation from which the analysis can arise. This chapter will demonstrate some pitfalls in critical thinking and reasoning.

Perhaps it is disputable whether humans have the legal rights to produce such a documentary of a naked human being because such observations are relatively invasive. The observations continually require the legal consent of more than one person. Arguably, the production of the documentary may violate anti-child pornography legislation, privacy rights, or other laws within certain jurisdictions at certain times.

Humans are also very secretive kinds of mammals, especially regarding what we conceal from other members of our own species, our own social groups and the law. Our laws and legal systems reflect these facts. Consequently, legal systems are often confronted with dilemmas that involve either reducing privacy rights individuals are afforded in a populace or increasing the security of the society (i.e., rather than both). This is often the case regarding legal systems' interferences and observations of previously private types of communications.

One key example of the sacrifice of personal privacy rights for security is the legal disallowance for any citizen in some legal system to commit suicide since the law functions to protect the lives of individuals and there is a denial of the private right to death. Likewise, the attainment of knowledge about the law, the legal system, or institution require observations, methods, techniques, and technologies that can be invasive and thereby illegally interfere with the communications and actions of the members of the legal institution and others. For example, some journalists interfere with police investigations.

The legal system involves the communications and actions of numerous people's ever-changing roles, many of whom we recognize as members of the legal institution (e.g., judges, police, lawyers, lawmakers, etc.), but some evade recognition, such as criminal informants (i.e., snitches) and undercover detectives and agents. Many of the latter individuals involved with the law and law enforcement are faced with the tasks of observing criminals' behaviors, evaluating evidence of criminality, arguing on behalf of or against criminal masterminds, legislating to reduce criminality, and playing many very different and important roles in society that affect the earth's environments and societal dynamics of human populations.

The difficulties ever-present for the researchers of legal sciences, such as the science of policing, include observing the observers of violent criminal activity or those who observe activities, which if known to the criminals, would likely result in violent retaliations against all the observers or the organization with which they are affiliated. An observer is a component of the environment in which the observer observes some object, which is the focus of the observation and the focus of the observation begins with a preconception of the object within an environment (Brant, 2013a, pp. 182–195; Beck, 1961, p. 7).

Before the analyst begins describing to herself and reporting to others what each significance of the observations and the measurements of what is observed are, say, even before the observations are made, a process of imagination, hypothesizing, theorizing, and predicting occurs regarding what the analyst accepts as valid observational data, without which the individual who both observes and analyzes would lack focus entirely upon the object about to undergo the analysis. William Brant (2013a, p. 151) maintains that:

> Typically, distinctions are made between (1) an individual's mental images of objects x, y and z etc., (2) an individual's sensory experiences of objects x, y and z, and (3) investigated objects x, y and z, concerning what is within and without the individual. However, the knower and the known are both implicated, and there is already a presumed cognitive process of realization occurring during observations and meta-observations (i.e., observations of observations), according to Francisco Varela (Luhmann et al., 2003).

Brant (ibid.) continues:

> Moreover, (3) concerns no more than a combination of (1) and (2), except that (3) also concerns multiple individuals' agreements about x, y and z as well as measurements. The significance of agreement regarding

> observation and analysis provides science with a form of intersubjectivity that may depend upon culture and involve anthropocentricism or false assumptions, resulting from the limitations of our observational and analytical skills, despite the aid of technology and measurements (Henrich et al., 2010).

Finally, Brant (ibid.) claims that:

> Less arbitrary assumptions for theoretic frameworks, that contribute to yielding testable scientific hypotheses, may very well consider the process of mental imagery formation as a necessary aspect of the cognitive process of realization (i.e., when something, like an object, outcome, or event, is recognized and/or confirmed as being real or unreal) rather than as a mental process with a nature that is inferior to other psychological phenomena.

Mental images involve both visualizations as well as thinking about sounds and other sensory perceptions of objects and are important for the formation of the preconception of the object of focus of the observer and analyst (Brant, 2013a). The realization of the level of analysis, which arises after the observations within the fitting level of observation still requires the formation of mental imagery for the legal analysis. If the objective is to investigate corporations within a country that have been indicted with violations of employees' labor contracts, the focus and the preconception already involve the legal researcher's mental images which direct the research toward observational data (e.g., the judgments of court cases on the matters).

Any agreements with the productions of other independent researchers provide fuller conceptions of corporations' violations of labor contracts within that country. If the object of study instead focuses upon the relationships of the latter corporations with judges and lawyers and decisions in favor of the corporations,[1] then the task of research is presented with a diverse set of obstacles that require the discoveries of clandestine relations and any unlawfulness the parties attempt to keep secretive.

The analytic difficulties obviously sometimes exceed the challenges of solely observing the observers and their observations. The legal researcher begins the investigation with a conception that even precedes the investigation

1 For example, consider the relationship between the Monsanto corporation and US Supreme Court Justice Clarence Thomas, who ruled on court cases concerning Monsanto, despite being one of Monsanto's lawyers before the Supreme Court cases.

(i.e., the preconception) and has a conception after the investigation (i.e., the fuller conception[2]), which are both different in various respects. The concepts are different especially in respect to the latter concept being a restricted but improved organization of knowledge of the object of study (Beck, 1961). The reported and reconfirmed improvements of the concept may later serve as the basis for some analyst's preconception of the object under repeated investigations. The fuller conceptions of the object have been filled with the knowledge attained from investigations. They are undertaken to restrict the range of possibilities considerable to the analyst investigating the matter (Brant, 2013a, pp. 137–138).

1 Integrative Levels: Classification Systems for Knowledge Organization and Law

The legal system is studied via various levels of analyses. On these levels, legal systems can be studied or particular subsystems may undergo observations, research, and analysis, such as criminal justice systems or police departments. The level of analysis focuses upon something regarding its entirety or focuses upon its parts or components (Singer, 1961, p. 77); herein lies a problem with integrative levels and their classifications.

Focus upon the entirety of something necessarily incorporates many other concepts that are necessary conditions for the entirety of some phenomena, whereas the components of something, upon which the analysis focuses, are,

2 The choice of terminology, "fuller conception," comes from the translation of Heinrich Beck's (1961) work and the fact that the observations, hypotheses, and theoretical aspects directed toward what has been observed is more developed or "fuller" in terms of historical content. However, the conception is less externally comprehensive when there are falsehoods, for instance, about generalizations of the phenomena observed. The aspect of comprehensiveness regarding the fuller conception that is more inclusive of the content provided by the observers also involves the amount of internal consistencies of the newly developed fuller conception. It is questionable how many internal consistencies of descriptions are externally consistent with real phenomena in the world, which also means that this amount involves being more or less externally comprehensive. This aspect of the conception that forms after the preconception is more internally comprehensive than the preconception because there have been more experiences with the phenomena. The methodological concern is whether the internal consistencies of the fuller conception are also accurately able to be described as external consistencies of reality or of a hypothetically most accurate set of descriptions of the phenomena with measurements. Certainly, after the observations are made, there is a more developed and more elaborate mental image that the former observer may have, especially if the observer is asked to recall his observation of the thing at hand, near or beyond an arm's length.

disputably, also made of other components. The problem permeates within most educational institutions, which are usually bureaucratically divided into departments with departmental privileges to access technologies for particular levels of observations for their specific levels of analyses. For example, physicists normally have access to different tools than microbiologists, which can become problematic for a biologist studying part of a cell and which is necessary to analyze its chemical compounds or atomic features.

Levels of scientific analyses and legal analyses almost invariably depend on observations performed at various levels (Brant, 2013b). Yet the access to tools and machines allowing for even gradual transitions to be made by observers from one level of observation to another[3] are bureaucratically restricted and divided for political reasons. This involves departmentalizations in education systems and hinders interdisciplinary investigations aiming to present different levels of analysis. Such investigations are often even required by theories. Some political reasons for restricting access and departmentalizing involve nepotism. There are increases in funding for universities' departments through government grants for politicians' friends and family.

Sometimes the theory is comparable to the model of, say, the shoe that appears to fit. However, if the shoe is the smallest or largest one of that model and appears to fit, there is still the possibility that a slightly smaller or larger one, respectively, would be even more fitting (Brant, 2013b, p. 297).

Social dominance theory, which is thoroughly applicable to law and almost invariably involves law, requires macroscopic investigations of multiple people in comparison to other groups of multiple people. Social dominance theory involves the macroscopic investigations of individuals, confirmations at entirely different levels, such as microscopic levels that demand analyses and observations at specific levels of analysis and specific microscopic observational levels that incorporate measurements of neurological activity, hormones, and behavior regarding social dominance (Summers et al., 2005; Anderson & Summers, 2007).

The law and legal systems arise from a group of people at an integrative level, which is a level of organization by which social phenomena appear because of the preexisting social phenomena at lower organizational levels. Here, the term "emergence" is meant to refer specifically to the arising of real phenomena at higher levels of organization from real phenomena at lower levels. Most common instances of emergence in scientific literature illustrate consciousness arising from the anatomy and physiology of organisms' central

3 These are also requisite for testing the legal analysis in important ways, like testing the model of a shoe for a large foot.

nervous systems and life evolving from chemical elements that are not alive (Blitz, 1992). The highly integrated levels are understood as always involving more complex phenomena due to the emergence of the phenomena later in the environment and system.[4]

From the level of non-living things to living things and from conscious living things to conscious human beings in a society with a legal system, we are confronted with a plethora of necessary conditions. These necessary conditions have, doubtlessly, amounted to sufficient conditions for the emergence of the law and legal systems. They are fundamental to such an extent that they may even appear to be irrelevant.

The fact that the chemical compound of water and its elements, hydrogen and oxygen, are requisite for the emergence of law, legal communications by members of the legal institution, and any legal system is largely ignored. This regards multiple levels of observation and analysis. The functions of water regarding legal systems are perhaps at best taken for granted but are also overlooked. Functions that involve mentioning the requirement of water may be discarded as irrelevancies. Water is necessary for consciousness of any human being, necessary as the life source of humans, and necessary for survival, societies, violence, sex etc.

Water is involved in legal ownerships of real estate. Yet water is just not an ordinary subject matter of discussion concerning the topic of law and legal systems, even though water is a necessary condition for the emergence of animal life, for consciousness from non-conscious animals, and for each human being who is a component of any society with law. Undoubtedly, water is important as a legal issue when water is observed, analyzed, and described in forms of ponds, lakes, rivers and oceans, as clean and treated or untreated, polluted, drinkable, and undrinkable.

One hypothesis about why knowledge about chemical compounds and molecules are absent from explanations and knowledge about law is that law is a higher emergent set of real phenomena. That is, knowledge of law resides at different levels of relevancy than other real phenomena, such as water.

Political decisions often determine the funding for research and development in the sciences (i.e., also legal science), which restrict the scholarly task of exploration of the plethora of variables involved in the rise, continuation,

4 There are examples of living organisms that have evolved and prey on other organisms that are even more complex than they are (i.e., many hosts of parasites are more complex). Such examples involve a different meaning of "emergence" and have different relations of dependence than integrated phenomena have on simpler phenomena, such as the integrated phenomena called "molecules." Molecules emerge from particles and atoms.

and fall of the law. Political decisions have legislated specializations in forms of departments, such as engineering, physics, chemistry, biology, psychology, sociology, and many other departments with many overlapping interests amongst those in them. Divisions are sometimes arbitrary, say, insofar as many social psychologists could work well or even better in sociology departments and vice versa. These legal and political divisions often prevent employment opportunities, which directly hinder the educated choices of research focal points as well.

The latter academic disciplines' sometimes have sharp divisions that may lead many researchers to presume that certain subject matters, such as water, are solely involved in the domains of knowledge of chemists or biologists, for instance. Such divisions strictly oppose ideas and classification schemes proposed by the theory of integrated levels. Divisions may prevent subject matters from entering research interests of those in legal studies and legal science.

The importance of water, and other necessary real phenomena (e.g., blood cells and neurons) may thus be taken for granted and overlooked. They certainly deserve critical analyses as an integral aspect of legal studies itself—so too does forming scientific hypotheses about impacts of hydration levels of lawmakers, judges, juries, potential criminals, criminals, police etc. Moreover, legal allowances of members of nations' militaries to engage in armed conflicts in certain areas depend on access to drinking water and future water resources for the economics of militaries. Water serves as one example of a component of more complex integrated phenomena, such as the law. The problem, however, arises about how exactly to incorporate real phenomena, such as water, into approaches of legal studies.

Necessary components for integrated phenomena, which are more complex, are requisite for more comprehensive presentations of the organization of any type of knowledge, including knowledge of the law. However, the focus, time, and lengths spent on components of law as integrated phenomena can, of course, be counter-productive. Thus, there is the need of a form of presentation that involves classification methods like those in fields of taxonomy and phylogenetic systematics in biology. They facilitate the classification of humans as *Homo sapiens* in one of several kingdoms, phyla, classes, orders, families, genera and species.

There are examples of systems of classification that are ever-developing. Some classify law, members of the legal institution, the legal system, crime, war, terrorism, violence, etc., yet they begin with the fundamentals. The Integrative Levels Classification and the Classification Research Group are two systems for the organization of knowledge derived fundamentally from the combined efforts of computer science, biology, library science, philosophy and then basically every other discipline. There are many more, including the Broad System of Ordering, Brown's Subject Classification, Bliss's Bibliographic Classification, and Dahlberg's Information Coding Classification.

The Integrative Levels Classification approach in 2015 represents concepts and phenomena that are the most fundamental via the lowercase letters at the very beginning of the classification sequence for any particular thing. The alphabet is utilized in the following manner so that a = form, b = spacetime, c = energy, d = particles, e = atoms, f = molecules, g = bodies, h = celestial objects, i = weather, j = land, k = genes, l = bacteria, m = organisms, n = populations, o = instincts, p = consciousness, q = signs, r = languages, s = civil society, t = governments, u = economies, v = technologies, w = artifacts, x = art, y = knowledge, and z = religion.

If we search, for instance, for what is further classified in c, i.e., energy, we are confronted with c1, which is electromagnetic radiation, and c11 is visible light, and c11c is the color violet. The latter classifications represent the concepts as subclasses insofar as the color violet is classified as visible light, visible light is classified as electromagnetic radiation, and electromagnetic radiation is classified as energy. The Integrative Levels Classification further classifies "bodies" at a higher complexity and integrative level than molecules, which are higher than atoms regarding complexity and the integrative levels, and atoms are higher than subatomic particles in the latter respects.

The terms "legal" and "law" are classified within governments and economies, although the concept of law is also classified within the concept of technology in respect to conforming to regulations as well as within the concept of knowledge in respect to texts of law. The classification of being "ruled by law" is t6 and includes the subclasses of contracts, law of torts, law of property, family law, succession law, corporate law, competition law, labor law, commercial law, intellectual property, penal law, constitutional, administrative, and international law.

Each of the latter types of law are symbolized as "t6" with an additional lowercase letter at the end. Relevant concepts, such as crimes, are classified nearby other relevant concepts (e.g., "crimes" are subclasses of t7). The symbols allow one to readily understand the level of abstraction and specificity in relation to other concepts as well as view the related concepts, which contributes directly toward the facilitation of the understandings of levels of analyses and levels of observations.

On the other hand, a compilation of numerous systems would allow for individual concepts to be classified as subclasses of multiple other classes (e.g., the subclass of horses can be classified within zoology and veterinary medicine as well as within animal husbandry, livestock, mammals, vertebrates, animals etc.). While a single system may have serious flaws, numerous systems lead the information to be categorized largely in arbitrary ways, especially when they are based upon politically divided departments. Departments are partially divided in terms of the technology and similar methods of observation, but the divisions of the technology for certain departments is based on the political divisions, which are reinforced partially by the levels of observation, for example, that the technology concerns.

The virtues of the latter types of systems, such as the Integrative Levels Classification, are more than encyclopedic because their aims are to reorganize knowledge for maximizing its usefulness, although they are still in their infancies. Rather than merely representing disciplines and their subfields (e.g., the history of contract law and the history of contract law in the 20th century), such classification systems represent actual phenomena within the world in which we live, instead, which signifies both practicality as well as increased consistency (i.e., the external consistency between concepts and real phenomena). The undertakings of classification systems therefore involve shifting away from the bureaucratic divisions of disciplines and replacing these discipline-centered approaches with systems of classes and subclasses of real phenomena, which is of great interest to researchers of law and has vast implications for library science and the innovative approaches available for reorganizing libraries.

Some legal theorists have naturally led themselves to classify the law via integrative levels and have been compelled to write about other disciplines like physics in relation to law and legal science, such as Hans Kelsen (1930 & 1939). Although late 20th century and 21st century research and contemporary theories very rarely include conceptualizations of levels of reality, the problems of the levels are included within many scientific writings, such as levels of analysis, levels of description, levels of explanations, levels of complexity, and levels of organization (Hartmann, 1940, 1942 & 1943; Poli, 2001, p. 281; Kim, 2006, p. 139; Dziadkowiec, 2011, pp. 95–96). The theoretic frameworks within sciences and philosophy of science that incorporate the latter types of levels are presented within the research of Conger (1925), Feibleman (1954), Bunge (1979), Blitz (1990, pp. 153–170; 1992), Poli (1998; 2001; 2008), Ellis (2004), Morowitz (2002), and Dziadkowiec (2011).

Law can be analyzed from various standpoints and points of view. Valerie Kerruish (1992) distinguishes between what Ronald Dworkin refers to as a "point of view," which is storytelling from a particular viewpoint rather than the way in which H.L.A. Hart and J. Finnis utilize the phrase "point of view" as the viewing of some object from some specific point or angles. Kerruish (ibid., p. 64) argues the latter distinctions involve totally distinct kinds of activities, and consequently:

> [T]he purpose of specifying a point of view is to draw attention to the fact that the narrative or view will vary according to points of view. So, this is one point on which they agree. It poses a problem: what kind of claims can be made for this narrative or for this account of the object viewed? Hart, Finnis and Dworkin are all telling us what law is and telling us somewhat different things. They do agree, however, unsurprisingly, that human actors are participants in law making and that their participation is intentional.

Beliefs about others' intentions and expectations and what lawmakers pass are important components in the comprehensive worldview of what the law is. Kerruish (ibid.) begins explaining the jurists' differences:

> Finnis and Dworkin think it appropriate to bring in another thing—the purposes of participants or of the practice. They want to talk not only about what participants think they are doing but why they are doing it. Hart uses a different method of generalising his theory as an assertion about the function of law and a classification of participants according to roles as officials or private citizens. So, for him the internal point of view is just a matter of official functionality, or to put that another way, a matter of conditions for the existence of certain kinds of rules basic to law.

Kerruish observes other agreements even after the point at which the legal scholars, Finnis and Dworkin, make their point of departure. Kerruish (ibid.) states:

> As a point of view of (all or some) participants in legal practices, the internal point of view concerns reasons for action and decision—not necessarily in the sense of reasons as motives for action but rather in the sense of justificatory reasons or reasons which support the rationality or soundness of an act or decision. In this sense the internal point of view is concerned with understanding the structuring assumptions and conventions of a discourse and with some form of commitment to them.

Some amount of thought about the way to participate in discourse is a requirement for the internal point of view to emerge. Such thought must also allow the participant to realize how the viewpoint applies to different situations and legal cases that have not yet occurred. The theoretical analysis of the point of view from the observer to the object of analysis in the environment is further analyzed by Brant (2013a, pp. 182–195).

Different points of view and systems of classification are important regarding the continued investigation of any real phenomenon. Points of view are crucial for knowledge management, especially fact checking. This naturally occurs during the process of research.

The organization of knowledge naturally arises through the research processes of those with diverse points of view. Some viewpoints coincide better with greater organizations of knowledge. Working in teams with diversely educated personnel is superior.

Disagreements especially allow for the point of view of each individual researcher to shape, elaborate, in terms of justifications against each side, and improve upon the viewpoint of each investigator regarding the set of observations and analyses. However, researchers' personalities that are high in agreeableness can stifle the latter benefits.

2 Methodological Concerns Regarding Legal Research

Methodology for researching the variety of specializations encompassed by legal studies has transformed dramatically within the latest information age of the 21st century, to wit, an age that has witnessed the ever-farther reaching World Wide Web, which reached outer space and the international space station in 2010. We are now confronted with the opportunity to store millions of books, articles, audio files, and videos of multiple disciplines and upon each of our very own personal computers, phones, and other devices.

The files can be saved in multiple languages and translated into multiple other languages instantly, even if they are only translated imperfectly. For *Beyond Legal Minds*, I have saved an e-library of thousands of books and articles as PDF files, with which I often searched for key terms and arrived immediately at every part of these texts where the desired terms are located. These are some of the research methods and techniques with technology that have led me to complete this book.

There are a few problems we face with such research methods for law. For instance, one problem here is that relevant research material, which is superior to what the researcher has at hand, is usually available either free of charge from the authors themselves or legal and illegal downloading online, such as the millions of books and articles available at the (in)famous Russian Library Genesis, which provides approximately 25 million textbooks, books, and research articles online for free (Cabanac, 2014). This source exceeds the number of volumes available via the access of most Western universities because universities restrict themselves to merely attaining information legally, according to their own legal systems, via means that generally require financial compensations for their accesses to the information. Library Genesis has around 42 terabytes of stored information of many of these documents, according to Cabanac (2014, p. 874).

Firstly, researchers confront the problem of laying aside materials on which they have focused much time and effort. Replacing research materials occurs when something is found that is similar but more concise, more consistent, comprehensive, or more practical, and more relevant for their purposes. The replacement of research materials with other sources requires the researcher to familiarize oneself with another style and different presentation of research. The replacement increases the likelihood that there will be wasted moments during which the new material presents the same information as the replaced material for the researcher.

Secondly, researchers for legal studies, depending on the legal system's jurisdiction in which they reside, are placed at serious advantages and disadvantages. Researchers no longer simply just borrow books. Researchers transfer readily accessible electronic libraries themselves with digitally displayed images and words. Contemporary problems with research involve its organization as an overlapping, messy monstrosity of information and misinformation that is always in want of greater methods of categorization with user-friendly devices via methods in ergonomics, human factors psychology, and library science. The latter task facilitates investigative methods for research teams rather than individual researchers.

Counter-opposing systems in philosophy (e.g., determinism and indeterminism) are important to understand for philosophers. Systems of thought offer potential argumentative solutions that contradict other potential argumentative solutions. Research teams benefit from the approach here insofar as socio-legal problems are presented in ways that illustrate their attempted solutions by means of multiple systems of thought rather than a single system. The strict advocacy of a single system (i.e., instead of the presentation of multiple systems) increases risks of errors since systems generally coincide with the creation or advocacy of subsystems or subdivisions of a single system utilized for problem-solving. Strictly advocating a single system disallows problem-solving to be directed toward other opposing systems of thought (Hartmann, 1936/1977).

Legal researchers are confronted with reconciling the latter problems regarding legal studies and law, which is why multiple disciplines, multiple systems of thought, worldviews and legal "problem-thinking" are included here. This book serves as an example of a philosophy book that is rife with other disciplines. They are represented by the quotes, ideas, comedy, lyrics, and citations of publications of experts in them, yet this book is unorthodox to the extent that no single discipline is given strict priority. The latter fact is indicative of problem-thinking.

Problem-thinking, as opposed to mere problem-solving,[5] is one line of thought presented throughout this book. Problem-thinking is the research approach that compares and contrasts different worldviews and counter-opposes systems of thought with one another, regardless of whether different types of system-thinking offer identical solutions to the same problems. An inherent risk subsists for any researcher to strictly advocate a system of thought and the creation of subsystems in it (ibid.). Creations of subsystems of thought in any faulty system are time and energy-consuming and inconsistent. At some point, they lack practicality as problem-solving methods or attempted solutions.

In each system and academic discipline, there are diverging stances regarding answers to inquiries about law. An observation and an analysis of something are not necessarily more accurate simply because they occur in closer proximity to what is observed and analyzed (e.g., an analysis of serotonin levels of a criminal via a microscope), even when the skills of the observers and analysts remain constant. Observations and analyses that occur at greater distances can be more accurate for several reasons. A police stakeout with a telescope is less invasive. According to Kurt Lewin (1951, p. 157):

> The first prerequisite of a successful observation in any science is a definite understanding about what size of unit one is going to observe at a given time.

More recently theoretical views of levels of analyses have been applied to international relations and sociology (Jepperson & Meyer, 2011; Yurdusev, 1993; Singer, 1961). Multiple levels of analysis of the law require observations, methodologies, and rationalistic means through which attempts are made to combine analyses at various levels with one another in consistent manners.

The law as a social system often involves various peoples. Historically, the latter peoples differ regarding the amounts that they observe and are observed by other peoples, especially in an official capacity. Generally, when people realize they are being observed and analyzed, they behave differently. This is a common type of response to observers and analysts. Individuals who know they are being observed may protest against it or act as if they do not realize

5 Problem-solving is practical. Problem-thinking involves intellectually structuring types of potential solutions to problems. However, the problems may not be solvable, such as the problems presented by the enduring questions in philosophy (e.g., What is morally good? What is causation? Etc.).

they are being observed, despite alterations of their behaviors. The latter factors contribute to the ease of misunderstanding what sizes of units are and about who or what undergoes the observations.

One may find the presumptions worthwhile that there are both positive and negative correlations concerning the greater and lesser proximities of the observers to the objects of observations and accuracies of the analyses. Such correlations depend on what Lewin (1951) called the realization of the size of the unit being investigated at particular times (Brant, 2013a, pp. 182–195; Brant, 2013b). When people are observed and analyzed, and people believe and perceive that they are being closely observed, they may respond typically in the following manners: (1) The observer, who the analyzed people (e.g., criminals) believe is likely closer to them—and who is thus in a more privileged position to attain more accurate information about certain events—tends to provide reason for the people to refrain from behaving in ways that they believe are socially unacceptable or illegal or, on the contrary, for the people who suspect they are being observed to pretend to act in illegal and socially unacceptable ways to elicit a response from their observer.

Social unacceptability is important regarding the fact that observations have the potential to play key roles in the transitions from what is alegal and socially unacceptable to what is illegal and socially unacceptable (i.e., when analyses of the observational information reach the right hands). For the latter reasons, the closer the people believe the observers are, the greater they tend to act in ways they believe will be perceived as socially acceptable, depending on whom they believe the observers are; this assumes they are not attempting to elicit a response from the observers.[6]

(2) When the analyst accurately portrays the members of a social group performing illegal or socially unacceptable acts, the members of the social group may deny or confirm any descriptions of wrongdoings or threaten, kill, or negotiate with the analyst. Members of the social group may also approach the potential publishers to prevent the publications of their social group's mistakes and flaws. The social group with members who realize that they are being observed may wait to discover whether the public disregards the findings,

6 There are exceptions to any sort of rule maintaining there is a tendency for social groups to refrain from acting in perceivably illegal and socially unacceptable ways. Some exceptions involve situations with conditions of utter desperation, significantly lower values placed on human life, or the use of violence for coercion. Exceptions occur in emergency situations and cases of extreme violence. Mexican drug cartels who behead, maim, and leave signs of tortured human bodies as scare tactics against those who may attempt to undermine their powers are examples of the latter types of exceptions (Pansters, 2012; Grayson, 2010). They torture and murder their observers.

perceives the social group as terrifying enough to refrain from actions against it, accepts, or tolerates the current status, or demands change.

The group which observes the other social group often assumes part of the role of the social indicator for planned social changes. However, the social indicator can be prone to corruption. Donald Campbell (1976, pp. 47–48) argues there ought to be a prohibition for social scientists to engage in social research, which would remove *ad hominem* attacks, especially for political gains and mudslinging.

Attacks against the person, and especially against the representative or representatives of any group (e.g., a low-status or high-status group), which can be presented in the form of accurate information about the worst characteristics of that group, are particularly risky. The accuracy of the information is coupled with the overrepresentation of the vices, misconduct, or annoying attributes of this group. The overrepresentation is a form of "targeting" people identified as members. It is questionable what sort of negative impacts the targeting has. Social research is strongly recommended to be justified on the gravity of the social problem at hand rather than the certainty of any particular answer to the social problem. Campbell's law (ibid., p. 49) asserts:

> The more any quantitative social indicator (or even some qualitative indicator) is used for social decision-making, the more subject it will be to corruption pressures and the more apt it will be to distort and corrupt the social processes it is intended to monitor.

When we consider the group of observers in (1) as a social group, such as Mexican police, Mexican journalists, and Mexican soldiers, we are confronted with social groups acting as social indicators for social decision-making. They often attempt to undermine the economic and social decision-making of drug and weapon dealers involved in a multi-billion-dollar black market industry. The law enforcement, journalists, and soldiers become ever more prone to pressures of corruption (Grayson, 2010; Pansters, 2012). Some journalists, law enforcers, and military personnel therefore lead double lives, working for two mutually oppositional organizations, receiving at least double the salary or wages, and typically becoming informers for the secretive black market business activity. Opposing the latter business would result in torturous and deadly retaliation against the individual and their families.

One important type of analysis demonstrates a social group (e.g., law enforcement agents in a precinct) has a serious defect that is both unnecessary and capable of being removed. The latter type of analysis is especially important when it is based on verifiable observations. Imperfections of social groups in the legal institution are discoverable from multicultural analyses via comparisons of legal systems' sets of employee-based hierarchies and each system's impact on the remainder of the populace. They are discoverable through a combination of self-examinations (i.e., legal institutional members analyzing themselves) and insights attained from those who are not members of any legal institution but are nonetheless affected by legal systems. Stephen Savage (2003, p. 645) writes:

> The justification of a particular perspective on legal contexts need not necessarily entail the denial of legitimacy of alternative frameworks for the analysis of law. It should be accepted that our appreciation of legal contexts is enriched by the proliferation of approaches to the subject, from varied disciplines and a multiplicity of conceptual and methodological paradigms. However, in the context of comparing, in our case, psychological with social scientific, or sociological, stances on the study of legal contexts, this tends not to be the case.

Savage (ibid.) continues:

> There is indeed a high degree of territoriality at work. Thus psychologists might deride the failure of sociology to satisfy the standards of the 'scientific paradigm' in its varied methodologies; sociologists, in turn, may attack psychology for 'naivety' in aspiring to apply the strictures of the natural sciences to human behaviour or for failing to see the wood (society and social processes) for the trees (human individuals).

Interdisciplinary works are highly important. They require an integrative levels theoretic approach. This greatly facilitates knowledge management, knowledge organization, and disregards arbitrary, bureaucratic divisions superimposed on the exhibitions of knowledge.

Conclusions of well-researched phenomena can increase public perceptions that the authorities (e.g., lawmakers, judges, and police) are rightfully legitimate. They may lead to focuses on aspects of societal subsystems that can cost-effectively undergo improvements. Moreover, the latter conclusions can be more easily drawn without as many of the hindrances of interdepartmental politics at universities and other research institutes. Funding for research projects combining multiple researchers in multiple departments have less impact on competitive struggles between the researchers who must compete for limited resources in the same spaces.

Legal systems that have modernized have also increasingly begun to recognize the role of legitimacy regarding law, governance, and their effectiveness (Tyler, 2006a, 2006b & 2010). The role of legitimacy includes the importance of widespread beliefs of the populace that the legal system and its subsystems (e.g., court and policing systems) are entitled to make decisions. Attributing legitimacy to the system supports the belief that the legal system ought to continue to pursue criminal justice. Alternatively, one option is appealing to some other party to gain compensation for being wronged (e.g., a mercenary or criminal organization that would retaliate against someone in return for payment).

Societies necessitate the maintenance and creation of legitimacy by the police (Tyler, 2010; Skogan & Frydl; Skogan & Meares, 2004). The role of legitimacy comes not only from the perception of fairness in the procedures of the justice system but also from the maintenance of a professional appearance that undergoes the process of modernization. This may involve uniforms or interiors and exteriors of the halls of justice, such as those in Paris undergoing renovation in 2011, which is shown in figure 7.

Methods of research are incredibly important in the legal sciences for the reduction of corruption. Methods, observational data, and units of observation need to be studied in addition to what conclusions researchers maintain about legal phenomena for reducing corruption. They further establish perceptions of legitimacy of the system. The roles of leaders are also required for the reduction of corruption to make headway.

FIGURE 7 Renovation of the Parisian Palace of Justice

Progress regarding the reduction of corruption might be occurring[7] in China under the presidency of Xi Jinping and an anti-corruption campaign. It maintains they will "hunt tigers and swat flies." Yet the reduction of corruption undermines certain power structures in place and legitimate businesses, such as those that offer luxurious products and benefit from the lavish lifestyles of corrupt officials and multi-millionaire Communist party leaders (Harrison, 2015; Denyer, 2015; Sudworth, 2014; MacLeod, 2014). The anti-corruption campaign might as well be interpreted as an ideological description given by the mass media.

One may consider policing and evaluative methods for individual police departments in certain jurisdictions and methods and data analyses concerning clearance rates (i.e., the rate at which the crimes are solved by police in the department) as a quantitative social indicator. The social and hierarchical pressures for particular police departments to reduce the overall amount of open cases and to have them solved has inevitably led to greater corruption in many jurisdictions.

Skolnick (1966) and Campbell (1976) maintain that such corruption includes failures to record the complaints of citizens, postponing the records of complaints for time periods after the cases they concern are already solved, and plea-bargaining. Plea-bargaining is an alegal process and custom whereby a court of law and prosecuting attorney agree with an alleged offender on the crime and penalization that will be implemented against him or her. The offender pleads guilty to one or more crimes and avoids expenditures of time, efforts and money for the trial. Additionally, other members of the legal institution may play crucial roles concerning some plea-bargain, such as homicide detectives and undercover law enforcement agents. Donald Campbell (1976, p. 51) writes:

> Crime rates are in general very corruptible indicators. For many crimes, changes in rates are a reflection of changes in the activity of the police rather than changes in the number of criminal acts (Gardiner, 1969; Zeisel, 1971).

Campbell portrays the research of Skolnick (1966) to demonstrate the flaw in any legal system utilizing plea-bargaining (e.g., the United States) to change

7 Perhaps a more realistic way of understanding the prosecutions, convictions, and executions of other Chinese leaders is the securing of political power by the president of China via consolidation.

unsolved crimes to solved ones. Regarding plea-bargaining, Campbell (ibid.) writes:

> While this is only a semilegal custom, it is probably not undesirable in most instances. However, combined with the clearance rate, Skolnick finds the following miscarriage of justice. A burglar who is caught in the act can end up getting a lighter sentence the more prior unsolved burglaries he is willing to confess to. In the bargaining, he is doing the police a great favor by improving the clearance rate, and in return, they provide reduced punishment. Skolnick believes that in many cases the burglar is confessing to crimes he did not in fact commit.

The rise and fall of crime rates coincide with ideological arguments put forth by lawmakers and potential lawmakers to increase their fame and legitimacy regarding public perception. Methodological concerns about legal research must involve methods for investigating methods of studying legal research. Social science research includes numerous academic disciplines.

Perhaps social psychology has the greatest access to laboratory equipment and utilizes laboratory settings for experimental conditions more effectively and/or frequently than other social science disciplines. Divisions between disciplines are largely bureaucratic. Working in a particular social science department (e.g., sociology, anthropology, political science, public administration, etc.) typically requires an academic degree in the discipline of the social science department to teach in it, despite whether the phenomena under investigation are the same. There are many other factors that contribute to the bureaucratic division of the social science disciplines, including the amount of political funds allocated for departments. This is often problematic when decisions for the distribution of public funds are decided by bureaucrats and those with vested political interests.

According to Max Weber (1864–1920), methodological concerns regarding bureaucracy are multifarious and generally involve the official and fixed areas of jurisdiction within which procedures are ordered as well as administrative regulations and rules.[8] The requirement of the implementation of commands to distribute duties is strict and provided by some authority figure who may or may not know anything useful about the social science research to which he or she allocates funding. Once funding has started, the continuation of funding

8 Weber's magnum opus, *Economy and Society* (i.e., *Wirtschaft und Gesellschaft* (1922)) describes the general characterization of bureaucracy, and his analysis endures and still directs research.

becomes a primary concern for the research on the side of the researcher, the researcher's department and crew. On the side of the public administrative bureaucracy, there is often very little concern for the direction of study or phenomena undergoing the investigation. Preferential treatment is often given to academics in certain departments that provide some of the social science research. Social and political philosophy professionals in philosophy departments may receive far less financial assistance than sociology and political science departments.

On both sides, precautions are methodically made to regulate and thereby provide continual fulfillments of official duties that are performed by those who are generally required to have regulations concerning their qualifications for employment. Management of offices of the departments with researchers (e.g., at universities) and public administrative offices are based on written documentation and filing systems. The fact that the bureaucracy is hierarchically ranked, and that the public administrative bureaucracy determines funds of the social science research leads to a dependency on the public administration relationship for academic departments.

The relationship of public administration to the academic disciplines is partially responsible for the divisions and subdivisions of the departments themselves and largely responsible for the perpetuation of the often-arbitrary divisions. Even socio-economic hierarchies at universities emerge in which professors of certain departments make significantly higher wages than researchers at comparable levels of experience and productions of research but in different departments. Methods and research of those earning less may, in many instances, be superior for the advancement of knowledge but may very well lack access to certain processes of popularization and publication even because the usefulness of the research for bureaucrats is negligible.

The research of many of individuals in social psychology has even been subdivided further into the discipline called "moral psychology." The research project of moral psychology produces much political research that even attempts to establish the moral superiority of certain types of lawmakers within major political parties. The designs of the experiments involve political symbols, such as national flags, and, in some instances, appear to aim to demonstrate that right-wing politicians with traditional values, concerning the society, have an extra moral dimension that others lack and oppose (Haidt & Graham, 2007; see Ch. 4.8). However, perhaps most research has leftist agendas in political philosophy, psychology, and sociology.

There are extensive and multifarious reasons why methodological concerns regarding legal research are paramount. Methodologies that do not fall prey to the aforementioned types of pitfalls of certain ways of researching social scientific topics are requisite for the advancement of knowledge of the legal system and of various systems interconnected with it within society.

3 Autobiographical, Biographical, and Historical and Sociological Ways of Thinking about Law

We find obvious value in the specifications of certain topics concerning particular aspects of the law, even if the observations, measurements, and analyses merely come from the standpoint of a subdivision of psychology or any other particular field of study. The present analysis focuses upon how people think differently about the law, which incorporates psychological, sociological, and cultural studies from various micro- and macro-levels of analysis and observation. How people think about the law involves sociologists, historians, journalists, psychologists, philosophers, anthropologists, and many other academics' thoughts and impacts upon others as well as the layman or average sort of person walking the streets, begging on the curb, or working on the corner of a busy avenue in addition to crowds and other social groups that behave in unison.

Insofar as those who affect the law, and who are affected by the law, think autobiographically about their own run-ins or reliefs concerning the law as well as about others' interactions with the law and historical perspectives about their entire society's or international communities' law, there is a growing need to develop accounts that consider each of these ways of thinking about the law and which are likely to be voiced regularly by individuals.

Figure 8 provides an example of how a person can smoothly transition from the introspective self-examination of him or herself via what may be called "autobiographical ways of thinking" and which may very well lead to other psychological or socio-historical ways of thinking about others. Additionally, figure 8 illustrates how an individual may consistently structure and transit from one thought to the next about members of the legal institution, such as police, and thereby begin to form an ideology because of the focus of his or her thoughts about law.

FIGURE 8 Transitions of thought about the law from oneself to others

Figure 8 furthermore shows that the socio-historical way of thinking, which directly concerns the "sociological imagination," is at a greater distance from the autobiographical way of thinking. Socio-historical thinking requires maturation. We may hypothesize that it is more challenging for one to think about one's own circumstances and then to consider the socio-historical and economic circumstances than it is for one to consider the circumstances of just one other human being. Moreover, it is hypothesized that it is easier for one's thoughts to transit from socio-historical and biographical ways of thinking to autobiographical ones than vice versa.

The study of ideology espoused by a single adult or adolescent requires describing not only beliefs, desires, motivations, and ideals of that individual but also how they manifest themselves at each level of analysis by means of thinking about the person, say, affiliated with the law in more or less stereotypical ways and thinking about entire social groups and the environment as a whole. Moreover, the interrelations of thinking at one level and then the next are dependent upon our prior experiences.

All three ways of thinking also require at times that one way of thinking overrides another way of thinking. When one's personal experiences are quite different from the accounts and shared experiences of others who are presented with the same sets of circumstances, comparisons between the conclusions drawn from autobiographic thinking and biographical thinking are made and may likely lead the critical thinker to investigate the sociological and historic events that have led to such circumstances to reconcile and understand one's own situation. When those people, with whom one is surrounded, are placed in fairly unique conditions in relation to the rest of the society, then again, the critical thinker likely investigates the sociological and historic events that have led to such circumstances for understanding one's own situation. This facilitates the improvement of one's social position in certain societal hierarchies.

Hans Georg Gadamer's magnum opus called *Truth and Method* (1960) conceptualizes humans as hermeneutically situated even prior to and regarding the "fore-structures" of understanding. These fore-structures are anticipatory structures and serve as necessary conditions for what becomes understood, grasped, or interpreted in a preliminary manner. Hans Georg Gadamer writes:

> An actual historical thinking must think for itself with its own historicality. Only then it will not chase after the phantom of the historical object, which the object of the progressive research is, but rather historical thinking learns to recognize the internalized other in the object and becomes with this one like the other. The true historical object is no object, but is rather the unity of this one and the other, a relation in which the actuality of the history similarly subsists like the actuality of

> the historical understanding. (Gadamer, 1990, p. 305) [Ein wirklich historisches Denken muß die eigene Geschichtlichkeit mitdenken. Nur dann wird es nicht dem Phantom eines historischen Objektes nachjagen, das Gegenstand fortschreitender Forschung ist, sondern wird in dem Objekt das Andere des Eigenen und damit das Eine wie das Andere erkennen lernen. Der wahre historische Gegenstand ist kein Gegenstand, sondern die Einheit dieses Einen und Anderen, ein Verhältnis, in dem die Wirklichkeit der Geschichte ebenso wie die Wirklichkeit des geschichtlichen Verstehens besteht].

Gadamer (ibid.) continues:

> A reasonable and non-fictional hermeneutics in the understanding of itself would have exhibited the actuality of history. I call this the required *effective history*. Understanding is its essence towards an effective historical process. [Eine sachangemessene Hermeneutik hätte im Verstehen selbst die Wirklichkeit der Geschichte aufzuweisen. Ich nenne das damit Geforderte >*Wirkungsgeschichte*<. Verstehen ist seinem Wesen nach ein wirkungsgeschichtlicher Vorgang.]

Investigations of legal research are undoubtedly impacted in a variety of manners via the autobiographical, biographical, and the historical and sociological ways of thinking. Interpretations of the content within these three aforementioned ways of thinking are naturally made, and one very important type of interpretation concerns the perception of legitimacy of the authority figures, such as the police within the jurisdictions that the individual, who has her thoughts represented within figure 8, also has in mind. With the three ways of thinking about oneself, the other, and the others, for instance, a primary causal factor that greatly shapes one's evaluations of the courts and police is procedural justice, which is the fairness involved in the means by which the authority is exercised (Tyler, 2007, 2008 & 2010). The perceptions of procedural justice are an aspect of legitimacy that is also crucial and plays a key role within the reduction of deviance. Tom Tyler (2010, p. 127) writes that:

> [T]he importance of understanding how individuals who deal with legal authorities experience their encounters is being more widely recognized, particularly how those experiences shape their judgments about the legitimacy of the police and the courts.

Of course, Tyler is presuming that the importance of understandings of these recognitions of individuals' experiences with legal authorities are occurring within the USA and other developed nations instead of nations within transitional and temporary periods of crisis, such as Somalia in the 21st century or developing nations. What seems evident is that the construction of a theory of law that incorporates interdisciplinary studies will need some principles of transition that efficiently enable one to think from one level of analysis to the next because those who come to understandings of some theory of law need not, or cannot, think of a particular human being simultaneously while thinking also about some social group.

One who just focuses and observes individual trees cannot simultaneously have focused the observations upon the whole forest since the units of measurements and focuses are very different. For these reasons, the theory of integrative levels and classification systems, especially within computer and library science and biology are necessary. Different levels of analyses are derived from different levels of observation and thereby also provide very different accounts and reconciliations of measurements as well as different focuses.

Levels of analyses appear to give analysts greater challenges for their research when, say, two different sets of observations at two distinct levels of analysis and distinct levels of observation call for the analytic approach to account for unknown and unobserved forms and the spatial or temporal periods between the two distinct levels. We may consider the challenges for analysts to present analyses of the unknown and unobserved forms and spatiotemporal points at which bundles of non-living chemical compounds became living beings, or, also at two alternative levels of analysis and alternative levels of observations, the points at which unconscious animals evolved, developed, and matured into conscious animals concerning some species (Brant & Brant, 2012, pp. 40–43).

There is a lack of observational information from which such analyses can rationally derive confirmed and practically-relevant descriptions. The emergence of social systems, such as societal, political, and legal systems, from the communications and actions of small social groups and the increase of the relevant human populace also present us with another example that evades our attempts to produce observational information with confirmable measurements and units of measurement, upon which researchers can agree. That is, how can we produce a rational analysis about social systems that enlightens us and realistically explains the distinctions between groups of people, larger groups of people, and society?

In the former two paragraphs, three different sets of questions regarding the integrated levels can emerge, to wit: What comes between non-life and life, between unconscious animals and barely conscious animals of the same species as well as between a non-societal group of people and the emergence of society?

Such principles of transitions that smoothly enable thinkers of a theory to appreciate each level of analysis and each level of observation, from which the theory originates, possess ontological importance, i.e., their significance concerns the study of the entities and patterns of actions as existents rather than figments of the imagination.

Some theorists have argued that there are different levels of reality, such as Nicolai Hartmann (1940) and Konrad Lorenz's neo-Kantianism (1978, pp. 56–64), whereas one may disagree via arguing that objects and events do not consist of various levels of reality, but rather we are only able to analyze them at different levels, i.e., from the common analysis with the naked eyes and ears to the microscope or telescope as well as the use of analytic methods of measuring time concerning these things under investigation.

Figure 9 roughly illustrates the levels of immediate observations or appearances as well as mediated observations, which usually involve the utilization of a tool or machine that also narrows the focus of the observation.

There are, of course, many other examples of mediated ways from which observational data can be collected. Indirect standpoints of observations, including surveys, questionnaires, and interviews are mediated by the time required to complete them. Psychological analyses involve both micro- and macroscopic vantage points as levels of observations of the individual human

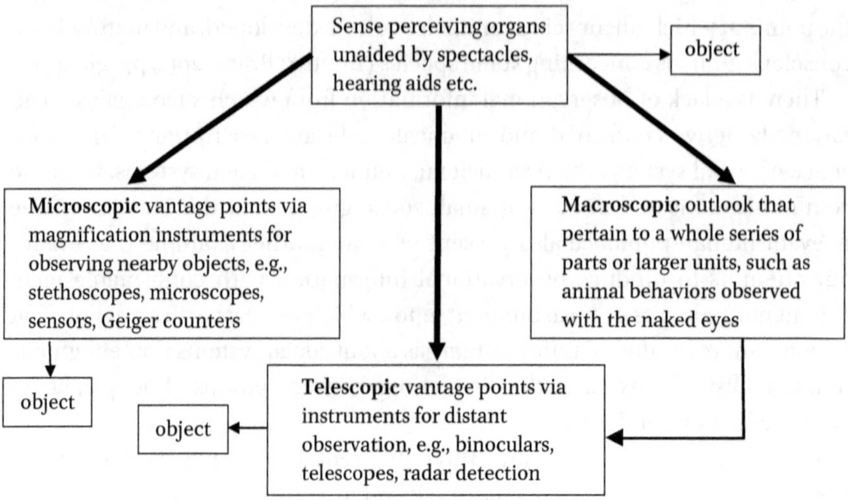

FIGURE 9 Levels of observations with and without magnifications

being as well as the group, within which the individual or the group under observations becomes analyzed. Sociological analyses lack a microscopic perspective and do not have the comparative methodology between control and experimental groups that reside within the laboratory conditions (Campbell, 1976).

Is reality leveled, or is there merely one level of reality, which we analyze and observe at various levels with multitudes of methods from different approaches? The latter inquiry will not be answered in relation to the structure of the real world as a layered world or not (i.e., perhaps layered from the essential and microscopic layers of the non-living atoms, the layer of the living beings, the layer of the conscious beings, and the layer of the society). However, such inquiry shall serve as a way of avoiding troubles that arise when one attempts to solve a substantial and particular set of problems (e.g., the attempt to reduce violence via coming to an understanding of the negative impacts of ideology) by means of the production of consistent descriptions that result from strictly advocating a certain system of thought.

The strict advocacy of a system of thought is called "system-thinking" (Hartmann, 1936/1977). The trouble with system-thinking is it often tends to ignore the universal nature of the problems that other systems also attempt to manage via various approaches, methods, and levels of analysis.

If we consider the example of H_2O, then we are confronted with a chemical compound that is essential for so many of the layers of the real world. Water serves as a necessary condition for life, biological or animal consciousness, humans as well as societies with governments and social systems, such as political and legal systems. Systems of thought may cast aside such real phenomena as if they are irrelevant to perpetuate their own accounts with their own terminology.

Systems of thought do not recognize themselves as such, but rather they focus on solutions to problems, which various systems of thought attempt to manage. Advocating one system over another system of thought via rational analysis involves the critique of both systems. A critique is a method of analysis that can be utilized for correcting, guiding, comparing, and contrasting numerous systems that attempt to solve the same problems in diverse ways.

Such a comparative analytic critique involves comparing systems of thought as worldviews that are advantageous or disadvantageous in relation to their characteristics of comprehensibility, parsimony, internal and external consistency, practicality, or the amount of interdisciplinary usages in comparison to other forms of system-thinking (i.e., a form of external consistency). Excellent critique and diction lead to enhanced clarity of the universal problems and superior approaches to problem-thinking, whereas system-thinking supports the evolution of one approach, which is one set of methods that may even rely upon one set of levels of observations. However, systems of thought are necessary for progress in science, and thus, fundamentally, the purpose of the present analysis is to inspire diverse ways of system-thinking.

Systems of thought are often attributable to social groups, may in some cases be ascribed as ideologies, and the present investigation seeks to critique and describe aspects of ideologies, which involves both an attack against their flaws as well as descriptions of their historical underpinnings or conditions that support their origins.

In the late 18th century, inquiries of Immanuel Kant were formulated. They concerned what the conditions of the possibility of knowledge are. Nicolai Hartmann (1935; 1938; 1940; 1950) further developed many Kantian ideas and raised new questions concerning what the conditions of the possibility of the history of philosophy are (Hartmann, 1936/1977).

Hartmann established a theoretical framework that combined diction with critique and distinguished between system-thinking and problem-thinking. This was accomplished via demonstrating the openness of metaphysics of problems and the constructive nature of the designed metaphysics of systems. The latter may be viewed as one criterion of insight in philosophy, according to Ingeborg Heidemann (Hartmann, 1936/1977, pp. 190–191).

Of course, the "openness of the metaphysics of problems" involves many of the overarching concerns of philosophers (Hartmann, 1977, p. 191). For example, are all events determined by prior causes or not? Are our voluntary behaviors or free choices caused and "out of our control"? Do they result from factors we must undergo? Can we choose freely and be held morally responsible for our intentional acts?

Can things exhibit potentiality? For example, a person is potentially sick or healthy at some specific time. A seed rots or develops into a mighty redwood. Does potentiality merely describe unreal alternatives we can imagine as being real? Are there many possible worlds or just one possible world, which is the actual world in which we live? Are time and space merely subjective aspects of minds? Are they required for one to have a conscious experience of any object or event? Are other characterizations of space, time, worlds, potentiality, choice, moral responsibility, and consciousness more accurate?

Metaphysics is an ancient field of philosophy in comparison to most of the philosophical disciplines, and metaphysics is a multicultural phenomenon that can be found as a field of study or inquiry in various geographical regions and cultures (Kim, Sosa & Rosenkrantz, 2009, p. xiii). The problems of metaphysics in the previous paragraph exhibit "openness" to the extent that there are several logically possible and relevant answers to each of them, which leaves much space for creativity. They exhibit indeterminateness, and the problems were presented as a problem-thinker would present them as opposed to a system-thinker. The constructive conceptual designs of certain systems of thought place strict constraints upon thinkers who persistently remain within the boundaries of a form of system-thinking to keep internal consistency at the expense of perhaps comprehensiveness, practicality, and parsimony.

There are many systems of thought that consistently describe the above-mentioned metaphysical problems. Yet often the individual advocates one type of system-thinking, which leads one to ignore or criticize the others. The other ways of answering certain related problems may be singly or collectively superior to the person's systematic approach. These manners in which eclectic approaches combine multiple types of system-thinking, or charitable explorations for advantages of other systems, are likely to contain elements that are more comprehensive, practical, and concise, perhaps even reducing levels of redundancy.

Assume that the triangle, square and gray circle in figure 10 each represent the entirety of a single but distinct theory regarding the illustrations, writings, and other representations of the facts, approaches, outlooks etc. of the theory. Assume that the triangle represents a theory that has more practicality, the circle explains more brute facts, the square is more concise, and descriptions of the square do not lead into as many contradictions as the other theoretical frameworks do (i.e., it has less external inconsistencies). Figure 10 shows the

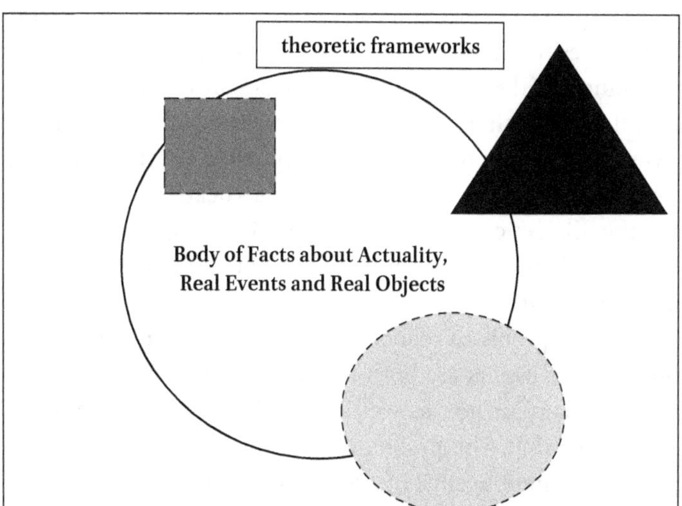

FIGURE 10 Facts and theoretic frameworks

relations of systems of thought to a largely unknown and comprehensive set of facts about reality.

For instance, libertarianism is one type of system-thinking, which contributes to answering the question about whether we can choose freely in a way that makes sense for us to be held morally responsible for our intentional actions. Libertarians thus consistently argue that if all events are caused, there can be no free will, but there is, however, free will, which involves events that are uncaused. Some libertarians argue for a liberty of indifference such that when two or more choices are equal, or do not matter in terms of their outcomes, the agent with free will can choose between them and select any of them.

Many libertarians argue that the agent with free will "could have chosen" one of the alternatives or that the act was not causally determined or that the action resulted from an act that was not causally determined (Clarke & Capes, 2017; Kane, 1996). So, the choice was not determined by events outside of the control of the person's will, according to this view. Such a worldview usually involves the advocacy of moral responsibility and the existence of many possible worlds, which we shall later realize within an analysis that applies the related concepts to law (See Ch. 5).

However, there are, of course, other systems of thought with well-developed answers to the same questions and which oppose the libertarian stance in many respects. The opposing stances of libertarianism are compatibilism, which holds that free will and causation are compatible with one another; so, the world can contain both free will and causation simultaneously and in respect to the same events and people, and the other opposing stance is hard determinism, which argues that there is no free will and every event is caused.

Another similar stance to the last one is the Megarean worldview about modalities, maintaining that all possibilities are realities, all realities are necessities, and everything that is unreal is also impossible (Hartmann, 1937; Hartmann, 1938, pp. 12–14). The Megarean stance, advocated by Diodorus Cronos and Philo the dialectic logician, is diametrically opposed to the Aristotelian conceptions of potentiality, contingent or coincidental reality, and contingent or coincidental unreality.

Basically, the universal problems concerning the latter theoretical approaches are whether some events are both real and unnecessary and some events are real and necessary or not, as well as which specific events those are and how we can know that. The problem relates directly to law because some acts that law enforcement agents, judges, victims, criminals, and advocates perform are presumed to be unnecessary, although they may very well be historical and situational necessities for certain strict ideological thinkers who act in accordance with their ideologies. Other behaviors are assumed to be necessary, although they may be considered "coincidental," in accordance with different systems of thought.

Interestingly, law functions in many respects according to each of the ways of thinking, namely, libertarianism, compatibilism, and hard determinism. The suspected thief may very well argue with an officer via maintaining that what he did was necessary for some sufficient reason. For example, if both know enough about the situation, and the thief exclaims: "I had to take that there, because if I didn't, I would've been shot in the head! Don't you realize that?" In this situation, the suspected thief may argue that he really had no other rational decision at all, and he certainly should not be held morally or legally responsible, because if he did not take the property, then another person would have killed him, which is a convincing argument insofar as the police officer realizes that the situation, with which he was confronted, is consistent with what the suspected thief said.

Significant uses of the libertarian, compatibilist, and hard deterministic worldviews in legal contexts occur during judicial trials. Some individuals have been convicted of murder, sentenced to life in prison, or death. Others have been found guilty of killing victims but are granted much more lenient sentences. In the latter situations, questions, statements, and arguments often revolve around the latter three worldviews.

The latter ideas regarding theories and decision-making are crucial regarding analyses of the law for judges, juries, jurists, lawyers, lawmakers, and various others who are important for the functions of the legal system, especially the criminal justice system. Such ideas are important to mention because they affect our ways of thinking and serve as examples of system-thinking (Hartmann, 1936/1977).

4 Psychological Levels of Analysis: Situations of Law Enforcement

Exponential growth of cities during the late 20th century resulted in multitudes of police officers witnessing horrid events during their duties. They experienced burnt bodies, child abuse, and murder victims. Suicide rates of city police officers rose in places, such as the United States, according to Aamodt and Stalnaker (2001), Aamodt and Werlick (1999), and Marzuk et al. (2002).

To reduce police suicides in the USA, changes occurred in police departments. Officers became increasingly encouraged to consult psychologists who were not affiliated with their own departments and who had no authority to evaluate whether police were fit for work or not. Non-partisan consultation and support groups for officers has decreased suicide rates of police officers, especially in places like New York City.

On the other hand, before non-partisan consultation services, many police departments in the United States during the late 20th century had specialized psychologists working in their precincts. They evaluate law enforcers' mental health and aid in their rehabilitations regarding negative impacts of traumatic events. Posttraumatic stress disorder is common for combat soldiers and city police. It likely results after being in the line of live gunfire, witnessing the aftermath of a fellow officer being murdered etc.

Psychologists had determined whether law enforcement agents in their own departments were mentally suitable for work. This gave some psychologists significant hierarchical power in police precincts. The latter practices resulted in many officers being reluctant to visit psychologists during their free time. Risk-assessments led them to avoid psychologists out of fear of losing their jobs. In many precincts across America, the creation of a relatively large culture of cops who felt strong urges to avoid psychologists emerged. Some police perceived the consultation of counselors' services as psychological weakness.

A few lessons can be learned from the history of police in America, especially since there is some transparency regarding access of information about them. Observers and analysts are crucial for feedback for the legal system. It is important psychologists, sociologists, anthropologists and others play roles that can both positively impact precincts and other organizations of the legal institution and remain impartial. For reductive measures, police need to refrain from favoritism and from showing disfavor toward certain law enforcers and certain organizations regarding impacts their work has on legal systems and institutions.

It is important to realize the diverse set of factors that place psychological stress on law enforcement agents. Many of the stress factors increase chances, frequencies, and intensities of maladaptive behaviors. These include alcoholism, suicidal thoughts, and suicidal behaviors of police.

Types of stress that law enforcement agents confront include their work-shifts at strange hours, overwork and overtime hours. They have a constant exposure to violence, threats of violence, and face life-threatening circumstances. Each can have negative impacts on their family lives.

Policemen and women also work in hierarchies and face problems concerning their managers, interdepartmental politics, bureaucracy with rigid, incorruptible coworkers. Some would rather oversee office procedures and follow orders than to help a coworker. Police must cope with common workplace issues, like authoritarian and other non-situational leadership styles of superiors, lack of recognition, lack of motivation from superiors, insufficient equipment and a lack of technology that facilitates 21st century police work (Loo, 2003).

For police officers, psychological stresses do not end there. Police are required to make courtroom appearances and be cross-examined by professionals. Police may feel stresses from the public when they are unappreciated by the public in the communities they serve. People file many sorts of complaints against police officers and assault them.

Violanti et al. (2015) have found that a sense of hopelessness in police officers coincides with the perception of their work as futile. Feelings that their police work is futile arise especially after long cases, on which the officers worked many hours. Feelings of futility intensify when cases are dismissed and criminals, about whom officers know are guilty, are released or released early from incarceration. Feelings of pointlessness of police arise when officers perceive or calculate their efforts to reduce or eradicate crime in certain areas are fruitless because of rising crime.

Police officers certainly undergo feelings of hopelessness, feelings of betrayal, especially when their organization does not stick up for them, anger, and frustration. These feelings as well as many others have impacts on their work and their personal lives.

Nevertheless, we need law enforcement agents in every society to be selected after undergoing psychological tests. They must undergo training to serve the public during times of peace and prosperity, times of crisis, emergency, and war. Those are times that can also create additional psychological stresses for police.

Because there are such diverse types of stresses police undergo, we would expect rates of police suicide to be thoroughly studied. However, most studies of police suicide are typically just short-term studies. They require meta-analyses to lead analysts to better understandings of the extent of psychological stress factors leading to increased chances of suicides.

Unfortunately, police departments typically retain no historical records of suicide rates of police officers from them (Loo, 2003). Police officers who arrive first on the scenes may be tempted to cover up evidence that strongly suggests that police officers committed suicide. Reasons for this include social, religious, and other stigmas. Violanti et al. (1996, p. 79) state:

> Police investigators are usually the first at the scene of any suicide and can readily control information to protect victim officers and their families from the stigma of suicide. If police suicides are successfully hidden,

> the validity of rates becomes suspect and may over time influence public policy and scientific research (Aldridge & St. John, 1991; Cantor & Dunne, 1990; Douglas, 1967; Hlady & Middaugh, 1988; Holding & Barraclough, 1978; Kitsuse & Cicourel, 1963; Kleck, 1988; Litman, Curphey, Shneidman, Farberow, & Tabachnick, 1963; Malla & Hoenig, 1983; McCarthy & Walsh, 1975; Monk, 1987; Murphy, 1979; O'Carroll, 1989; Pescosolido & Mendelsohn, 1986; Phillips & Ruth, 1993).

Indubitably, some suicides are extremely likely to have been concealed by departments. Feeling the need, moral obligation, or desire to give favors to families to conceal the fact that the deaths are police suicides certainly increases stresses of officers. Stresses arise because they cover up systemic problems in illegal manners. More stress arises because they witness the aftermath of fellow coworkers who took their own lives.

Violanti et al. (1996, pp. 81–82) describe four obvious cases of suicide originally evaluated as "undetermined" deaths. They were later reevaluated by a panel of medical examiners and labeled as "suicides." Concealments of suicides of police officers by police suggests officers may feel the need to save colleagues from stresses of facing greater frequencies and intensities of suicidal thoughts. It perhaps suggests forms of self-deception arise where police officers suppress their doubts and come to firmly believe they were not, in fact, suicides, even though they were. This is like parents who may undergo psychological processes of self-deception and form beliefs their children are not drug addicts, although they are. John Violanti (2004, p. 766) writes:

> The fact that the rate of suicide among police officers is about 80% of that of the general population may speak to the enormous stresses associated with police work, and the more proper conclusion may be that being a police officer greatly increases the risk of suicide in individuals suffering from no significant preemployment psychopathology.

The reasoning demonstrated by Violanti (ibid.) rightly presumes the society contains many elements of diagnosed psychopathology within it already. Police have undergone diagnoses that suggest that they do not have a diagnosable psychopathology. Moreover, police officers are also employed. So, it behooves us to compare the suicide rates of police officers to populations of other service industry professionals who have been psychologically tested already and employed after there were no findings of psychopathologies.

Police suicide rates are understudied. When they are studied, comparisons with other populations' suicides are typically inappropriate. The comparisons mislead analysts to assume that the police suicide rates are not problematic when, in fact, they are.

Divorce rates, health problems, alcoholism, other addictions, and suicide rates of police officers have led to some public demands for change. These involve creations of support groups for cops, introducing psychologists and their services during police academies' training phases, and encouraging police to overcome the socio-cultural stigma of being psychologically analyzed. Since there are such elevated levels of stress that police experience during their duties and vast differences in the lifestyles of police as service workers of different shifts, it is argued by some that stress explains statistics of police being more than twice as likely to become divorced as the average citizen, during the 20th century in the USA (Cheek & Miller, 1983).

It is both humane and cost-effective to promote the mental health of law enforcers. Promoting officers' mental health is accomplished only after knowing what the risks are concerning the aftermath of the experiences they undergo. Understandings of latter analyses, involving both psychological consultation and sociological and statistical studies, are necessary for officers who have young children. Some police are required by duty to witness the aftermath of parents killing their children, child abuse, and parricide.

What this brief psychological analysis has covered so far is one small aspect of a type of relevant and practical set of analyses regarding prominent figures of law, the law enforcers. Psychological analyses cover increasingly large levels of analyses with focuses on humans as determinants of actions and on the individual as a single unit of measure for each analysis. Psychological levels of analysis often involve assuming one's responsibility of being a causal agent of the actions that create, shape, and change legal systems (Greene et al., 2007; Carson & Bull, 2003).

Psychology of law is a general focus on impacts of judges, parole officers, expert witnesses, juries, victims, cops, lawyers, defendants, prison guards, and others, as individuals, on legal systems. One attempt of psychology of law is to find a close approximation of the average or median description of each of these figures' roles. This includes moral dilemmas they face and psychological stresses they undergo. Another attempt involves goals to transform and improve legal systems via changing legal institutions' members' interactions, communications, and situatedness in their hierarchical positions of employment. It involves constantly improving institutionalization processes and selection processes for human resources for law.

One key presumption of psychology of law is that the traits of those interacting in legal systems directly impact the operations of these social systems. The law likewise instantiates changes on individuals' behaviors, traits, and mental states (i.e., beliefs, desires, disgusts, expectations etc.). This is readily observed via communications of their feelings, recordings of their behaviors, and associated characteristics. The latter changes are important to understand and analyze. They are not unique. These changes, presumably, point to psychological tendencies which similar professionals face under relatively similar circumstances. This is evident when we utilize the sociological imagination or socio-historical ways of thinking (See Ch. 3.3).

The psychological level of analysis deserves a fuller overview and application in respect to each of the distinct types of members of the legal institution. This level of analysis is always relevant when one analyzes legal systems or can be shown to have a high-level of relevancy. Of course, psychological analysis may result in a focus that is too specialized or too specific for that which is needed for an investigation. Therefore, an analysis of groups is preferable via sociology, anthropology, history, and other interconnected social studies.

5 Sociological Levels of Analysis: Legal Systems as Changing Sets of Communications

Cultures, especially in different societies, have different laws and different morally permissible actions. However, other cultures, especially those which study practical sciences, work continuously with the concept of morality. The concept of morality is inseparable from knowledge in the society (Parra, 1921, p. 563).

Legal sciences and other sciences are applied to the law. This includes sociology of law where sociologists apply knowledge of society with the concept of morality. Different legal codes exist in different nations. The law still tends to apply societal knowledge to create predictable order in society, though.

Knowledge coinciding with understandings of other societies and laws elsewhere, especially during the late 20th and 21st centuries, can create "social stresses." Social stresses coincide with challenges of law to serve as the legitimate authority that establishes order. Laws and norms, or communications of them, from one nation may appear arbitrary to some group in that nation because the laws are different elsewhere. The laws elsewhere have significantly greater advantages for some, which may lead to social stresses for those people who recognize this.

Elites may use their powers, influences and connections with lawmakers to facilitate certain advantages for their high-status groups in societies. This is partially accomplished through lawmaking of legal but socially unacceptable products, services, or behaviors (i.e., socially unacceptable for the subordinated groups within society) and illegal but socially acceptable ones (See Ch. 2.5).

Although laws of multiple nations overlap for some people in geographic regions, which is called "legal pluralism," they can be complicated with multiple layers (Berman, 2012). Law is presumably crucial in the process of diminishing societal complexity. This is an enduring social problem.

Law produces some amount of order partially by organizing and stabilizing expectations for society. It reduces the chaos of impulsive behaviors by criminalizing or illegalizing some types of actions in certain types of situations. It utilizes law enforcement to maintain that certain behaviors are only infrequently exhibited at most. Complexity describes the set of actions of any type of social system, for instance, which has parts that interact repetitively and follow rules that are not given by a higher authority. All social systems are communicative.

The legal system is complex because it has a variety of parts that interact with each other in a multitude of ways. The subsystem of lawmakers, legal courts, and policing systems interact communicatively and partially form a more complex system, to wit, the legal system. A legal system can be characterized in distinctly different ways than subsystems of the legal system can be. So, the legal system is not reduceable to its subsystems.

Intercommunications between law enforcers, lawmakers, and judges cannot be reduced to communications of any single category of legal workers or any subsystems of the legal system. They need to be described as interwoven together with communicative interactions with emerging properties (i.e., like the emergence of water and emerging properties of wetness, liquidity, etc. from the atoms of hydrogen and oxygen).

The legal system can also be described as a social system that rhetorically and culturally persuades the populace (Verenich, 2003). The legal system has its own distinct sociological analyses at levels of analyses that proceed beyond boundaries of the subsystems of the legal system. New properties emerge, such as legalities and illegalities that are communicated through various societal subsystems.

The legal system is at a higher level or scale than the criminal justice system. Properties are non-existent in the elements at the lower level or scale. Properties emerge from interactions between elements of criminal justice systems and other social systems (e.g., mass media systems). When social interactions generate novel information, emergence happens, and social systems that are more complex arise, such as the legal system.

The law imposes restrictions, interferes with communications. The law does many things that reduce societal complexity. Laws make it riskier to break promises regarding contractual agreements and easier or less risky to attain compensations for wrongdoings, etc. Despite efforts to reduce societal complexity, the modern world has been growing exponentially. This is true of the 20th and 21st centuries regarding human environments. For analysts like Jürgen Habermas (1975), the assimilation of the people is opposed to the tendency of the modernizing world to individuate.

With increases in populaces and the human global population, societies become increasingly complex and require greater organizations of legal institutions and legal systems. A social problem becomes even greater when parts of society assert social claims and expect these claims to receive non-standardized responses with sufficient amounts of consideration. Members of the legal institution are expected to tolerate and accommodate many of these new claims for recognition. They regard sexualities, third genders, minority groups trying to gain compensations for wrongdoings against them etc.

People who compose legal institutions include police officers, judges, legal clerks, jurors, federal investigative agents, lawyers, criminal informants, military police, international police through Interpol, mediators, lawmakers, etc. Many play adversarial roles with the interferences of each other's communications. Many of members of the legal institution play adversarial roles against each other in certain situations, too. This includes prosecutors versus defense attorneys, and police officers set against multiple groups, including prosecutors, defense attorneys, judges, and criminal informants and others. These people with many of their straightforward communications are also psychologically opposed to each other in many distinct situations.

For understanding social violence and finding reductive solutions, we need analyses of groups as wholes, groups' tendencies, and their interactions forming systems. Despite insights offered by psychological analyses and closer understandings of the propensities to behave and think in certain, even predictable, manners by members of the legal institution, the problem of understanding and promoting social order cannot take place via understanding psychological tendencies of people. Social order cannot be reduced to psychological tendencies. This includes multiple or single autopoietic systems that can reproduce themselves if the concept of autopoiesis appropriately characterizes legal systems (See Ch. 1.4).

It is argued by some systems theorists that legal systems just consist of communications like all social systems do (Luhmann, 1986). The organization of the legal system is what allows the system to reproduce. Systems are measurable regarding their complexity and information (Gershenson, 2015).

Sociologist, Niklas Luhmann, argues for the following definition of social systems. It combines various ideas in biology and psychology as part of a general systems theory. Luhmann maintains that individuals who compose the legal system and many of their actions are not at all what compose the legal system. Luhmann writes:

> A social system arises always when an autopoietic communicational interrelation emerges, and this interrelation establishes boundaries via a reduction of the suitable communication against an environment. Accordingly, social systems do not consist of people, and also not of actions, but rather of communications. (Luhmann, 1986, p. 269) [„Ein soziales System kommt zustande, wenn immer ein autopoietischer Kommunikationszusammenhang entsteht und sich durch Einschränkung der geeigneten Kommunikation gegen eine Umwelt abgrenzt. Soziale Systeme bestehen demnach nicht aus Menschen, auch nicht aus Handlungen, sondern aus Kommunikationen."]

"Autopoietic systems" are systems that do not merely serve as inputs and outputs. They have important internal processes of self-reproduction. They ensure the conditions necessary for the reproduction of the system itself are in place. Autopoietic systems cannot be replaced by other systems.

Other systems are necessary for an autopoietic system to subsist. The other systems are considered to be inputs, outputs and also the environment of the autopoietic system. Legal systems can be studied as types of social systems with relations to various social groups. Such investigations involve focus on communications of legal institutions and their interrelated communications with other systems. These include mass media, political, and education systems.

What needs further analysis is Luhmann's conception of social systems and just exactly what it means to communicate and what the establishment of boundaries is regarding communication "against an environment." The communication itself is part of the environment, in Luhmann's view.

Communications can range from types of seductions to informative emails to threats. Social systems, such as military systems, implement threats, which are communicative. Militaries implement violence against other societies during certain time spans during which the legal systems communicate with other societal systems. Controlled violence is thereby legally permitted to occur in jurisdictions (i.e., legalizing the conditions for war).

Violence can result from miscommunications, failures to engage in diplomacy, negotiations, compromises, agreements, and non-deceptive communicative relationships. Many deceptions are types of communications or miscommunications.

What can appear even more important in a society than the communication of law and legality is the lack of communication with certain groups concerning written laws establishing the illegality of actions that these certain groups have the tendency to perform and the illegality of commodities that these people want to buy, sell, and/or possess. Official and unofficial communications of the legal system, which are communicated to itself and others, provide a wide assortment of interpretations, including miscommunication, deception, sincerity etc. Such interpretations may be clarified as being "mentalities."

Although the phrase "legal system" is commonly used, the phrase itself is misleading and involves much debate about just what is incorporated in a single legal system. System theorists debate whether the legal system is a subsystem of the political system or not and whether the legal system functions merely as the political system's output channel in a nation (Sigler, 1968; Parsons, 1990; Luhmann, 1993).

For our purposes, the legal system includes the criminal justice system, judicial system, and communications of politicians and others who propose bills, pass laws etc. The "legal system" of a nation is the authorized, self-legitimizing, and leading system of important and practical labels of actions of certain groups, i.e., as "legal" and "illegal." It is an establisher of legal and illegal objects or property. The legal system is, according to this view, not merely the political system's output channel in some nation. Any non-fragmented legal system contains portions of the executive, judicial, and legislative branches of government that, respectively, involve enforcing policy via policing, interpreting and judging policy, and passing policy in some polis or polity.

Clearly, without social groups, families, communities, etc., there would be no legal system. Legal systems change in accordance with the union of new generations, composing the new additions of legal institutions. They incorporate innovative ideas and manners of acting, which they partially integrate through the education system. The education system is crucial for the legal system (e.g., law schools). Legal and education systems create, indoctrinate, and systematically produce legal-minded communications between people.

It is unclear how relevant mental states are to legal systems. Dynamically changing governmental systems and social movements are certainly impacted by people's mental states that shift during times of stress and fortune in societies. The enduring question is how we conceptualize ways of thinking and behaving beyond legal minds.

The concept of the legal system as a social system arises from people without legal minds, in some relevant sense. Larger systems must first be composed of smaller social groups without any government.[9] Insightful investigations

---

9 There is no example of any known society, ancient or modern, in which ruling via direct democracy was exercised by every person old enough to vote in the society. Societies with approximately 2,500 inhabitants with political systems and legal systems have apparently reached the upper limitation for socio-political decision-making via consensus within direct democracies that necessitate participation with social interactions with interpersonal, face-to-face communications (Bodley, 2011, p. 219).

going beyond legal minds would therefore enlighten us regarding the emergence of legal systems.

From observations of smaller human populations, like tribal cultures, we are confronted with less laws than the laws in larger cultures and societies.[10] So, there is a positive correlation between the number of laws, laws enforced, and human populations. Archaeological findings of towns and villages with more than 2,500 inhabitants present us with no or little evidence for preexisting governments and societies with social classes. This includes examples, like the prehistoric Lillooet, Neolithic Middle Eastern villages, including Abu Hureya, Cyprus during the Bronze Age, and the Anasazi in America (Bodley, 2011, p. 219; Moore et al., 2000; Keswani, 1996).

Bodley (2011, p. 219) maintains that such examples demonstrate the possibility of living in a society that is socially complex without tremendous inequality. The society may lack a hierarchy. This needs to be reconciled with the social dominance theory's proposal that each society is a human group-based type of social hierarchy with low-status groups on the bottom and high-status groups maintaining control by various means, such as legal systems.

Heterarchy and homoarchy are the alternatives to social hierarchy, according to anthropologists (Crumley, 2001; Bondarenko, 2006). Carole Crumley (2006, p. 11) states:

> Hierarchy (the classic, pyramidal organizational form) is a structure composed of elements that on the basis of certain factors are subordinate to others and may be ranked (Crumley 1979: 44, 1987b: 158). Another way of viewing the meshwork of dimensions and levels in large societies is as a heterarchy, the relation of elements to one another when they are unranked, or when they possess the potential for being ranked in a number of different ways depending on conditions. Understood from a heterarchical perspective, sources of power are counterpoised and linked to values, which are fluid and respond to changing situations.

Crumley's (ibid.) points are better considered regarding hierarchical analyses of employees of legal institutions and regarding societies at large and the populations of the so-called "lower status groups" who have disproportionately larger population sizes in prison populations of the societies. Theories of

10 However, as legal pluralism suggests, some of the tribal cultures must abide by the laws of multiple legal systems, such as the tribal cultures in Colombia and Panama, which may have their own laws, prisons, governments etc. They are compelled to act in legally permissible ways with laws of those nations.

social heterarchy are best reconciled with social dominance theory. Such communications are important for attaining fuller understandings of the counter-opposed ideas and research focuses from the sociological levels of analyses.

Any individual is difficult to hierarchically rank. An individual likely has a status in his or her own family, a status at work, a status in his or her culture, socio-economically and so forth. The ranking of one in one's own family can change on a day-to-day basis perhaps if such a ranking is even feasible. Quantitatively and qualitatively, identifications of ranked and unranked groups and individuals are important for sociological analyses of law.

6 Chemical and Neurobiological Levels of Analysis: Aspects of Law

Interpretations of chemical and neurological activity of human brains before and after decision-making processes appear increasingly problematic for many researchers who study moral and legal decision-making. When intentions of the accused party are under legal examination for determining guilt or innocence of the person in or outside of a court of law, decisions that coincide with wrongdoings are analyzable at two distinct levels of analysis.

Firstly, the level of analysis drawing conclusions from macroscopic observations with unaided human eyes has allowed us and our ancestors for perhaps millions of years to recognize another person's ability to make decisions. This level of analysis and observation allows us to blame the person for decisions he or she makes. Secondly, the level of analysis that draws conclusions via the microscopic observations of chemical compounds and neurons with brain imaging technology is gaining popularity.

Recent interpretations of chemical and neurobiological findings favor the presumption that culprits of crimes are not morally responsible for their own actions. Relieving criminals of guilt with courts opposes criminal justice systems' evidence for the guilt of criminals in some cases. This happens because some claims in neuroscience maintain, seemingly authoritatively, that choices are predetermined by brain activity. They argue brain activity determines relevant behaviors that are legal or illegal (Streng, 2007).

A long trend in the history of law illustrates why criminals have less severe penalties. They are judged "criminally insane" or "temporarily insane" (Hermann, 1983; Emanuel, 1989; Streng, 1989). In the United States, the case of *People vs. McQuillan* (1974) provided reasonable grounds to introduce a new type of verdict, namely, "guilty but mentally ill." The system contained three other verdicts, guilty, not guilty, and not guilty but insane. The fourth type of verdict was adopted due to an absence of a guilty plea involving the judgment that defendants potentially have serious mental health problems that prevent rational decision-making under certain conditions.

Serious misconceptions remain concerning concepts of guilt, responsibility, blameworthiness concerning illegality, being at fault and wrongful action, culpability, and even innocence. In certain jurisdictions, for one to plead on behalf of one's mental handicap, one must be represented by another individual who understands whether that involves the plea of guilty or not guilty, depending on the jurisdiction, unless the region has all four options (i.e., guilty, not guilty, guilty but mentally ill, and not guilty but mentally ill). These opposing pleas for mentally impaired people arose relatively recently.

Two judgments must be made by juries concerning their own assessments of the evidence for the status of mental health and for the evidence for culpability. Roles of neurological investigations making distinctions between guilt and innocence, mental health, and mental illnesses regarding judicial decisions is incipient. Levels of analyses of neurobiology only dubiously draw conclusions about guilt, innocence, mental health and mental illnesses. Court cases can proceed without evidence that illustrates what realistic types of conclusions are possible from such levels of analyses. For justice, it is superior to extract what can be induced and deduced from observations at the chemical and neurobiological levels.

Innocence is a concept that is closely correlated with the process of aging and psychological development during the human lifespan. Babies are typically conceived of as being innocent (i.e., against ancient doctrines of original sin), and so are toddlers and most children. Certainly, there are less innocent adolescents and adults, proportionally speaking, than infants and children.

A baby handling a gun and shooting and killing somebody is not considered murderer. A young adolescent, say, a fourteen-year-old boy, who behaves in the same ways as the baby, will probably confront years of juvenile criminal system processes concerning justice, rehabilitation, punishment etc. She or he can be prosecuted as an adult. This partially depends on whether the individual and perpetrator is a member of a dominant or subordinate societal group. There are tendencies to favor members of dominant groups in societies. There are tendencies to disfavor members of lower status groups.

What is problematic for making consistently precise judgments about blameworthiness for the application of law concerns those children who have learnt to repeatedly kill (e.g., child soldiers in the South Sudan and other parts of Africa), adolescents who have killed just once, and how a just system treats these individuals. Chemists and neuroscientists may argue the developmental differences necessarily result from increases in amounts of hormones during puberty and neural networks involved in prediction, planning skills and higher order decision-making processes. Chemical imbalances, reactions to drugs, drug withdrawal symptoms, and irregular neurological activity may provide rational grounds for us to knowledgeably recognize mental disorders of certain individuals.

What remains strikingly problematic concerns the most recent interpretations about those identified as criminals, especially those about whom we lack evidence for any mental disorder. Some criminals are potentially considered guilty and neither morally responsible nor blameworthy for their actions.

> Recent findings in brain research call into question the idea of free will, at least in respect to our rational notions of human decision-making. Initially, it was demonstrated by Benjamin Libet that in the subjects there was a definitively pronounced action based on the brain waves, with which the measurable readiness potential already existed a half second before the correspondent and active conscious decision was firmly established. (Duttge, 2009, p. 97) [Neuere Befunde der Hirnforschung stellen die Idee der Willensfreiheit, zumindest aber unsere rationalistischen Vorstellungen von der menschlichen Entscheidungsfindung in Frage. Erstmals von Benjamin Libet wurde aufgezeigt, dass bei Versuchspersonen das eine Handlung definitiv ankündigende, anhand der Hirnströme messbare Bereitschaftspotential im Durchschnitt bereits eine halbe Sekunde vor dem Fassen des entsprechenden bewussten Handlungsentschlusses vorlag.]

There are several necessary conditions for decision-making. They include the environment, positions of the human body, behaviors, and other important, associated concepts. They contribute to the development of the concept of the decision. The concept of free will was not originally derived from brain research.

Insofar as exercising free will requires behaviors, its exercise can, at best, only be partially observed from brain research. A "decision" is not something that we would reduce to or call "mere brain activity." The meaning of the concept came well before brain research began to augment the concept and to measure certain relevant phenomena in the periphery. The interpretations that free will is undermined by findings in brain research are thoroughly dubious and dangerous, as we shall see.

For arbitrary reasons, classifications or reductive attempts to undermine free will, as an illusory phenomenon, drastically change the perceived relevance of levels of observations, levels of analyses, and the previous conception of free will. We should consider certain scientists' aims to uplift brain research to the forefront. Presumably, free will cannot be observed from levels of observations made during the progression of brain research.

Observations of others' making decisions and the experiences of our own decisions occur at very distinct levels of observations. Observations of brains, neural networks, neurons, and chemicals are at different levels from them. Recognizing a decision of another individual requires quite ordinary observations at ordinary levels of observations, regardless of whether the decision is investigated in brain research. If a criminal decides to steal one product versus another, the product that was taken still always resides entirely outside the realm of chemical and neurobiological levels of analysis. No observation of the brain can reasonably demonstrate that the criminal stole one product as opposed to the other.

There are differences in levels of observations and levels of analyses of brain research and free will research (Brant, 2013b). Questions remain exactly how, when, where and why brain researchers and free will researchers can analyze observations of neural networks, brain imaging, etc. and apply phenomena, such as neural correlates of consciousness, to the concept of free will to undermine it.

Defense attorneys have vested interests in undermining the role of free will when they defend guilty criminals. Defense lawyers argue that events, especially concerning human choices, are either necessary or coincidental. Both attributes of necessity and coincidence negate the existence of moral blameworthiness of individuals for making choices they do (See Ch. 5.5). Yet Duttge (2009, p. 98) continues:

> If, in other words, by becoming conscious (and "giving one's blessing") of the questionable impulses, the resolving action as decision has already been established, then what emerges is the question about whether our free will constitutes suggestible consciousness and a mere illusion. Substantiated doubt becomes realistic introspective perception concerning our decision-making process and freedom of choice through experiments, which would trigger actions via direct stimulation of certain brain regions of the immediate and organic subject concerned; subsequently the subjects have interpreted their actions as willful ones based on them being free choice effected actions. (Duttge, 2009, p. 98) [Wenn also bei Bewusstwerden (und „Absegnen") des fraglichen Impulses die vorzunehmende Handlung als Entscheidung bereits feststeht, ergibt sich die Frage, ob unser Willensfreiheit suggerierendes Bewusstsein eine bloße Illusion darstellt. Erhärtet werden Zweifel an einer realitätsnahen introspektiven Wahrnehmung unserer Entscheidungsprozesse und Entscheidungsfreiheit etwa durch Experimente, in welchen durch direkte Reizung von bestimmten Hirnregionen Handlungen der betreffenden

> Versuchsperson unmittelbar organisch ausgelöst wurden; nachfolgend haben die Versuchspersonen ihre Aktionen dann als willentliche, aufgrund freier Entscheidung getätigte Handlungen interpretiert.]

Much focus has been on the prior expectations of brain researchers that decision-makers being investigated would be conscious of their decisions or exhibit certain neural correlations of consciousness of a decision before the decisions could be predicted accurately by scientists. Perhaps their prior expectations are irrelevant, though. Why should it matter whether consciousness, which is currently scientifically immeasurable, arises at any point that is earlier than, simultaneous with, or later than the choice of the subject, according to any third party?

Scientists claim to have found disconfirming evidence that consciousness about the decision-making arises before or during the decision. They claim the decision is predetermined by neural activity. Accordingly, scientists have maintained that subjects were not consciously aware of their decisions before the decisions could be predicted by the scientists. There is a foundational problem here with categorization. Neither the concept of decision nor observations of actual decisions can be attained from brain imaging or from any mere observations of any brain.

The epistemic problem subsists when knowledge of real phenomena at one set of levels of analyses, which was derived and understood from one set of levels of observations (e.g., ordinary knowledge of decision-making processes), is augmented, ignored, or misunderstood because of knowledge of associated and connected real phenomena derived and understood from a separate set of levels of observations and levels of analyses (e.g., specialized knowledge of neural events). The everyday sorts of experiences we have when we recognize other people's decisions are typical observations. They happen over durations that generally differ from atypical observations in controlled settings, like types of decisions during brain imaging studies.

Ordinary observations of the decision-making processes, even by the decision-makers themselves, may require seconds, minutes, hours, days, weeks, months, years, or even decades. Observations of decision-making processes with brain imaging techniques do not involve any observations that last for even hours or longer. Timings of the observations from the ordinary and unordinary levels of observations, at which decision-making processes are observed, are generally different with and without brain imaging. The settings are also unfamiliar ones within strange types of human environments (e.g., labs with fMRI machines) in which people are generally also not used to making decisions.

Only observations that involve our ordinary experiences of another's decisions enable us to determine whether a decision is being made since we need to understand what the objective is for the decider. Giving the person an objective detracts greatly from the decision-making, too.

Observations of brains and brain research never could have allowed the formation of the concept of the decision to emerge without our common observations of choice-making. For instance, the actual object (i.e., as opposed to an illusion) or objective, at which the decision-making is directed, is absent from, or at least unobserved in, the set of levels of observations of the brain (Brant, 2013a, pp. 182–195).

Choosing to go one direction versus another or choosing to retrace one's steps to find a set of keys both require an objective or an object that is separate and distinct from the individual and, of course, from the individual's brain. One may argue that the objective or object is represented neurocognitively.

An individual's choices are conceptualized via objects that are apart from the individual dealing with them. There can be no reliance on the memory of the agent. Accurate memories can only be confirmed via the state of affairs being handled by the individual. For legal and moral philosophy, this means we must know already that a wrongdoing has occurred, such as a rape, before we can analyze an individual's neural activity and question the individual about being responsible for the rape.

The importance of this research extends to legal ideology, legislation, and criminal law. The research and many interpretations of the research suggest human decisions are determined by neural events outside the control of the individuals making the decisions. The use of certain arguments can certainly be in favor of criminals and impulsive decision-makers as well as savvy defense attorneys. They can wield legal arguments that direct juries or judges toward blamelessness for illegal actions.

> Since the German criminal law appears to be committed to the underlying idea that guilt is proof of freedom of the will, which is what the profiling brain researchers Wolf Singer and Gerhard Roth opine, the new insights point toward a task of the criminal law of obligations, which is in favor of a criminal purpose of law. (Duttge, 2009, p. 98) [Da das deutsche Strafrecht hinsichtlich der zugrundeliegenden Schuldidee einer Beweisbarkeit von Willensfreiheit verpflichtet scheint, meinen etwa die profilierten Hirnforscher Wolf Singer und Gerhard Roth, die neuen Erkenntnisse sprächen für eine Aufgabe des Schuldstrafrechts zu Gunsten eines Zweckstrafrechts.]

The law of obligations is in mixed legal systems and civil law legal systems[11] and is a branch of private law whereby the rights and duties that emerge between individuals are organized and regulated by the body of rules called the "law of obligations" (Zimmermann, 2005). For civil law legal systems, the system of reference becomes the foundational source of law. It is argued that the systems of reference within civil law legal systems are advantageous for the objective of criminal law, which requires legitimizing, making sense and showing the purpose of penalizations as functions of these criminal justice systems.

It remains problematic with issues of guilt and free will whether brain research can be incorporated within the law of obligations so that legitimation, sense-making, and the showing of purpose are necessitated for a verdict of guilty to be established because multiple levels of observations and multiple levels of analyses are utilized with the concepts that can become equivocated. That is, the concepts of guilt and free will that are derived from neurological investigations may be distinctly different than those same concepts derived from ordinary investigations regarding observations via the utilizations of the investigator's sense perceptions with the aid of simple tools (e.g., spectacles, hearing aids, etc.).

The concepts of free will and guilt that are derived from observations coming from brain research of subjects versus the concepts of free will and guilt that are derived from observations made from watching persons who make decisions are sometimes contradictory. Regarding neurological analyses and observations of guilt, we always lack information about what happened beforehand and about what happened during the act of the victimization because the neurological observations always come afterwards, according to Niels Birbaumer, an Austrian neuroscientist.

The high mental competency of the guilty criminal coupled with neurochemical studies of subjects, who also have high competencies, have resulted in neuroscientists interpreting the results of the delayed conscious awareness

---

11 Civil law (i.e., Roman law and the kind of law of legal systems in continental Europe, most of Central America and South America) originated in Europe. Civil law legal systems generally possess and assert key principles with codification (i.e., a collection process that involves restating the law made within a relevant jurisdiction and forming legal codes). On the other hand, common law legal systems (e.g., most of the United States, Canada, England, Ireland, Australia and New Zealand) have intellectual structures by which judges render legal decisions and precedents are set. The precedents become the authority and set of rules or principles from these earlier legal cases that either persuade or bind the decisions of future cases that have similar circumstances and relevant facts (Reimann & Zimmermann, 2006).

of choices (i.e., delayed in comparison to measurable brain activity that is utilizable for predicting what the choice will be) as involving a lack of guilt that could be utilizable for moral blameworthiness concerning, for instance, a verdict of guilty in a court of law.

The suggestion that there is an absence of blameworthiness and guilt has resulted from a few different conceptions that have not been proven to be entirely relevant. The first conception is: An individual can only be blamed for what happens, if what happens could have been different and is, therefore, not necessary. In other words, some maintain that if an event is necessary, then one cannot be rationally blamed for it in any moral sense because necessary events could not have occurred in any other way, which means the events have an inevitability. To say the least, the latter claim is dubious in accordance with many systems of thought in philosophy, though.

What we are confronted with in such cases, concerning decision-making, are the currently irreconcilable differences in respect to levels of observations and levels of analyses. Coupling physiological, chemical, and neural events within the brain with the legal conception of guilt directly concerns attempts to interpret indirect observations of events at the neurochemical levels with events at levels of observations we directly make with our unaided auditory and visual sense perceptions.

Moreover, the indirect observations of the events are also not the relevant events that involve the court cases, but rather they are typically cerebral events that occur in subjects who have undergone diverse types of brain scans. The guilt cannot be established by any brain research, although brain researchers can discover the guilt of an individual by having access to other types of evidence, such as video and audio footage of a robbery where the individual can be observed to have committed the felony and to be cognizant. However, brain research may be used to give them some amount of confirming evidence.

Competency, guilt, and blame are all simple types of judgments we make on daily bases, especially concerning articles about wealthy CEOs, corporations filing for bankruptcy, armed conflicts and other human choices that impact the world. Although they are simple for us in the latter respects, such judgments involve incredibly complex sets of perceptions, neurological activity, chemical reactions, and hormonal influences on behavior. Thus, an overwhelming amount of literature, experimentation and research on competency, guilt, and blame concern the macro-levels rather than micro-levels of analyses and observations. Nevertheless, the prediction of an individual's choice before the individual consciously experiences making the choice involves yet another level of analysis and observation with various methods of computation and neurological imaging.

Coupling of concepts that have been developed in different fields, levels of observations, and analyses shows we need more complicated methodology that takes multiple layers into consideration. We need methodology that accounts for distinctly different levels of analyses and observations. We need competing theories that account for, describe, and explain events at the microscopic but multicellular levels in the most efficient and relevant ways to our most familiar events at macroscopic levels to make more sense to us, regarding what we already know.

Consider that the competent criminal (i.e., where there is great supportive evidence of her guilt) is, indeed, blameworthy, concerning our most well-known and utilized levels of observations and analyses. People construct interpretations via combining neuroscience with evaluations of neural levels (i.e., microscopic neurons and networks) and viewable behaviors (i.e., at a macroscopic level) as either determined and necessary or arbitrary and coincidental.

Because of attributions of inevitability of the action, people who claim that the act was necessary also tend to claim that the performer of the action cannot be held morally or legally blameworthy for it. Contrarily, because of attributions of the act being unintentional, unforeseen, and unplanned, people who claim that the act was coincidental also tend to claim that the performer of the act cannot be held morally or legally blameworthy for it. This problem is discoverable in some sciences and intensifies in courts of law with highly skilled attorneys (See Ch. 5.5).[12]

Overstatements in neurosciences appear to involve indiscriminate conclusions made about some macro-level of analysis or observation drawn from evident conclusions coming from some micro-level of analysis and observations. This entails there is something like a misguided set of evaluative claims or a neuro-pseudoscience that seeks to combine categories of entirely different levels. Problematically, they have completely different relations of dependency, different principles, and require different types of observations and analyses.

Basically, it is as if we have two separate and distinct categories, reasons to believe the categories are linked, and lack evidence for the links. However, people still make conclusions about one category from observations about the

12 Of course, neuroscience and the conclusions we attain from it are not entirely able to alter our legal judgments about morality, immorality, criminality, innocence, obedience, and deviance. Neuroscience involves techniques, technology, computational, and statistical methodologies that are only common to small groups of academics and practitioners. They involve undiscovered territories that inform us about ourselves. The importance of the findings during the beginning phases of the techniques can certainly be overstated.

other category. The categories are separate and distinct from the perspective of the attainment of knowledge. Herbert Spiegelberg (1982, p. 310) describes problems of categories in Nicolai Hartmann's theory of the levels of reality:

> The second error of traditional philosophy is the propensity, stemming from the monistic need for unity, to transfer the categories or principles of one province to another that differs from it in kind. Illustrations are the application of mechanistic principles to the sphere of the organic, of organic relationships to social and political life, and, conversely, of mental and spiritual structures to the inanimate world.

The problematic insistence of scientists superimposing conclusions of neurological investigations on mental activities and social concepts leads to some false but persuasive conclusions in arguments. This includes in courts of law. There are great dangers in lacking philosophic methodologies in sciences. The worst lack ethics, of course. Dangers are more apparent when sciences form interdisciplinary studies where two types of knowledgeable scientists, say, biologists and psychologists, draw speculative conclusions about each other's realms from insights about their own realms and simple agreements between them. Spiegelberg (ibid.) continues:

> This infringement of categorial boundaries, as Hartmann calls the theoretical encroachment of one province of being upon another, must be eliminated by rigorous critical analysis; yet the categories must preserve their relative validity for the domain from which they were taken originally. From the standpoint of a critical ontology, the totality of beings then turns out to be a far more complicated structure than finds expression in the traditional metaphysical formulas of unity.

"Infringing the categorial boundaries" or intruding on another domain of knowledge includes the application of concepts regarding the inorganic and organic levels and superimposing concepts and descriptions from these microscopic levels of intense magnification onto interactions of molecules in the brain. Likewise, interactions of molecules in the brain are observed and analyzed. Next, the concepts and descriptions are used with the desire to apply them to social, legal, and political life. Social life involves the level at which we discover choices, guilt, and moral blameworthiness. The brain research does not discover choices, guilt, and moral blameworthiness nor does it teach us these feelings or experiences in choosing, undergoing guilt and being blamed.

Improving procedural justice involves forming understandings of these complex phenomena we piece together with bits of information.[13]

The concept of guilt in a court of law, involving decision-making and circumstances, cannot directly carry over and enlighten us regarding decision-making processes and circumstances we uncover during neurocognitive real-time fMRI studies. Why is there a dogmatic tendency to think that the chemical and neurobiological accounts will enlighten us regarding our concept of guiltiness in a court of law?

Results yielded from neurocognitive studies require critical analyses and further investigations before we can acquire reasons to contribute to or reconstruct our concepts that we formed as products from our experiences concerning our interrelations with one another in societies and cultures. Doubtlessly, cognitive neuroscience contributes to the production of fuller concepts, yet interconnections of concepts at totally different levels are not obvious, especially when they involve concepts formed outside of neuroscience. The concepts of decision, belief, and desire will continue to be used for practical purposes, despite conclusions in neuroscience.

7 Logical Levels of Analysis: Philosophy of Law

Philosophy, like mathematics, involves painstaking and constant attention to proofs of validity and to the methods used to evaluate argumentation. Philosophy is at least sometimes a mathematical application of the rules of inference, derivation, and replacement to the language being used with logic. What hinders both legal sciences and philosophy of law is the inability to come to agreements on the terminology that shall be consistently used for investigations of legal matters. For the latter reason, logics are absolutely crucial for this

13 Consider neuroscientists and other professionals using findings from their area of expertise and applying those findings to important testimonies in courts of law. With generally a lack of humbleness, they intrusively suggest their domain of knowledge extends to the next domain. This is treacherous theoretical territory. Knowing both domains of knowledge at the level of an expert guarantees no knowledge about connections, fundamentally share principles, or the status of unobservable aspects of objects, even though the objects are roughly known at both levels of observations. Scholars ideologically impose ideas about choices, free will, and moral blameworthiness to assess judgments of guiltiness in courts of law. One way they do this is by focusing on chemical and neurocognitive levels.

field because each logic demands that each variable remain consistent (e.g., "p" is always defined consistently with itself).

There are many different logics, including classical binary logic, ternary logics, modal logic and other multi-valued logics, such as fuzzy logic. All these logics contribute to advancements in the attainment of knowledge. The ones that were historically derived before the others are also able to contribute to such progress. These logics inform us of systems that philosophers of different eras utilized for different presentations of thoughts.

Systems of logic are beneficial to researchers' purposes, despite whether the systems allow for derivations of conflictual conclusions. Binary, ternary, and other multi-valued logics all provide interesting additions to sciences of law and philosophy of law. Historical emergences of logics are relevant to analyses that demonstrate influence of logical developments of philosophy of law. Logical rules of derivation and inference provide philosophers with mathematical tools for systematically and methodically applying, comparing, and critiquing many arguments. They develop speed and greater validity in their arguments with practice. Such skills have scientific value.

Pitfalls in human reasoning generally hinder research. The proper usage of the aforementioned argumentation and rules of replacement provides consistency and naturally prevents inconsistencies. They are ideals toward which to strive. They are not expected structures of thought for most people (Mannheim, 1929/1995). Fallacies are also noteworthy regarding constructions of arguments for deceiving evaluators in courts of law and during proposals of bills by lawmakers. The multiplicity of fallacies facilitates the derivation of invalid (and unsound) conclusions.

In courts of law, one common type of situation involves the presentation of an expert witness who testifies under oath about his extensive knowledge concerning some realm. Mechanical engineers testify about motor vehicles involved in car wrecks. The use of the expert involves the expectation that jurors and judges will believe what the expert says is true. The expert is credible. So, there are desires and expectations that people will commit the fallacy of appealing to authority. This happens frequently in the US court system.

The expert is paid by one of the legal parties. The opposing party argues that the so-called expert is less credible or untrustworthy. In some cases, two expert witnesses from the opposing legal parties are presented to the court in session. Both may fundamentally disagree regarding basic facts of the case, say, with regard to the speed and locations of the vehicles at the point of impact, whether the individuals were fastened in seatbelts, etc. Of course, not all legal systems allow for communications to occur in the same ways.

The position of the lawyer is quite often the position of the arguer who seeks to win arguments, according to evaluations of other people who the lawyer does not know. Lawyers also do not typically attempt to produce the best arguments for uncovering facts of the case. They construct arguments that best suit the interests of their parties (i.e., the lawyer, the law firm, and the clients). For these reasons, it is extraordinary for the same law firm to accept and provide their services for both the accuser and the accused, the plaintiff and the defendant. It would pose an opposition of interests.

Philosophy is distinctly different in the latter respect. Two philosophers from the same department could decide on the issue of, say, academic fraud and handle the accuser and the accused. They can likely proceed without fear of conflicts of interests.

Many lawyers also refrain from asking revealing questions about illegal behaviors of their clients. Some prefer not to know irrelevant details that may demonstrate to the lawyer that the defendant has a deplorable moral character or is the culprit of the crime at issue. Lawyers may inquire whether the clients performed certain actions and said certain things that were overheard by law enforcement agents. Arguments are constructed as shortcuts for winning and to represent their clients as having the highest values for society that can be constructed from what the lawyer knows. Lawyers can mislead the jury or judges to believe in some alternative story that only partly describes what happened, too.

Sometimes arguments are constructed to suggest that the opposition has the lowest moral values for society. The arguments are also constructed to be consistent with the accessible evidence, which requires an understanding of the evidence. Many different alternative arguments that even contradict each other can remain consistent with the evidence. Evidence does not demonstrate a complete picture of what happened concerning the case. Constructions of arguments need not possess conclusions that are externally consistent and that are assertions concerning the case. External consistency involves only descriptions of what really happened.

The logical level of analysis often permits recognitions of ideologies. Such analyses expose convincing but invalid arguments. This level of analysis involves methods of evaluations, constructions of arguments, and critiques with the guidance and corrections for ideal ways of analyzing legal issues and other sets of facts, information, and misinformation. Logical rules of derivation and replacement are necessary for both the logical analysis of legal philosophy, law, and legal sciences and the historical analysis of the philosophy of law. This level of analysis is fundamental for progress in science. Chapter 5 includes several forms of logical analyses.

8 Historical Levels of Analysis: Philosophy of Law

Writing a history of philosophy of law requires the historian to be a philosopher of law. Doubtlessly, the historian of mathematics can contribute to the history of mathematics, yet such a historian could only attempt such an endeavor with vain efforts if the historian was no mathematician. Likewise, historians of philosophy are also required to be philosophers to successfully write an intellectual achievement of a history of philosophy. The same is true for a history of philosophy of law.

Challenges of producing an accurate historical and philosophically adequate analysis of law involve the development of the following: An understanding of what was meant, seen, and recognized via others' works. Conceptualizations and achievements left by thinkers and systems of thought, which thinkers strove to support with their teachings, need clarification (Hartmann, 1977, pp. 10–11). Concepts, which are represented by words and phrases, are crucial to recognize with or as operational definitions, in their usages in the work's entirety.

Even the meanings change from one thinker to the next, despite the usages of the same phrases and word; one of these words with changes in meaning is "law." Another one is "justice." The logical divide can be quite staggering, ranging from one set of thinkers who maintain some laws are just and some laws are unjust. Another set of thinkers ascertain that a so-called "unjust law" is not a law at all.

Nicolai Hartmann (1936/1977, p. 18) describes writings of history of philosophy like either the written history of religion or the written history of art opposed to how one writes history of science or branches of knowledge. There is no universally accepted history of philosophy. There is no unanimous agreement on history of philosophy of law.

There is no known set of beliefs on which philosophers have a consensus. The amount of disagreement is staggering amongst philosophers (Bourget & Chalmers, 2014). The amount of disagreement in the academic discipline of philosophy, according to the *PhilPapers Survey* of a sample of 3,226 people in 2009, includes respondents answering with all fourteen possibilities for each of the thirty questions posed to them (ibid.). The greatest amount of agreement regarding all thirty questions concerned the question, "God: theism or atheism?," to which 1,710 out of 3,226 respondents (i.e., ~53%) answered "Accept: atheism." The remainder of the respondents answered with all of the other thirteen alternative answers.[14]

---

14 The other thirteen responses included "accept: theism, lean toward: atheism, agnostic/undecided, lean toward: theism, reject both, accept another alternative, the question is

The amount of discord in the field of philosophy, confrontations with various systems of thought and teachings, and lack of recognition of the state of philosophy by philosophers is no new phenomenon. Any overestimations or underestimations of the amount of consensus in the field quite strongly suggests that the accuracy levels of interpretations of philosophy, its history, and accomplishments of prior generations of philosophers are thoroughly disconcerting.

What is particularly confusing and disturbing about the lack of consensus in philosophy on so many philosophic issues[15] is the absence of the organization of knowledge offered from teachings of the discipline of philosophy. This is coupled with the nominal amount of content from other academic disciplines that incorporate rational argumentation and logical analyses from philosophy, too. Additionally, the amount of philosophical research concerning themes in other disciplines, such as philosophy of perception, very often excludes the latest scientific research. It excludes the research and knowledge from biology and psychology that we have known for decades.

A strict divide between philosophic research and scientific research has occurred in some circles. Scientific research involves measurable units, measurements, techniques for observations, experimental alterations of conditions, and comparative analyses and measures with unaltered or controlled conditions. It involves systematic answers to preconceived questions based on prior observations.

Philosophic research involves raising questions that are so challenging to answer, and they are so perplexing that we confront the problem of whether the inquiries are even answerable. We question whether philosophic questions are sufficiently phrased to lead thinkers to systematic answers rather than superfluousness (Grimm, 2008).

Philosophy is a complicated task, which appears evident from the fact that philosophers, unlike scientists in certain respects, may create their best written works and publish them only to have the methods, concepts, and phrases used and analyzed centuries later. It is as if methodologies, conceptualizations, and systems of thought were ahead of their times when they were written philosophically. Aristotle's works provide one example. The 18th century philosopher and historian, David Hume, provides another example of such an author. Hume's philosophic writings lacked popularity during his lifespan,

too unclear to answer, accept an intermediate view, there is no fact of the matter, skip, other, accept both, and insufficiently familiar with the issue" (ibid.).

15 They range from religion to choice-making, mind, time, physicality, logicality and morality.

despite his well-received historical writings during the 18th and 19th centuries. Hume's writings about English history lost its popularity amongst later historians. Hume's philosophic works continue to gain in popularity after his death. There is much continued Humean scholarship during the 21st century.

The anticipations of exceptional philosophers, utilizations of systematic methods with rational arguments, and highly organized logical analyses yield ground-breaking results whenever both content and practical relevance suffice. The latter factors play crucial roles in scientific discoveries and technologies. They range from the prediction of the solar eclipse during antiquity by the philosopher Thales in approximately 585 BCE and the biology of Aristotle to the algebraic coordinate system of Descartes, the calculation machine and calculus of Leibniz, and the reckonings of Kant for his discovery of the forces of lunar gravitation on the tides.

Philosophers investigate the entirety, the fundamentals, and the end of the phenomena beneath the scope of philosophy. Philosophy always tends to direct attentions mostly toward unrestrained appendages. It creatively assembles pieces of works of other branches of knowledge. Philosophy continually speculates in multiple directions and sometimes exhausts all logical possibilities of a realm with its classification systems. Philosophical investigations so often are strongly enticed to focus on the most inaccessible objects or happenings. They impose constructive and critical thinking skills. Nicolai Hartmann writes:

> Place one of the learners, as the circumstances require, not just before the multiplicity of systems and doctrines, but also before the interpretations and perceptions of them, and so one takes every possibility in this boundless manifold to find one's bearings; one brings oneself directly toward despair in all understanding and to premature disillusionment and avoidance instead of proceeding toward the orientation and the understanding. (Hartmann, 1936/1977, p. 4) [Stellt man den Lernenden, wie es die Sachlage erfordert, nicht nur vor die Vielheit der Systeme und Lehrmeinungen, sondern auch noch vor die der Deutungen und Auffassungen, so nimmt man ihm jede Möglichkeit, sich in dieser uferlosen Mannigfaltigkeit zurechtzufinden; man bringt ihn, statt zur Orientierung und zum Verstehen, gerade zur Verzweiflung an allem Verstehen, ja zu vorzeitiger Ernüchterung und Abwendung.]

Nicolai Hartmann describes how the situation for learners in the field of philosophy can easily lead them to relinquish their desires to study philosophy. Philosophy of law is no different but does include a different starting point

(See. Ch. 5.7). The history of the philosophy of law is obviously faced with the task of selecting the systems of thought it mentions and describes in detail or not.

The historian of philosophy may even present the teachings of opinions and interpretations and perceptions of them to construct a historically accurate and coherent set of ideas. This is amid a disorganized clutter of stances that proceed in all logically possible different directions. *The Historical Dictionary of Philosophy* published from 1971 to 2007 in German (i.e., *Das Historisches Wörterbuch der Philosophie*) is perhaps the best attempt at an organized publication of philosophic concepts placed in an historic manner. It formed from the efforts of multiple historians and philosophers.

Each generation of academic philosophers begins the learning process in quite different circumstances. Each generation is confronted by various systems of thought, different worldviews and teachings strictly opposed to other systems, views, and educations. Systems, views, and teachings can be comparatively analyzed and evaluated based on their comparative comprehensiveness, internal and external consistency with relevancy and practicality, and parsimony.

Nevertheless, any of such comparative analyses first require the knowledge of these systems, views, and teachings. Such knowledge is probably lopsided, increasing the chances of favoritism toward some sides and hindering the impartiality of the decision-making process. So, certain directions are taken and are necessary from the outset of the learning process. Again, we are confronted with challenges concerning a history of the philosophy of law in the latter respects.

Pursuing and attempting to discover each direction, which one would later face, leads to utter confusion. The directions require quite different pathways and contradict one another on some issues. From the perspective of one view, another view may lack comprehensiveness. This entails that the former view lacks parsimony from the perspective of the latter view (e.g., theism and atheism, respectively). Intellectuals naturally tend to uphold forms of ideological thinking rather than remain skeptical.

One alternative, which involves at least temporarily refraining from the strict advocacy of some system of thought, is the creation of an outline of contents about subject matters that is handled quite differently via alternative systems. This sort of undertaking promotes the indecisiveness and involves the withdrawal of intellectual worldviews based on decision-making. It involves withdrawing processes involved in the achievement of knowledge. Despite the shortcomings, outlining the content of the subject matters does prevent one from going astray. It prevents the investigator from going down the many tunnels of endless mazes of deep research.

The latter type of creation is quite commonly utilized in philosophy of law and jurisprudential teachings insofar as syllabi of professors often incorporate multiplicities of systems for intellectual digestion of legal scholars. One frequently used pedagogical method involves the presentations of multiple systems of legal thought. They are slightly opposed to each other, or they can be opposite-ended systems for learners to study and come to superficial understandings before any direction of research is deeply solidified in one system. Subject matters may divide the syllabus of a course instead. The problem arises that the themes are grasped and taught in the encompassing role of some system of legal thought or several, even if inadvertently.

9 History of Philosophy and History of Philosophy of Law: System and Problem-thinking

Nicolai Hartmann asks what the condition of the possibility[16] of the history of philosophy is. Such a condition is the same condition for the history of philosophy to be a reality (Hartmann, 1936/1977, p. 190). Hartmann (ibid., p. 3) first concludes that, doubtlessly, the history of philosophy, as it is viewed as being the object of research, teachings, and representations, repeatedly becomes a concern for research.

History of philosophy has been viewed differently during various times. During the early 20th century, many scholars were convinced of the historical accuracy of ideas presented in their histories of philosophy. Some of them, as Hartmann (ibid.) points out, asserted there was already a path being paved by means of these philosophic thoughts for the future of philosophy.

Despite optimism of historians of philosophy, conflicts of opinions and stances against the undertaking of any definitive history of philosophy arose. Nothing emerged as anywhere near a universally accepted work. Nothing arose describing, explaining, or denoting the entirety or even what is undoubtedly factual as the scholars commonly understood.

From standpoints of evaluations, interpretations of meanings, and combined efforts of constructions, the construction of a history of philosophy was conditionally disputed regarding the times. Even during the beginning of the 21st century, the impact of Georg Friedrich Wilhelm Hegel (1770–1831) is readily observable. It is observable in many parts of Eastern Europe and in

16 In Nicolai Hartmann's works, including *The Philosophical Thoughts and their History* (1936/1977), Hartmann proceeds from the Kantian-inspired question about what the conditions of the possibility of knowledge are.

East Germany, too. For these sorts of reasons, what becomes apparent is the popularization of ideas and philosophic thought. The impact that philosophical thought has on other domains of knowledge in other disciplines remains disputable.

Apparent connections and giving the appearance of unification of directions in philosophy during certain time periods seems one-sided. Boundaries of facts of the matters and reconstructions seem hopelessly ambiguous. The grand endeavor was to complete a whole picture of philosophy. It began anew after Hegel's death failed to meet the desired goal. The result was a great divide in almost all historic research with the objective to write a history of philosophy, according to Hartmann (ibid., pp. 3–6).

What followed in the academic field of philosophy was an abundance of systems and focuses upon subsystems of thought. Philosophic teachings often incorporate opinions about opinions. There is no foundation from which to determine any one enduring philosophy. Critical thinking and rational argumentation only can lead theorists, philosophers and analysts to borders of content under investigation and as far as what the content allows.

William Brant (2013a, pp. 107–117) describes the problematic historical period in the field of psychology during the early 20th century when the concept of mental imagery involved discussions in major scientific journals that amounted to opinionated assertions and opinions about other psychologists' opinions specifically regarding mental imagery. Here, too, the lack of measures and absence of clear direction and motives of researchers, coupled with abstract content, led to a search for methodologies and experimental processes. The methods and processes were repeatable and thereby led to similar conclusions for different groups. Consequently, approaches of classical conditioning and operant conditioning became prolific in many institutions for psychology. The literature about mental imagery waned for about half a century.

Philosophy of law and jurisprudence involve much of the same advocacy of systems which taught as subdisciplines in universities. Many universities require basic knowledge of readings of scholars who advocate different systems of thought. Historically, these include natural law theory, legal positivism, legal formalism, legal realism and legal constructivism. Philosophies are described as belonging to philosophers. They may take on the personas of certain individuals who are important in the field, such as Oliver W. Holmes, H.L.A. Hart, Richard Posner and Ronald Dworkin. Many identify them as legal scholars who have amassed tens of thousands of citations in others' works (Shapiro, 2000, p. 424).

Multiple books and articles are entirely dedicated to describing and explaining some of the opinions of philosophy of law of these men. Books often incorporate opinions about opinions. Thus, the history of the philosophy of law is confronted with the troublesome task of filtering out opinions about opinions and teachings of them. Opinions and meta-opinions about law and teachings of systems as solutions to philosophic problems of law[17] provide distractions from aspects of theoretic frameworks that facilitate generations of scientific hypotheses for legal science.

If we consider the American philosophers of law, namely, Walter Wheeler Cook, Karl Nickerson Llewellyn, Jerome Frank, Underhill Moore, and Herman Oliphant, to be both denouncers of the common legal tradition at the turn of the 20th century based on its conservatism and formalism and consider them advocates of forms of legal realism,[18] we may criticize considerations here in several respects. Instead, we may endeavor to interpret systems of thought, against which legal realists argued from the perspective of legal realism, and then provide a comparative analysis of the system of thought known as legal realism.

The abovementioned legal realists argued against a type of legal anti-realism in which the law was viewed as an independent and complete system including consistent rules, principles, and conceptions. For self-identified realists, legal anti-realism mostly viewed law insofar as it was the strict involvement of applications of logically consistent rules with inevitable consequences for law to be applied. According to legal realists, legal anti-realism maintained judges discover determinations of law via strict adherence to rules of order for judicial decisions.

Despite descriptions of the current US associate Supreme Court Justice, Neil Gorsuch,[19] which maintain he supports textualism, originalism, and natural

17 Oppose this with teaching them as parts of problems of law in need of reconciliation and with other systems via comparatively analyzing them.

18 Legal realism maintains legal certainty, regarding judicial decisions, is almost always unattainable and perhaps would not even be ideal regarding desirable social consequences.

19 Judge Gorsuch replaced the Associate Supreme Court Justice Antonin Scalia who served from 1986 until his death in 2016. Scalia held similar views of textualism and originalism. Originalism maintains a stance in which the Constitution can be interpreted as stable from the period during which it originated. So, meanings remain the same, despite societal changes and different eras. Right-wing conservative theorists in the United States are often accredited with espousing such a stance in favor of corporate microeconomies, including the latter two judges and Supreme Court Justice Clarence Thomas who favored the corporation Monsanto and others with his originalism.

Legal formalism (i.e., a form of anti-realism) is a system of thought that is the antithesis of legal realism. Textualism is a subsystem of formalism. Textualism maintains interpretations of laws be based foremost on meanings of texts rather than any other considerations, such as considering purposes for passing laws. The formalist system includes arguments for applying socially acceptable principles to facts of cases for judicial decisions. Formalists argue that judges make decisions in those ways and that they should

law theory in philosophy of law, at least one of Gorsuch's positions can be characterized as the latter type of anti-realist stance. Judge Gorsuch claimed as the dissenting judge in *No. 15-9504, TransAm Trucking, Inc. v. Admin. Review Bd., U.S. Dep't. of Labor*:[20]

> It might be fair to ask whether TransAm's decision was a wise or kind one. But it's not our job to answer questions like that. Our only task is to decide whether the decision was an illegal one... And there's simply no law anyone has pointed us to giving employees the right to operate their vehicles in ways their employers forbid ... [M]aybe someday Congress will adorn our federal statute books with such a law. But it isn't there yet. And it isn't our job to write one—or to allow the Department to write one in Congress's place.

We may interpret the judge's decision siding with the trucking corporation, his justifications as well as many of the points he made repeatedly during his 2017 US Senate confirmation hearings to be fitting examples of the legal anti-realism against which many of the philosophers of law argued at the turn of the 20th century. The judge's responses in other settings also demonstrate that

---

make decisions in those ways. It is a descriptive and prescriptive system. Formalists also oppose the legal realist subsystem of thought known as legal instrumentalism. Legal instrumentalism proposes law be used as an instrument with which creative interpretations of laws allow promotions of social justice, improved public policy, protections of rights, and social interests. These systems have been largely developed in the American legal system, and functions and counter-opposing tendencies arise differently in common law legal systems as opposed to civil law legal systems.

20 Judge Gorsuch was the only dissenting judge on the case, which is likely surprising because of the facts. In January 2009, Mr. Alphonse Maddin was transporting cargo in temperatures that were well below freezing. He pulled over to the side of the highway at about 11:00 p.m. His gas gauge was below empty, and he had not found the gas station mandated by TransAm, his employer. Subzero temperatures caused his brakes to freeze. Mr. Maddin reported the problem to his superiors. He was instructed to wait by the highway.

The truck's auxiliary heater did not work. After hours of waiting and a phone call at 1:18 a.m. from his cousin, Gregory Nelson, Mr. Maddin was informed that his speech was "slurred" and that he appeared "confused." Mr. Maddin reported the additional problems to his dispatcher, telling the dispatcher that his feet and torso were numb, he waited an additional thirty minutes after the dispatcher told him to "hang in there," and then he contacted his supervisor, Larry Cluck, who he informed that he could not feel his feet and that he was also having breathing problems from the coldness. Mr. Cluck told Mr. Maddin to either drive the truck to the nearest gas station with the cargo, or to wait for Road Assist to help. The first option given by the supervisor was considered very dangerous by Mr. Maddin. Mr. Maddin unhitched the cargo trailer from the truck and drove to the nearest station. He was dismissed shortly thereafter from TransAm.

this newly appointed Supreme Court justice is willing and able to uphold apparently unethical and unfair laws to support judicial decisions, especially in favor of corporations. The main qualification appears to be that the decisions cannot be illegal ones.

The facts of the case that place the situation into a context in which moral values and immoral values and actions can be extracted from the impartial evaluator are ignored. The system of thought ignores these values. The system favors evaluations of acts purely regarding the legality and illegality of them, according to relevant written laws. On the other hand, judges who advocate opposing systems of thought give the societal system the risk of arbitrarily deciding cases based on factors that are separate from written laws.

Legal anti-realists' systems of thought confront problems when the law appears incomplete as a system and contains inconsistencies, contradicts principles it upholds in certain areas, and possesses misconceptions. Thus, upholding the law in each case, according to the counter-opposed system of thought, will certainly lead to unfairness, injustices, and failures for people to stabilize their expectations about the law regarding procedural justice. Alternatively, legal realism is presumably a system of thought that considers flaws, incompleteness, arbitrariness, hidden conflicts of interest, and other sorts of unfairness that are communicated by the legal system and superimposed on the people by members of the legal institution.

Jurisprudence of legal realism may be viewed as being superficial and abstract. Many analyses of fairly obvious social facts were well-known during that same time period. They were known by certain minority groups. However, legal realists' system of thought seemed to play no practical and significant role regarding recognitions of unfairness toward low-status groups. Most perhaps favored the opulent and dominant groups, giving disadvantages to lower status groups.

Judges were viewed by both social psychologists and legal realists as failing to consistently apply rules that were logically consistent. Implementations of inconsistent rulings were plainly noticeable to low-status group members who underwent greater disadvantages regarding aspects of such rulings. In their jurisprudence, perhaps legal realists deserve recognition for their lines of inquiry leading social analysts to investigate inconsistencies of judgments regarding inconsistent applications of legal rules, concepts, and principles applied to people because of different ways of thinking that impact the process of decision-making and outcomes in courts of law.

Perhaps legal realism can inspire focus on general legal decision-making for lawmaking and law enforcements. Decision-making is affected by unconscious biases at all levels. This is apparent in legal decision-making of lawmakers, judges, and law enforcement professionals in any history of any legal system and laws of any society. There are disproportionately more negative consequences on lower status groups, comparatively.

People, such as judges in courts of law, have unconscious biases including racism. This affects their decision-making outcomes for even significant judgments (Macrae & Bodenhausen, 2000; Greenwald & Krieger, 2006; Kang, 2005; Lane, Kang & Banaji, 2007; Adams et al., 2007; Dovidio, Glick & Rudman, 2005; Greenwald, Oakes & Hoffman, 2003).

Joris Lammers and Diederik Stapel (2011, p. 375) found judges can suppress their racist tendencies during the decision-making process and judge in fairer ways. They can do this via focusing on justice throughout the decision-making process. It is worthwhile for judges to be continuously reminded by impartial individuals that they should focus again and again on justice.

Decision-making processes during policing are negatively impacted via the social identification of race and racially biased decisions of police officers to discharge their weapons or to refrain from doing so. Empirical studies and anecdotal evidence published by multiple mass media outlets suggest that suspects' ethnic identities play important roles regarding tendencies for police to fire their weapons at them (e.g., Payne, 2001; Correll et al., 2002; Correll et al., 2007). Consider the shooting of the unarmed teenager, Michael Brown, in Ferguson, Missouri on August 9, 2014 (Brown, 2014; Lee, 2014; ACLU of Missouri, 2014).

Well-known or obvious examples for many people of inconsistencies regarding the law include its rules, penalizations, and procedures that come from: (1) Judges, who tend to make unfairer decisions when they fail to consider justice frequently during the decision-making processes; and (2) Law enforcers, like police officers, who sometimes behave unfairly when they fail to consider justice during incidents that require decisions. Inconsistencies involve unequal applications of rules and laws to certain groups of people. Unfairness is identifiable via statistical analyses of high and low-status groups.

All this undermines the practicality of legal realism regarding claims that it states merely obvious facts, especially regarding the obviousness that politics affect legal decisions. The system of thought described as legal realism is perhaps best attributed to many others before those who are self-identified legal realists. It is a system of thought of others who were suppressed and oppressed and disadvantaged, regarding being excluded largely from the system of exchanges. It involves legal ideas of realpolitik and cynicism regarding the law and legal systems.

Low-status group members have noted all these sorts of latter injustices. Their knowledge is identifiable by the fact that they do not merely always engage in system justificatory behaviors. The recognitions of injustices can be viewed in their music, other arts, and comedy of low-status groups. In some cases, alternative histories develop, such as different interpretations of history proposed by some African Americans of the probable assassination on December 11, 1964 of the great musician, composer, and producer, Samuel Cook known as Sam Cooke. He had been performing enduring songs for the Civil Rights Movement, such as "A Change is Gonna Come."

Cooke promoted societal change by requiring his audiences to blend the ethnic groups. The alternative history was written and accepted by many that Mr. Cooke was killed in self-defense or as a "justifiable homicide." Many questions remain unanswered. No autopsy was performed. Circumstances of his whereabouts with his Ferrari at a cheap motel were very much out of character for him. His case was not properly investigated.

The latter alternative histories demonstrate two opposing systems of thought that aim to describe the American society. The legal realists and legal anti-realists propose two other opposing systems. Perhaps it is best to further understand what is meant by the philosophic use of the concept of a system.[21]

In the field of jurisprudence, many systems oppose others to greater or lesser degrees, such as legal realism, legal positivism, natural law theory, legal constructivism, legalism, and legal formalism. There would be no progress in philosophy or any other discipline without the constructive works of system-thinkers. System-thinkers are those who advocate and develop systems of thought. They are opposed to other systems of thought.

The construction of each system is a gradual and tedious process. It undergoes the production of rational arguments in agreement with each other. Deconstructive and rational argumentation tests the consistency of the system and refutes some lines of valid but unsound argumentation. So, systems of thought are constructed and then reconstructed after counter-arguments refute the subsidiary arguments and rebuttals are analyzed. Subsidiary arguments support the basis of subsystems of thought in many cases and are

21 Nicolai Hartmann writes: A system is no beginning, but rather an end for the philosophical knowledge. This end is never there, never finished; therefore, philosophical knowledge is never finished. A system indicates the ideal totality of this knowledge. Its methodical meaning for the handling of the individual problems is thus impossible to prohibit because it resides only in the relation of the ideal, intentional end of the knowledge. (Hartmann, 1912, p. 23) [System ist kein Anfang, sondern ein Ende für die philosophische Erkenntnis. Dieses Ende ist nie da, nie fertig; denn philosophische Erkenntnis ist nie fertig. System bezeichnet die ideale Totalität dieser Erkenntnis. Seine methodische Bedeutung für die Behandlung einzelner Probleme kann daher unmöglich eine unterbindende sein; denn sie besteht nur in der Beziehung auf die ideale Endabsicht der Erkenntnis.]

sometimes invalidated via counter-arguments. Hartmann characterizes the differences in approaches.[22]

One way of thinking depends on the consequence of the system, which is sought after rather than forced or insisted upon; unanimous agreement is reached to some extent. This is how stances in philosophy (e.g., determinism, compatibilism, and libertarianism) are formed and how other related philosophy of law stances (e.g., natural law theory, legal realism etc.) are formed. What is unavoidable is the oppression or suppression of the problems. When the problems fail to fit in the system, they may be classified as falsely phrased questions and assertions and poorly phrased demands for solutions. System-thinking allows the enforceable solutions to be validated.

Problem-thinking slowly follows from the consequence of the problem. No worldview is presumed or even anticipated as both an option and decision. It need not lead somewhere toward a solution. So, it all remains undecided regarding the content. With problem-thinking, the reversal of any decision can occur or recur at any time.

Problem-thinking does not provide principles. Problem-thinking searches for principles. Such a way of thinking proceeds from problems at hand. Problem-thinking either relies on the oppositional content of at least two systems of thought or involves the crossing or exceeding of one system of thought to

---

22 Hartmann writes: Nevertheless, allow us without difficultly to distinguish between two types of thinkers throughout all times: suchlike the prevalent system-thinkers are, and suchlike the prevalent problem-thinkers are. The first are superior in number. The masters of scholasticism belong here almost without exception, firstly breaking the oppositional tendency into two parts in late nominalism; during antiquity Plotinus (~204–270 CE) and Proclus (412–485 CE) were of this type, and Bruno (1548–1600), Spinoza (1632–1677), Wolff (1679–1754), Fichte (1762–1814), Schelling (1775–1854) and Hegel (1770–1831) during modern times. (Hartmann, 1936/1977, p. 6) [Dennoch lassen sich durch alle Zeiten hin unschwer zwei Typen von Denkern unterscheiden: solche, die vorwiegend Systemdenker sind, und solche, die vorwiegend Problemdenker sind. Die erstere sind in Überzahl. Die Meister der Scholastik gehören fast ohne Ausnahme hierher, erst im späten Nominalismus bricht die Gegentendenz durch; im Altertum waren Plotin und Proklus von dieser Art, in der Neuzeit Bruno, Spinoza, Wolf, Fichte, Schelling, Hegel.] Hartmann continues to describe the distinctively rare type of thinker in philosophy as the problem-thinker: The problem-thinkers are fewer. One can see their type relatively purely represented in Plato (~428- ~423 BCE) and Aristotle (384–322 BCE), but also Descartes (1596–1650), Leibniz (1646–1716) and Kant (1724–1804) allow one to clearly discern. Their signature is that their thinking does not at all fit in a system, or it constantly exceeds it and breaks it in two parts. (ibid.) [Der Problemdenker sind weniger. Man kann ihren Typus in Platon und Aristoteles relativ rein repräsentiert sehen; aber auch Descartes, Leibniz und Kant lassen ihn deutlich erkennen. Ihr Signum ist, dass sich ihr Denken entweder überhaupt nicht in ein System fügt oder doch es ständig überschreitet und durchbricht.]

the development of the preliminary. The latter may end with the relinquishment of both systems. It may also end with the reconciliation of systems. It may lead to further developments of one system as opposed to another via system-thinkers who favor it.

Problem-thinking involves the outright persistence of investigation and uncertainty regarding the discovery of a solution to the problem. Every direction is taken related to research focal points as options. No solutions to problems are ever completely validated. Either an opposing system of thought disallows the validation, or such validation amounts to something unproblematic with which problem-thinking is unconcerned.

From the standpoint of a system of thought, the consequence of the problem appears to be characterized by a lack of logical sequence. However, problem-thinking dismisses absolutely no problem. It repeatedly divides the structures of thoughts. Consider Immanuel Kant's (1783) antinomies where statements and their oppositions are coupled. For example, one statement claims that all the events in the real world occur coincidentally. The opposing statement claims that there is some event that occurs necessarily.

System-thinking produces the temporal conditions and the ephemeral structure. Problem-thinking produces the lasting intellectual achievements of knowledge. Problem-thinking is potentially everlasting.

Fundamentally, systems change and shift, acting like houses of cards of thoughts. The quietest, gentle shake enables collapses. Realization of the research of problems with its structural design remain intact for problem-thinkers. They utilize rises and falls of systems.

Popularity of the adherence to any system of thought lacks historical continuity of the philosophic problems themselves. Historical continuity of problem-thinking is crucial for the endeavor of constructing any history of the philosophy of law with any consensus.

Philosophical problems are inscrutable. They may appear to one as if one is attempting to solve them via a discovery in an abyss. We fail so easily to achieve a real solution. The philosophic problems usually escape the grasp of most thinkers. However, opposite-ended thinkers during completely different time periods manage to combine the content of them. Positions of problems or their settings (framings or situatedness) are arbitrary and artificial, to some extent. Philosophic problems are important regarding limitations in attainments of knowledge, content and meanings.

As philosophical enduring problems, jurisprudence and philosophy of law are concerned with justice, mind, and goodness. They are unable to be dismissed. Jurisprudential philosophic problems repeatedly impose themselves, despite time periods and focuses of interests. Legal philosophic problems are independent regarding systems of thought. They concern many of the most basic questions and assumptions for attempts at solutions.

Of course, problems, such as the philosophic problems of law, may be temporarily ignored, missed, or taken for granted in assumptions by one, despite many of the assumptions lacking truthfulness. Therefore, "mind" is crucial to understand along with other problems of the philosophy of law. Problems are phrased in numerous ways, languages, and in multiple centuries.

In forms of questions, philosophic problems of law[23] involve requests and inquiries regarding their definitional meanings. Philosophical problems of law are posed in many alternative ways by alternative systems of legal thought. They can only be represented as examples, which are disputable: What is justice? What is mind? What is society? What is goodness?

Alternatively, philosophic problems of law may be posed in terms of location and temporal presence also regarding their contiguity in space and time (e.g., When and where will justice occur (for them)?). The latter notion of contiguity is quite disputable but allows one to form philosophical questions as examples in the following manners: What precedes justice and follows from justice? Where can justice occur?

Issues of such problems involved in jurisprudence lead to another fundamental philosophic problem, to wit, substance. Inquiries ask about problems regarding the real world in which we live. Comprehensive classification systems contain the concept of substance. Answers and solutions to such problems appear to require something "substantial" to both fit in the locations and to be contiguous with anything or to impact things. Substance, forms, space-time, and energy are conceived as real phenomena by some systems of thought from which the abstract conceptions of substance, forms, space-time, and energy are drawn, used, and which are concerned in assumptions, raising

23 One basic skill of philosophers is constructing and extracting information from non-philosophical questions to form philosophic ones (e.g., The question, "What time is it?," can be changed to form the philosophic question, "What is time?"). Questions are not straightforward (e.g., The question, "What is time?," could be interpreted as a question about translations into another language, i.e., What is "time"?, and answers could range from *Zeit* in German to *tiempo* in Spanish etc.). Questions require a philosophical outlook. They demand conceptual analyses. Philosophy of law includes many enduring questions: What is law? What is legal system? Some philosophic questions demand conceptual analyses to be constructed: What are the necessary conditions for a society to possess a legal system? Are some laws unjust, and if so, then what suffices to make them unjust? The latter skill of philosophical question-forming and conceptual analyses must therefore be applied by the historian to craft any worthwhile history of philosophy of anything, including law.

parallel and related problems, about which philosophy of law is concerned at various levels of analyses.

To make matters even more difficult for the task of philosophy of law and its history, there are many other lower level classes and subclasses from which phenomena, such as societies and law arise (See Ch. 3.1). Problems may also be phrased as lines of inquiry concerning their functions, their emergences, and who the problems concern the most, to wit: How does justice function and arise? Who primarily concerns themselves with justice? Under what conditions is justice considered? These are merely examples of questions approaching philosophic problems of law. They are best emphasized as coming from a single author's system of thought, but the commands, descriptions, and explanations of the philosophical problems remain unlisted here.

Correct answers to these problems are ambiguous. The problems are enigmatic and thereby result in the serious challenge for any thinker attempting solutions in forms of descriptions and explanations. System justification theory has involved the generation of an abundance of testable psychological and sociological hypotheses, which have tested social dominance theory. Social dominance theorists and many system justification theorists maintain criminal justice systems function in similar ways to terroristic organizations. Such systems also impose controlled violent acts and orchestrated threats. Criminal justice systems commit violent acts and make threats disproportionately more against low-status groups. They dominate subordinates.

However, many people may assume those who are most concerned with justice are those in the criminal justice system. However, histories of civil rights movements demonstrate minority group activists or activists from disadvantaged groups (i.e., lower status group members) are crucial for the attainment of progress toward a more just society and legal system, which was certainly true for women's suffrage in 1920 in the USA (Clift, 2003; Lerner et al., 2006, p. 17).

Despite whether people can live without philosophic problems arising in their own thoughts during their lifespans, the problems cannot ever be cast out of the world. They linger and repeatedly resurface. Hartmann (1936/1977, p. 8) concludes that the world with our lives in it, even just as it is at one single time, gives us these philosophic problems. The problems cannot be evaded. We are powerless regarding changing any of them.

When we take the latter factors into consideration, it is worthwhile to consider what the written history of the philosophy of law has achieved. What sorts of lasting advantages have come from the history of legal thought, and what are its realizations and achievements? What has the history of legal thought discovered? Obviously, any intellectual achievements of knowledge will come in a list of the content as a whole. The latter questions inquire whether epistemic achievements are distinguishable in the momentary work of the systems of thought.

There are multiple levels of analyses of law and multiple systems of thought that are present at the same levels. It is questionable whether intellectual achievements, which amount to knowledge and concern law and its relations to the philosophic problems, have amassed in systems of thought, at any moment. Problematically, the way in which philosophic problems of law are phrased is different at different times from the peripherals of alternative systems of legal thought. Problems of legal philosophy never truly become the focus of the investigation because a solution is the creation of an alternative system of legal thought. A history of legal thought focusing on a specific time is advantageous. It may involve the discovery and the beginning of the construction of new systems of legal thought.

10 Dual Roles of Historical Occurrences

Historical literature and documentation often involve circulation and popularization. From the popularization of documented events, it follows that there is a sort of "dual role of each historical event." There is the occurrence of the event during a specific amount of time. There is also the episode of the popularization of the descriptions of that very same event. That is, we consider the event as opposed to its accounts. Its accounts may expand over much longer periods than the event itself and be continuously documented.

Historical theory, philosophy of history and the philosophy of historiography confront various ways of thinking about the task of evaluating and measuring the significance and relevance of dual roles of historical events. There is concern for events that are relatively unimportant and irrelevant in relation to their documentations. However, their documentations may yield greater significance regarding overall impacts and subsequent consequences and changes.

The dual role of an historical event concerns natural ramifications of the event itself and its relation to the consequences of the popularization of the event's descriptions circulated via images and words or communications. Communications are circulated via conversations and mass media outlets etc. They generally involve varying degrees of inaccuracy.

Fundamental distinctions between the first and second roles are, respectively, a deterministic role involving causes[24] as opposed to consequences

24 They are causes as necessary and/or sufficient conditions for naturally arising ramifications of the event.

arising from another event or source that are inessential and may appear as unintended or unexpected consequences. Often these dual roles are reinterpreted by means of historical analyses and various methodologies.

Historical accounts of pregnancies of women before the 20th century involve natural consequences and presumptions about sexual reproduction, two parents, their socio-economic relations etc. However, historical accounts of the pregnancy of Mary, the mother of Jesus of Nazareth, provide entirely different conclusions concerning assumptions about pregnancies' natural consequences. The second role of the historic event includes presumptions about biological processes of sexual reproduction and parenthood being rescinded. Historical accounts state Mary was a virgin impregnated by God with the "son of God."

Accounts of Mary's pregnancy are opposed to natural consequences (i.e., the first role of the historical event). They contradict principles of and consistent observations about causation concerning sexual reproduction. Natural consequences are also able to be studied indirectly via numerous levels of observation (e.g., microscopic observations of spermatozoa and fertilization processes). They concern natural processes, such as the biological process of pregnancy. So, natural history is crucial concerning the first role of the historical event (Tucker, 2009, xii). On the other hand, historical accounts of Mary's pregnancy are consistent with the second role of the popularization of the event's descriptions. They shape ideologies via the second role.

Methodologies of philosophy of history and philosophy of historiography include incorporations of varying levels of doubt. This includes doubt whether events that occurred, which were recorded, were as significant for that zeitgeist compared to other events of that same period and perhaps even those with which we are totally unfamiliar. We may be led to believe in their importance based on their popularizations. The degree of the uncertainty or skepticism about the significance of the event undergoing investigation is problematic. The possibility remains that the record, circulation, and popularization of the event are far more significant than the event itself in virtue of the natural ramifications for societies.

The problem of evaluating the significance of the particular event with the event of the recording of that particular event is troublesome during the 21st century with mass media systems. Systems may coincidentally or intentionally publicize recordings of some events with lesser social impacts than perhaps other events would have had. Media systems sometimes aim to deceive or distract away from major events. Instead, if events had occurred without being documented, circulated, and popularized to such a degree or without the same images or words being used in their broadcasts, there might have been very little impact from them, in the society.

Oftentimes, historically significant events, concerning some legal system and law, include a stark contrast between what is legally allowed but socially disallowed, what is legally prohibited but socially acceptable and alegality (See Ch. 2). These contrasts involve two forms of permissions and prohibitions, namely, legal and social permissions and legal and social prohibitions. However, acts of publicizing cases of behavior that involve these combinations of permissions and prohibitions, by different groups by some of the legal institution and another social group, excite the judgmental nature of even the most impartial human beings in the society.

The following concepts have persisted for thousands of years because they involve logical possibilities concerning any legal judgment about crime and the judiciary court system:

> (1) Presumed innocence until guiltiness is proven; (2) Assumed guiltiness by means of being under suspicion; (3) Presumed guiltiness by means of being associated or affiliated with the guilty party; and (4) Assumed guiltiness until innocence is proven.

All four concepts illustrate aspects of human error in respect to knowledge, initial presumptions, prejudices, and judgments. They often have greater significance when they are official. The concept of one being "guilty until proven innocent" is generally contraposed to the more famous phrase "innocent until proven guilty."

The contraposition usually involves two different relations. First, the innocent person who has been wrongly convicted of a crime is considered guilty until proven innocent by a court of law. Second, the individual who committed the crime is considered innocent until proven guilty in a court of law. The 19th century US Supreme Court case of *Coffin v. United States, 156 U.S. 432 (1895)* maintains that "the presumption of innocence is evidence in favor of the accused, introduced by the law in [their] behalf." Vicki Helgeson and Kelly Shaver (2006, p. 276) discovered that it is very likely that the presumption of innocence is a false assumption:

> Because juror biases might impede realization of this guarantee, the law provides a protection for defendants–the presumption of innocence. Three experiments were conducted to assess presumptions of innocence directly. In the first two experiments, subjects were given written descriptions of the defendant and charge; the level of judicial instructions was varied. Results failed to show a presumption of innocence and suggested that biases can be induced by the manipulation of crime congruence to defendant occupation.

We may hypothesize that the appearance of the individual (i.e., his or her phenotype) who has been accused or indicted is important regarding the presumption of innocence. Hypothetically, those perceived as "warm" as opposed to "cold" and "incompetent" as opposed to "competent" are likelier to be granted something like the presumption of innocence until proven guilty. Those who are identified as being members of the "in-group," as opposed to the "out-group," are likelier to be presumed innocent until they are proven guilty. The latter hypotheses might be drawn from social cognitive psychology research, such as Cikara and Fiske (2012).

In courts of law, we may hypothesize that men closer to their peak reproductive potentials from approximately fifteen to fifty years of age are more likely to be presumed guilty until proven innocent. The latter hypothesis is partially drawn from prison data demonstrating that throughout the 21st century so far well over 90% of prisoners are men, according to the World Prison Brief in 2017. Helgeson and Shaver (ibid.) continue:

> In addition, biases were not counteracted by specific judicial instructions, and crime congruence affected males and females differently. In a third experiment, the same biasing variable was incorporated into a simulated trial. Subjects viewed videotapes of the trial from jury boxes in a law school's model court room. With the full trial setting, crime congruence did not influence presumptions of innocence. Sex differences were noted again, with females giving higher ratings of guilt, but showing less confidence in their judgments compared to males.

Concepts (1) and (4) above are fundamental concerning legal decision-making processes and other groups' choices to pursue whether the court system convicted or relieved the appropriate individuals. The concept expressed in the phrase "guilty by suspicion" is closely related to "guilty by association." The individual can be suspected guilty because she is associated with another individual or group. Moreover, she can be considered "guilty by association" because she faces suspicion.

The 1991 film, "Guilty by Suspicion," was directed by Irwin Winkler and starred Robert De Niro. De Niro played the role of a director during the 1950s at the peak of the red scare in the USA. Hollywood directors and actors were often accused of being communists or communist sympathizers during the 1950s. The latter accusations were enough during the "red scare" to presumably lead to more frequent occurrences of presumptions of guilt because of suspicion of the association with communism.

The dual roles of historical occurrences can negatively impact the willingness to make fair decisions, especially when events (e.g., gatherings of communists) are utilized for mass broadcasts on TV and in other mass media. Dual roles give politicians capabilities to further impact the second role of historically significant events. Politicians focus on consequences of popularizations of events' descriptions circulated via images and words or communications.

The second role can influence the concepts of presumed innocence until guiltiness is proven, assumed guiltiness by means of being under suspicion, presumed guiltiness by means of being associated or affiliated with the guilty party, and assumed guiltiness until innocence is proven. The society can change rapidly from the former forms of presumptions to the latter forms via mass media systems and politicians. Such was the case with witch hunts and the Salem witch trials[25] in colonial Massachusetts in the 1690s.

Politicians often acquiesce during social phenomena, like witch hunts. Others exacerbate the problems, such as in former US Senator Joseph McCarthy's alleged search for communists during the second red scare in the USA (~1947–56). Hunts appear to involve willing members who fabricate lies to increase their own publicity. They, like parts of the crowds of panicking people, turn their energy into stampedes, trampling, ruining careers, relationships, and lives.

Witch-like hunts generally happen in legally permissible or alegal manners and have taken the form of hunts for Muslims and Arabs during the 21st century. These hunts have occurred because of the popularization of negative imagery and wordings against the latter people. They have been associated more closely with terrorism in Western Europe and America via mass media systems. Reinforced surges of anti-Muslim and propagandizing anti-Arab sentiments have been reconfirmed by politicians and public policy since the attacks of September 11, 2001 in New York City and the Pentagon. The latter occurrences compose a set of events that have been continuously replayed via various media outlets for almost twenty years and form some of the propaganda material utilized to invade Middle Eastern countries, such as Afghanistan, Iraq, Syria, and Pakistan during the 21st century.[26]

---

25 Trials resulted in mostly executions of women. 165 people were accused in Salem of being witches. Serious charges were brought against 39 people of mostly women under twenty-three years old (Pavlac, 2009, pp. 140–141). Many of the women may have been at least inadvertently targeted in Salem because there was a relatively widely held belief that women should not hold property (ibid., p. 138). The more frequently occurring punishments and executions after the cross-examinations of younger women in the late 18th century for witchcraft illustrates that presumptions of guiltiness until innocence is proven is culturally dependent. It depends on many other factors, such as sexual selection.

26 The 21st century technology used for many of the invasions are remote controlled missile launching planes called "drones" that are operated by the United States Central Intelligence Agency Special Activities Division.

11 Comedic Levels of Analysis of Law: Laughableness, Booing, and Applause

The comedic level of analysis of law involves observations and measurements of laughing, booing, applauses, standing ovations, and other reactions of audiences to comedy and humor about law. Forms of comedy of law include stand-up routines, theater acting, films, music etc. Comedy about the law offers a platform from which aspects of the law can be observed and measured.

The comedic level of analysis is pertinent and attainable via methodologies traditionally used in social psychology, sociology and cultural anthropology. Units of measurement include volumes of sounds of audiences, lengths of times of audiences' responses, types of responses (e.g., laughs, tears, smiles etc.), associations with content, especially about police, judges, crimes, etc.

Previously, levels of the chemical and neurobiological analysis of the law were investigated (See Ch. 3.6). It was argued that ordinary observations of decisions are made at entirely different sets of levels of observation and levels of analyses than those provided and involved in brain research. It remains disputable whether the individual is relieved of legal and moral responsibility and blameworthiness when findings suggest consciousness of decisions arises only after certain neurological determinants. Comedy can be studied at levels of neurological observations. Many types of reactions to comedy are readily observable with videos, naked eyes and ears for scientific investigations.

Comedy and comedy about the law are probably as old as history itself. Athenian Old Comedy and New Comedy was represented, respectively, by Aristophanes (446–386 BCE) and Menander (~342–290 BCE) and consisted of vast amounts of material concerning the legal system (Buis, 2011; Buis, 2014). Perhaps the usage of the law as comedic material is as old as any legal system. Emiliano Buis (2014, pp. 325–326) informs us that:

> Aristophanes, then, provides a wealth of legal vocabulary that is used with accuracy and paralleled by the orators; occasionally, he uses a term in a legal context or a procedure not found elsewhere—and we have seen no reason to discredit these as true representations of legal procedure.

Buis (ibid.) then raises some questions:

> But how does Old Comedy really use this legal armature? It is not rare to find passages in which Aristophanes relies on the legal knowledge of the audience (i.e., its juridical encyclopedia) to understand a joke. But if humor requires a distance between the comic reference and everyday experience, how is this gap achieved in Old Comedy?

For the sake of comprehensiveness and to evaluate the consistency of legal theories, it is arguably crucial to include even disrespectful, comedic, and humorous evaluations of the law. Consider judgments of members of the legal institution in ways that portray them as racists, sexists, and domineering. They may invoke or provoke the most negative opinions and ideologies of the law of any land. Indeed, there are probably no means that are more efficient, entertaining, and pleasurable for the presentations of series of thoughts about unfairness and injustices in the legal system than comedy. Comedy is incorporated in music, film, and many venues. Buis (2014, p. 330) writes:

> Women are also given in comedy an unusual legal personality. In the "real Athens," an Athenian woman could only take part in a trial through the agency of closest male relative or kyrios (in general, her father if unmarried, husband if married, or son if widowed). In the "feminine" comedies, women assume power in environments traditionally controlled by men.

Although Harvard University and many other universities are famous for comedic performances for their graduation ceremonies. The lines and actions, which famous comics decide to utilize for creatively influencing people to laugh and applaud, appear to evade legal studies regarding investigations of the law. There is much to be learned from comedy via investigations.

David Khari Webber "Dave" Chappelle (1973-present) is an American actor, writer, and comedian who is famous for his outlandish, grotesque, and exaggerated descriptions of American society and the legal system. This includes jokes and other comedic effects of the political and policing systems and court system. Usually the presentation of members of the legal institution are incorporated in unexpected ways in his material and often are depicted as mistreating Chappelle's choice of black characters. They are represented by Mr. Chappelle via various African American vernacular English accents, and other American characters have various accents. David Chappelle's 2004 Stand-up comedy called "For What It's Worth" presents a contrast between what he calls a mistake (i.e., his own "untrained eyes" lead him to believe that Asians look alike) and people who think that all blacks look alike. Chappelle calls those people the "police."

> The only people that Asian people have beef with is other Asian people, like if you call a Korean guy Chinese. I've done this. They will flip out. (Chappelle speaks with a different accent) 'Hey, what makes you think I

> am Chinese!? I am Korean! Do I look Chinese?' Yes, motherfucker you do look Chinese. That's why I said it. It was an accident. To the untrained eye you all look Chinese to me. It was a mistake. I wasn't trying to offend you. Some people say that all blacks look alike. We don't get bent out of shape. We normally just call those people 'police,' okay? (audience laughter and applause)

What is relevant for the comedic analysis of law is that there are varying levels of laughter in terms of volume, which is measurable. There are also distinct types of laughter, such as uncontrollable laughter. The accompaniment of applause is another qualitative factor that is measurable quantitatively regarding volume. Another set of measures could include the numbers of people, races, and genders of those who laugh and clap compared with the whole crowd. Scientific analyses would most likely be directed toward reactions of audiences and signals, especially regarding language and actions of performers. Chappelle (ibid.) continues to perform:

> Just learn to live with it. That's all I can tell you. Everybody's afraid of police,—scared to death of these police. I am nigga. I got a police scanner with the first money I got. It's the first shit I went out and bought—bought me a police scanner. I just listened to these motherfuckers before I go out—just to make sure everything is cool. You hear shit on it. (Chappelle speaks while cuffing the microphone) "Calling all cars, calling all cars be on the lookout for a black male between four (foot) seven and six (foot) eight." (Audience laughter) Staying in the crib tonight. Fuck that. (laughter) Gotta work on that alibi for a minute. (laughter)

Chappelle uses many hyperboles with which many of his audience members can identify perhaps regarding their own exaggerations about members of the legal institution. This may be the case when they have friends and family members who are also afraid of police or believe they need alibis. Chappelle says:

> Every black person needs an alibi. I do those impromptu though. If I'm by myself and need an out, I'll just open up the windows in the apartment and turn all the lights on, start beating off right in the window. Look at me! (light laughter increasing intensity) Hey everybody, look! It's me. Dave Chappelle, crazy. I'm jerking off. Note the time motherfuckers. It's 2:35. Look at me. I'm jerking off in the window. Comedian, Dave Chappelle. It's June tenth. Note the time! (laughter)

Chappelle need not directly describe the fact that there are lopsided numbers of black people in the US who are falsely accused, arrested and incarcerated to the extent that blacks suffer more than other racial groups in certain respects. He need not mention that the acts of the criminal justice system are best scrutinized for accountability. The hyperbole that "every black person needs an alibi" demonstrates indirectly that black people tend to have greater fears of being falsely accused of crimes and tend to be falsely accused more often. Chappelle continues:

> That shit could save my life. (Chappelle speaks with another accent) 'Officer, Dave Chappelle couldn't have done that. I saw him in his window masturbating from 2:35 to 2:37. (laughter) I'm certain of it. He was standing on a clock and holding a calendar and today's paper.' (laughter and light applause)

In the latter half of his performance, Chappelle makes a comparison between three fifteen-year-olds and a seven-year-old. Chappelle argues that the American people are really undecided about whether fifteen years of age is an age of innocence or not. He compares the case of the kidnapping of Elisabeth Smart who was fifteen and submissive to her captors to the thirteen-year-old, Lionel Tate. Lionel Tate performed a wrestling move on his neighbor. He had seen the move on TV. Chappelle calls attention to the court case of Lionel Tate who was sentenced to life in prison at the age of thirteen for the indictment of first degree murder. Chappelle (ibid.) maintains:

> I know I sound mean, and I know what people are thinking when I'm saying this. Dave, she is only fifteen. Alright, but that's the discrepancy because when you talk about a little girl, like Elisabeth Smart, then the country feels like fifteen is so young and so innocent.

Mr. Chappelle uses the case of Elisabeth Smart who was held by her kidnappers for about six months to compare the similar ages of the adolescents.

> On the flipside, here comes fifteen again. Now, we're talking about a fifteen-year-old black kid in Florida. This black kid accidently killed his neighbor who was practicing wrestling moves that he saw on TV. Now, was he a kid? No. They gave him life. They always try our fifteen-year-olds as adults.

The latter statements of Chappelle are serious accusations and focus on ongoing social problems. In 2000, Chapelle says the following in a comedic acting performance called "Killing Them Softly":

> One thing that I'm seeing—you'll be walkin' down the street, and you'll see like a group of black dudes walkin'- Not just any ole black dudes. We're talkin,' you know, thugs. (laughter) We're talkin,' you know, there'll be some thugs. In the group they've got like one or two—sometimes as many as three white guys will be with them. Have you ever seen that shit? (audience laughter)

Chappelle utilizes observational humor to illustrate that even violent delinquents regularly accept other racial groups in their own groups and respect them as members. Chappelle suggests that under such circumstances the group consisting mostly of violent black men can benefit from the presence of even more violent white men in their group. They are useful because of their interactions with law enforcement agents. Chappelle (ibid.) claims:

> Let me tell you something about those white guys. (laughter) Those white guys are the most dangerous mother fuckers in those groups. (laughter and applause) It's true. It's true man. It ain't no tellin' what they've done to get them black dude's respect. (laughter) Well, them black dudes have seen them do some wild shit. I'll tell you that. (laughter) I've been trying to tell brothers that. Every group of brothers should have at least one white guy in it. (laughter) I'm serious—for safety. (laughter) 'Cause when the shit goes down someone's gonna need to talk to the police. (laughter and applause)

David Chappelle proceeds to explain some cultural facts about blacks in America to the extent that they have greater fears of police, which is a fact that is supported by social dominance research (Sidanius & Pratto, 1999b, pp. 220–221). Chappelle (ibid.) jokingly says:

> I mean that's when that white friend comes in handy. Uh oh, Ernie, Ernie, do you wanna get this one? Come on. Come on now. Do something. You see black people are very afraid of the police. That is a big part of our culture. (audience clapping) It don't matter how rich you are—how old you are? (clapping and yelling) We just afraid of them. We've got every reason to be afraid of them.

Chappelle continues to explain the racial differences in the perceptions and emotions of the police by sharing a hyperbole with a person of a different race than his, a white lady. Chappelle exclaims:

> (Dave Chappelle looks at a person in the audience) You know what I mean, like you're a white lady. Have you ever been pulled over before? You know. What they say? Let me see your driver's license and your registration, right? See. See. I'm just guessing. (laughter and light clapping) That's not what they say to us. (laughter) You wouldn't believe what they say to us. (shouting audience member) Spread your cheeks, and lick your sack. (laughter and applause)

Trevor Noah is a former actor and radio disc jockey who performs comedy around the world. He was born on February 20, 1984. His mother is South African with heritage from Xhosa people. His father is Swiss from the German-speaking area of Switzerland. In 2013, Trevor Noah performed some stand-up comedy in South Africa called "It's My Culture" in which he gave the following performance:

> We're driving through Lusaka, the capital, and Ali looks over at me in the car and he goes, "Trevor, you know here in Zambia we're a very God-loving nation, huh?" I said, "Oh okay Ali, that's a good thing to know." (speaking with perhaps a Zambian accent) "Yes. So, while you are here, don't be gay." (audience laughter) I said, "What?" He said, "I know it can be tempting sometimes, but don't do it. Don't be gay." (speaking with comedian's usual accent) Don't be gay? I've never been warned of this in my life. Don't be gay? (Using a different accent) "Hey bro, don't be gay. Don't be gay." (Trevor's accent) Don't be gay? Crazy!

Mr. Noah utilizes comedy to demonstrate how communications of the legal system are communicated to tourists by people who work in the transportation industry. Noah (ibid.) continues:

> Crazy warning skits, but then I found out why Ali was warning me. It turns out that in Zambia being gay is illegal. If you are found to be gay, you will be arrested and sent to prison for more than thirty years, yeah which is a bit of a weird punishment (confused facial expression by Noah and audience applause) when you think about it. (laughter) … I couldn't believe this. Gay is a crime in Zambia, which got me thinking, if gay is a

> crime, that means the police have to monitor it. They actually have to police gay.

Trevor Noah shows the absurdity in the practice of the utilizing the policing for such nonviolent behaviors that coincide with sexual activity in private. Behaviors associated with homosexuality have been severely criminalized in Zambia.

> Yeah, which means that in their police force, they have a gay division. (laughter) It's a crime. It's a crime. So, that means they've got a murder unit, got a robbery unit, got a White Collar Crime Unit, and then they've got a Gay Unit, huh? (laughter) Yeah, they've got a little G Unit in their police force (laughter) that's responsible for all things gay. (laughter) That must be the most fun police force to be in in the world. (laughter) You get to go undercover, dress really nice, get in touch with your flamboyant side, have a good time. (laughter)

Margaret Cho is a female Korean American comedian from San Francisco. She is outspoken about lesbian, gay, bisexual, and transgender rights, has won several humanitarian awards, and has a background in acting, singing, song writing and fashion design. In Cho's stand-up comedy called "Beautiful" on July 3, 2009, she comically inquired and informed her audience in Long Beach, California that:

> Why is that people in Washington who are elected to create laws governing our sex lives—Why are they the unsexiest people in the world? Like the guy who heads the FDA board on reproductive drugs—He's the guy named Dr. David Hager—unsexy? He actually counsels women who suffer from PMS to read the Bible. (laughter) Oh, he is a special kind of asshole. (laughter and clapping).

Many articles have been written about the accusation that David Hager repeatedly raped his wife while she slept and had the condition of narcolepsy. Ms. Cho (ibid.) continues to describe legal issues involving the gynecologist, David Hager:

> So, he's in a big divorce with his wife. She is divorcing him, and she is suing him for having anal sex with her while she was sleeping. (loudness of laughter increases, then decreases and increases again) I know, and I am

> such a light sleeper. (very loud laughter) I'm like what kind of mattress do you have? (very loud laughter) Was there a full glass of red wine next to you that didn't spill? (loud laughter) You didn't wake up at all. (laughter)

The previous excerpts serve as pieces of analyzable material concerning the law, members of the legal institution, but especially the social acceptability and unacceptability concerning the law and the actions of its members. The video and audio footage involve genuine audience members' responses of uncontrollable laughter, yelling, screaming, clapping, and crying. They reveal much about what people think and what surprises people. The disgust, anger, sadness, contempt, surprise, joy, and perhaps even fear are all present in the performances.

The law is a very common variable in comedy. It is worthwhile to consider that the comedy represented here is representative of a particular perspective and that other comedians present very different outlooks. Before an inquiry can intelligently be answered about why law is so common in comedy, it is far better to provide objective measurements of observational data. Thus, the analysts and scientists who seek knowledge about how people think about the law may consider focusing upon the correlations between the legal content of the comics, the types of reactions, and the reaction times and intensities. More audio and video footage can be utilized to discover what audiences think about the law by observing audiences and comedians alike.

12 Measurements and Observations Concerning the Comedic Level of Analysis of Law

There is much potential for the science of comedy. Observable and measurable factors that are verifiable through audio and video recording technologies include: Lengths of time of individuals laughing, their gazing behaviors with focus upon the presenters of comedy about the law, the lengths of times of the audiences laughing, booing, and applauding, and the auditory volumes of the laughter, booing, and applauses. Observations for legal research and comedy include observations of those behaviors of comics and observations of members of their audiences. Audience members' behaviors can be subdivided into their proximities to the comic performing and audio or video output devices.

Multiple observational focal points can provide easily distinguishable and measurable units. This allow for the collection of data that is analyzable via inferential statistics. For instance, a unit of measurement for comedy with legal material may be the smile. It is largely analyzable via video equipment, although some smiles can be covered by the hands. This may provide another unit of measurement (i.e., covering the face with a hand or two). The length of time of each smile in relation to the comedic material about the law may provide an analyst with revealing sociological data. It could enable researchers to better understand the acceptance of law, lawmakers, verdicts in courts of law, and intolerance of the latter issues.

Contexts of comedy about the law are important. Contexts can be associated with several types of units of measurement (e.g., the loudness and length of time of audiences standing up and clapping). Contexts can also serve as units of measurement. Contexts concerning comedy of law include police and their roles in racial discrimination, judges, verdicts, celebrations after verdicts are publicized (e.g., the O.J. Simpson verdict and celebrations of black people in Los Angeles). Contexts concern behaviors of politicians (e.g., the denial of President Clinton that he had sexual relations with Monica Lewinski), and crimes (e.g., admitting to violating the law and police, judges, and politicians breaking the law and receiving special treatment for their relations to the law, and frivolous lawsuits). The comedian, Dave Chappelle in the last section includes all the latter content in his comedy routines.

Contexts of comedy about the law are associated with the aforementioned measurable units. Contexts serve as measurable units themselves regarding lengths of time the legal content is presented, the number of words on the legal subject matter, etc.

Reactions to comedy of law are multifarious because of various other factors, including sounds of different accents, dialects and foreign languages, hyperboles, metaphors, irony, sarcasm, and other insincere forms of speech. Body language, miming, impersonations, coordinated acts, acting in uncoordinated ways, laughing, and smiling contribute to presentations of comedy of law. They impact procedures of measuring. Measurements still work without measuring the latter contributing factors to the associations between the content and context of the comic material about law and the behaviors of laughing, smiling, booing, and applauses.

Measurements of humor need not always involve audiences with whom comedians, cartoon characters, etc. have identifiably similar senses of humor. Failed attempts to make intended audiences laugh and applaud are relevant to the comedic level of analysis. The comedic analysis of law is also necessary for enlightening us about legal ideology. It may serve as a way of associating emotional reactions of audience members to material about law. It may introduce practical solutions to valuable concerns, like the law's dual role in the reduction of violence and threats and implementations of them.

CHAPTER 4

Psychosociological Relations of Law

1 Leadership Characterizes Successful Terrorizers as "Cowards": Upsides and Downsides

In 1983, US President Ronald Reagan responded to the bombing of the US embassy in Beirut, Lebanon by claiming that the terrorists involved were "cowardly." Fifteen years later President William Clinton maintained that the terrorists in both Dar es Salaam, Tanzania and Nairobi, Kenya were "cowardly." Probably the most impactful usage of the term that describes terrorists with the vice of "cowardliness" was spoken by President George W. Bush concerning the attacks of September 11, 2001.[1]

Studies have demonstrated that individuals' perceptions of authority figures as legitimate ones tend to increase the likelihood of individuals' voluntary acceptances of the figure's decisions and obedience to rules that such figures make (Tyler & Lind, 1992; Tyler, 2006b). People will also support their leaders with system justificatory behaviors. In an oppositional response to President Bush, the political satirist, Bill Maher, on the television series *Politically Incorrect* on September 17, 2001 maintained, contrary to the latter three presidents and agreeing with his guest, Dinesh D'Souza, that:

> We have been the cowards, lobbing cruise missiles from two thousand miles away. That's cowardly. Staying in the airplane when it hits the building, say what you want about it. It's not cowardly.

Bill Maher lost most of the funding for his program for making the latter comments and was persuaded to apologize on the network (Bohlen, 2001). Maher's comments and oppositional defiance against the nationalistic American ideology, which peaked shortly after the September attacks, provide perhaps partial reasons why Maher's nine-year long program terminated just months later. Bill Maher's September 17, 2001 assessment of motivational factors and determination of each terrorist appears to be more accurate because the September

1 Scholars of criminology and violence have argued that since there are focuses during certain times on certain types of violent groups or types of situations of violence, other types of violent groups and situational violent acts are less likely to occur during those times because they lack motivation to act to get heightened infamy. So, school shooting rates decreased during the years following the September 11th attacks and the terrorism scare, likely, because of the decrease in the potential for inflating the importance of school terrorizers.

 | DOI:10.1163/9789004385955_006

hijackers were not fearful cowards. It undermined the assertion of the president at the height of the American populace's elevated level of system justificatory behaviors and presented dangerous levels of backlashes. This included stirred emotions, death threats, and other risks.

The more one perceives oneself to be dependent on systems in which one lives, the more one feels that the world is more unpredictable and uncontrollable, which is what increases the motivation to justify and defend these systems, hierarchies, and governments, according to Laurin, Sheperd, and Kay (2010), van der Toorn et al. (2014), and many others. The American people likely considered the hijackings and attacks to be both unpredictable and uncontrollable. They likely felt dependent on societal systems in which they lived. So, one fair assumption is that their motivations to justify and defend their systems amplified. This led to disdain and ridicule against anyone who spoke out against the president or any other government official with enough perceived legitimacy.

Mistaking those who intentionally perform violent attacks as "cowards" appears dangerous. Cowards are submissive to threats and violence. Those who are less cowardly are also less submissive. It is questionable whether dubbing attackers as cowards has been intentionally deceptive. Mistaking individuals or groups as being "fearful" or "cowardly" seems to involve misunderstandings of their goal-directed behaviors, beliefs, desires, and expectations.

Misrecognitions of fears would lead misrecognizers to presume that groups or individuals will, or would, respond to threats and dangers via forfeiting their goals. Misidentifications and misrecognitions, concerning cowardliness, seem to impede the accuracy of predictions of future behaviors. They are important predictions because they facilitate preventions of violence.

One alarming fact is: In experimental conditions, those individuals who identify themselves as dominant as opposed to submissive tend to act in more domineering ways. They overemphasize their views of themselves when others inform them that they are submissive rather than dominant (Burke & Stets, 2009). Vice versa is also true. Individuals who identify themselves as submissive but who are labeled by others as being "dominant" tend to act in more submissive ways in response.

The suggestion here is that calling terrorists "cowards" probably increases danger. They would, hypothetically, act out in more domineering ways via overemphasizing their views of themselves by recklessly acting. These reckless acts are heroic or courageous acts, according to their ideology. They may successfully attempt more often to reach their goals, despite obstacles.

Whether terrorists have overemphasized their reckless, domineering, and destructive behaviors based on the latter factors that contribute to the productions of meanings (i.e., remaining consistent with their standards of their own identities) is worthy of much further consideration. This is true for reducing numbers of provocative mass media messages ideologically evaluating identities of so-called terrorists. Burke and Stets (2009, p. 72) write about the experimental results measuring the functions of social identity, dominance, and submissiveness:

> Those who saw themselves as dominant but were told they were submissive acted in a very dominant fashion, even more than the dominant persons who received self-consistent feedback. Those who saw themselves as submissive but were told they appeared dominant acted in a more submissive fashion than the submissive persons who received consistent feedback. Thus, in each case, those with discrepant feedback acted in a manner that overemphasized their self-view. Overall, then, for these participants, we see them acting to manipulate the meanings in the situation.

Participants in the experimentation of Burke and Stets (ibid.) denied and refuted false claims that confederates of the experiment made about them when claims were about their false identities as dominant (or submissive) people. They additionally acted in more dominant ways (or even more submissive ways), presumably, based on the mistaken identification they were given. Increases in behaviors that they were falsely described as lacking may be viewed as the participants' attempts to reverse descriptions attributed to them so that new descriptions would consistently coincide with their self-identities. This occurred via the dominant participants, who were described as "submissive," increasing their behaviors exhibiting dominance.

Likewise, submissive persons, who were described as "dominant," increased their behaviors exhibiting subordination. All participants with self-identities, which were different from descriptions given to them, accounted for these inconsistencies via acting more dominantly or more submissively than earlier. Results are based on the opposite characterization, given by others, of the characterization they self-identify. Opposite characterizations are provocative.

Applying the latter social psychology experimentation about dominance and submissiveness to sociological observations of violent groups appears straightforward, especially if we consider that the output of messages from the mass media and politicians about cowardliness (i.e., the mistaken identifications) are interconnected with the future motivations of the violent groups. Basically, the theory of false descriptions of the submissive of dominant people can well be hypothesized to be closely associated with the theory of false descriptions of the cowardly terrorists. So, the sorts of descriptions that the US presidents, Reagan, Clinton, and Bush are viewable as provocations of more violence. The mass media systems' roles should also not be underestimated.

Some researchers maintain that the mass media outlets' messages contribute to increased amounts of terrorism, which is explained via the theory of the self-fulfilling prophecy (Zulaika, 2009). The predictions by the mass media that violence and terror will continue to be wrought by some terrorists or that there is an elevated level of danger of terrorism can lead people to act like they are in states of crisis. False descriptions of the circumstances can lead to new behaviors that appear to render the original conception of the circumstances as being true. So, people have tendencies to believe the original predictions were correct. The mass media outlets can surely facilitate the increase in the amount of terrorism via the dual nature of the historically significant events, too (See Ch. 3.9). Zulaika (2009, p. 1) thereby maintains that "[c]ounterterrorism has become self-fulfilling, and it is now pivotal in *promoting* terrorism."

It is questionable why the relationship between the role of terrorism and cowardice or the characterization of terrorists as cowards is as strong as it is, at least, within significant amounts of mass communication rhetoric connecting these concepts. Undoubtedly, such messages take on an enhanced amount of significance when they are broadcast on television by extremely influential politicians. Around the world, watching television is the most popular activity for leisure time (Kubey & Csikszentmihalyi, 1990; Harris, 2004, p. 1). Politics is the most often viewed form of news content, comprising approximately twenty-five to forty percent of news stories within China, Columbia, Germany, India, Italy, Japan, Russia, and the United States (Straubhaar et al., 1992; Harris, 2004, p. 229).

There are, doubtlessly, different uses of the terms for the vice of cowardliness, which we may consider for the interpretations of mass media messages. For instance, a man who assaults a child can easily be called a "coward." However, calling one who beats a child a "coward" appears to presume that the man would refrain from assaulting another man of a more or less equal physique because he would be afraid to do so, but the latter presumption can certainly be a false one.

The misattribution of cowardice to the man who engages in assault, even who assaults children, may lead others to focus upon the judgment of his character as a cowardly one, which is false, rather than focusing on the possibilities that the child knows things that the man does not want anyone else to know, for instance (i.e., since the child is in the position to know more about the victimization as the victim). That is, the man may not want anyone to know the explanation for the man's violent outburst. The violence may have resulted from either the impulsivity of the man or, contrarily, from an appraisal of the situational variables and emotional response to the child's actions or the presence of the child after the man considers his lowered social status, reduction of power, or lower self-confidence. The violent treatment could also be habitual, though. If the child relinquishes the information to others, the man's social status, power, and confidence may reduce. There appears to be no benefit in the description of the man as a "cowardly one," though.

The attribution of cowardice to people who assault those who are unable to defend themselves might be thought of as an attempt to reduce the aggressive and abhorrent type of behavior via associating it with fearfulness that coincides with cowardliness, but such thoughts are ideological and idealistic at best. The synonyms of cowardice could be descriptively used as an insult against one who hits a child and thereby serve as a positive punishment, decreasing the likelihood that the man will hit children in the future.

However, the meaning of the latter type of attribution of cowardliness does not appear to provide the reason why US presidents and others make such attributions to whom they call "terrorists," though.

The three American presidents appeared, rather, to attribute cowardliness to the style of the attack performed by the attackers and hijackers. The attackers directly engage in the violence via secretly and repeatedly attacking, retreating, and gradually weakening the stronghold of the opposition while testing the borders and extent of its security. Otherwise, the use of the insult of cowardice might be used to encourage additional aggression, which would likely be impulsive, reckless, and prone to mistakes. That is, additional aggression could be provoked from the terrorists as a means of identifying them once the law enforcement, military, and other agencies are ready.

The above-quoted evidence suggests that describing the fearless, reckless, and courageous people as being "cowards" will result in those people acting in ways that exhibit the opposite of cowardice. The latter tendency perhaps occurs as a sort of compensation for their mistaken identities since one's identity of self is intersubjectively formed because of third parties' judgments and treatments of the person. From a cognitive dissonance theoretical perspective, the amount of time, effort, or money expended by the individuals on fearless, reckless, and courageous endeavors (or at least thoughts, expectations, and desires about themselves behaving in such manners), may be crucial as parts of the formations of their self-identities, and the latter factors may lead to greater psychological tensions when others describe them as "cowards." Actions tend to be taken by certain individuals to reduce the psychological tensions, to support the former characterizations they gave themselves, and to thereby publicly reconfirm their self-identities somehow as far from cowardly.

Those who believe that they are described falsely as "cowards" may act in more intrepid ways based on the insecurities that arise with the attacks against their fragile identifications of themselves, especially if they are people who demand attention from others who reconfirm the desired descriptions of them. What is questionable are the differences between their behaviors in social groups of strangers, including those who they believe they will interact with in the future and those who they believe they will likely never see again, and social groups with which they are familiar.

This latter point is important in relation to circles of friends, family members, coworkers, and within other human environments with which people often spend their time. It behooves researchers, therefore, to provide experimental conditions with groups of friends, groups of family members, and groups of coworkers for better understanding the social interactions and the attributions of such mischaracterizations of the individual within each type of the latter groups, respectively, sociologically and psychologically observing and analyzing. These are methodological requirements for attaining knowledge from the realm of the psychosociological levels of analysis.

Sometimes thinking of the methods in sciences, the conditions required with unknowing experimental subjects, and the like are sufficient to guide our understandings of the matters for the formations of worthwhile hypotheses. At present, the concern is extracting the evidence from the slightly relevant descriptions of the social sciences and applying the evidence to the most important aspect of law, the intercommunications of the legal system, and violence. The concern is whether the actions of the mass media system broadcasting incongruent descriptions of "terrorists" (i.e., incongruent with their own self-identifications) spoken by some of the most impactful leaders during the late 20th and early 21st century were actions that promote peace, actions that were by and large neutral, or actions that provoke more violence.

In the latter cases of the three US presidents' addresses to the American people, the vice of cowardice was unreasonably attributed to terrorists since terrorists are better described as reckless, desperate, and likely vengeful rather than cowardly because they were determined to accomplish their objectives, they overcame their fears, and ignored dangerous obstacles to accomplish the violent September attacks. In 2001, the terrorists successfully met most of their intended goals since three of their four hijacked planes were crashed into the two World Trade Center towers and the Pentagon, starting off the American experience during the new millennium with a state of emergency on the very day and month that are represented as the numbers for calling American emergency services (i.e., 911 calls are made for police, fire fighter, and ambulance services), and the date of the occurrence as written by Americans is "9/11" or 9/11/01.

The latter sort of description and reasons, which would explain why the terrorists and their directors performed such destructiveness, would obviously result in very different public reactions toward the presidential messages, if the presidents had instead broadcasted the destructiveness as being caused by reckless, desperate, and vengeful people rather than cowards. Firstly, the individuals of the populace would likely agree with the attribution of recklessness to the hijackers but raise public inquiries why the hijackers or planners were described as being desperate and vengeful. However, the attributions of desperation to the hijackers via mass media outlets may have been considered as a potential means for increasing the amount of sympathy for the hijackers as desperate men with families. The hijackers' families probably attained a sufficient amount of financial support from the group responsible for the planning of the September 11th destructive mass murders.

Any attributions of vengefulness to the hijackers by the mass media may likely lead to lines of questions that presume that some social group or individuals are responsible for provoking the attacks and that they have reasons for seeking revenge. However, people who are regularly exposed to the mass media images and words generally do not act reasonably during such times of crisis, they search for answers from leaders who, apparently, automatically are perceived with peaking amounts of increased legitimacy, and the people may encounter emotional barriers that hinder their intellectual capacities to raise intelligible inquiries.

It is doubtful that describing the violent and destructive people as "vengeful" would likely reduce the overall amount of patriotic and nationalistic behaviors of the populace. Perhaps the description of vengefulness being broadcast by the mass media instead would lead to more serious political disputes. It is doubtful also that there would be an increased tendency to face violent confrontations within the populace after such a description after the attacks, unless the reasons for revenge are directly related to the politicians in power.

Research shows that individuals are motivated to reinforce and defend their social arrangements as well as to view the social systems in which they live as just and fair ones in relation to others (Jost, Banaji & Nosek, 2004). The latter individuals who offer psychological support or justifications for some system intensify their supports and justifications when either threats are made against their system, the system is undermined, the individuals perceive the system as being inevitable, or the individuals think they are controlled by the system or believe they are dependent on it (van der Toorn, et al., 2011; Jost & van der Toorn, 2012).

The virtue of bravery or courageousness is often misunderstood as being the polar opposite of cowardice. However, cowardice is typically viewed by virtue scholars as a deficiency of the virtue of bravery, whereas the excessive amount of the virtue of bravery (i.e., the opposite of cowardice at the far end) is recklessness, like the fire fighter who rushes into a burning building without his protective gear or the police officer who hastily arrives at a gunfight and refuses to take the time to put on a bullet-proof vest.

The attributions of cowardliness and other vices that are really misattributed to those who wreak devastation certainly increase the overall amount of ideology and increase the amount of disrespect by the international community concerning leaders who deceptively or falsely describe the culprits and their actions. Moreover, the use of deception by leading politicians likely exacerbates the problem of increasing cynicism toward government officials and the society's ways of life.

On the other hand, misattributing cowardice to an entire social group may lead other groups to believe that the cowardly social group can more easily be defeated or beaten in competition. So, there is a practicality in the misattributions of cowardliness to some extent. The practicality probably resides in the propagandizing of those who will be selected and some who will be used for counter-terrorism. That is, perhaps more people would be willing to sign up for military service with successful propaganda that asserts the "enemies" are cowards. The branches of militaries are then better able to select from those who can be unhesitant in following the general plans of the command.

Cowardliness involves fearfulness, which involves a lack of determination of the will of the coward to accomplish his or her desired goal. Courageousness and bravery involve the individual's determination to perform the act, which perseveres, despite the emergence of fear. Courage is also generally viewed as a moderate character trait, whereas cowardice is a deficiency of courage and moderation. Contrarily, recklessness is excessiveness in relation to courage and exceeds the upper limits of moderation because recklessness involves surpassing dangerous obstacles haphazardly and thoughtlessly, paying no attention to risks or fears. Recklessness entails the steady determination of the will of the individual to complete some goal, despite the risks, and involves both a lack of rational fear and lack of a moderate amount of attention to dangers. Thus, reckless individuals, much like suicide bombers, tend to die or become injured more often during their reckless activities.

The 9–11 hijackers demonstrated a suicidal reckless abandonment of their own lives, which should neither be mistaken for cowardliness nor courageousness. The hijackers were unwaveringly determined to meet their goals (i.e., unlike cowards) and lacked a moderate amount of attention toward dangers (i.e., unlike the courageous). Courageous individuals are more thoughtful than reckless ones at least concerning the acts in question.

The goal-directed behaviors of reckless people sometimes tend to involve less realistic desires since their beliefs and expectations about achieving their goals tend to lack the incorporation of the dangers arising from the obstacles they must confront to accomplish their goals. Alternatively, the reckless individuals may tend to act impulsively like the common archetype of the career criminal. However, it is also possible that recklessness does not fittingly describe the hijackers of the planes.

Since there is general agreement that the 9–11 hijackers implemented a strategically planned attack, they are typically not considered impulsive. That might be a false assumption in some of the nineteen individual's particular cases. Thus, there has been much accord concerning the explanations that the hijackers believed in an afterlife. They may have believed they would be martyrs for their organization's cause. However, the latter explanations may not convincingly account for the fact that the hijackers realized that most of the members of their organization, contributing to the cause of the catastrophe, would not be required to sacrifice their own lives. Those who are chosen by the planners of terrorism (i.e., to wreak massive destruction and mass murders) might very well be a mixture of desperate individuals who need protection and finances for their direct families, individuals who support the cause and who have been diagnosed with untreatable cancer or other illnesses, suicidal people who support the cause, and individuals who have been successfully indoctrinated religiously, politically, legally, economically, militarily, etc.

The coward is one who often fails to achieve goals because fear interferes with the coward's decision-making process, thereby preventing the coward's volition from determining the coward's desired performances. What the coward wants to occur tends not to happen because of his or her fearfulness and lack of determination of the will when the coward considers the risks and since the performance requires some degree of courage and willpower, which all cowards lack to some degree.

Cowardliness sometimes involves the indecisiveness of the individual, concerning the performance of an action, or the hesitation of the individual to act as the individual desires to act because one's recognitions of risks that arise. The recognitions and focuses on risks allow fear to emanate, to increase, to tend to lead the individual to reevaluate potential consequences as well as to increase considerations of alternative forms of action. Considerations of alternative forms of action tend to alter the intentions of individuals to act because individuals become more undecided about what they realistically want to occur and thereby alterations of goal-directed behaviors are made more frequently, which involve cognitive processes that incorporate strategies to reduce risks or dangers, even if the same goal is sought after.

The misrecognitions of groups, or of an individual, as being "cowardly" is akin to either denying that they remain steadfast when they attempt to achieve their goals, despite their fears, or the judgments involve overlooking their fearlessness in addition to their determination, resolution, or firmness of their purposes as well as their lack of attention to risks and dangers concerning their unwavering attempts to accomplish their goals. Typically, as a positively attributed character trait, "courageousness" involves desired goals that should be accomplished and that are performed, whereas "cowardliness" involves objectives that should have been performed but were not performed, and "recklessness" involves goals that are unlikely to be completed but are sometimes, despite risks. Moreover, the successful completion of goals takes place less frequently with those who exhibit recklessness than bravery.

In general, those who identify themselves with terrorists (e.g., those who aid or embed them or simply have like-minded goals) will tend to judge terrorists as if the terrorists are brave and courageous individuals. The terrorists demonstrate their willpower to accomplish their goals despite their fears. However, those who identify terrorists as opponents or members of out-groups would more accurately judge terrorists as reckless. They are heedless, showing a lack of regard for the dangerous consequences, and carelessness for innocent bystanders.

An organized terroristic group obviously implements secretive strategies, concealments of their own behaviors, possessions, and identities. They escape detection once they have attempted to perform some destructive act against another group considered their "out-group." Since terroristic acts are performed by social groups, which plan and implement strategies, requiring the avoidance of detection, secrecy or hidden behaviors, terroristic group members who run away from law enforcement agents cannot accurately be described as "cowards." The evasion from detection involves acting on behalf of their devious strategies.

For an individual's behaviors to be accurately described, accompaniments of accurate descriptions of the social context and groups with which one identifies oneself are required. This typically involves peer pressures, crowd behaviors, motivational influences of groups and potential threats and punishments for divergent behaviors against the groups' main interests. Considering the social contexts and groups, it is conceivable that some of the September 11th terrorists feared the wrath of their own organization (e.g., violently torturing and murdering them or their family members and friends).

The previous analysis of the character traits, virtues and vices (e.g., bravery, cowardice, and recklessness) is opposed to some of the research that maintains there is no evidence that people have such character traits. Research suggests that situational variables are more important (Harman, 1999). It is perhaps best to consider the analysis of the character traits in relation to the public perceptions of them and directions that the mass media thereby leads audiences.

Some of the hijackers may have acted against their own individual interests but in favor of the interests of their family. In this latter and specific sense, terrorists may indeed be viewed by some as "cowards" because they would be unable to perform certain desired actions because of their fears. However, if the hijackers are viewed as "cowards" in this context, they would also be consistently characterized as being loyal to friends and family members. Hijackers would be characterized as determined to prevent the terroristic organization from retaliating against their friends and families.

Possible solutions to problems that mischaracterizations give may focus on behaviors of planners rather than character traits of the deceased hijackers. Focusing on planners and others who were responsible for the destruction and mass murders should undermine their moral integrity and status. Their integrity is best undermined by their own standards, too. Describing planners as displaying recklessness for their own cause may feasibly lead to the risk that the planners will plan their future attacks more diligently. Displaying that they murdered other Muslims and Arabs would be one way to start the undermining of the moral structure of the social group. The idea is that the planners would be rightfully identified as morally inferior.

Instead, however, the US government reacted to the situation by placing travel bans on the Muslim family members of the victims who were not allowed to fly to see their loved ones' memorial services. The travel bans were reactionary and thoughtless political moves. In fact, the video and audio footage of Muslims and Arabs visiting the victims could have been utilized by the mass media system to broadcast the images and words that would certainly be a better attempt at demoralizing the relevant social group of the attackers, if there had not been travel bans on the family members.

We may learn from the methods of civil rights activists how to destabilize the power structure of the opposition via demonstrating that the opposition is morally inferior in accordance with their own moral standards (See Ch. 2.3).

The attempt to bring some of the people over to the other side by systematically weakening their motivations to murder can be accomplished by describing the attackers properly and carefully selecting the extent of their group's image with which they are most likely to disagree. According to this philosophy, the latter methods are ideal for reducing violence in comparison to the propagandizing and implementing threats, which may create a form of counter-terrorism that promotes violence.

2 Ways and Reasons of Propagandizing for the Retaliatory Society: Brave Heroes versus Villainous Cowards

One obvious psychosociological relation of people to the law involves the initial influence of the broadcast of political messages via the mass media system about being under attack. Thereafter, the applications and enrollments of people to serve in the police academies and branches of the military tend to increase. Insecurities wrought by means of political messages often result in increased time and efforts of audiences watching TV or utilizing other sources of information. Increased efforts and insecurities of people are quite obvious during political messages broadcasted to briefly describe incidents of intentional destructions (e.g., the Oklahoma City bombing by Timothy McVeigh and Terry Nichols in 1995 or the Nigerian massacre by Boko Haram in Baga during January 2015), unless the incidents are perceived as being isolated ones after the culprits are captured. The efforts include psychological tensions, such as increases in anger, disgust, contempt, hatred, sadness, surprise, and vengeful thoughts.

The psychological feeling of security ordinarily requires that one knows about one's circumstances and surroundings to some extent, yet one may feel safe without actually being safe, of course. The broadcast of any type of destructive or violent event, which is still unknown to the media's audience member, greatly increases the probability that the viewer or observer will seek more information about the incident, its causes, impacts, and about whether more similarly destructive events will happen in the near and relevant future and proximity. When individuals do not know the status of their localities' securities or believe that the status of the security of their family, friends, neighbors, fellow countrymen, etc. is endangered, then psychological tensions or cognitive dissonance arise, and individuals are thereby motivated to assuage the tensions and reduce the feelings of insecurity they undergo. There are thereby increases in those motivated to join the armed forces, clandestine agencies, and other security forces.

Individuals are inevitably faced with a dilemma, which is either to flee from what one perceives as a problematic situation of some place and to arrive at a different location (i.e., either known or suspected to have less danger), or, alternatively, one engages in the physical struggle to attain some level of security, to reduce others' insecurities with whom one identifies oneself, or to increase the insecurities of the oppositional forces, at least. Situations of emergency and relevant political messages call for individuals to "stand their grounds," in a manner of speaking, to protect what the people have as a collective group. They call on them to restore levels of security to a status that surpasses what it was before the event occurred.

Stabilizing societal expectations concerning security, compensations, and fairness are principal functions of the legal system. Sometimes restoring the level of the psychological feeling of security to its prior state is not possible or is at least not feasible insofar as actually having security requires knowledge. Knowledge about violence within the society can destabilize societal expectations about security and prevent the return of the psychological feelings of security in the individuals. One reason for this is that the occurrence of the prior destructive event, as an unexpected one, demonstrates the lack of knowledge and forethought within some locality, of course, because there was no successful prevention of the destruction. Moreover, publicized demonstrations of knowledge, exhibits of professionalism, etc. would be required to restore the level of individuals' psychological feelings of security.

The state of security (i.e., as opposed to the psychological feeling of it) requires that the legal forces and military forces have some extent of knowledge in addition to willingness and readiness to act unhesitantly on behalf of the society. The members of the legal forces and military forces endanger the society when they lack a certain amount of knowledge about the destructive powers' relations to their society. However, members of legal and military forces can also endanger the society when they possess too much knowledge of the destructive powers' relations to their society since they may begin to form jealous affixations to members of their own society, violate their privacy rights, and increase the overall amount of the distrust in the society.[2] For example, young attractive and fertile females in society may tend to be watched by members of

2 Societies that have growing maldistributions of wealth, developing countries, and underdeveloped countries appear to be at greater risks concerning this relation of knowledge about violent groups. Of course, the members of the military and legal institution who know the most about the dominant violent group within society, which is opposed to the law, are the ones who are already members of the violent group as well as the legitimate institutions.

the legal institution more frequently as well as their potential mates. Moreover, members of legal and military forces can be compelled to join destructive groups, which has happened in Mexico where hundreds of police have been arrested after they had served drug lords while they had also retained their positions within the legal institution during the 21st century.

Without knowing the number of potential attackers, strengths, or locations of potential future attacks, the security of a populace that underwent an attack is already thoroughly compromised. Nevertheless, fears of potential future destructions or mass murders also carry reasons for weariness, reluctance, hesitation, cynicism etc. Herein lies some rational rhetoric and logic of the ideologues through propaganda. The propagandizing strategically aims to overcome as much hesitancy, cynicism, fear, and reluctance as possible via images and words from people perceived as being legitimate leaders. These perceptions of legitimacy of leaders are psychologically prompted by perceptions of the threat itself for various reasons. Some reasons are included in political psychology of system justification theory and cognitive dissonance theory.

Cognitive dissonance theory may be reformulated to explain why certain underprivileged social groups at least temporarily reverse their disapprovals for lawmakers and other leaders and decidedly approve of them instead, i.e., after these groups have already endured the unwanted time and efforts made by the leaders who were also involved before the recognition of the threat to the society, which enters a state of emergency. In the latter sort of case, the threat serves as a mutual threat against the underprivileged social groups and against the leaders who may be perceived with extra approval and legitimacy since the leaders serve the purpose of eradicating the greater threat at hand. So, during times of crisis or emergency, the members of the lower status groups temporarily approve of the leaders and hierarchy in place (i.e., as external justifications) because the leaders serve as the means to end the threat. With the greater approvals of their leaders, the psychological stress is reduced in the individuals, according to a psychosociological application of the cognitive dissonance theory.

The latter explanation for the actual increase in the approval ratings of leaders (e.g., approving of the work of members of congress or parliament, heads and chiefs of state, police, court systems, emergency workers, etc.) can lead to very dangerous displays of power. Thus, threats and partial destructions of the society can absolutely ruin legal systems. For instance, during the Great Depression in the 1930s, the Germans had very high approval ratings for Chancellor Adolf Hitler who easily restored much of the land that had previously belonged to Germany and attained approval for invading many neighboring countries and for waging war at massive levels; moreover, this occurred without a rational level of public outcry and disdain to dissuade the plans of the NAZIS (i.e., the NSDAP or *Nationalsozialistische Deutsche Arbeiterpartei*, the National Socialist German Workers' Party) during the late 1930s and early 1940s.

The public broadcast of the political message of "being under attack" avows sorrow for the dead and injured, disgust and disdain for the attackers but, most importantly, involves the labelling of the attackers with the doubly dichotomized role for the leaders of the society to advance the retaliatory efforts. The attack need not be one that occurs with military force, but rather may include hacking websites, financial or economic attacks, or the persuasive appeal to the populace that some attack has nonetheless happened (i.e., the so-called "attack" can also be a mischaracterization).

The first dichotomy within the political message about being under attack is that the attackers are given the concise, descriptive roles of "villains," which inevitably raises the question about where and who the "heroes and heroines" are. For the part of the populace, which consists of able-bodied men and women, the political message of being under attack subtly calls for the forthcoming of candidates for heroism, ready to be trained for services, for duty, for honor, for patriotism, and for justice, according to the mass psychology message. The first dichotomy also creates heroes or heroines who are sometimes given the official status of nationalistic martyrdom.[3]

A few good candidates are memorialized as heroes with the view of their deaths as exhibiting honor, bravery, strength, and determination. Yet the latter ideological status gives absolutely no individual with such a status the opportunity to behave dishonorably or unfavorably in the future since death offers the finality and permanence of heroism via the propaganda. The finality of death and process of memorialization of the dead and attributing honor to the dead can lead to individuals becoming mythologized figures of legends. Unnamed streets and buildings are given their names, and plaques and statues may be erected in their honors. President Bush's speech "Justice Will Be Done" on September 20, 2001 begins as follows:

3 It is important to note that the individuals who showed some courage are glorified, probably never acted with any idea or ideals about the nation as a whole or protecting the nation, and the propagandizing presents them as protectors of the whole nation regardless. Along with great athletes and winning national teams, they become key components of the advertising to promote the nation or nationalistic ideology. The ideologies of nationalists are relatively recent and probably began during the early 18th century in Europe and increased because of reactions of people to the French Revolution. Globalization is one concept that people may use to undermine nationalistic ideologies.

> Mr. Speaker, Mr. President Pro Tempore, members of Congress, and fellow Americans, in the normal course of events, presidents come to this chamber to report on the state of the Union. Tonight, no such report is needed. It has already been delivered by the American people. We have seen it in the courage of passengers who rushed terrorists to save others on the ground. Passengers, like an exceptional man named Todd Beamer. And would you please help me welcome his wife Lisa Beamer here tonight?

A park, a high school, a post office, and a student center have all been named after Todd Beamer. Mr. Beamer posthumously received the Arthur Ashe Award for courage as did Mark Bingham, Tom Burnett, and Jeremy Glick who are all held responsible for successfully preventing Flight 93 from meeting its target for destruction and mass murders on September 11, 2001. With the role of technology, such as in-flight telephone calls, there is often less need during the 21st century to fabricate the performances in virtue of guessing who provides the most help for preventions of even graver catastrophes. The people on Flight 93 sufficiently overpowered the four hijackers on September 11th to prevent the plane from crashing into a populated area.

While the latter men probably did perform courageous actions, and respecting them as role models for such acts is ideal to the extent that they were helpful intentionally and realistically, the propagandizing focuses instead more abstractly on the ideology of the nation. The nation can then draw from its potential human resources by using and exaggerating the courageousness of a few selected people who serve the roles of advertising.

Through the propagandizing, the men who exhibited moments of courageousness at some locality become "national heroes," which is official and bureaucratically set forth. The ideology assures that they are not merely local heroes of the part of the community that was actually saved. The mass media broadcasting publicizes the excessive statuses of the men thereby advertising the ideology of the nation. The nationalistic ideology reinforces itself with the notion that the heroes helped save the whole nation. The lack of dispute of the extended use of the images and words representing "heroism" and the nation leads to common societal presumptions, which are irrationally based on the propaganda.

The political rhetoric does, indeed, give people reasons to believe that one can be recognized and memorialized for patriotically defending the national interests. The tributes to those who are officially recognized as "heroes and heroines" also increase the desires of others to place themselves in situations where they could patriotically defend the national interests, too. One hypothesis is that those who live in the areas where the bridges, streets, buildings, etc. are named after heroes are more likely to enroll in the military, law enforcement, or other similar industries in the service sector of the national economy, depending on their ages and exposures to the propaganda.

The second dichotomy is given as a political message to the people. The political message is that the culprits, lawbreakers, wrongdoers, evildoers, enemies, and villains are also "cowards." The second dichotomy reinforces the first, which is viewed as "cowardly versus courageous." The second dichotomy provides us with often well-strategized political messages about having endured the worst that the cowardly villains can do. There appears to be a tendency for the propaganda to attribute the opposite descriptions to the opposition, which may be one reason why the wordings for the opposition involve cowardice since it is opposed to the heroism of those from the society under attack.

The double dichotomy emphasizes the rhetoric of "us versus them" where we have "the brave heroes" on our side as opposed to the others' "cowardly villains." So, dichotomy-one redefines the roles of those already involved, to wit, "heroes versus villains," which remain officially and bureaucratically permanent. Dichotomy-two redefines the character traits of those same individuals, namely, "the brave versus the cowards."

The second dichotomy is by far the most ideological one since it often involves calling people, who are apparently fearless attackers, the "cowards." One reason for calling the attackers "cowards" is to repeatedly reinsure the potential hesitators on the leaders' own side that they are also meant to battle the fearful enemies who would rather flee than fight them. The propaganda maintains that the villains would rather give up their plans and goals out of trepidation.

The political strategy is interwoven within the ideological messages because the legitimized leaders strongly and unwaveringly assert that the enemies are cowards. People who waver with reluctance or motivations for evading their duties to serve the armed forces or to aid in the retaliation tend to be indoctrinated with the idea that the retaliatory efforts will be easy because the enemies are weak-minded, apprehensive, cowardly enemy combatants.

3 Real Phenomena: Energy as Legal, Alegal and Illegal Forms of Power

Energy is a fundamental ontological entity or real phenomenon for the theory of integrative levels and various classification systems (see Ch. 3.3). The form of energy concerning legal theory, legal science, and sociological relations is called "power." Bertrand Russell (1948, p. 10) maintains:

> [T]he fundamental concept in social science is Power, in the same sense in which Energy is the fundamental concept in physics. Like energy, power has many forms, such as wealth, armaments, civil authority, influence on opinion. No one of these can be regarded as subordinate to any other, and there is no one form from which others are derivative. The attempt to treat one form of power, say wealth, in isolation, can only be partially successful, just as the study of one form of energy will be defective at certain points, unless other forms are taken into account.

Bertrand Russell (ibid., p. 12) continues:

> Power, like energy, must be regarded as continually passing from one of its forms into any other, and it should be the business of social science to seek the laws of such transformations. The attempt to isolate any one form of power, more especially, in our day, the economic form, has been, and still is, a source of errors of great practical importance.

There are difficulties of accounting for the social hierarchies and changes of individuals' statuses within them from low to high or vice versa. Such accounts concern the independence between the actual social hierarchies and where any particular individual desires to be placed within social hierarchies. The sadist and the masochist may, for instance, be similarly ranked within many relevant social hierarchies within a society, community, church, mosque, or synagogue, and corporation during their first year together at the same company.

However, the sadist may exert power over the masochist via producing her intended effects, whereas the masochist may allow and want this to happen, undergoing humiliation and subordination, yet simultaneously producing the intended effects. Despite both of them achieving their desired goals in certain respects, the sadist may rise within the company hierarchy, relinquish social relations with the aforementioned masochist, and achieve many other aspirations, including early retirement, financial goals, having more children, and providing them with greater opportunities to increase their socio-economic statuses as well.

System justification theory ascertains that human motivations are in many instances directed toward the support, justification, and defense of the status quo. Under certain conditions this involves people holding such favorable attitudes toward the overarching social order that their attitudes more greatly favor their systems than their social groups and themselves. System justifications, defenses, and supports supplied by a populace can override their particular social group's justifications, defenses and supports as well as override the defense and support of their own needs for their own personal safety.

A more comprehensive definition of "power" hereinafter focuses not only upon the intended effects but also on the placement within real social hierarchies. Power for an individual is the instantiation of his or her realistically intended consequences in addition to one either retaining the same social status overall or increasing the social standings within one or more of the social hierarchies, to which he or she is placed in relation to others in some ranking orders. Power is defined as more than attaining what one wants, especially if what one wants is realistic or even unrealistic and if what one wants is actually harmful to the individual.

The person who plays the lottery for millions of dollars and who wins also achieves the production of an intended effect because, of course, one typically does not play to lose. The attainment of power is realized through the increase of the person's socio-economic status. Other increases in power are also possible, especially if the lottery winner works as a fortune teller or psychic. This may increase the social standings of the individual within that field as a so-called accurate predictor of the future, according to certain social groups.

In China during the 21st century, the industry of teaching English as a second language has allowed many native English speakers to legally enter China with work visas and employment contracts that allow them to make approximately five to ten times the amount of the average salary of Chinese citizenry within multiple cities. English language instructors in China may earn less than their American or Europeans counterparts. The instructors may have greater opportunities to purchase more goods, travel more, and be ranked higher in respect to social status within the Chinese society than their counterparts are ranked in other societies.

Even merely describing the hierarchical relations of an individual is complicated. Comparing an individual in China with his or her educational background, work experience, etc. to someone else within a different society but with an otherwise very similar educational background and work experience is vexing. Sometimes, however, sociological data is accumulated and allows for measurable units to form based on observations, which permit comparative analyses.

One form of isolation of power is soft power versus hard power. Soft power can be cultural warfare via the implementation of ideas and their representations as opposed to hard power, which can be military warfare via the implementation of violence with weaponry and usages of threats to wield against adversaries to sway them via coercion.

4 Soft Power and Hard Power

To reduce violence by means of systematically understanding opposing ideologies, the usage of different sorts of power better be first understood. During the 21st century, the challenge to identify social groups with clandestine systems of communications, which terrorize and aim to support certain political, religious, or cultural agendas etc., is problematic. These social groups largely utilize hard power for attacks and a combination of hard and soft power for recruitment.

The ideas of hard power and soft power might well be applied to the problem with terrorists and extremists. Some extremists identify themselves with Islam, other religious groups, racial groups, or political groups.

Hard power involves not only the physical destructions by means of bombings, shootings, knifings, strangulations, arrests, interrogations, financial penalizations, searching people, etc. but also the implementations of threats of violence to coerce others into obedience. Imposing soft power against one's adversary is far subtler than the implementation of hard power.

Soft power is implemented via replacing the values, understandings, norms, traditions, customs, and ways of thinking with alternatives, for instance. Soft power can be implemented quite abrasively via seductions as well as the desecrations of revered and sacred objects and via disrespecting beliefs or desires of another social group. Soft power can be implemented ever more subtly via the replacement of these glorified objects, beliefs, and desires with alternatives, especially if the alternative objects, beliefs, and desires increase the perceived likelihood that greater numbers of opportunities will arise for the people who replace their sets of beliefs and desires as well as replace the revered objects with other objects that are honored by a more dominant social group, such as the beliefs in the education system of France in northern Africa (See Ch. 2.2).

Many 21st century legal systems fail to fairly and justly protect the reverence and sanctity of objects or possessions, unless there are distinguishable characteristics about the object that may somehow relate to the price of the object, such as the age (e.g., stolen antiques sometimes bring harsher penalties than newer commodities). Holy books, however, have undergone relatively drastic changes regarding their statuses as sanctified objects within many 20th and 21st century courts of law in developed countries, or, at least, the extent to which a certain object is honored with a sacred status is both uncertain and likely differs quite greatly from one judge and jury to the next (Nordland, 2012).

The status of the consecrated object, such as the *Holy Bible*, is baffling because in one case an individual may be allowed to urinate on or burn the *Bible* in accordance with law and under the protection of the law insofar as the law defends one's right to treat one's own possession this way via the amendment that protects one's freedom of speech, religion, etc. (e.g., the first amendment of the Constitution in the USA). On the other hand, one may also be required to "solemnly swear" with one's hand upon the Bible before providing some official testimony, which may even be presumed to provide the court of law with more truthful attestations. The refusal to take such an oath may also be interpreted as a disobedience or an act of defiance against some system, which is a system that jurors, jurists, or judges may support. Moreover, in some legal systems holy books have been used for the affirmations that individuals will tell the truth, all the relevant truths, and nothing else, except for the truth via the religious oaths with the accompaniment of sacred books.

What is the importance of soft power concerning the formations of understandings about violence and how to reduce violence? In many instances, terrorists implement attacks with hard power against those who attack their social groups via the usage of soft power. In certain situations, the implementation of soft power against a social group leads to even more violent attacks against their adversaries via the use of hard power than the use of hard power against the social group prompts them to react.

The fact that the use of soft power, even inadvertently, against another group can lead to extremely violent reactions has been duly noted by militaries in Afghanistan. Militaries in Afghanistan during the 21st century have witnessed intransigent, blood-sickening reactions toward them after their disrespectful treatments and destructions of Islamic holy books (Holmes, 2012). Afghans have responded with extreme violence that is often reckless regarding their utter disregard for their own safety and lives.

One may conclude that we live in a globalizing world with hundreds of countries displaying nationalism via the soft power coming from mass media broadcasts and cultural wars. If one compares the Afghani group's response of hard power because of the usage of soft power against them and compares the usage of hard power against the same group, one is confronted with what appear to be a disproportionate, reactionary responses. For instance, the wrongful killings of several Afghan people may result in less violent reactions from others in their social groups than the desecrations of their holy books, which are replaceable with holy books containing the same content.

We see the imposition of soft power utilized against various social groups, especially through the use of images and words that undermine, disrespect, and propose alternative sets to their sets of systematic and ideological beliefs held by members of the social groups. During the 21st century, Danish, French, and other political cartoonists have published works that may be well-interpreted as disrespectful toward Islam, such as focusing upon the hypocrisy of Muslim extremism and on the usage of hard power wrought by the extremists against those who undermine their customs, clothing, religious beliefs, etc. That is, these cartoonists from developed countries have been wielding soft power against Muslims and Arabs.

Soft power can be incredibly subtle and lead multitudes to fail to consider multiple crucial factors regarding historic events. Hollywood film production companies are major world producers that continuously wield soft power, too. One interesting film displaying the realization of Hollywood's soft power, which portrays the United States government during the mid-20th century, is "Guilty By Suspicion," which illustrates the intolerance of many governmental officials toward communistic ideologies.

Consider Hollywood's portrayal of the bombings of Pearl Harbor on December 7, 1941 by the Japanese. The portrayal of the event generally depicts the Japanese military as completely unprovoked by the USA and yet totally belligerent toward the USA. The entertaining productions use soft power that aims to fortify the moral stature of the US government and its actions during World War II while simultaneously weakening the moral structure of the enemy combatants.

The US had already used hard power against the Japanese before 1941, though. The American bank accounts of Japanese citizens were frozen, Japanese people in America were placed into internment camps, and sanctions against Japan were upheld before Pearl Harbor and the US base in Guam were struck. It is important to understand that restoring the ideologically given status of a strong moral character to the USA was especially important after the obliteration of Nagasaki and Hiroshima during the summer of 1945 by US bombers.

The uses of soft power contributed to the process of the restoration of the ideology that the USA has a high moral standing amongst nations. The hard power imposed by the US government replaced the Japanese legal system with an entirely new constitution, but soft power changed Japanese legal ideologies. The soft power was used in combination with the subordination of the

Japanese (i.e., via hard power), and the soft power implemented against the Japanese still lingers during the 21st century via multiple sources for outputs of ideology, such as nationalistic and patriotic ones.

What we are confronted with concerning soft power is a much more complicated set of multi-layered approaches through advertising, testing, experimenting, persuading, seducing, and overshadowing the sets of ideals, beliefs, desires, motivations, etc. with many sorts of goods and services. Soft power is too complex to analyze separately from hard power and requires massive efforts to reveal the underlying assumptions and historical reasons for the ideologies it creates, replaces, and attacks. As we have seen, especially with the violent responses (i.e., implementations of hard power) against the use of soft power, soft power is crucial to understand for deriving valuable solutions to the enduring problem of how to reduce violence.

5 Psychosociological Analyses Concerning Law: Reasons for Greater Fears

Fear is a fundamental emotion. It can be recognized in many of the behaviors of people and other species. Fear may promote many rapid reactions.

Prolonged fears in society can lead to massive social unrest and prolonged violence. In societies, we may hypothesize that lower status groups tend to have greater fears than higher status groups.

Additionally, the fears may take two different forms or a combination of them, such as more or less intense fears when one is extremely afraid or slightly afraid or startled and when one has more or less prolonged fears, which is when one is scared on a daily or weekly basis versus a monthly or yearly basis, for instance. Fear may lead one to avoid leaving the house or office.

Fear can involve one refraining from going out at night or at various times during the day. Fear can impact the behavior of the individual who interacts with his or her social group. With fear, one may refrain from traveling around the neighborhood, city, country, or to other nations, unless one is accompanied by one or more people.

Fear can ruin the real opportunities that individuals have in the world for careers and all the facets of life. Fear impacts the heartrate, blood pressure, digestion, and many other aspects of the human organism, preventing higher levels of intelligence and decision-making when the fear is intense enough. It is thus important to understand what the research on fear suggests about the people in the society, what the research evidently suggests about the legal system, criminal justice system, and members of the legal institution, such as law enforcement members, in relation to the fear they instill in people, threats of violence, and implementations of violence that they produce largely during their service hours toward certain groups, to wit, the lower status groups of the society.

The psychological and ethological study of fear has many forms, including the "flight or fight response," which has become an adage. The facial expression of fear is also a major focal point for comparative studies of cognitions of race, sex, age, and species, especially visual cognitions. The expression of fear can be worn in ways that are far more expressive than the most flamboyant clothing, yet Bestelmeyer et al. (2010, pp. 13–14) write:

> Adaptation to angry faces of one race and fearful faces of the other race simultaneously caused faces of the first race to appear less angry and faces of the other race to appear less fearful in the postadaptation test than in the preadaptation test.

Imagine that a society consists of higher status groups of people (e.g., based on race) who display facial expressions of anger toward members of a lower status group (e.g., based on race) within society and that the lower status group members display more facial expressions of fear in response. The latter findings by the team of scientists would suggest, sociologically speaking, that the groups would be less prone to noticing the negative emotions of anger and fear and perhaps, under the changing circumstances of economic declines and other obstacles societies undergo, the negative emotions could be expressed in more extreme forms, leading to increases in violence and destruction.

The latter thought-experiment, however, does not mention any history of the enslavement, oppression, struggle for human rights, or the attainment of social equality from a legal perspective, which all gradually take away the legal rights of the dominant group to own slaves, to oppress the subordinate group, and finally to do things that the lower status group is not legally permitted to do. However, the instilling of fear in the others is a form of oppression. Bestelmeyer et al. (ibid.) continue:

> These findings complement previous findings for race contingent aftereffects following adaptation to faces that had been varied on feature spacing (Jaquet et al., 2007; Little et al., 2008), since we observed race-contingent aftereffects following adaptation to faces differing in facial expressions. Our findings also complement previous studies of expression aftereffects

(Hsu & Young, 2004; Webster et al., 2004) by demonstrating that adaptation to expressions can bias subsequent expression perception.

The highest rates at which individuals report having greater fears of the police are expressed in reports of surveys by low-status groups. Low-status group members' reports of relatively more fears are hypothesized to be directly related to the proportionately higher amounts of threats, arrests, and violence used against low-status groups. Much research concludes that threats, arrests, and violence by the police occur proportionately more often than they do for higher status groups (Sidanius & Pratto, 1999b, pp. 220–221). The fact that the poorer socio-economic classes and other low-status groups report "more fear of the police" on average than high-status groups report it, if given surveys, is confirming evidence for the theory of social dominance. Social dominance theory maintains that there are higher rates of searches, arrests, excessive uses of violence, and convictions of lower status group members with greater frequencies and intensities (i.e., greater likelihoods to receive the maximum penalties) in proportion to their population size in the society.

According to Dr. John Lamberth (Harris, 1999), who represented the American Civil Liberties Union in a court of law, 5,741 motor vehicles and their passengers were the focus of a rolling survey study. The study consisted of observations of the driving behaviors, vehicles, and the identifications of the races of the drivers during an approximately forty-two-hour period. The study maintained that the observations of 5,741 people allowed for the verifiable identification of 96.8 percent of the racial identities of the drivers of the vehicles. The number of white drivers totaled 4,341, which was about 75.6 percent of the total number of drivers, and the number of black drivers was shown to amount to 16.9 percent.

The analysis of the observations showed that 5,354 drivers violated the traffic laws during the observation period. Thus, approximately 93.3 percent of the drivers were legally allowed to be stopped and questioned by the State Police of Maryland. The number of lawbreakers determined by the study were 74.7 percent white people, and 17.5 percent were black people. This data thus very strongly suggested that there was very little discrepancy regarding the race of the driver and the likelihood that the driver would violate some traffic law.

However, from January 1995 until September 1996 the reports given by the Maryland State Police showed that 823 motorists north of Baltimore on Interstate 95 were searched. 600 of the people searched, which is about 72.9 percent, were black people. 661, which is approximately 80.3 percent, were either Hispanic, black, or other members of a racial minority group. The number of white drivers who were searched amounted to only 19.7 percent. 646 of the searches, or about 85.4 percent, were performed by the same thirteen state troopers.

The evidence examined within the statistical analysis very strongly suggests that the racial discrimination negatively impacted black motorists and other minorities because of the law enforcement agents' behaviors upon Interstate 95 in Maryland. The initial forty-two hour study was used to demonstrate with a statistically significant sample (i.e., 5,741 drivers) that the majority of drivers violate some legal code at some point while they drive (i.e., 93.3%), and race can easily be determined within the vast majority of cases (i.e., 96.8%). The study illustrates how many violators are black (i.e., 17.5%) and white (i.e., 74.7%) at a specific time on the highway to compare the statistics in accordance with the law enforcement statistics.

The law enforcement statistics illustrate that there is a tendency to search minority groups disproportionately more than whites (i.e., regarding their population sizes). Whites within the study were searched only 19.7% of the time, despite the much greater probability that any given violation of the law was performed by an individual who is white regarding the conclusions of the analysis of the forty-two-hour observational study.

Such sociological studies offer supportive evidence for the theories that maintain there is a tendency for the law enforcement and criminal justice systems to systematically refrain from stopping, searching, and penalizing higher status group members with the same frequency of other groups. Simultaneously, such analyses offer support for theories that ascertain that there is a systematic tendency to stop, search, and penalize lower status group members more often in respect to the proportion of their population sizes (Harris, 1999).

Subordinate social groups within legal systems are treated fundamentally differently than other groups and sometimes are fundamental for key transitions to legislation to happen. Generally, subordinate social groups are easily recognizable because their national population is historically overrepresented within the nation's prison system at hand, according to social dominance theorists. Their fears of law enforcement are greater, and they tend to lack trust in the procedures of the criminal justice system more often than other groups.

These low-status groups include blacks in the US, aborigines in Australia, Arabs in Israel, and foreigners in Greece, Spain, and Holland during the early 21st century, for instance. The latter peoples make up a relatively small percentage of the population within each of those countries at large, i.e., in comparison to other social groups, but nevertheless they compose an excessively high percentage of each country's prison population in comparison to the other social groups. According to Leung, Woolley, Tremblay, and Vitaro (2005, 289–290) in respect to the United States:

> Some people are more likely to be convicted of a crime than others. Men, those of African descent, aboriginals, the economically disadvantaged and the mentally ill are convicted of more crimes than are women, whites, the affluent and the mentally healthy (Carrington, 1998; Chesney-Lind and Sheldon, 1998; Harris, 1999; Jernigan, 2000; Rowe et al., 1995; Weitzer, 1996). There is wide-spread agreement on facts. For example, in the US, a young African-American male is more likely to spend time in jail than go to college (Weitzer, 1996; Wordes and Bynum, 1995).

Statistics concerning the expression of social inequalities within the United States illustrate social conditions and inequalities worsened for African Americans, the poor, Native Americans and those with mental disorders during the last decades of the 20th and the beginning of the 21st century. Roughly half the world's prison incarceration population is in the United States, China and Russia, which suggests that these societies that dominate the world in certain respects also dominate their own low-status groups.

The World Prison Population List provides the numbers of people held in 223 prison systems around the world. According to Roy Walmsley (2016, pp. 2 & 14), the data available demonstrates that there were 10.35 million prisoners around the world on October 31, 2015 when the world was estimated to have about 7.2 billion people. This shows an increase in the world prison population by approximately 1.7 million people since 2000 when the world was estimated to have a human population size of about 6.1 billion.

The prison population of the Americas was 3.78 million on the same date in 2015, and the Americas contained a human population size of approximately 977 million. The United States contains a prison population of more than 2.2 million people, which means that US prison facilities contain well over twenty percent of all the prisoners in the world, despite having a population of less than 350 million inhabitants, according to Walmsley (2016) and the World Prison Brief. Walmsley (ibid., p. 2) maintains:

> Since about the year 2000 the world prison population total has grown by almost 20%, which is slightly above the estimated 18% increase in the world's general population over the same period. The total prison population in Oceania has increased by almost 60% and that in the Americas by over 40%; in Europe, by contrast, the total prison population has decreased by 21%. The European figure reflects large falls in prison populations in Russia and in central and eastern Europe.

The Russian Federation has tremendously decreased its prison population from 1.06 million prisoners in 2000 to 0.642 million prisoners as of October 1, 2015, and Russia has had a decrease of about 417,934 prisoners or about 40% (ibid., p. 12). Walmsley (ibid., p. 2) continues:

> In the Americas, the prison population has increased by 14% in the USA, by over 80% in central American countries and by 145% in South American countries. The female prison population total has increased by 50% since about 2000, while the equivalent figure for the male prison population is 18%. The female total has increased proportionately more than the male total in every continent. Consequently, the proportion of women and girls in the total world prison population has risen from 5.4% in about 2000 to 6.8% in the latest figures available.

Most of the incarceration is handled within government-run prison systems, yet companies are beginning to prosper and to handle minimum, medium, and maximum-security prisons, detention centers, mental health centers as well as centers for immigrants, such as the GEO Group, Inc. in Australia, North America, South Africa, and the United Kingdom.

Drastic changes in the United States prison system with the incorporation of privatizations of prisons has taken place quite recently. The rise of corporate systems handling the incarcerations of the US population mostly involves two companies, namely, the Corrections Corporation of America (now CoreCivic) and Group 4 Securicor, which became the second largest employer in the world with well over half a million employees in the 21st century. Since the 1970s, the United States legal system transitioned from having a government-run set of prisons that handled prisoners to a system that grants contracts to privately owned prisons that allow profit-making for shareholders to enter this highly important aspect of the legal system.

The result of corporate incarceration is a system of profit-making for shareholders from increased amounts of bondage. The bondage is largely the bondage of black people since companies have realized that young black men and adolescents both have less chances of winning lawsuits against the corporations and have lower tendencies to file lawsuits against the corporations because they have less trust in the US penal system for criminal justice than other age groups and racial groups of the population.

Lobbyists act to influence political decisions in respect to the creation of laws. International companies providing privately owned prisons, the Corrections Corporation of America, and GEO Group, had, respectively, 179 state lobbyists and 63 state lobbyists from 2003 through 2010, which greatly affected the 2004 US Presidential election since the final decision was determined in

Florida where the Corrections Corporation of America and GEO Group had 30 lobbyists (Ashton & Petteruti, 2011, p. 25). The federal lobbying total expenditures of GEO and Corrections Corporation of America for 2004 was over $3 million, and more funding was donated to the United States Republican Party, which narrowly won the presidential election with George W. Bush in 2004 (Ashton & Petteruti, 2011, pp. 24–25). According to The GEO Group (Vargas-Vargas, 2005, p. 41):

> We typically refrain from pursuing contracts that we do not believe will yield attractive profit margins in relation to the associated operational risks. For example, *we have avoided* operating certain juvenile and female correctional facilities which we believe may be prone to increased operational difficulties that may result in increased litigation, higher personnel costs and *reduced profitability*.

The latter practices of avoiding admittance of certain types of people are enhancing factors of social hierarchies within the society because those admitted based on their physical descriptions (e.g., race, age, and sex) are given systematic disadvantages within the societal system, regardless of the crimes committed, which is, respectively, racist, ageist, and sexist, in accordance with social dominance theory. Alarmingly, many corporations have realized that the decriminalization of nonviolent crimes and any reductions of the rates of crime within the society would have negative impacts upon these corporations' abilities to attain profit because these corporations produce goods and services for criminals.

Thus, corporations and shareholders have interests in maintaining or even increasing the criminalization, illegalization, and imprisonment processes within society, and, of course, when they act in ways that support their latter interests, this has negative impacts upon the society which thereby increases the social hierarchy enhancing factors. Communities can also develop and form great dependencies on the local prison for jobs and other economic benefits for the surrounding businesses. The GEO Group (ibid., p. 42) continues:

> [A]ny changes regarding the decriminalization of drugs and controlled substances or a loosening of immigration laws could affect the number of persons arrested, convicted, sentenced and incarcerated, thereby potentially reducing demand for correctional facilities to house them. Similarly, reductions in crime rates could lead to reductions in arrests, convictions and sentences requiring incarceration at correctional facilities.

With such a system in place, the United States has placed itself at great risks for even higher rates of incarcerations, which are already amongst the highest in the world, as well as record rates of convictions, etc. because there are vested interests in the increases in imprisonment, which really needs to be a public rather than a private service. As private services, the prisons rely entirely on the high crime rates, conviction rates, and incarceration rates for profit, and they may attempt to increase the latter rates for their businesses. For example, if groups from other nations are interested in the decline of the American society via having the society increase its incarceration rates to even more than the record highs, they could easily invest in the stock corporations that profit from incarceration, which would allow lobbying to increase their chances of gaining support from winning politicians who would allow increases in incarceration. These private prison corporations are thus detrimental to the American society as well as others.

Another alarming aspect of the privatization of prisons in America is that black "[m]ales between 18 and 24 years of age demonstrated the highest propensity for criminal behavior and the highest rates of arrest, conviction, and incarceration," according to the Corrections Corporation of America (Vargas-Vargas, 2005, p. 41). Such corporations have financial incentives for supporting measures that increase crime rates so that their facilities will receive more criminals. In the United States and the United Kingdom, the criminal justice systems have witnessed the increase of punishment-based policies with "zero-tolerance" policing, 'three-strikes' sentencing, registrations of sex offenders, and curfews for youth with the increases in the public-private partnerships between the governments and private prisons (Jones & Newburn, 2005). Advantages exist for criminals under the age of eighteen as well as females within the criminal justice system. The greatest disadvantages are for young adult black males.

In the USA, greater disadvantages for young adult black males occur because of increasing corporate profitability from government contracts that pay for each day of the housing of convicted criminals. Additionally, losing profits from lawsuits is minimized because the incarcerated groups are less likely to win lawsuits for several obvious reasons, including the lack of education, resources to fund a good defense attorney, and, of course, racism. The US Department of Justice (Bonczar, 2003, p. 1) states that:

> About 1 in 3 black males, 1 in 6 Hispanic males, and 1 in 17 white males are expected to go to prison during their lifetime, if current incarceration rates remain unchanged. For women, the chances of going to prison were

> 6 times greater in 2001 (1.8%) than in 1974 (0.3%); for men, the chances of going to prison were over 3 times greater in 2001 (11.3%) than in 1974 (3.6%).

The latter data is restricted to state and federal prisons rather than private prisons (Bonczar, 2003, p. 11). Such restrictions of information provided by the US Department of Justice of the criminal justice system contribute to misconceptions that can exacerbate problems of inequality. The theory of social dominance focuses on the development of a system of thought that demonstrates the ways in which group-based social hierarchies are maintained and developed. This can enlighten us in respect to the reasons, extents, and give us ideas for workable solutions to the problem of social inequality. Any interpretation of the latter statistics provides us reasons to explain why black people fear police more in America. This is represented in comedy and in music (See Ch. 3.11 & Ch. 1.3). Pratto, Sidanius, and Levin (2006, p. 272) write:

> Unlike most other theories of prejudice, stereotypes, and discrimination in social psychology (e.g., realistic group conflict theory, social identity theory, self-categorisation theory, stereotype content model), social dominance theory assumes that we must understand the processes producing and maintaining prejudice and discrimination at multiple levels of analysis, including cultural ideologies and policies, institutional practices, relations of individuals to others inside and outside their groups, the psychological predispositions of individuals, and the interaction between the evolved psychologies of men and women (e.g., Pratto, 1999; Sidanius, 1993; Sidanius & Pratto, 1999; Sidanius, Pratto, van Laar, & Levin, 2004).

Social dominance theorists also discuss the ways in which multiple processes function at distinct levels with each other to yield systemic effects since social dominance theory upholds that societies of humans are systems. Social dominance theory, cognitive dissonance theory, social identity theory, and system justification theory are all sociological and psychological theories, theories of motivation, theories of perceptual cognition, and theories of desires and beliefs. First and foremost, the latter theories and self-fulfilling prophecy theory are theories of perceptual cognition. As theories of perceptual cognition, they require and presume ways and types of real and unreal phenomena that individuals perceive and cognitively process.

Social dominance theory contains a psychological theory of perception and cognition. With this theory, the hypothesis is established that the individual perceives and recognizes oneself, one's social group, and others' social groups as being hierarchically ranked from high to low. This is based on their relational statuses within the society via numerous instances of dominations and subordinations. The dominations and subordinations are power relations involving both hard power and soft power.

Cognitive dissonance theory is a psychological theory of perception and cognition. The hypothesis is generated from cognitive dissonance theory that the individual perceives and recognizes real and unreal phenomena and perceives stress, anguish, or psychological tension (i.e., cognitive dissonance). There is cognitive dissonance when certain relevant types of inconsistencies arise in thought.

System justification theory is also a psychological theory that hypothesizes that the individual perceives and recognizes oneself, one's own social groups, and the system in which one and one's social groups as well as others are situated and altogether form the status quo. Other systems are cognitively perceived via various means, such as numerous media outlets, especially if an opposing system threatens one's system.

Social identity theory is a psychological theory of perception and cognition as well, with which the hypothesis maintains that one perceives and recognizes oneself within social groups as what gives one a social identity as opposed to the perception and recognition of deviance that coincides with being socially excluded or outcast. The individual is argued to have a self-concept that is partially derived from the individual's perception that he or she belongs within some relevant social group (Tajfel, 1978). Social identity theory includes many assumptions that are largely presumed to be major contributing factors within social dominance theory and system justification theory (Burke & Stets, 2009, pp. 69–73). The perception of the various statuses of social groups, the perception of the stability and legitimacy of their statuses, and perceptions of movements from a certain social group to another one are aspects of social identity theory utilized by social dominance theorists (Burke & Stets, 2009).

As a theory of motivation, system justification theory maintains that an individual's motivation to justify, support, and defend the status quo (i.e., system justificatory behavior) can take priority over one's motivations to support and protect oneself (i.e., ego justification) as well as override one's motivations to support and defend the social group (i.e., group justification) of which one is a member. Moreover, the fact that system justifications sometimes supersede both group justifications and ego justifications has led researchers to find, observe, and measure the situational variables that lead to vast numbers of people supporting systems, especially during emergency situations, in which the systems themselves are perceived as being threatened, in ways that can result in great costs to individuals and their social groups thereby lending support to the systems, which may suppress or oppress these very individuals.

As a theory of motivation, system justification theory is a psychological theory, which may indeed allow an observer to describe and explain the behaviors of an individual within a group and a system differently from the behaviors of the others, especially if the individual was reared and lives within a system that he or she perceives to be in danger, and the other group members come from entirely different systems (e.g., the individual comes from a jurisdiction within the political and economic systems of the US and the others are from China but belong to some common social group).

One theory of motivation, from which system justification theory developed, is cognitive dissonance theory, which maintains that the desires and beliefs of individuals are greatly affected by the prior and forthcoming expenditures of time, effort, or money upon some given task (Lee & Schwarz, 2010). Cognitive dissonance theory ascertains that when a person expends time, effort, or money on a task, psychological tension (i.e., dissonance) arises, which will naturally and typically be assuaged.

According to cognitive dissonance theory, while reducing psychological tension, the individual forms either an internal or external justification for his or her expenditures on the task. Cognitive dissonance is the mental stressfulness that an individual undergoes when he or she realizes at least two of his or her ideas, beliefs, values, or desires conflict with each other or when his or her view contains a contradiction (Festinger, 1957). Whether cognitive dissonance theory and system justification theory can be combined to generate hypotheses that can test and confirm both theories is a worthwhile inquiry to contribute to changes or progress to both theoretic frameworks.

Perhaps system justification theory can assert consistently that humans have motivations to sacrifice time, energy, or money for the attempt to support the systems in which they live. One may thus treat both theories as psychological or sociological theories regarding distinct levels of observations and analyses. Theories of motivation interplay with theories of emotion. Expending time, energy, or money on some item or activity can either bring great frustration or extraordinary joy. The support of a system, such as the political or legal system, can also lead to opposite-ended emotional states. The important emotional and motivational cues for maintaining peace, order, and reducing violence are worthy of consideration in the latter respects.

Schachter's theory of emotion is often cited to maintain that when violence comes from anger and angry aggressiveness, anger and angry aggression are derived from a twofold source of excitation and cognition (Schachter, 1964; Nisbett & Schachter, 1966). Berkowitz (1974) maintains that impulsive aggression can come about as a result of undergoing pain, which regularly leads to reactions that are apparently immediate, like reflexes (Zillman, 1988, p. 53). Lazarus (1966) focused upon the processes involved with coping with various psychological stresses and maintains that that aggression need not be impulsive since it can involve appraisals, may be attenuated by means of considerations of morality, sympathy, and forgiveness.

Moreover, aggression may assume different forms within human environments. The latter form is probably most relevant to at least some of the associations we make about those who perform the violent destructions of terrorism because terrorism is, theoretically speaking, generally planned rather than impulsive. Zillman (1988, p. 53) maintains:

> Moral considerations, for instance, are capable of liberating extreme agonistic emotions. Recognition of having suffered an injustice is a uniquely human form of endangerment. Actions by others are seen as unwarranted and, therefore, as hostile attempts to lower power, status, or self-esteem. A secure, just world is in jeopardy, for example, when colleagues get salary raises that they do not seem to deserve; and those who assess matters in these terms experience agony and fury to a degree that would be difficult to produce by physical pain and minor injury.

The reassurance of the focus and duty of legal systems to be fair and just is crucial, especially when people perceive that their standards of living are decreasing in relation to those around them. The perception that standards of living are decreasing is a growing problem that the worldwide internet connections have exacerbated. The focuses on fairness and justice need to be systematic and procedural to attain the greatest mutual benefits (Tyler et al., 1997). The realm of morality, moral reasoning, moral judgments, and the like are necessary means in order for legal systems to advance to stages at which procedural justice and fairness are norms.

Not every individual is capable of remaining consistent regarding his or her moral reasoning. Most people are, indeed, inconsistent to some degrees regarding applying the moral principles that they claim to uphold.

The newly emerging discipline of moral psychology consists of many studies that support current political parties. We might well maintain that the discipline has been diluted with investigations of phenomena that may best be described as concerning emotional states, such as disgust, surprise, anger, and contempt, rather than moral phenomena such that concern the system of moral values of being morally right and morally wrong, moral permissibility, and moral impermissibility. Moreover, while it may be easy to attain information about people's alleged moral values on issues that concern things that surprise, disgust, and anger people, the ease with which the data is collected and the lack of thoughtfulness which the experimental subjects place into their evaluations may allow us to question whether the experiments and survey methods are really testing moral evaluations at all.

6 Moral Psychology: Problems Concerning Models' Combinations of Multi-leveled Observations

The social intuitionist model has become a dominant model within the field of moral psychology over the last decade. Many social intuitionist models presume certain philosophical stances, e.g., moral subjectivism, moral skepticism, and determinism. Social intuitionists suggest that the ability to make moral decisions via free will is absent.

The role of moral psychology appears to be growing during the 21st century and often involves many ideas that contribute to particular political stances and which are important for the roles of members of the legal institution. The following sections describe the social intuitionist model and explain why advocates of social intuitionism lean toward the philosophical stances subjectivism, skepticism, and determinism in respect to morality. Moreover, the importance of such philosophical stances for legal studies and juridical verdicts within courts of law and judgments made during mediations is illustrated.

It is argued that the social intuitionist model fails to provide a workable model that incorporates the range of moral judgments, moral reasoning, morality, planning, and control as well as what social cognitive psychologists call "theory of mind" within the field of moral psychology. The social intuitionist model confronts a widespread problem. Multiple levels of observation are utilized by the model to explain phenomena that require a level of analysis from which conclusions, which are drawn from distinct levels of observation and which require computational neuroscience, are unable to innovatively influence. Moreover, the overall importance of a focus upon the moral dimension via the levels of observation and analysis in the fields of psychology and sociology can contribute significantly to legal decision-making.

7 Introduction to Moral Psychology

Moral psychology is a relatively new subdiscipline of psychology and is multidisciplinary. Moral psychology involves fields as diverse as learning and memory, developmental, abnormal and social psychology, philosophy, history, linguistics, biology, anthropology, cognitive neuroscience, and feminist studies. The latter fields focus upon moral psychology insofar as they concern the psychology of moral issues, ethics, and moral development as well as conditions (e.g., brain damage) that play central roles in the loss of moral reasoning or moral intelligence (Doris & Stich, 2012).

As a new field of study and line of experimental research, moral psychology has not yet made an impact upon legal studies and legal practitioners in any significant and noticeable ways. However, some researchers in the field called "moral psychology" do observe the potential influence that their line of studies may have upon political and legal systems as well as cite political and legal books and journals (Haidt & Graham, 2007; Haidt & Hersh, 2001; Haidt et al., 2011).

8 Social Intuitionism's Role in Moral Psychology

Intuitionist research models concerning moral judgments focus primarily upon two different types of systems they claim are responsible for moral choices, namely, the "intuitive system," which is argued to be quick, automatic, and unintentional, and the "reasoning system," which is relatively slow, consciously accessible, and controllable (Bargh, 1994; Wegner & Bargh, 1998; Wegner & Wheatley, 1999).

Certain researchers argue that, despite the access and control humans have over moral reasoning, moral reasoning generally occurs after moral judgments are already made (Haidt et al. 2000; Haidt, 2001), and moral reasoning is *post hoc*, largely influenced by emotions and social influences (Sherif, 1935; Berger & Luckman, 1991; Haidt, 2001). According to Haidt (2001, 814), "[m]oral reasoning is usually an *ex post facto* process used to influence the intuitions (and hence judgments) of other people."

Thus, the role of moral reasoning is argued to be a residual effect of the intuitive moral judgment, a justification of moral judgments already decidedly made, and it is even argued to be a type of reasoning that rarely persuades others, although it is utilized, especially in social situations, to influence others' intuitions, according to Haidt (2000; 2001 & 2004). It is hypothesized that the persuasions of others via moral reasoning are new, emotionally responsive intuitions of the listener.

Haidt (2004, p. 286) gives the following definitions for "moral reasoning" and "moral intuition" after defending his stance against Saltzstein and Kasachkoff (2004) and claims that:

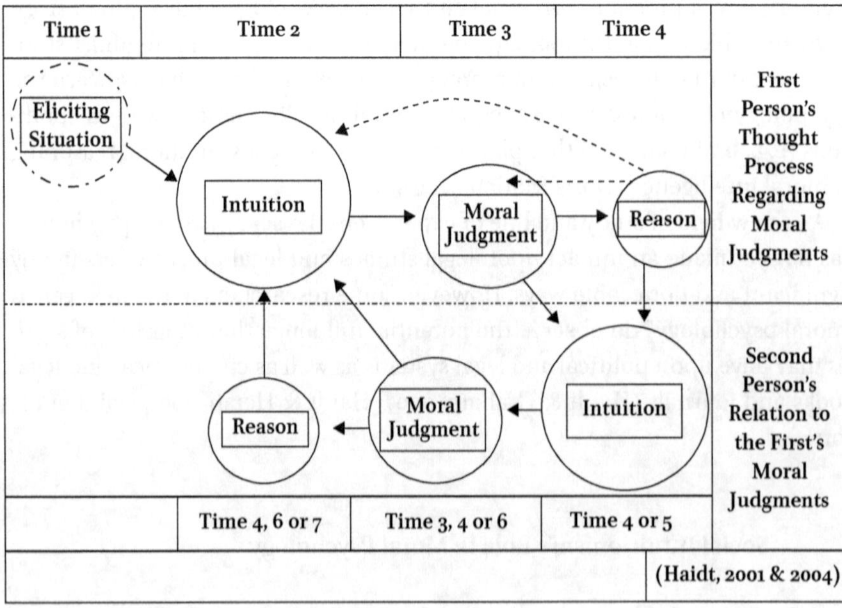

FIGURE 11 Social intuitionist model of moral decision-making

> The critical feature of reasoning is that it occurs in sequential steps, at least a few of which must be performed consciously. I defined moral reasoning as '*conscious mental activity that consists of transforming given information about people in order to reach a moral judgment*' (Haidt, 2001, p. 818). I contrasted moral reasoning with moral intuition, which I defined as '*the sudden appearance in consciousness of a moral judgment, including an affective valence (good-bad, like-dislike), without any conscious awareness of having gone through steps of search, weighing evidence, or inferring a conclusion*' (Haidt, 2001, p. 818). Reasoning and intuition are both forms of cognition.

Figure 11 illustrates Haidt's stance regarding some situation in which a moral judgment is brought about by some eliciting situation. Haidt's social intuitionist model is a model of at least two people, in which case one individual is illustrated to be influenced by another person or group, for instance. The social intuitionist model of moral judgments approximates the sequential pattern of mental processes.

Haidt (2001, 2004 & 2011) argues that the link called the "reasoned judgment link" (i.e., with the dotted line from reason to moral judgment) and the "private reflection link" (i.e., the dotted line from reason to intuition) are relatively "rare" in relation to the other links. The moral reasoning system, according to Haidt (2001, 818), is a process that "is intentional and controllable ... consciously accessible and viewable ... (and) [s]ymbol manipulation (where) thought is truth preserving." Haidt (2004, 286) writes:

> Let's look more closely at what happens when two people discuss a moral issue. If person A makes a statement and person B offers a counterargument, either of two things might happen in person A's mind. Person A might understand the counterargument, consider it against her original position, decide that the counterargument is right, and change her mind. In such a case, as long as there was "conscious mental activity" with at least two steps, I am perfectly willing to say that person A engaged in moral reasoning.

Haidt (2004) does not argue that every case of moral reasoning is post hoc, but rather he argues that the occurrence of moral reasoning outside of social interactions is post hoc the vast majority of the time because people are required to facilitate our recognitions of other people's viewpoints. Haidt (ibid., p. 287) continues:

> But let's look at another possibility. Sometimes person B responds to person A and all at once, even as person B is still talking, person A "gets" it, sees the issue in a new light, and changes her mind. Going by the terms as I just defined them, this is a perfect example of intuition, not reasoning. Person B has triggered a new intuition in person A, without person A engaging in moral reasoning for herself. Yet if we look at the dyad as a single entity, then their discussion does involve "transforming information about people" in steps.

Regarding conversations with a few people about moral issues, Haidt maintains moral reasoning is often only used post hoc to "explain" the positions that are "intuitively felt" for the conversationalists. As opposed to the aforementioned characterization of Haidt's work, one may opposingly argue it is insufficient and undesirable to merely describe the "discussion of a moral issue" regarding moral reasoning. The prescriptive aspect of moral reasoning or moral imperatives are underrepresented by Haidt (e.g., "You should not hit your sister!" and "Be fair to people of other races!"). These commands demand for people to respect freedoms of others.

Arguably, moral reasoning takes place when an individual, such as a teacher, assesses the situation in a classroom, on a bus, or outdoors, and then gives a moral command to students, parents, or other teachers. Moreover, the continuation of a misbehavior may give the teacher further reason to think of a fitting punishment that deters the repeated misbehavior of the person, especially when misbehaviors result in unfairness.

Moral reasoning thus appears to involve discovery of unfairness, producing a descriptive account of it and forming a reasonable and prescriptive moral judgment that may consider the severity of the action and the severity of pontential punishment, especially if actions are repeated. Moral reasoning that occurs with the mention of moral issues, adult human behaviors, and discussions of relevant moral issues, is required for moral decision-making to make effective determinations. Many of these moral decisions are crucial in the field of law, especially in courtrooms where thinking about justice can play major roles in fairness of decisions.

9 Moral Judgment and Action Require Attention, Intention, Memory Capacity, and "Being in Control"

One moral and psychological view is that whenever a moral decision is made, the decision-making process involves a certain amount of freedoms. By "freedoms" one can mean that when we make moral judgments, there are lacks of types of controls during these processes. Moreover, any individual who is completely controlled and determined is not an individual who is making a "moral decision" at all. That is, what we must do cannot be what we should not do; however, one may argue that there are exceptions to the latter claim insofar as the neurological and psychological events requisite for the decision-making process or determinations are excluded from the claim that "what must be done cannot be what should be done." The latter exception is noteworthy for neurological studies (see Ch. 3.6).

For starters, one may maintain that moral decision-making occurs only after events are understood in some sense, and they often involve people, animals, the environment, etc. "Understanding an event in some sense" means that we use our sensory perceptions, and we perceive objects and events, which are categorized by us, first and foremost, as being "possible," and then we classify them as either "real" or "unreal." Finally, we make a determination about whether the events are necessary or coincidental before we make some moral decision, which involves the comprehension of some event within the environment, sensations, and voluntary behaviors or volition to refrain from taking action. The event that is understood as being a coincidental one is also one that cannot be blamed upon the intentions, plans, or decisions of another person (see Ch. 5.3–5.6).

It appears obvious to us that any event must first be established (or cognitively categorized) as being "possible" by a person who is about to make a moral decision before that person (i.e., moral agent) can act intelligibly (or with moral intelligence) in relation to the event with goal-directedness. However, the mere attribution of possibility for some event is insufficient for "moral decision-making" since much more cognition must occur.

For instance, consider a roommate named "Albert" who knows the following facts: it is "possible" that Mary took the trash outside, she took it out the last three weeks in a row, although Albert should carry the garbage out every other week. Albert, in this scenario, is in need of more knowledge about what he views as a "possible event," which is, namely, that the trash was possibly taken out by Mary again. What Albert is morally responsible for is quite plain and simple, i.e., "assuring that the garbage is outdoors" so that it can be collected by a couple of sanitation workers early in the morning.

Perhaps Albert hopes the garbage is already outside, and he is lying in bed with back pains, or perhaps he dwells over some strange event that happened during his long day at work (i.e., types of "controls" that make him less likely to check the status of the trash), which all decrease the likelihood that he takes out the trash (i.e., when his thoughts about taking out the trash would be less important than a number of other things with which he is preoccupied). Moreover, there are so many decisions for him to make regarding just the trash. He could call Mary and ask her if it is already outside, look out the window, or walk outside, or even go directly to the bin to remove the waste just as if he realized that Mary did not do it for them again. However, our analysis is concerned with what is "necessary" in order for Albert to make a moral judgment and act accordingly.

Of course, Albert must have the ability to *remember* (or recollect) certain facts and thoughts as well as practice and utilize this ability, think about the facts attentively, and act to make the moral decision or, perhaps, refrain from making a slightly immoral decision (i.e., by removing the waste from the bin). Obviously, if Albert falls asleep from utter exhaustion, the whole process of moral decision making is automatically ended quite abruptly, but perhaps if his last will and effort and intention to reach the trash was not good enough, and his exhaustion caused him to pass out with the garbage sack in hand as he lied by the door upon the floor. If Mary saw this strange situation and what appears to be an attempt to remove their waste from their home, then Mary would probably not hold Albert morally responsible for failing to remove the trash because she could see that he intended to do so. She may hold him morally blameworthy for something else or consider the event to be a coincidence, i.e., an unintentional event brought about by Albert's need of sleep.

One may emphasize that the type of example of Albert's recognitions, certain duties for which he and his partner are responsible at home, and the lack of desire to perform some action is a typical case concerning moral duty, actions, and moral decision-making of able-bodied adults, although it is not studied in accordance with the methods of moral psychology. The methods of moral psychology are likely unable to observe and analyze these typical situations that involve the moral virtues of responsibility and thoughtfulness. Moreover, the example, and similar ones, can be applied to major ethical theories.

10 Virtue Ethics and Consequentialism

Virtue ethicists may consistently maintain that by performing such duties, Albert is preventing laziness (i.e., discouraging a vice), acting diligently (i.e., promoting a virtue), and his act to remove the bin disallows Mary from being servile (i.e., preventing a vice). Perhaps the virtues of cleanliness, patience, respectfulness, etc. are relevant here, too. The promotion and encouragement of virtues and prevention and discouragement of vices coincide with the ethical decision-making for virtue ethicists, and there are certainly moral reasons that are involved, but the practice of becoming a virtuous person might well be described by Aristotle in terms of practicing the virtues over and over until they become habits. It is also worthwhile to note that such encouragement and the recognition of it by others in society sometimes play important roles within courts of law.

Consequentialists may argue that his action produces the best consequences, if Albert does what is best, say, in respect to Mary, himself, neighbors, and the sanitation workers, whom we may argue would have to displace twice as much stinky garbage the following week and handle insects or rats, if both fail to be responsible with their waste. The advocacy of consequentialism and the practice and recognition of it involve doing things that result in the best consequences. However, the practice of people fallibly applying the principles of consequentialism may involve a focus upon just the environment, people, short-term goals that may have negative consequences on some course of events that happen decades later, on just animals or even just the citizens of one's own society, in which case the different focuses that people have regarding what they think the "best consequences" are at some time are important regarding legal decision-making at all levels, such as law enforcement, law-making, and legal judgments and verdicts in courts of law.

11 Duty Ethics: Deontology

Duty ethicists would argue that there is a moral worth in Albert fulfilling this duty, which is even greater when Albert really does not want to fulfill his duty to remove the bin. Failing to fulfill his duty is immoral because if we were to form a maxim to fail to properly remove and separate the waste (i.e., universalization principle of Kant's categorical imperative), there would be total chaos, more frequent disease outbreaks, the inability to form social groups within a city, etc., and no universal law could be formed from this failure. For the same reasons, the duty ethicist, Immanuel Kant, argued that "breaking promises" is immoral because as intelligent beings, we can imagine what would happen if breaking promises were no longer considered "unethical" since we know that this would result in an extreme lack of trust, many webs of lies, and perhaps the inability to form legal and justice systems or even to live with any security at all. Those who are intelligent enough to imagine what would happen are intelligent enough to be held responsible for their actions, too.

Of course, in Albert-type cases where duties are not fulfilled, there is often a use of reasoning to convince others that the moral agent is not morally responsible for failing to fulfill some duty. Sometimes reasoning is used in order for a person, who places blame on another, to view the events from a closer perspective to the person who receives the moral blame.

However, sometimes people express guilt, regret, moral accountability, and realize their moral blameworthiness. So, moral reasoning is used to construct sincere apologies in certain cases and is crucial in order for one to change one's habits, views, beliefs, and desires to those that are more reconcilable with others' rational wishes.

Moral reasoning is quite interesting from the perspective of the individual who attempts to combine motivational theories in psychology with the view of what has a moral worth for duty ethicists. Consider a lawmaker who contributes the most to passing a bill that becomes a law, which benefits virtually everybody within the society, especially the underprivileged. Does he deserve moral praise?

He does not deserve any moral praise, according to duty ethics, since the lawmaker was inclined to pass the bill. Attempting to pass bills is a part of his job. If, on the other hand, the new law would negatively impact him and his family, for instance, and he only begrudgingly put forth his efforts to make the new law, then the lawmaker would deserve moral praise. The latter points present difficulties for moral psychology when there is a consideration of measurements and experimental conditions. These methods in science may be needed for one to develop an understanding of moral reasoning via Kantian or deontological ethics.

From a developmental psychological perspective the latter use of moral reasoning is what allows children to quickly learn "how they should treat others." Moral reasoning is, therefore, an aspect of the learning process that aids in our abilities to understand what others' needs, beliefs, and wants are in relation to our own, and it includes what we must morally do about others' needs, beliefs and wants. Moral reasoning is perhaps better used as a way to understand other wants and needs in the environment and to improve one's behaviors so as not to interfere as much. The latter explains the intimate interrelations between what we call "theory of mind" and "moral reasoning" in the following sections.

12 The Social Intuitionist Model Describes "Out-of-Control" Moral Decisions

The characterizations of morality, moral judgments, and moral reasoning, which social intuitionist models illustrate, are opposite-ended in respect to the aforementioned viewpoint in the previous section. According to Schnall et al. (2008, p. 1097):

> [M]oral reasoning is an important part of moral life, but for most people, most of the time, most of the action is in the quick, automatic, affective evaluations they make of people and events.

Schnall et al. (2008) argue in accordance with the social intuitionist model, claiming that when people make moral judgments, it is unlikely these people make moral judgments via ways in which they are "in control" of making these judgments. Moreover, people tend not to be consciously aware and tend not to make the judgments via intentional processes that are viewable, in some sense, for the people making moral judgments (Haidt, 2001). There are some similarities with emotivism in philosophy, which asserts that moral judgements of being right, virtuous, wrong, and morally deplorable are basically positive and negative attitudes of approval and disapproval, respectively. Emotivists argue that these moral terms express emotions and can elicit similar emotions in others (van Roojen, 2016).

Haidt and company argue that the *intuitive system* is responsible for the vast majority of moral judgments that humans make. Haidt (2001, p. 818) claims that the general features of the intuitive system are:

> Fast and effortless; Process is unintentional and runs automatically; Process is inaccessible; only results enter awareness; Does not demand attentional resources Pattern matching; thought is metaphorical, holistic; Common to all mammals; Context dependent.

In combination with the social intuitionist model, moral foundation theory (Graham, Haidt, & Nosek, 2004) incorporates what it calls five established sets of moral intuitions, which include: in-group/loyalty, authority/respect, purity/sanctity, which tend to be emphasized by "political conservatives" more, and harm/care and fairness/reciprocity tend to be emphasized to a greater extent by liberals on the political psychological spectrum.

The latter conclusions are dubious and place certain parties and social groups at possible risks if the research is generalized in such manners. For instance, we may ask Graham, Haidt, and Nosek whether more political liberals are unfaithful to their spouses than political conservatives are insofar as loyalty, respect, and purity are presumed to be emphasized to greater degrees by political conservatives (ibid.; Haidt & Graham, 2007). Any answer to such inquiries, however, without studying the phenomenon of infidelity based on political beliefs is misguided. On the other hand, the latter researchers are, presumably, not emphasizing the actual behaviors of the political liberals and political conservatives because they lack access to them, except in terms of what they say and write, but rather the researchers claim that liberals emphasize fairness and conservatives emphasize loyalty more often.

13 Disbelief in Free Will and Dangers and Influences of Social Intuitionist Models May Reduce Feelings of Moral Responsibility

Perhaps it is worthwhile to hypothesize within a theoretical framework for moral psychology that there is no such thing as an "out-of-control" moral judgment, an out-of-control moral decision, or out-of-control moral action. What is meant by an "out-of-control moral judgment" is an irrational judgment that is determined by intuitions, tastes, and other subjective qualities rather than the process of categorizing an event as "possible," then "real" or "unreal," and directing one's goal-oriented actions toward such an event based upon what one believes, desires, and what the "matter of fact" about reality is. Young, Scholz and Saxe (2011, p. 302) state that the "[m]oral judgment depends critically on theory of mind (ToM), reasoning about mental states such as beliefs and intentions."

"Theory of mind" is the ability to attribute mental states, such as beliefs, desires, and expectations, to others that are different from one's own mental states. Such an ability means that the practical use of theory of mind involves recognizing what others' needs are in addition to what they merely wish or want. The recognitions of what others truly need places demands upon us as actors who should not interfere with the autonomies of others and should not disrespect them as they pursue what they need and some of the things they merely want.

The latter points are quite easy to understand regarding children who may want to hit their friends or eat candy all day. Adults and adolescents who practice moral reasoning would prevent the latter behaviors and might also offer reasons why the children should not perform those behaviors. Young and Saxe (2008, p. 1913) claim:

> By the time they are five, children reliably pass the false belief test. This capacity appears to precede rather than to coincide with the capacity to use belief information in the context of moral judgment. Five year olds can make moral distinctions based on mental state distinctions only when consequences are held constant (Karniol, 1978; Nelson Le Gall, 1985; Nunez and Harris, 1998; Siegel and Peterson, 1998; Wellman et al., 1979).

The ability for children at the age of five to recognize that others have beliefs and desires that are different from their own appears to develop before the children begin to apply their ability to the context of moral decision-making. Perhaps the ability is better recognized as being a "skill" since the practice of it almost certainly leads to improvements and could even involve greater applications to the contexts of moral judgments. Moreover, the lack of practice almost certainly leads to arrested developments with regard to theory of mind. Young and Saxe (ibid.) continue:

> Even though they can represent beliefs, these children continue to base their moral judgments primarily on the action's consequences rather than the actor's beliefs, when these two factors conflict (Hebble, 1971; Piaget, 1965/1932; Shultz et al., 1986; Yuill, 1984; Yuill and Perner, 1988; Zelazo et al., 1996).

The age of the subjects within the latter experiments is important. Four-year-olds often do not attribute the correct false beliefs to others. Five-year-old subjects attribute false beliefs most of the time, except in cases where they have disorders, such as autism, but even in cases with disorders, the six-year-olds with low levels of autism are likely to attribute the correct false beliefs to the characters. The experimentation concerning the ages of the children and the sophistication levels of their developing theory of mind abilities are important for court cases concerning witnesses who are children as well as children who are raped, especially because it is important to know what their abilities to form webs of lies are like.

Most of the experiments, however, do not involve the alteration of the independent variable regarding the desire or dislike of the object that the subject actually has and the desire or dislike of the object that the character has and to whom the subject attributes the false beliefs (Ziv & Frye, 2003, p. 859). That is, there could be significant differences concerning the children's attributions of the false beliefs of others about objects when those objects are liked, disliked, or the children making the attributions are indifferent about them, for instance.

What is also important for people, as moral decision-makers, is to understand that their webs of interconnected beliefs can and do, in fact, change regularly, and moral agents can freely decide upon multitudes of choices and ways in which they go about executing these choices. Rigoni, Kühn, Sartoni, and Brass (2011, 616) write that "we demonstrated that weakening the belief in free will affects brain processes underlying early stages of motor preparation." Many psychologists and neuroscientists argue that the individual's feelings of being in control of his or her own actions are illusory along with free will and argue that the intense subjective experiences of being in control are illusory rather than veridical.

However, the crucial fact of the matter is that these feelings and subjective experiences are not observable, in principle, from the observational levels involved with fMRIs and observations of the brain. Rigoni et al. (2011, p. 613) discover that when people begin to disbelieve in free will, their motivations and performances are affected, and they maintain:

> Recently, it has been shown that undermining free-will beliefs influences social behavior. In the study reported here, we investigated whether undermining beliefs in free will affects brain correlates of voluntary motor preparation. Our results showed that the readiness potential was reduced in individuals induced to disbelieve in free will. This effect was evident more than 1 s before participants consciously decided to move, a finding that suggests that the manipulation influenced intentional actions at preconscious stages. Our findings indicate that abstract belief systems might have a much more fundamental effect than previously thought.

Jonathan Haidt publicly advocates the position that morals are subjective features that animals have evolved. The role of evolution here is interesting and undoubtedly important, but the reduction of morality to the subjective features of animals appears to be excessive because it fails to take the social learning process into consideration. Moral reasoning involves and demands consistency, which can be improved along with each individual's critical thinking skills. Moral intelligence is a set of skills that is honed and undergoes developmental processes as it develops within the individual as an incipient ability during the first years of the human lifespan.

As Kant maintained, there is no contradiction in the denial of morality, but once the notion of freedom or liberty is concerned as a real phenomenon, morality can no longer be denied. Liberty is also required by law, and law undoubtedly requires liberty. Even the development of laws in newly developed societies have been argued to advance and form states only based on moral principles of fairness and justice for the decision-making of protection agencies that also compete against each other partially based on having the fairer system (See Ch. 1.2).

An interconnected set of problems arises when individuals persuade others that freedom, liberty, or free will are illusory and persuade others that morals are entirely subjective because the advocating of such stances fails to be based upon observational data. Decision-making, like consciousness, is not observable from numerous levels of observations, like other real phenomena are, such as water (e.g., observable via taste, with the naked eyes, microscopically, etc.). Thus, convincing arguments for the illusory nature of humans' control over their own actions and persuasive arguments for the subjective nature of morality tend to be fallacious when they are presented in such ways. There are tendencies to fail to account for the levels of analyses and levels of observations that are relevant to the study of liberty, freedom, free will, morality, and decision-making.

The levels of observations that are relevant to morality and decision-making are the levels of observation that we ordinarily make when we observe others. We observe others' morals and decisions with our visual, tactile and auditory sensory experiences that are unaided or aided by things, such as spectacles, rather than observe microscopic levels or levels involved with fMRIs, for instance. The relevant levels of analysis follow from the appropriate levels of observations.

The law is based within each society under the assumptions that people typically refrain from acting immorally. In societies, we may consider there to be immorality at least to the extent that people infringe on freedoms of others. Research in the field of neurobiology, which fails to account for the importance of conclusions from studies remaining relevant to the levels of observations and analyses from which the conclusions are derived, tends to draw conclusions about concepts of liberty, freedom, free will, morality, and choices in ways that are not operationally defined; thereby they allow for irrational generalizations to be made.

Moreover, the process, which is coupled with the sharing of these ideas and misinformation within courts of law, can have dire consequences. The misguided conclusions of scientists about individuals' choices can never really be drawn from the levels of observation and the levels of analysis used in neuroscience, which can lead to the wrong conclusions in courts of law. For example, the fMRI machine cannot identify a human choice and cannot produce an image that even the greatest neuroscientist could use to identify any human decision. Also, the idea that choice-making is illusory is not identifiable and has no more evidence to support it than the opposite idea does.

However, the data collected over decades from infancy to adulthood for numerous people may be requisite to produce useful observational data about human decisions that provide us with conclusions with which we can begin to gauge the amount of control or freedom of their actions. The data collected over the course of a few hours each for many participants is perhaps insufficient to provide any gauge of any amount of control or freedom one may have over one's actions. The miniscule amount of data provides no reason for believing that a human being lacks control over her own actions. The questions about control and decisiveness are enduring philosophical questions. We can form valid arguments for and against each side on the issue, forming opposing systems of thought.

If we consider motivation theories, such as Abraham Maslow's hierarchy of needs or Frederick Herzberg's theory of motivators and hygiene factors, we view the human being as one who has more freedom and control once the basic physiological needs or hygiene factors are fulfilled. Yet such considerations are absent within the scientific studies concerning the neurobiology of choice-making. There appears, again, to be an assumption that choice-making is a short-term and observable process that is thereby able to be investigated with brain imaging techniques and also with observations of responses of many people to the same stimuli that all occur for each person within the course of a single day.

However, decision-making is a complex process that develops over time and is a skill rather than a mere ability because it is learnt and improves with practice. Moreover, it is applicable to many types of situations, and greater exposures to any certain type of situation will likely allow the individual to form decisions with greater displays of skill. Perhaps this is most easily viewed in sports where greater exposures to certain aspects of the game allow the person to decide more professionally.

The reason why Haidt (2000, 2001, 2004 & 2011) fails to take a single moral stance on any particular moral problem in his latter works is that his niche within the research on moral psychology merely concerns the descriptive moral aspect rather than the prescriptive aspect of morals, imperatives, and moral psychology. For instance, Haidt does not claim that it is moral, amoral, or immoral for a brother and sister to have safe sex with one another (Haidt, 2000 & 2001). However, Haidt assumes that others will make those moral judgments when he observes them as subjects answering psychology survey-type questions after they have read several sentences about a brother and sister having sex with each other. Haidt often merely describes participants' moral judgments about "hypothetical cases." Moreover, he provides no insights about what is morally right or morally wrong and does not explain why he refrains from offering any moral evaluations.

The type of method of Haidt involves what is descriptive of subjects' superficialities and ideologies because only their webs of beliefs in respect to spoken and written communications are studied rather than goal-oriented actions and duties. The skills attained from the practice of moral reasoning and decision-making are not investigated by Haidt in any thorough way, and the experimentation within the latter works often involve stimuli that are surprising and disgusting for subjects. So, we might expect for people to react in ways that present difficulties for them to apply moral reasoning and decision-making skills that are consistent and thoughtful.

Investigating the social psychological phenomena involved in a thorough manner in Haidt's (2000, 2001, 2004 & 2011) experiments must involve greater alterations of the independent variables in them. They answer the survey questions differently regarding the amount of time spent on reading and reflecting on the material, the intensity of the events described in the material, and the amount of material the informants read. The experimentation needs to include "concomitant variations" to draw reasonable and probable conclusions, assuring that the independent variables are sufficiently altered (Mill, 1843). Having participants produce moral judgments of some action after entering a place that smells bad must include different intensities of "bad smells" and the presence of other smells that are neutral and pleasant ones.

Haidt appears to be more interested in generalizing about morality than thoroughly investigating the social psychological phenomena to draw conclusions that are more specific and that yield higher levels of relevance and certainty. There are several problems in Haidt's approach. First, his research largely focuses on examples that could involve moral problems but actually do not (Haidt, Koller, & Dias, 1993; Haidt, 2000). For instance, Haidt (2001, p. 817) makes it abundantly clear that the purpose of Haidt et al. (1993) is to examine:

> American and Brazilian responses to actions that were offensive yet harmless, such as eating one's dead pet dog, cleaning one's toilet with the national flag, or eating a chicken carcass one has just used for masturbation.

The responses are not actually responses to "actions" but rather are responses to hypothetical descriptions of actions. They suffice to make these sorts of examples more superficial. Participants may respond based on how they want to be perceived by experimenters, and experimenters from institutions may be feared in so far as they can report signs of disobedience to the government, like defacing the flag. One may consider numerous situations where it might be considered "morally permissible" for one to eat one's own dead pet dog, the chicken, and clean the toilet with a flag. The Uruguayan rugby team had players who had to eat their dead teammates to survive in the Andes Mountains after their plane crashed in 1972.

Haidt et al. (2000; Haidt, 2001), however, does not produce contexts that involve serious moral problems, but rather he asks questions as if the contexts involve moral problems, but rather the contexts generally involve things that disgust and unpleasantly surprise subjects (e.g., selecting subjects who walked through an area with greater or lesser amounts of "fart spray" before asking them questions about cousins getting married and having sex). Haidt is, in at least one sense, probing or encouraging his subjects to answer questions irrationally, and then he uses their irrational responses as supporting evidence for intuitionism via generalizations.

The moral dimension or aspect of much of the research is certainly undermined to some extent via the participants' trust for the researchers, too. However, the role of the research, the funding of the research and the focus upon certain political stances, in which case a certain political group is to some extent glorified at the expense and in relation to others, is alarming and should be well-considered within any evaluation of the validity and soundness of the research in moral psychology.

The relevance of moral psychology research to the law is quite great. Psychologists and psychiatrists often serve as paid experts to testify and to undergo cross-examinations. In fact, psychologists have largely led to the increases in the number of verdicts in many courts of law, including the verdicts of "guilty but insane" and "not guilty but insane." Also, much of the research in the field of moral psychology appears to coincide consistently with the research presented by Duttge (2009) insofar as the idea of moral decision-making is undermined to the extent that it is viewed, ideologically, as being illusory and involving a lack of conscious control (See Ch. 3.6).

CHAPTER 5

Comprehensive Conceptions of Possibility: Legal Theory

Possibility and its negation (i.e., impossibility) compose two all-pervasive concepts involved implicitly in every other concept or idea. As modes, they are suitable as starting points from which law, legal theory, probability, socio-political, and economic theories, hypotheses, and facts become analyzed. Moreover, possibility theory may well have developed in many important respects from the practices, theories, and teachings of law. This chapter presents an analysis of three different conceptions of possibility that provide a comprehensive analysis of the scope of possibility theory and its relations to legal systems and law.

The category and mode of possibility is illustrated to be conceptualized as follows: disjunctively possible, which means greater than reality with regard to the size of the content included with reality; really possible, which means equal to reality in respect to the size of their content; or recollectively possible, which means less than reality in relation to the sizes of their contents. I argue that recollective possibility functions as a more viable conception for further investigations. Recollective possibility treats the concept of possibility as a mere but important aspect of the cognitive process of realization, during which events, locations, and time spans of things or processes are recognized as real and unreal.

Recollective possibility utilizes disjunctive and real possibility in a ranking order for memory, memorization, and methods of categorization. Recollective possibility incorporates possibility theory for AI, regarding information's meaning rather than merely transmissions of bits of information. Recollective possibility also maintains that disjunctive possibility and real possibility provide a framework for human problem-solving that creates complicated sets of expectations and grounds them within frameworks that utilize cognitive realizations, which allow for the groundwork of social, political, and legal theory insofar as expectations of expectations arise for individuals in these manners. Altogether the three conceptions provide a comprehensive framework for philosophic and methodological investigations, specifically in relation to decision-making and general problem-solving.

Such decision-making, especially within methodology, and general problem-solving are directly applicable to law (i.e., as far as theories generate practical

DOI:10.1163/9789004385955_007

and testable hypotheses). Possibility theory is applicable to law because the different concepts of possibility encompass what law is, what law will become as well as what law could be, despite whether the latter possible or potential law is actualized. In virtue of law as the legal rules made by legislatures, possible laws include those laws that are necessary for any political economy and nation (e.g., tax laws that cover the costs of the legal system, laws against violent crimes, etc.) as well as laws in place that are unnecessary or arbitrary (e.g., laws governing the side of the road on which one is obligated to drive).[1]

Moreover, there are possible laws that undergo decision-making processes within legislative bodies but that are rejected by the legislatures. Other laws can be easily passed with negligence. Lawmakers are rarely aware of each detail of each bill they pass or reject. Legislators are certainly unaware of the impact that their lawmaking will have upon their society and other societies. They are not truly tested over such matters after they are elected. There is no requirement for testing them over such matters before or during their tenures. They are tested in some ways by journalists, though.

1 Although we may speak about law and society separately, law is inseparable from society, which also includes tribal cultures, even though tribes may lack what we generally refer to as legal systems. Laws themselves can be categorized in accordance with what they regulate as subject matter, such as criminal law, contract law, property law, and tort law. Laws are also classified by means of what they establish as norms, such as permission-granting, duty-imposing and penalization-imposing law. Laws can also be classified in accordance with the legal system that makes or enforces them. If we inquire whether there is such a thing as a universal or worldwide law, we may immediately consider the differences in written and enforced laws between different legal systems.

We may think of such legal systems involved with the creation and implementation of Chinese law, ancient Greek law, French, or German law, and consider that there is instead a multiplicity of laws (Ehrlich, 1922, pp. 130–131). The suggestion that there are indeed commonalities in respect to all the various legal systems is less dubious insofar as we will likely find marriages, legal contracts, inheritances, families where parents have legal rights that impact them as legally responsible caretakers, laws involved with buying and selling goods and services, renting, loaning, and possessing. According to Eugen Ehrlich (1922, p. 132):

> Those who proclaim a multiplicity of Laws understand by "Law" nothing other than Legal Provisions, and these are, at least today, different in every state. On the other hand, those who emphasize the common element in the midst of this variety are centering their attention not on Legal Provisions but on the Social Order, and this is among civilized states and peoples similar in its main outlines. In fact many of its features they possess in common even with the uncivilized and the half-civilized.

The latter distinctions made by Eugen Ehrlich are important to the extent that progress is hindered in sociology of law amongst academics who understand two very different sets of facts about what the law is, unless those sets of facts are elaborated.

The aspect of law that concerns rules, norms, and regulations is argued by Timasheff to be a real part of the culture and neither merely evaluative nor disjunctively possible. According to Timasheff (1937, p. 226):

> In both analytical and historical jurisprudence the comparative method may be applied: legal norms are studied with regard to a group of countries the social structures of which present or presented some similitude. This is the task of comparative jurisprudence. Finally, the structure of the legal norms presents, at all times and places, some unchangeable features which may be considered as belonging to the very essence of law. Studying this unchangeable form of patterns, their natural elements, is the task of theoretical jurisprudence.

The comparative method of jurisprudence is also often undertaken by philosophically-minded travelers who spend sufficient amounts of time in other countries. Timasheff (ibid.) continues:

> In all these cases the norms of conduct as such remain the object of study. This is, in spite of the opinion of many scientists, a study of actuality, and not a study belonging to the domain of evaluation—for the social patterns of behavior included in law actually exist, forming a part of culture. Rules of evaluation are the object of jurisprudence, but in their relation to actuality. Finding out the logical interdependence between various individual norms is the main task of this science; logical analysis is therefore its chief method.

Comparisons made in the discipline of jurisprudence are comparisons between real phenomena. This includes the patterns of behaviors of social groups with law. For the latter reason, an ontology of law is important. Timasheff (ibid.) maintains that what are not studied in jurisprudence are the human behaviors determined by the legal norms, in society.

Perhaps some differences held in the current investigation maintain that certain social phenomena related to the law, such as comedy about the law provide means with which real phenomena of the law can be compared and measured. This includes whether their intensities increase or decrease from time to time and general social behaviors, which may implement dominance and subordination. Thus, the investigation of *Beyond Legal Minds* includes much methodology for the attainment of knowledge about the law and mixes analytical, historical, and theoretical jurisprudence. In this chapter, multiple forms of logical analyses are explored in relation to the law and its consequences as human social phenomena in legal systems.

1 Modal Theory and Possibility Theory: Social Implications

Laws or legal rules do not necessarily limit the possibilities of actions for people. Laws are not always accompanied by informative means that provide realizations of legal consequences for violating the law. Legal systems provide an extra element, dimension, or aspect that is considerable and that increases the complexity of society itself. With this, expectations for individuals become simpler insofar as the society's legal system serves to stabilize expectations (Luhmann, 1987). People in relatively successful legal systems live in societies with efficient legal procedures that produce increasing perceptions of legitimacy via procedural justice (Tyler et al., 1997). In such societies, people generally expect others to tend to behave in ways that do not violate the law. In such societies and circumstances, humans tend to behave as if there is less bribery, extortion, contract violations, blackmail, etc.

In any legal system, the range of possibilities for human action and inaction depend on multiple factors. These include the diversity of ranges of elevations that cities or their outskirts have and ranges of temperatures. These factors contribute to different treatments of different types of crimes in different regions. The mountainous country of Afghanistan and the desert nation of Libya have harsher penalties for rape.

Archaic-like legal systems sometimes allow for victims of rape to be killed to rid families and villages of what they consider to be dishonor and shame. They kill the rape victims in these cultures' geographic regions (Metz, 1987). Moreover, concerning certain ranges of temperatures and taking such factors into consideration, such as night and day, there is a positive correlation between the increase in temperature and the amount of violent crimes (Anderson, 1989; Cohn & Rotton, 1997; Rotten & Cohn, 2001; Butke & Sheridan, 2010).

The complexity of the society with a legal system possesses greater organization. They serve to better stabilize expectations. The complexity of the society is, arguably, understood as there being many more possibilities than can become real there, during any actual duration.

For people, the society thereby provides systems in which human decision-making is simpler. They reduce chaos and destruction that accompanies lawlessness. The society as a whole is greatly shaped via the environmental conditions. These place limitations and change expectations for legal systems.

2 Presumptions Concerning the Critique of the Concepts of Possibility

"Possibility" is often utilized as a concept with which one categorizes a wide-ranging set, within which a vast load of content fits (e.g., events, objects, and attributes fit as members of this purportedly largest set). At least a few different philosophic approaches and arguments conclude that the category of possibility is greater than the category of reality (i.e., or greater than actuality, being, or existence) with regard to the sizes of their contents or in relation to the extensiveness of them as sets or conceptions. The latter type of concept of possibility, which maintains a greater amount of content than reality, is referred to in several ways, including "logical possibility" and "inclusive disjunctive possibility."

Within this chapter "reality" is utilized in the same manner as some use the words "existence," "being," and "actuality." This chapter provides critical and systematic arguments that form three distinct concepts of possibility. The latter concepts are often equivocated and are generally presumed to form counter-opposing and philosophically problematic systems. All three concepts of possibility, i.e., inclusive disjunctive possibility, real possibility, and what is referred to here as "recollective possibility," are illustrated to function together within cognitive processes of realization, decision-making, attention, and memory (i.e., in accordance with the most recent conception of possibility). Each concept is described as functioning within scientific methodology concerning observations and formations of testable hypotheses for general problem-solving.

General problem-solving and methods are directly applicable to law, and the concepts of possibility encompass everything that is the law. Possible laws include those that are necessary for so many of the functions of civil society as well as laws in place that are unnecessary, which are different within various legal systems. Possible laws in the forms of bills, which undergo the process of legislative decision-making, are sometimes restricted by the legislature. In some cases, legislators may better understand the impact of potential laws upon their constituents because of their outspoken desires to pass or reject such relevant bills. Recollective possibility is a conception that offers further insights into the decision-making process as well as the attribution of possibilities, which impact decisions about the law.

3 Inclusive Disjunctive Possibility: Possibility as an Indifferent, Abstract, and Broad Conception

Inclusive disjunctive possibility is the most inclusive conception of possibility. The catchphrases for this conception are well known and include: "Anything is possible," "Nothing is impossible," and "All things are possible." It is argued that some things are possible, even if they never happen, according to this conception of possibility. Generally, the only restriction (i.e., for those who are in the position to utilize the concept of inclusive disjunctive possibility, say, in contract law) is contradictoriness insofar as it is impossible for something, simultaneously, to be and not be or to happen and not happen at the same time. Likewise, arguments that are deduced from impossibilities are generally presumed to have the highest validity regarding law (Garner, 2004, p. 5263).

The concept of inclusive disjunctive possibility is important as it can misguide theorists and practitioners since the focus upon the false statement within a disjunctive claim may lead to impractical analyses regarding, for example, the deductive consequences of such a false statement, especially when the falsehood is not known to be false. The concept of inclusive disjunctive possibility appears to be at odds with mathematical possibility theory of fuzzy sets and artificial intelligence possibility theory insofar as intelligent systems must attribute meaning to remembered or stored information, which is viewed as "possibilistic" and structurally framed via artificial intelligence possibility theory. However, the inclusive disjunctive possibility concept includes too much. For example, if a discussion of potential legislation includes a series of legal penalties for committing violent acts, the inclusive disjunctive conception of possibility would also have the discussion include no legal penalties and legal rewards in response to people who commit violent acts.

Organizations have arisen for legal knowledge management, such as the International Association for Artificial Intelligence and Law and the Foundation for Legal Based Knowledge Systems during the late 1980s. The organizations formally manage legal information for supporting legal decision-making and facilitating the search and retrieval processes of legal knowledge (Casellas, 2011, p. 1). The integrative levels theoretical approach and knowledge organization systems for classification of real phenomena can also greatly benefit from these other knowledge management systems (see Ch. 3.1).

The requirements for the transmission, coding, detection, communication, and reception of information are viewed as "probabilistic" and thus are dealt with via statistics and probability theories. The characterization of an event as one that never happens is akin to characterizing that event as an impossible one for that finite system; this is where the apparent contradiction resides between artificial intelligence possibility theory and the conception of the inclusive disjunctive possibility, yet artificial intelligence is concerned with the analysis of rare events (Zadeh, 1978/1999; Dubois & Prade, 2001). Thus, problematic questions remain about how humankind can construct artificially intelligent systems in ways that allow them to attribute wide ranges of inclusive disjunctive possibilities, for instance, especially for things that are characterized as "never occurring" rather than "rarely occurring" within finite systems.

Consider either the application of a single law or set of laws, like those involved in the Soviet Union regarding illegalizations of types of private property via communistic laws, establishing public property instead (i.e., state, cooperative, and social ownership) (Feldbrugge, 1989, pp. 297–338). Sizes and standings of black markets in the USSR often counteracted the transformations of private property to public property. Black market growth changed expectations about impacts of communistic laws.

What neither occurred in the Soviet Union nor occurred in other so-called communist countries, such as Soviet Georgia, is an efficient legal system that implemented a well-governed communist economic system. Shortages of goods and services and bureaucratic delays for exchanges generally led to the enlargement of the second economy or black market (Sampson, 1987). Nevertheless, what is exceedingly problematic is the representation of the social facts, expectations, real impacts of the laws, and lack of any occurrence of communism in a political system. The communistically intended laws strengthened the roles of black market systems, which meant more private property or at least less legal control. This suggests that a communist legal system and national economy is only a possibility in the inclusive disjunctive conception and is thus ideological and unrealistic.

Recent attempts have been made to measure the sizes of black markets (i.e., underground and informal economies). Measurement systems of governmental agencies may fail to notice large and developing portions of the underground economy (Feige, 1989, p. 14). The Havocscope limited liability company runs a research-based website (www.havocscope.com) dedicated to organizing data regarding illegal trade and the global black market. It provides a ranking order of industries estimated to have goods and services valued at the following prices in 2017: (1) $200 billion of counterfeit drugs; (2) $186 billion of prostitution; (3) $169 billion of counterfeit electronics; (4) $141.8 billion of marijuana; (5) $140 billion of illegal gambling; (6) $85 billion of cocaine; (7) $72.5 billion of prescription drugs; (8) $68 billion of heroin; (9) $63 billion of software piracy; and (10) $50 billion of cigarette smuggling (Havocscope, 2017).

The underground economy permeates probably every known political economy, despite the guise or actual implementation of communism via law, in which case communistic laws are now generally known by researchers to be associated with the black market that becomes known as an enlarged "second economy" (Feldbrugge, ibid.; Sampson, ibid.). In China, the role of the underground economy is staggering with even the Communist political party officials amassing tens of billions of dollars of goods and monies with the ideological and deceptive guise of the support for the economic system of communism. However, the Chinese Communist Party evidently contributes or is positively correlated with the placement of its members in elite jobs, such as managers (Jacobs, 2015; Osburg, 2013; Walder, Li & Treiman, 2000, pp. 194–195).

The representation of information (e.g., about the law in relation to communism and the black market) is complicated by misinformation, especially regarding facts concerning rare social phenomena at certain social levels (e.g., certain social groups may collectively practice communism, yet the introduction of ever more people within the social group may inevitably lead away from presumed attenuations of certain types of hierarchical structures within the economic system, which naturally either never allows or else dismantles the communistic economic system over time).

The concept of inclusive disjunctive possibility maintains that absolutely nothing is insurmountable regarding negating the possibility of something, except for the propositional report's own logical contradiction. Even something that never occurs but lacks a logical contradiction is disjunctively possible. Therefore, not only despite the rarity of the effectiveness of communistic laws upon the "colored economy" (i.e., the black, gray, and white market economies within some political social system) but also, in spite of the fact that substantially sized political economies have never had effective communistic laws, the concept of inclusive disjunctive possibility allows for the inclusion of the system of communism as a possibility for the functions of even the largest human economies. Katsenelinboigen (1977, p. 62) writes:

> The Soviet experience so far has shown, in contrast to Marxist anticipations, that the planned socialist system requires market elements. Indeed, one may speak of a whole range of markets in the USSR .... I distinguish markets from the standpoint of their legality.

Katsenelinboigen (ibid.) continues:

> If the government and the people openly support a particular kind of market, it is a *legal* kind. I will indicate it by bright, light colours: *red, pink, white*. If the people want a market and the government does not like it but at the same time 'closes its eyes' (the government makes a compromise), that is a *semi-legal* kind, which I will colour *grey*. If the people (or some of them) like a kind of market which the government tries to abolish, that means an *illegal* kind for which I will use dark colours—*brown, black*.

One may question whether the Soviet system ever underwent any time period during which the communistic laws were effectively enforced, and whether the Soviets successfully abolished the market on which it focused elimination efforts. The latter inquiry suffices for the utilization of the entrance of the inclusive disjunctive possibility of the communist economic system into the logical realm (i.e., along with all other, at least, internally consistent fantasies about political economies with legal systems).

When the possibility of communism as an economic system is coupled with ideology and equivocations with, say, communist political parties or communistic laws, the denial of social facts and misapprehension of social phenomena stifles research. Afterwards, alternative idealistic models of societal systems arise with greater consideration than they deserve, which is a risk of the overuse of the inclusive disjunctive concept. Basically, the serious considerations of communism as forms of government (i.e., of any economic, political, and legal, societal system) come from misunderstandings of how people work together and form social hierarchies. Even if communism has or will function temporarily as a form of government, there are, overwhelming, instances in all political economies of people striving to attain competitive advantages. There are also black markets, which also result from motivations to gain competitive advantages. Black markets form in all political economies as well, which directly undermine any communist system.

The following is a propositional report: The state can be perpetually functional as a communistic system, and the state can also fail to be such. The latter propositional report is problematic because it provides what appears to be two strictly contradictory statements, but which are understood instead as possibilities via the concept of indifference in accordance with the inclusive disjunctive concept of possibility. The propositional report that "S can be P" is problematic insofar as the counterpart and opposing propositional report is entirely open, which is, namely, "S can also be not P." Inclusive disjunctive possibility remains totally indifferent toward the status of any problematic propositional report (McKay & Nelson, 2010). The latter quoted statements are both logical possibilities rather than contradictory statements, according to the inclusive disjunctive conception of possibility, which maintains an indifference regarding any propositional report of them (Hartmann, 1938, p. 48).

Any focus upon the latter problematic propositions via the concept of inclusive disjunctive possibility, however, is still a restricted logical propositional report insofar as other modal propositional reports regarding S and P are absent as long as they fail to be included within the realm of the given connection (i.e., necessity, coincidence and impossibility are disallowed to enter this realm). Contradictoriness also fails to become analyzed within the latter two examples in quotations, concerning the inclusive disjunctive concept of possibility, because the expansiveness of this concept of possibility allows for both real things and unreal things to be possible and thus for S to possibly be P and to also possibly be not P, which is why this concept of possibility incorporates inclusiveness and disjunction.

Yet the propositional reports "S cannot be P" and "S must be P" contradict, merely respectively, the first two problematic propositional reports and they contradict each other as well. These logical contradictions concern any conception of possibility since the assertion of the possibility of something is contradicted by the assertion of the necessity of that very same thing's negation (i.e., what is necessarily unreal is also called an "impossibility").

The propositional report of the necessity of something is contradicted by the propositional report of the impossibility of that same thing. Moreover, the latter propositional reports in quotes about impossibility and necessity are withheld at least during the initial phase of the report or judgment during which the propositional report of possibility is given (i.e., with the concept of inclusive disjunctive possibility).

The statements, "S must be P" and "S cannot be P," remain outside the realm of connection until they are introduced within it. Once the latter statements are introduced, the concept of exclusive disjunctive possibility enters the realm for consideration. One is a possibility, or the other one is a possibility but not both in the case at hand, according to the exclusive disjunctive conception.

"S can be P" and "S also can be not P" remain general focal points until the more specified and restricted conception of exclusive disjunctive possibility is coupled with a reason to exclude one of the propositional reports as a viable option and possibility, like certain combinations of pieces of a puzzle are no longer considered possible combinations at later points. Likewise, in a court of law a defendant's guilt is likely considered a possibility in addition to the possibility of the defendant not being guilty, until further information solidifies the judicial decision.

When the latter modalities of necessity and impossibility are introduced into the logical realm with two types of possibilities (i.e., of something and of its negation, e.g., P & ~P), two additional types of disjunctive possibilities arise regarding the first problematic propositional report. One comes from the affirmation of either "S can be P" or "S is P" in addition to the negation of "S must be P," providing the disjunctive possibility of "S need not be P," which is the proposition of coincidence.

The next disjunctive possibility arises from the affirmation of either "S can be not P" or "S is not P" coupled with the negation of "S cannot be P," which provides the disjunctive possibility that "S need not be not P." Consequently, one may apply the concept of inclusive disjunctive possibility to all the following statements and thus maintain that all the following are possible propositional reports, albeit in a different realm of logical judgment than that within which (2) and (3) are solely and initially made:

---

(1) S must be P (i.e., it is necessary that S is P)
(2) S can be P (i.e., it is possible that S is P)
(3) S can be not P (i.e., it is possible that S is not P)
(4) S need not be not P (i.e., it is unnecessary that S is not P)
(5) S need not be P (i.e., it is unnecessary that S is P)
(6) S cannot be P (i.e., it is impossible S is P)

---

(1) asserts necessity, (2) and (3) assert possibility, (4) and (5) assert coincidence, which is either real but not necessary or unreal but not impossible (i.e., that which could have been otherwise, need not be, or must not be), and (6) asserts impossibility.[2] (1) through (6) are the propositional reports derived from "S can be P" and "S can also be not P," which are inclusive disjunctive possibilities. (1) through (6) ideally provide the framework from which the latter two quoted statements and similar ones transit from inclusive disjunctive possibilities to exclusive disjunctive possibilities via methodologies, observations, and measurements for problem-solving.

For some metaphysicians, only (1) and (6) are informative. (4) and (5) describe conceptual generalities that often involve discrepancies and their relations to specific traits of an example of that concept. For example, a triangle "need not be" one with a 35° angle, but any specific triangle with a 35° angle needs that angle to be a triangle because if the angle were discarded, say, via one line segment being discarded, then no other angle could form to join the two remaining line segments and still create a triangle.

(2) and (3) are not informative enough since they remain neutral about "S is P" and "S is not P" (i.e., neither of the latter statements is able to be derived by (2) or (3)). Yet (2) through (5) are important for moral judgments, attributions of moral praise, and moral blameworthiness, which are crucial for legal decision-making, understanding justice, and implementing fairness.

2 Within this chapter what remains consistent concerns the translations of the German words *Zufälligkeit* as "coincidence" and *Kontingenz* as "contingency" within Immanuel Kant and Nicolai Hartmann's philosophies and refrains from using the word "contingency" with its connotations of dependency, conditionality, emergency, and eventuality.

The propositional reports, (1) through (6), arise as logical considerations, about which the concept of inclusive disjunctive possibility remains indifferent. However, the disjunctive possibilities have logical consequences (e.g., (1) requires (2) and (4) and that (3), (5), and (6) be negated). The disjunctive possibility of (2) contradicts (6) and allows for (1), (3), (4), and (5) to remain open as disjunctive possibilities. The latter analysis demonstrates further analysis of the problematic aspect of the propositional reports "S can be P" and "S can be not P," which arise from the concept of the inclusive disjunctive possibility.

One may utilize the concept of disjunctive possibility via limiting it to a single concept or to every concept. For instance, inclusive disjunctive possibility is treated as an *almost* all-encompassing mode, in which case the modes of necessity, reality, coincidence, and unreality are all encapsulated by this single modality or, at least, all their content fits within the category of possibility, except for some of the content of unreality. Only impossibility (i.e., necessary unreality) remains outside of the boundaries of the category of possibility as the opposing mode of possibility. For these reasons the concept of inclusive disjunctive possibility is analyzable as that which has a greater outreach than the concept of reality since it extends from (1) to (5) and includes all of reality and part of unreality.

The propositional report of the lack of impossibility of certain types of unreal things is, arguably, derived from the idea that certain unreal things or events, even which do not ever occur, are still describable in the three following ways: without any necessity, without being coincidentally real, and without logical contradiction. So, some unreal objects or events are viewed as being logically possible still in accordance with various theoretical frameworks since they either "could have occurred but did not occur," "could have been but never arose," "might be the case but are not the case," or "might arise or subsequently occur but will never happen."

The latter quoted types of attributions of possible occurrences or of possible states of being, which are free from logical contradiction, provide them with a form of internal consistency in accordance with such frameworks, even if such attributions lack external consistency. For law, the internal and external consistency are more complicated since a law may very well be consistent with all other laws (i.e., internal consistency), and yet the internally consistent law might not be enforced ever or often. For example, a newly reduced speed limit on the Interstate 10 highway from 70mph to 55mph northwest of San Antonio, Texas in the USA during the late 1990s was rarely enforced and perhaps did not reduce the speeds of the vehicles on the highway.

Law enforcement is necessary to put laws into effect. The presence of unenforced laws within legal books is a potential danger for society because some laws can be enforced by police officers when police choose to enforce them selectively. So, in the latter cases police officers have the authority to issue citations to those who exceed the 55mph speed limit, even if this is only rarely enforced.

(1) through (6) may describe laws insofar as "S" stands for "some specific action" at a certain location within the jurisdiction of a legal system, and "P" stands for "prohibited or illegal." An action can thus be described in accordance with the legal system, criminal justice system, constitution, or contract as: (1) what "must be" illegal; (2) what "can be" illegal; (3) what "can be" legal; (4) what "need not be" legal; (5) what "need not be" illegal; and/or as (6) what "cannot be" illegal, for instance, at some time period within a certain jurisdiction.

Logical possibility and physical possibility are crucial concepts within any court of law. Defense attorneys defending guilty culprits (i.e., defendants) are likely to create logically possible but fictional stories that are consistent with the facts presented by the prosecutor and themselves. Creations of fictional and plausible stories presented by defense lawyers give reasons to jurors to doubt the guilt of defendants.

The presentations of descriptions of fictional actions performed by or around the defendants usually also must be physically possible. Even the presentation of a plausible alternative description, say, in an automotive accident can be demonstrated by experts (i.e., accident reconstruction professionals, mechanical engineers, etc.) to be physically impossible, if the remains of the vehicles (e.g., unburnt vehicles with forensic evidence) show structural damage that is inconsistent with the alternative description. For defendants, the demonstration that their defense involves physical impossibility can be devastating, especially if the physical impossibility is recognized by all the jury members or judges.

The concepts of logical and physical possibility are by no means only relevant to the latter specialized sorts of cases. They apply to any legally-binding contracts, such as employment contracts. A legal contract can very well contain contradictions as well as be open to multiple interpretations, which may raise questions about fairness concerning the parties involved and who are legally obligated under the contract.

Likewise, an individual may have several beliefs that are contradictory when the content of the beliefs is, say, written as descriptions. Moreover, beliefs are necessary for contract law to be interpreted. The inclusive disjunctive concept of possibility is important for all the latter factors because it enables the consideration of each factor that is not strictly determined to be contradictory. Yet even in the cases of contradictions, the inclusive disjunctive conception of possibility allows for each of the alternative, contradictory claims to be analyzed separately.

4 Possibility and Impossibility in Relation to Logicality, Physicality, and Law

Often the idea proposed by logical or inclusive disjunctive possibility is paired with the idea that everything that is real is less than everything that is possible. The common view maintains that which is real is always possible, and that which is possible is also not always real. According to the common view, all real things are undoubtedly possible, and some unreal things are possible, which, presumably, makes the concept of possibility a modal concept rather than a merely epistemological one. It is precisely this latter meaning of the term "possibility" that involves possibility being greater than reality in virtue of the sheer amount of content encapsulated by the concept. Roughly speaking, the relational sizes of the concepts of possibility (i.e., logical possibility or inclusive disjunctive possibility and physical possibility) are presented in comparison to the concept of reality within figure 12 on the following pages.

For legal theory, the concept of logical possibility is the least restrictive for any logical analysis of legal facts. For legal practitioners, the concept is quite obvious insofar as contradictions either require reconciliation or are generally disallowed. Logical possibility can be enlightening in a court of law since if the defendant maintains that he or she was in one place at some time, and evidence from a video or witnesses places the individual in a different place at that same time, the prosecutor may easily illustrate the implausibility of the arguments of the defense based on the logical impossibility of being in two places simultaneously. Only one of the two given logical possibilities can remain since they are contradictory, which influences the legal decision-making. Moreover, the testimony of one witness may logically rescind the contradictory testimony of another witness, leaving the jurors or judges to at least further suspend their judgments on the matter or side with the more charismatic witness etc.

The propositional report that "there is more than one possible world" coincides with the concept of inclusive disjunctive possibility. The latter report concerns one logical possibility amongst two other logical possibilities: namely, that "there is less than one possible world" (i.e., albeit also requiring complete indifference) and that "there is just one possible world." The latter two logical possibilities complete the latter sphere of connection (i.e., the logical realm containing all the relevant logical possibilities), upholding three possible disjunctions that are relevant to the theme about any one of them being logically possible. It remains possible, in accordance with the inclusive disjunctive conception of possibility, that there is only one possible world, that there is less than one possible world (i.e., the theoretic denial of the givenness of reality (Hartmann, 1931)), and that there is a plurality of possible worlds, although not simultaneously.

The latter application of the concept of inclusive disjunctive possibility illustrates the utter lack of restriction regarding the logical realm. Theorizing about what hypotheses to construct for legal theories and critically analyzing the differences between legal theories (i.e., in virtue of perceived comprehensiveness, internal and external consistency, concision, and practicality) rely upon assumptions regarding the latter three disjunctive possibilities about possible world theory to some extent.

The form of each of the latter logical possibilities (i.e., only one possible world, nothingness, and the plurality of possible worlds) demands absolutely no external consistency, but rather only internal consistency. Without external consistency there is also a lack of practicality and relevance, but there is a means through which the direction of the philosophy, even aimed at the application of legal theory or application within a court of law (e.g., the Scope's Creationism Trial), likely results in a purely speculative endeavor with unrealistic objectives and totally untestable claims.

For legal theory, the number of possible worlds, or lack thereof, has not become a principal issue from which theoretic frameworks begin. The idea that there are multiple possible worlds that are virtually identical to the real world, in which we live, but which differ in respect to the future and thus differ regarding legal consequences, legal decision-making, verdicts decided by jurors and judges, concerning guilt and innocence, is an idea that seems to presume an arbitrary nature and unpredictable status of the legal system. It appears to fail regarding the creation of a foundational theoretic framework (i.e., based upon conceptions of possibility) supporting legal theories that generate testable hypotheses for legal sciences. One reason for this is that the generation of descriptions of all the logically possible laws, legal systems, penal systems, etc. would be endless and arbitrary.

With only a requirement of internal consistency, inclusive disjunctive possibility may be relationally defined via affirmation, negation, and familiar distinctions between logicality and physicality. Allow "LP" to stand for "logical possibility" or "logically possible," "PP" means "physical possibility," "PI" stands for "physical impossibility," and "LI" means "logical impossibility." Sentence (1) below is properly read: Logical possibility is the negation of logical impossibility and is either physical possibility or physical impossibility, but not both physical possibility and physical impossibility (i.e., "$\oplus$" is an "exclusive-or" symbol, i.e., EXOR, and "v" is an "inclusive-or symbol").

We are confronted with the four following statements about the relationships of the concepts of logicality, physicality, possibility and impossibility: **(1) LP = ~LI & (PP $\oplus$ PI); (2) PP = LP & ~(LI v PI); (3) PI = ~PP & (LP $\oplus$ LI);** and **(4) LI = PI & ~(LP v PP).**

The concept of inclusive disjunctive possibility, i.e., logical possibility, is requisite for our series of overlapping propositional reports about the differences concerning the (epistemic) statuses of unreal things. It contains exclusive disjunction as a subconception within it. So-called unreal objects that are physically possible tend to be hierarchically ranked more viably as objects, i.e., ones with which we will have to deal in the future, than unreal objects that are merely ranked as logically possible (i.e., concerning our propositional reports of them); this describes a practical way of using the concepts that are observable from a listing of many of the examples used by multiple philosophers and logicians. The practicality involved therein is typically not considered an aspect of the concept of logical possibility. Logical possibility involves a reservation of judgment about whether what at hand is physically possible or not. As such, examples of logical possibilities change with the times, technologies, sciences, and legal systems.

Bad blood and bad air are no longer typically considered to be logically possible phenomena that allow us to provide sufficient reasons for illnesses. We now have understandings of microscopic aspects involved with the blood, lungs, and air pollutants. Thus, in multiple legal systems medical procedures that involved bleeding patients to rid them of bad blood causing their illnesses (i.e., as opposed to blood transfusions) are outdated, although legally permitted in the past. Bleedings, as procedures for most ailments, could result in medical malpractice lawsuits in some legal systems.

During the 17th century, bad blood and bad air were also considered physical possibilities. During the 21st century, modernized legal systems typically require descriptive terms that are far more precise than the adjective "bad" to suffice for any sort of professional medical explanation in a court of law. Attributions of physical impossibility retain disjunctive possibility in an abstract form. Attributions of logical impossibility are reserved for various sorts of contradictions and things that can never be or happen (Brant 2012: pp. 220–243).

Physical impossibility usually involves something or some event that is insurmountable to a certain extent. For example, logistics involved in a massive migration movement from multiple regions of the world into a particular political economy and legal system may indeed be physically impossible under the conditions for the legal system to legally account for all newcomers. The legal system may place annual or monthly or weekly limitations on the number of migrants with legal documentation rather than allowing what the bureaucratic system may consider to be an excessive number of immigrants.

Although thousands of immigrants may migrate to Canada from China each year, hundreds of thousands of Chinese migrants each year would be insurmountable for the legal system and border patrol to bureaucratically handle in addition to the regular flow of people, which involves one definitional sense of physical impossibility but not logical impossibility. The controversy superimposed and intensified by the mass media is largely not because such a type of migration is logically possible, but because the audiences of the mass media fail to recognize the limitations of physically and humanly possible migration patterns, bringing about two very different stances that exhibit irrational and emotional, counter-opposing opinions.

The opinionated presenters either offer public support of the migrants to enter the country for some years or offer disdain for the migrants to enter the country. In accordance with the mass media's selections, the bickering, shouting, and persuasive and emotional arguments are chosen over indifference and attempts to realistically inform and educate the populace about the real limitations for migration. Mass confusion occurs.[3] Professional politicians take stances on the issue, which their teams perceive as offering them the greatest competitive advantages at the time, and the public becomes uninformed and thereby frequently votes against its own best interests with their ideologies. Those who fall under one or the other ideology have no understanding of the physical limitations and limits of human possibilities in the society concerning immigration, but rather they realize the logical possibilities, which are often irrelevant for the advancement of the society.

An alternative definition of "physical possibility" involves any instantiation of an event that occurs within the unity or totality of the physical world. Physical events affect one another in multifaceted ways. The possibility of a particular physical event may be viewed as depending upon its occurrence at some point, spatially or temporal, within the physical system.

In part, the unity of the physical world may lack a physical possibility that another part of the physical world contains, in which case physical possibilities are conceptualized as merely composing the entirety and unity of the physical world or reality; this is in contrast to figure 12 on the following pages insofar

3 The mass confusion is intensified by people who are financially compensated for offering their alleged opinions to the public via mass media broadcasts. The public is further persuaded by these people who sometimes offer support for stances that they privately oppose, yet they are paid to support those stances because they are articulate and charismatic presenters. For instance, members of minority racial groups, who would be expected to support a different political party than the conservative one, are used for the latter purpose, which deceives much of the populace to vote against their best interests or causes indifference and thereby failures to vote. Moreover, once an issue becomes enough of a concern for the public to inform itself, there is a complete shift from that issue to another one with the transition of the news cycle, basically treating the public, although sociologically, like a hyperactive child with an attention deficit disorder.

as physical possibility is strictly viewed as consisting of both real events and objects and some unreal events or unreal things without the latter distinction about parts of the physical world, unless reality is understood as the entirety of the physical world. Some may insist, however, that there are multiple physically possible worlds. Others may insist that there are necessarily multiple logically possible worlds. Yet others may dispute the latter attributions of necessity and inquire whether it is logically possible that there is only one logically possible world or physically possible that there is only one physically possible world.

Regardless of one's stance regarding physically or logically possible worlds, the generation of hypotheses that can undergo testing in such ways that allow us to confirm or disconfirm evidence for and against theories is an efficient means of attaining knowledge. Yet it appears to be superfluous to attempt to generate testable hypotheses for multiple possible worlds since they involve a set of irrelevancies, impracticalities, and they lack at least some external consistency with the real world insofar as only one possible world could be externally consistent with the real world in which we live. Moreover, they are untestable, hypothetical, and speculative statements, which are made as conjectures about what, at best, could be tested in some other world, say, that is isolated and distinctly different from our own (i.e., not another planet or galaxy, but rather a hypothetical alternative universe) or what is speculatively testable in some fantasy-driven alternate world.

Consider the brief socio-anthropological analysis and conceptual distinctions between hierarchy, heterarchy, and homoarchy (see Ch. 3.5), and consider the sorts of laws that may be implemented or that may be totally unnecessary within such types of societies. Some of the views concerning multiple possible worlds would appear to allow for such laws to be passed and for societies to make such changes within the near future. However, such theorizing that fails to consider the supporting evidence for theories, like social dominance and system justification theories, redirects the research. Social dominance theory is dependent upon the idea that human societies are formed as hierarchically structured systems regarding dominant and subordinate social groups instead (Pratto et al., 2006, pp. 272–273).

Sociologists attempt to identify and measure hierarchy enhancing and attenuating factors within society, which largely appear to many to support social dominance theory or system justification theory (Jost, 2001; Jost & Sidanius, 2004; Jost et al., 2009). Social dominance theory also has implications for legal theory insofar as legal systems are argued by social dominance theorists to institutionally select law enforcement trainees who tend to have higher social dominance orientations. The policing system is argued to institutionalize the law enforcement agents so that their social dominance orientations tend to increase throughout police training, in which case law enforcement agents tend to implement controlled threats and violence against low-status group members more often than high-status group members as a matter of institutional practice within criminal justice systems (Pratto et al., 2006, p. 295; Pratto & Walker, 2004). Understanding human nature or the nature of human social groups as well as human behavioral patterns cannot benefit from the arbitrary and unguided generation of problematic propositional reports, which often appear with the overuse of the concept of inclusive disjunctive possibility.

An analysis of the concept of inclusive disjunctive possibility entails a type of symmetry coinciding with the idea and argument that there are the same number of truths as falsehoods. The ideological reason given for the latter claim is that the negation of any truth is a falsehood, and the negation of any falsehood is a truth. Likewise, the formation of a logical possibility and its counterpart (i.e., the opposing logical possibility) sometimes form a logical necessity e.g., $(p \rightarrow q) \vee (p \rightarrow \sim q)$, which can be negated to form a logical impossibility, $\sim((p \rightarrow q) \vee (p \rightarrow \sim q))$. So, with negation and all the relevant disjunctive possibilities, regarding some realm, the formations of both logical possibility and logical impossibility are always inclusively disjunctively possible. No one utters and writes the same number of truths as falsehoods or the same number tautologies as logical contradictions throughout the lifespan, and the ways of thinking, which the previous ideas of numbering the amounts of truths and falsehoods, etc. involve, do amount to an ideology of symmetry of truths and falsehoods.[4]

Scientific hypotheses often proceed after observations and formulations of propositional reports of physical impossibility since any scientific experiment that tests whether a phenomenon is physically impossible only requires one successful trial to refute such propositional reports. A successful trial refutes a propositional report by means of affirming physical possibility and, most importantly, by providing a description of the thing as a real phenomenon. A sufficient amount of refutations of physical impossibilities may also very well override the characterization of something relevant and interconnected as a "logical possibility" or "logical impossibility."

Physical impossibility is either logically possible EXOR logically impossible, and physical impossibility necessitates the latter characterization, according to the disjunctive concept of possibility. For the latter reasons the study of the history of concepts in science is crucial, although social epistemology may utilize historical studies to relativize advancements of science from

---

4 Nicolai Hartmann (1935, p. 37) argues against the idea of using the concept of truth and the concept of reality in their plural forms because, although there is much that is true, the truth itself in the many is one and the same, and although there are many real things, the reality in them (or actuality) is the identical mode of being.

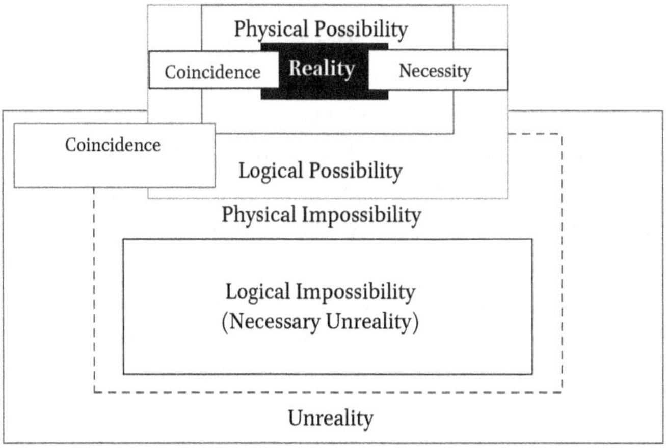

FIGURE 12 Rough depiction of all logical, physical and modal relations

contextualists' perspectives. The study of the outbreak of the bubonic plague during the 17th century in England and the misguided concept of "bad air" and usage of smoke to deter its spread were misconceptions wrought by the legal and political system themselves. Ignoring such concepts and refraining from attributing certain modes to them (e.g., ignoring the concept of „bad air" and not attributing logical possibility to it) coincides with scientific advancements.

Figure 12 illustrates a rougher way of conceptualizing the various hierarchical and ranking orders of the modal categories in respect to logicality and physicality. Several categories overlap. The category of unreality contains every logical impossibility, every physical impossibility, portions of both logical possibility and physical possibility in addition to the type of coincidence that is possible yet unreal. Coincidental unreality could be portrayed as a more significant portion of what is unreal and could be conceptualized alternatively as larger than the category of logical impossibility.

Consider it to be a coincidental unreality (i.e., logical possibility and physical possibility) that the law does not state that it is illegal to drive on the right side of the road rather than the left side within the US legal system. Perhaps during some historical period before American cars had driver seats on the left sides, decisions could have been made for American drivers to drive to the left of oncoming traffic. However, investments in productions of cars facilitating driving on the right side of the road and placements of road signs involve two types of massive investments. They made it more likely that the law would only legally permit driving on the right side of the road.

Consider the same time period these investments, productions, and placements were made. Arguably, legal permission to drive on the right is not a mere chance or coincidence at all. The legal permission and the side of the road on which one drives in relation to oncoming traffic is predictable and probable on some day, month, year, decade, or century. The Americans will only legally drive on the right side of the road by and large.

Henceforth, the concept of the coincidental unreality for Americans to legally drive on the left side may be considered by some to be physically impossible instead insofar as such a legal decision contradicts human motivation theories, economic, and sociology theories, etc. as soon as we incorporate knowledge concerning the investments, productions, and placements of signs. Insofar as coincidental unreality concerns what is physically possible in some finite timeframe (e.g., a few hours), it may be physically impossible instead to make the change from right to left in any other manner, except for passing legislation. The law enforcement's issues of citations for the new law would logistically require much time. So, one may view a law, potential law, or change in law as coincidentally unreal and physically possible in some limited timeframe and physically impossible or logically impossible outside of that timeframe.

A portion of physical impossibility is also logical impossibility. Everything that is physically impossible is also unreal. Part of what is physically impossible is coincidentally unreal and logically possible.

The category of physical possibility contains reality, the necessarily real, and the coincidentally real but also contains some of the content of the category of unreality (i.e., only the coincidentally unreal), although physical possibility is smaller than physical impossibility, i.e., in accordance with figure 12. The latter relations form a model that suffices to illustrate how the concept, category, and mode of possibility, albeit via inclusive disjunction, is consistently viewed as being greater than reality regarding their contents, which is why figure 12 illustrates logical possibility as containing a greater amount than all of reality.

The category of reality has been characterized in metaphysics as really, or possibly, consisting "entirely of necessities," "entirely of coincidences," or "a combination of necessities and coincidences" by thinkers, such as Spinoza, Kant, Aristotle, and Leibniz, which are characterizable as "metaphysical possibilities" at least insofar as they are disjunctive possibilities. Physical possibility is a more restrictive rendition of logical possibility because it negates physical impossibility but not the coincidentally unreal, according to some metaphysicians. One maintains an indifference regarding whether what is physically possible is real or unreal and also whether some things, which are physically possible, ever occur or never occur. Figure 12 above is a very rough illustration of the modal categories regarding their overlapping placements and comparative sizes.

Consider the representations of "unreality" (U), "reality" (R), "coincidence," (C) and "necessity" (N) below with "logical possibility" (LP), "physical possibility" (PP), "physical impossibility" (PI) and "logical impossibility" (LP) and their relational sizes in accordance with the following popular stance within metaphysics: (U > PI > LI) & (LP > PP > R ≥ C v N).

The latter popular stance is counter-opposed to the concept of real possibility advocated by Megareans, Spinozans and perhaps Parmenides who maintained that the being cannot succumb to any change and does not involve coming into being (i.e., no becoming) because the being continuously remains within the eternal moment of the present (i.e., neither past nor future, but rather solely now) so that all emerging and vanishing is absent, and being just involves eternality (Hartmann, 1938). The latter logical conceptions for some far less popular stances may best be represented via: (U = PI & LI) & (LP = PP & R & N).

Figure 13 illustrates the complex interrelations of dependence and independence of logicality, physicality, and possibility in relation to unreality and reality. Figure 13 roughly illustrates the logical relations between the modes wherein the dotted lines represent weak conceptual relations in one direction. For instance, physical possibility is weakly related to reality insofar as only some, rather than all physically possible events and objects, are real. Solid arrows represent necessary relations between the concepts. For example, every coincidental reality and coincidental unreality is logically possible. The concepts of necessity and coincidence on the left side respectively represent necessary unrealities (i.e., impossibilities) and coincidental unrealities, whereas necessity and coincidence on the right side represent the concepts of necessary and coincidental events and objects that are real.

Various claims become problematic for popular metaphysic stances, such as U > LP, LP > U, PI > PP, PI > R, R > PI, R = PI, etc. regarding their sizes. Applications of the latter concepts and ways of thinking about possibility and impossibility regarding the relational sizes of logicality and physicality being greater than, equal to, or lesser than another concept regarding the content, are multifarious for the development of legal theories. They are crucial to the practice of critical thinking and problem-solving in legal practices.

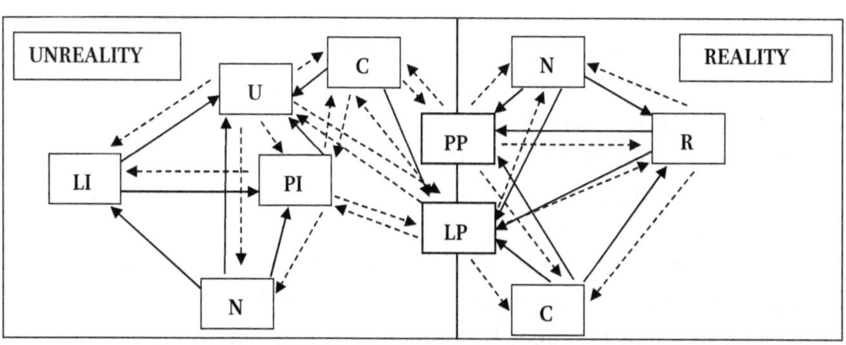

FIGURE 13 Strength of relations between the logical, physical and modal concepts

5 An Application of the Concepts of Physicality, Logicality, and Modalities for Courts of Law

Consider briefly the vast number of ways a defense attorney might utilize the concepts of necessity and coincidence for a solitary case within some legal system and in which a defendant is facing a criminal indictment of murder in the second degree instead of a lesser charge of vehicular manslaughter. Imagine that the defendant had a volatile relationship with a woman concerning a shared bank account that the woman closed and drained before they separated, and two reports of domestic violence had been reported by her against the defendant. Furthermore, the man and woman were driving in two separate cars that collided and resulted in the fatality of the woman, the incident for which the man is undergoing a murder trial.

Consider the important and selected events to either be argued by the defense attorney to be coincidental or necessary. The defense lawyer may choose to argue either via the concepts interconnected with the conception of coincidence or by means of concepts interconnected with the conception of necessity.

The defense via the concepts connected with the conception of coincidence is one way to view the direction of arguments in relation to physical possibility (i.e., since no decent lawyer would argue for any logically possible defense that could be interpreted as physically impossible). Moreover, in each alternative case of the defense attorney arguing either via the concepts interconnected with coincidence or those with necessity, the defense rationally concludes that the defendant is neither morally blameworthy nor guilty of any criminal act, despite what is held as evidence.

Let us first consider some types of arguments we may derive from the concept of coincidence. The application of the concept of coincidence to the aforementioned murder case for the defense can become crucial because the defense may very well argue that the event was "coincidental" and utilize the same language as Hartmann (1938, pp. 36–37) for this. Hartmann's philosophy on the subject has also been translated as "contingency" rather than as "coincidence" within the first full translation of Nicolai Hartmann's magnum opus in English (Hartmann, 2013).

The defense lawyer may decide to argue and describe the event as a "tragic coincidence," which was unintentional, unforeseen, and unexpected by the defendant, and which involved impartiality. For example, the attorney may argue that if the vehicles had collided slightly differently, moving the center of impact just a couple of inches away, then the man would be deceased rather than the woman. So, it may be argued by the defense that the man had absolutely no control over the main consequence with which the case is concerned.

A set of valid arguments that also coincide with the concept of coincidence include those that conclude that the man could neither have planned nor decided to kill the woman via such means, unless he was suicidal, for instance. Subsidiary arguments can be constructed to maintain that there is no evidence and no reason to believe that the man had any suicidal tendency. Causing the death of the woman while remaining uninjured, via the defendant slamming his car into hers, would therefore neither be something that the man could have planned, nor could it have been his intention since it was coincidental.

In order for the defendant to be judged as "not guilty" or "not proven" (i.e., the latter judgment is a type of Scottish verdict) it is insufficient for the outcome to be solely argued to be an unintentional one since many behaviors, for which humans are morally and legally blameworthy and responsible, are unintentional but still may have been foreseen or planned, despite culprits' hesitations and attempts to prevent the outcomes during the events' last moments. So, a successful defense may result from a set of descriptions, arguments, and evidence, which strongly suggests to jurors and judges that the incident, and especially the outcome, were unwanted, unintentional, unexpected, unplanned, and accidental in relation to the defendant who was impartial.

A successful defense may argue (i.e., via the concept of coincidence being applied to the incident) that even if the defendant had wanted the outcome to take place, he was an impartial observer of the event who could not have determined the outcome. Experts within the field of accident reconstruction, engineering, and private investigation may be funded by the defense to attest, as expert witnesses, that the driving skills and the choices of the man were insufficient to cause a collision that resulted in the other driver's death without resulting in serious injuries, death, or at least the elevated risk of injuries or death to both of them. The man is thus argued to be "lucky" to have survived with such minor injuries but "unlucky" to have to face criminal prosecution for killing his wife as well as being "unlucky" because he lost his wife.[5] "Luckiness" and "unluckiness" are partial meanings or aspects of the concept of coincidence with either positivity or negativity as a coinciding attribute based on desires, expectations, and surprises.

When the concept of coincidence is applied effectively within a court of law (i.e., via the multiple ways that the concept is equivocated (Hartmann, 1938, ibid.)), the set of arguments, concluding that some event in question is coincidental, mutually support one another and presume at least the momentary

5 It behooves the defense attorney to argue that the husband is a relatively unlucky person because this will likely increase the sympathies exhibited by the evaluators of the case.

innocence of the individuals involved with the results of the event. There is a very common presumption that it is unfair and unjust to hold an individual morally and legally blameworthy and responsible for an event that is coincidental at least in respect to a combination of all the aforementioned meanings of "coincidence." One cannot provide an intelligent, moral response and answer to some series of events that precede a coincidence to intentionally prevent the coincidental event from happening, if the event is unexpected and unforeseen or if the individual does not have ample time to react.

Consequently, the defense may simply argue via the concepts interconnected with coincidence that the events in question were coincidences, and, therefore, the defendant is not guilty. The subsidiary arguments of the defense basically aim to satisfy the conditions of meeting each of the aforementioned ways of defining the coincidence for each of the particular aspects of the incident that may lead jurors to decide upon the guilt of the defendant. Since there are several descriptions of events within the case that may lead a jury or judges to consider the defendant to be a criminal, the ways of reducing the attributions of criminal behaviors to the defendant by the jurors and judges well involves arguments for the coincidental nature of the defendant's situatedness at certain times.

The facts of the case, involving the two reports of domestic violence against the defendant, may lead several jurors to decide that the defendant tends to act violently like a criminal. The reduction of the psychological factors that contribute to the latter sorts of decisions made by jurors can also be approached by the defense lawyer via arguments with brute facts and statistical data that are utilized again to reemphasize the coincidental nature of the series of events. So, the two domestic violence reports against the defendant may be compared with any other domestic violence reports the deceased woman may have made against others, which thereby makes the domestic violence reports appear to be more like coincidences or even previous habits of the deceased as opposed to signs of delinquency on part of the defendant.

The defense may present statistics that show the likelihood of false domestic violence reports, statistics concerning the likelihood of murder after domestic violence reports (i.e., if the likelihood is low), the lack of evidence of any injury directly before and after the reports, and any evidence of the deceased having made false claims, especially about bodily harm. The amount of time spent by the defense alleviating any tarnishing of the defendant's character is best calculated in relation to the amount of time the defense considers to be best for the jury to focus on the perception of the character of the defendant. Instead, the defense may seek to tarnish the character of the deceased spouse, although this may result in indirectly diminishing the credibility of the defendant as the other spouse.

The lawyer may build the defense via encouraging witnesses, before they take the witness stand, to describe certain personality characteristics of the defendant to humanize him in addition to describing certain virtuous traits for that purpose, which also may increase the likelihood that the members of the jury will consider the domestic violence reports to be coincidental and, therefore, less important regarding their judgments for the verdict. Describing certain vices of the defendant to the jury and judges can also humanize the defendant so that the evaluators become acquainted with him on a personal level and thereby increase the probability of judging the events to be out of character for him. They may thereby judge the events to coincide with his choices coincidentally.

Some of the vices that can humanize the person and could also serve in the defense are unpunctuality or being overly punctual, servility, laziness, or a tendency to overwork oneself, overindulgences in food, etc. The creation of any story that coincides with the patterns of behavior of the defendant, especially which focus on the target character traits for the jury that lead them to believe in the coincidental nature of the incident, is ideal.

Of course, the defense should consider wisely selecting the best jury members, if given the opportunity, and providing informative instructions for the jury. Many researchers agree with Kassin and Wrightsman (1988, p. 61) who maintain that "contrary to the worst fears, scientific [jury] selection procedures cannot reliably tip the scales of justice." However, social cognitive psychology experiments concerning schadenfreude do strongly suggest that if people, including jury members, identify a person, such as a defendant, as being cold rather than warm, competent rather than incompetent, and as a member of their out-group, then they are far more likely to experience malicious joy when something at least slightly bad happens to the defendant. The extent of the schadenfreude as well as the extent or range of damaging factors happening to the person, who they judge, and which still gives them joy, is currently unknown but undergoing scientific investigations (Chiao & Mathur, 2010; Cikara et al., 2010; Cikara, Botvinick & Fiske, 2011; Cikara, Bruneau & Saxe, 2011; Cikara & Fiske, 2012).

On the other hand, it remains possible for the defense attorney's lines of argumentation to take an entirely different direction. The lawyer for the defense could instead decide to refrain from using the concept of coincidence as frequently (or at all) as part of the defense. The defense attorney may argue that the incident resulting in the death of the woman was a necessary one.

The defense lawyer also needs to remind or inform the judge and jury that any event that must occur also cannot be used reasonably to hold one morally and legally blameworthy and responsible. Such a reminder can surface within the lines of questions and cross-examinations (e.g., If there is something that has to happen, is it reasonable to expect you to prevent it from happening? Is it reasonable to hold you blameworthy for it?). The applicable idea here for court cases and legislation is simply that what anyone must do also cannot be what the individual should not do. If the defendant must do something, which is known to be necessary, then it is unreasonable to conclude that the defendant shall be held legally responsible solely for such a performance.

Basically, arguments for the defense, which either conclude that the incident in question was coincidental or necessary, are likely to relieve the defendant of moral guilt, moral blameworthiness, and legal culpability. This is a major aspect of the neuroscientific research that is in favor of the criminals' behaviors (See Ch. 3.6). The analysis of the modal relations (i.e., with or without supportive conclusions from neuroscience) to the moral realm requires much attention to the concepts of freedom of choice and the possibility for some alternative action with less risky consequences. Arguments for prosecution cannot allow the defense's arguments for the coincidental or necessary nature of the incident (or crime) in question to override the defendant's moral blameworthiness for the act when the defendant had the freedom of choice and the possibility for some alternative action to occur with less risky consequences.

Again, the defense's arguments may be entirely consistent with the idea that the incident occurred out of necessity. This is, of course, a metaphysical stance for the defense attorney for the interpretation of the relevant events of the case, which can be interpreted, metaphysically speaking, as ontic necessities or ontic coincidences (i.e., respectively, completely necessary events or completely unnecessary events (Hartmann, 1938, pp. 35, 46 & 48)). If the point of impact and destruction of two cars was a necessary event because of the road conditions and limitations of steering of the vehicles or any other circumstances beyond the control of the defendant, then the conclusion that the defendant should have prevented the collision from happening is utterly unreasonable.

Of course, there may be juries who would be persuaded that the events were necessary ones but who later determine that the defendants are, nonetheless, legally and morally responsible for those incidents either because the persuasiveness of the arguments for what necessitates the events are overshadowed by other factors (e.g., judgments of the freedom of decisions and possibilities for alternative actions with less risky consequences that the defendant should have chosen) or because the juries are unreasonable or are partial toward plaintiffs, etc. Logically valid and sound arguments are not always persuasive for juries, and fallacious arguments are often very persuasive, such as arguments that appeal to the authority of individuals who have well-recognized credentials (i.e., expert witnesses).

The concepts of necessity and determinism are embedded within psychological debates, which concern the various systems of thought that range from explaining behaviors of humans and other species in respect to nature or nurture or some combination of the two. Opposite-ended theorists lean toward either nature, such as Sigmund Freud, or nurture, such as John Watson and B.F. Skinner. The explanations, regarding those who lean toward human behaviors being performed because of, and just as, natural occurrences, often place greater emphasis upon genetics, hormones, instincts, etc. regarding the major contributing factors for why the behaviors are performed. The explanations, regarding those who lean toward human actions being performed as a result of and largely as learnt behaviors, tend to place greater emphasis upon learning, short-term and long-term memory, declarative memory, motor memory, operant and classical conditioning, etc. in virtue of the major reasons why the behaviors are performed.

There are, indeed, verdicts that arise after situations with supporting evidence that have led juries to lean toward nature or toward nurture as the ultimate explanation for the verdicts and which coincide with the given reasons and rational argumentation that concludes why some heinous or criminal action was performed. In many legal systems, defendants have been found "guilty but insane" for numerous reasons and have been given reduced sentences as a result. Yet if the judgments maintain that defendants are temporarily insane instead, defendants tend to have reduced sentences for their crimes or are given the verdict of not guilty.

Defendants have also had the verdicts of "not guilty but insane," yet such a verdict probably does not arise from the judgment that one is temporarily insane (e.g., with crimes of passion), despite whether jury members tend to believe that the diagnosed mental disorder of the defendant can be overcome or will be overcome at some future date. Crimes committed by those with mental health disorders often lead to their placements in mental health centers in developed nations. Each of the latter factors contributes to the complications involved with judgments of coincidence and necessity. Evidence for seeking rehabilitation can contribute to the defense as well because rehabilitation functions like a safe refuge in developed countries for lessening the severity of the sentences. The latter arguments for necessity and for psychological determinism are utilized to suggest that the relevant decisions made by the defendant were out of his or her control.

The legal defense of Robert Durst in Galveston, Texas demonstrates the frequent use of the notion of coincidence and the infrequent use of the concept of necessity. The usages support legal arguments of Durst's defense against the prosecution's suggestion that Robert Durst murdered his first wife and a friend. His wife had been a missing person for twenty years during the court case. However, Mr. Durst admittedly shot his neighbor in the face. Durst then decapitated and dismembered his body inside Durst's rental home.

Robert Durst's defense attorneys responded to suggestions and indirect accusations against him via consistently maintaining that Durst was "unlucky" and unfortunate. They described Durst as being the "victim" since his wife had disappeared and his friend had been murdered. Robert Durst's attorneys asserted that Durst was coincidentally placed in such circumstances.

Additionally, the concept of necessity for legal argumentation on behalf of Robert Durst was utilized to suggest that Robert Durst had struggled and fought with Morris Black over a pistol that allegedly, accidentally fired and killed Mr. Black. Moreover, the fight and struggle for the pistol were argued to be necessary for Mr. Durst to defend himself. The firearm's discharge was argued to be coincidental insofar as it was accidental, unintended, unforeseen, and unplanned.

For the dismembering of the body of Morris Black, the defense maintained that Robert Durst had a coincidental loss of memory such that the whole series of questions asked by the prosecution (e.g., what limb did you cut off first? Did you chop off Morris Black's right arm before his left arm or vice versa?) were all answered by Durst with the statement, "I don't remember."

The verdict was that Robert Durst was found to be not guilty. Since the verdict, however, there has been a 2015 six-part HBO documentary called "The Jinx: The Life and Deaths of Robert Durst," the content of which has led many to believe that Durst's not guilty verdict was largely the result of high-priced lawyers providing a more sophisticated, surprising, and well-argued defense than the opposing prosecuting attorneys did. At the end of the documentary, Durst comes strikingly close to a confession or at least close to an audible and recorded self-confession while he is using the restroom and appears unaware that he has taken the recording device with him while he appears to speak to himself. Durst says at the end of the sixth part of the documentary, "There it is. You're caught. You're right, of course, but you can't imagine. Arrest him ... What the hell did I do? Killed them all, of course."

The utilization of the concepts of necessity and coincidence, which were consistent with the facts, presented by the evidence given by the prosecution in the 2003 murder trial of Robert Durst, were intelligently placed by the defense attorneys regarding the selection of real and perhaps unreal events to which they were attributed. For instance, the attribution of the concept of necessity had a practicality regarding its use for explaining the fight and struggle for the handgun at least insofar as Durst allegedly wanted to protect himself.

This was easier for people in the court to believe or at least more viable since Morris Black was shot in Durst's apartment.

The dismemberment of the body and decapitation of Morris Black were argued by the defense to be a coincidental event insofar as it was unplanned and unforeseen. The loss of memory of the defendant concerning the dismemberments of Mr. Black's body was also at least presumed to be coincidental (i.e., unintended, unforeseen, impartial, unplanned, and accidental), which would otherwise require more explanation, psychologically speaking, for the jury to tend to form beliefs that the loss of memory was necessitated.

The brilliance of the defense was that it maintained an internal consistency regarding the well-established and known facts of the case. The defense also utilized many different conceptions of coincidence that are typically overlooked in respect to their differences, and which tend to be equivocated, too; this allowed for a simple argument to be constructed, namely: the disappearance of Durst's wife, murder of his friend, and killing of Mr. Black out of self-defense were all coincidental.

Coincidental events are events that are not intended, not foreseen, and not planned. Coincidental events are also not necessitated by the will or volition of an individual for his or her actions. So, one cannot be held morally blameworthy for the outcome of any coincidence, accordingly. Therefore, it is unfair to hold a person legally responsible for any such event. Overall, the defense also utilized the concept of coincidence regarding the events being inessential and accidental.

The judgements about events being necessary or coincidental are tendencies of thinking about the modal relations of actions from metaphysical standpoints rather than tendencies of thinking about the moral relations of actions from ethical standpoints that require the freedom of the will and the opportunity for some alternative decision with less risky consequences, which the prosecution likely failed to present to the jury.

The fundamental moral and legal problem heretofore is that if one can neither be held morally responsible nor legally responsible for a coincidence or a necessity, then how can such concepts be intelligently and pragmatically utilized within a court of law for verdicts and within daily life for decision-making about blameworthiness and praiseworthiness?

6 Coincidence as Inessentiality or Accidence: Abstract Concepts and Particulars

In the previous section, we observed how the modal analysis of events, especially events that are legally, judicially, and morally problematic and relevant for decision-making, can mislead decision-makers from making rational choices based on conceiving the actions of individuals from within the moral realm and applying concepts, such as freedom of volition, to the likely state of affairs. The difficulty that coincides with unwise decision-making is often a tendency to misattribute the modalities, especially the modes of coincidence and necessity. However, the interpretation of such a difficulty can be considered a way of thinking metaphysically because there is no criterion for proper as opposed to improper decision-making. Moreover, these misattributions can happen both at the moral realm as well as the social realm, which can promote racism, ageism, sexism, and other forms of discrimination that make negative impacts.

Coincidence, as what is inessential, regards the application of abstract ideas or concepts to what is given to us via the senses (i.e., representations of objects and events) to the extent that our abstract concepts allow the incorporation of a wide variety of representations of things to become particular instances of some abstract concept. For instance, the particular representation of some object, such as a triangle, can be any length and any color, and the triangle could have many different angles as long as it is an enclosed three-sided figure with three inside angles that are equal to 180°. The abstract concept of a triangle is the representation of a triangle that fits any particular case or example of a triangle. The unnecessary features that may be associated with the concept of the triangle are the inessential and coincidental aspects, such as the size and any specific angle.

Concepts include basically everything about which we think, including people, friends, laws, sex, violence, plants, planets, stars, tables and chairs, pets, and mammals. The abstract concept of people involves different skin and hair colors and may be associated with clothes, names, large and small numbers of people, noises, and sounds they make, and the other things that people do. Of course, those people who are born blind and deaf have concepts of people too. So, there are abstract concepts of people that do not involve what others may conceptualize as race, noisiness or music, and colorful designs that accompany people as coincidences of inessentiality.

Race, as an example in the latter sense, is an accidental or coincidental and an inessential characteristic of people. Races do not define our concepts of people. However, what is essential to our concept of people is the notion of plurality, being more than one human or person. So, various other concepts are essential or necessary to the concept of people, such as biological life, mammals, and lifespans, food consumption, excretion, but not any specific age, no specific art of cooking, and no particular material of defecation because of a range of diets, etc.

People often act based on what they perceive to be two distinctly different races, themselves and others, in-groups and out-groups, etc. Moreover, there is mutual agreement amongst many people about there being differences in human racial groups. Some differences are argued to be biologically based rather than culturally based (Hooton, 1946). Enough members of a group entering mutual agreements, concerning some classification, functions as goal-oriented actions when the misattribution of modes provides the reasons from which: (1) group members convince their other group members that the misattributions of modes are really correct, especially when misattributions provide the group with some mutual benefit and social cohesion.

A group may tend to argue that a certain race of people is less intelligent, diligent, and skilled or as able as one's own race or that another race is better suited for manual labor or lacks important skills or abilities; and (2) the organized agreements of misattributions of modes (i.e., attributing reality to unreal commonalities amongst a group or race of people) serve as a basis for social dominance of one group over some group undergoing the processes of subordination.

The latter facts explain how it is possible that racism functions in virtue of a principle of agreement, which escalates the organization of a higher status group (i.e., based on a misattribution of modes to some other race). The misattribution of a mode to some range of behaviors performed by a "race of people" requires the implantation and indoctrination of the idea that the dominant group, which tends to be the majority, is "better" or "superior" in certain respects than the other group, which is either mentally or physically superior or both. The challenge for members of a group about to engage in domination is to implant racist ideas, despite the evidence of "social contradictions," such as interracial marriages, friendships, and outstanding achievements of the targeted racial group (i.e., targeted for racism and subordination or even extermination, such as the Tutsi in Rwanda during 1994) in sports and academic achievements, and reasonable movements and speeches, such as those given by Dr. Martin Luther King Jr. and musical compositions and performances of Sam Cooke in the 1960s.

Perhaps the greatest social contradiction within the American society occurred with the first world boxing champion of African descent, Jack Johnson, on July 4, 1910 in Reno, Nevada when the society realized that Mr. Johnson surpassed the boxing skills of intellect and physicality of the former champion of European descent and won the world championship boxing match fairly in front of tens of thousands of white spectators. Africans Americans across the nation celebrated. However, the following weeks led to great increases in violence, especially led by white Americans who murdered many African Americans across the country, asserting their dominance as a racial group (Kent, 2013).

The escalation of the organization of a group may easily intensify racist tendencies of that group toward another as well as dominance and superiority in certain respects. Real and observable domination then functions as an actual and present reason from which people understand others as subordinates and consider themselves to be more sophisticated regarding overall intelligence. That is, the group's social agreement about "their own" characteristics in comparison to others tends to increase the misattributions of modes, which, in turn, serves that particular group's best interests, i.e., an interest to dominate the other group systematically with the tendency to provide high-status members with advantages and the tendency to provide greater disadvantages to subordinates.

The tendency to provide particular groups with advantages and other groups with disadvantages is systematic and serves to describe one aspect of societal systems that consist of social groups that are able to communicate effectively to establish mutual agreements about commonalities of other social groups, which are underrepresented within the societal system. When the mutual agreements about another social group involve the misattributions of modes concerning the underrepresented social group's abilities, social dominance occurs, which likely involves an overrepresentation of the subordinate social group within the prison population. Mutual agreements may even include the subordinate group members misattributing negative characteristics to themselves and the dominant group also doing so to them.

The concept of intelligence is often viewed ideologically by dominant group members and is misconstrued as being positively correlated with the more dominant racial groups' cognitive abilities within the society insofar as people conceive of subordinate racial groups as having limitations regarding their intelligence, which is lower than other racial groups. The moral and philosophical concept of freedom (i.e., lacking certain controls necessary to be a moral agent) is associated in many ways with intelligence. Real limitations are placed upon moral agents from subordinate racial groups partially because they are misapprehended as having lower intelligence levels.

The acts of racism (i.e., "racism" being a concept that partially forms from the misattribution of the mode of reality concerning races' abilities) thusly restrict the freedom of moral agents of subordinate racial groups. Members of lower status racial groups are thus led to actually face barriers that tend to decrease scores of measurements of intelligence for such groups. Thereby the misunderstood reasons for lower intelligence levels, according to certain measures, become the rational means of denying particular groups' autonomies to increase the autonomy of at least some dominant group. The reason for the lower outcomes concerning intelligence scores concerning any racial group is that the lower status racial group undergoes emotional stresses that are significantly worse than those stresses faced by higher status groups, which impose the psychological stresses on more members of the lower status groups. Moreover, the stresses imposed on lower status (e.g., racial) groups can come in many forms.

Disallowing individuals to purchase goods in certain places based on their race is one such example of the restriction of racial group members' autonomies. Of course, a "rational" aspect still resides in such examples and concerns people organizing their behaviors and like-minded ways of thinking based on a principle of agreement. The agreements serve to direct actions toward increasing the freedom of the domineering group, which systematically diminish the freedoms of the subordinated group via institutions, organizations, and social systems, such as racist families, the Ku Klux Klan in America, Neo-Nazis around the world, and other racist organizations, and the criminal justice system for penalization and imprisonment, which is formed by members of the legal institution who are largely members of the dominant group of the society.

A dominant group's ability to form a mutual agreement (i.e., based upon misattributions of modes), to organize its members, to indoctrinate them through successful institutions, and to overcome the challenges to their racist ideology presented by social contradictions, is already a hegemonic power that need not rule entirely by force (i.e., hard power) since the entire (national or societal) system functions to reinforce the ideology (i.e., soft power; See Ch. 4.4). Institutions often function as organized employee-based hierarchies that indoctrinate both dominant and subordinate group members with the racist renditions of mutual agreements; this occurs through the process of institutionalization, which reinforces subtle but effective racist tendencies.

The institutions primarily employ members of the dominant racial group, and organizations tend to promote members of the dominant racial group to higher positions than the subordinate racial group, allowing for the dominance to be perpetuated systematically. The racist renditions of mutual agreements thereby become contractual. The employment contracts legalize the latter process, and the lower status racial group is continually subordinated as lower level employees or lower status members of the institutions.

Additionally, the latter process occurs because people realize and understand that dominance and subordination are real and necessary for certain hierarchies to exist. As part of the institutionalization process, people search for justifications for these human (as well as other species) social hierarchies. Actual domination also functions within the formations of racist arguments to preserve the principle of mutual agreement amongst large numbers of dominant group members.

Domination reinforces dominant group members' mutual agreements about subordinate groups (i.e., racist, ageist, sexist, and other discriminatory ideologies about which large numbers of dominant group members agree) because the realization of domination provides a main reason why the dominant group members are viewed as superior to subordinate group members. Domination serves as a primary reason why the dominant group is superior, despite the instances of domination and subordination relations of the people. So, although there are instances of lower status racial group members in society who are managers and employers, for example, the overall domination of the higher status group serves higher status group members as the reason why they are superior and why they deserve to be dominant in their society. The dominant group's status as the majority, for instance, may also serve to reinforce the principle of agreement, which creates the ideology of racism, enabling rule via soft power.

One honorable academic opinion maintains that any particular person from any race actually can be a person who is more skilled, in any or all respects, than any other person from another race since race has nothing to do with the concepts of skill and intelligence. However, the academic attribution of that fact is suppressed or ignored by stronger, more dominant institutions, such as the criminal justice and law enforcement systems and military establishments, which attack other races of people.

Dominant groups are given systematic advantages, which tend to be overlooked by members of dominant groups. Subordinate groups are given systematic disadvantages, which tend to be overlooked by members of dominant groups. Moreover, the status of subordinate groups being disadvantaged also provides ideological reasons to believe that dominant social groups' races are superior in certain respects; the reason for this ideology is that race is easily perceived and associated with the low-status rather than the process of subordination itself being associated with the lower status, which requires social and historical understandings. Therefore, subordination is a complex process that involves the formations of ideologies via mutual agreements about derogatory claims about some group.

Socio-historical thinking is requisite to oppose the mutual agreement of the racist ideology but is exceedingly difficult to acquire early in life and without formal education that refrains from indoctrinating preferences toward particular groups (See Ch. 3.3). A side effect of domination and the institutionalization of the racist principle of agreement as well as the suppression of low-status group members' achievements (e.g., undermining the achievements of the black boxing champion, Jack Johnson, before he won his match on July 4, 1910) is the formation of groups, which are radical, and which take the misattributions of the modes more seriously. For instance, a side effect is the creation of extremist groups (e.g., the Ku Klux Klan and Neo-Nazis).

Of course, social dominance theory or system justification theory, coming from such older and newer thinkers as Karl Marx, Max Weber, Jim Sidanius, and John Jost, is relevant in respect to metaphysics, or any of the other academic disciplines, since academic institutions, money, subordination, preferences, and privileges are often interrelated. Philosophers, scientists, and other departments' members form groups at universities that function to decrease other group members' chances of being published, attaining full-time jobs, and tenured positions. Some even outcast or end communication with certain members to influence their decisions to leave universities and allow the other group to increase its chances of attaining more members. The subtleties of such acts by university professors are deviously ingenious and provide much difficulty in virtue of their detections since they are constantly hidden and naturally secretive.

The latter social dominance behaviors were likely an aspect of the first ideology department in France during Napoleon's rule. Napoleon Bonaparte played a key political role in the transformation of the meaning of the word "ideology" from "a study of ideas and their interrelations" to a more dogmatic meaning which later incorporated "false consciousness" within the Marxist usage of the term (Rehmann, 2007). Knowledge about those who are potential political opponents is necessary for political strategy to unfold through practice. Political stances of academics are often obvious in respect to the nation's major political parties. The associations of concepts are negatively impacted by institutionalization at multiple levels in virtue of their susceptibility to incorporate coincidences of inessentiality within them.

The academic faculty members composing the "university department of ideology" or college around the turn of the 19th century tended to have very similar beliefs, systems of thought, methodologies, and tended to behave as professors behave with their vaster amounts of free time needed and granted for philosophical reflections. Such a department perhaps did not efficiently function as one that could amass new knowledge without the methods and discoveries of scientific studies. Studying ideas or concepts is fruitful to the extent that scientific investigation is widespread enough to be directed through channels that filter out arbitrary speculation, which prevent them from overloading science with strict subjectivism, despite science lacking complete objectivity and being sometimes misdirected for financial, political, and personal purposes.

Concepts are also susceptible to the latter misdirection in respect to incorporating coincidences that are inessentialities. For example, when a person from a social group thinks of people, his or her concept of people may very well involve only people from his or her racial or social group at least regarding the representations or images he or she conjures up. We have already observed how Australians ignored the status of aborigine people as people insofar as they were not legally classified as "people" before 1967 at least to the extent of reckoning the size of the population (See Ch. 2.3). The formations of our concepts require the representations we receive via our sense perceptions and memories (Kant, 1781). So, they are not immediately formed but rather require multiple experiences and representations of parts or aspects of those experiences for their formations.

The process of thinking requires the abstractness of concepts and the particularity of sensations and experiences to which the concepts are applied, and which may enhance certain aspects of the experiences and sensations regarding deepening the understanding. Coincidence as inessentiality basically involves the characteristics and relations of objects and events that are unnecessary but, nevertheless, tend to be attributed to our abstract concepts via arbitrary associations with other concepts, which can be mistaken as forming elaborations of the abstract concepts, but which really lead to misconceptions. Thus, the abstract concepts of racism and sexism and misconceptions that many people have about another race, people in general, or a biological sex are simultaneously possible, and their conceptual statuses arise with the modal concept of coincidence as inessentiality, according to this view.

The following subsection illustrates why the popular stance in metaphysics (See Ch. 5.5) is problematic for further metaphysical and methodological investigations and shows why a stance that maintains strict relational comparisons between the modes, which are accompanied with logicality and physicality, does not serve well as a mainframe or foundation for scientific theoretic frameworks.

7 The Starting Point of Legal Studies: Reality's Givenness, Theoretic Doubt of the Real World, and Theoretic Consideration of Multiple Possible Worlds

For legal theory, legal practices, and philosophy of law, the relevancy of the starting point of legality is questionable but worth the inquiry. Any jurist who already knows the precise starting point from which one best begins the analysis of legal theory or praxis is also already at the forefront. Such a jurist is set for directing legal scientific and legal philosophical investigations.

Legal analysis is initiated with or after the presumption of the givenness of reality. There are a variety of so-called metaphysical and ontological investigations of law. It appears that all legal theory begins with the presumption that the theoretic negation of reality is entirely irrelevant. It is irrelevant as a starting point regarding the philosophy and science of law.[6]

Consider difficulties of the discussion of fiction and non-fiction in the formal manners with which the topics arise in courts of law. One example is the Scopes trial with the defense attorney Clarence Darrow, concerning biological evolution and creationism. It involved stories of fiction and tales of non-fiction, and the majority opinion greatly differed from the professional and expert opinions of biologists (Shapiro, 2013). Indeed, a vast number of court cases concern incorporations of fictions, intentionally or unintentionally. They influence decision-making within each judicial, legislative, and executive branch of government.

People often misidentify, forget, exaggerate, mislead, or lie to escape punishment and penalties from penal systems. So, perhaps even the vast majority of court cases involve at least some fiction within them.

Disobedience and lying come from a natural developmental process. Performances of lies begin at approximately the age of three (Talwar & Lee, 2002 & 2008). Much developmental psychology research has become important regarding rehearsed lies of children. Often these lies are coached by adults before the children are asked to give their testimonies within courts of law (Talwar et al., 2006).

The absence of knowledgeable people and legal decisions with common pitfalls in human reasoning and logical fallacies demonstrates a gap in procedural justice. Lying and fallacies are sets of problems that logical analyses may attempt to solve after decisions and verdicts have already transpired. They can

6 Almost no one remains doubtful of the reality of the world within which one lives. Yet even with such practicality, the theoretical negation of the foundation or grounding of the reality of the world is never eliminated (Hartmann, 1931, p. 7). Theoretic discussion about ontology, direct and indirect realism, and the givenness of reality as well as the discussion about the point of departure (i.e., a period during which one refrains from doubting the reality of the world) are relevant at least insofar as there is still subjectivism, idealism, skepticism, relativism, even solipsism and pragmatism. The propositional report that "something is real" is almost invariably accepted. The propositional report that "nothing is real" or "nothing exists" is generally denied, if at least such propositions are not entirely ignored. However, the proposition that "nothing is real" is not at all self-contradictory like the proposition "no proposition is true" is self-contradictory (McTaggart, 1921, pp. 58–59). It follows that the negation of the claim that "nothing is real" cannot be logically derived since it is not self-contradictory.

measure factors concerning justice in judicial systems. Logicians and critical thinking experts may partake in discovering formal and informal fallacies that involve persuading laymen, judges, and jurors through irrational arguments that appear rational.

The previous section argues that the conception of coincidence or necessity can be utilized to guide the logical conclusions and decision-making processes of jurors. Neither the affirmation nor negation of the proposition "nothing is coincidental" can be logically derived since it is neither self-evident nor self-contradictory. The proposition that "something is necessary or coincidental" confronts the same consequence as the proposition "something is real." The same is true for the claim "nothing is necessary."

One is inclined to claim that we have knowledge of reality because reality is given with any experience. The "givenness of reality" requires perception and experience or remembrance, no matter how faulty. Even if our descriptions are mistaken, or if we lack veridical perceptions or have totally inaccurate memories, the mistaken descriptions, false memories, illusions, hallucinations, etc. still allow us to have the "givenness of reality." The givenness of reality coincides with any of the latter perceptions.

Any lengthy trial concerns theoretic denials of some things that are real. The practical problem in law is that we frequently do not know the distinction between the serious denial of something that is real and the serious denial of something that is unreal. From the example of the Scopes trial, we are confronted with a form of the theoretic denial of certain aspects of reality, the serious denial of some real process, and the serious denial of some unreal process by advocates of biological evolution, creationism or both (Shapiro, 2013).

The skepticism that is basically a focused set of doubts upon the legal domain (i.e., legal systems, laws, legal institutions, lawmaking, law enforcement, etc.) is an attempt to localize skepticism. Localizing skepticism is an impossible endeavor without excluding the interconnected social phenomena and maintaining skepticism about the other social phenomena as well. For example, skepticism about the mass media system, education system, intercommunications, etc. needs to be upheld to place the skepticism regarding the legal system into a more appropriate context from which to lay doubt (Maitzen, 2006).

The act of consciousness must exceed and transcend the conscious agent for the recognitions of the objects, including objects and evidence in courts of law. The transcendence must happen for the formation of knowledge of the relevant facts of the case at hand and in order for justice to occur. Moreover, the transcendental acts of consciousness need to occur with multiple people who evaluate the case in virtue of the evidence for there to be any fairness. With any recognition, there is room for doubt.

Ethics is required in these evaluations, especially honesty, as well as attention to the facts during the case which can last for hours, weeks, or months. Afterwards, a weighing of the facts and application of concepts, such as freedom, blame, and illegality are required for justice as fairness in a court of law. Nicolai Hartmann describes the relations of mere thinking with recognizing via the transcendence of the act of consciousness with the recognizer and the objects that exist independent from the recognizer's perceptions of them.[7]

That which the act of consciousness must exceed during recognition involves the objects that exist independent from the perceptions of them, but which allow for the perceptions of them to arise (i.e., representational realism). Within legal systems, in courts of law, amongst lawmakers, during policing situations and during ordinary perceptual recognitions, there are recognitions of legal proceedings, objections sustained and overruled, verdicts, laws passed and rejected, criminals and others questioned, searched, apprehended, arrested, convicted, fined, jailed, imprisoned, and even executed.

The latter recognitions of the law, members of the legal institution, and what they do also involve thoughts and imaginations, but the events are real and thereby allow for recognitions of them to sometimes arise. Insofar as the objects of knowledge and consciousness require acts of transcendence and real relations to the recognizer, the recognizer attains knowledge of only some of them. Others are misapprehended.

The recognitions of legal acts and legal systems are requisite for the emergence of the legal point of view since the circumstances of the individual lead one to this attitude. The legal viewpoint presumes that there are both recognizable and recognized legal events rather than mere imaginations, fantasies, thoughts of legal events, and beliefs about the law. The legal point of view assumes that solipsism is false and maintains a stance opposed to idealist philosophies. From the viewpoints of the lawyers, judges, and juries, the admissible evidence for the existence of things and evidence for the occurrences of events lead individuals in courts of law to recognize facts. Some of these facts lead toward sound argumentation and judgments, and justifiable and/or just verdicts.

---

7 Hartmann writes: Indeed, however, the act must exceed it insofar as it should be an act of object recognition. Here the distinction opposing mere thinking, imagining, and fantasizing is tangible. The distinction lies in the transcendence of the act, in which the connection is on a real oppositional link. The consequence reveals itself immediately with the concept of the object. (Hartmann, 1931, pp. 9–10) [Wohl aber muss der Akt es überschreiten, sofern er gegenstandserfassender Akt sein soll. Hier ist der Unterschied gegen blosses Denken, Vorstellen, Phantasieren greifbar. Er liegt in der Akttranszendenz, in der Bindung an ein reales Gegenglied. Die Konsequenz zeigt sich sogleich am Gegenstandsbegriff.]

If the latter viewpoints of those involved with the law did not presume that such objects and events were recognizable, the set of proceedings for courts of law would be completely undermined. The set of presumptions and circumstances surrounding the legal viewpoint, against which solipsism and idealist philosophies are faced, present us with a practical philosophy, a philosophy of law. From this practical philosophy, decisions and problem-solving methods (e.g., legal verdicts and legal argumentation) aim to provide solutions giving defendants, culprits, accusers, and the accused a chance for a fair and just legal decision to be made.

Such legal decisions and legal problem-solving are necessary for legal systems to continue stabilizing expectations of people of the society. The philosophy of law supports a form of realism and involves the relinquishment of various types of skepticism (e.g., global and perceptual skepticisms).

Legal practitioners would be hard-pressed to find a solipsistic or idealist account (i.e., a solipsistic legal theory or a theory of legal idealism) that could contribute to the generation of testable hypotheses. What we are in search of are methods that facilitate recognitions and attainments of knowledge of the law. The law is a set of real phenomena or events that is independent from the observer. The law thereby in no way depends on an observer's perception of law since it arises socially along with other social phenomena via intersubjective communications, agreements, etc. Knowledge-acquisition requires a knower and often an observer.

The objects of knowledge are completely impartial regarding whether they are ever known. An object is not dependent on knowledge to subsist since any object must be indifferent regarding being known or knowable. This is consistent with the legal point of view. Legal decision-making is typically made with the realization that there is even more available evidence, which would also be admissible, but the verdict is decided under the limitations of time for the sake of practicality. There are inferences made toward the best limitations under conditions that are never the most desirable temporal ones regarding evidence.

Knowing that one knows obviously plays a major psychological role amongst players in legal systems regarding lawmakers, enforcers, judges etc. The knower who knows that he or she knows can withhold or divulge one's knowledge of one knowing that one knows. The knowledge of having knowledge may be accepted by the others as what one believes, likely believes or deceives others into thinking that one believes. What the audience takes from the interaction often depends on the presentation of the story rather than the listing of facts.

Epistemic theory is rooted as a second consideration along with an ontological one with regard to the basis of givenness. The carrying capacity of the given conditions that convey to us the knowledge of reality determine the standing or falling of the outcomes of every ontological reflection (Hartmann, 1931, p. 8). Methodology is intricately connected with these conditions that convey knowledge.

Theories are involved in such methods that are invariably included with attainments of knowledge. Theories involve presumptions that often fall short as outcomes of ontological reflection. Sometimes presumptions are analyzed separately as if they are theories themselves (i.e., involved with the formations of test-worthy or testable hypotheses for attaining knowledge), and yet they fail both in the methodological endeavor to form testable hypotheses and even hypotheses that are worthy of being tested.

If it is theoretically and ordinarily viewed that there is definitively a real world,[8] views of skeptical alternatives and doubt about the real world are altogether absent. The definitude results in presumptuously discarding one metaphysical possibility and one level of skepticism at a theoretic level of analysis that is beneath the amount of intensity of global skepticism (Brant, 2013b). Problematically, no sufficient reason for lowering the level of systematic doubt would be provided. This would hinder methods, too. So, theoretic analysis must begin without the use of an incredibly important tool from the philosopher's toolkit, namely, intense analytic suspicion.

The theoretic starting point thus begins with doubting the real world, and then understanding two more logically possible alternatives as systems of thought. The plurality of possible worlds thesis within the field of metaphysics appears to some to have a number of advantages as a system, from which methodological analyses are yielded. The plurality of possible worlds is usually just compared to the thesis that there is only one possible world, though. One expense of the latter common comparison is what we may call a "relinquishment of the denial of the thesis that there is no real world and no possible world at all." The nonexistence of any possible world is one metaphysical possibility, one logical possibility, and, according to some systems, a physical possibility (Hartmann, 1931).

The plurality of possible worlds thesis is presented at the expense of the, at least, tacit presumptions that the givenness of reality entails that "there must be at least one possible world" and that "there is at least one real world." The failure to apply skepticism in this logical realm has led many philosophers to uphold that there is a plurality of possible worlds. Next, it is argued that some of those worlds contain similar social systems as the social systems in the real

8 The use of the phrase "real world" refers to either the mind-dependent or the mind-independent world or both.

world and that the other possible worlds are viewed as having similar but alternative actions. The possible worlds are imaginatively described as including social systems, such as legal systems, in societies.

Legal systems are amazingly complex. There have been hundreds if not thousands of them throughout history. When the major worldly legal systems are described, they have been placed in three families, which some scholars argue are uncontested, namely, the "Romano-Germanic family, the Common law family and the family of Socialist law" (David & Brierley, 1985, p. 22).

The latter systems are argued by some not to incorporate the contemporary legal conceptions. There are many exceptions that fall outside of the latter three types of legal systems, although legal systems in the late 20th century have taken elements from one or more of the latter three families of legal systems. The extent of the differences between legal systems from the three families can be drastic, though. For example, in the Far East, many of the traditional views of law maintain that law is for "barbarians" only (ibid., p. 30). Rene David and John Brierley (ibid., p. 30) write:

> For the Chinese, law is an instrument of arbitrary action rather than the symbol of Justice; it is a factor contributing to social disorder rather than to social order. The good citizen must not concern himself with law; he should live in a way which excludes any revindication of his rights or any recourse to the justice of courts. The conduct of individuals must, unfailingly, be animated by the search for harmony and peace through methods other than the law. Man's first concern should not be to respect the law.

The diversity of legal systems is quite great and may inexorably be involved in the lack of application of the dogma of the multiple possible worlds thesis, regarding social systems. The idea is that in these so-called other possible worlds there are entirely different legal systems, despite having societies that have remarkably similar cultures otherwise. We may hypothesize that the plurality of possible worlds thesis lacks relevance to the philosophy of law. It is thereby arbitrary regarding any application to law or legal systems.

The analysis of the proposed unity of sense perceptions, consistent scientific observations, results, and conclusions made by scientific communities are theoretically compared and contrasted with the unity of reality. The analysis is complicated by a dogma that the givenness of reality necessarily leads to the notion that there must be at least one possible world and that there is one real world. The level at which the analysis is undertaken is already ambiguous.

Modes are tacitly but presumptuously superimposed on the possibility of the real world. There is a common view that maintains that it is necessary to describe the possibility of the real world but never the theoretic unreality or theoretic impossibility of the real world. There is a difference between a scientific investigation aiming to describe aspects of an extant legal system via measurements and one with philosophic postulations that the legal system has a range of entertaining possibilities that never came to fruition (e.g., unnecessary or coincidental unrealities or logical or physical impossibilities). The problem is a matter of irrelevancy for such philosophic postulations. Appeals should be made to practical sciences.

The inclusive disjunctive possibility of the plurality of worlds is at least apparently given greater credence when the theoretic denial of the real world is absent from the discussion. The greater credence of the plurality of worlds thesis is much like the case with the under and overrepresentation of information from the mass media system regarding law. The theoretic denial of the real world is underrepresented if not entirely misrepresented.

The momentary popularity of the multiple possible world stance has culminated in the debate concerning possibilism and actualism. Arguably, the possibilism and actualism-debate presents an "extreme stance" that is comparable to another stance that would entertain the idea called the theoretic doubt of the real world.[9] The outlying nature of the plurality of possible worlds thesis can undergo deep consideration. Consider its relation to the idea that the concept of possibility is merely an aspect of cognition that serves no role other than allowing us to attain knowledge or understanding of the real world (Kant, 1781; Hartmann, 1938; Lorenz, 1941/1984 & 1977; Zadeh, 1999).

Various metaphysical possibilities have been presented over the course of roughly two millennia and allow us to theoretically consider and doubt that the real world consists of:

> (1) just coincidental events; (2) just necessary events; or (3) both coincidental and necessary occurrences; and a fourth version that is almost always absent: (4) maintains that the real world neither consists of coincidences nor of necessary events. (4) is also consistent with the theoretic doubt of the real world but may involve some neutral interpretation of events, describing the modal attributions of necessity and coincidence or the unnecessary as irrelevancies.

(1), (2), and (3) remain philosophically problematic and controversial, whereas the aspect of (4), regarding the theoretic doubt of the real world, is

9 The serious doubt of the real world is sometimes called "Cotard syndrome." Cotard syndrome is a form of psychosis with which people claim to be dead or rotting or claim that they do not exist, and which is often associated with schizophrenia and bipolar disorder (Young & Leafhead, 1996, p. 155; Pearn & Gardner-Thorpe, 2002, p. 1400; Brant, 2013b, p. 302).

uncontroversial insofar as we consider the givenness of reality. Contra the theoretic doubt of reality and (4), for us, reality is a "given." Some even presume that reality's givenness is necessary. (4) may be doubted but also considered as a way of thinking about objects and events so that their alleged statuses as either necessary or coincidental are merely descriptive of ways of describing or thinking rather than descriptive of the objects and events themselves. The latter point has serious implications for the analysis of the neurobiological realm in Ch. 3.6 as well as the application of the modes of necessity and coincidence to court cases, which both lead to the denials of moral blameworthiness and legal blameworthiness that seriously impact verdicts (See Ch. 5.5).

The epistemic theoretic concern is that if what we maintain of the real world is not real, then what we call "knowledge" is not knowledge at all; it is closer to pure thought, imagination, dreaming, and fantasizing. The modal view of reality, which dichotomously holds that reality is necessary EXOR not necessary, is a prime candidate for epistemic theoretic concern.

Brant (2013b) maintains that if the least skeptical argument, which is able to defeat the alleged knowledge-claim undergoing the analysis, is also equivalent to a form of global skepticism (i.e., the most skeptical arguments[10]), then such a claim is embedded within the theoretic framework itself from which the theorist functions. As an embedded claim, the alleged knowledge-claim is not knowledge. It is, rather, a presumption of the system of thought itself that is, at best, utilized to attain knowledge in other respects.

Often the presumptions embedded in the system's framework pertain to many alleged knowledge-claims about possibility as a concept and to alleged possibilities of different events and objects. Figure 12 is greatly undermined by such an analysis. Figure 12 can be considered as categorizations of different types of unreality (e.g., unnecessary unrealities and impossibilities) and different modal types of reality or real things (e.g., necessarily and coincidentally real things) that are arbitrary, theoretic constructions able to misguide theorists and practitioners, even regarding legal studies.

At least one interpretation holds that one metaphysical possibility about the world is that there could be absolutely no physical possibility at all. This illustrates just how indifferent metaphysical possibility is toward physical

10 The most skeptical arguments propose that the memory of the alleged knower is faulty and thereby the premises and conclusions of the arguments the individual makes are unable to be remembered and are unknown to anyone. Moreover, the skeptical scenario proposed by the arguments illustrates that the real world has only existed for a few milliseconds.

possibility and reality. The latter level of analysis is more fundamental than the level of analysis from which we begin our investigation of law, though.

8 The Concept of Metaphysical Possibility: Inclusive Disjunction and Possibility Concerning Metaphysic Content

There are overlapping differences between all that is properly categorized as "logically possible," LP, and all that is fittingly categorized as "metaphysically possible," MP. Differences between LP events, regarding the legal system, and MP ones are less relevant to our analysis regarding the law and reducing violence.[11]

11 "Metaphysical possibility" (MP) is a type of inclusive disjunctive possibility that often involves the content of metaphysics (i.e., philosophical issues concerning determinism, indeterminism, time, space, theism, causation, ontology, etc.). The broad definition of MP maintains that the possibility of unreal things, which are PP EXOR PI not LI (i.e., physically possible or physically impossible but not both and not logically impossible) is MP. MP is conceptualized, in this sense, as being greater than reality and physicality insofar as MPs include everything real and physical as well as what is unreal but not logically impossible and what is merely PI and unreal (i.e., PI but not LI). So, anything that is real is also MP, anything PP is MP, and many unreal and PI things are MP, according to the broad view of MP.

Broadly speaking, metaphysical possibility thus includes both that which is within the unity of the physical world as well as disjunctive alternatives concerning even what never has happened nor ever will occur within the real physical world, i.e., just as long as the MP events are free from contradictoriness. However, there are alternative views of the concept of MP, and some of them rely upon making specific distinctions between what is "actual" and what is "real." (See Ch. 5.13; Lewis, 1986).

The broad and narrow views of MP both maintain that it is MP for any particular event to happen that falls within "the *range* of the events that have happened," even if the particular event never actually occurs, for instance. So, for example, if the two fastest one-mile runs by humans are, respectively, three minutes and thirty seconds long and three minutes and forty seconds, then it is still MP for a human to run a three minute and thirty-five second mile, even though no human *ever* runs that time or speed (i.e., where speed equals the distance divided by the time). Likewise, if the highest amount of weight ever lifted for the clean and jerk Olympic lift (e.g., within or outside of the Olympic games) is 700lbs., and 650lbs. is never hoisted above the head by any weightlifter, then it is MP to lift 650lbs. despite such a feat never being or becoming fulfilled.

Given the former presumptions, it can be PP for the mile-run to be completed by a human in three minutes and thirty-five seconds, if it is the case that the fastest runner could have slowed down. For example, perhaps the runner could have decelerated because he or she decides to do so or because of environmental factors. Some environmental factors are the wind speed and directions of the wind during the race.

Moreover, if any of the slower runners could have trained more efficiently and run that swiftly, the conditions for the physical possibility of the event would be fulfilled. Physically possible events are restricted via the occurrences of other physical events. However, metaphysically possible events are, presumably, free from the latter restrictions, since they, conceptually speaking, transcend physicality.

Metaphysical possibility is unquestionable in the latter regard since the conceptual content of metaphysical possibility includes much of what is physically impossible. For instance, it is MP for a human and even a snail to complete a mile in three minutes and twenty seconds, according to the broad view of MP. Any amount of weight being lifted over one's head is MP, too, according to this view. The former presumptions are questionable regarding the PPs, though.

It remains questionable whether running a mile in three minutes and thirty-five seconds is PP. An affirmative answer may greatly undermine motivational theories in human psychology and sports psychology. Such theories utilize the concept of PP in their analyses of what is humanly possible, too. For instance, how could an athlete train for so many years at the Olympic level, be the fastest runner ever on the planet, and simply choose to run significantly slower during the main event, according to any theory of motivation?

The greater range of possibilities, concerning the decision-making of the runner, gives us at best a more comprehensive theory of possibility. This range, however, perhaps includes too much at the expense of parsimony and consistency. It provides us with a possibility theory that is less practical in relation to its affects upon our motivational theories' abilities to yield testable scientific hypotheses.

For these reasons, when an Olympic committee maintains that an athlete has shattered the current world record in a sport, the introduction of certain inclusive disjunctive possibilities is senseless and seemingly baseless. For instance, when the Olympic committee claims that a male high jumper cleared the bar at over eight feet high, and one maintains that "possibly he did not clear even six feet on that same jump," we are provided with an irrelevancy as a logical possibility since arguably, "it's not possible that he did not even clear six feet because he reached over eight feet."

It might well be argued that the weightlifter who hoisted 700lbs. could have lifted 650lbs instead, but if this never happens, then it is merely a mathematical conclusion that involves a specific instance that is, in principle, unobservable and unknowable. Moreover, such a conclusion—that the lifter can always lift less weight than what the lifter actually lifted—assumes a metaphysical stance that presumes the falseness of any stance that maintains that specific real events are necessary and tends to presume that it is true that many or all such events are coincidental and unnecessary. Besides, many weightlifters have even become injured after attempting lifts with lighter weights than their maximum lifting performances for those same lifting exercises.

Propositional reports about what is MP are totally indifferent, apart from excluding what is contradictory, but the attribution of MP may very well be restricted to what is real or lack such a restriction. There is neither a list of generally agreeable things or events that are logically possible but not MP, nor MP but not logically possible, nor both MP and LP. The concept of MP is therefore abstract, ambiguous, and dubious in relation to its contribution as a subdivision of the concept of inclusive disjunctive possibility, although it can be useful in describing the opposing alternative sets of possibilities when they present strictly metaphysical problems, such as the concepts of freedom and determinism as they are applied to the same situations.

Arguments against the alleged knowledge of what is MP only concern globally skeptical arguments. For the latter reason, the only arguments that are able to cast doubt upon alleged knowledge claims about what is MP are the most skeptical arguments (i.e., global skepticism). However, the globally skeptical arguments are also, simultaneously, the least skeptical arguments that are able to cast doubt upon alleged knowledge of what is MP, which is thoroughly problematic (Brant, 2013b). Globally skeptical arguments are the least skeptical arguments regarding alleged knowledge-claims of MP of things since there are no arguments that are less skeptical than global skepticism that cast doubt upon such alleged knowledge-claims. For instance, perceptual skepticism produces a vast array of doubt but gives no reason to doubt any attribution of MP.

MP is inclusive disjunctive possibility that remains indifferent regarding metaphysical alternatives, such as idealism, direct realism, and representationalism. So, the systems of thought that altogether complete some conceptual realm are each considered MP. The broad view of MP also involves certain instances of PI events and things, such as a whale flapping its fins and flying through the air or into outer space. As such fantastical alternatives to the way things are, MP alternatives are often purely imaginative attributions of possibilities contributing to science fiction rather than scientific methodology, except in some cases where the relevance involves observational data, e.g., concerning decision-making, determinism, free will, liberty of indifference, and spontaneity, say, that coincides with the metaphysical possibilities of libertarianism, compatibilism, and hard determinism (Soon et al., 2008).

The latter ways of thinking inevitably involve the law and legal systems when such analysts begin analyzing the social realm and society as a concept. For instance, alternative verdicts from the ones that already happened in courts are hypothesized to have happened in similar but other possible worlds. Each aspect of the society and its subsystems is viewed alternatively. They are viewed in ways that differ from what really happened with multiple social systems. However, such ways of thinking about the social systems, hypothetically speaking, leave so much to be desired. These ways of thinking, arguably, reach nowhere regarding the attainment of knowledge about any society and social systems, such as legal systems.

One might bet that the latter methods of attributing PP, LP, and MP to unreal events and objects have never been demonstrated to be effective, apart from in philosophy. It remains questionable whether they are effective within philosophic works, too. Nonetheless, there are strict ways in which the attribution of modes is applied before the scientific experimentation begins. For instance, the sociology of law can be tested by hypotheses pertaining to the police in a jurisdiction regarding what is physically possible for them to do, such as the approaching of a building occupied by masked gunmen, as quickly and cautiously as possible from the precinct.

Methods of attributing PI and PP vastly change the role of the "hypothesis" in theoretic frameworks since hypotheses are generally formed to test theories. One could attribute PI and PP without any record or memory of prior attributions of LP, MP and LI, for example. If a theory entails that a certain type of event is PI, the instantiation and observation of that type of event would at least produce a serious reason for the theory to undergo structural changes within its framework. The theory's ability to yield hypotheses becomes ever more questionable.

The narrow usage of MP above seems to involve the analysis of systems of thought (e.g., Islamic, Jewish, or Christian philosophy). It involves such systems' interpretations of physicality, nature, the supernatural, and what is possible in accordance with such

9 Real Possibility: Requiring Real Fulfillment and More Exclusive Disjunctions

There are certain applicable ideas that expand across multiple fields but may receive greater consideration in one field than another. Murphy's law is an example of this. It applies to both engineering and legal systems.

Murphy's law is often applied in physics and engineering. The law maintains that "anything that can go wrong will go wrong." Murphy's law is used specifically to refer to design flaws with the structures of things, such as buildings, aircrafts etc. (Mathews, 1995). Murphy's law is a subconception of the concept of real possibility.

Structural flaws in machinery will not continuously function to any ideal standards in any ongoing way. They cannot continuously work via coincidences referred to as "luckiness." Instead, flaws will lead to functional problems over long enough durations. The events of failures of functions of machines and systems are confirming evidence for the predictive power of Murphy's law. This is true when the law is attributed to some proposed design flaw of a vehicle regarding its unbalanced structure, for example.

Murphy's law can be applied to laws within legal systems as well. If the laws are dysfunctional and are enforced accordingly, then what can become wrong will actually go wrong. In the latter sense, a law is tested or undermined with each instance of its violation. Those who conceived of what is lawful can reduce their ideological thinking about what lawfulness is or should be, too.

So, like a structure that has a flaw, a law that is flawed (i.e., where something can go wrong) will demonstrably show its dysfunctional characteristics, according to this view (Matthews, 1995). The same problem of the lack of functionality regarding structural flaws can be applied to the methods of enforcement and the methods of evaluating or judging, respectively, within the executive and judicial branches of government.

---

systems of thought. Their attribution of MP to an event or object is made once the metaphysical content (e.g., God and His abilities) arises (Chalmers, 2002, 145–146; Chalmers, 1996). Gilbert Fulmer (1978) describes the dubiousness of such attributions of the supernatural. A common type of attribution of the mode of MP is that something traveling a billion meters per second is MP. The attribution is in accordance with such systems of thought, which is why we may call the consistent attributions of MP, such as this, the "narrow view of MP."

What appears to be ignored within modal logic and metaphysics, concerning modality, is the real function of modal attributions (i.e., of possibility, reality, necessity etc.) at the outset, which is, namely, their epistemic functions for the individual, especially regarding the attainment of knowledge in an environment in which one lives and that is, of course, applicable to societies with legal systems.

Murphy's law, as a subsidiary concept of the conception of real possibility, is applicable regarding laws within courts, legal systems, and criminal justice systems. Consider the "separate but equal" laws before the Brown v. Board of Education court case in 1954 in the United States (Lerner et al., 2006). The latter court case undermined the Jim Crow laws of the South in the United States in a manner that is like the overuse of a machine with a flaw or the additional stress purposely placed on a flawed machine.

This conception of the law and the analogy of a flawed machine might well be analyzed further. Consider whether the creation of a totally different machine is better for functionality or whether the improvements of the machine from the more fundamental parts of its structure (i.e., its infrastructure) is best. Likewise, law or the legal system can be considered similarly regarding the total replacement or the improvements of the law or legal system.

The concept of law conveyed in relation to Murphy's law is one which conceives of the law like a social scientific experiment of the society. Changes in law often fundamentally impact the cultures of the society. Changes in law can determine the legitimacy of business and change the relations of power, too.

Perhaps though, the aspect of law or legal systems that is analogous to the infrastructure of the machine with flaws, and from which the improvements are most easily made, is the pre-establishment of power relations. The power relations are problematic regarding violence, in accordance with social dominance theory. The power relations demonstrate unfair, and unjust ways of systematically subordinating lower status human groups in societies. The unfairness in power relations is evident historically from the devastation of the ways of life of indigenous peoples and evident in the systematic disadvantages of subordinated groups who are incarcerated more frequently.

"Real possibility" excludes each inclusive disjunctive possibility that fails to ever become instantiated but includes the remainder of possibilities. Real possibility is a conception that requires more than the mere lack of logical contradictoriness (i.e., coinciding with the inclusive disjunctive concept) for something to be possible. Otherwise, the concept of contradictoriness incorporates a wider domain for the association of the concept of real possibility to be made (See Ch. 5.10).

From the concept of real possibility, regarding problematic propositional reports (e.g., S can be P, and S can also be not P), only one option is a real possibility. The sheer absence of logical contradictions generally does not suffice in courts of law for some alternative description of the relevant facts. There are far too many of that sort of possibility for there to be practicality when presenting them.

Real possibility instead requires the attainment of the thresholds for all the necessary conditions that suffice to make something happen. Reaching each threshold for each necessary condition composes a sufficient condition for the real possibility of that event. The failure to fulfill any of such thresholds (e.g., even attaining all of them, except for one) suffices for such an alleged event to be impossible. The concept of real possibility is descriptive of what necessitates the fulfillment of every condition that suffices for something to be real and to happen.

The conception of real possibility is indifferent regarding when and where some possible event actually occurs. The timing and the location of any type of event that happens, but which rarely or barely suffices to become instantiated, still involves real possibility. That is, if the event ever occurs or occurs even once at any duration and in any place, then the event amounts to a real possibility. Such an event is really possible in accordance with the fulfillment of its conditions for instantiation. Thus, what is irrelevant, and the aspect about which the concept of real possibility is indifferent, concern the time and the location at which the event, which is really possible, happens. The same is true for Murphy's law since the law states that what can go wrong will go wrong. As a subsidiary concept of real possibility, Murphy's law neither informs us when, where, or how the event (i.e., failure) will happen.

Hartmann (1938, p. 45) explains that while the perfect geometrical and spherical form of a body lacks logical contradictoriness, for example, no such body is really possible. The form cannot subsist in the real world whenever the series of real conditions fail to be met sufficiently. For example, during the absence of the balance of the mass or the lack of any other governing factors (e.g., the gravitational effect of other masses, the internal heterogeneity of the specific weight, the rotation, etc.), there can be no existence of the form. So, the status of a being requires that each necessary condition for existence be met to meet the sufficient condition for its real possibility.

"Real possibility" is a far more restrictive concept than inclusive disjunctive possibility. Real possibility is foremost a denial that the concept of coincidental unreality describes anything whatsoever. Anything veridically characterizable as "unreal" is thus also always characterizable as "impossible" (i.e., necessarily unreal).

Theoretic frameworks advocating the concept of real possibility deny that there are different types of unreal things and unreal events. Their reasoning is that everything that is unreal is also impossible. For the latter reason, the concept of real possibility requires an additional conception of contradictoriness. In the next section, the importance of the coinciding conception of contradictoriness with the concept of real possibility is presented with its relations to law.

The concept of real possibility is serviceable in courts of law. For example, the concept can be applied when evaluating violence that happened with deliberately inflicted, serious physical injuries to others (i.e., grievous bodily harm in the UK). Charges of grievous bodily harm, sexual assault, breach of a domestic violence order and torture are four separate charges in legal systems' criminal justice systems (e.g., in Australia).

The four charges may involve the same incident that lasted two minutes long or could involve four different incidents by the same person or up to four different people. This latter point utilizes the concept of real possibility concerning four charges. These charges arose in combination with the preceding violence and violated order.

Generally, bills concerning unreal or physically impossible things do not become laws. This suggests that legislation generally involves consistency with (or stricter adherence to) the concept of real possibility and its coinciding concepts. Legal studies and philosophy of law also tend to utilize the concept of real possibility, although not explicitly.

Nevertheless, the concept of real possibility plays a vital role concerning methods for attaining knowledge, including the social causes of violence. Much of our data concerning the social causes of violence derives from our courtroom records, records of verdicts, indictments, unofficial charges and accusations shown via the mass media etc. Data illustrates that those who experience procedural injustices after committing violent acts are more likely to become repeat offenders.

Understanding and then ultimately reducing social causes of violence also require attention to the criminal justice system's process of domination of lower status groups. With the concept of real possibility, attention to the so-called coincidental is minimized to zero. Focus on the necessity is brought to the forefront.

10 Contradictoriness for Real Possibility and Logical Possibility: Exclusive and Inclusive Disjunction and Legal Maxims

Social contradictions arise when the limitations of our human understandings lead us to identify people as performing certain roles because of their relations with us in society.

For example, in marriages, the in-laws can strengthen and support or meddle and weaken the marital ties. Such social relations appear contradictory.

The descriptions given by high-status and low-status groups of the criminal justice system often appear contradictory. Each criminal justice system executes violence and controlled threats. Each criminal justice system reduces violence and controlled threats. It lessens some types of the same real phenomena that it increases, namely, the societal violence.

Each criminal justice system measurably increases the frequency and intensity of violence. For example, the number of police shooting people annually and number of yearly fatalities from this violence is measurable. There are also methods for measuring the decreases in societal violence. It becomes difficult to fittingly attribute the decreases in violence to the police. Our understandings are challenged by the mass media's over and underrepresentations of the polices' roles as increasers and decreasers of violence. That illustrates what might be called a social contradiction of policing.

The societal relations appear contradictory regarding the criminal justice system. Consider that prosecuting attorneys and police sometimes oppose the ones who are not responsible for the violent crimes for which they stand accused. Consider the civil liberty groups, lawyers, and police who are protecting the guilty. The latter people's behavioral patterns are diametrically opposed to those of the lawyers and police opposing those who are responsible for committing the violent crimes.

Ideally, civil liberty groups protect the innocent from false accusations of crimes. However, there are tendencies to protect the non-criminals and tendencies to protect the criminals. There are tendencies to oppose such protections and also to be offensive.

Defense and prosecuting attorneys, police, judges and others make these just and unjust decisions, too. Family members and friends often defend their people in their own social groups, despite whether they committed wrongdoings or not. Each type of member of the legal institution makes the same sorts of actions that coincide with justice and acts of injustice. Social contradictions arise at times when the members are assumed to strictly take one role in one direction and those members instead take another role in the opposing direction (e.g., increasing conflict and violence).

Any incident that actually happens, even the rare ones, are real possibilities. The real possibilities also concern the changing relations of power and cohesion. The social contradiction is not a concern when the concept of real possibility is applied because the concept of identity is conceptually different during its use. For example, a carpenter, a judge, and a criminal are not a carpenter, judge, and criminal when they sleep because no carpentry, judging, and criminality are happening from them during the sleeping state.

With the conception of logical possibility, the behavioral tendencies of woodworking, judging, and stealing, the occupational titles etc. lead people to overextend the identities as if the identities take precedence over other behavioral tendencies. A carpenter could very well destroy more furniture than he or she ever makes. A police officer could destroy more than he or she protects. For the use of real possibility being conceptually applied, the concept of a carpenter involves that which is identified as creating the carpentry, ignoring the notion of personhood as if the body of carpenter is entirely different each moment that no carpentry is being accomplished. According to the concept of real possibility, the same is the case for the police officer who would cease to be such during those moments and places that do not involve policing.

In the society, relations of power and social cohesion regarding the social groups are changing (Berkman et al., 2014). For instance, gang members are lost, leave, join another gang, but ultimately there are social reasons for gangs to remain intact. Social cohesion may refer to the presence of bonds and absence of social conflict between the members of the social group.

Two families in one neighborhood may change their relations of power to each other based on an election. For example, the social cohesion can be lost with group members' inequalities regarding wealth, racial differences, and even when there are great differences regarding political participation (ibid.).

When a social group has a higher social cohesion, a member who deviates from the group's actions will quickly be communicated with to change his or her behaviors. When the deviant fails to change his or her behaviors, the group with higher social cohesion tends to refrain from giving that member any social approval. That member's choices for group activities become less impactful. There are tendencies toward ostracism from the social group with high social cohesion (ibid., p. 302; Homans, 1958). The social group begins dominating the member who deviates from their norms.

In society, actively lowering the frequency and intensity of dominating lower status groups can be accomplished in two different manners. Firstly, it is strategic to attempt to reduce the number and intensities of legal disadvantages of lower status groups to levels of higher status ones. Secondly, it is strategic to attempt to increase the number and intensities of legal disadvantages of higher status groups to the levels of lower status groups. The strategies may best be implemented gradually. Criminal justice systems are confronted with these strategies as logical possibilities.

Herein lies the apparent social contradiction. Lessening the intensity and frequency of the so-called social contradiction is likely to show us more about the social causes of violence and reduce violence. There is an opposition of societal tendencies toward hierarchy enhancing means of domination of low-status groups. They are opposed to the tendencies toward hierarchy attenuating means of domination.

The latter two strategies are interferences of hierarchy enhancing means of domination for reducing the number and intensity of legal disadvantages for lower status groups. The latter interferences are types of social contradictions. They arise as well from the criminal justice systems themselves.

Real possibility provides an alternative conception of contradictoriness. One reason for this is that the two following types of statements are contradictory for real possibility but not for disjunctive possibility: (1) S can be P; and (2) S can also be not P.

For real possibility, the amount of contrast and contradictoriness of (1) and (2) is essentially the same for (1) and the following statement: (3) It is not the case that S can be P. If (1) is true, then S is or will be P, and (2) and (3) are both false in accordance with the concept of real possibility. If (1) is false, then (2) and (3) are both true.

In each case, the truth, falsity, and contradictoriness never depend upon any specific knowledge of it. They describe a relation where one disjunctive possibility must be false (i.e., (1) EXOR (2)). The necessity of either (1) EXOR (2) brings forth the conception of real possibility via an exclusive disjunctive principle. That is, (1) or (2) but not both.

The attainment of scientific knowledge happens through a methodology that, roughly, confirms and disconfirms each contradictory statement. Hypotheses' descriptions being contradicted by the descriptions of observations form the disconfirming evidence. Hypotheses as statements differ regarding their specification levels. They are constructed to contradict a presumption held by the scientist and similar presumptions held by previous scientists who investigated similarly.

For instance, if a plaintiff injured his left leg in a car wreck, the confirmation and disconfirmation of the two following contradictory statements also further specify the problem:

> (i) His left knee is injured; and (ii) It is not the case that his injured left knee is fractured. (i) and (ii) differ slightly regarding their specification levels. (ii) needs more specificity regarding the type of injury so that the scientific line of inquiry and testing allow for progress to be made regarding the knowledge attained. Knowledge is acquired partially from confirming or disconfirming evidence for (ii).

Realizing the plaintiff had an injured left knee may lead to no prior assumptions about the plaintiff's muscles, tendons, ligaments, etc. before the investigation. The sphere of connections only involves the status of the claimant's left knee. In sport science, the question whether the injury might not be a sprain is either confirmed or disconfirmed with evidence. The testing methods already presume that the appropriate limb is injured. This thereby limits the range of disjunctive possibilities that are expected by investigators, jurists, judge, jury etc.

Logical possibilities of injuries to all other limbs are thereby ignored because of their irrelevancy. The possibility of the lack of a sprain[12] is argued against once some ligament is observed and analyzed to be twisted or partially torn. Using the concept of real possibility places limitations on what becomes considerable as a possibility.

Real possibility is necessary for methodology and the advancement of science like logical possibility is. Logical possibility may involve utter irrelevancies that necessitate the placements of limitations on concepts, such as limiting them to what is merely physically possible. We limit the range of logical possibilities in some realm when we have knowledge of real phenomena regarding that realm. The concept of real possibility is used in the court of law for the plaintiff who maintains a stance for the seriousness of the injury and for the defense attempting to undermine the significance of the injury. The concept is applied to influence the verdict of the case.

Real possibility demands the fulfillment of truth via a principle of exclusive disjunction but requires a methodology for the attainment of such knowledge. One knows that (i) EXOR (ii) is true, and partially derives this from the observation of the reduced performance, the reduced mobility of the left knee, swelling, reported pain around the joint, etc. (i) is mistaken if the pain is psychosomatic or the injury is largely or entirely feigned (i.e., a disjunctive possibility that broadens the range of concepts involved) but (ii) is not. (ii) is formed as a contradictory statement that is confirmed via any disconfirmation of (i), despite the amount of irrelevancy of (i) and (ii) regarding the reported pains of the plaintiff.

In accordance with real possibility, only one alternative is really possible whereas the other is inadequate, despite its logical and physical possibility. When the concept of real possibility is utilized within methodology for the attainment of knowledge, such as during the process of the medical doctor x-raying the plaintiff to test (ii), it involves the use of the scientific method, which is applicable to the legal sciences as well.

Several legal maxims are relevant here regarding the conceptions of real possibility and disjunctive possibility, and to the issue of contradictoriness. Three are presented. After the presentation of the legal maxims comes a brief analysis of how the inclusive disjunctive concept of possibility can be overused and how it oversteps the boundaries of relevancy regarding content.

---

12 It may replace (ii), especially once knowledge in favor of (ii) or contradicting (ii) is had (e.g., x-rays).

Bryan Garner (2004, p. 5262) asserts the following legal maxim: "*A non posse ad non esse sequitur argumentum necessarie negative, licet non affirmative,*" which is translated as "from impossibility to nonexistence the inference follows necessarily in the negative, though not in the affirmative." This is a legal maxim and a principle in modal logic.

There is indeed disagreement between such a maxim and a logical principle within certain philosophies. The conclusion of the nonexistence of something allows for the derivation of an impossibility for that so-called thing, i.e., within Megaric and Spinozian philosophies. The latter philosophies lack or discard the conception of a contingent or coincidental unreality.

The latter legal maxim is based upon valid arguments that maintain that each impossibility is also an unreality. That is, anything that is impossible is also unreal. However, the maxim also means that something that is unreal is not necessarily impossible.

The first legal maxim is perhaps shortsighted regarding the consideration of timing, placement, and the concept of real possibility. For example, when something really did not happen at some place, we may claim that it is impossible that it happened at that time and place. With the concept of real possibility, the investigator or scientist progresses with records of measurements of what happened at that time and place as well as from other relevant expectations (Beck, 1961).

For instance, consider that the plaintiff claims that something happened at a certain time and place (i.e., something unreal). The courtroom watches a video of that spot at that time. It is used as evidence to show that the event did not occur. The defense can very well argue that it is impossible that the event happened at that place and time.

The first maxim is consistent with the concept of inclusive disjunctive possibility but is, in part, inconsistent with the conception of real possibility. For instance, the defense attorney may even decide to pause the film every minute of the relevant time period. He or she may ask whether it is possible that the event in question happened during that minute, and then the next minute, and so on. The defense attorney presumes and persuades the court that the event would have been physically impossible to have happened without being detected by the camera. The prosecutor may call into question the quality of camera and flaws.[13]

13 It depends on the prosecuting lawyer's research conclusions about the customer feedback about that camera and its ranking as an older or newer product, records of its purchase etc.

A second legal maxim that Garner (2004, p. 5263) also maintains is that: "*Argumentum ab impossibili plurimum valet in lege*," which means that "an argument deduced from an impossibility has the greatest validity in law." The second legal maxim is perhaps applicable at times when lawyers are listing their major arguments on behalf of the clients they are defending or for prosecuting a defendant.

An argument that may destroy the credibility of a witness of a crime, an expert witness, or a defendant who has been cross-examined is often stated by a prosecuting attorney. The prosecuting attorney claims that the person said something contradictory (e.g., being at one place at 13:00 on one day and being in another place at the same time and date). The presentation of this contradiction could establish the untrustworthiness of the person who stated it under oath. The lawyers deduce that the individual who spoke under oath said something that is false in at least one instance.

The second legal maxim can be used in combination with the concept of real possibility from the previous example where the idea is established that anything that did not happen at some time and place also could not have possibly happened. That is, the event in question is an impossible one based on the lack of the fulfillment of the conditions for its instantiations at that time and place. Unreal events at prior times and locations are conceivably impossible ones, too. The example of the video shows evidence that an event in question did not happen at that time and place. Such evidence is best used for the formation of an argument that is deduced from the physical impossibility of the crime in question.

Again, the second legal maxim can be utilized specifically with the conception of real possibility. For example, many vehicles are tested to assess their performances and estimate what drivers had abilities to perform in them. The latter assessments of performances affect the outcomes of court cases. For instance, the maximum speed of a vehicle and ability of the vehicle to stop as quickly as possible within the shortest distance after reaching a certain speed are sometimes valuable information within courts of law for accident reconstruction experts, mechanical engineers, and private investigators. Of course, the conditions of the roads and tires as well as other factors will likely be taken into consideration within sufficiently important cases.

Any physically difficult performance, unlikely occurrence, or physically impossible feat for a vehicle to perform, which the defense attorney claims to have happened (i.e., a lawyer perhaps working for the manufacturer), can be utilized by the prosecuting attorney to either show the improbability of this or the impossibility of it (i.e., via the conception of real possibility). It becomes obvious that when one attorney has been overstating the performance of a vehicle under the relevant conditions, the opposing attorney can use this to his or her advantage via constructing an argument from the deductive consequences of the impossible performance of the vehicle in those relevant conditions, which has already been stated by the adversary to have happened. Even fictitious court cases in films (e.g., in "My Cousin Vinny") show lawyers who make false assumptions about the facts of a case, such as the tire marks of a vehicle belonging to the wrong one, whereas the defense is able to argue that the getaway vehicle had to be a different one to lay the tire marks.

A third legal maxim regarding contradictoriness is "*A l'impossible nul n'est tenu*" means that "no one is bound to do what is impossible," according to *Black's Law Dictionary* (Garner, 2004, p. 5260). The latter legal maxim is quite vague and shows, at least, the attempt to make a precedent to establish the limitations of legal obligations upon subjects required to act or refrain from acting, in accordance with the law. The idea that one is never legally required to perform some act that is impossible to perform is an important one.

The third maxim concerns the inclusive disjunctive conception of possibility. Obviously, a person who is expected to appear within two different courts in two different cities at the same time cannot be legally required to do so because this is physically and logically impossible. Such an expectation can readily be argued to involve a contradiction in accordance with the inclusive disjunctive concept of possibility.

The third maxim also concerns the concept of real possibility. A person cannot be legally required to make a courtroom appearance given the circumstances. A couple types of circumstances are if the person is overseas and the notification for the appearance in court either does not provide enough notification time or the notification does not ever reach the person.

If a bank's employees have made it exceedingly difficult for the bank to receive payments it is owed by certain customers, especially those who have taken loans from the bank and who have placed very expensive property (e.g., houses) down as their collateral, then, given the appropriate evidence that the bank clientele have attempted to provide the bank with timely payments, the bank customers may be allowed to escape negative legal and financial consequences because the customers and their legal advocate may argue against the bank advocates that it was "impossible" to make their payments during appropriate time periods before their deadlines. The financial interest of the bank is also shown to be a motivation for increasing the difficulties with deposits.

Real possibility is conceptually concerned in the latter case because the fact that a bank customer attempted to pay within an appropriate time period and was unable to pay is the demonstration of the negation of the real possibility of the payment being made at that point (i.e., it was really impossible for the bank customer to pay at that point). The bank's legal representation is, of course, likely to argue that it was (inclusively disjunctively) possible for their customer to make the payment, in which case the lawyer may reference many time periods during which the bank customer could have paid but did not.

However, the combination of evidence and the negation of the real possibility of paying at some appropriate times gives the bank customer the opportunity to escape the legal and financial penalties (e.g., the repossession of the bank customer's house) within a court of law. The third maxim states that no individual is legally required to do the impossible, and when the customer has sufficient evidence to provide the court with enough instances of well enough attempted payments that were either rejected or unable to be made for some other reason, such as the bank closing because of harsh weather, the maxim provides the grounds from which the customer can be given a fairer opportunity.

The neurological research for decision-making processes has been in favor of relieving the guilt and moral blameworthiness of criminals (See Ch. 3.6). Moreover, the reliefs of guilt occur, regardless of whether they are known to have committed the crime at hand for which they are undergoing the procedures of the justice system.

One argument is that the impulsivity of a person can be viewed at the neurological level. Furthermore, at some point before a decision is made or before an action is performed, the person is totally unable to choose or behave differently.

Again, the third maxim can be applied by the defense attorney who may argue consistently with neuroscientists that for the defendant, it would have been impossible for him or her to have chosen to perform any other action. Moreover, because no one is bound to do the impossible (i.e., the third maxim), the defendant is, arguably, relieved of guilt, blameworthiness, and legal responsibility. Such arguments have certainly been used within court cases.

These latter arguments are dubious and technically and ethically problematic. To the defendant, they fail to apply the concepts of freedom, moral blameworthiness, and decisiveness, which is derived from the ordinary level of observation with which we are familiar. We can only determine that a choice has been made from the ordinary level with our naked eyes or spectacles, naked ears, etc. Otherwise, we would be hard-pressed to use only a set of fMRIs to determine that another person has chosen anything. No one can determine the independently-made decision of another person with just a machine.

The guilty criminals who escape the justice of the penal system (i.e., guilty people given the not guilty verdict) tend to have savvy lawyers who hire experts. However, in countries with relatively high incarceration rates, like the United States, people who are not guilty for the crimes are often convicted when prosecutors utilize neuroscience research (Denno, 2017). The experts in the field of neuroscience (e.g., medical doctors) argue for the impossibility or necessity of making a certain decision at a certain time period based on levels of analysis and levels of observation. The latter levels are, however, irrelevant at least to the levels of analyses and observations from which the concept of the decision was derived (See Ch. 3.6 & Ch. 5.6).[14]

The law cannot function according to standards regarding the attainments of truths of the matters since judgments and legal decision-making are performed by humans, which inevitably involves fallibility. Neuroscience research does not inform us of anything significant about legal or moral philosophy or moral judgements, apart from claims about emotions (Patterson & Pardo, 2016). Neuroscience will neither answer enduring philosophical questions (e.g., What is justice?) nor answer normative questions about morality (e.g., What moral standards should be used and developed?).

In many courts of law, probabilities and statistics are frequently used. In the best-case scenarios, legal judgments are frequently made based on what is likely to have happened. However, the presence of an authority figure, like a

14 Consider the neuroscience research of 800 criminal cases in the United States by Deborah Denno (2017). Denno (ibid.) illustrates that the use of brain scans in court cases is common to demonstrate the extent of the injury of the victims. However, the neuroscience research tends to be utilized to a far greater extent than its purpose in showing injuries. Brain scans are typically used by prosecutors.

Approximately half of the cases involve expert testimony from medical practitioners who claim the victims suffered from shaken baby syndrome. This syndrome is abusive head trauma and is one of the primary causes of death of children in the United States. Denno (2017, p. 323) claims that shaken baby syndrome is:

> [A]medical diagnosis with controversial scientific underpinnings and distorted legal ramifications. The diagnosis often successfully serves as the sole foundation for a prosecutor's case, with no proof of the defendant's act or intent beyond the victim's brain scan and the accompanying medical expert testimony. Shaken baby syndrome cases thus portray a troubling phenomenon in which the key element of mens rea is either unclear or overlooked altogether and prosecutors are permitted to concoct intent out of brain scans that were admitted for the sole purpose of presenting the victim's injury.

Denno (ibid.) continues to describe hundreds of United States court cases:

> My study further reveals that shaken baby syndrome cases are merely the more transparent examples of the criminal justice system's failure to deal adequately with the surging influx of neuroscience evidence into the courtroom. Shaken baby cases thus represent a microcosm of prosecutorial misuse of victim neuroscience evidence more generally, particularly when the evidence is employed to determine a defendant's mental state.

medical doctor, with demonstrations of brain scans to jurors or jurists tends to lead to verdicts in favor of the side of the authority figure utilizing higher level technology (i.e., the prosecution in the United States). Evidence for the theory or hypothesis that some set of actions occurred (e.g., as stated in a court of law) is partially what makes it less reasonable to doubt as a matter of fact, although there are exceptions to this latter point, such as lying, lying under oath, and tampering with evidence.[15]

The third maxim appears to have tendencies of overuse. This is true regarding defendants who committed the crimes, of which they were accused, and who are argued to be relieved from guilt based on so-called evidence from brain scans.

Contradictions between some logical possibilities (i.e., contradictory according to the concept of real possibility) are not always apparent. The fallacies in critical thinking of appealing to authority, reliance on technology for conclusions etc. should lead our tendencies toward skepticism regarding conclusions of guilt or innocence.

11 Real Possibility: Supporting Arguments, Historic Origins and Law

The employment of the concept of real possibility is prolific in legal reasoning. Arguments that support the concept of real possibility often involve appeals to our intuitive judgments. They may involve propositional reports regarding the absence of possibility for unreal things. They sometimes emphasize the reality and necessity for any possible thing.

Those advocating only real possibilities argue in ways that are consistent with the idea that: That which did not happen also did not possibly happen. If an event did not occur a few days ago, we may presume, in accordance with the concept of real possibility, that the event also did not possibly happen a few days ago as well.

For instance, a common line of thinking is that a verdict that failed to happen also did not possibly happen. Judicial, legislative, and law enforcement decisions and events are arguably similar in that respect. The latter way of thinking is prolific.

---

15 Tampering with evidence is often a theme about the law within movies, although it remains a clandestine and illegal tactic in societies. The relevancy of tampering with evidence also may behoove many opposing attorneys to imply or suggest that it is in the best interests of the adversaries to secretly tamper with evidence. Attorneys may point out that the opponents have the financial capabilities to do so when their opponents do, and they can undermine the trustworthiness of their opponents within certain legal systems.

On the other hand, if the latter utilization of the concept of real possibility is employed commonly by legal practitioners, another aspect of the concept is utilized to much lesser extents. Consider these ideas: What does not happen also does not possibly happen, and what will not occur also will not possibly occur, accordingly.

Like real possibility, inclusive disjunctive possibility is a concept involved in the process of verification itself. The concept of inclusive disjunctive possibility might be used to broaden the ranges of possibilities but risks irrelevancies. Inclusive disjunctive possibilities also involve attributions, made by humans, to events, things, and others. The cognitive processes are always limited by time, energy and the capacities of people or others to imagine and attribute them from the outset.

For attributions of real possibility, the reason why such determinations of the absence of possibility are so important concerns the propositional reports themselves and their uses concerning the attainment of knowledge. Attributions of real possibility are supposed to exclude the largest set of logical possibilities, i.e., the unreal possibilities or coincidental unrealities.

The real possibilities are what happen at some time or times and place or places. A propositional report involved in the attainment of knowledge cannot remain problematic. At some point, the modal attributions of "S can be P" and "S can be not P" are relinquished in favor of a decision that, at least implicitly, supports one more than the other.

The determination that the individual makes via the modal propositional report does not give the same amount of credence to all the disjunctive possibilities (i.e., at some level of relevancy) within the realm of their connections. No determinate propositional report could ever be made otherwise or create a solution (See Ch. 5.3). That is, some propositional report cannot continuously maintain that something can be X and also maintain that the same thing can also be not X without the emergence of a contradiction and impossibility.

The Megaric school utilized the concept of "real possibility" (Beck, 1961; Hartmann, 1938; Hartmann, 1937). The Megaric school maintained that anything that is possible is real, and anything that is real is necessary; therefore, anything that is possible is also necessary. Accordingly, nothing that fails to happen (or to exist) is possible. Nothing is coincidental, and everything that is unreal is also impossible.

The Megaric system advocates a form of logical determinism that is reached conclusively via sets of modal arguments. Logical determinism of Megareans is derived as a conclusion that logically follows the requirements for the possibility of something to always form a necessary condition via meeting a series of fulfillments to be possible. Otherwise, there is an inadequacy regarding being really possible, which Epictetus describes from the arguments of Diodorus. The master or ruling argument derived by Diodorus Cronos has a revolutionary appeal as an argument regarding the concept of possibility, especially concerning knowledge and judgments or propositional reports about the past. According to Epictetus (Long 1877: pp. 162–163) in book II and Chapter XIX:

> [T]here is in fact a common contradiction between one another in these three positions, each two being in contradiction to the third. The propositions are, that everything past must of necessity be true; that an impossibility does not follow a possibility; and that thing is possible which neither is nor will be true. Diodorus observing this contradiction employed the probative force of the first two for the demonstration of this proposition, 'That nothing is possible which is not true and never will be.'

The statement "if some crime C did not happen at some time and place, then it is true that C did not possibly happen at that point" has some very intuitive appeal. People typically do not assume that a presumably honest speaker believes that some event C possibly happened when, in fact, the speaker claims that C did not happen. However, the replacement of the quoted statement with its logical equivalent seems to lack at least some of the intuitive appeal: Either C happened, or it is true that C did not possibly happen.

The second claim that "impossibilities do not follow possibilities" is a claim that is crucial to certain types of logic. We may assume that some legal action A is possible, but B follows from A, and B is an impossibility. With such realizations, it is common to presume that A is also not possible. However, as we have seen, there is a difference between inclusive disjunctive possibility and exclusive disjunctive possibility.

So, if we consider the exclusive disjunctive possibility that either A or C, but not both A and C (i.e., also where D follows from A and B follows from C), then we are confronted with a reason why B would be an impossibility. B would be an impossibility because C did not happen (e.g., it was an impossibility at some prior point).

The exclusive disjunctive conception (i.e., the concept of real possibility) is more time sensitive than the inclusive disjunctive conception. Let us assume that A is a legal action that reoccurs and so is legal action C, in which case the situation may arise such that legal action A occurs, which leads to D. Now, assume that legal action C occurs later, which leads to B. Thus, there is a reason for thinking that an impossibility may follow a possibility, chronologically speaking.

Consider the presence of these arguments about the world as suggestions that the use of the concepts of possibility provide different advantages for argumentation concerning law. They play crucial roles regarding the attainment of knowledge. This will become more apparent with the third concept of possibility in the next section (i.e., recollective possibility).

The claim that "if something Q is neither true, nor happening, nor will ever happen, then Q is impossible" is a claim that denies or restricts the concept of inclusive disjunctive possibility. The latter claim appears to be intuitively false concerning our realizations about the range of our abilities. For example, let us assume that Q means "the man stole 20kg of quartz from the jewellery shop," and the man really stole just 10kg of quartz from the jeweller.

To remain consistent with the latter assumptions, Q must be impossible if the man will also have never stolen 20kg of quartz, according to a Megaric logical analysis. However, it appears obvious that the man could have simply stolen 10kg more than he did steal to fulfill the requirements of Q. For this latter reason, the last claim appears to be dubious to some thinkers and their systems of thought.

Additionally, for law, it is important to realize that when a plaintiff has been victimized, he or she may tend to be vengefully dishonest and is thus more likely to report more losses than what was lost. Epictetus (Long 1877: pp. 162–163) describes more ancient philosophy within book II and Chapter XIX:

> Now another will hold these two: 'That something is possible, which is neither true nor ever will be': and 'That an impossibility does not follow a possibility,' but he will not allow that everything which is past is necessarily true, as the followers of Cleanthes seem to think, and Antipater copiously defended them. But others maintain the other two propositions, 'That a thing is possible which is neither true nor will be true': and 'That everything which is past is necessarily true'; but then they will maintain that an impossibility can follow a possibility.

It is maintained that it is impossible to uphold the three aforementioned propositions since these lead inevitably to some contradiction. The logical proof of Diodorus maintains that nothing is possible, except for the actual or real, because nothing can follow from the impossible (Eisler, 1912, p. 131). In any situation, where there are two preclusive instances in which only one event can occur, one is real and the other is impossible insofar as it is excluded as a possibility since if it were possible, then a possibility would arise from an impossibility (Eisler, 1904, p. 579).

For Diodorus, a possibility can neither be derived from nor follow from an impossibility, and an impossibility also cannot be derived from or follow from a possibility. It is important to treat the latter arguments as a system of thought that has been derived from the concept or real possibility. Aspects of it are opposed to the concept of inclusive disjunctive possibility, from which other systems of thought have been derived.

According to Diodorus Cronos, if we construct statements about the past, and the statements accurately describe what happened, then the statements are necessarily true. Moreover, if an event is possible, no event that occurs as a result of it can be an impossible one. Likewise, a statement that is possibly true cannot have an impossibility be derived from it. Therefore, nothing is possible which has never occurred and never will happen, according to this Megaric system of thought. Such a system might be understood better in relation to a system with coincidences (i.e., instead of none) as well as comparing the systems' abilities to yield hypotheses.

Consider the idea of the necessity of the truth of statements about the past. Now, consider practical ways of legal thinking and judging in courts of law where verified and authentic video footage has captured past events, and judges and juries were listening to accurate descriptions of the video footage by the attorneys.

The latter descriptions may very well be understood and accepted as necessary truths by juries, lawyers, and judges. They can become the basis for their decisions regarding the verdict, decisions for putting forth certain lines of questions, and sustaining and overruling objections. Moreover, within the investigation of an incident, which is important within a court case, there are unknown factors, such as whether a traffic light was red during the time of the impact of two vehicles. The possibility of the latter event cannot result in an impossibility regarding judgments that are based upon it, unless they are irrationally made or deceivingly accepted.

The system developed by the Megareans maintains that something is not possible if it neither is true nor will be true because the lack of fulfillment of any necessary condition for something to be instantiated and thus to really occur is also an insufficiency for its real possibility. Change and movement do not occur within the Megarean system. Change and movement are illusory, in this system of thought. Anything that is possible, according to real possibility, definitely takes place at some temporal and spatial point, or else it is impossible

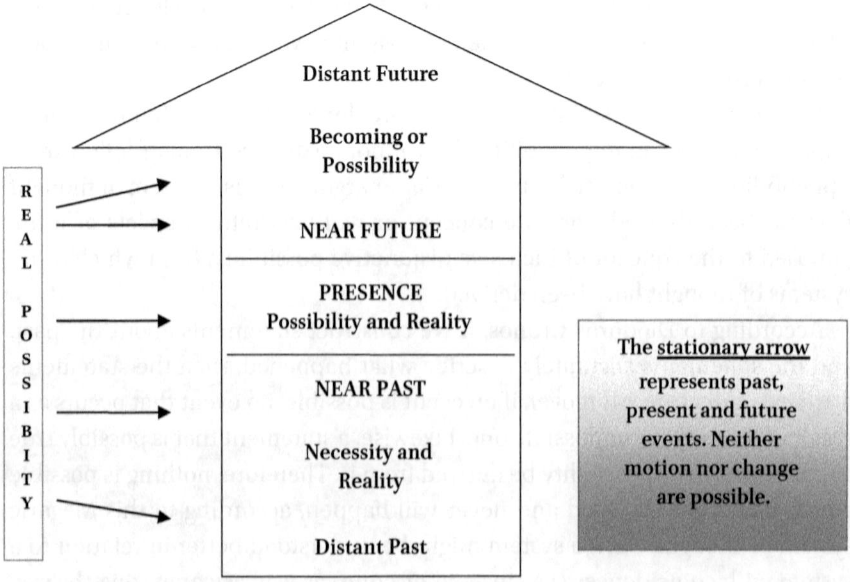

FIGURE 14 Megaric concept of real possibility

This is viewable within figure 14 by means of the Megarean conception of possibility and time.

Regarding physical limitations and an example that partially clarifies the concept of real possibility, we may imagine that an Olympic athlete runs a mile in three minutes and thirty seconds. Imagine further that he is the fastest human runner everlastingly for that distance (i.e., let us presume), and the second fastest runner ever, for the mile-race, completes the mile-run in three minutes and forty seconds.

Coinciding with the concept of real possibility, given the latter conditions and presumptions, it is impossible for anything else to happen, apart from what does happen. Something cannot be possible if it is insufficient regarding meeting the conditions for becoming. Insufficient conditions for events are the failures to fulfill necessary conditions for the events' instantiations. That which never becomes true (e.g., a human running a three minute and thirty-five second mile) amounts to such an insufficiency; it lacks the necessary conditions for the possibility for it to become.

Despite the tendencies to maintain that the fastest runner could have merely slowed down because of some physical constraint or a psychological motive to have done so, the concept of real possibility ascertains that these tendencies involve misguided applications of conceptions and misunderstandings. Moreover, they are generally overly abstract and fail to account for specificities.

Consider the obvious fact that the abovementioned fastest runner could not suddenly develop the new motive to run significantly slower during the last couple seconds of the race to complete the mile-run in three minutes and thirty-five seconds. His momentum would carry him over the finish line at a faster finishing time. Thus, some specific timeframe that is earlier would have to be analyzed in virtue of explaining an inclusively disjunctively possible motivation for an Olympian to run slower than he did.

Generally, the concept of motivation would be applied without any further analysis, superficially. People would dogmatically agree that the Olympian could have run five seconds slower, *prima facie*. The understanding of Megaric philosophy allows for such dogmas to easily be elucidated.

Examples concerning legal systems, executive, judicial and legislative acts are just as relevant concerning the application of the conception of real possibility. The failure of some legal event to occur still amounts to a lack of fulfillment and sufficiency for the event to be instantiated. This thereby provides skeptical reasons to attribute any possibility to the failed legal act. There is also reason to attribute impossibility to the failed legal act via describing the reasons for the impossibility as failing to fulfill certain conditions.

Skepticism for attributing possibility to the legal event should enter the critical thinking process, even if the legal event appears to fall within the boundaries of possible conditions that have been fulfilled. Skepticism is easier to apply if the alleged legal event resulted in similar occurrences that also may appear to exceed the upper and lower limitations of the conditions required for the event to have occurred.

12 Recollective Possibility: Expectation and Recognition of the (Un)-Real via Possibilistic Rather than Probabilistic Cognitions and Knowledge

This section is more theoretical than the previous sections. The role of the concept of recollective possibility to problem-solving is demonstrated. The cognitive process of realization is described along with the recognition of objects and the usage of the concepts of inclusive disjunctive possibility and real possibility. The concept is an aspect of the methodology used in the analysis of the previous sections.

Contrary to inclusive and exclusive disjunctive possibility, not all real things are undoubtedly possible. Anything that is real, but which also fails to be considered by one, fails to be given the attribution of possibility for the process of realization. For instance, if there is a job opening with the police in Mumbai, India for one with the credentials that a specific person has already, that person has no possibility of having that job if he or she never realizes it or never encounters others who realize the opportunity.

The real possibility of something may have no impact on the realization and decision-making processes of the individual. There is absolutely no attribution of possibility to any unknown opportunity. Recollected possibilities are those with the attributions of possibility and are more relevant in the decision-making process.

The concept of recollective possibility maintains that the concepts, modes, and categories of possibility and reality are not identical. Yet everything is included within the expansiveness of the concept of reality (i.e., every existent, every event, etc.) (Quine, 1948, p. 1). Thus, the major distinction between the concept of reality and the concept of possibility, which are viewed as categories, entails that possibility has less content than reality does.

So, the possible, according to this conception, concerns a relatively small portion of reality, such as just the cognitions and what is recollected. The reason for this is that reality encompasses so much more than merely every cognitive formation of what is possible, according to the concept of recollective possibility. Recollective possibility therefore functions as a concept and category that includes less content than the concept and all-encompassing category of reality.

Real objects and events often lack the attribution of undoubted possibility (i.e., lacking the attribution of their possibilities that undergoes doubt, for instance) as well as the attribution of undoubted impossibility because the range of possible solutions for problem-solving, say, for a court case or finding a job, are limited by the total amount of possibilities that are realized by the problem-solver or problem-solvers during the process of problem-solving rather than after the process.

What fails to be considered by the individual is neither attributed as being possible nor impossible. Moreover, the consideration that "everything or anything is possible" only allows for a system or individual to consider the range of events and things recalled, perceived, and expected, for instance, to establish them as possibilities. The problem-solver may realize there are multiple options for winning a court case but not realize what any single one of these options is. They are options that are not being considered for problem-solving but that may occur during the attempt of the solution. They are not viable possibilities of solutions during the case, if they are never recollected or considered. In a consistent manner, Niklas Luhmann writes:

> The human being lives in a meaningfully constituted world, within which relevance for one is not clearly defined via one's organism. The world

> shows the human being, consequently, an abundance of possibilities of experiences and actions, which only confront a very limited potential for momentary conscious perception, information processing, and action. In the ever-present and thereby evident and given content of experience, one consequently finds references to other possibilities, which are likewise complex and contingent. (Luhmann, 1987, p. 31) [Der Mensch lebt in einer sinnhaft konstituierten Welt, deren Relvanz für ihn durch seinen Organismus nicht eindeutig definiert ist. Die Welt zeigt ihm dadurch eine Fülle von Möglichkeiten des Erlebens und Handelns, der nur ein sehr begrenztes Potential für aktuell-bewußte Wahrnehmung, Informationsverarbeitung und Handlung gegenübersteht. In dem jeweils aktuell und damit evident gegebenen Erlebnisinhalt finden sich mithin Verweisungen auf andere Möglichkeiten, die zugleich komplex und kontingent sind.]

Luhmann accurately describes the conception of recollective possibility insofar as the world is involved with the arising of attributions of possibilities. The world, of course, includes the entire situation and the whole individual with all of one's cognitions and attributions. Conscious perceptions are momentary and have limited potentials. This is why the concept of recollective possibility incorporates less than the concept of reality or actuality.

Experiences that one has during one's life span and realizations about others' experiences being different than one's own (i.e., the ability called "theory of mind"; See Ch. 4.13) and realizations about one's own actions and actions of others lead to suggestions that there is an abundance of possibilities. However, there is a much more limited amount of information processing and conscious experiences. Expectations set boundaries for decision-making and problem-solving as well.[16]

---

16 Niklas Luhmann continues but begins with the description of the concept of complexity via the incorporation of the conception of inclusive disjunctive possibility:

> Under *complexity* we want to understand that there are always more possibilities than can become actualized. Under *contingency* we want to understand that the indicated possibilities of further experience can turn out differently than were expected: the indicator therefore can deceive while it makes reference to something that is not contrary to expectations or is unattainable, or, if one has taken the necessary provisions for some recent experience (for example, to have gone somewhere), that is no longer there. Complexity practically means necessitation of selection, and contingency practically means disappointment resulting from danger and the necessity of embarkation amid risks. (ibid.) [Unter *Komplexität* wollen wir verstehen, daß es stets mehr Möglichkeiten gibt, als aktualisiert werden können. Unter *Kontingenz* wollen wir verstehen, daß die angezeigten Möglichkeiten weiteren Erlebens auch anders ausfallen

For the individual, particular signals may lead one to expect a certain outcome, but the concepts of coincidence or contingency allow one to understand that something different from one's expectations may occur. This shows perhaps one advantage of the incorporation of modes of Aristotle and traditional and historical modal analysis (Hartmann, 1938).

Recollective possibility is a type of conception that does not generally involve an indifference to problematic propositional reports, unlike real possibility and inclusive disjunctive possibility. Recollective possibility demands that the individual focus some attention on something expected. It demands for one to remember such expectations to change one's web of beliefs. This is in relation to whether his or her expectations were met or unmet based on the object of knowledge that becomes comprehended.

More than a mere object of knowledge is required for the use of recollective possibility. The act of grasping the object in itself requires a connection with a real oppositional link. The link is to a real object or event that allows for realization to occur and which resides independent from the act of realization in the first place. Theoretic realism enters the conception of recollective possibility. What remains relevant to the individual is the sort of being that can become something that is made into an object of knowledge, even though any object is entirely and obviously indifferent regarding whether and to what extent it can become an object of knowledge.

Regardless of whether expectations are met or unmet, the individual frequently remembers those expectations and comparatively contrasts remembrances of the older expectations with newer expectations. This happens after the realization of whether the older and more, supposedly, important expectations were met EXOR unmet. Consider an alleged solution to some problem the individual attempts to solve. Problem-solving is ever-present in the latter respect since the processes involved in realization demand energy in

können, als erwartet wurde: daß die Anzeige mithin täuschen kann, indem sie auf etwas verweist, das nicht ist oder wider Erwarten nicht erreichbar ist oder, wenn man die notwendigen Vorkehrungen für aktuelles Erleben getroffen hat (zum Beispiel hingegangen ist), nicht mehr da ist. Komplexität heißt praktisch Selektionszwang, Kontingenz heißt praktisch Enttäuschungsgefahr und Notwendigkeit des Sicheinlassens auf Risiken.]

The process of decision-making of an individual tends to be far less complex than a group's decision-making processes since more possibilities for alternative decisions tend to be considered by the group instead. However, group members may refrain from sharing their attributions of possibilities with the group because of embarrassment, time constraints, etc. The concept of complexity concerns the inclusive disjunctive conception of possibility as well for Niklas Luhmann, especially within his sociology of law.

certain forms. Forms of attainments of energy are more or less scarce, depending on the environmental conditions (Brant, 2013a: pp. 136–170).

Realization is a relatively small set of processes within an environment and thus a minuscule part of the real world, i.e., for theoretic frameworks that are opposed to idealism, solipsism, etc. Realizations are involved with problem-solving, decision-making, and the attainment of knowledge. Realizations occur when an individual recognizes events, objects, decisions, solutions, etc. as real and unreal ones. Realizations occur at multiple levels of analysis and multiple levels of observation from realizations at the microscopic level concerning the recognitions of the roles of stress hormones upon members of the legal institution and at macroscopic levels concerning the realizations of the racial bias of a jury member and the social realizations of the greater fears of the poverty-stricken and other low-status group members directed toward law enforcement professionals. Such occurrences of realizations can be applied to multiple levels of analyses of multiple disciplines, sciences and arts alike (Brant, 2013b).

When the concept of possibility is exclusively utilized as an aspect of the cognitive process of realization, the conceptions of inclusive disjunctive possibility and real possibility still arise cognitively. They arise with limitations upon the amount of awareness that the individual has regarding them. The individual's awareness is based upon the capabilities of information processing, the momentary conscious perceptions, memory constraints, etc.

The ordinary realization of something often starts as a process involving expectations via the utilization of inclusive disjunctive possibility (i.e., expecting that something can happen and that it may not happen at that same place during a timeframe). Even before the recognition of something as real EXOR unreal (i.e., real or unreal but not both), the individual discards, ignores, or establishes the irrelevancy of many of the earlier disjunctive possibilities; this happens like the prior combinations of puzzle pieces are discarded or ignored or established as irrelevant for the solution. Often before realizations occur, the individual only attributes possibilities and potentials (i.e., to the phenomenon being recognized) that are as close to real possibilities as observations and trial and error processes allow (i.e., only certain combinations of puzzle pieces are selected and become the collection of possibilities (Brant, ibid.)).

Henri Bergson (1946: pp. 20–22) argues that there is a negative and positive meaning of "possibility." For Bergson, "inclusive disjunctive possibility" is negative insofar as it includes the possible but unreal. Bergson provided a positive meaning of possibility that is different from the Megaric concept of real possibility and presented this concept of possibility within his September

24, 1920 lecture called "*Le possible et le réel*" (i.e., The Possible and the Real). According to Bergson, the positive sense of possibility is one that considers it absurd for possibility to precede reality regarding anything. For him, the positive meaning of "possibility" involves realization and decision-making. For instance, no such possibility could ever exist for a Shakespearean play to already be totally in the mind of William Shakespeare before he ever wrote it since writing and the process of completion requires both decision-making and realizations at various stages. We could similarly maintain the same thing for the constitution or the laws of the land.

Solving a jigsaw puzzle involves the cognitive processes of realization and decision-making, attributions of disjunctive possibilities, which sometimes even conflict with each other, not unbeknownst to the problem-solver, and requires attributions of real possibilities. In the first stages of the problem-solving, some pieces are placed together as (inclusively disjunctively) possible parts of the solution, even though they will not (and really cannot) fit within the larger picture in that particular combinatorial form. Yet some of those disjunctive possibilities are real possibilities, which will fit, i.e., albeit unbeknownst to the individual who only later solves the puzzle and gradually comes to realizations about them for moments. The problem-solver appears not to dwell on the realizations, too.

The individual does not, in the first place, recognize which partial solutions are merely inclusively disjunctively possible and which are real possibilities, according to our first two conceptions of possibility. That is, the meanings of "possibility" for the conceptions of inclusive disjunctive and real possibility are meanings that both involve a sort of independence from mind, knowledge, conceivability, and realization. For these reasons, one is allowed to consistently make problematic propositional reports about possibilities that are unbeknownst to the reporter of them. So, the threshold for reaching contradictoriness requires something more obvious because the concept of contradiction from the inclusive disjunctive possibility is utilized.[17]

The solely inclusively disjunctively possible solutions are established with the attempt (i.e., the solver's trial, attempt, or test) to more quickly satisfy the individual's desire to solve the entirety of the problematic puzzle. The

17 Yablo and Chalmers (Gendler & Hawthorne 2002: p. 6) emphasize: "The idea that conceivability is a guide to metaphysical possibility is extremely problematic. According to current orthodoxy, metaphysical possibility can neither be reduced to, nor eliminated in favour of, linguistic rules and conventions; it constitutes a fundamental mind-independent subject-matter for thought and talk. Given this picture, it is rather baffling what sort of explanation there could be for conceiving's ability to reveal its character. It seems clear that the causal explanation for the reliability of perception is quite unsuitable here—and it is profoundly difficult to see what to put in its place."

inclusively and disjunctively possible solutions are attributed because the individual expects for "some" of these disjunctively possible combinations to fit (i.e., all the real possibilities). Realizations allow the individual to attribute impossibility (i.e., in accordance with theoretic frameworks utilizing the concept of real possibility and its associated concept of stricter contradictoriness) to certain combinations for the final solution so that solely inclusively disjunctively possible solutions are considered impossibilities because they are no longer attributed as real possibilities for the problem-solver. The reason for this resides in the latter section within the philosophy of Diodorus Cronos, namely, that an impossibility can never follow from a possibility.

We may in some manners conceive of the law as a set of problematic puzzles with which to attempt to construct and distribute the roles, rules, penalizations, etc. that contribute to the reduction of violence and increase the potentialities for people to pursue what brings greater happiness, peacefulness, and prosperity. With the latter view, since the process of realization is utilized multiple times for problem-solving about law, it is practical to understand the process and the obstacles that impede it, especially concerning the intercommunications of the legal system and other societal systems.

Some inclusive disjunctive possibilities are later characterized within the process as "impossibilities" for solving the task at hand, and yet they were the original considerations of logical combinations and completely viable for the problem-solver at some earlier stage. In the latter sense, law may very well be attributed as having the set of characteristics of a social experiment. Consider communism and communistic laws in the latter manner (i.e., as disjunctive possibilities of the past that were later characterized as impossibilities for large societies because of the creation of black and gray markets and their impacts on hierarchies based on private property) since it appears difficult (i.e., without socially experimenting with the promotion of an economic system) to determine whether the implementation of laws and penalties that contribute to the formation of the new economic system will work harmoniously within the society (See Ch. 5.3).

The latter process involves the transition of thinking from the logical sphere to the sphere of the real (i.e., or transiting from the ideal sphere to the real sphere) since the combinations that are considered are not logical impossibilities and generally would not be considered physical impossibilities either (See Ch. 5.4). The social experimentations with communism have not been exhaustive though, which can be readily viewed from any characterizations of the laws of communism in comparison to the number of possible laws available for legislation as shown within the logical structure of legalization (See Ch. 2.5).

Additionally, the concept of *lex imperfecta* is employable here. *Lex imperfecta* maintains that laws may have been written and may have undergone the legislative processes with lawmakers, but the laws may also lack a type of impact on the society since the laws are not able to be enforced. The penal system is thus unable to penalize for offenses against these laws. They are a set of incomplete laws.

Lex imperfecta legislation only rarely has legal consequences attached to legislative violations. In early 21st century Greece, for example, there has been a problem regarding tax laws since taxes are generally paid by honest people. Many others refrain from paying taxes and often escape penalization. For many types of laws, it remains at least an inclusive disjunctive possibility that they too are *lex imperfecta* legislation.

The remembrance and collection of all these logical considerations of combinations (i.e., inclusive and exclusive disjunctive possibilities) as well as the remembrance and collection of the smaller number of them that are real possibilities, arising during the task of the completion of a puzzle or even legislation, for instance, are the recollective possibilities. The concept of recollective possibility utilizes only every consideration of inclusive disjunctive possibilities and only each and every real possibility that cognitively arise throughout the process of completing the task at hand. Completing the task coincides with realizations, decision-making, the timeframe, and problem-solving.

Presumably, if two people worked on two identical puzzles (i.e., two puzzles with the same number of pieces, same solution, overall picture, etc.), there would probably be more considerations of disjunctive possibilities that undergo the process of trial and error and which later become ignored at subsequent times before the finishing point. Likewise, if the intercommunications between two governmental systems worked on the completion of legislation that is enforceable, there is obviously more considerations of inclusive disjunctive possibilities that undergo the process of trial and error and which later become ignored or discarded, although there is no foreseen finishing point. The logical structure of legalization allows for there to be dozens of alternatives regarding whether acts or products are merely minimally or partially legal or completely legalized (See Ch. 2.5).

Recollective possibility concerns the specific process of realization for a single individual (i.e., since memory involves an individualistic process) and thus only concerns the inclusive and exclusive disjunctive possibilities that arise for that individual during the completion of the task. With the puzzle, some of the inclusive disjunctive possibilities result partially from the unforeseen ways in which the pieces fall and gather together upon the table. In hindsight, we may find that many or even most of the various logically possible combinations are never considered by the individual. They are not attributed as partial solutions or anything concerning the puzzle at all, which is how and why recollected possibility only incorporates a finite number of disjunctive possibilities. Only the portion of inclusively and exclusively disjunctively possible combinations of pieces that arise via cognition during the process of the completion of the puzzle are recollective possibilities.

Even before the problem-solver realizes the final solution, the solver has disassembled some of the disjunctively possible puzzle combinations, ignores them, and often forgets those combinations thereafter, and establishes them as "irrelevant" for the final solution. Some of the disjunctively possible puzzle combinations are considered to have the same possible fate as those which were already discarded, and yet they will either be undone EXOR left assembled to be slid into the place where they fit (i.e., one or the other but not both), presuming that the puzzle will be completed.

It is possible to utilize some of those inclusively, disjunctively possible solutions, say, by constructing another 9,900 puzzle pieces and creatively making 100 actually fit as a part of another puzzle, which would disallow both puzzles to be simultaneously solved. Resources are finite, and the problem-solver typically comes to the table with the presumption that there is only one solution or a best solution to the problem. The attributions of possibility to solutions for the problem necessarily involve the individual thinking of a finite number of solutions, which excludes much.

There is an exclusion of some solutions as the result of their lack of consideration by the problem-solver; this finite number of considerations might best be described as what concerns the "possibilistic" rather than the probabilistic (Gaines & Kohout, 1975). The "possibilistic" refers to the meaning of information in addition to the ability to answer questions or solve problems related to stored information, say, within a database. Alternatively, the "probabilistic," refers to the transmission of information as something that is statistical in its very nature as well as measurable. Lofti Zadeh (1999, p. 10) writes:

> The interpretation of the concept of possibility in the theory of possibility is quite different from that of modal logic in which propositions of the form 'It is possible that…' and 'It is necessary that…' are considered (Hughes & Cresswell, 1968).

In modal logic, alternatively, the concept of necessity is treated in such a way that the necessity of something x means that it is not possible that not x, and the possibility of something y allows for y to be either necessary or unnecessary. The notion of the possibilistic allows for a more restricted definition since at least some of those things or events that fail to be considered are things and events that are not possibilistic. Zadeh (1999, p. 10) continues:

> The importance of the theory of possibility stems from the fact that – contrary to what has become a widely accepted assumption – much of the information on which human decisions are based is possibilistic rather than probabilistic in nature. In particular, the intrinsic fuzziness of natural languages – which is a logical consequence of the necessity to express information in a summarized form – is, in the main, possibilistic in origin.

Probability theory may contribute to the ability for an investigator to analyze part of the duration of the completion of a puzzle, which involves measurements concerning hand-eye coordination with the pieces, the frequency during which separate pieces are moved and organized closer together as fitting pieces, etc. Alternatively, possibility theory in artificial intelligence research and mathematics contributes to the analysis of the meaning of the information already remembered or stored within the system so that the system is viewed as dealing with a finite amount of data. For instance, the system may consider that there is only one solution to the puzzle, that the pieces are all present, that the individual has the ability to complete the puzzle, that the pieces being organized contribute to solving the puzzle faster, and that each individual piece fits within the picture, even if a puzzle piece appears during an early part of the completion time to be entirely unfitting.

Yet not all systems are alike. Let us assume that we want to predict the average number of minutes that will elapse for a group of individuals to each solve one's own puzzle. One individual may have a possibilistic framework that includes solving some puzzle via creating new puzzle pieces for the final solution. That individual would never end up solving the puzzle, according to the statistical analysis that requires only one solution to be possible, and the alternative solution thus ruins the statistical analysis via being discarded as a non-solution or as lasting an infinite number of minutes. Such cases generally fail to be measured. So, the qualitative concerns as well as the structural frame for the information's analysis are possibilistic since the range of possibilities for the problem-solvers are viewed as limited by the statisticians.

The quantitative concerns, quantifiable information, transmissions, and receptions of data are best dealt with via probability theory. How could even the best statisticians with the most advanced statistics software and theories contribute to the analysis of problem-solvers for puzzles, if the problem-solvers in their sample intend to expand, reduce, or create something entirely different from the ordinarily presumed puzzle solution, though? How do we handle the information about the individuals who solve the puzzle in the most common way but accidently damage certain pieces? Should they also be discarded from the data undergoing statistical analysis for similar reasons to those who provide alternative solutions? Moreover, we may have absolutely no way of knowing when the solution is completed for some because it may appear to be vaguely finished, or the individual may consider the goal of completion to be around the half-way mark and be determined to complete the puzzle the following day or week or month, etc.

Exclusive and inclusive disjunctive possibilities are viewed as finite insofar as only limited numbers of them arise cognitively for any individual with a lifespan and limited duration for any given task. That is, both concepts are used within the concept of recollective possibility, the concept of finiteness regarding thinking of the possibilities is applied, and instead of the advocacy of a system of thought that is largely derived from the concepts of inclusive disjunctive and real possibility, the associated systems with the latter concepts are sometimes withheld. Inclusive disjunctive possibility is a subsidiary concept for recollective possibility, which requires cognitive processes involved with attention, decision-making, and memory. Real possibility is also a subsidiary concept for recollective possibility.

Recollective possibility thus does not involve the consideration of logically consistent solutions as being possibilities, for instance, if those logical solutions are never actually considered. So, an event is not recollectively possible if it fails to be considered. Time constraints, energy constraints as well as other limiting factors prevent more inclusive disjunctive possibilities from cognitively arising for the individual who makes reality tests via trials and errors. Figure 15 illustrates a rough characterization of recollective possibility as an aspect of the cognitive process of realization via the conceptions of reality, realization, recognitions, and recollections occurring across a certain span of time with trials or attempts at tasks that can be recognized and remembered as errors by the learner.

The role of the concept of recollective possibility within the process of realization is important both before something is realized (e.g., an object is recognized as being located at a certain location at some time) and afterwards. Before a specific object is recognized as being or moving at a certain location within some timeframe, an individual may attribute a whole range of disjunctive possibilities to that object, which may very well include the actual location of the object at that time (i.e., the real possibility) in addition to many inclusive

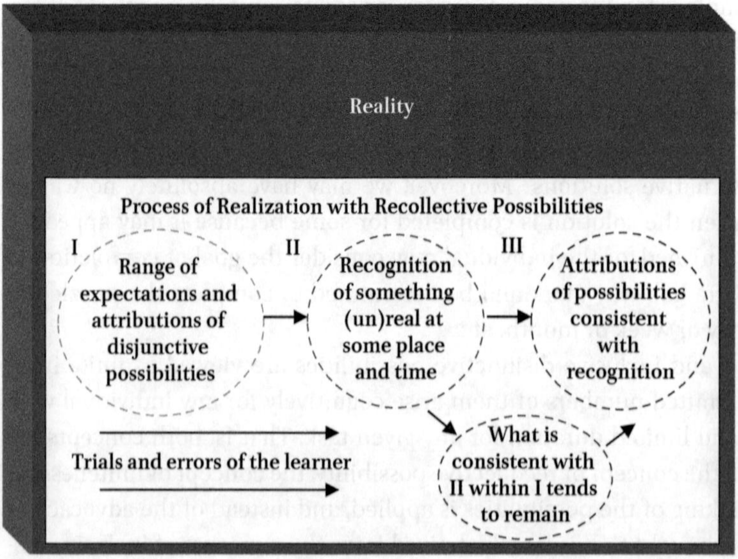

FIGURE 15 Concept of recollective possibility for the realization processes

disjunctive possibilities, i.e., inaccuracies; this suggests the possibilistic rather than the probabilistic nature of cognitive process of realization. That is, the possibilistic nature of the object involves the attribution of the meaningfulness of the information concerning the object rather than the attributions of series of probabilities about the location, timing and characteristics of the object.

After the object is recognized with its specified location at some time, another range of disjunctive possibilities may be attributed to the object regarding the previous and subsequent locations of it. As it often occurs, part of the latter range of disjunctive possibilities may conflict with part of the prior attribution of the range of disjunctive possibilities, which were attributed to the object and event before the recognition of the object's location within some time frame (i.e., before the recognition of the real possibility). The subsequent attributions take precedence and sometimes involve surprises that arise when expectations have been changed.[18]

Attributing disjunctive possibilities to the movement and placement of some object at some time prepares one for quick recognitions of its actual locations. For the realizer and rememberer, the realization of the discrepancy

18 This analysis is relevant to the thinking and communications involved with legal systems as well as the expectations about extant laws and newly developing laws, expectations in courts of law, expectations concerning policing, lawmaking, and interpretations of laws.

between attributions of the inclusive disjunctive possibilities and the real possibilities of its location at a time likely increases the probability of the formation of a memorable object with movement.

Attributions of the inclusive disjunctive and exclusive disjunctive possibilities regarding the same object allow for there to be remembrances of the discrepancies between the first attributions of ranges of disjunctive possibilities (i.e., the imagined movements and placements of the object) and the actual movements and placements of it within a time frame (i.e., an act of transcendence of consciousness allows for realization or recognition and reconfirmation of the object) (Hartmann, 1931).

An ongoing process of the attribution of disjunctive possibilities to something and the recognition of it as real EXOR unreal and the final attribution of additional, augmented, or of the same possibility (i.e., reconfirmations) facilitates how one learns to make predictions. Predictions are accomplished via trial (e.g., forming the original attributions of disjunctive possibilities of the direction and final location of the object at some time) and error (i.e., the attributions of different disjunctive possibilities and discrepancies concerning what really happens and did not meet expectations).

Felipe De Brigard (2014) argues that the system of memory does not generally malfunction even when an individual misremembers since individuals often remember past events as "what could have happened" instead of "what really did not happen." This serves as predictive constructions of possible future events, i.e., "what may really occur in the future." According to the conception of recollective possibility, the recognition of the possibility of something before the realization of it as a real event also becomes recollected in various cases, which may suffice to provide the intelligent organism with a three stage process of realization shown in Figure 15:

> **(I)** the cognitive report of inclusive disjunctive possibilities of the event, involving expectation (i.e., logical possibility); **(II)** the recognition of the event as a real one (i.e., also physically possible); and **(III)** the recollection of (II) following (I) successively in addition to the validation of part of (I) via (II), the replacement of logical possibility with physical possibility as a categorization of that part, and repetitive categorizations of possibilities consistent with (I) and (II) so long as trials and errors happen with the capability of recognizing errors and attempts at the tasks or trials. This describes the learning process and actual realizations.

(I) is the formation of ranges or more specified inclusive disjunctive possibilities, i.e., all those considered by the individual in the time frame of completing the task or the attention span. (II) is the recognition of whether (I) demonstrates a set of real possibilities or whether they are unreal and inaccurate (i.e., a realization of what is real EXOR unreal but also relevant regarding the task or focus, which involves discovering the impossibilities in accordance with the concept of real possibility); and (III) is the attribution of additional possibility (or possibilities) after (I) and (II), which regards the appearances and realizations attained from (I) and (II). (III) tends to be consistent with the recognition process of intelligent organisms and involves a focus upon the discrepancies between (I) and (II).

(I) provides us with an additional way of thinking about how "conceivability entails possibility" (i.e., during the initial phase of the process of realization) because the first expectations that occur before an individual realizes something (e.g., the solution to a puzzle) may suffice to show that the individual's original considerations are characterizable as "disjunctively possible," even if they fail to be real possibilities. What the individual conceives within (I) concerns some range of disjunctive possibilities, and nothing that is independent from cognitively conceiving of possibilities is a recollective possibility, according to this conception. Thus, the conception of conceivability is crucial to the concept of recollective possibility. (II) concerns the act of the transcendence of consciousness, which will (exclusive disjunction) or will not (inclusive disjunction) happen (Hartmann, 1931).

(II) typically provides the grounds for discarding much of (I) from both the consideration and memory of the individual who realizes something, except for cases coinciding with De Brigard's (2014) insights. (III) is akin to the cognitive formation of a set of real possibilities since the formation relies upon the trials and errors involved first with the cognitive formation of expectations (i.e., (I)) and second with the recognition of what actually arises. Resultantly, (III) arises as a set of attributions of possibilities after ideas about what will happen and recognition of what does happen are remembered and are used within this process. Yet many of the possibilities of (III) are both real possibilities and inclusively disjunctive possibilities since other disjunctive possibilities naturally form even after the realization of the solution to the task but before its completion.

Overall, the concept of recollective possibility distinguishes itself from the concept of reality or actuality as well as the concepts of logical possibility and real possibility. The concept of reality includes absolutely everything, including realization. The concept of recollective possibility is only used within the process of realization.

Therefore, the concept of recollective possibility maintains that the category of possibility is less than the category of reality. Recollective possibility is the most feasible conception of possibility in comparison to inclusive disjunctive and real possibility, although the latter concepts are utilized within the process of realization. Recollective possibility is a cognitive-based conception, which involves possibility only arising as an aspect of what occurs within the cognitive process of realization and which involves organisms' recognitions about things within their environments. Since the recognitions involve the concept of recollective possibility in application, and all recognitions are based upon real physical substrates, the content of reality is larger and accounts for the emergence of the cognitive-based conception of possibility, which is smaller regarding its content.

Logical possibility, real possibility, and recollected possibility may be conceived, according to this view, as a mere portion but also an important aspect of the process of realization since they arise often before one realizes that something is real or unreal. The individual may recognize the thing as being inclusively disjunctively or really possible first and foremost, which is prior to the recognition of the real thing.

In many respects, the latter characterizations of possibility theory, especially with emphasis upon the concept of recollected possibility, offer legal theory and legal practice a theoretic framework. The theoretic framework encompasses legal theory and practice within a structure from which the decision-making process can be analyzed regarding policing decisions, judges' decisions, verdicts of jurors, lawmaking decisions, and prior desires, prior expectations, and then how the outcomes are analyzable by journalists, for instance.

The main concern with the conceptions of possibility is effective problem-solving, which requires well-directed methods. Thus, a form of methodology arises from the attributions of the concepts of logical possibility, real possibility, and recollective possibility. This methodology is directly applicable to law.

13 Methodological Problems for the Conceptions of Possibility

In this chapter, the arguments began by describing some of the foundational assumptions that are applied to theories. The foundational assumptions regard the systems' uses of the concept of inclusive disjunctive possibility and the concept of real possibility. Skepticism is generally focused in the direction of the assumptions of the system of thought that is opposed to the one with dogmas.

William Brant's (2013b: pp. 297–302) methodological analysis briefly critiques both the concepts of inclusive disjunctive possibility and real possibility. Brant maintains that the strict usage of either of these concepts within logical argumentation may lead one to mistake presumptions about possibility, which is coming from one's theoretic framework, as being knowledge-claims about possibility. Instead, they are tautologically derived from the theoretic framework itself.

During the process of acquiring knowledge, understanding and deriving the differences between the gradations of skepticism is important. Globally skeptical argumentation can involve arguing against such alleged knowledge-claims about a concept of possibility's status or functions. Less skeptical argumentation fails to cast serious doubt because a concept of possibility is so theoretically fundamental.

The concept of possibility must be involved within any argument that attempts to undermine it, except for a conception that incorporates the usefulness of the other concepts of possibility. This section aims to show the utility of other concepts of possibility as they are combined as aspects of the process of realization, according to the concept of recollective possibility and the methods developed by Brant (2013b).

Drawing a distinction between the levels of skeptical arguments is important for both the analysis of knowledge-claims and approximating levels of relevancy (ibid.). The least skeptical type of argument that is nevertheless able to defeat alleged knowledge-claims, regarding the meaning and use of the concept of possibility, is the globally skeptical argument.

Globally skeptical arguments are also the most skeptical types. The form and content of globally skeptical argumentation can vary greatly. They may involve casting doubt on the ability to remember. They can focus on forgetfulness.

Brant's (ibid.) methodology insists that there are three important types of arguments. They are constructed for a more systematic analysis of the relevancy and certainty levels of alleged knowledge-claims via systematic doubt.

These three types of arguments that are applicable to the alleged knowledge-claim are: (1) the globally skeptical argument; (2) the least skeptical argument that defeats the alleged knowledge-claim; and (3) the most skeptical argument that fails to defeat the claim and which thereby offers support for it.

We may treat the idea of the plurality worlds as a claim which lacks a recognizable distinction between (1) and (2) when the idea undergoes analyses (Lewis, 1986). We may also, in this light, compare the adoption of the thesis of the plurality of worlds and attribution of serviceability to it with a model of shoes of various sizes. However, consider a situation where the customer for the shoes is unable to try on a smaller size of that model to observe whether that model's smallest available size fits her feet.

When one purchases the smallest size of a model and is unable to test something smaller, then one fails to understand whether the range of sizes for that model are best-suited for one's wear. One can wear the shoes. One can adopt the thesis. It remains questionable whether they are fitting, though.

When one analyzes alleged knowledge-claims, and only globally skeptical arguments are suitable for casting doubt upon them, as opposed to something less skeptical, the relevance of the claims appears to regard the model itself. The alleged knowledge-claims are more like descriptions of the theoretic framework from which the thinker works.

Each theoretic framework comes with some specific size, form, and functions. The theoretic framework, like the model of shoes, is unable to be evaluated properly. The less skeptical arguments are unfitting and so are the feet that developed only until they reached a smaller size than that model covers.

A model and size of shoes might still be practical. This can be one difference between theoretic frameworks and frameworks of shoes. Shoes that are not too large can often still be useful. However, the problem with a theoretic framework, which only submits to global skepticism, is precisely that it yields no other upper limitation than the limitation of the highest skepticism.

Theorists who advocate frameworks, which only succumb to global skepticism, may never even acknowledge that global skepticism even suffices to shed sufficient doubt upon their system of thought. The skepticism reveals the irrelevancy of the thesis. Because global skepticism suffices to shed sufficient doubt on every thesis, it may be ignored, unfortunately, for this reason.

Skeptical hypotheses raise differing levels of doubt for all legal theories and examples of legal cases, police actions, policies, etc. For example, without reliable observations of dominations and subordinations, the social dominance theory's stance on criminal justice or penal systems is irrelevant.

The relevancy of the latter facts concerns the capability for a methodology to distinguish between alleged knowledge-claims that are vulnerable to levels of skepticism below the level of global skepticism. Arguments less skeptical than global skepticism present knowledge-claims with distinguishable levels of relevancy from claims that are embedded and fundamental to the framework from which the claimer works.

Many claims do not involve any relation to anything observable or even accommodate something real or actual. The existence of such types of claims can be explained in terms of what Thomas Metzinger (2003: p. 43) argues, namely, that "human brains can generate phenomenal models of possible worlds."

14 Synopsis and Future Directions of Research: Possibility Theory for Law

There are at least three equivocations of the word "possibility" regarding content, concepts, modes, and categories: (1) disjunctive possibility, which is the category of possibility that is greater than the category of reality; (2) real possibility, which is the category of possibility that is equal to the category of reality; and (3) recollected possibility, which is the category of possibility that is less than the category of reality in terms of content, and is based upon the finite and possibilistic nature of cognition.

Inclusive disjunctive possibility, metaphysical possibility, logical possibility, and indifferent possibility are concepts that hold that the category of possibility or range of possibilities, which fit into these conceptions, are greater or wider than the category of reality to the extent that they include possible unreal things that never happen or never come into being. Events that never happen are not necessarily impossible by the standards of the four former conceptions of possibility. Even those things that exceed the limitations or boundaries of what is physically possible or real are possible in accordance with inclusive disjunction, metaphysics, logicality, and indifference as concepts applied in relation to the conception of possibility. From the perspective of real possibility, the latter inclusive disjunctive possibilities, which all the latter types of possibilities may be called, are "virtually" possible but are only "really" possible if the events to which they are attributed ever occur.

The study of ontology perhaps favors the idea that there is only that which is real (i.e., there is nothing else besides that which is, that which exists, that which is actual, or that which has being), and so the study can be viewed as focusing on nothing else than the real. For this reason, there is also a general and presumed distinction between what is possible and what is real in the field of ontology. The advocacy of the concept of disjunctive possibility as opposed to the concept of real possibility may lead one to maintain that all sorts of fantastical events that never happen are, nonetheless, possible, which is akin to upholding system-thinking in ways that apply the concept of disjunctive possibility across an entire realm of discourse (e.g., a theory in physics, a legal theory, economic theory, ethical theories etc.).

The attributions of possibilities during the course of the cognitive process of realization are crucial in order for the distinction between the possible and the real to ever be made within the study of ontology. Any study, such as biology and law, requires realizations that are verified and that are thus cognitive in nature. One interpretation of possibility, therefore, is that the concept is solely an aspect of the realization process.

What has been provided here is a treatment of the concepts of possibility as crucial aspects of systems of thought themselves and as what involves tendencies to form presumptions for problem-solving, decision-making, and methodologies. The formations of the concepts of logical possibility, real possibility, and recollective possibility coincide with their own systems of thought that may or may not be adopted for various reasons and which are frequently equivocated with each other. It would be premature to ignore any of the three concepts of possibility as to avoid certain undesirable conclusions, such as the conclusion, which is detrimental for legal systems, that "there cannot be any moral responsibility" because each conception is applicable to such statements in very different ways.

The concept of inclusive disjunctive possibility incorporates the occurrences of both coincidentally and necessarily real and unreal events. The modal concepts of coincidence and necessity can be implemented within courts of law by defense attorneys to relieve the moral blameworthiness of the accused regarding the views of the judges and jurors (See Ch. 5.5). The concept of real possibility might be ignored for the latter reason, regarding a lack of moral blameworthiness as well, yet Baruch Spinoza utilized the concept of real possibility as at least a subsidiary one in application within his *Ethics*.

The concept of recollective possibility deserves much more attention because it combines both disjunctive and real possibility conceptions in a manner that treats cognition as a necessary condition for the application and emergence of modal propositional reports (McKay & Nelson, 2010). Recollective possibility is a concept that may yield many more testable scientific hypotheses, which would demonstrate its serviceability.

Future research questions may inquire how the concept of possibility best functions for artificial intelligence and whether the concept solely functions for the cognitive process of realization or for the understanding. That is, how would artificial intelligence utilize the concept of possibility in relation to realization? How would artificial intelligence attribute possibility to ambiguities within certain time frames concerning locations toward which the intelligent system maintains its focus?

Many questions remain about how this applies to legal systems, lawmakers, and decreasing societal violence. How might the concept of recollective possibility be applied to legal studies in other ways for the attainment of goals and increases in the efficiencies concerning the processes and procedures of legal systems and their performances regarding justice and fairness? How can we also begin to understand how people think about the law and their statuses within society and why people make choices to commit violence?

The closing chapter, The F-Problem, focuses on the latter question regarding the fundamental human problem of the 21st century, which is the problem of balancing the human birthrates with the human death rates to reduce the likelihoods of war, poverty, disease, famine, unfairness, and ruthless competitiveness, especially competitiveness for mates for sexual reproduction.

CHAPTER 6

The F-Problem

Two sorts of problems threaten the human species with endangerment and extinction, to wit, nuclear holocaust and degradations of environments around the earth. The F-problem concerns the latter because it is the absence of balance between the birthrate and death rate of humanity. The latter problems have been problems of the 20th and 21st centuries, have been wrought by human beings, and continue to be problems that are exacerbating. While the gradual destruction of the planet or the nuclear obliteration of the human species are violent in their own ways, the common human experience of violence is local and personal.[1]

1 Domestic violence is an ongoing problem and likely involves a set of learned behaviors so that those who have undergone domestic violence as children may have increased tendencies of choosing partners who abuse them or selecting partners who they abuse because parents or caregivers are the role models for children and adolescents and who they will likely follow when they become adults. Methodologically speaking, in the field of sociology, murder rates are the most worthwhile statistics to follow because other violent crimes greatly lack the transparency, such as rapes, police brutality, and assaults perhaps because the general ease with which dead bodies are found and the vast ways of presenting evidence that allows homicide detectives, for instance, to determine the causes of deaths versus the tendencies to hide the statistics with other violent crimes.

Excessive amounts of publicity on the national level by mass media broadcasts (e.g., with the copycat phenomenon and the motivation of killers to seek infamy and inflated importance), the maldistribution of wealth, especially the increases in poverty and realizations of it, and the access to guns, especially handguns, are factors that explain the high rates of murders in societies. In societies with high murder rates, such as the USA, immigration has been shown to have the opposite impact, namely, lowering the murder rates in areas, according to Jack Levin in a 2011 lecture, "Trends in Violence," at Emmanuel College in Boston. However, increased tourism in cities can lead to increases in violence, too.

Levin also maintains that familicide is characterized as increasing in rates during economic crises, in which cases the husbands and fathers tend to take the roles of the murderers/victimizers, and the wives, partners, and children tend to take the roles of victims, especially when there have been great losses to the killers (e.g., divorces, bankruptcy, etc.). Many cases involve premeditated murders where the direct family members are selected, oftentimes suicidal tendencies coincide with them, and ideologies concerning the afterlife, heaven etc. have been used by many of the suicidal killers as motivations to commit their victimizations and suicides for protecting them, ideologically speaking, from the suffering of the living world.

Parents kill their own children below the age of five more than friends, acquaintances, other families, and strangers kill the children of other parents combined, in large civil societies, according to Levin. Some societies have subcultures of violence, such as the rural areas

 | DOI:10.1163/9789004385955_008

The 21st century already includes the coupling of extremely violent attacks that are being operated from remote locations by professionals who decide when, where, and at whom to lead missiles. The experiences of the victimizers, these professionals, are vastly different than the soldiers of war during the 20th century because the commanders of unmanned aircrafts pull the triggers that cause violence and then return to their homes, families, children, etc. after their days at work (Marlantes, 2011). The experiences of war now include those of people who live like civilians. They may never even leave their own countries and also may, coincidingly, fight a war from their home countries via technology.

Obviously, war impacts populations around the planet and devastates the environments. War can certainly become ever more frequent and ever more intense regarding violence when there are increases in the sizes of populations. The exponential growth rate of human populations and frequencies of human births are intertwined with the needs for more resources as well as the needs for more places for human waste materials. For these reasons, the investigation shifts to a more fundamental problem, the F-problem, which directly concerns the human species and other species that sexually reproduce their offspring.

A major change in the growth rate of the human population will occur during the 21st century. The combination of the currently high global birthrate, the amount of devastation to the environments, and falls in the amount of global food production and drinking water will occur with the sufficient deteriorations of the environments. Nevertheless, humans will continue to have uncontrollable desires to find, select, compete for mates, and to sexually reproduce; the F-problem is the problem of balance for sustainability of human mating practices and our species in its entirety.

The fundamental set of questions concerning the reduction of violence during this century is: How do we balance the global human birthrate and global human death rate, despite humans' overwhelming desires to copulate, to expand the territories of ownership, and to procreate human offspring? How will legal-mindedness be impacted by these human sexual desires, especially the thinking of lawmakers who tend to make decisions based on their constituents' interests? Presumably, legal systems and institutions will continue to be intricately involved in policing, legislating, and judging for and against crimes

of the South in the USA, which behave violently to protect their alleged honor and their identifications as being masculine or macho. Mass murders, alternatively, are premeditated and may tend to occur with individuals who have no family nearby and no sense of community to help them through troubling times with support and encouragement, and many killers tend to feel isolation and loneliness, according to Levin as well.

of sex and reproduction. Feasibly, members of the legal institution (e.g., police, politicians and judges) may tend to give advantages more often to people who they find sexually attractive when lawmen and women are seduced, even unwittingly. It behooves us to consider the latter range of issues as well as the history of our species regarding procreation.

In the prehistoric past, the human species was probably faced with the problem of the struggle for its own existence. Some prehistoric people likely had trouble sexually reproducing enough offspring to populate certain areas. People were scarce in most regions. Over 12,000 years ago there were not many people on the planet in comparison to the amount on the planet at any time during the last 200 years. One estimate is that the Earth had a population of four million humans in 10,000 BCE (Ortiz-Ospina & Roser, 2016; Kremer, 1993). Prehistorically speaking, the human species faced a problem of struggling to balance the human birthrate with the human death rate because the human death rate was relatively high in comparison to the birthrate over 12,000 years ago. Now, we are faced with the opposite danger concerning the frequency of our species procreating.

The reasons for the risks of the human species becoming endangered or extinct are complex and do not merely concern our species. Many species, which sexually reproduce, undergo time periods when they reproduce too many offspring. A species can thereby overpopulate a region. The resources, which the species needs, dwindle under such circumstances. Competition becomes fiercer for nutrients. Competitions for mates escalate. Aggression increases as well as killings, diseases, and famines. Individuals with more resources have advantages in respect to procreating more offspring. Domination more easily occurs and is implemented by individuals and families with greater access to resources, especially when the individuals are motivated to do so.

The human species no longer faces the same circumstantial problems regarding the struggle for the continued existence of the human species. Before 1800, the human global population growth rate never surpassed 0.5% per year (Ortiz-Ospina & Roser, 2016). After 1800, a new trend happened in the growth of the global human population, which reached one billion during the early 19th century (ibid.). During the first half of the 20th century, another drastic trend occurred insofar as the global human population growth rate exploded from 0.8% to 2.1% per year (ibid.).

Even just a 1.0% population growth rate per year can be excessive because, continually speaking, this amount of growth allows for a population to double its size in less than 70 years. The continuation of a population doubling its size once or twice each century is often deadly for the environments where the populations live and therefore is often disastrous for the populations, too. How do the legal systems begin to handle these challenges of sex and reproduction without the escalations of violence for our species?

The F-problem needs to be divided into smaller, more manageable problems, such as considering the divisions of generations and focusing on the impacts that one generation will have on the others throughout its diverse lifespan (i.e., the concept of a generational lifespan and its impacts). One problem for humanity is the challenge of balancing the human birthrates that occur for each generation with the death rates of every generation. Each generation of human beings has its own special concerns with education, the workforce, breadwinners providing for families, upholding traditions, etc. The latter concerns are typically more relevant to any particular generation than the problem of balancing the birthrate of the population with their death rate for energy and resource optimization. This balance problem is also called the "F-problem" because human desires are often sexual in their nature, which exacerbate the balance problem of the stability of our species and sustainable human practices. Sometimes when people realize that problem-solvers have attempted to lower the rate of sexual reproduction, the F-problem is exacerbated.

Regarding the seriousness of a set of problems, the F-problem stands uncouthly for the "fucking problem" or the "sexual intercourse motivated and fertilization-related problem," which is the apex of the set of problems discussed whenever the problems involve sexual reproduction as a necessary condition for the emergence of the set of problems from the outset. The human consequences of a drought, for instance, can be described in many ways to be one member of this set of problems, which involves sexual reproduction as a necessary condition and is thereby an F-problem. Sex and sexual reproduction exacerbate the problem of the drought. Moreover, the previous occurrences of sexual reproduction are also necessary for the drought to be a human problem in the first place and tend to be necessary for the drought to be an F-problem, and occurrences of human sexual reproduction and sex certainly worsen the problem of a drought during the drought, especially if the drought lasts longer than the gestation period of nine months.

Other examples of F-problems are more interesting. For instance, feminists have sought to undermine the ideas of Amir (1971). Amir (1971) argues that approximately 20% of women facilitate the occurrences of their own rapes by leading them to happen prematurely, in accordance with the police data in his study. Other questions concern the role of masochism and sadism as well as sex that is forced on one partner, like a rape is, but it differs from a rape insofar as the one in the role of the "victim" either does not perceive it as a rape after the occurrence or comes to enjoy the sexual encounter, for instance. Another F-problem concerns the impact on sexual reproduction that ritualistic scarring of the genitals and forced circumcisions have on the victims or on the youths who undergo these so-called “rites of passage.” In this chapter, the births of babies of ten to fourteen-year mothers and forty-five to forty-nine-year mothers are also analyzed in addition to societal practices regarding reproduction in the USA, South Africa, and other countries.

1 The Economic Problem, the F-Problem, and Human Overpopulation

Some of the most basic problems of humanity are economic problems. There is the lack of access to humanly needed resources, especially clean water and nutrients, such as proteins, iodine, and iron, and the absence of knowledge of how to attain the resources repeatedly. There are obviously not fulfillments of each human’s wants and needs on our planet. The earth contains many hundreds of millions of human inhabitants who are undernourished in the 21st century.[2]

In essence, there are problems that humans face regarding the scarcity of the four factors of production, namely, land, labor, capital, and entrepreneurship, which are, respectively, the resources of nature, human resources, manufacturing resources, and the resources of knowledge of combining the former resources and risk-takings for business activities (i.e., the enterprises). The latter problems will always persist since humans have unlimited needs and wants, and there are also limited resources, which are insufficient for the fulfillments of our wants and needs; this is our “economic problem.”

The economic problem coincides with the presence of human diseases, violent conflicts, wars, famines, and poverty; each of the latter human problems are greatly exacerbated with the overpopulation of humans in the environment and with dwindling resources. Also, the diminishing access to the resources or expectations of the diminishing access to them generally cause increases in the problems’ intensities and frequencies.

Conceptually speaking, the frequency of sexual reproduction remains an even more fundamental factor that is necessary for both overpopulation and

2 Approximately 793 million people were undernourished in 2015, according to the Food and Agriculture Organization of the United Nations in 2017 (www.fao.org). In fact, even the latest “Millennium Development Goal” targets of the United Nations and the World Food Summit for nourishing people around the planet are set at levels that would still leave hundreds of millions of human beings undernourished.

the economic problem to occur.[3] The human species is one that sexually reproduces, and the recurrences of problems that inflict our species must be analyzed in relation to sexual reproduction for an understanding of them, especially overpopulation.

Ultimately, a solution to the F-problem is necessary in which professionals find how to stabilize, balance, and manage the birthrates and death rates of populations in environments where resources may be in great abundances or shortages. Any solution to the F-problem requires an understanding of sexual reproduction from STEEPLE analytical perspectives (i.e., social, technological, economic, environmental, political, legal, and ethical analyses). This chapter aims to enlighten readers so that they attain understandings of the concepts of sex partners who are statistically shown from ten to forty-nine years of age, sex partners of different races and who have diverse levels of genetic relations to one another as well as to their parents, which are presented with statistics in the following sections. Moreover, sociological, anthropological, and historical analyses (i.e. widely interdisciplinary analyses) are required to enlighten us with regard to the changes in the patterns of age, race, and sexual reproduction rates for various generations (e.g., generations X, Y, Z and so on).

Sexual reproduction is a fundamental factor for a scientific understanding of the concept of society. Sexual reproduction is necessary for the existence of poverty, famine, much disease, and violence. The famous Jonathan Swift wrote an essay and satirical solution to the problem of famine in Ireland, and "A Modest Proposal" in 1729 presented the idea that there was no famine problem because the presence of babies shows that fresh meat is readily available. So, there is potentially no hunger problem for adults and adolescents at least. Yet human social practices, ethics, behavioral tendencies, and laws disallow any similar form of problem-solving to be utilized or taken seriously.

Each of the problems, namely, the F-problem, the economic problem, poverty, famine, and disease, are related intricately to the problem of violence. Only the F-problem is entirely unable to be relieved by violence because it requires a solution of balance that offers stability and sustainability of human practices that can be assimilated into human cultures. Alternatively, poverty, famine, and some diseases can be alleviated by violence to the extent that killings may easily allow the wealthy to eradicate the poor or the poor to take over the possessions of the wealthy, including food, shelters, and positions of power.

3 The relationship between procreation and the economic problem is most obvious when humans are conceptualized as property (e.g., of the state or coinciding with slavery) and the wants and needs of elites and others are considered foremost to be insufficiently fulfilled.

Diseases can be contained and vastly reduced concerning their risks when the diseased are obliterated. The economic problem may at least be partially eliminated with killings since ending lives leads to the reduction of needs and wants as well as more resources that are available for the living (e.g., natural and artificial or manufactured resources), except for human resources and entrepreneurship, of course. Moreover, each society remains capable of the latter sorts of violence, especially with the onset of worsening conditions for certain groups coupled with mass ideology.

Even war must be understood in relation to the F-problem and sexual reproduction with war's associated concepts of patriotism or loyalty to the nation and other ideologies that lead warriors to kill people from, typically, less closely related families than those of their fellow soldiers. From a biological standpoint, we may consider whether "war" can be viewed consistently as a phenomenon that persists as human social tendencies that fundamentally but inadvertently or unconsciously include the killings of people who are less closely genetically related or of people who have dissimilar phenotypes regarding skin, eye, and hair colors, other facial features, somatotypes, etc.

Some conceptualizations of war maintain that war is only a problem for the human species, like the problem of poverty. However, the increased violence and the possessions of less resources per individual on average are general results of the overpopulation of any species in an area. The study of the balance problem between the human global birthrates and death rates would thusly benefit from ethological analyses.

The presence of human overpopulation depletes natural resources and replaces them with waste while polluting the air, lands, waters, and even outer space. The concept, however, of human overpopulation is not well-defined and can very well be based upon a series of factors that can also be applied to studies of droughts. Overpopulation depends upon the amount of resources available in the environment. So, one region may have more inhabitants than another region that is overpopulated. The former region may even be underpopulated. Similarly, an area with lower moisture might not be experiencing a drought, although other regions with greater moisture could be undergoing droughts.

With droughts, the increase in technology can reduce the negative human consequences of these prolonged periods without sufficient moisture that comes from the reduction of precipitation over a certain time. For example, rain water collection systems, distribution services for water, water pipe infrastructures, water storage and treatment systems, etc. can prevent many of the negative impacts upon humans. Much of the literature on droughts discusses at least six categories of definitions of the term "drought," which include the agricultural, atmospheric, climatological, hydrologic, meteorological, and water management (Wilhite & Glantz, 1985). Similarly, human overpopulation can be studied from multiple perspectives and disciplines, including ecology, economics, sociology, anthropology, water management, and agriculture.

The presence of reduced moisture or a drought may very well signify human overpopulation in some areas, especially where desertification occurs. Humans disturb the amount of moisture in certain areas by building dams, roads, neighborhoods, and redirecting waterways, which may drastically increase or decrease the amount of moisture in regions. Technology can also reduce the negative human consequences of high population densities at certain times (e.g., more efficient transportation, water treatment, food distribution systems, etc.). Perhaps the potential for natural or human-caused disasters should raise the likelihood for a region to be considered as "overpopulated." Such an analysis first needs measurements, though.

Contrarily, a STEEPLE analysis of the social, technological, economic, environmental, political, legal, and ethical issues involved with any group of people may lead one to argue that some regions lack human overpopulation insofar as the increase in the efficiencies of one or a few of these factors would prevent or relieve the aftereffects of overpopulation considerably. However, overpopulation is an F-problem because it is also the result of the procreation of a maldistribution of generations of populaces insofar as the experiences and education necessary for the prevention of the effects of overpopulation are highly unlikely due to demographical factors, especially the ages of the people.

Underdeveloped nations with human populations where the median age is under twenty years old are typically unable to educate their populations regarding family planning, which concerns practices that control the frequency and number of births per family, especially with products (e.g., contraceptives) and services (e.g., voluntary sterilizations). Developing nations are also likely unable to educate their populaces regarding family planning. On the other side, many developed nations even have negative population growth rates. The reasons for the differences in education regarding issues concerning the F-problem can be understood in virtue of the types of professionals within the distinct types of nations.

Underdeveloped nations have most of their professionals within the primary sectors of their societies, managing the industries for mining, fishing, forestry, and farming. So, they concern themselves mostly with the management of the extraction of natural resources primarily, except for some subsidiary F-problems, such as droughts. Developing nations have most of their professionals within the secondary sector, managing the industries for construction, packaging, and factory work, transforming the raw materials extracted by the primary sectors' business activities to produce goods, finished or unfinished products, etc. So, the latter professionals concern themselves typically with the management of manufacturing and the processes of industrialization. Overall, the underdeveloped and developing countries tend to have and to require cheaper human resources for development.

Of course, there are various other professionals outside of the former types of specific industries and the former sectors of the economies within underdeveloped and developing nations, especially in major cities that have greater developments. However, the professionals within the service sectors of the non-developed countries tend to lack the level of professionalism, the amount of salaries, proportionately speaking, and the benefits from employment contracts that developed nations have for their service sectors' professionals. So, there tend to be shortages of professionals within the tertiary sectors of underdeveloped and developing countries, and these sorts of professionals are important because professionals concerned directly with family planning are tertiary sector employees of societies. Moreover, developed nations have larger and more efficient public sectors of their economies, which allow for some professionals to further develop their skills for the public service of family planning. Thus, any solution to the F-problem that involves family planning is likely to be shortsighted if there are expectations and assumptions about underdeveloped and developing countries controlling their populations through strategies in family planning via the usage of their own professionals.

Another F-problem is violence, especially violence that is initiated by males. It is very questionable, for instance, whether violence in many cases would have occurred if the male or group of males would have had better access to females to whom they were attracted or not. Competition between males for the access to females (i.e., intrasexual selection) is one reason for violence, even if females are not directly in the vicinity, and this reason for violence is not just violence that is directed from human males to other human males but involves multiple species, especially those where the males are not required to expend as much time and effort regarding caring for their own offspring. Moreover, the competition among males and among females intensifies with overpopulation or when the amount of sexual reproduction has greatly increased.

Sexual reproduction is the biological fertilization process that occurs with the development of fertilized eggs amongst millions of species that sexually reproduce as opposed to the asexually reproducing organisms. However, for our purposes, we are primarily concerned with the species that sexually reproduces and forms social groups that direct violence against other social groups that are members of the same species as opposed to the sexual reproduction of plants and fungi, for instance. The frequency of the former processes become social F-problems when and where overpopulation occurs, and especially when environmental conditions are also drastically altered because of the impacts of the overpopulated species on the distribution of resources and waste materials.

Overpopulation results in the diminishing sustainability of the environment to maintain the conditions with which the members of the population reside. Environmental conditions, such as droughts, are also F-problems. Humans are either led into areas that undergo extended periods without rain or the environment, in which humans already dwell, has been significantly changed by the presence of the species, which has led to the drought with depleted aquifers and lakes. The F-problem also arises when the sexually reproducing species has a higher death rate than birthrate for a long enough time or intensely enough to endanger its existence. The frequency of the sexual reproduction and intensity of sexually motivated or intended acts become F-problems when and where diseases arise as the result of overpopulation as well as when and where poverty arises because of human overpopulation.

Human overpopulation is an abstract concept about which no certain range of measurable limitations is present since there are so many factors that contribute to it, apart from the sheer number of human organisms in some region during some time. So, currently there is neither an upper limitation nor a lower limitation for the concept. However, we may maintain that the increasing presence of competitiveness of the members of the same species, increasing populations in certain areas, increasing intensities and amounts of violence, increasing poverty, decreasing resources or increasing numbers of individuals who lack knowledge of how to collect or select resources, and increasing cases of diseases "greatly signify" the overpopulation of some region.

Additionally, any such society with overpopulated geographical regions typically has many other human-caused and related problems, such as air, land, and water pollution, diseases, and epidemics or droughts. Air, land, and water pollution, diseases, and droughts are also F-problems, although they are subsidiary F-problems, because they result from the overabundance of sexually reproduced (human) organisms but not immediately so, and such problems are exacerbated by human undertakings, especially business activities.

War, poverty, and typically famine are also F-problems. Famine can result from the harshness of the environment (e.g., deserts and tundra) or from a lack of knowledge about what is edible regarding an environment. Increases in waste materials, diseases, droughts, competitiveness for land, shelter, food as well as violence are all reasons for discouraging the increase in birthrates and promoting the balance of the birthrate and the death rate globally. Promoting the balance of global human birthrates and death rates is crucial for the continuation of our species, it is important for the sustainability of environments on earth. It is ethical from multiple perspectives, including environmental ethics so that other species are not placed in jeopardy and face extinction because of overconsumption by humans and degradations.

As sexually reproducing animals, the average amount of time necessary for individuals of a species to sexually reproduce, the luck of the selection of mates, the luck of the extant resources and the environments in which individuals live as potential partners, the demands of the potential sexual partners before sex and before reproduction, the search for mates, and the competitiveness against others that find the same mates simultaneously or at similar times are all characteristics of the situations that sexually reproducing species face as opposed to species that reproduce asexually.

In recapitulation, the F-problem is a pervasive problem that concerns the birthrate and its relation to the death rate, especially for the global human population but also for populations of any species that rely upon sexual reproduction. The fundamental issue to solve for problem-solvers of the F-problem is the creation of a sustainable balance of the birthrate and the death rate within environments, globally and otherwise. Without having balance and stability as the key notions from which to solve the F-problem, humans will be confronted with the consequences of increased violence and increased death rates. If the death rate remains higher than the birthrate, our species is faced with becoming endangered and then extinct, but if the birthrate remains higher than the death rate, our species will confront a rapidly increasing death rate.

Wars and diseases have the capacity to endanger our species or drive it extinct, but they usually serve as ways to reduce the population and typically result in periods of peace and lower occurrences of outbreaks. However, late 20th and early 21st century types of warfare and diseases of the late 20th century (e.g., HIV, SARS, malaria, and Ebola) have the capabilities of wiping out entire populations or substantial portions of them. The outbreak of new strains and new diseases increases with the increases in the industrial meat production partially because the animals are fed antibiotics. Microorganisms become resistant to the antibiotics, and thereby they become deadlier for humans and other species. Pandemics become ever more likely, and these uncontrollable outbreaks of diseases have the potential to drive humanity to extinction.

On the other side of the scale, if the birthrate remains higher than the death rate, then the needed resources dwindle, competitiveness for resources rises, violence occurs more frequently as well as diseases (i.e., where greater numbers of members of the same species are closer together for longer periods), environments deteriorate, living conditions worsen, poverty increases, and war, as far as we know, becomes inevitable. The death rate tends to rise after the birthrate has exceeded it long enough or intensely enough. Yet no one sanely wants to live amid such violence, unfairness, death, destruction and disease-ridden areas. So, utilitarian and consequentialist ethics offer support for the balance of the global human birth and death rates.

Systems are in place which control birthrates to some extent and control death rates, too, but the systems change with the changes of societies. Legal systems and criminal justice systems control birthrates in multiple ways, which include the obvious separations of people of the opposite sex from each other in jails and prisons. Political proposals of any organization for creating balance in the global human population cannot feasibly be made on the global stage since those involved would have the power over the life, birth, and death of many members of our species.

2 Legal Encouragement and Discouragement of Fertilization and Corporate Impacts on the Planet

Legal systems in some societies reward and encourage some people to increase the national birthrates (e.g., tax breaks are provided to families), especially if those societies are developed and have a negative population growth rate (i.e., if the societies have higher death rates or migration rates than their birthrates). The Child Support Grant of South Africa implemented during the late 1990s is an example of national support wrought by the legal system for the support of families with births that took place over the span of about a decade (Lund, 2008, pp. 59–79).

Contrarily, legal systems within other societies discourage and penalize people for exceeding their legal maximum number of births, which can be calculated via the number of births per female or per family (e.g., the One-Child Policy of China (Goh, 2011)). Those societies with legal systems, within which legislators have dubbed the society's population within certain regions as "overpopulated," may very well implement such penalizations to contribute to the decrease of the birth rate in relation to the death rate.

With the author's Taiwanese colleague, Yawen Cheng, William Brant conducted primary research on a village of Chinese people within the Sichuan province in Liangshan (i.e., "barren mountain" in English) from February through June 2016. In this remote mountain village near the town of Sha Ba and another neighboring village about two hours away from Yu Ma Shan by foot, approximately 800 people live in the mountains. The living conditions of the village are generally quite harsh and are extremely harsh during the winter. There are absolutely no public services in the village.

There are millions of Chinese people who are in similar circumstances, although the Chinese government has been making efforts to alleviate poverty during the 21st century. From 1981 to 2004, China successfully reduced poverty by 500 million people, which accounted for about 70% of the global poverty alleviation (Yan, 2016, p. 1). Public services, such as in universities, are required to care for villages: to assess, evaluate, report, and relieve poverty.

In the mountain village, there are absolutely no public services for electricity, police, water, postal services, roads, education, or transport. My colleague and I were informed by people in the nearby town of Sha Ba that the villagers were dangerous thieves who often transported drugs, which presented an ideology that the Han Chinese ethnic group held against their poverty-stricken neighbors from the Yi minority ethnic group.

In the mountain village, there is one school, and the teacher is compensated by a corporation for which he worked in the past with approximately $20 per month for his full-time services as a teacher. He is required to show the progress of the students to the corporation regularly. One charity group from Chengdu has donated school uniforms for the children and visits them a few times per year. There are approximately 200 children and babies in the village and just one school with one classroom and one teacher, Mr. Zhang, who teaches different age groups of children altogether.

Villagers attain water from just a few wells outside their homes and must hike back to their homes with the water, and there are some streams from which most of the villagers carry their water before boiling and drinking it in their homes. Several of the homes have solar panels that supply a little electricity. They must hike to and from Yu Ma Shan to receive mail, which is about a two-hour hike and can be exhausting. There are no paved roads, and for a few weeks during each year the main route to the neighboring village is submerged beneath water. I was almost stuck in the village after a rain in late June of 2016.

Figure 16 is a photograph taken during June of 2016 of the terrace farming in the village. The image shows several houses as well as one with solar panels.

FIGURE 16 Terrace farming of Chinese village in the Sichuan province

The village does have a few horses, but largely people travel on foot through goat trails. For some children, the hike can last well over an hour to reach their school.

The villagers are one of the 56 Chinese ethnic groups called the "Yi" people and the majority of them in this Sichuan village only speak the Yi language, and thus, the villagers cannot communicate effectively with the people in the nearby towns who speak Mandarin. Perhaps most the villagers and probably most of the children have no legal Chinese identification or passport. Villagers' opportunities are extremely limited partially because they have been significantly impacted by the One-Child Policy. So, the children are "illegitimate children," despite having both their parents as caregivers, in many cases.

In the Sichuan village shown in figures 16 through 20, some of the young men have each sexually reproduced with more than one woman. I visited one young man's older partner and younger partner with whom he had procreated and impregnated, respectively. His older partner had three children, a baby, a larger house in the village, comparatively speaking, and she was skilled at cooking and farming. We ate pork fat, plums, and a leafy vegetable stew.

The village receives donations, including over 1,000 pounds of wheat flour and rice that were sent by our group, China Charity Crusaders, which I managed with Ms. Cheng and a few others through the WeChat social media. The clothes and toys they received from our unregistered organization were probably sold to compensate for purchases, such as solar panels, electronics, farming materials, etc.

FIGURE 17 Chinese village children without identification

Many of the villagers gathered around one of the sick villagers in figures 19 and 20. Her home was the only home out of over 50 I visited that hung eggs and feathers at the top of the doorway (i.e., shown in figure 20), which perhaps signifies rebirth or something superstitious along these lines.

Legal systems in many societies hinder the birthrates of particularly targeted social groups, which are typically low-status groups (e.g., poverty-stricken and low-status racial groups). The villages housing perhaps millions of Chinese people from ethnic minority groups, such as the Yi people in Figures 16 to 20, have vastly diminished opportunities within the Chinese society because they have more than one child, and there are generations of people who lack Chinese identification documents. For more pictures and information, visit the author's website.[4] The births of generations of people in China, going against the Chinese legal permissiveness of the one or two-child policies of the 20th and 21st centuries, lead them to live in remote areas like outcasts of society.

4 http://williambrant.weebly.com/travels-with-photography.html It is questionable what sort of impact, positive or negative, our organization had on this village of people who would at least appear to benefit more from the creation of greater numbers and more diverse business activities and less births per household. Our organization certainly created a set of artificial stimuli that were presented within the economy of their village, which may have increased the likelihood for them to sexually reproduce. They certainly sold and traded the items that were given to them, such as toys, clothing, and perhaps even some of the education materials. The education given to a village that creates sustainable practices, largely including business activities with renewable resources, is certainly a superior form of charity.

FIGURE 18 Inside a village hut

FIGURE 19 Villagers gathering around a sick woman

For those who live in accordance with the Chinese rules of law, there are hindrances regarding the number of children they are legally permitted to beget. Hindering the birthrate of selected individuals can well be viewed as an institutional form of artificial selection, social dominance, and sexual dominance. Such hindrances are also commonplace within developing countries at certain times as well as some developed countries, although less frequently. Lombardo (2011, p. ix) writes:

FIGURE 20 Sick woman in a village with no public services

> In 1907, Indiana passed the first involuntary sterilization law in the world based on the theory of eugenics. In time more than 30 states and a dozen foreign countries followed Indiana's lead in passing sterilization laws; those and other laws restricting immigration and regulating marriage on "eugenic" grounds were still in effect in the United States as late as the 1970s.

One of the latest landmark court cases in the United States was *Relf v. Weinberger* (1974), in which the legitimacy, authority, and constitutionality of the rules and regulations of the Department of Health, Education and Welfare, as a governing body for the implementation of human sterilization, were decided upon within a court of law (Ordover, 2003, pp. 168–170). Within the case, it was argued that within a few years prior to and leading up to 1974, an estimated 100,000 to 150,000 low income people had been sterilized each year, and between approximately 2,000 and 3,000 of them were under twenty-one years old each year. Many of the people, who were irreversibly sterilized, were told beforehand that a failure to cooperate would cause them to lose their welfare benefits from the social welfare programs that provide financial benefits to underprivileged and poverty-stricken people, and people of African descent were also targeted (Ordover, 2003).

The F-problem is of the utmost concern for legal systems since legislation concerns the legal allowance or even legal necessitation of abortions and irreversible sterilizations. Abortions also carry the risk of irreversibly sterilizing women and adolescents unintentionally. Legislation directly impacts the birthrates and death rates of sexually reproducing species.

Legislation also funds research on puberty, menstruations, pregnancies, and postpartum phenomena, childbirths and women's mental health issues regarding reproduction, and menopause (Barnes, 2014). Another subsidiary F-problem concerns the time periods during which lawmakers serve their terms as elected officials, which are relatively short in relation to the length of time of the human lifespan and even a human generation, which will be further analyzed within this chapter. The constituencies of lawmakers also matter, about which John Glad (2006, pp. 46–47) maintains:

> It is a simple fact that current state policies – both domestic and foreign – already influence differential fertility patterns. Since future generations by definition represent a zero constituency for any politician, the public sphere is largely defined horizontally – between those who are currently living – whereas vertical or longitudinal effects are mostly relegated to the private domain and thus ignored. Eugenicists oppose this horizontal/vertical opposition, maintaining that, since the unborn constitute a vastly greater potential population than do the currently living, their rights take precedence.

Most politicians are elected for short terms in office and do not expect to remain in office for several decades. It is worthwhile to inquire how the length of political terms and expectations play roles in the decision-making of legislators regarding important long-term policies that make impacts upon future generations. While public sectors, especially in developed countries, tend to provide affordable public services and goods, such as transportation, medicine, education, defense, etc., the private sectors of the economies, regarding ownership, or voluntary sectors, are challenged with the task of protecting the rights of future generations, which are rarely even considered to have primary importance, although the protection of future rights entails sustainability, self-sufficiency, and independence.

Likewise, hindering the ability for future generations to use the same amount of resources, which generations of the past used, gives certain disadvantages to humankind's continuation as an extant species. We may form goals for humanity to include the preservations of our non-violent cultural practices, developments of knowledge, technologies, constructions, preservations of the earth via sustainable practices with our waste materials, promotions of biological diversity, and much more.

Stock corporations are seemingly beginning to shift their focuses upon corporate social responsibility and doing STEEPLE analyses, which provide social, technological, economic, environmental, political, legal, and ethical analyses of the impacts of many of their business activities. Changes are coming from stakeholders and societies that demand that corporations change their practices of combining the factors of production (i.e., natural, human, and artificial resources and enterprise) to create a sustainable future on the planet. Legal systems are faced with the tasks of controlling, to certain extents, the pathways and timings of our main goals as societally concerned human beings.

However, laws of many countries legally permit the vast and gradual degradation of our planet's environments. The reason for the latter legal permissiveness concerns the decisions that are made to maximize the profits of the shareholders and vast incomes of CEOs, especially via corporations in developed countries. Dunlap and Jorgenson (2012, §1) write:

> Generally speaking, the populations of wealthier and more militarily powerful countries are positioned advantageously in the contemporary world economy, and are thus more likely to secure and maintain favorable terms of trade allowing for greater access to the natural resources and sink (or waste-repository) capacity of areas within less developed countries.

Dunlap and Jorgenson (ibid.) continue:

> These structural relationships allow the wealthy and powerful nations to partly outsource or shift the environmental costs and burdens of their extremely high consumption levels, which ultimately contributes to the depletion of natural resource stocks in less developed countries. In short, these types of ecologically unequal exchange relationships are structural mechanisms that enable the high-consuming populations of affluent and militarily powerful nations to treat poorer nations as their supply depots.

These are tendencies that are greatly beneficial regarding competitive advantages for dominant societies (i.e., the developed countries). Groups, especially within developed countries, have inherited much wealth resulting from ancestors who took advantage of slavery (and afterwards the laws, like the Jim Crow laws in America) as a form of human resources in their business activities to sustainably produce goods and services. The latter tendencies are also F-problems in multiple respects because, for instance, slaves (or employees with curfews under Jim Crow-like laws) are placed at great disadvantages regarding being able to provide resources, wealth, and security for their offspring, whereas slave masters, employers, majority shareholders, CEOs, etc. are able to better provide resources, wealth, and security for their offspring.

Large corporations function as microeconomies within societies and as totalitarian and tyrannical, legally independent persons that send branches of themselves across borders to exploit the poorest working conditions of other societies (i.e., within underdeveloped and developing countries), to create employment contracts with the least number of benefits, and to form systems of dependency for low wage workers oftentimes. Many scholars and political dissidents describe stock corporations similarly, such as Noam Chomsky through multiple books and via forums, such as Democracy Now!, which is a news program on the internet, TV, and radio.

Corporations become the constituents of politicians who gain much financial support from them in return for expectations to return their political donations in the forms of policies that positively impact corporate shareholders, regardless of their negative impacts on far greater numbers of stakeholders and environments. Negative impacts on environments will always certainly negatively impact future generations of humans and other species. Glad (2006, p. 47) continues:

> Politics is, by definition, a struggle among the currently living, and what may well be a victory for some faction in their midst may well be a disaster for their children, just as the disasters of the parents may be to the children's good fortune.

Consider the legal restrictions of certain amounts of waste, which are implemented with legal penalties when businesses, organizations, or individuals produce too much waste. It may well be argued that we should not produce so much waste that it hinders the ability for future generations to produce the same amount of waste, i.e., advocating a form of sustainable development. Restrictions of the amounts and types of waste are examples of challenges of what either will be placed upon the extant populace or future generations.

Wealthier nations and their citizens have vastly higher ecological footprints, causing much more massive environmental degradation around the earth (Dunlap & Jorgenson, 2012; York, Rosa & Dietz, 2003). The middle class and upper class households in cities, especially in developed countries, continue to unethically produce unsustainable amounts of waste with plastics, acids (e.g., sulfuric acid, battery acids, and fertilizers), electronic waste, etc. for the earth's environments to handle via replenishing itself. There are positive correlations between household income, the number of members per household, and the amount of waste that households produce (Bandara et al., 2007; Sankoh et al., 2012). According to Daniel Hoornweg, Perinaz Bhada-Tata, and the World Bank's report (2012, p. 8):

> Generally, the higher the economic development and rate of urbanization, the greater the amount of solid waste produced. Income level and urbanization are highly correlated and as disposable incomes and living standards increase, consumption of goods and services correspondingly increases, as does the amount of waste generated. Urban residents produce about twice as much waste as their rural counterparts.

It may also be easier for lower classes of societies to adapt to practices that would greatly reduce strains on our planet, such as water collection systems on rooftops. Overall, we may very well argue that virtuous people (e.g., thoughtful and efficient) make impacts on the planet that are largely neutral and rarely negative, whereas unethical people are thoughtless regarding the extent of the destruction they cause on our planet with their unsustainable lifestyles, which lessens the number of opportunities for future generations and which is promoted by corporate outputs regarding their products, services, and advertisements.

3 The F-problem, Eugenics, and Misconceptions about Human Sexual Reproduction

Social problems can rarely be described without ways of outlining or considering viable solutions for them. Any solution to the F-problem requires more than merely reducing the birthrate of the global human population since our goal as a species is the continuation of our species or lineage, presumably, and the decrease in the birthrate of the human population comes with many obstacles. Obviously, the initial reduction of births must begin with a particular generation of people.

One challenge, regarding the reduction of human birthrates, comes at the national level, at which political economies must pass and implement laws that reduce the rate of births for some specific generation before other generations. National security becomes a problem once the generation that has been reduced in size has reached the age of maturity to join the workforce. Although the decrease of a single generation's birthrate may not, from the outset, have drastic negative impacts upon the society (e.g., affecting, at first mostly, companies that supply baby products, and then primary school employees, etc.) the latter decrease will certainly lead to challenges for the society once that generation's population has reached the age of the workforce on which the society depends for labor and business-related outputs, goods and services.

The reduction of a generation's number of overall births requires the generation of fertile females (i.e., who are responsible for giving or refraining from giving those births) to be motivated in one direction, i.e., to refrain from bearing a child at least temporarily, unless the society places itself at risk via legally allowing human rights violations to reduce the birthrate in uncivilized or inhumane ways, such as abortions that adolescents and women are legally obligated to undergo. For civilized reductions of birthrates, political motivations or encouragement from politicians are generally insufficient and so are ideological arguments that maintain that refraining from child birth will benefit the society since, for instance, any individual may always consider the fact that one more, or even three additional lives, will not impact the society or planet much at all. The motivations of those females (i.e., who are presumed to be fertile) to give or refrain from giving birth can also be concealed.

Motivations for controlling birthrates must come from multiple sources to effectively manage the human population of Earth, yet there is still no reason to believe that any such motivations will impact the amount of sexual intercourse. So, motivations are needed for sexual intercourse to more frequently become unsuccessful regarding procreation, which is the essence of the F-Problem. There are still distinct reasons to believe that motivating people to refrain from sexual intercourse is maleficent for human social relations. People's relationships can become destructive sometimes when they refrain from sexual contact with each other.

Efforts to increase or decrease population growth rates are global F-problems. When the efforts are political in nature, they may greatly support or destroy the political careers of lawmakers or potential lawmakers. The ill-informed politicians during the early 20th century in Germany and the United States passed laws that were implemented to decrease particular sectors of the populations within their own societies, which specifically involved programs in the field of eugenics.

The ill-informed German politicians ideologically supported the sexual reproduction of a single race, purportedly, without people from multiple races copulating and producing offspring, which to some degree is more incestuous than the reproduction of offspring of parents from multiple racial groups. Moreover, incest is well-known to decrease the diversity of genes and to tend to result in weaker immune systems of offspring. Many Germans still have an ideology concerning race and will refer to themselves as being "racially pure" (i.e., *reinrasig*, and the author has asked a few dozen Germans whether they are "racially pure" in German), especially if they are white and have white ancestors with German family names as far back as they know or are willing to tell. Alternatively, the production of human offspring from multiple racial groups and with greater diversity increases the chances for stronger immune systems of offspring within the population. According to John Glad (2006, p. 10):

> The eugenics movement, which can be understood as human ecology, has long considered itself a lobby for future generations, arguing that while it is true that we should not be presumptuous in our ability to predict the future, we can define what we want – healthy, intelligent children who will grow up to be emotionally balanced, broadly altruistic adults.

Glad (2006) argues that if the majority of a species has its members living past their childbearing years, then the important characteristic of those who will populate the planet in the future is fertility and the number of offspring they will procreate. This is considered a revolutionary change in our species. Now, we have a selection via fertility instead of selection by means of mortality. Eugenics movements have been implemented in ways that homogenized human societies to some degrees. Multiple legal systems supported them. Homogenization involves inbreeding to some degree. Glad maintains (2006, p. 47):

> We are now able to separate sex from procreation; either may occur without the other. It is now even possible for women to bypass the male's sperm. Thus, while leaving the right to sexuality within the private sphere, eugenicists argue that procreational rights – inasmuch as they define the very nature of future people – can be ignored by society only to its own detriment.

Sexual reproduction is often misunderstood. Many misunderstandings about sexual reproduction likely happen because there are a number of taboos associated with sex and with procreation. For instance, all humans are related to each other, and sexual partners, especially parents, typically do not research how closely they are related to one another. So, many married people and parents of the same offspring do not know how closely related they are to one another, and they may even be repelled from researching the extent of their genetic relationships. Moreover, the extent to which we are genetically related to one another is different for different couples.

Offspring born from two biological parents, who are more closely related to one another, are more closely related to their parents than two other parents are when the biological parents are not as closely related to each other. Except for rare exceptions (e.g., chimeras or sisters giving natural birth to their nieces), this is a biological fact that is frequently overlooked by partners who sexually reproduce. Consider horse A and horse B that procreate offspring that is more closely related to A and B than the offspring procreated by horse A and a donkey or a zebra is related to horse A. In fact, all the horses in an area might be more closely related to horse A than the offspring of horse A, which is a mule.

Apply the latter fact to humans. Now, consider the impact that the less closely related offspring have had on societies that have enslaved and battled against other peoples. We may inquire whether the extent and intensity of the slavery and battles would have been less brutal if the dominant groups had been more closely related to their subordinates from the outset.

Humans have migrated, especially over the past 500 years. Humans have interbred with other humans who have been more distantly related to them, especially between European and African parents procreating together, Native Americans and European settlers as well as people of African decent and Native Americans. There may very well be many unforeseen consequences that arise when two parents have offspring who are more distantly related to each of the parents than the parents' other offspring who are more closely related to the parents.

Consider the horrid institution of slavery in the United States during the 19th century and the treatment by fathers who were slave masters of their own slave-children. Their slave-children were less closely related to them than their non-slave born children, but fatherly behaviors differed. The institution and roles of slavery generally took precedence over fatherly roles as caregivers to their own children (Hughes, 1897; Douglass, 1855 & 1892).

In Great Britain and the United States during the late 18th century and early 19th century, sexual partners, who were slaves and selected for parenting by and with their slave masters, were chosen differently than other sex partners, who were not slaves. The latter non-slave parents had many more of the same genes, alleles, etc. and were labeled as being of the same race. According to John Relethford (2012, p. 49), the common way of thinking about the uniqueness of parenthood, ancestors, and the diversity of the human population is vastly misguided:

> [Y]ou have two ancestors one generation in the past—your biological parents. Because each parent also has two parents, this means that you have four grandparents. Extending this back means that you had eight great-grandparents, 16 great-great grandparents, and so on. In mathematical terms, we can express the number of ancestors as 2^n (2 raised to the nth power), where n is the number of generations in the past. The number of ancestors thus increases exponentially into the past.

Relethford (ibid.) argues that no human has completely unique ancestors that extend beyond 30 to 40 generations because at 30 generations the number of ancestors that one would have would amount to 1,073,741,824 people but at 40 generations one has had approximately 1.1 trillion ancestors, even though 40 human generations only extends 1,000 years in the past (i.e., when we generously grant that there are 25 years per generation). That is, no human being can have completely unique ancestors since the reproduction performed by anyone's ancestors must involve some of the direct lines of ancestors parenting with sexual reproductive partners who were related to them (e.g., some of the ancestors were certainly not such distant cousins). Thus, our ancestors must have been sexually reproducing with individuals with whom they were already genetically related. This also likely occurred without parents knowing how closely related they were from the outset.

Many factors complicate people's understandings about human genetic relationships and contribute to ideological views about the characteristics of persons who are most closely related to them. Ideologies and taboos also concern sex before marriage, incest, and sex and sexual reproduction with non-marital partners during the marriage. It is unfortunate that the best partnerships for sexual reproduction are unlikely to form naturally, and the relationships, which have the strongest bonds with much trust, are unlikely to be the best for yielding the offspring with the strongest physiological and anatomical traits that are genetically inheritable.

The ideas of the "best partnerships for sexual reproduction" and "strongest physiological and anatomical traits" do not involve measurable phenomena, although they may be comparatively measurable, and these ideas are largely abstract concepts, which suggests at least a somewhat arbitrary nature with which the offspring are procreated. For instance, we know that siblings are unlikely to make the best partnerships for sexual reproduction and are unlikely to give birth to offspring with the strongest physiological and anatomical traits in comparison to healthy parents who are less closely related than siblings are. Moreover, environmental factors, including diet, location, shelter as well as the age of the parents typically play crucial roles regarding sexual selection and procreation, although these factors largely need not play roles in sexual reproduction since technology allows for preservations of sperms and eggs, and diets, locations of the parents, and shelters can be altered as well.

Governments often encourage the homogenization and some degree of inbreeding within societies. In South Africa, the period of Apartheid lasted from 1948 until 1994. When Nelson Mandela began his presidency (1994–1999), South Africa had a history of legislation that racially segregated people via the Immorality Act of 1927. This act disallowed extramarital sex between white and black people (Guelke, 2005, p. 25). In 1949, the legal act of prohibition against mixed marriages disallowed blacks and whites to marry each other legally in South Africa, and the following year a legal act was passed to prevent racial groups from entering the neighborhoods of other racial groups.

Legal systems contribute to the artificial selection process via institutionalized means of providing benefits, threatening violence, penalizing, and disproportionately implementing violence against social groups. This is accomplished via the acts of legislation for the encouragements of births, penalizations of births, sterilizations of citizens, programs for breeding, and programs for separating social groups to decrease the frequency of intergroup sexual intercourse or procreation. Indeed, even incarceration reduces the birthrate for targeted social groups (i.e., generally, the poor and racial minority groups) and is implemented more frequently against low-status groups regarding population sizes and especially more frequently against those who are more prone or who have increased sexual vigor regarding their reproductive organs. There is discrimination based on ages of sexual maturation.

From a philosophical perspective, it is questionable whether the promotion of biodiversity for the human species is the best alternative because it leads to different races and produces a discriminate sexual selection process based upon race, which is racist. Consider other species, for instance, the horse and the donkey. Sometimes, but very rarely, they give birth to fertile offspring, which could possibly become a new species. Promoting a non-racist situation of less biodiversity would involve the artificial and sexual selection of the animals that result in a single and perhaps hybrid species, consisting of ever less horses and donkeys and instead consisting of ever more mules[5] and hinnies[6] as well as ever less hybrids of horses with mules and hinnies and donkeys with mules and hinnies. So, less equine hybrids or equine races would exist, less biodiversity would exist, and less racism or races as well. This latter situation of less biodiversity is the non-racist artificial and sexual selection of horses and

5 These are the offspring produced by mares with jackasses.

6 A "hinny" is the offspring of a stallion and jenny, a female donkey.

donkeys that involves the eradication of the horse and donkey species in favor of just the hybrid species.

On the other hand, the promotion of biodiversity demands that the three lines, races, hybrids or species remain intact, which requires selective breeding with those that are more closely related to each other. So, horses will breed with horses the vast majority of the time, donkeys with donkeys, and mules with hinnies if possible, i.e., whilst keeping the horses and donkeys as separate species, which involves almost exclusive breeding, and thereby biodiversity is promoted. Nature allows for such biodiversity to arise as a possibility, but such biodiversity is improbable since the vast majority of the equine hybrid offspring are infertile.

Obviously, the implications for human populations similarly means that people who are more closely related to each other would almost exclusively sexually reproduce with one another to create different races that largely remain separate from each other regarding sexual reproduction. The sexual selections of closely related sexual partners promote both biodiversity and separate lines of races in the latter respects, which supports the continuation of the various equine species (e.g., ponies, donkeys, wild asses, zebras, and horses) as opposed to their hybrids (e.g., zebras bred with donkeys produce "zebrasses" and zebra stallions and horse mares can procreate "zorses") because the latter hybrids are more closely related to one another and are therefore less diverse.

Many governments have produced legislation that results in racist promotions of biodiversity for the human species, such as South Africa during apartheid and the practice of "ethnic cleansing" in Germany during the early 20th century. Germany performed the opposite practice during the late 20th century by legally allowing large numbers of Turkish migrants to settle, assimilate, and gain citizenship. However, there are large cultural segregations of the peoples still in the early 21st century.

Germany has also legally allowed many hundreds of thousands of refugees from Syria, Iraq, and Afghanistan to reside in Germany with societal support, offering education, shelter, food, etc., which has involved circumstances in 2015 and 2016 that resulted from the decisions of the United States government to go to war with Afghanistan in 2001 and Iraq in 2003. The decisions made by the US governmental officials led to a massive exodus from the Middle East into Europe several years later. Many of the governmental decisions deserve to be made transparent for public access to analyses of the social, technological, economic, environmental, political, legal and ethical issues that concern the steps taken during the process of the decision-making of government officials.

4 Violence Directed toward Intersexuals, Transsexuals, and Non-heterosexuals as a Form of Social Dominance

A social theory of heterosexism, homophobia, biphobia, lesbophobia and transphobia probably best begins with a set of hypotheses concerning relations of humans with differing sexual orientations, violence, and social dominance. This involves relationships between dominant and subordinate groups, respectively, heterosexuals and non-heterosexuals. Moreover, the perceived biological sexes of individuals are obviously important, especially perceptions of people who typically think that there are only two sexes.

The heteronormative presumptions fail to make certain distinctions, such as there only being male and female sexes as opposed to another sex, the intersex. For example, intersexuals may appear to us to be male or female through our ordinary perceptions of them with our naked eyes, even if we perceive their naked bodies. Intersexuals have different internal anatomy, such as people with ambiguous genitalia or with external female anatomy (e.g., a vagina) but internal male anatomy (e.g., testicles). Consider the condition of androgen insensitivity syndrome (Blackless, et al., 2000).

Transsexuals include people who continually experience gender identities that are different from their assigned sexes by the culture, law, and medical communities, for instance, and sometimes would prefer to undergo sex change operations. More violent tendencies are directed toward all these people who either do not neatly fit within the category of male or female (i.e., in accordance with significant numbers of people within the society) or who perform non-heterosexual sexual behaviors with others, apart from theatrical performances.

There are abundant signs of social dominance in societies regarding the subordination of open non-heterosexuals via policies (i.e., LGBT people who do not hide their lifestyles). In several countries, such as Zambia, homosexuality has been outright criminalized (see Ch. 2.10 & 6.6). Perhaps it is more accurate to claim that the criminalization is focused upon sexual behaviors of those who engage in non-heterosexual behaviors with other people, but this can also depend upon anatomy, sex toys, etc. Moreover, legal systems disallow homosexual marriage rights between members of the same sex in multiple nations, visitation rights in hospitals and other institutions, and they are often disallowed the rights to protest and parade.

The Lesbian, Gay, Bisexual, and Transgendered (LGBT) people tend to be targeted for violence more frequently and intensely than heterosexuals in proportion to their population sizes, and research suggests that police have historically tended to investigate crimes directed against LGBT people less than violence against heterosexuals in proportion to the number of violent acts each group undergoes (Chakraborti & Garland, 2015). There are multiple reasons for the latter facts. People in the LGBT community often mistrust the police. There are enforcements of laws against males having sexual relations with one another and overpolicing against homosexuals in multiple nations, e.g., the United Kingdom and the United States (ibid., pp. 46–60).

During June 2016, the bloodiest set of murders wrought by a single perpetrator in US history occurred, during which 49 people in a nightclub, which was frequented by non-heterosexuals, were murdered by a gunman and 53 others were wounded. Some of the first attempts to explain the tragic incident by mass media broadcasters involved the killer's sexual orientation and other arbitrary factors. The act targeted a group, arguably, for subordinating them with the use of hard power and the fear of the threat of death, violence, and destruction that coincides with the use hard power. Yet the fact about whether the mass murderer was a non-heterosexual or a heterosexual, etc. makes no difference in respect to the major issue of subordination because homophobic non-heterosexuals and homophobic heterosexual people are potentially just as dangerous as each other.

The direction of the mass media broadcasts and lines of questioning that were directed at the killer's sexual orientation may have very well overshadowed the importance of the main societal problems involved and thereby hindered the process of problem-solving, creating a greater challenge for reducing the amount of overall violence in society. The broadcasts certainly led mass audiences to consider irrelevant facts (i.e., unrelated to the problem of reducing societal violence at least), misinformation, and information that was over and underrepresented.

There appears to be a social phenomenon that alleviates fears of dominant groups after extremely violent acts of subordination. The alleviations result from the societal perceptions or beliefs about one or more members of the low-status or subordinate group committing the violent acts against one's own group or their own groups. A set of false justifications and misguided explanations arise and are perpetuated by the mass media systems. These acts of societal violence are not viewed the same way as other acts of societal violence. The violent acts are explained away as concerning a specific social group, which happens to already be subordinated but has been attaining recognition, more rights, and has come to the forefront for being a primary example of a group in need or in demand of human rights. As such, the group greatly shapes the language and range of concepts associated with human rights.

The phenomenon we may call "the social phenomenon of the dominant group's alleviation of fear" emerges when people simplify their understandings of violent acts by maintaining the acts are wrought "by the others and against the others," which basically means that the members of the dominant group's outgroup, who are subordinate group members, are committing acts of violence against themselves. There is also a tendency here for dominant group members to think their outgroup is therefore disinterested in committing violence against their ingroup. Many of the members of dominant groups in society dehumanize outgroups.

With the misunderstandings that the subordinate group's members largely or exclusively commit violence against themselves and that there is a lesser tendency for the subordinate group's members to commit violence against the dominant group members, the dominant group members may facilitate the emergence of an ideology of disrespect, which is directed toward the subordinate group. Two reasons for this are that any group and any culture can be rightfully and reasonably criticized for implementing gratuitous violence, especially against itself. Secondly, a dominant group may promote a feeling of superiority experienced by its members over the subordinate group members to the extent that dominant group members tend to believe that the violence is directed less toward dominant group members. This altogether may increase the likelihood that dominant group members commit acts of hate more frequently and intensely against the subordinate group members. Dominant group members tend to disrespect subordinates and also have less fear of retaliation from them under such circumstances.

Acts of hate and violence suggest that there is an absence of types of education and absence of mass media systems within society that encourage acceptance, demand toleration, and that promote peace, wellbeing, and improvements of the conditions for subordinate groups via their communications. It has often been proposed that hate crimes need not involve hate, but rather the group, with which the victim is affiliated, is more important for a crime to be labeled as such (Gerstenfield, 2013, p. 11; Chakraborti & Garland, 2015). The violence does indeed add to the overall amount of societal violence, suggests a greater intensity of insanity and psychological disorders in the society, and should be approached differently by the media for reducing violence.

Dominant groups' fear alleviations after acts of extreme violence are often preceded by the overrepresentations of irrelevant information that redirects the focus from the violence to the possible motivations for the violence. Overrepresentations of irrelevant information about the reasons for the violence also misdirect the understandings of people, especially those from dominant groups. They view themselves as being less negatively impacted by the violence.

Such overrepresentations of irrelevance sway their understandings away from a more comprehensive conception of the violence as a larger arising part of the set of all violent acts within the society. Overrepresentations of irrelevant information are spread via word-of-mouth and images and words broadcast by mass media systems.

The key points in the latter incident concern the facts that during the 2016 Florida nightclub murders, the peak of murderous violence reached a high point in that region and within the whole society. The act of violence was perpetrated against a subordinated group that only very recently began attaining the status of recognition for human rights, which involved legalizing certain acts and processes and redefining institutions, such as marriage. Moreover, increased fears arose within the subordinated group after the tragedy. On the other hand, the media's portrayal of the event involves a great amount of coverage of two types of outgroups for most members of the dominant groups within the American society, namely, the homosexual outgroup and the outgroup which is not well-defined but abstractly involves Muslims or Arabs who are violent male adults (i.e., generally, as opposed to women and children who are Muslims or Arabs).

The homosexual outgroup is also not well-defined because the widest spread of content is the daily news content that is broadcast, and which bases its content upon what will result in greater viewership and readership. So, the information often involves presentations that seek to entertain, lower fears, raise fears, and shock audience members into watching, listening, and reading more. Enlightenment is rarely an aspect of news coverage that is mass broadcast. It would require more intelligent professionals who would demand better working conditions and benefits concerning their employment contracts and is, of course, far more challenging (but also more rewarding) to uphold. Mass media systems, therefore, often base their content upon what presumably or predictably will result in greater viewer and readership instead of enlightenment (See Ch. 1.4).

The range of biological sexes from male to female are misunderstood by the general populaces, and there are also many misconceptions of sexual orientations from heterosexuality to homosexuality, bisexuality, bestiality, etc. Sexuality also concerns the range of behaviors from promiscuity to prudery. Sometimes "sexuality" is defined in virtue of behaviors and at other times is defined in respect to desires, beliefs, and choices.

For instance, a person who has only been surrounded by members of the same sex who also engages in sexual intercourse may or may not be labeled as a "homosexual," and a person who has a spouse and children, and who has never had sex with anyone of the same sex as he or she is, may nevertheless fantasize and frequently desire to have sex with someone of the same sex, and again the person may or may or may not be labeled as a "homosexual." Additionally, there is the range of characteristics from masculine to feminine ones that partially characterize the conception of sexuality. The concept of sexuality is misconceived by the general public, is often discussed unintelligently when it becomes relevant enough for attention by means of mass media broadcasts, and it is especially misunderstood by the masses in relation to its role with violence and the threats of violence because the general public typically has no accurate understanding of evolution, artificial selection, and the types of sexual selection.

Social dominance theory can be reformulated as one framework through which the F-problem can be approached. As a theory that states that societies are human group-based social hierarchical systems, in which there are dominations performed against low-status groups, multiple invasive but testable hypotheses are easily formulated regarding the many ways that societal institutions implement systematic hindrances and advantages to subordinate the low-status groups and allow the high-status groups a continued state of domination through artificial and sexual selection processes. According to Charles Darwin (1859, pp. 87–88):

> Inasmuch as peculiarities often appear under domestication in one sex and become hereditarily attached to that sex, the same fact probably occurs under nature, and if so, natural selection will be able to modify one sex in its functional relations to the other sex, or in relation to wholly different habits of life in the two sexes, as is sometimes the case with insects ... Sexual Selection ... depends, not on a struggle for existence, but on a struggle between the males for possession of the females; the result is not death to the unsuccessful competitor, but few or no offspring.[7]

One may also hypothesize whether homophobia is largely an aspect of the ideologies associated with the latter processes. Darwin's research should be developed to include other types of competitions concerning the sexes, including intersexuals, for all types of sexual partners. Darwin focuses on males competing against other males for females rather than focusing on males competing against other males for other males for sexual intercourse and females competing against other females for males (i.e., easily observable in parts of Yunnan, China, such as the Women's Kingdom) and for other females for sexual intercourse.

7 Darwin (ibid.) continues: "Generally, the most vigorous males, those which are best fitted for their places in nature, will leave most progeny. But in many cases, victory will depend not on general vigour, but on having special weapons, confined to the male sex. A hornless stag or spurless cock would have a poor chance of leaving offspring. Sexual selection by always allowing the victor to breed might surely give indomitable courage, length to the spur, and strength to the wing to strike in the spurred leg, as well as the brutal cock-fighter, who knows well that he can improve his breed by careful selection of the best cocks."

Consider whether heterosexual males, who are in the same social groups as male homosexuals, are typically placed at advantages regarding their selections of mates of the opposite sex if the heterosexual males continue to have heterosexual behaviors and desires. Obviously, if one thousand people live in an isolated area with 500 men and 500 women, and 100 of the men are homosexuals, then the heterosexual men would appear to have an advantage regarding choosing an unattached mate of the opposite sex successfully in some sense. Why would there be any homophobia with such advantages?

Social dominance theory and its relation to the F-problem may offer explanations for the homophobic ideology of heterosexual males, which is applicable to females as well. If a small society has a dominant and a subordinate group within it, say, a majority ethnic group consisting of 7,000 people, which is the dominant group, and a minority ethnic group with 3,000 people, which is the low-status group, and the groups are typically, visually distinguishable via certain characteristics, such as skin color, then the fact that either group has individuals who refrain from sexual intercourse with the opposite sex and sexual reproduction actually contributes to the relationship of domination and subordination between the groups.

The hypotheses formulated here thereby state that: (1) homophobic heterosexuals tend to focus their fears or hate toward homosexuals within their own groups with which they identify, especially based on race, age, or socioeconomic class; (2) homophobic heterosexuals from lower status groups within societies tend to have greater amounts of fear and hatred regarding their focuses upon homosexuals within their own low-status groups; (3) homophobic heterosexuals from lower status groups within societies tend to have less fear and hatred for homosexuals in higher status groups; (4) homophobic heterosexuals from higher status groups tend to have less fear and hatred for homosexuals in lower status groups. The latter two hypotheses are constructed because the lower status groups are at increased risks of being more intensely dominated by higher status groups already, especially if the lower status groups' population sizes continuously increase at comparatively slower rates. Moreover, (3) and (4) hypothesize that group members tend to support the growth of their own groups in relation to the growth of other groups in their societies.

Other factors may play large roles with the intensity and frequency of homophobia, including the comparative ages of the higher and lower status groups. Another hypothesis may be formulated: (5) if dominant groups' population sizes are aging populations, consisting of comparatively greater numbers of higher status group members beyond the years of their sexual primes (i.e., in comparison to the lower status groups), then the frequency and intensity of homophobic expressions and violence will tend to increase by heterosexual dominant group members against other dominant group members who are non-heterosexual people. The latter hypothesis illustrates a possible role of human generations regarding the ideology stemming from social dominance and the F-problem. The five hypotheses are testable via various methods, in which cases any statistically significant data that undermines any one of the hypotheses would likewise enlighten us regarding sex, sexuality, and social dominance.

5 Opposing Concepts of Human Generation: Importance of Adolescent Pregnancies

There are ranges of ways of thinking and focusing on research concerning human generations. The concept of the human generation is a concept directly concerning the procreation of human offspring, resulting from at least one parent who gives birth at a certain age and another parent who impregnates at a certain age. Some of the research, especially in developed countries, tends to lead researchers to focus on the concept of any single human generation as lasting longer, say, 25 or 30 years long. Other ways of thinking and investigating lead researchers to focus on the human generation as lasting shorter spans, such as 10, 15, or 20 years of age. It may well be argued that any specific number is arbitrary for the length of time for the concept of human generation. However, explanations that include calculations and discussions of human generations will benefit from the presumption of a specific number that signifies the length of any human generation in years because they facilitate understandings of the concept.

One way of thinking about a single human generation has involved a change over the centuries that largely focuses on the increases of the life spans and life expectancies of human beings. The increases in human life expectancies and life spans has led many researchers to argue that a single human generation during the 20th and 21st century lasts longer than the span of the human generation during previous eras. The latter way of thinking and researching human generations involves the attribution of an age that is varied but still finite insofar as the life span is finite and to the extent that the variance in the human generation has resulted in an increase in the average ages of populaces, especially because of 20th and 21st century medical technologies and the onset of developed countries with public sector healthcare programs. The idea that the number of years, with which we should conceive of a human generation, is greater than in the past is an idea stemming from scholars from developed countries and does not reflect the circumstances of underdeveloped nations and developing nations (Henrich & Norenzayan, 2010).

Another way of thinking about the human generation concerns a focus upon the multiplicity of human generations of people who may even live in a single household, neighborhood, or city as the youths of the family and their surviving ancestors, in which cases the actual parent-offspring relations first allow for the analysis of two generations (i.e., the parent and the offspring), then three generations (i.e., the grandparent, the parent and the grandbaby), etc.

Contrarily, the latter way of thinking about the human generation provides a focus that may lead one to ascertain that, despite increased life spans, a human generation is perhaps better viewed as lasting a shorter period than during previous eras. The reason is that young adolescents give birth from the ages of ten years old. So, it is even possible to have six or seven human generations in one household. Thus, it makes less sense to maintain that a generation lasts for 25 or 30 years if there are six generations in any household because that would suggest that the oldest family member in the household would be, respectively, 125–150 or 150–180 years of age.

Human males and females have increasingly, sexually reproduced offspring at ever younger ages. This is "the age at first reproduction" (Leonetti & Nath, 2009). The increasing frequency and younger ages at first reproduction lead one to rationally consider that the human generation during the 20th and early 21st centuries lasts a shorter amount of time than during previous eras instead. Global and even national statistics that describe the fertility and birth rates of humans take ten-year-old girls into account, and pregnancy tests have become commonplace within many clinics to assess some of the impacts of rape on girls even younger than ten years old. Regarding the United States data for births in 2013, Martin et al. (2015, p. 4) write:

> The number of births to teenagers aged 15–19 was 273,105 in 2013, down 11% from 2012 (305,388) and 47% from 1991 (519,577). Birth rates for teenagers aged 15–17 and 18–19 in 2013 were 12.3 births per 1,000 for the younger age group and 47.1 births per 1,000 for the older group, down 13% and 8% from 2012, respectively, and record lows for both groups. Since 1991, the rates for these two groups have fallen 68% and 50%, respectively. The birth rate for teenagers aged 10–14 declined to 0.3 births per 1,000 women in 2013, a record low, from 0.4 in 2012.

At times, some countries have very high rates of adolescent pregnancies. From 1970 to 2004 in the United States, the age group from ten to fourteen years old consistently gave birth to a higher number of newborns than the age group of women from forty-four to forty-nine. In these cases, there have been declines in the rate of births of ten to fourteen-year-old adolescents and increases in the rate of births of forty-four to forty-nine-year-old women (Martin et al., 2015, p. 19).

From 1970 through 2013 in the USA, birthrates of ten to fourteen year old adolescents has ranged from 0.3 to 1.4 births per one thousand, and birthrates of forty-five to forty-nine year old women has ranged from 0.2 to 0.8 per one thousand, but the upper limitations of births is probably better understood via realizing the highest frequencies of births of some minority groups, such as the rate of 5.1 births per one thousand black mothers from 10 through 14 years old in 1989 and 1.5 births per one thousand Pacific Islander or Asian mothers from 45 to 49 years old in 2013 (ibid., pp. 19–21). Basch (2011, p. 614) writes about teenage pregnancies in the United States and upholds that:

> A recent analysis of the National Longitudinal Survey of Youth indicated that, after adjusting for other risks, daughters of teen mothers were 66% more likely to become teen mothers (Meade, Kershaw & Ickovics, 2008). In all likelihood, an unmarried teen mother and her child will live in poverty (Amato & Maynard, 2007), further perpetuating a cycle of poverty and subsequent nonmarital teen births (Meade, Kershaw & Ickovics, 2008).

The notion of the human generation, especially regarding the latter data about the recurrence of teenage pregnancies, involves a reduction of the amount of time concerning the duration of human generations since a single household may have six generations living within it, for instance. When the household consists of family members who have given birth at relatively young ages (e.g., fifteen-year-old mothers), in which case a newborn, a teenage mother, a grandmother in her late thirties, a great-grandmother in her mid-fifties, a great-great-grandmother in her seventies, and a great-great-great grandmother in her nineties, then the family is regarded as having six living generations, however infrequent that is.

Even within developed nations it is possible for the number of teenage pregnancies to reach rates that exceed one-third of the teenage population (Hamilton, Martin & Ventura, 2007). Because the rate of pregnancies for adolescent girls varies quite greatly from generation to generation, and since the latter pregnancies at the beginnings of the life spans of the generation of females are often unintended, unwanted, or haphazardly decided, adolescent pregnancies are extremely important regarding the formation of understandings of any society and legal system. Such understandings play crucial roles regarding the possible legal actions families make, whether they be legal or illegal abortions, legal or illegal adoptions, statutory rape indictments, etc.

Perhaps the two ways of thinking about human generations are best combined regarding the analyses of human population. Consider both ways of thinking about human generations with the increases in life spans during the 20th and 21st centuries and frequencies of preteen and teenage motherhood so that a human generation is conceptualized as being significantly longer than ten years but shorter than thirty years of age.

Let us assume that each generation is twenty years. So, during any era the vast majority of the human population is describable regarding five generations at any point in time, which each last twenty years long. The generation from birth to twenty years of age, twenty to forty, forty to sixty, sixty to eighty, and the generation from eighty to one hundred years old account for more than 99% of the human population of any nation at any time.

Politically speaking, the youngest living human generation is almost entirely insignificant in respect to being a constituency. A very small percentage of them have reached the voting age and can vote. From a political and legal perspective, the youngest generation may also be hypothesized to consist of the best candidates to focus upon for the task of lowing the birthrate. The birthrate of the youngest generation of the population, involves increases in the likelihood of unintended or unwanted pregnancies, depression, lower education levels, increased delinquency, and higher incarceration rates for the offspring born to preteen and teenage parents.

According to Speidel, Harper, and Shields (2008, p. 197), approximately thirty-eight percent of all human pregnancies on earth are unintended, which amounts to about eighty million unintended pregnancies per year. In the United States in 2001, there were approximately 6.1 million pregnancies, about half of them were unintended, and over eighty percent of the 800,000 pregnancies of the teenagers for the year were unintended, which impacted the decisions of the resultant 1.3 million abortions and four million births, one-third of which were also unintended, and the remaining 800,000 were miscarriages (Finer & Henshaw, 2006; Speidel, Harper & Shields, ibid.).

The impacts that specific generations with greater numbers of adolescent pregnancies have upon the society, culture, and law are multifarious. Their impacts may be best observed and measured regarding the finance, banking, legal, education systems, labor production and joblessness, for which they account. Their impact on the unemployment rate is calculated with special emphasis upon the second and third living generations. The second and third extant generations (i.e., 20 to 60 years of age) are more frequently incarcerated, especially in accordance with data of the incarceration rates of those born to teenage and preteen mothers.

The workforce and labor production for the society are produced foremost by the second and third generations. Relatively and significantly smaller amounts of labor are produced by the first, fourth, and fifth generations. In some underdeveloped and developing countries, the labor produced by the first and fourth generations may be enough to support the first or fourth generations. It is probably insufficient to support the first and fourth generations in developed countries, especially where the fourth generation has a comparatively large amount of people from 70 to 80 years of age.

Under what conditions should we take measures and prevent violence? When the second and third generations have a high unemployment rate or high rate of underemployment, this should happen. We should further consider measures for preventing violence when the second and third generations are not actively continuing their education. Under the latter conditions, a recipe for social protestation and unrest is present.

During the early 21st century within the Middle East and northern Africa, the rate of unemployment has remained high. The rate of unemployment for the living second generation is extremely high. Moreover, significant portions of the latter generation discontinue their education. *The Economist* (2016) maintains that in 2010 the unemployment rate for the Arab world was 10% and the youth unemployment was 27%, which certainly contributed to the Arab uprising beginning in 2010.

Presumably, the absence of work and education opportunities have great impacts upon the birthrate since the rate of employment and the intensity and amount of labor and continuation of education are negatively correlated with the birthrate. Results in the Middle East and northern Africa involved many social uprisings and protestations during the early 21st century. This largely concerns the F-problem regarding increased opportunities for sexual reproduction because of the decrease in career opportunities. Cultures are shaped by the dynamic changes from generation to generation through either work and progress with excessive births or increased births, reduced opportunities, and greater competition for resources.

6 Increasing the Number of Competitors for Resources Increases Amounts of Competition

The human population of the Earth continues to exponentially grow. The global human population reached approximately one billion humans in 1820, two billion in 1930, three billion in 1960, four billion in 1974, five billion humans in 1987, six billion in 1999, and seven billion humans were alive on the planet in 2012 (CIA World Factbook, 2017). Humans are mammals within the animal kingdom. As mammals, we populate the planet via means requiring a variety of physiological and basic needs to be met. The basic needs are food, water, mother's milk for newborns, air, shelter, defecation, and homeostasis.

Humans populate the planet via sexual reproduction, which requires fertility. Fertility and birth require extra amounts of food consumption, healthy digestion, defecation, and other physiological needs being met. Many variables contribute to the increase or decrease of contaminations of the resources that humans need to survive, including sewage treatment.

The increase in the population of humans is positively correlated with the increases in the sizes of deserts and the populations of other mammals and birds. For example, cats, dogs, rats, cows, pigs, chickens, ducks, rabbits, sheep, and goats increase. Such increases hinder the ability for future generations to extract the same quality and quantity of resources from the environment that predecessors were able to take. Increasing populations of human beings are negatively correlated with sizes of rain forests and the amounts of unpolluted air, water, vegetation, and livestock (Vitousek et al., 1997).

Human population increases require extra demands for increases of the complexity of organized, sustainable societal systems (e.g., waste management, political, economic, and legal systems). Increases in populations of specific types of mammals and birds and certain species of insects in regions (e.g., cockroaches in many cities relatively near the earth's equator) reduce the likelihood for sustainable development, too.

Definitions of "sustainable development" are naturally humancentric as opposed to demonstrating more ecological awareness. However, it is exceedingly challenging to consider the multitude of species in environments and the natural resources utilized by them all. Definitions regarding sustainability and development inevitably include human-centered worldviews.

Sustainable development directly regards waste management insofar as extant human generations are producing excessive amounts of waste materials and pollutants that continuously decrease the ability for future generations of humans to produce as much waste in their environments as we can, which hinders the sustainable development of human ecosystems and multiple other environments. Sustainable development is the systematic plan for the frequency and means through which human generations acquire environmental resources in ways that allow future generations to take the same amounts of resources at the same frequencies as previous human generations.

The F-problem regarding the growing global human population and the shrinking amount of biodiversity exacerbates many other problems on Earth. Conserving biodiversity is becoming an ever-larger problem. Human actions have already led to the consumption of about forty percent of the earth's annual gross terrestrial primary productivity. This is the biomass produced via photosynthetic processes (Cincotta & Gorenflo, 2011). According to Cincotta and Gorenflo (2011, p. 1):

> Our species has already converted almost one-third of the terrestrial surface to agricultural fields and urban areas (United Nations Development Program et al. 2000; Vitousek et al. 1997). And this wholesale transformation of our planet's biosphere is anticipated to continue at an alarming rate ... According to their most recent revision, UN demographers project that by 2050, the human population will range between 7.8 billion (the UN low fertility variant) and 10.8 billion (high fertility variant), with a best guess of about 9.2 billion (the UN medium fertility variant).

Consider the degradation of the 21st century. Much of the growth of human populations will happen in tropical environments that provide the habitats for the greatest concentration of species (Cincotta and Gorenflo, ibid; Cincotta and Engelman 2000; Cincotta et al., 2000). Cincotta and Gorenflo (ibid.) predict that the legal rights of people to attain access to nutrition, shelter, energy, drinking water, and ways to participate in the political economy will overshadow future efforts to preserve populations of nonhuman species and save them from extinction.

Figure 21 displays the exponential growth of the human population from the 19th to the 21st century, according to 18th century predictions of Thomas Malthus. Malthus argued that human overpopulation would lead to war, poverty, disease, and starvation. Humankind has already experienced the actual onset of devastating wars, poverty, and disease.

Certain consequences of overpopulation, namely, famine and malnourishment, result either from a lack of macronutrients (i.e., proteins, fats, and carbohydrates) or from a lack of micronutrients (i.e., vitamins and minerals). They ultimately lead to starvation as the result of the lack of organically diversified diets, such as iodine deficiency, which is preventable with iodized salt, vitamin A, and iron deficiencies. Their deficiencies lead to irreversible health problems and deaths in hundreds of thousands of humans each year. They mostly impact pregnant women and the first generation, according to the World Health Organization in 2015. According to Per Pinstrup-Andersen and Peter Sandøe (2007, p. viii):

> According to the World Hunger Map, every seven seconds a child under the age of 10 dies – directly or indirectly of hunger – somewhere in the world. The UN's Food and Agricultural Organization (FAO) has recently estimated that the number of undernourished people around the world has increased to 840 million: comprising 799 million in developing

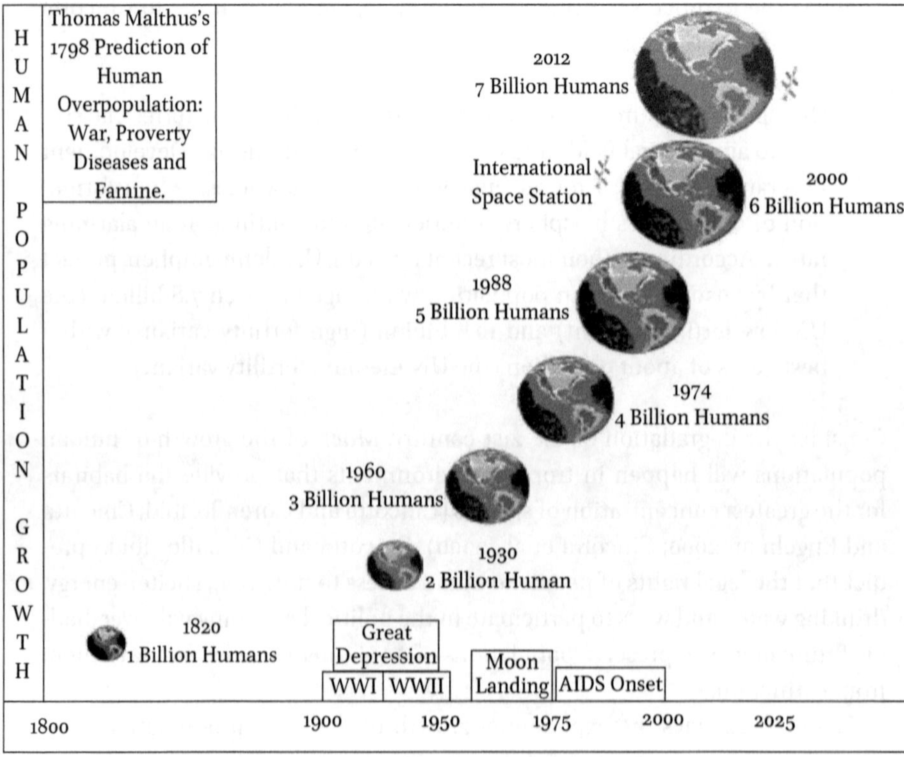

FIGURE 21 Problems related to exponential human population growth

countries, 30 million in countries in transition, and 11 million in industrialized countries.

Over two billion humans suffer from malnutrition resulting from the lack of micronutrients. This frequently leads to the failure of children to develop "normal" physical and mental capabilities (Pinstrup-Andersen & Sandøe, 2007). Within many regions of the world there are overabundances of nutritious foods and drinking water. The problem remains that millions of humans starve every year and undergo malnutrition and either the loss of mental capabilities or the failure to develop them.

The lack of these resources greatly contributes to the problem of poverty. This increases chances for starvation and undernourishment. Malnutrition occurs in all types of countries, even developed countries, which is also partially due to the legal policies that are implemented. Companies are legally permitted to lower many types of nutrients in food products and to replace them with addictive ingredients, such as corn syrup and sugar.

Epidemics, such as HIV and AIDS, have increasingly negative impacts because of poverty and famine. Good nutrition slows the effects of diseases. Malnutrition also hinders the ability to acquire an education.

One of the impacts of education is that the generation that follows from more institutionally educated parents tends to become older parents at first birth. Those who tend to have less institutional education or perhaps less education, in general, tend to impregnate or give birth earlier and more frequently, even though malnutrition also hinders impregnations, pregnancies, prenatal developments, and births to some degree. So, the result of each of the latter factors involves vast increases in conditions of desperation.

There are ideologies that involve enhanced competitiveness (e.g., ones with higher social dominance orientations), which impact certain living generations more than others and shape the whole culture. Competitiveness from sexual selection manifests itself in the search for partners who tend to reach some perceived threshold of health insofar as they appear to lack certain types or certain conditions of diseases and malnutrition.

The human overpopulation of a region increases the frequencies of disease, famine, poverty, and the discontinuation of education. Results include decreases in planning, such as family planning. This leads to losses in considerations for future consequences of actions. Losses in considerations of consequences allow greater numbers of preteen and teenage births (i.e., for those who gain access to sufficient resources). This increases the overall birthrate of the population to such an extent that the societal and governmental systems are unstable and unsustainable.

The lack of stability and unsustainable development are hallmarks of societies with dominating powers as opposed to hegemonies. The human social hierarchy is enhanced with ever greater discrepancies between the affluent and the poverty-stricken. Dominant and subordinate groups involve a small minority of powerful people enforcing hard power via the control of military and policing forces.

Democracies are not immune to instability and unsustainability. Democracies continually demonstrate that the role of propaganda leads to uninformed societies and voters and mass media systems that focus on less important social issues. The soft power wrought by "propaganda" basically plays a similar role to the hard power wrought by "military and policing forces." Soft power hegemonically produces instability and unsustainable cultural practices through thought-control and indoctrination.

Under the conditions of the dominating powers, individuals and families seek temporary relief. They increasingly attempt to acquire the satisfactions of their basic needs and needs for security whilst conflicts, social uprisings, and warring are ever more likely under the latter conditions than with a hegemony. In an unstable society, the first and second generations attempt to satisfy physiological and security needs and become more competitive, committing theft and violent acts more frequently.

Competitiveness increases, and the population sizes of the fourth and fifth generations greatly diminish. The first generation is greatly victimized, which are reasons for the conditions that allow child soldiers and sex slaves to arise. The predominant form of thought-control of the child soldiers and sex slaves comes from hard power, demanding that children shoot and kill other human beings, drugging, torturing, and threatening them and sex slaves with brutal violence.

People increasingly migrate when given the opportunities under the latter conditions. When ideologies of competitiveness, desperation and ways of behaving by means of thievery and violence remain, there are increases of global terroristic actions.

The access of information about any area of the globe is inexpensive and requires very little investment of time. The access to transportation routes is facilitated once people are outside of the unstable society. Desperate and competitive people attempting to fulfill basic needs and needs for security and safety are more likely to have learned to implement destruction and violence against fellow competitors for resources, especially those who are perceived as having many more resources.

The ideology of competitiveness is separate from the concept of fairness, although some people may engage in competition according to the fairness of rules. However, sometimes the annihilation of the opponent or destructions of many opponents' chances increase the range of opportunities for the competitor. This partially explains how people could have acquired terroristic and violent tendencies within developed civil societies through observing or participating in such destructiveness. For the latter reasons, the increase in the number of competitors for resources also increases the amount of competition for security and safety as well as the victimizations of people that contribute to dismantling the organizations of societal systems.

7 Victimizations and Contributing to the Disorganizations of Societal Systems

Presumably, increases in frequencies and intensities of competitions lead to increases in frequencies and intensities of victimizations. Increasing the amount of competitiveness raises the need for divisions of compensations for the victimizations of others. The divisions of compensations are, however, not based on the intensities of the experiences of the victims, but rather they are based on the locations, objects, and events that are present during the victimizations. The divisions facilitate the presentations for the confirmations and disconfirmations of evidence for policing, judging, and legislation.[8]

Generally, compensations are not made to those who have just been secretly victimized. Compensations are sometimes granted to those who have been victimized and who are willing to undergo the steps through the legal system and await procedural justice. Otherwise, some victims have friends or family members who handle their victimizations forcibly by victimizing their victimizers and taking compensations with haste. This is often separate from the procedures of the legal system.

Competitiveness naturally arises within civil society because of population growth rates that exceed societal systems' abilities to incorporate the dynamic changes in the age structure and the growing ratio of dependency of the young or elderly. Increased competition also arises when the society has a continually higher birthrate than death rate. Many nations have higher death rates than their birthrates because the environmental conditions are harsh (e.g., with greater risks of infectious diseases). Some societies have extremely high population growth rates of two or three percent per year. Their needs for divisions of compensations for victims usually cannot become actualized in ways that stabilize expectations of justice and fairness via the legal system.

Consider several African nations, such as Angola, Burkina Faso, Cameroon, Mali, Niger, Uganda, and Zambia. They are estimated to each have human population growth rates of over 2.5 percent per year. At least half of their populations consist of people who are younger than twenty years of age. These nations' birthrates exceed thirty-five births per one thousand. Their death rates exceed ten deaths per one thousand (CIA World Factbook, 2016).

---

8 The objects of importance for evidence are related directly to the cases, such as knives and guns for violent offenses and objects that have been stolen for cases of theft. The appearance of weapons at certain locations, such as schools, can increase the judgment of the severity of the crime and the event of a video recording of the crime can as well. So, for instance, theft at a school with a gun can be judicially recognized as a more severe criminal offense than theft at a convenience store with a gun, especially if guns are permitted to be concealed and brought into the convenience store. The value of the products stolen are important for the cases, especially insofar as a threshold is reached, because once some threshold has been reached, which could be $50, $100, or $1,000, the severity of the type of crime and potential penalization increase. The latter aspect of procedures shows the arbitrariness of penalization, for example, to the extent that if the value of some theft had been $0.01 less than reaching the threshold, the type of crime and potential penalization would be greatly reduced. Hence, there is an arbitrariness regarding the penalizations of culprits for their crimes, which occurs to facilitate the procedures for justice and decision-making and is inherently unfair to some degree.

Angola, Burkina Faso, Cameroon, Mali, Niger, Uganda, and Zambia are estimated to have very small populations of people who are sixty-five or older who compose less than 3.5 percent of each nation's population. Their average age of mothers at first birth is in the teenage years. The CIA World Factbook (2017) estimates the number of children between five and fourteen years of age who produce labor is twenty-four to forty-three percent in these nations; this is based on estimates from 2001 and later.[9]

Angola, Burkina Faso, Cameroon, Mali, Niger, Uganda, and Zambia have very high risks of major infectious diseases and have histories of military coups, dictatorships, and refugee camps. There was a twenty-seven-year civil war in Angola (1975–2002). The countries have histories as colonies of Portugal (i.e., Angola), France (i.e., Cameroon, Burkina Faso, Mali and Niger), and Britain (i.e., Uganda and Zambia). The latter countries all gained independence from their colonizers during the 1960s or 1970s.

The F-problem is apparent within these African nations in multiple forms. The nations lack the medical and legal technology to account for births of new citizens. Women and maternal families of the infants and youths bare most of the time, energy, and money to rear, school, and teach the children how to help their families.

Fathers can easily escape the financial responsibilities. Such responsibilities are considered by legal-minded people to be legal obligations in many political economies (e.g., each of the developed countries). Pregnancies become endemic. Many result from rapes and deceptions. Some women falsely believe their children will be cared for or supported by fathers. Yet many men and adolescent boys have impregnated more than one woman, preteen, or teenage girl each. They live in unstable societies and political turmoil.

Poverty can naturally increase political turmoil and societal instability. Scientific research illustrates that decreasing the number of births of

9 These estimates appear exceedingly low concerning labor, though, but they may refer to white market business activities as opposed to gray and black market labor because we may very well maintain that in countries that are underdeveloped and in countries that are at war, such as Syria in 2017, the children are typically working once they have reached an age where they have developed the abilities to carry items, such as drinking water, to locations that they can remember in virtue of instructions and directions. Moreover, the work of individuals, such as homemakers and children who do regular housework, are vastly underestimated in terms of their impact and the extent to which they are investigated, except perhaps in the fields of home economics and family and consumer sciences. The regular production of food, balancing the accounts, financial planning, paying taxes, cleaning, etc. are all tasks that are performed as forms of labor but which typically only receive job titles for those who do such work for people as service sector employees within developed countries (e.g., cooks, accountants, maids etc.).

unmarried people and strengthening marriage lead to reductions in poverty (Amato & Maynard, 2007). Within Angola, Burkina Faso, Cameroon, Mali, Niger, Uganda, and Zambia, the legal systems lack the structural components to encourage marriages as formal and legal bonds, especially between those who have reproduced. The child support laws that demand for both parents to offer support for their children are ineffective under the conditions of the societies.

Much of the economic activity is also not recognized as such by the state. Moreover, male members of the legal institutions directly place themselves at risks, concerning the enforcements of child support laws. Male legal workers undoubtedly contribute to the number of births of adolescent and adult women who remain unmarried in underdeveloped and developing countries. This includes most of the world.

Providing genuinely effective aid to the latter African societies would require developed nations to perform tasks that will most probably be met with resilient oppositions. There would likely be unwelcoming members of many different institutions and defiance that results from clandestine interests if the aid from developed nations concerns population control, for instance. Contrarily, providing aid that merely appears to be effective can increase the amount of achievements for short-term political gains. People from developed nations bring food and medical supplies (e.g., medicines, wheelchairs, condoms, contraceptives, etc.) or other goods (e.g., prescription eyeglasses) into underdeveloped nations as aid without expectations of reasonable compensation. This often leads to the inability for many of such industries to develop in the latter countries.

A wheelchair manufacturer cannot afford to produce wheelchairs in a city that has been given many wheelchairs for free to many consumers. This contributes to a higher supply and lower demand for such a product. The average price for the product is lowered by free ones. A developed nation providing food and drinking water that is produced through systems outside of the underdeveloped nation can sporadically increase the birthrate and create even longer lasting dependency upon those external systems. Such donations can lead to massive social problems when those external systems cease to produce goods for the underdeveloped nation that fails to develop the relevant and sustainable systems of production.

The artificial stimulation of some external economy can lead to a great dependency on external stimuli that exacerbate the F-problem and further destabilize the societal system in ways that are temporarily unapparent. The behaviors of giving things and providing services only superficially appear to be generous. Such behaviors often fail to contribute to the creation of sustainable systems (i.e., systems that continuously produce or allow for the attainment of commodities and the emergence of services) via practices of reasonable compensation and stable systems of payment.

The result of unplanned and unconditional aid leads to well-disguised factors that contribute to the disorganization of societal systems. This is akin to parents caring for children and adolescents in such ways that the parents cook and clean for them as well as perform many other tasks. This disallows the youths to attain the skills and good habits, and their offspring may never learn to cook, clean, and perform other tasks for themselves before they leave home. This greatly increases the difficulties for their adaptations and increases arrested developments. The parents may never even realize that they have contributed to the problems of their children attaining independence and may view themselves as helpful and generous parents instead of servile ones. Servility can even prolong the dependence of the ones who attain short-term benefits from those who are both servile but independent. They yield to the needs of their loved ones.

The short-term and long-term political and societal goals are often opposed to one another both within the same society and regarding others as well. A man (i.e., one who the author met on a flight from America) flew to Africa to give away spectacles with a non-governmental organization to the poverty-stricken with poor vision. He was probably confronted with happy and appreciative people. Such a man may view himself as generous until he has a run-in with a salesperson, distributor, or producer of eyeglasses. The likelihood of the latter run-ins is very low, whereas the probability of meeting satisfied and appreciative people is very high.

The person from the developed nation who provides the goods at his or her own expense may identify him or herself as thoughtful and generous or even sanctimonious. Of course, the latter mental states and the ideology of generosity for giving to the poor are dangerous, especially when political economies make massive efforts to artificially and unconditionally stimulate regions of undeveloped cities and nations. Developed economies refrain from contributing to the establishment of the means of production for those things and processes. The donations are stimuli that are produced by much stabler systems of production (i.e., autopoietic systems).

The opportunities for newly emerging businesses that sell and distribute products and services decrease along with employment, financial security, and the stability of the political, economic, and legal systems in the undeveloped city getting the donations because artificial stimuli from outside of the societal system are brought into it and cheapen the products and therefore present problems for paying laborers who are employed to produce such products. The same is true concerning volunteer work. Volunteer work, apart from government-funded or nonprofit companies, for instance, lowers the price of labor because it is performed without wages. Volunteer work can be performed by a sustainable system and contribute to sustainability.

Banking systems also produce difficulties for such nations. Those who open bank accounts with lesser amounts of money are subjected to more frequent financial penalties as well as "service fees." This may typically exceed any interest that accrues within the bank accounts of poor people.

The affluent typically escape many of the service fees. They hold enough to exceed the thresholds for penalties and service fees. Banking systems function in ways that stabilize the preexisting socio-economic hierarchy within the society. The hierarchy ranges from the affluent to the poverty-stricken. The interest that accumulates in an individual's account with much money is exponentially greater than the interest from the one with little money. The idea that more labor is required more often from those with less wealth must also incorporate an intensification with the onset of extant money and banking systems.

Banks also typically make no efforts to cooperatively combine the money from the accounts of indigent people to allow them to attain higher levels of interest from their financial investments. For instance, something that would be close to equal with the level of interest that those with vast amounts of money in bank accounts make.

Ideologically speaking, the wealthy have even attempted to utilize the term "earning" instead of "making" in ways that lead people to believe that the money of the affluent is well-deserved. There is a way of thinking or having faith that wealthy people are "entitled" to the money that is made via the accumulation of interest in bank accounts. The money accumulates without the individuals producing labor, though. For these reasons, bank robbers and burglars may reasonably feel no sympathy for the banks themselves. They are part of banking systems, which are systematically unfair for the poverty-stricken.

Banking systems currently exacerbate the F-problem insofar as those who inherit more and who already have or earn more are placed at unfair advantages. The banks protect more property for them and more frequently penalize those with less property. The banking systems thereby increase the abilities of the affluent (i.e., very often with family members who share financial resources) to acquire resources. They hinder the abilities of the indigent to acquire resources, except for certain ways of financing the poor, such as microloans. Microloans are relatively new and infrequently used sources for finance. The unfairness of the global financial system climaxes with the inheritances of the coming generations at their extremes, who are either born with fortunes, nothing, or debts.

The banking system in the latter manner increases the instability for the indigent and increases the stability of the affluent. The hierarchy-enhancing way of the system leads to very different dynamic changes regarding the behaviors involved with sexual selection. Theoretically speaking, the affluent tend to mate less often in ways that lead to births but select mates that vary quite greatly regarding their desirability.

For example, the wealthy may select their mates based on having wealth, beauty, power, fame, great talents, or holding certain ideologies, etc. On the other side, indigent people tend to mate more often in ways that lead to births, tend to sexually reproduce at younger ages at first reproduction, and tend to select mates under social conditions within the same socio-economic class.

We may even hypothesize that people from lower socio-economic classes have sexual intercourse more frequently. There is a dependence on their conditions (e.g., provided that they have access to nutritious foods, clean drinking water, and free time). Sex can be a form of entertainment as opposed to more costly ways of entertaining themselves. We may further hypothesize that indigent people tend to have sex more often (i.e., than the affluent) without contraception to increase the tactile sensations and feelings of life-altering risks. Of course, wealth and poverty cannot be determined with certainty when one only knows about the total amount of money or income individuals have in banks. Real estate, stocks, other assets, and debts often surpass the wealth within accounts and income.

All the latter factors contribute greatly to the structure of social hierarchies within societies. They are of the utmost importance regarding potential solutions to the F-problem. They impact both the frequency and the sexual selection of partners for sexual reproduction. Many of the latter problems regarding victimizations are slow and gradual and hardly noticeable, such as the systematic unfairness of banking systems around the world, and yet they contribute to the disorganizations of societal systems. Slow, gradual, and barely noticeable problems are difficult to change when the entire systems require changes.

8 Relations of the F-Problem to Victimization as a Form of Theft

Most, if not all, of the offenses wrought by prosecutors against defendants basically amount to accusations of theft of some sort. Most offenses, which lead to indictments, amount to the general action of a victimizer unlawfully taking something away from a victim as it is stolen by the victimizer. What exactly that thing is, which is taken away from the victim, greatly determines the divisions of compensation. The divisions of compensation are further divided into measurable units that allow for victims to have the chances to regain what was taken in some cases. The divisions partially determine an aspect of the penalizations of the victimizers.

Victimizing is performed by one or more culprits against one or more victims. The victimization occurs via the change in the roles of the people who enter the relationship and the process of domination and subordination. Thereby something is taken away from the victim by means of the victimizer. The victimizer acquires what is taken or not (i.e., the victimizer may steal from the victim or destroy what the victim has).

Murder, arson, rape, contract violations, assault, battery, spousal abuse, animal abuse, and sexual harassment can be viewed as taking away time, effort, money, or the ability to use one's own decision-making processes to make choices. Taking such things away is the "stealing" or "theft" of one or more of these things. So, most convictions basically amount to formal judgments being rendered against the accused and alleged victimizer for what principally amounts to some form of theft (i.e., of time, effort, money, or choices).

Each victimization interferes with the process of sexual selection and the frequency of sexual intercourse or intimacy. This suffices to make each victimization an F-problem. The victimization could involve taking away either time, effort, money, other resources, or the ability to make decisions over some time span. The latter types of interference of victimizers against victims, which leads to the F-problem, is best hypothesized as decreasing the birthrates of victims and increasing the birthrates of victimizers. Victimizations are transient moments. We may assume that victimizers tend to benefit from the disadvantages they impose upon their victims, even if the advantage is merely or largely a psychological experience of taking control of the domination and subordination relation.[10]

---

10 On the contrary, certain species that sexually reproduce can be induced to reach sexual maturity and maternity faster when they have undergone increased amounts of stress hormones. For humans, much of the research concerns the segment of populations who want and attempt to become pregnant and how stress hormones may, in fact, hinder their abilities to become pregnant. So, for those who are educated and planning families, any victimization will likely lead to increases in stress hormones and hinder their abilities to procreate. On the other hand, research concerning stress and stress hormones may very well be considered regarding the increased chances in pregnancies of preteenagers in underdeveloped, developing, and developed countries.

Penal systems for criminal justice often reverse the relationships of domination and subordination to provide fairer chances for victims to become the legally dominant parties and for the victimizers to become the legally subordinated. In any society, social dominance theorists maintain that low-status group members are more likely to be victimized by the criminal justice system and members of law enforcement and legal institution. This systematic process of dominating groups via controlled threats and violence tends to be implemented against lower status groups more frequently and intensely. The latter subordinate groups are identifiable via their overrepresentations within any society's prison population. Dominant group members are identifiable via their underrepresentations within any society's population of prisoners.

We may thus hypothesize that the low-status group members also have less chances to reverse the relationships of domination and subordination against them when they are victimized, especially by members of higher status groups. This is consistent with social dominance theory. Moreover, we may further hypothesize (i.e., if the latter hypothesis is true) that segregations of low-status groups and high-status groups naturally arise within societies as a legal process to decrease the amount of social injustices. Isolating low-status groups reduces the overall amount of victimizations of low-status group members by means of high-status group members and may at least temporarily reduce the overall amount of victimizations in the society. So, segregations of black and white people in America and South Africa during the mid-twentieth century, for instance, are best viewed as legal systems (man)handling racist social dominance and victimizations via legally requiring the separations of the races in diverse ways. This would have temporarily reduced the number of victimizations, given the truths of the latter hypotheses.

Legal systems and political systems may support the legalization of segregations of races, religious groups and others. This can include those groups that are distinguished by high and low statuses within any society. This may reduce demands for legal services and dependencies upon the legal system to reverse the roles of victimization, domination, and subordination and for reducing the overall number of social injustices. Although unjust, the legal segregations of racial and religious groups are implemented via the legal institution.

They serve an initial function within society. They temporarily reduce the overall amount of social injustice and illustrate progress regarding the relation of dominance wrought by the high-status groups for the subordinations of the low-status groups. It is reasonable to consider legal segregations of subordinates to be signs of advancement within the society as one that is diminishing social injustices, especially directly after nations have undergone periods of slavery, genocide, or other types of massive human rights violations of the subordinate groups.

It is noteworthy that the segregations of people via the legal system with police enforcements is inherently unfair, unjust, and thoroughly unethical. The segregations of peoples via legal systems disrespect subordinate groups and place others on pedestals.

On their ideological pedestals, many of the dominant group members can facilitate the development of ideologies of belonging to groups with superiority. This creates forms of servility and ideologies of inferiority in the subordinate groups.

One form of necessary segregation in societies is the segregation of the prison systems. One newly developed form of imprisonment that enhances the social hierarchy of dominance and subordination, especially in the United States, is the private prison system.

In the United States, private prisons largely consist of populations of blacks between the ages of eighteen and thirty-five (Weitzer, 1996; Wordes and Bynum, 1995; Vargas-Vargas, 2005, p. 41). Corporations that own the prisons profit from the incarceration of this group. This is largely because the young black men and adolescents of age have already been incarcerated at higher rates than Hispanics and Whites in America (Bonczar, 2003, p. 1).

Taxpayers fund the prisons, and stockholders have been making profits from the private prisons and increases in crime rates. Thereby law enforcement agents and criminal justice workers have financial motivations to frequently and intensely enforce the laws when they are also stockholders of the corporations that operate private prisons. There are financial motivations for some criminal justice workers (i.e., the stockholders) to victimize young, black men. The latter group yields higher profits for them as stockholders.

The United States has the highest incarceration rates out of developed countries. The United States Justice Department also does not even include the private prison population within their statistics of the incarceration rate for the public. Prison populations are mostly people who would be part of the workforce. Statistical analyses for the unemployment rate are impacted so that prison populations are neither counted as unemployed nor underemployed.

Prison workers earn wages below minimum wage while they are imprisoned. In the United States at the end of 2010, well over two percent of the population of the United States were within the United States Department of Justice corrections population (i.e., 7.1 million people) and were either on probation, parole, in jail, or in prison. This excludes private prison populations and detention centers within its account, too (Glaze et al., 2011, pp. 1–3).

One function of the criminal justice system is to deter certain types of victimization. Another function is for the criminal justice system to stabilize the societal expectations. So, compensations for wrongdoings and the deterrence of victimizations must be ongoing, legal and systematic processes. They should enable fair and just decisions to be made on behalf of a third party that was initially uninvolved in the incidents of the victimizations.

Based on evidence, expectations of enabling fair and just decisions fall in favor of the victim. Couple these with expectations that the third party, which evaluates the evidence and forms a verdict, consists of one or more individuals who are neutral and impartial observers of the evidence brought forth. The evidence directly relates to the victim, who plays the role of the accuser, to the victimizer, who plays the role of the accused, and to the accusation of the victimization. The victimization is basically a form of theft (i.e., a taking away of something, to wit, time, effort, items, or the decision-making ability of the victim).

Murder takes away the decision-making process of the victim permanently and instantly ends the period of the individual's lifetime. Murder is simply the victimizer taking away the life from the victim in an unlawful way. As such, murder is a form of theft and an F-problem. It makes the victim entirely unable to sexually select and sexually reproduce. The ability has been taken away from him or her.

A penalty that would allow for a fairer compensation to the victim, according to this view, would be for modern medical technology and justice systems to allow for the victim to reproduce after the murder and for the victimizer to support the offspring of the victim through labor, which would present, at least, a theoretically fairer set of circumstances. However, increases in populations during the 21st century already contribute greatly to the F-problem as a problem of stabilizing the rates of human births and deaths in globally sustainable ways.

Arson may result in a victim's loss of time, effort, money, other items, and choices regarding several matters. The word "rape" also contains the meanings of "taking away" and "forcefully seizing" within its modern definitions. It can be defined as the victimization performed by a victimizer who dominates a victim.

For clarity and for future solutions to the F-problem, rape may be categorized in two different manners as "that which may lead to sexual reproduction" and "that which will not result in sexual reproduction" so that greater emphasis is placed upon rapes of women involving vaginal sexual intercourse without protection (i.e., an unbroken condom). Yet the latter distinctions fail to consider the fact that rape results in the loss of time and energy of the victim as well as the risks of infections, psychological trauma, and even suicidal tendencies that may result. They are important for measurements and attaining understandings of the role of rape, sexual and social domination, and procreation.

Again, legal systems are involved in two fundamentally different ways with regard to the processes of victimization in societies. First, legal systems and legal institutions function in ways that contribute to the victimizations of human populations. They do this via forms of systematic and institutionalized threats and violence and by producing victims.

Second, legal systems and institutions even reverse the roles of the victims and victimizers. The victimizations of murder, arson, and rape make impacts upon people regarding their sexual lives, future choices for mates, and contributions, or lack thereof, to the development of the human population. Legal systems, again, offer the opportunities to reverse the roles of the victims and victimizers. So, legal systems play important roles for humans to engage in sexual intercourse. Legal systems prevent some and facilitate others' sexual reproductions.

The importance of the latter facts appears to be greatly underestimated within the scientific literature. Buildings constructed as prisons and jails and rules of legal institutions strictly divide the sexes. They prevent procreations by the legally and systematically chosen inmates.

The latter processes include dividing both prisoners and prison guards by sex as well as the roles of others in "correctional centers" (e.g., male guards are placed less often with female prisoners). "Imprisonment" and "conviction" are only understandable as means through which individuals' potential procreations are artificially and institutionally selected out of the population. This is accomplished via members of the legal institution.

This provides a crucial way to understand the legal process. Certain types of people are more likely to be convicted and wrongly convicted, such as African Americans. They have been wrongfully sentenced to death historically more frequently than other racial groups in the United States.

During the early twenty-first century, globalization regarding legal systems is undeveloped regarding the F-problem. Typically, it remains legally permissible for adolescents and men to impregnate females within other nations (i.e., as foreigners) without having the legal requirement to financially support their own offspring. The attainment of information concerning biological fatherhood is at a low level. Information about the public relationship statuses of the offspring of fathers is vastly dwarfed by the amount of information regarding the public relationship statuses of marriages. The knowledge of mothers, about who fathers of children are, is crucial for solutions to the F-problem and attaining an understanding of the problem itself.

Only modernized legal systems and institutions have begun to reverse the victimization process of females. Females would otherwise be left with the burdens of rearing their own children without any support from their children's biological fathers. Underdeveloped and developing countries have mothers who are left with the burdens of rearing their children without a father-figure. They lack child support payments as mandatory aspects of their societal systems.

In modernized legal systems and institutions, biological fathers are required to financially support their own children if born to a mother who has the right citizenship. Globalization has not at least yet significantly allowed the F-problem to be further realized. There is a problem of finding the reversal of the victimization process for pregnant women who were raped and who were abandoned by biological fathers of their offspring before or after births. Pregnant rape victims are victimized directly whilst their decision-making processes are forcefully taken away from them. There are reasons to assume rape victims are typically from low-status groups (Amir, 1971, p. 44). Ethically speaking, children deserve parental support at least from all capable parents who are responsible for their births.

9 War as an F-Problem and Peace: Sexual Selection and Rites

The greatest victimization process related to the F-problem involves lawmaking for violent conflicts. Michael Walzer (2006) argues that "war" is a legal condition during which two or more groups are equally permitted to continue conflicting with one another via armed forces. Wars require vast amounts of financial resources, time, energy as well as large risks of human resources.

Impacts of wars on the changes in the natural process of sexual selection and breeding are largely unknown. Victors of war procreate with a different set of circumstances for sexual selection than their defeated opponents do. This is true for victors of wars who tend to spare the lives of fertile females and kill males at the peaks of their reproductive potencies. The amount of intergroup and interracial procreation that occurs before, during, and after wars is largely unknown as well.

It has been estimated that from the years 1500 to 1860 there were at least 8,000 peace treaties signed, all of which aimed at continuous peace, but they only lasted an average of two years (Stevens, 1949, p. 221; Fromm, 1955, p. 4). The 20th century involved even greater amounts and intensities of violent conflicts than the previous centuries. According to Wilhelm Grewe (1982, p. 104):

> Legally, the main purpose of a peace treaty is the termination of a state of war and the restoration of normal friendly relations between the former belligerents based on a settlement of matters arising out of the war. But a peace treaty is not the only way to terminate a war; there are other means to bring about this effect. Quincy Wright, who tried to count all wars and peace treaties from the end of the 15th century on, concluded that overall, less than half were ended formally by a treaty of peace.

Grewe (ibid.) continues:

> But with increasing frequency until World War I, wars were ended by peace treaty: one-third in the 16th and 17th centuries, half in the 18th century, two-thirds in the 19th century and six-sevenths in the first two decades of the 20th century. Since 1920, however, when the concept and the practice of war changed radically, wars have usually begun without a declaration of war and ended without a peace treaty.

Consider whether the concepts of war and peace deserve vast reconceptualizations. "War" and "peace" are typically not defined as directly involving the natural consequences of human overpopulation and reducing human populations via increasing death rates. "War" is not ordinarily defined as directly involving sexual selection processes that change from warring conditions to conditions of peace. "War" is often not defined as direct changes in both in-group and out-group domination that may differ within times of war and peace.

The reconceptualization of war may best incorporate the increasing number of human perceptions of needs for more resources because of the increasing perceptions of human population growth and realizations of these needs. This coincides with John Malthus's predictions of the consequences of exponential human population growth (See figure 21). Increases in population naturally increase the number of conflicts that arise. This fact tends to largely explain conflicts between groups that occupy territories near one another.

Reconceptualizing the concept of war to account for differences regarding the process of sexual selection is complicated. One hypothesis is that there have been more frequent deployments of low-status group members to war in proportion to their population sizes at large. Other facts, for which to search, are whether low-status racial groups tend to be placed in harm's way during wars more often (i.e., in respect to their population sizes compared to high-status groups). Consider whether there are greater war-time employment opportunities for high-status racial group members. Also, consider their jobs for the productions for wars and battles rather than dangerous positions of infantry and other combat soldiers.

The result of the latter reconceptualization of war would thus provide us with the *realpolitik* of the leadership of one society that tends to support policies that reduce the size of its own low-status groups. Consider that leaders support reductive measures regarding males of the subordinate group who are at the peak of their sexual potencies. Leaders have, simultaneously, sought to dominate another group (i.e., the out-group) and foreign society via reducing its population of males who are at the peak of their sexual potencies, too.

One result of the latter tendencies could be (the hypothesis) that the victors of war also tend to be victors of procreation. The victors of war and procreation tend to be the males of the high-status groups within the warring society, which increases the proportion of females within its own society. Also, it increases the proportion of females in the defeated opponents' society.

The male members of the dominant groups of victorious societies are thus hypothesized to tend to increase the frequency of their own procreations within both their own society and the opponents' societies. There is probably an increase in the pregnancy rate of the defeated societies' females who are impregnated by the males of the victorious societies.

Consider prolonged wars, such as the French and American occupations of Vietnam during the 1950s through the 1970s. Many of the women from Vietnam became naturalized citizens of the USA and birthed their offspring with the support of American fathers. Consider the hypothesis that fathers performing their familial duties were most likely members of the high-status group (i.e., white males in higher socio-economic classes). Hypothetically then, American non-white and indigent males were less likely to both father and support their offspring with Vietnamese mothers. Some procreated more frequently with Vietnamese women than the women in American low-status groups.

Presumably, in America, veterans of the high-status groups could afford to father and support their offspring with Vietnamese mothers. The latter men likely sexually selected their mates based on their skills, attractiveness etc. For continued societal dominance, the high-status group could also still afford the development of heterogeneity offered by the Vietnamese mothers' offspring with American men. Lower status groups may have tended to act according to intense ideologies that strongly opposes fathers of lower status groups offering themselves as fatherly caregivers to their offspring with Vietnamese mothers. The reason for this could involve tendencies for lower status group members to strengthen their population size.

The concept of war involves the intensification of the processes of sexual selection of the higher status groups from the dominant warring society. Higher group-status-men from the dominant society become more frequently able to select and procreate with the more desirable women from the warring society. This happens gradually before and during the society being defeated undergoes subordination greater than lower group-status-men of the victorious society undergo subordination.

The victors of war would thus be interpreted as the warring societies with the most men who have impregnated the most women from the other warring societies. The remaining males of the victorious societies likely return to their own societies' geographic locations after periods of wars and tend to provide far less support for the women they impregnated as well as their offspring within the defeated societies. They tend to have less resources. Additionally, we may hypothesize that males from the high-status groups of victors increase the pregnancy rate of the women within their own societies and are more likely to provide support to these offspring than their others. They tend to be caregivers for their offspring who are likelier to be more closely related to them than offspring they fathered in other societies, against which they went to war.

Historically speaking, people who live closer to one another tend to be more closely related by kinship. Societies tend to promote marriages and sexual reproductions of members of the same-status groups (e.g., racial and socio-economic groups). Victors of war thus contain higher status group members who more frequently, sexually select their partners. Such high-status group members further select their partners based on their roles as potential caregivers with partners they have sexually selected.

Especially during and after wars, high-status group members have procreated with mothers from their own society and with foreign mothers. So, they further select their own children to whom they provide greater fatherly care. From the theoretic concept of war as a F-Problem, consider whether in Afghanistan and Iraq there have been more intense or prolonged US and ally military battles because, unlike past wars, far less procreation between US and Afghan and ally and Afghan people happens.

Consider the F-problem of war as an enduring problem. We may discover that – given that the latter hypotheses are true concerning the victors of war and procreation the – coming times of peace tend to approach faster, thereby ending the violent conflicts between the warring societies, when the soon-to-be victors begin to have significant impacts upon the rates of pregnancy within the society that is becoming defeated.

The latter hypothesis about the reasons for peace presumes certain things about the locations of wars. Ongoing conflicts may, therefore, involve less frequent impregnations of the women within the occupied territories by military forces. Wars that involve fronts that are between the opponents may tend to involve the coming terminations of war and then longer periods of peace when more marital relations are made or arranged between males in the dominant society and many of the females of high-status groups in the subordinated society. Without such relations, more intense or prolonged conflicts may occur.

War has been historically terminated via legal peace treaties. They are typically initiated by the victors via the suspension of hostile actions. This occurs via improvements in diplomatic relations or recognitions of other treaties.

War may be ended with the defeat of the opponent in such a way that the opposition's territory is acquired by the victors and the "legal existence" of the sovereign state is dismantled (Grewe, 1982). This involves the termination or replacement of leadership. Peace treaties are no longer used in the same manner that they were used in the 19th century and more distant pasts.

Warring societies focus on the lawful killing of their out-groups' most sexually potent males. Wars have become ever more violent regarding the intensities of violence. One undeniable similarity concerning all wars is the overall impact on the populations of males who have matured to levels that are at their peaks concerning sexual potency and their abilities to procreate.

Consider the impact of war on the birthrates and sexual selection with special emphasis on victors. Males on victorious sides of wars are more likely to procreate. Instead, the focus on the concept of war has historically involved far greater attention to death rates. The reasons for the disproportionate focuses on death rates during wars is that the number of dead bodies for each side is far easier to count than the number of impregnations caused by each side.

It is challenging to calculate and estimate the number of impregnations wrought by males of victorious societies and those particular births of their offspring that occur from the defeated society. Their offspring almost certainly receive less fatherly care. They undergo harsher living conditions and may contribute to the process of peace via the processes of social and sexual domination.

The F-problem reaches its height during or around the onset of war. War tends to result from increases in human population growth. War may involve suspensions of hostility that partially result from a natural process of sexual selection. The defeated society tends to care for larger numbers of offspring who are the descendants of the victors.

Hypothetically speaking, increasing intensities of violence and destruction during the wars of the late 20th and 21st centuries, especially wrought by developed nations, have resulted partially from the decrease of males from victorious societies who impregnated females from the conquered societies. A consistent hypothesis maintains that conquered nations, which have had many of their female citizens impregnated by the males of the victorious nations, are less likely to undergo prolonged and intense violence via the victorious nation. At some threshold, war becomes pointless for dominations when the defeated have populations of babies that had been fathered by males from the victorious nations.

Surviving males from the defeated society impregnate far less women from the victorious society than their counterparts. However, it is worthy to research what the rates of impregnations and births are for females who remain in the defeated societies when they are impregnated by the males from their own society. Women in the defeated society who were impregnated by the soldiers of the victorious one can find men in their own society as caregivers for their children. They may be described as being "mixed races."

Men and women from conquered societies may sexually reproduce at higher rates after wars. Men and Women in developing and underdeveloped countries reproduce at higher rates than in developed ones. Males of victorious militaries sexually reproduce more often with the defeated society's females than the defeated society's surviving warriors do with the victors' females.

In the latter ways and relations, the processes of peace-making theoretically tend to involve the process of sexual and reproductive domination, procreation, and the greater spread of the genes or alleles of the male victors of the more fortunate society. There are violent destructions of the resources and genes of the defeated societies' people, especially able men.

Carlos Navarrete and Melissa McDonald (Shackelford & Hansen, 2014, pp. 99–100) write that human violence is evident in historical and prehistorical times and was probably relatively more frequent and intense in the distant past:

> Archeological evidence affirms that this state of affairs likely characterized prestate societies predating civilization, with evidence stretching back to at least the Upper Paleolithic (e.g., Keeley 1996; Kelly 2005). This intergroup aggression has almost exclusively been perpetrated by groups of males against other males in contexts ranging from small-scale coalitional skirmishes to regional and geopolitical conflicts (for reviews, see Daly and Wilson 1988; Keegan 1993; Wrangham and Peterson 1996).

The Upper Paleolithic period was between 10,000 and 40,000 years ago and is a prehistoric period about which researchers maintain that archeological evidence as well as genetic evidence confirms that opposing groups of males exerted more violence against each other and also acted violently within a range of groups of varying sizes. Carlos Navarrete and Melissa McDonald (Shackelford & Hansen, 2014, p. 100) continue:

> Evidence for male aggression, going back from deep time to the present, can be inferred from genetic studies comparing the global and regional distribution of the Y-chromosome DNA (inherited from male ancestors) relative to mitochondrial DNA (inherited from female ancestors) in extant humans. Researchers find less variance among Y-chromosome DNA, indicating the presence of fewer male ancestors relative to female ancestors ...

Makova and Li (2002) present confirming evidence that all humans are related to a male ancestor who lived between about 30,000 and 50,000 years ago and a female ancestor who lived between 150,000 and 200,000 years ago. It is argued that the higher mortality rates of males during the Upper Paleolithic were the reason for the stronger selections of Y-chromosome DNA in comparison to mitochondrial DNA. The evidence is also inferred from studies that are made from populations that had invasions from comparatively smaller groups of males that sexually reproduced with females from the larger population. Carlos Navarrete and Melissa McDonald (Shackelford & Hansen, 2014, p. 100) write:

> For example, extant South American Indian populations show little to no evidence of the persistence of Y-chromosome DNA from native populations in the New World from their most common male ancestor who lived only a few centuries ago (Mahli et al. 2008). However, native mitochondrial DNA is well represented among extant peoples throughout Latin America (e.g., Makova and Li 2002), suggesting strong selection for European male invaders in the last few centuries. Thus, genetic evidence is consistent with both anthropological and historical data suggesting that intergroup violence displacing natal populations has been primarily perpetrated by males against other males.

It is very likely that sexual selections of the human species have been largely guided by a smaller number of males sexually reproducing than the number of females who reproduce. Alternatively, males tend to kill the male offspring of other males more frequently than killing females or may tend to prevent the sexual reproduction of other males via numerous means, including castrations. Removing either the penis or testicles obviously reduces the frequency of sexual reproduction by neutered males. Some rituals involve scarring genitals or circumcising and may destroy certain reproductive functions.

In South Africa, multiple ritualistic circumcisions are performed on thousands of young men every year, which often end in deaths or mutilations of their sex organs (Fogg, 2014; Der Spiegel, 2015, 2013a & 2013b). Chamberlain (2009, p. 6) writes:

> Circumcision today perpetuates and institutionalizes a righteousness that permitted authorities of earlier times to dictate tribal markings and sexual mutilations and to force parents to comply. It is only recently in human history that genital cutting has been identified as "sexual abuse."

Thousands of young men have died because of these primitive ceremonies in South Africa. Perhaps millions have died worldwide in various cultures through similar means. Fogg (2014) writes that female elders do condemn the events at least in respect to what happens to their own sons. The tribal leaders vilify these women. The first successful penis transplantation was performed on a South African man in 2014 after his penis was cut off during a traditional circumcision ceremony by untrained circumcisers for what is typically a medical procedure within the developed world (*Der Spiegel*, 2015). Zabus (2008, p. xi) writes:

> Why not the earlobe? The fleshy and apparently useless appendage that hangs from the ear – the earlobe – has never been considered an outlaw appendage or invested with symbolic significance in the way sexual organs have been.

The ritualistic circumcision ceremonies are supported via their history as customs, whilst many male adolescents and children undergo the cutting of their sex organs involuntarily. From a medical standpoint, female circumcisions mutilate females arbitrarily and hinder the sensitivity of their sex organs. This has some impact on human sexual selection for procreation.

Male circumcisions that are successfully performed are beneficial when they reduce the frequency of the transmissions of diseases, improve cleanliness, etc. (Fox & Thomson, 2009). Sexual selection is important regarding the underlying motivations for such rituals insofar as a much larger proportion of males who undergo ritualistic circumcisions are mutilated to the extent that they are unable to sexually reproduce. Female circumcisions generally do not result in the mutilations of the sex organs to such an extent that sexual reproduction is disabled like it is with the males.

Hunting other males and giving forcible circumcisions are forms of social and sexual dominance. In many cultures, such as in the nation of Uganda, younger males are hunted and forcibly given circumcisions in many cases

(Fogg, 2014). Forcible circumcisions resulting in mutilations of the sex organs involve the selection of individuals of the male sex. Older males focus on the sex organs of the youth and realize the circumcisions or mutilations result in inabilities of younger males to have sex for some amount of time. Thereby older males' chances of sexual reproduction during that period increase. So, the sexual selection of the older males by females may temporarily increase for procreation.

The extent of the sociological problems associated with rites of passage from adolescence to adulthood via traditional circumcisions are unmentioned in much of the anthropological literature. Frank Salamone (2004, p. 348) writes:

> Circumcision is common, and it is considered a principal element of puberty rites. The operation is performed by the circumciser, who is supported by close family members of the initiate. In some cultures puberty rites are performed collectively, whereas in others rites are performed individually. An initiate is expected to demonstrate a great deal of confidence and endurance in the face of the painful removal of the foreskin of the penis.

There are legal, ethical, and cultural issues with the removal of skins from sex organs. Removals sometimes involve deaths and mutilations of sex organs that render it more difficult, if not impossible, to sexually reproduce. The ages of the boys matter; it is questionable in some cultures and jurisdictions whether boys are selected by other males for cutting their penises during the beginning stages of the sexual maturity of the boys. It is questionable to what extent this lowers the competition for the adult males regarding sexual access to females and impregnation. The competition is thereby greatly increased for the male youths undergoing circumcisions. They feel the need to wait until they heal before they can copulate. This is intrasexual selection since they must compete with the older males for access to females.

In some cultures, the circumcisions are performed by a ritual elder. Salamone (ibid.) continues:

> Circumcision is performed during the wet season, as the dry season is considered harsh on the wound and the heat often causes bleeding of the wound since the circumcision is done without western medical treatment, to reduce pain and bleeding. Adrenaline, found in snail slime which is supposedly recommended by spiritual beings, is applied. In other cases the ritual specialist, circumciser, impersonates ancestral spirits by putting on masks while performing the operation.

Another reason why the circumcisions may be performed during the wet season is that sexual intercourse may occur more frequently and intensely then. The wet season can lead to greater amounts and frequencies of males' ejaculations during vaginal intercourse since vaginal fluid levels and hydration levels of both sexes are greater on average.

Processes involved in intrasexual selection are likely to peak during the wet season for the latter reasons. That is, the males compete against one another for mates more intensely during the wet season. An aspect of the competition concerns mandatory circumcisions. The role of specialists who perform the same procedures of circumcisions probably add control to the rituals and tends to result in less frequent malpractices. Again Salamone (ibid.) continues:

> Among the Ndembu people, when a group of boys from a cluster of villages approaches puberty, the leaders of the villages hold a rite of circumcision in a camp that is set up for the purpose, and circumcisers are invited. The parents of the boys live in the camp, where a fire is lit and will continue burning for the length of the rites. On this fire the mothers of the boys prepare food for the boys during their seclusion. On the night before the circumcisions people beat drums and dance wildly, led by the circumcisers.

Types of rituals that involve entire families, who offer support for boys, also probably lower the likelihood of botched circumcisions. Salamone (ibid.) writes more:

> The boys are carried from the camp in such a way that they do not touch the ground. The next morning each mother feeds her son a big meal by hand. The boys are grabbed by their fathers and guardians and stripped of their clothes. The boys dash off into the woods, down a newly cut path to the circumcision place, known as "the place of dying." The mothers, chased back into the camp, begin to wail at the announcement of a death. After the operations and some herbal medical treatment, the boys are fed by men and are given beer.

Rites of passage involve circumcisions and education during the process of healing. Afterwards they enter manhood. Next, the men assume different roles in the village than before the rituals. Salamone (ibid.) maintains:

> The boys then are secluded in a lodge until their circumcision wounds are healed. During their seclusion they are taught lessons relating to

> adulthood. Masked dancers beat them with sticks. They are taken to a stream and washed and then sent into the bush to trap animals. Then they return to their parents' camp in painted bodies, disguised in such a manner that their identities are not easily known. The boys return to their villages and participate in adult life.

Consider a couple hypotheses concerning the involuntary circumcisions performed by adult men, especially those who are not supported by the family members of the youths who will undergo the circumcisions: In many societies, the frequency of sexual intercourse of older males increases, especially those who force the circumcisions directly after the traditional circumcision ceremonies. The frequency of intercourse of younger males decreases.

The latter hypotheses concern the cultures with rites of passage with circumcisions. In some cultures, such as German cultures, there is a tendency to refrain from circumcising. This can also lead to a form of sexual dominance and selection against males. The males with circumcisions during the late 1930s and early 1940s in Germany were hunted and victimized by the German military and others. Those with uncircumcised penises did not have to hide their genitals from German men and women.

Some social groups victimize those who are circumcised. Some victimize those who are uncircumcised. The function of the violence is still the same since there is a victimization in which the outgroups are controlled by their fears to evade detections of their sex organs. This temporarily reduces chances of sexual reproduction. The circumcisions themselves result in the refrainment of sexual intercourse most likely for a few weeks, which provides ample time for older males to impregnate more women, especially during certain seasons.

Often there are negative consequences for those who fail to undergo the ritualistic circumcisions. Tom Lansford (Salamone, 2004, p. 39) argues that the Australian aborigines also utilize circumcisions as rites of passage and have the oldest continuing practices of rituals for their religions. Regarding initiation ceremonies Lansford (ibid., p. 40) writes:

> During these large gatherings some of the most important ceremonies and rituals revolve around the initiation of the young into the tribe. For young males the first stage of initiation involves a ritual circumcision prior to puberty. The initiation ceremony varies slightly from tribe to tribe.

Consider another hypothesis that may link social dominance theory with sexual dominance. It is practiced within rites of passage and involves the implementation of intrasexual selection. Hypothesis: there are greater numbers or more intense hierarchy enhancing factors within the tribes that have larger numbers of mutilations of genitals and deaths resulting from rituals. Lansford (ibid.) continues:

> For instance, the Yoingus call the initiation "Dhapi" and circumcise youths at about age eight or nine, whereas the Walbiri wait until the boy is between eleven and thirteen. During the ceremony the males of the tribe carry the boy away from the females and form a circle. While two tribesmen hold the initiate, a third removes the foreskin in a series of cuts. The boy is then conveyed, or carried, over a fire as a means of spiritual purification.

By the age of thirteen years, most human males are sexually fertile. We may inquire why the Walbiri tribal people wait until this developmental stage of the youth to implement the rites of passage. Why don't the Yoingus wait quite as long. We can hypothesize that Walbiri communities implement forms of sexual and social dominance differently and perhaps to greater extents in terms of the amounts or intensities. Finally, Lansford (ibid.) explains the consequences for failing to undergo the rituals:

> Some tribes also use ritual scarring as a later part of the initiation process. For example, the Walbiri practice subincision (or ritual scarring of the genitals). After being circumcised at an early age, male youths are subincised in a ceremony at about age seventeen. Within the tribes who practice circumcision and subincision, failure of a boy to go through the ceremonies means that the boy cannot marry, enter an elder's lodge, or participate in other religious ceremonies.

Many questions remain concerning the knowledge that comes from these practices. The knowledge is attained in a largely asymmetrical way. The older males realize the sizes, shapes, healthiness, and unhealthiness of the genitals of the younger males but not vice versa.[11] Regarding the latter rites involving

11 The asymmetrical access to information regarding knowledge about the health, size, and shape of the genitals of others is also becoming ever more accessible regarding the quaternary or knowledge-based sector of economies, which has led to at least partial reasons why workers in that sector (e.g., Edward Snowden) have become outspoken proponents of increased privacy rights of citizenry. Of course, the information can be used by some to humiliate their opponents of the same sex, which is a means of intrasexual selection (e.g., via threatening to expose pictures of individuals' genitals). However, it can be used

circumcisions and subincisions, the roles of dominance and subordinance are questionable as well.

We may form another hypothesis concerning social and sexual domination: Botched circumcisions and subincisions occur more frequently and severely with males who tend to be more distantly related to their circumcisers or who are perceived to provide more competitiveness regarding attaining mates for sexual intercourse and reproduction. In relation to sexual selection, roles of circumcisions and subincisions are forms of sexual violence. This tends to be the case when they are performed by non-medical professionals or those who would face relatively minor consequences after occurrences of deaths and mutilations of other males' sex organs.

Regarding circumcisions, the role of violence is an ancient phenomenon. The first book of the Old Testament, *Genesis*, includes a chapter called "Revenge against Shechem," in which the role of rape, sexual selection, murder and one possible usage of traditional circumcisions are described. *The New Living Translation* of *Genesis* (34: 1–3 & 11) states:

> One day Dinah, the daughter of Jacob and Leah, went to visit some of the young women who lived in the area. 2 But when the local prince, Shechem son of Hamor the Hivite, saw Dinah, he seized her and raped her. 3 But then he fell in love with her, and he tried to win her affection with tender words… Then Shechem himself spoke to Dinah's father and brothers. "Please be kind to me, and let me marry her," he begged. "I will give you whatever you ask."

The behaviors that exert dominance and subordination are both demonstrated by Shechem, the rapist of Dinah, which illustrates the exertion of hard power by the male of an alien culture, and this man is seduced by the victim of his rape. The seduction is the exertion of soft power that makes Shechem susceptible. Shechem then pleads to Dinah's male family members to allow him to marry Dinah in return for what they ask of him. This shows the extent of the effectiveness of the soft power exerted by Dinah. There is also a need for the consent of the parents before marriage for Shechem. The father of Dinah, Jacob, learns after this about how Dinah had been dishonored and awaits his sons' advice on the matter. *The New Living Translation* of *Genesis* (34: 13–16) maintains:

---

by an individual against someone of the opposite sex to blackmail the person into sexual relations or even for multiple purposes of war.

> But since Shechem had defiled their sister, Dinah, Jacob's sons responded deceitfully to Shechem and his father, Hamor. 14 They said to them, "We couldn't possibly allow this, because you're not circumcised. It would be a disgrace for our sister to marry a man like you! 15 But here is a solution. If every man among you will be circumcised like we are, 16 then we will give you our daughters, and we'll take your daughters for ourselves. We will live among you and become one people" ...

The family of Dinah could exert domination over Shechem and his family via soft power. Their display of deceit allowed them to demand for the men of Shechem's group to be circumcised while proposing a mutual benefit for both of their groups. Leonard Glick (2005, p. 24) maintains that the circumcisions of alien adults are portrayed clearly as acts of aggression and exclusion insofar as the group that circumcises the other group is dominating, humiliating, and maiming them. *The New Living Translation* of *Genesis* (34: 24–26) continues:

> So all the men in the town council agreed with Hamor and Shechem, and every male in the town was circumcised. 25 But three days later, when their wounds were still sore, two of Jacob's sons, Simeon and Levi, who were Dinah's full brothers, took their swords and entered the town without opposition. Then they slaughtered every male there, 26 including Hamor and his son Shechem. They killed them with their swords, then took Dinah from Shechem's house and returned to their camp.

The use of deception by a different social group led uncircumcised males to undergo traditional circumcisions. This made them temporarily more vulnerable because of their soreness from the surgeries. It also provided temporary reductions or preventions of them from impregnating females. The exertion of hard power by Jacob's sons to avenge their sister involves the implementations of both soft and hard power to deceive Shechem and his group. They had to convince them to undergo a ritual circumcision that is atypical for adults. They murdered each of the males from Shechem's group and brought their sister home. *The New Living Translation* of *Genesis* (34: 27–29) reads:

> 27 Meanwhile, the rest of Jacob's sons arrived. Finding the men slaughtered, they plundered the town because their sister had been defiled there. 28 They seized all the flocks and herds and donkeys—everything they could lay their hands on, both inside the town and outside in the fields. 29 They looted all their wealth and plundered their houses. They also took all their little children and wives and led them away as captives.

The latter selections from the *Bible* clearly illustrate a different motivation of traditional circumcisions for males and competition for females. There is a motivation to maim outsiders slightly and to kill them later. Sexual selection is easily viewable from such tales and anthropological accounts of ritualistic circumcisions. Intrasexual selection is displayed in its most socially dominant form insofar as males are competing against one another to sexually reproduce or at least decrease other males' access and increase their own access to females. Intersexual selection is also displayed with the choice of Shechem to mate with Dinah.

Circumcisions function for Jacob's group for cleanliness, ritualistic, and religious purifications before adulthood. Circumcisions are beneficial to the extent that the males' sex organs are easier to keep clean. This reduces the risks of infections and diseases.

Since young men have strong sexual desires, convincing them to reduce or refrain from masturbation probably increases the amount of their vaginal sex performances as well as their number of offspring, to whom they can pass the taboo. Circumcisions tend to make masturbation more difficult but do not hinder vaginal sex. The latter factors increase the likelihood that male circumcisions are passed along as memes, involving transfers of cultural practices and taboos to others (Lynch, 1996; Blackmore, 1999, p. 135; Denniston, 2006, p. 3).

Yet circumcisions are also used as a clear sign of domination to subordinate male outsiders (Glick, 2005). Sociological and anthropological analyses can focus on the frequency and extent of mutiliation from botched circumcisions and the role of social dominance that coincides or stems from the focus of males on sex organs of other males for sexual competitiveness for females. This kind of violence is sexual. The roles of ageism, racism, and kinship are multifarious but, hypothetically speaking, are controlling factors.

Older males may tend to focus on dominating younger males. Minority racial group members may tend to have their sex organs more frequently mutilated when majority racial group members are their circumcisers. Kinship likely leads more frequently to successful circumcisions. African American males may undergo more mutilations of their sex organs from Anglo American circumcisers than they do from African American circumcisers.

The role of the law is not entirely clear. There is reason to view underdeveloped nations as failing to diminish the frequency of non-medical personnel from demanding and implementing ritualistic circumcisions as rites of passage. In the United States and the United Kingdom, unwanted circumcisions given to infants in hospitals have led to lawsuits. They are ordinarily successfully defended in court and do not typically lead to verdicts in favor of the plaintiffs that exceed the court costs significantly (Fox & Thomson, 2009). Most industrialized nations, except for the United States, United Kingdom, Canada, and Australia, do not have high rates of neonatal male circumcisions (ibid., p. 17).

An aspect of the sexual selection processes of mammals is viewed as males competing for females for the storage of their genes (i.e., during gestation periods) and the future spread and support of them (i.e., births, nursing, and rearing) rather than the death of the competing males. Yet the rituals for circumcisions in many cultures are known to competitively result in the decrease in the rates of sexual reproduction of younger males by older males. Many times they inadvertently lead to deaths.

These latter sorts of examples and sterilizations add complications to Darwin's (1859, pp. 87–89) definition of "sexual selection" as the struggle of males for the possessions of females, which do not result in the deaths of unsuccessful competitors. Some rituals that increase the chances of death can be the same rituals that are struggles of males for possession of females.

It appears likely that partial causes of wars concern perceptions of overpopulation regarding others who are more distantly related. Partial causes for the ends of wars concern the perceptions of the destructions of the other population, their resources, and the increased numbers of the victors' impregnations of females in the conquered society. That is, the conquered society is often socially and sexually dominated.

There are naturally occurring struggles for sexual selections of mates, especially amongst primates (e.g., monkeys, apes, and humans). Male intrasexual selection and female intrasexual selection are phenomena that may occur in different ways in provinces and nations, (e.g., the Women's Kingdom in the Chinese province of Yunnan). These selections are descriptive of the frequency of human sex-motivated actions of males to lower the chances of other males to spend time and sexual energy on selected females and of females to decrease the chances of other females to spend time and libido with selected males. Adults, adolescents, and even children "block" others of their same sex from interacting with selected potential mates. Blocking, discouraging and prevention are implemented via soft or hard power.

The law is traditionally a male-dominated institution regarding most legal systems insofar as judges, lawmakers, and law enforcement agents are primarily males. Prisoners are primarily males of subordinate groups (i.e., proportionately speaking, in comparison to their population sizes at large) based on race, age, and socio-economic class. Minority racial groups of males at peak ages for reproduction and fatherhood in the lower socio-economic classes are faced with greater risks. They are hypothetically greater targets of threats and violence resulting from intrasexual selection. One question from the F-problem that emerges from this is: To what extent does male and female intrasexual selection politically manifest and otherwise show itself within the law as an institution and system?

10 Conclusion

The concept of legality was argued to be ideologically placed in a binary code communicated via legal systems for multifarious purposes. Largely the purpose is to stabilize expectations of various peoples of societies. The legal system is an autopoietic system of communication that also tests itself via breaking down some of its own component parts to better control environmental factors hindering its efficiency as a societal system that brings order, stabilizes expectations and contributes to legal ideologies.

Systems test themselves via weakening chosen portions of themselves. Legal systems test themselves via increasing crime or the allowance of crime, for instance, during undercover operations. Clandestine law enforcement agents commit or allow crimes to occur to uncover the leadership of criminal organizations. Such tests on law enforcement systems allow feedback to provide analysts with better understandings of social causes of violence. One solution to reduce violence is offered with mock trials of judicial systems, unbeknownst to juries and jurists. They can lead groups to verdicts in ways that allow for predictions of unjustified and unethical decision-making.

These clandestine sorts of acts of legal systems and institutions are neither legal nor illegal. They are alegal acts. These acts challenge distinctions between legality and illegality.

The legal system imposes the binary distinction and encoding of "legality" and "illegality." This imposition impacts emotional states, decision-making processes, predictions, etc. of the masses. Legal obligations create social relations of intersubjectivity by means of multiple ways and forms of communication in multiple systems (e.g., political, mass media and legal).

The latter systems function to stabilize sets of expectations about elections, nationhood, currencies, and crimes. Intersubjective agreements about the existence, value, and desire for elected leaderships, border crossings, statehood, currencies, and criminal disobedience are foundations of the emergence of political, economic, and legal ideologies.

Legal ideologies are best viewed via the cultural anthropological analysis of a society's reactions to behaviors of people who act in "legal but socially unacceptable ways" and in "illegal but socially acceptable ways." The successful society with hegemonic powers enables a legal ideology to emerge. It reduces attention to such categorizations of behavior. Increased uses of propaganda from mass media systems do carry problems concerning the facilitations of escalations of violence from within and outside the society. Understanding social causes of violence requires more thorough investigations of the legal but unacceptable and illegal but acceptable ways of treating products and behaviors. Solutions come last.

The encoding of things as "legal and illegal" is paradigmatically problematic. So, the concept of "egal or alegality" must arise. The concept of alegality accounts for the impossibility of consistently distinguishing between certain acts that challenge the distinctions made between the legal and illegal acts. Legal and illegal acts are established via the legitimate authority. The more sophisticated process of encoding (i.e., legal, illegal, and alegal codes) develops later.

The original alegal act is the emergence of the legal system itself. Initially, the system lacks the authority, perceptions, and intersubjective agreements of legitimacy to encode its own foundational acts as legal ones during its emergence. Many other actions are alegal. These acts have not been illegalized. They include the number of immigrants from some nation into another nation. The maximum limit of immigrants legally permitted also changes. It depends on how many immigrate from each nation to the other.

Alegal acts include sales of homework, theses and dissertations. The latter gray market online services facilitate false authorship and fraud. They contribute to the destruction of education systems, especially ones with growing numbers of temporary workers and worsening conditions of labor contracts (e.g., temporary and part-time professors). Detriments to the education systems have negative impacts on legal and political systems and multiple other societal subsystems. Such injustices, already ever-present in education systems and rampant at universities and law schools, certainly motivate violence. Another social cause of violence comes from cheaters attaining education titles, finding their ways of being promoted in hierarchies of employment.

Another binary code arises for judicial verdicts in courts to coincide with the foundational code of the legal system. The legal system provides the exclusive verdicts of "guilty" and "not guilty." Most judiciary systems' binary codes are insufficient for consistent and systematic approaches to procedural justice. Most verdicts of guilty and not guilty are unaccompanied by a Scottish-type verdict of "not proven" and American verdicts of "guilty but insane," "not guilty but insane," etc. Such verdicts are infrequent. Infrequencies of verdicts demonstrate systemic flaws in the legal process of encoding and attributing judgments and blameworthiness. Lacking understandings of alternatives to the latter approaches and presenting false dichotomies (i.e., the insistence upon binary codes) in political, economic, and legal systems are reasons for arising political, economic, and legal ideologies.

Some social causes of social violence come from exposures and active and passive learning of violent behaviors. Youths learn to act violently from films, TV, music, music videos, computer, cellular phone and video games. These causes of social violence are preventable and measurable, ranging from increases in homicide rates to increases in pupils shoving, hitting and biting (Villani & Joshi, 2003, p. 235).

During the analysis of the second chapter, the social causes of violence caused by desperation, worsening social conditions, and social violence of mercenaries are discussed in relation to the September attacks of 2001 in the United States. One solution to reduce social violence is given that requires analysts to focus on the planners and others involved in the attacks and undermining their moral integrity according to their own moral standards. This solution could have been implemented if the deaths of the Arabs and Muslims in the attacks and the anguish of their families had been fittingly broadcast.

Another factor that provokes violence is a certain type of mischaracterization of how they self-identify. One solution to reducing social violence involves refraining from characterizing terrorists as "cowards" via broadcasts. Such mischaracterizations may provoke them to act in ways that are more domineering (Burke & Stets, 2009). Instead, attacking the moral integrity of their ideology in strategic ways facilitates reductive measures. This can be shown via broadcasting images of people that the terrorists impacted murderously and with whom they would most closely identify based on religion, ethnicity, sex, age, their family relations etc.

It is healthy to proceed from an understanding that the 21st century has involved vast social inequalities.[12] During the second decade of this century, the development of the finance and banking systems has led to the emergence of almost 2,000 billionaires who can subsist because of the relations of law. A few people in a country (e.g., the USA in this decade) can own more than the bottom half of the entire populace. Financial, political, and legal domination continue and play major roles regarding the development and sexual selection of the human species.

12 Harvard professor, Steven Pinker, argued that the percentage of extreme poverty, nuclear weapons, wars and autocracies of the world have decreased significantly from 1988 to 2017.

Social injustices come in many forms. They are identifiable via overrepresentations and underrepresentations of high and low-status groups, in many respects. The social causes of violence are best discovered via investigating injustices coinciding with the latter groups' interactions. Solutions to violence motivated by vengeance against prior injustices may appear obvious when investigating interactions of high and low-status groups.

A low-status group of people is identified by its greater presence as a percentage of the population of prisoners in society, especially private prisons, than the presence as a population in society at large. Low-status groups have far less major owners of properties or millionaires and billionaires in society. Low-status groups are victimized more often via higher status groups and victimized more frequently by the legal system and members of the legal institution, proportionately. Lower status groups are less likely to have the criminal justice system function to allow them the same chances of compensation after they have been victimized. The latter evidential facts impact the natural process of sexual selection for sexual reproduction within societies.

A society has various institutions and systems of domination. They focus on identifiable low-status groups to give these groups systematic disadvantages both within and outside of these systems and institutions. These include: (1) policing or law enforcement systems and institutions questioning, interrogating, searching, arresting, imposing soft and hard power more frequently and intensely against the lower status groups; (2) judicial systems and institutions convicting, giving harsher penalties for the same crimes, and sentences of death more frequently and intensely against lower status groups; and (3) law and policy-making or legislative systems, which pass laws that segregate for voting, as racist legal ideologies, etc. The latter system allows killings, warring, and even genocides in extreme cases, but also deportations, convictions without criminal trials etc., during states of emergency and via enacting such policies as plenary laws.

Another form of domination and subordination involves both the latter acts of the legal institution and legislation, verdicts, and enforcements of laws hindering intergroup and interracial sexual reproduction. Legal systems enhance social hierarchies and domination. They give subordinate groups systematic disadvantages regarding their population growth and birthrates. Some social causes of violence likely hinder subordinate groups' populations from reaching sizes of dominant groups.

There are psychosociological tendencies for people in society to support the status quo and to refrain from retaliating or speaking out in opposition to social injustices. These are system justificatory behaviors. Members of the legal institution undergo the same emotional states of insecurity as others in society. They are required to provide stability, too. With the increased emotional tensions of a crisis, whether financial, from attacks, or natural disasters, the members of the legal institution gain greater social approval. Their soft power allows them to escape legal consequences of using hard power more frequently, especially when it is implemented against low-status or targeted groups. Leadership gains larger amounts of attributions of legitimacy and authority. Thereafter, they can wield hard and soft power at more frequent and intense rates. Herein lies another social cause of violence.

The mass media system contributes to chaotic states of affairs via reporting controversies. The masses are generally informed via daily and weekly produced information outlets of the mass media system (i.e., as opposed to critical analyses that demand knowledge of theories, methodologies, and relevant statistical analyses). Masses are more prone to side with the leadership via opposing statements in disagreement with leadership.

Opposing the opponents of the shared leadership is an important type of system justificatory behavior. It intensifies during times of crisis. Dissenters who disagree with leaders are given disapproval during times of emergency. Ideology spreads and facilitates the exercise of domination via hard and soft power.

Importantly, the contribution of the political, mass media, and legal systems, especially during states of crisis, or perceived conditions of emergencies, intensifies in relation to the F-problem. Thereby natural processes of sexual selection and sexual reproduction are altered via ways of thinking. There are increases in support of certain social groups as opposed to others. The roles of intergroup exchanges, legal marriages, interracial interactions, and intergroup sexual reproductions may greatly diminish. High-ranking members of low-status groups and middle-ranking members of high-status groups are sometimes ideologically swayed from positive and constructive human interactions with each other. This is especially the case regarding sexual intimacy, marriage, and procreation.

The consequence is a homogenization of the human population within regions undergoing such social problems. This is exacerbated by increases in incarceration rates of males of lower status groups. Their chances are lowered regarding sexual reproductions.

Decreases in interracial and intergroup sexual reproductions contribute to the continuous formations of social group identities via a more incestuous process of in-group sexual reproductions. Legal and political systems are confronted with ever more challenging F-problems in many forms. Consider the ongoing increase in global human overpopulation and underpopulated political economies. Another form of the F-problem includes the length of the political terms of politicians. Terms conflict with long-term goals for societies to create better conditions for the people via increasing the quality of life, decreasing the birth rate of adolescents, increasing the role of family planning, etc.

Overall, human societies are conceptualized as hierarchical in ways that change over time from generation to generation. This greatly involves the inheritance of hard and soft power passed from ancestors to descendants. The inheritance of commodities (i.e., including money) directly involves laws that direct the transfer of money and other forms of property to descendants.

Inheritance facilitates the change in political and legal powers from ancestors to descendants. It exacerbates the F-problem in respect to the frequencies of procreation of different social groups. Inheritance makes a drastic and immeasurable impact on the sexual selection process. This can be interpreted as having a negative impact. The inheritance of descendants is an entirely arbitrary factor regarding the quality of offspring, the genes of the affluent, and genes of the non-affluent able to be procreated.

The sexual selection process is clandestinely observable and analyzable and largely involves intrasexual selection. With intrasexual selection, victimizations occur, especially during the search for mates and attempts to secure mates. The sexual selection process is further complicated in human populations because of a variety of sexualities ranging from promiscuity to prudery or celibacy, homosexuality, bisexuality, heterosexuality, bestiality, pedophilia, sadism, masochism, etc.

With legal systems, the initial task of reducing violence involves clarifications of victimizations, social dominance, sexual dominance, and the role of the legal institution regarding them as well as the F-problem. The latter task requires that considerable progress be made in relation to overcoming misconceptions that are facilitated by the legal, mass media, and political systems themselves. Overcoming these misconceptions requires advancements beyond ideologies and beyond legal minds.

Bibliography

Aamodt, M.G. & N.A. Stalnaker. (2001). "Police officer suicide: Frequency and officer profiles." In *Suicide and Law Enforcement*. D.C. Shehan, & J.I. Warren (Eds.) Washington, D.C.: Federal Bureau of Investigation.

Aamodt, M.G. & N.A. Werlick. (1999). "Police officer suicide: Frequency and officer profiles." Paper presented at the FBI Conference on Suicide and Law Enforcement, Quantico, VA.

Ackerman, B. (2004). "The emergency constitution." *Yale Law Journal*. 113, 5: 1029–91.

ACLU of Missouri. (2014). "Annual Report: October 1, 2013-October 31, 2014." American Civil Liberties Union of Missouri. 454 Whittier St. St. Louis, MO 63108 USA.

Agamben, G. (2004). *The state of exception*. Chicago: University of Chicago Press.

Aldridge, D. & K. St. John. (1991). "Adolescent and preadolescent suicide in Newfoundland and Labrador." *Canadian Journal of Psychiatry*. 36: 432–436.

Allen, Austin. (2006). *Origins of the Dred Scott Case: Jacksonian Jurisprudence and the Supreme Court, 1837–1857*. Athens: University of Georgia Press.

Amato, P.R. & R.A. Maynard. (2007). "Decreasing nonmarital births and strengthening marriage to reduce poverty." *The Future of Children*. 17, 2: 117–141.

Amir, Menachem. (1971). *Patterns of Forcible Rape*. Chicago: Chicago University Press.

Amnesty International. (2016). "A Year on China's Crackdown on Human Rights Lawyers." https://www.amnesty.org/en/latest/campaigns/2016/07/one-year-since-chinas-crackdown-on-human-rights-lawyers/ accessed May 20, 2017.

Anderson, Craig A. (1989). "Temperature and aggression: Ubiquitous effects of heat on occurrence of human violence." *Psychological Bulletin*. 106:74–96.

Anderson, William D. & Cliff H. Summers. (2007). "Neuroendocrine Mechanisms, Stress Coping Strategies, and Social Dominance: Comparative Lessons about Leadership Potential." *The ANNALS of the American Academy of Political and Social Science*. 614: 102–130.

Ashton, Paul & Amanda Petteruti. "Gaming the System: How the Political Strategies of Private Prison Companies Promote Ineffective Incarceration Policies." *Justice Policy Institute*. June 2011.

Associated Press. (2010). "Pa. accuses debt company of deceiving consumers." *Business Week: Financial News*. October 29.

Augustine-Adams, Kif. (2005). "The Plenary Power Doctrine After September 11." *UC Davis Law Review*. 38: 701–745.

Australian Bureau of Statistics. (2013). "Aboriginal and Torres Strait Islander population nearing 700,000." *3238.0.55.001 – Estimates of Aboriginal and Torres Strait Islander Australia*. August 30. Commonwealth of Australia. Accessed: http://www.abs.gov.au/ausstats/abs@.nsf/Latestproducts/3238.0.55.001Media%20Release1

June%202011?opendocument&tabname=Summary&prodno=3238.0.55.001&issue=June%202011&num=&view=.

Australian Bureau of Statistics. (2016). "Aboriginal and Torres Strait Island Characteristics." *4517.0–Prisoners in Australia, 2016*. Commonwealth of Australia. Accessed: http://www.abs.gov.au/ausstats/abs@.nsf/Lookup/by%20Subject/4517.0~2016~Main%20Features~Aboriginal%20and%20Torres%20Strait%20Islander%20prisoner%20characteristics~5.

Bakan, Joel. (2005). *The Corporation: The Pathological Pursuit of Profit and Power*. New York: Simon & Schuster.

Baldwin, Thomas. (1996). "There might be nothing." *Analysis*. 56.4: 231–38.

Bandara, N., J. Hettiaratchi, S. Wirasinghe & S. Pilapiiya (2007). "Relation of waste generation and composition to socio-economic factors: a case study." *Environmental Monitoring Assessment*. 135, 1–3:31–39.

Bandura, Albert. (1979). "The social learning perspective: Mechanisms of aggression." In H. Toch (Ed.), *Psychology of crime and criminal justice* (pp. 298–336). New York: Holt, Rinehart & Winston.

Bandura, Albert. (1988). "Social cognitive theory of moral thought and action." In W.M. Kutines and J.L. Gewirtz (Eds.), *Moral development: Advances in theory*. Hillsdale, NJ: Erlbaum.

Bargh, J.A. (1994). "The four horsemen of automaticity: Awareness, efficiency, intention, and control in social cognition." In J.R.S. Wyer & T.K. Srull (Eds.). *Handbook of social cognition*. (2nd ed., pp. 1–40). Hillsdale: Erlbaum.

Barnes, Lynn Diana. (2014). *Women's Reproductive Mental Health Across the Lifespan*. Heidelberg: Springer.

Baron-Cohen, S., A. M Leslie & U. Frith. (1985). "Does the autistic child have a 'theory of mind'?" *Cognition*. 21, 1: 37–46.

Basch, Charles E. (2011). "Teen Pregnancy and the Achievement Gap Among Urban Minority Youth." *Journal of School Health*. 81, 10: 614–618.

Bauman, Z. (1998) *Globalization: The human consequences*. Cambridge: Polity.

Beck, Heinrich. (1961). *Möglichkeit und Notwendigkeit. Eine Entfaltung der ontologischen Modalitätenlehre im Ausgang von Nicolai Hartmann*. (Possibility and Necessity. An Elaboration of the ontological teaching of modalities in the outcome of Nicolai Hartmann) Pullach, Germany: Berchmanskolleg.

Benjamin, Walter. (2007). "Critique of Violence (Reflections)." In B. Lawrence and A. Karim (Eds.), *On Violence: A Reader*. Durham: Duke University Press.

Bennett, J. 1991. "How to read minds in behavior: A suggestion from a philosopher." In A. Whiten (Ed.) *Natural Theories of Mind: Evolution, development and simulation of everyday mindreading* (pp. 97–108) Cambridge: Blackwell.

Bennett, Stephen E. (1973). "Consistency among the public's social welfare policy attitudes in the 1960s." *American Journal of Political Science*. 17: 544–570.

Berckenmeyer, Paul Ludolph. (1711). *Vermehrter curieuser Antiquarius, das ist, allerhand auserlesene geographische und historische Merckwürdigkeiten: so in denen europäischen Ländern zu finden.* (Increasingly curious antiquities, that is, all kinds of select geographical and historical noteworthiness: to find in these European lands) Hamburg: Benjamin Schillern.

Bergad, Laird W. (2007). *The Comparative Histories of Slavery in Brazil, Cuba, and the United States*. Cambridge, England: Cambridge University Press.

Berger, P. & T. Luckmann. (1991) *The Social Construction of Reality*. London and New York: Penguin Books.

Bergson, Henri. (1921). *La pensée et le mouvant. Articles et conférences datant de 1903 à 1923*. (Paris: Les Presses universitaires de France, 1969) Translation by Mabelle Andison, *The Creative Mind*, (New York, New York: Philosophical Library, 1946).

Berkman, Lisa F., Ichiro Kawachi & Maria M. Glymour. (2014). *Social Epidemiology*. New York: Oxford University Press.

Berkowitz, L. (1974). "Some determinants of impulsive aggression: Role of mediated associations with reinforcement for aggression." *Psychological Review*. 81: 165–176.

Berman, Paul Schiff. (2012). *Global Legal Pluralism: A Jurisprudence of Law Beyond Borders*. Cambridge: Cambridge University Press.

Bestelmeyer, P.E.G., B.C. Jones, L.M. DeBruine, A.C. Little & L.L.M. Welling. (2010). "Face aftereffects suggest interdependent processing of expression and sex and of expression and race." *Visual Cognition*. 18, 2: 255–274.

Bishop, George F. (1976). "The effect of education on ideological consistency." *Public Opinion Quarterly*. 40: 337–348.

Blackless, Melanie, Anthony Charuvastra, Amanda Derryck, Anne Fausto-Sterling, Karl Lauzanne, and Ellen Lee. (2000). "How sexually dimorphic are we? Review and synthesis." *American Journal of Human Biology*. 12: 151–166.

Blackmore, S. (1999). *The Meme Machine*. Oxford: Oxford University Press.

Blinder, Alan. (2015). "Alabama Judge Defies Gay Marriage Law." *The New York Times*. February 8, 2015.

Blitz, David. (1990). "Emergent Evolution and the Level Structure of Reality." in Paul Weingartner & Georg J.W. Dorn. *Studies on Mario Bunge's Treatise*. Amsterdam: Rodopi.

Blitz, David. (1992). *Emergent Evolution: qualitative novelty and the levels of reality*. New York: Kluwer Academic Publishers.

Bodley, John H. (2011). *Cultural Anthropology: Tribes, States and the Global System*. Lanham: AltaMira Press.

Bohlen, Celestine. (2001). "THINK TANK; In New War on Terrorism, Words Are Weapons, Too." *The New York Times*. September 29th.

Bonczar, Thomas P. (2003). "Prevalence of Imprisonment in the U.S. Population, 1974–2001." Bureau of Justice Statistics Special Report. U.S. Department of Justice: Office of Justice Programs.

Bondarenko, Dmitri M. (2006). *Homoarchy: A Principle of Culture's Organization. The 13th–19th Centuries Benin Kingdom As a Non-State Supercomplex Society*. Moscow: URSS.

Borgatta, Edgar F. & Rhonda J.V. Montgomery. (2000). *Encyclopedia of Sociology*. New York: Macmillan Reference.

Bourdieu, Pierre. (1997). *Pascalian Meditations*. Translation by Richard Nice. Stanford: Stanford University Press.

Bourget, David & David J. Chalmers. (2014). "What do philosophers believe?" *Philosophical Studies*. 170: 465–500.

Brant, William. (2012a). *Critique of Sarcastic Reason: The Epistemology of the Cognitive Neurological Ability Called "Theory of Mind" and Deceptive Reasoning*. Saarbrücken, Germany: Südwestdeutscher Verlag für Hochschulschriften.

Brant, William. (2012b). "Improving Global Education: Reducing Systematic Contract Cheating via Cyber Pseud-Epigraphy." Lecture given at the Fulbright Association 35th Annual Conference in London. October 20, 2012.

Brant, William A. (2013a). *Mental Imagery and Creativity: Cognition, Observation and Realization*. Saarbrücken, Germany: Akademikerverlag.

Brant, William A. (2013b). "Levelling the Analysis of Knowledge via Methodological Scepticism." *Logos and Episteme*. 4 (3): 293–304.

Brant, William A. (2016). "Improving Global Education: Conflicts of Interest. " Philosophy Dialogue Series. Texas State University—San Marcos. September 28th.

Brant, William A. & William A. Brant. (2012). "Engineering Ethics: Consciousness and Neuroethics." 1–77. Professional Development Hours Online: PDH Course G389. http://www.pdhonline.org/courses/g389/g389content.pdf (last access: 07.25.2015).

Brown, Emily. (2014). "Timeline: Michael Brown shooting in Ferguson, Mo." *USA Today*. December 2, 2014.

Brown v. Board of Education of Topeka, 347 U.S. (1954).

Bruhns, U. (1972). "Neuere Literatur zum Negerproblem in den USA Review." (New Literature about the Negro problem in the USA Review). *Jahrbuch für Amerikastudien*, Bd. 17: 240–248.

Buis, Emiliano J. (2011). "(En)acting law on stage: Time, Comic Rhetoric and Legislative Language in Aristophanes' *Acharnians* (vv. 676–718)." *Revue Internationale des Droits de L'Antiquité*. 3 Série Tome LVIII: pp. 13–38.

Buis, Emiliano J. (2014). "Law and Greek Comedy." Editors Michael Fontaine & Adele C. Scafuro in *The Oxford Handbook of Greek and Roman Comedy*. pp. 321–339. Oxford: Oxford University Press.

Bunge, Mario. (1979). *Treatise on Basic Philosophy, vol. 4, Ontology II: A World of Systems*. Dordrecht: Reidel Publishing Company.

Burawoy, M. (1979). *Manufacturing consent: Changes in the labor process under monopoly capitalism*. Chicago: University of Chicago Press.

Burke, Peter J. & Jan E. Stets. (2009). *Identity Theory*. Oxford: Oxford University Press.

Butke, P. & S.C. Sheridan. (2010). "An analysis of the relationship between weather and aggressive crime in Cleveland, Ohio." *Weather, Climate, and Society*. 2: 127–139.

Cabanac, Guillaume. (2014). "Bibliogifts in LibGen? A study of a text-sharing platform driven by biblioleaks and crowdsourcing." *Journal of the Association for Information Science and Technology*. 67, 4: 874–884.

Campbell, Donald T. (1969). "Reforms as experiments." *American Psychologist*. 24, 4: 409–429.

Campbell, Donald T. (1976). "Assessing the Impact of Planned Social Change." Paper no. 8. *The Occasional Paper Series*. Hanover: The Public Affairs Center, Dartmouth College.

Campbell, Gwyn. (2004). *The Structure of Slavery in Indian Ocean Africa and Asia*. London: Frank Cass.

Cantor, C.H. & M.P. Dunne. (1990). "Australian suicide data and the use of 'undetermined' death category (1968–1985)." *Australian and New Zealand Journal of Psychiatry* 24: 381–384.

Capozza, Dora & Rupert Brown. (2000). *Social Identity Processes: Trends in Theory and Research*. London: Sage Publications.

Carrington, P.J. (1998). "Factors affecting police diversion of young offenders: a statistical analysis." Report to the Solicitor General Canada. (accessed on 06.22.2013 http://www.sgc.gc.ca/epub/pol/e199802/e199802.htm).

Carson, D & R. Bull. (2003). *Handbook of Psychology in Legal Contexts*, 2nd Edition. John Wiley & Sons. West Sussex, England.

Casellas, Núria. (2011). *Legal Ontology Engineering: Methodologies, Modelling Trends, and the Ontology of Professional Judicial Knowledge*. Dordrecht, Germany: Springer.

Chakraborti, Neil & Jon Garland. (2015). *Hate Crimes: Impact, Causes & Responses*. 2nd Ed. Sage: Los Angeles.

Chamberlain, David B. (2009). "Delusional Psychologies of Circumcision and Civilization." In G. Denniston, F. Hodges & M. Milos. *Circumcision and Human Rights*. New York: Springer.

Chalmers, D. (1996). *The Conscious Mind: In Search of a Fundamental Theory*. New York and Oxford: Oxford University Press.

Chalmers, David. (2002). "Does Coceivability entail Possibility?" In T. Gendler & J. Hawthorne *Conceivability and Possibility*. Oxford University Press.

Cheal, David J. (1979). "Hegemony, Ideology and Contradictory Consciousness." *The Sociological Quarterly*. 20, 1: 109–117.

Cheek, F. & M. Miller. (1983). "The experience of stress for correction officers: a double-bind theory of correctional stress." *Journal of Criminal Justice*. 11, 2: 105–120.

Chesney-Lind, M. & R.G. Sheldon. (1998). *Girls: Delinquency and Juvenile Justice*. (2nd Ed). Pacific Grove: Wadsworth Publishing Company.

Chiao, J.Y. & V.A. Mathur. (2010). "Intergroup empathy: How does race affect empathic neural responses?" *Current Biology*. 20: R478–R480.

Chisholm, Hugh. (1911). *Encyclopædia Britannica: A Dictionary of Arts, Science, Literature and General Information*. Vol 15.8. (11th ed.). Cambridge: Cambridge University Press.

CIA World Factbook. (2017). www.ciaworldfactbook.org.

Cikara, M., M.M. Botvinick & S.T. Fiske. (2011). "Us v. them: Social identity shapes neural responses to intergroup competition and harm." *Psychological Science*. 22, 306–313.

Cikara, M., E.G. Bruneau, & R. Saxe. (2011). "Us and them: Intergroup failures of empathy." *Current Directions in Psychological Science*. 20, 149–153.

Cikara, M., R.A. Farnsworth, L.T. Harris & S.T. Fiske. (2010). "On the wrong side of the trolley track: Neural correlates of relative social valuation." *Social Cognitive and Affective Neuroscience*, 5, 404–413.

Cikara, Mina & Susan T. Fiske. (2012). "Stereotypes and Schadenfreude: Affective and physiological markers of pleasure at outgroups' misfortunes." *Social Psychological and Personality Science*. 3, 1: 63–71.

Cincotta, R.P. & R. Engelman. (2000). *Nature's place: human population and the future of biological diversity*. Washington, D.C.: Population Action International.

Cincotta, Richard P. & L.J. Gorenflo. (2011). *Human Population: Its Influences on Biological Diversity*. Berlin: Springer.

Cincotta, R.P., J. Wisnewski & R. Engelman. (2000). "Human population in the biodiversity hotspots." *Nature*. 404: 990–992.

Clarke, Randolph & Justin Capes. (2017). "Incompatibilist (Nondeterministic) Theories of Free Will." *The Stanford Encyclopedia of Philosophy* (Spring 2017 Edition). Edward N. Zalta (ed.), URL = <https://plato.stanford.edu/archives/spr2017/entries/incompatibilism-theories/>.

Clift, Eleanor. (2003). *Founding Sisters and the Nineteenth Amendment*. New York: Wiley.

Cohn, E.G. & J. Rotton. (1997). "Assault as a function of time and temperature: A moderator variable time-series analysis." *Journal Personality and Social Psychology*. 72: 1322–1134.

Cohrs, J., B. Moschner, J. Maes & S. Kielmann. (2005). "The motivational bases of right-wing authoritarianism and social dominance orientation: relations to values and attitudes in the aftermath of September 11, 2001." *Personality and Social Psychology Bulletin*. 31(10): 1425–34.

Coffin v. United States, 156 U.S. 432 (1895).

Conger, G.P. (1925). *The doctrine of levels. Journal of philosophy*. 22, 12: 309–321.

Converse, Phillip E. (1964). "The nature of belief systems in mass publics." pp. 206–261 In David Apter. *Ideology and Discontent*. New York: Free Press.

Cook, Phillip. (1980). "Research in Criminal Deterrence: Laying the Groundwork for the Second Decade." Editors Norval Morris & Michael Tonry. *Crime & Justice: An Annual Review of Research*. Chicago: University of Chicago Press.

Correll, J., B. Park, C.M. Judd & B. Wittenbrink. (2002). "The police officer's dilemma: Using ethnicity to disambiguate potentially hostile individuals." *Journal of Personality and Social Psychology*. 83: 1314–1329.

Correll, J., B. Park, C.M. Judd, B. Wittenbrink, M.S. Sadler & T. Keesee. (2007). "Across the thin blue line: Police officers and racial bias in the decision to shoot." *Journal of Personality and Social Psychology*. 92: 1006–1023.

Crooker, Richard & Zoran Pavlovic. (2010). *Cuba*. New York City: Chelsea House.

Crumley, Carole L. 2001. "Communication, Holism, and the Evolution of Sociopolitical Complexity." In *From Leaders to Rulers*, edited by Jonathan Haas, pp. 19–33. New York: Kluwer Academic.

Crumley, Carole L. (2006). "Historical Ecology: Integrated Thinking at Multiple Temporal and Spatial Scales." Editors Alf Hornborg & Carole Crumley in *The World System and the Earth System: Global Socioenvironmental Change and Sustainability Since the Neolithic*. Walnut Creek: Left Coast Press.

Dalbert, Claudia, Isaac Lipkus, Hedvig Sallay & Irene Goch. (2001). "A just and an unjust world: structure and validity of different beliefs." *Personality and Individual Differences*. 30(4): 561–577.

Darwin, Charles. (1859). *On the origin of species by means of natural selection, or the preservation of favoured races in the struggle for life*. London: John Murray.

David, Rene & John Brierley. (1985). *Major Legal Systems in the World Today*. London: Steven & Sons.

DeCremer, D. & T. Tyler. (2005). "Managing group behavior: the interplay between procedural justice, sense of self, and cooperation." In Advances in *Experimental Social Psychology*, ed. M Zanna, pp. 151–218. New York: Academic.

De Brigard, Felipe. (2014). "Is memory for remembering? Recollection as a form of episodic hypothetical thinking." *Synthese*. 191, 2: 155–185.

Deetz, S. & D.K. Mumby. (1985). "Metaphors, information, and power." In B. Ruben (Ed.), *Information and Behavior*. (Vol. 1, pp. 369–386). New Brunswick, NJ: Transaction.

Deetz, S. & D.K. Mumby. (1990). "Power, discourse, and the workplace: Reclaiming the critical tradition." In J. Anderson (Ed.), *Communication Yearbook*. (Vol. 13, pp. 18–47). Newbury Park, CA: Sage.

Denniston, George, Pia G. Gallo, Frederick Hodges, Marilyn F. Milos & Franco Viviani. (2006). *Bodily Integrity and the Politics of Circumcision: Culture, Controversy and Change*. New York: Springer.

Denno, Deborah W. (2017). "Concocting Criminal Intent." *Georgetown Law Journal*. 105: 323–378.

Denyer, Simon. (2015). "Without corruption, some ask, can the Chinese Communist Party function?" *The Washington Post*. February 11, 2015.

Der Spiegel. (2015). "21-jähriger Patient: Chirurgen melden erste erfolgreiche Penis-Transplantation." (21 year old patient: surgeons announce first successful penis transplantation). *Der Spiegel*. March 13th.

Der Spiegel. (2013a). "Südafrika: Beschneidungen fordern 30 Todesopfer." (South Africa: Circumcisions claim 30 victims' deaths). *Der Spiegel*. July 7th.

Der Spiegel. (2013b). "Mordermittlungen in Südafrika: Bis zu 23 Tote bei Beschneidungen." (Murder investigations in South Africa: Up to 23 deaths from circumcisions). *Der Spiegel*. May 17th.

Dillon, Conor. (2013). "Tempting PhDs lead politicians into plagiarism." *Deutsche Welle*. February 13th.

Di Viggiano, Pasquale Luigi. (2011). "Evolutionary Forms of Law and Social Systems." *The Juridical Current*. 45: 102–112.

Doris, John & Stephen Stich. "Moral Psychology: Empirical Approaches." *The Stanford Encyclopedia of Philosophy*. (Winter 2011 Edition). Edward N. Zalta (ed.), URL = <http://plato.stanford.edu/archives/win2011/entries/moral-psych-emp/>.

Douglass, Frederick. (1855). *My Bondage and My Freedom*. New York: Miller, Orton & Mulligan.

Douglass, Frederick. (1892). *Life and Times of Frederick Douglass*. Boston: De Wolfe & Fiske Co.

Dubois, Didier & Henri Prade. (2001). "Possibility Theory, Probability Theory and Multiple-valued Logics: A Clarification." *Annals of Mathematics and Artificial Intelligence* 32:35–66.

Duff, P. (1999). "The Scottish criminal jury: A very peculiar institution." *Law & Contemporary Problems* 62: 173–201.

Dunlap, Riley E. & Andrew K. Jorgenson. (2012). "Environmental Problems." *The Wiley-Blackwell Encyclopedia of Globalization*. http://onlinelibrary.wiley.com/doi/10.1002/9780470670590.wbeog174/full.

Duttge, Gunnar. (2009). *Das Ich und sein Gehirn: Die Herausforderung der neurobiologischen Forschung für das (Straf-)Recht*. (*The ego and its brain: the challenge of neurobiological research for (criminal) law*). Göttinger Studien zu den Kriminalwissenschaften. Göttingen: Universitätsverlag Göttingen.

Dutton, Donald. (2007). *The Psychology of Genocide, Massacres, and Extreme Violence: Why "Normal" People Come to Commit Atrocities*. Westport, USA: Praeger Security International.

Dworkin, Ronald. (2011). *Justice for Hedgehogs*. Cambridge: Harvard University Press.

Dyzenhaus, David. (2006). *The Constitution of Law: Legality in a Time of Emergency*. Cambridge: Cambridge University Press.

Dziadkowiec, Jakub. (2011). "The Layered Structure of the World in N. Hartmann's Ontology and a Processual View." in Roberto Poli, Carlo Scognamiglio & Frederic Tremblay. *The Philosophy of Nicolai Hartmann*. Berlin: Walter de Gruyter.

Eckstein, Harry. (2004). "Theoretical Approaches to Explaining Collective Political Violence." in John Jost and Jim Sidanius *Political Psychology*. New York: Psychology Press.

Eisler, Rudolf. (1904). *Wörterbuch der philosophischen Begriffe*. (Dictionary of philosophical concepts). Berlin: E.S. Mittler und Sohn.

Eisler, Rudolf. (1912). *Philosophen-Lexikon; Leben, Werke und Lehren der Denker*. (Philosophers-Lexicon; Life, Work and Teachings of the Thinkers) Berlin: E.S. Mittler und Sohn.

Ellis, George F.R. (2004). "True Complexity and its Associated Ontology." in John D. Barrow, Paul C.W. Davies & Charles L. Harper Jr. *Science and Ultimate Reality, Quantum Theory, Cosmology and Complexity*. Cambridge: Cambridge University Press.

Emanuel, A.S. (1989). "Guilty but mentally ill verdicts and the death penalty: an eighth amendment analysis." *North Carolina Law Review*. 37.

Epictetus. (1877). *The Discourses; with the Encheiridion and Fragments*. Translation by George Long. London, England: George Bell and Sons.

Farnsworth, Allan. (2010). *An Introduction to the Legal System of the United States*. New York: Oxford University Press.

Fatovic, Clement. (2009). *Outside the Law: Emergency and Executive Power*. Baltimore: The John Hopkins University Press.

Feibleman, James K. (1954). "Theory of integrative levels." *British journal for the philosophy of science*. 5, 17: 59–66.

Feige, Edward L. (1989). *The underground economies: Tax evasion and information distortion*. Cambridge: Cambridge University Press.

Feldbrugge, F.J.M. (1989). "The Soviet second economy in a political and legal perspective." in E. Feige *The underground economies: Tax evasion and information distortion*. Cambridge: Cambridge University Press.

Ferro, Marc. (1997). *Colonization: A Global History*. London: Routledge.

Field, John O. & Ronald E. Anderson. (1969). "Ideology in the public's conceptualization of the 1964 election." *Public Opinion Quarterly*. 33: 380–398.

Finer, L.B. & S.K. Henshaw. (2006). "Disparities in rates of unintended pregnancy in the United States, 1994 and 2001." Perspective Sexual Reproductive Health. 38: 90–96.

Finn, J.E. (1991). *Constitutions in crisis: Political violence and the rule of law*. Oxford: Oxford University Press.

Fitzgerald, Jacqueline. (2009). "Why are indigenous imprisonment rates rising?" *Crime and Justice Statistics: NSW Bureau of Crime and Statistics Research*. Issue paper no. 41: 1–6.

Fogg, Ally. (2014). "The death and deformity caused by male circumcision in Africa can't be ignored." *The Guardian*. August 25th.

Forbes, Graeme. (1995). "Realism and Skepticism: Brains in a Vat Revisited." *The Journal of Philosophy*. 92, 4: 205–222.

Foskett, Douglas J. (1970). "Classification for a general index language : a review of recent research by the Classification research group." London: Library Association.

Fox, Marie & Michael Thomson. (2009). "Reconsidering 'Best Interests': Male Circumcision and the Rights of the Child." In G. Denniston, F. Hodges & M. Milos. *Circumcision and Human Rights*. New York: Springer.

Franke-Ruta, Garance. (2009). "Palin flirts with Obama birth certificate question." *The Washington Post*. December 4, 2009.

Frederick, Howard H. (1987). "Electronic Penetration." in Thomas S. Walker, ed., *Reagan versus the Sandinistas*. Boulder: Westview.

Freedman, L. (2003). "The concept of security." In M. Hawkesworth (ed.), *Encyclopedia of government and politics*. London: Routledge.

Fromm, Erich. (1955). *The Sane Society*. London: Routledge.

Fulmer, Gilbert. (1978). "The Concept of the Supernatural." *Analysis*. 37, 3: 113–116.

Gadamer, Hans-Georg. (1990). *Gasammelte Werke Band 1: Hermeneutik I: Wahrheit und Methode: Gründzuge einer philosophischen Hermeneutik*. (Collected Works Volume 1: Hermeneutics I: Truth and Method: Fundamentals of philosophical hermeneutics). Tübingen: J.C.B. Mohr (Paul Siebeck).

Gaines, B.R. & L.J. Kohout. (1975). "Possible automata." *Proceedings of the International Symposium on Multiple-Valued Logic*, University of Indiana, Bloomington, IN: 183–196.

Gallant, Kenneth S. (2009). *The Principle of Legality in International and Comparative Criminal Law*. Cambridge: Cambridge University Press.

Gardiner, J.A. (1969). *Traffic and the police: Variations in law enforcement policy*. Cambridge: Harvard University Press.

Garner, Bryan A. (2004). *Black's Law Dictionary*. 8th ed. St. Paul: West.

Gendler, T.S. & J. Hawthorne. (2002). *Conceivability and possibility*. Oxford, England: Oxford University Press.

Gershenson, Carlos. (2015). "Requisite variety, autopoiesis, and self-organization." *Kybernetes*. 44 (6/7): 866–873.

Gerstenfeld, P.B. (2013). *Hate Crimes: Causes, Controls and Controversies*. 3rd ed. London: Sage.

Giddens, Anthony. (1971). *Capitalism and Modern Social Theory*. Cambridge: Cambridge University Press.

Gifford, Donald. (1997). *Understanding the Australian Legal System*. Sydney and London: Cavendish Publishing.

Glad, John. (2008). *Future Human Evolution: Eugenics in the Twenty-First Century*. Schuylkill Haven: Hermitage Publishers.

Glaze, Lauren E., William J. Sabol, Todd D. Minton, Ann E. Carson, Paige Harrison & Sheri Simmons. (2011). "Correctional Populations in the United States, 2010." U.S. Department of Justice. *Bureau of Justice Statistics*. December edition.

Glenn, Patrick H. (2006). "Aims of comparative law." in Jan M. Smits Elgar *Encyclopedia of Comparative Law*. Cheltenham: Edward Elgar.

Glick, Leonard B. (2005). *Marked in Your Flesh: Circumcision from Ancient Judea to Modern America*. Oxford: Oxford University Press.

Goebel, Nicole. (2011). "Second German politician resigns over plagiarism allegation." *Deutsche Welle*. Editor: Chuck Penfold. May 5th.

Goh, Esther C.L. (2011). *China's One-Child Policy and Multiple Caregiving: Raising little suns in Xiamen*. London: Routledge.

Graham, Jesse, Brian Nosek, Jonathan Haidt, Ravi Iyer, Spassena Koleva & Peter Ditto. (2011). "Mapping the Moral Domain." *Journal of Personality and Social Psychology*. 101, 2: 366–385.

Gray, Christopher B. (2010). *The Methodology of Maurice Hauriou*. Amsterdam, The Netherlands: Rodopi.

Grayson, George W. (2009). *Mexico: Narco-Violence and a Failed State?*. New Brunswick: Transaction Publishers.

Green, E., Kirk Heilbrun, W. Fortune & M. Nietzel (2007). *Wrightman's Psychology and the Legal System*, 6th Edition. Thomas Wadsworth. Belmont, California.

Greene, Edie, Kirk Heilbrun, William Fortune & Michael Nietzel. (2007). *Psychology and the Legal System*. Belmont: Thomson Higher Education.

Greenwald, A.G. & L.H. Krieger. (2006). "Implicit bias: Scientific foundations." *California Law Review*. 94: 945–967.

Greenwald, A.G., M.A. Oakes & H.G. Hoffman. (2003). "Targets of discrimination: Effects of race on responses to weapons holders." *Journal of Experimental Social Psychology*. 39: 399–405.

Greenwald, Glenn. (2009). *Drug Decriminalization in Portugal: Lessons for Creating Fair and Successful Drug Policies*. Washington D.C.: Cato Institute.

Grewe, Wilhelm G. (1982). "*Peace Treaties*." in Rudolf Bernhardt ed. *Encyclopedia of Public International Law: 4 Use of Force, War and Neutrality, Peace Treaties*. Amsterdam: North-Holland Publishing Company.

Grimm, Patrick. (2008). "Philosophy of Mind: Brains, Consciousness and Thinking Machines." The Great Courses: Audio Cassette; Publisher: The Teaching Company.

Guerin, Frances. (2005). *A Culture of Light: Cinema and Technology in 1920s Germany*. Minneapolis and London: University of Minnesota Press.

Haass, Richard N. (1998). *Economic Sanctions and American Diplomacy*. New York: Council on Foreign Relations Press.

Habermas, Jürgen. (1975). *Legitimation Crisis*. Boston: Beacon Press.

Haidt, Jonathan. (2007). "The new synthesis in moral psychology." *Science*. 316: 998–1002.

Haidt, Jonathan & Jesse Graham. (2007). "When morality opposes justice: Conservatives have moral intuitions that liberals may not recognize." *Social Justice Research*. 20: 98–116.

Haidt, Jonathan & Matthew A. Hersh. (2001). "Sexual morality: The cultures and emotions of conservatives and liberals." *Journal of Applied Social Psychology*. 31: 191–221.

Haidt, J., F. Bjorklund & S. Murphy. (2000). *Moral dumbfounding: When intuition finds no reason*. Unpublished manuscript, University of Virginia.

Haidt, J., S. Koller & M. Dias. (1993). "Affect, culture, and morality, or is it wrong to eat your dog?" Journal of Personality and Social Psychology, 65, 613–628.

Hallaq, Wael B. (1997). *A History of Islamic Legal Theories*. Cambridge: Cambridge University Press.

Hamilton, B.E., J.A. Martin & S.J. Ventura. (2007). "Births: preliminary data for 2006." *National Vital Statistics Report*. 56, 1: 1–18.

Harman, Gilbert. (1978). "Studying the chimpanzee's theory of mind." *Behavioral and Brain Science*, 4: 576–577.

Harman, Gilbert. (1999). "Moral Philosophy Meets Social Psychology: Virtue Ethics and the Fundamental Attribution Error." *Proceedings of the Aristotelian Society*. 99: 315–331.

Harris, David A. (1999). "Driving while black: racial profiling on our nation's highways." An American Civil Liberties Union Special Report. *Minnesota Law Review*. 84: 265–326.

Harris, Richard J. (2004). *A Cognitive Psychology of Mass Communication*. Mahwah: Lawrence Erlbaum.

Hart, H.L.A. (1994). *The Concept of Law*. 2nd ed. Oxford: Clarendon Press.

Hartmann, Nicolai. (1912). "Systematische Methode." (Systematic methods) *Logos*. 3 (2): 22–60.

Hartmann, Nicolai. (1921). *Grundzüge einer Metaphysik der Erkenntnis*. (Basics of a metaphysics of knowledge). Berlin, Germany: Walter de Gruyter.

Hartmann, Nicolai. (1931). *Zum Problem der Realitätsgegebenheit*. (Toward the problem of the givenness of reality). *Philosophische Vorträge*, veröffentlicht von der Kant-Gesellschaft, 32. Nördlingen: C.H. Beck'schen Buchdruckerei and Berlin: Pan-Verlagsgesellschaft.

Hartmann, Nicolai. (1935). *Zur Grundlegung der Ontologie*. (Toward a grounding of the ontology: Volume 1 of 4 of Ontology) Berlin: Walter de Gruyter.

Hartmann, Nicolai. (1936/1977). *Der philosophische Gedanke und seine Geschichte*. (The philosophical thought and its history). Stuttgart: Reclam.

Hartmann, Nicolai. (1937). "Der Megarische Und Der Aristotelische Möglichkeitsbegriff. Ein Beiträg Zur Geschichte Des Ontologischen Modalitätsproblems." (The Megaric and the Aristotelian concept of possibility. A contribution to the history of the ontological problem of modality). Abhandlungen der Preussichen Akademie der Wissenschaften, Philosophisch-Historische Klasse 10.

Hartmann, Nicolai. (1938). *Möglichkeit und Wirklichkeit*. (Possibility and actuality: Volume 2 of 4 of Ontology) Berlin: Walter de Gruyter.

Hartmann, Nicolai. (1940). *Der Aufbau der realen Welt: Grundriß der allgemeinen Kategorienlehre*. (The structure of the real world: layout of the general teaching of categories: Volume 3 of 4 of Ontology) Berlin: Walter de Gruyter.

Hartmann, Nicolai. (1942). *Neue Wege der Ontologie*. (New ways of ontology). Berlin: Walter de Gruyter.

Hartmann, Nicolai. (1943). *Systematische Philosophie*. (Systematic philosophy). Stuttgart: Kohlhammer.

Hartmann, Nicolai. (1950). *Philosophie der Natur: Abriss der speziellen Kategorienlehre*. (Philosophy of nature: brief outline of the specific teaching of categories: Volume 4 of 4 of Ontology) Berlin: Walter de Gruyter.

Hartmann, Nicolai. (2013). *Possibility and Actuality*. Trans. Alex Scott & Stephanie Adair. Berlin: Walter de Gruyter.

Hartung, Gerald & Matthias Wunsch. (2014). "Studien zur Neuen Ontologie und Anthropologie." (Studies toward the new ontology and anthropology) Berlin: Walter de Gruyter.

Havocscope. (2017). "Havocscope Global Black Market Rankings." http://www.havocscope.com/products/ranking/ Copyright © 2017 Havocscope, LLC. (Last accessed 05.18.2017).

Hermann, Donald. (1983). *The insanity defense: philosophical, historical, and legal perspectives*. Springfield, Illinois: Thomas.

Hasday, Judy L. (2007). *The Civil Rights Act of 1964: An End to Racial Segregation*. New York: Infobase Publishing.

Hebble, P.W. (1971). "Development of elementary school children's judgment of intent." *Child Development*. 42: 583–588.

Heil, John. (1998). "Skepticism and Realism." *American Philosophical Quarterly*. 35, 1: 57–72.

Helgeson, Vicki S. & Kelly G. Shaver. (2006). "Presumption of Innocence: Congruence Bias Induced and Overcome." *Journal of Applied Social Psychology*. 20, 4: 276–302.

Hennig, Willi. (1950). *Grundzüge einer Theorie der Phylogenetischen Systematik.* (Grounding of a theory of phylogenetic systematics). Berlin: Deutscher Zentralverlag.

Henrich, J., S. Heine & A. Norenzayan. (2010). "The weirdest people in the world." *Behavioral and Brain Sciences.* 33, 2–3: 61–83.

Herman, Edward S. & Noam Chomsky. (1988). *Manufacturing Consent: The Political Economy of the Mass Media.* New York: Pantheon Books.

Hlady, W.G. & J.P. Middaugh. (1988). "The underrecording of suicides in state and national records, Alaska, 1983–1984." *Suicide and Life-Threatening Behavior.* 18: 237–244.

Holding, T.A. & B.M. Barraclough. (1978). "Undetermined deaths-suicide or accident?" *British Journal of Psychiatry.* 133: 542–549.

Holmes, Catherine B. (2012). "Quran Burning and Religious Hatred: A Comparison of American International, and European Approaches to Freedom of Speech." *Washington University Global Studies Law Revue.* 11, 2: 459–481.

Homans George. (1958). "Social Behavior as Exchange." *American Journal of Sociology.* 63 (6): 597–606.

Hoornweg, Daniel & Perinaz Bhada-Tata. (2012). "What a Waste: A Global Review of Solid Waste Management." The World Bank Urban Development and Local Government Unit. No. 15. https://siteresources.worldbank.org/INTURBANDEVELOPMENT/Resources/336387-1334852610766/What_a_Waste2012_Final.pdf.

Hooton, Earnest A. (1946). *Up from the Ape.* The Macmillan Company: New York.

Hsu, S.M. & A.W. Young. (2004). "Adaptation effects in facial expression recognition." *Visual Cognition.* 11: 871–899.

Hughes, Louis. (1897). *Thirty Years a Slave: From Bondage to Freedom.* Milwaukee: South Side Printing Company.

Hughes, Caitlin & Alex Stevens. (2007). *The Effects of Decriminalization of Drug Use in Portugal.* London: The Beckley Foundation.

Hughes, G.E. and M.J. Cresswell. (1968). *An Introduction to Modal Logic.* Methuen, London.

Ingram, A. (1994). *A political theory of rights.* Oxford: Clarendon.

Jacobs, Harrison. (2015). "Here's The Ridiculous Loot That's Been Found With Corrupt Chinese Officials." *Business Insider.* January 22, 2015.

Jacobs, Ronald N. (2004). *Race, Media and the Crisis of Civil Society: From Watts to Rodney King.* Cambridge: Cambridge University Press.

Jaquet, E., G. Rhodes & W.G. Hayward. (2007). "Opposite aftereffects for Chinese and Caucasian faces are selective for social category information and not just physical face differences." *Quarterly Journal of Experimental Psychology.* 60: 1457–1467.

Jaspers, Karl & Kurt Rossmann. (1961). *Die Idee der Universität: Für die Gegenwärtige Situation.* (The idea of the university: for the present situation) Berlin: Springer-Verlag.

Jeffreys-Jones, R. (1979). "Theories of American Labour Violence." *Journal of American Studies*. 13, 2: 245–264.

Jepperson, Ronald & John Meyer. (2011). "Multiple Levels of Analysis and the Limitations of Methodological Individualisms." *Sociological Theory*. 29, 1: 54–73.

Jernigan, A.S. (2000). "Driving while black: Racial profiling in America." *Law and Psychology Review*. 24: 127–138.

Jones, Trevor & Tim Newburn. (2005). "Comparative Criminal Justice Policy-Making in the United States and the United Kingdom: The Case of Private Prisons." *The British Journal of Criminology*. 45, 1: 58–80.

Jost, John. (2001). "System Justification Theory as Compliment, Complement, and Corrective to Theories of Social Identification and Social Dominance." Research Paper Series. Research Paper No. 1672. Stanford: Stanford University.

Jost, J.T., M.R. Banaji & B.A. Nosek. (2004). "A decade of system justification theory: Accumulated evidence of conscious and unconscious bolstering of the status quo." *Political Psychology*. 25: 881–919.

Jost, John T., Aaron C. Kay & Hulda Thorisdottir. (2009). *Social and Psychological Bases of Ideology and System Justification*. Oxford: Oxford University Press.

Jost, J.T. & J. van der Toorn. (2012). "System justification theory." In P.A.M. van Lange, A.W. Kruglanski, & E.T. Higgins (Eds.). *Handbook of theories of social psychology*. London: Sage.

Jost, John T. & Jim Sidanius. (2004). *Political Psychology*. New York: Psychology Press.

Kane, Robert. (1996). "Responsibility, Luck, and Chance: Reflections on Free Will and Indeterminism." *Journal of Philosophy*. 96: 217–40.

Kang, J. (2005). "Trojan horses of race." *Harvard Law Review*. 118: 1489–1593.

Kant, Immanuel. 1952. *The Critique of Pure Reason*. Publisher, William Benton Encyclopedia Britannica, Inc. Chicago, Illinois.

Kant, Immanuel. (1781). *Kritik der reinen Vernuft*. Johann Friedrich Hartknoch. Riga.

Karniol, R. (1978). "*Children's use of intention cues in evaluating behavior.*" *Psychological Bulletin*. 85: 76–85.

Kassin, S.M. & L.S. Wrightsman. (1988). *The American Jury on Trial*. New York: Hemisphere.

Katsenelinboigen, A. (1977). "Coloured Markets in the Soviet Union." Soviet Studies. 29, 1: 62–85.

Kearney, Richard. (2003). *Continental Philosophy in the 20th Century*. Routledge. New York.

Keeley, L.H. (1996). *War before civilization: The myth of the peaceful savage*. New York: Oxford University Press.

Kelly, R.C. (2005). "*The evolution of lethal intergroup violence.*" *Proceedings of the National Academy of Sciences*. 102: 15294–15298.

Kelsen, Hans. (1930). *Der Staat als Integration: eine prinzipielle Auseinandersetzung.* (The state as integration: a principle examination). Vienna: Springer.

Kelsen, Hans. (1939). "Die Enstehung des Kausalgesetzes aus dem Vergeltungsprinzip." (The emergence of the law of causation out of the principle of retributive justice). *Erkenntnis*. 8, 1: 69–130.

Kelsen, Hans. (1943). *Society and Nature: A Sociological Inquiry*. Chicago: University of Chicago Press.

Kent, Graeme. (2013). *The Great White Hopes: The Quest to Defeat Jack Johnson*. Stroud: The History Press.

Kerruish, Valerie. (1991). *Jurisprudence as Ideology*. London: Routledge.

Keswani, Priscilla Schuster. (1996). "Hierarchies, Heterarchies, and Urbanization Processes: The View from Bronze Age Cyprus." *Journal of Mediterranean Archaeology* 9: 211–50.

Kim, Jaegwon. (2006). "Emergence: Core ideas and issues." *Synthese*. 151: 547–559.

Kirsher, T., J. Nelson, & H. Burdo. (1985). "The autopsy as a measure of the accuracy of the death certificate." *New England Journal of Medicine*. 313: 1263–1269.

Kitsuse, J. & A. Cicourel. (1963). "A note on the use of official statistics." *Social Problems*. 11: 131–139.

Kleck, G. (1988). "Miscounting suicides." *Suicide and Life-Threatening Behavior*. 18: 219–36.

Klein, P. (2008). "Skepticism." In E. Zalta (Ed.), The Stanford encyclopedia of philosophy. http:// plato.stanford.edu/archives/fall2008/entries/skepticism/.

Köbler, Gerhard. (1995). *Deutsches Etymologisches Wörterbuch*. (German Etymological Dictionary) Mohr, Tübingen.

Kremer, Michael. (1993). "Population Growth and Technological Change: One Million B.C. to 1990." *Quarterly Journal of Economics*. August: 681–716.

Kubey, R. & M. Csikszentmihalyi. (1990). *Television and the quality of life: How viewing shapes everyday experience*. Hillsdale: Lawrence Erlbaum Associates.

Kugler, Matthew B., Joel Cooper & Brian A. Nosek. (2010). "Group-Based Dominance and Opposition to Equality Correspond to Different Psychological Motives." *Social Justice Research*. 23: 117–155.

Lammers, Joris & Diederik Stapel. (2011). "Racist biases in legal decisions are reduced by a justice focus." *European Journal of Social Psychology*. 41: 375–387.

Lane, K.A., J. Kang & M.R. Banaji. (2007). "Implicit social cognition and law." *Annual Review of Law and Social Science*. 3: 427–451.

Lansford, Tom. (2004). "Australian Aboriginal." In F. Salamone. *Encyclopedia of Religious Rites, Rituals, and Festivals*. New York: Routledge.

Laurin, K., S. Shepherd & A.C. Kay. (2010). "Restricted emigration, system inescapability, and defense of the status quo: System-justifying consequences of restricted exit opportunities." *Psychological Science*. 21: 1075–1082.

Lazarus, R.S. (1966). *Psychological Stress and the Coping Process*. New York: McGraw-Hill.

Lee, Trymaine. (2014). "Eyewitness to Michael Brown shooting recounts his friend's death." *MSNBC: Microsoft and the National Broadcasting Company*. August 12, 2014. Updated August 19, 2014.

Leon, Mark. (1988). "Realism, Skepticism (and Empiricism)." *Metaphilosophy*. 19, 2: 143–157.

Leonetti, Donna L. & Dilip C. Nath. (2009). "Age at First Reproduction and Economic Change in the Context of Differing Kinship Ecologies." *American Journal of Human Biology*. 21: 438–447.

Lerner, K. Lee, Brenda Wilmoth Lerner & Adrienne Wilmoth Lerner. (2006). *Human and Civil Rights: Essential Primary Sources*. Detroit: Thomson Gale.

Leung, Ambrose, Frances Woolley, Richard E. Tremblay & Frank Vitaro. (2005). "Who gets caught?: Statistical discrimination in law enforcement." *Journal of Beahavioral and Experimental Economics*. 34, 3: 289–309.

Levin, S.L. (1996). *A social psychological approach to understanding intergroup attitudes in the United States and Israel.* Unpublished doctoral dissertation. Department of Psychology. UCLA.

Levin, S.L. (2004). "Perceived group status differences and the effects of gender, ethnicity, and religion on social dominance orientation." *Political Psychology*. 25: 31–48.

Lewin, Kurt. (1951). *Field Theory in Social Science: Selected Theoretical Papers*. Harper, New York.

Lewis, David K. (1986). *On the Plurality of Worlds*. Oxford, England: Blackwell Publishing.

Lindahl, H. (2008). "Border Crossings by Immigrants: Legality, Illegality, and Alegality." *Res Publica*. 14:117–135.

Lipschultz, Jeremy H. (2008). *Broadcast and Internet Indecency: Defining Free Speech*. New York: Routledge.

Litman, R.E., T. Curphey, E.S. Shneidman, N.L. Farberow, & N. Tabachnick. (1963). "Investigations of equivocal suicides." *Journal of the American Medical Association*. 184: 924–929.

Little, A.C., DeBruine, L.M., Jones, B.C. & Waitt, C. (2008). "Category contingent aftereffects for faces of different races, ages and species." *Cognition*. 106: 1537–1547.

Lombardo, Paul A. (2011). *A Century of Eugenics in America: From the Indiana Experiment to the Human Genome Era*. Bloomington: Indiana University Press.

Loo, Robert. (2003). "A Meta-Analysis of Police Suicide Rates: Findings and Issues." *Suicide and Life-Threatening Behavior*. 33 (3): 313–325.

Lorenz, Konrad. (1941). "Kants Lehre vor Apriorischen im Lichte gegenwärtiger Biologie." (Kant's teachings on the apriori in light of current biology) In Lorenz & F. Wuketits (1984). Die Evolution des Denkens. (The evolution of thinking) R. Piper & Co. Verlag: München & Zurich.

Lorenz, K. (1977). *Die Rückseite des Spiegels*. (The backside of the mirror) Zweiten Auflage. Piper Verlag. München.

Lorenz, K. & F Kreuzer. (1988). Leben ist Lernen: Von Immanuel Kant zu Konrad Lorenz: Ein Gespräch über das Lebenswerk des Nobelpreisträgers. (Life is learning: from Immanuel Kant to Konrad Lorenz: a conversation over the life's work of the Nobel laureate) Piper Verlag. München.

Louis, Errol. (2009). "Obama's critics launch the birth of a nutty nation." *Daily News*. New York. July 22, 2009.

Lowe, E.J. (1996). "Why is there anything at all?" *Aristotelian Society Supplementary*. 70: 111–120.

Luhmann, Niklas. (1970). "Soziologie des politischen systems." (Sociology of the political system). In Luhmann, *Soziologische Aufklärung. Aufsätze zur Theorie sozialer Systeme*. (Sociological Enlightenment. Compositions toward the theory of social systems). (pp. 154–177). Cologne: Westdeutscher Verlag.

Luhmann, Niklas. (1981). *Ausdifferenzierung des Rechtsystems. Beitrage zur Rechtssoziologie und Rechtstheorie*. (Differentiation of the system of law. Contribution to the sociology of law and theory of law). Frankfurt am Main: Suhrcamp Verlag.

Luhmann, Niklas. (1987). *Rechtssoziolgie*. (Sociology of Law) 3. Auflage. Opladen: Westdeutscher Verlag.

Luhmann, Niklas. (2000). *The Reality of the Mass Media*. Trans. Kathleen Cross. Stanford: Stanford University Press.

Luhmann, Niklas. (2004). *Law as a Social System*. Oxford: Oxford University Press.

Luhmann, Niklas, Maturana, Humberto, Namiki, Mikio, Redder, Volker & Varela, Francisco. (2003). *Beobachter: Konvergenz der Erkenntnistheorien*. (Observer: Convergence of Theories of Epistemology) Wilhelm Fink Verlag. Munich.

Lulat, Y.G.-M. (2005). *A History Of African Higher Education From Antiquity To The Present: A Critical Synthesis*. Westport: Greenwood Publishing Group.

Lund, Francie. (2008). *Changing Social Policy: The Child Support Grant in South Africa*. Cape Town: HSRC Press.

Lynch, A. (1996). *Thought Contagion: How Belief Spreads Through Society*. New York: Basic Books.

MacLeod, Calum. (2014). "China targets widespread corruption, but doubts remain." *USA Today*. September 2, 2014.

Macrae, C.N. & G.V. Bodenhausen. (2000). "Social cognition: Thinking categorically about others." *Annual Review of Psychology*. 51: 93–120.

Mahmood, Z. (2009). "Contract Cheating: A New Phenomenon in Cyber-Plagiarism." *Communications of the IBIMA*. 10: 93–97.

Maitzen, Stephen. (2006). "The Impossibility of Local Skepticism." *Philosophia*. 34: 453–464.

Makova, K.D. & W.-H. Li. (2002). "Strong male-driven evolution of DNA sequences in humans and apes." *Nature*, 416, 624–626.

Malhi, Ripan S., Angelica Gonzalez-Oliver, Kari B. Schroeder, Brian M. Kemp, Jonathan A. Greenberg, Solomon Z. Dobrowski, David G. Smith, Andres Resendez, Tatiana Karafet, Michael Hammer, Stephen Zegura & Tatiana Brovko. (2008). "Distribution of Y Chomosomes Among Native North Americans: A Study of Athapaskan Population History." *American Journal of Physical Anthropology*. 137: 412–424.

Malla, A. & J. Hoenig. (1983). "Differences in suicide rates: An examination of underreporting." *Canadian Journal of Psychiatry*. 28: 291–293.

Mann, Michael. (1970). "The social cohesion of liberal democracy." *American Sociological Review*. 35: 423–439.

Mannheim, Karl. (1929/1995) *Ideologie und Utopie*. (Ideology and Utopia). 8. Auflage Frankfurt/Main : Klostermann.

Marlantes, Karl. (2011). "What it is like to go to war." New York: Atlantic Monthly Press.

Martin, Charles H. (1997). "Internationalizing "The American Dilemma": The Civil Rights Congress and the 1951 Genocide Petition to the United Nations." *Journal of American Ethnic History*. 16, 4: 35–61.

Martin, Joyce A., Brady E. Hamilton, Michelle J.K. Osterman, Sally C. Curtin & T.J. Mathews. (2015). "Births: Final Data for 2013." *National Vital Statistics Reports*. 64, 1: 1–68.

Martinez, Theresa A. (1998). "Race and Popular Culture: Teaching African American Leadership Styles through Popular Music." *Teaching Sociology*. 26 (3): 207–214.

Marzuk, P., M. Nock, A. Leon, L. Portera & K. Tardiff. (2002). "Suicide Among New York City Police Officers, 1977–1996." *American Journal of Psychiatry*, 159: 2069–2071

Maslow, A. (1943). "A Theory of Human Motivation." *Psychological Review*, 50, 370–396.

Matthews, R.A.J. (1995). "Tumbling toast, Murphy's Law and the Fundamental Constants." *European Journal of Physics* 16 (4): 172–176.

Maturana, Humberto R. & Francisco J. Varela. (1980). *Autopoiesis and Cognition: The Realization of the Living*. Dordrecht: D. Reidel Publishing Company.

McCarthy, P.D. & D. Walsh. (1975). "Suicide in Dublin: I. the underreporting of suicide and the consequences for national statistics." *British Journal of Psychiatry*. 126: 301–308.

McClelland, Kent A. & Geoffrey P. Alpert. (1985). "Factor Analysis Applied to Magnitude Estimates of Punishment Seriousness: Patterns of Individual Differences." *Journal of Quantitative Criminology*. 1, 3: 307–318.

McKay, Thomas & Michael Nelson. "Propositional Attitude Reports." The Stanford Encyclopedia of Philosophy (Winter 2010 Edition), Edward N. Zalta (ed.), URL = <http://plato.stanford.edu/archives/win2010/entries/prop-attitude-reports/>.

McNeese, Tim. (2007). *Plessy v. Ferguson: separate but equal.* New York: Infobase Publishing.

McTaggart, J.M.E. (1921). *The Nature of Existence.* Cambridge: England. Cambridge University Press.

Meade, C.S., T.S. Kershaw & J.R. Ickovics. (2008). "The intergenerational cycle of teenage motherhood: an ecological approach." *Health Psychology.* 27, 4: 419–429.

Meri, Josef W. (2006). *Medieval Islamic Civilization: An Encyclopedia, Vol. 1, A–K.* London: Routledge.

Mesritz, George D. (1975). "Guilty but Mentally Ill: An Historical and Constituional Analysis." *Journal of Urban Law* 53: 471.

Metz, Helen Chapin. (1987). *Libya: A Country Study.* Washington D.C.: GPO for the Library of Congress.

Metzinger, Thomas. (2003). *Being No One: The Self-Model Theory of Subjectivity.* Cambridge, Massachusetts: MIT Press.

Middleton, John. (2002). *Africa: An Encyclopedia for Students. Leakey – Rwanda. Vol. 3.* Princeton, New Jersey: Charles Scribner's Sons.

Mill, John Stuart. (1843). *A System of Logic, Ratiocinative and Inductive, Being a Connected View of the Principles of Evidence, and the Methods of Scientific Investigation.* London: John W. Parker, West Strand.

Monk, M. (1987). "Epidemiology of suicide." *Epidemiologic Reviews.* 9: 51–69.

Moore, A.M.T., G.C. Hillman, and A.J. Legge. (2000). *Village on the Euphrates: From Foraging to Farming at Abu Hureyra.* New York: Oxford University Press.

Moreira, Maria, Brendan Hughes, Claudia C. Storti & Frank Zobel. (2011). *Drug Policy Profiles: Portugal.* Luxembourg: Publications Office of the European Union.

Moretti, Luca. (2013). "Global scepticism, underdetermination and metaphysical possibility." *Erkenntnis*: 1–23.

Morowitz, Harold J. (2002). *The Emergence of Everything: How the World Became Complex.* Oxford: Oxford University Press.

Morris, Thomas D. (1996). *Southern Slavery and the Law, 1619–1860.* Chapel Hill: University of North Carolina Press.

Mühlen, N. (1964). *Die schwarzen Amerikaner: Anatomie einer Revolution.* (The Black American: Anatomy of a Revolution). Stuttgart, Kohlhammer.

Mumby, Dennis K. (1997). "The Problem of Hegemony: Rereading Gramsci for Organizational Commuication Studies." *Western Journal of Communication.* 61, 4: 343–75.

Mumby, D.K. (1987). "The political function of narrative in organizations." *Communication Monographs.* 54, 113–127.

Mumby, D.K. (1988). *Communication and power in organizations: Discourse, ideology, and domination.* Norwood, NJ: Ablex.

Murphy, G.K. (1979). "The undetermined ruling: a medicolegal dilemma." *Journal of Forensic Sciences.* 24: 483–491.

Muskal, Michael, Timothy M. Phelps & Matthew Teague. (2015). "Alabama same-sex couples get marriage licenses as legal confusion swirls." *The Los Angeles Times*. February 9, 2015.

Natapoff, Alexandra. (2009). *Snitching: Criminal Informants and the Erosion of the American Justice*. New York: New York University Press.

Navarrete, Carlos D. & Melissa M. McDonald. (2014). "Sexual Selection and the Psychology of Intergroup Conflict." In T. Shackelford & R. Hansen. *The Evolution of Violence*. New York: Springer.

Nelson Le Gall, S.A. (1985). "Motive outcome matching and outcome foreseeability—effects on attribution of intentionality and moral judgments." *Developmental Psychology*. 21: 332–337.

Nichols, John S. (1985). "The Media." pp. 183–199 in Thomas S. Walker, ed., *Nicaragua: The First Five Years*. New York: Praeger.

Nie, Norman H. & Kristi Andersen. (1974). "Mass belief systems revisited: political change and attitude structure." *The Journal of Politics*. 36: 540–587.

Nisbett, R.E. & S. Schachter. (1966). "Cognitive manipulation of pain." *Journal of Experimental Social Psychology*. 2: 227–236.

Nordland, Rod. (2012). "When Koran Burnings Incite Riots and a Mass Murder Doesn't." *The New York Times*. A4 March 15, 2012.

Nozick, Robert. (1974). *Anarchy, State and Utopia*. New York: Basic Books.

Nunez, M. & P.L. Harris (1998). "Psychological and deontic concepts: separate domains or intimate connections." *Mind & Languange*. 13: 153–170.

O'Carroll, P.W. (1989). "A consideration of the validity and reliability of suicide mortality data." *Suicide and Life-Threatening Behavior*. 19: 1–16.

Ogungbile, David. (2004). "Puberty Rites." In F. Salamone. *Encyclopedia of Religious Rites, Rituals, and Festivals*. New York: Routledge.

Oliphant, James. (2011). "Obama: Donald Trump's birth certificate talk helps me." *Los Angeles Times*. April 15, 2011.

Oliver, Pamela E. & Gerald Marwell. (1988). "The Paradox of Group Size in Collective Action." *American Sociological Review*. 53: 1–8.

Ordover, Nancy. (2003). *American Eugenics: Race, Queer Anatomy, and the Science of Nationalism*. Minneapolis: University of Minnesota Press.

Ortiz-Ospina, Esteban & Max Roser. (2016). "World Population Growth." Published online at OurWorldInData.org. https://ourworldindata.org/world-population-growth/.

Osburg, John. (2013). *Anxious Wealth: Money and Morality Among China's New Rich*. Stanford: Stanford University Press.

Page, James S. (2004). "Cyber-pseudepigraphy: A New Challenge for Higher Education Policy and Management." *Journal of Higher Education Policy and Management*. 26, 3: 429–433.

Pansters, Wil G. (2012). *Violence, Coercion, and State-Making in Twentieth-Century Mexico: The Other Half of the Centaur*. Stanford: Stanford University Press.

Parra, Porfirio. (1921). *Nuevo Sistema de Lógica Inductiva y Deductiva.* (New system of inductive and deductive logic) Tercera edición. Ciudad de México: Librería de la Vda. De Ch. Bouret.

Paternoster, Raymond. (2010). "How Much Do We Really Know about Criminal Deterrence?" *The Journal of Criminal Law & Criminology.* 100, 3: 765–823.

Patterson, Dennis & Michael S Pardo. (2016). "The promise of neuroscience for law: 'overclaiming' in jurisprudence, morality, and economics." Patterson & Pardo (eds), *Philosophical foundations of law and neuroscience.* pp. 231–247. Oxford: Oxford University Press.

Pavlac, Brian A. (2009). *Witch Hunts in the Western World: Persecution and Punishment from the Inquisition Through the Salem Trials.* Westport: Greenwood Press.

Payne, B.K. (2001). "Prejudice and perception: The role of automatic and controlled processes in misperceiving a weapon." *Journal of Personality and Social Psychology.* 81: 181–192.

Pearn, J., C. Gardner-Thorpe. (2011). "Jules Cotard (1840–1889): his life and the unique syndrome which bears his name." *Neurology.* 58, 9: 1400–1403.

People vs. McQuillan. 392 Michigan 511, 221 N.W.2d 569 (1974).

Pescosolido, B.A. & Mendelsohn, R. (1986). "Social causation or construction of suicide? An investigation into the social organization of official rates." *American Sociological Review.* 51: 80–101.

Peters, William. (1987). *A Class Divided: Then and Now.* New Haven: Yale University Press.

Phillips, David P. (1974). "The Influence of Suggestion on Suicide." *American Sociological Review.* 39: 340–354.

Phillips, D.P. & Ruth, T.E. (1993). "Adequacy of official suicide statistics for scientific research and public policy." *Suicide and Life-Threatening Behavior.* 23: 307–319.

Phillips, David P., Katherine Lesyna & David T. Paight. (1991) "Suicide and the Media." In Ronald W. Maris, et al., eds. *Assessment and Prediction of Suicide.* New York: Guilford.

Philpot, Tasha S. & Ismail K. White. (2010). *African American Political Psychology: Identity, Opinion and Action in the Post-Civil Rights Era.* New York: Palgrave MacMillan.

Piaget, Jean. (1965/1932). *The Moral Judgment of the Child.* New York: Free Press.

Pidd, Helen. (2011). "German defence minister resigns in PhD plagiarism row." *The Guardian*, Tuesday 1 March.

Pierce, John C. (1970). "Party identification and the changing role of ideology in American politics." *Midwest Journal of Political Science.* 14: 25–42.

Pinstrup-Andersen, Per & Sandøe, Peter. (2007). *Ethics, Hunger and Globalization: In Search of Appropriate Policies.* Dordrecht: Springer.

Poli, Roberto. (1998). "Levels." *Axiomathes.* 9: 197–211.

Poli, Roberto. (2001). "The Basic Problems of the Theory of Levels of Reality." *Axiomathes* 12: 261–283.

Poli, Roberto. (2006). "The Theory of Levels of Reality and the Difference Between Simple and Tangled Hierarchies." pp. 715–722. in G. Minati, E. Pessa & M. Abram. *Systemics of Emergence: Research and Development*. New York: Springer.

Popitz, Heinrich. (1992). *Phänomene der Macht*. (Phenomenons of Power). Tübingen: Mohr.

Prätorius, Rainer. (2008). "Entkriminalisierung und alternative Sanktionen." (Decriminalization and alternative sanctions) pp. 325–341 in Hans-Jürgen Lange. *Kriminal-Politik*. Wiesbaden: Verlag für Sozialwissenschaften.

Pratto, Felicia, Jim Sidanius & Shana Levin. (2006). "Social dominace theory and the dynamics of intergroup relations: Taking stock and looking forward." *European Review of Social Psychology*. 17: 271–320.

Pratto, F., Sidanius, J., Stallworth, L.M. & Malle, B.F. (1994). "Social dominance orientation: A personality variable predicting social and political attitudes." *Journal of Personality and Social Psychology*. 67: 741–763.

Pratto, Felicia & Angela Walker. (2004). "The bases of gendered power." In A.E. Beall, A.H. Eagly, & R.J. Sternberg (Eds.), *The psychology of gender*. pp. 242 – 268. New York: Guilford Press.

Prebble, John. (2008). "Justice Hill and the Autopoiesis of Income Tax Law." Victoria University of Wellington Legal Research Paper. No. 32/2011: 1–25.

Premack, D. & G. Woodruff. (1978). "Cognition and Consciousness in Nonhuman Species – Reply." *Behavioral and Brain Sciences*. 1(4): 616–628.

Quine, Willard V.O. (1948). "On What There Is." in Quine *From a Logical Point of View*. Cambridge: MIT Press.

Rabinowitz, Joshua. (1999). "Go with the Flow or Fight the Power? The Interactive Effects of Social Dominance Orientation and Perceived Injustice on Support for the Status Quo." *Political Psychology*. 20, 1: 1–24.

Raz, Joseph. (1980). *The Concept of a Legal System: An Introduction to the Theory of Legal System*. Oxford: Oxford University Press.

Rehmann, Jan. (2007). "Ideology Theory." Trans. by Peter Thomas. *Historical Materialism: Research in critical marxist theory*. 15: 211–239.

Reimann, Mathias. (1996). "The End of Comparative Law as an Autonomous Subject." *Tulane European and Civil Law Forum*. 11: 49–72.

Reimann, Mathias & Reinhard Zimmermann. (2006). *The Oxford Handbook of Comparative Law*. Oxford, England: Oxford University Press.

Relethford, John H. (2012). *Human Population Genetics*. Hoboken: Wiley-Blackwell.

Relf v. Weinberger. (1974). CIV. A. NOS. 73–1557, 74–243.

Rieppel, Olivier. (2006). "On concept formation in systematics." *Cladistics*. 22: 474–492.

Rigoni, D., Satori, G., Kühn, S. & Brass, M. (2011). "Inducing disbelief in free will alters brain correlates of preconscious motor preparation." *Psychological Science*. 22: 613–618.

Rodriguez-Pereyra, Gonzalo. (1997). "There might be nothing: the subtraction argument improved." *Analysis*. 57.3: 159–166.

Rosen, M. (1985). "Breakfast at Spiro's": Dramaturgy and dominance. *Journal of Management*. 11, 2: 31–48.

Rosen, M. (1988). "You asked for it: Christmas at the bosses' expense." *Journal of Management Studies*. 25: 463–480.

Rossiter, Clinton L. (1948). *Constitutional Dictatorship*. Princeton: Princeton University Press.

Roth, Tanya. (2010). "Debt Collectors Use Fake Courtroom on Debtors." *FindLaw: Law and Daily Life*. November 1, Thomson Reuters Business.

Rotton, J. & Cohn, E.G. (2001). "Temperature, routine activities, and domestic violence: A reanalysis." *Violence and Victims*. 16: 203–215.

Rowe, D.C., Vazsonyi, A.T. & Flannery, D.J. (1995). "Sex differences in crime: do means and within-sex variation have similar causes." *Journal of Research in Crime and Delinquency*. 32: 84–100.

Russell, Bertrand. (1948). *Power: A New Social Analysis*. London: George Allen & Unwin.

Salamone, Frank A. (2004). *Encyclopedia of Religious Rites, Rituals, and Festivals*. New York: Routledge.

Salinger, Lawrence M. (2005). *Encyclopedia of White-Collar and Corporate Crime. Vol. 1*. Thousand Oaks: Sage Publications.

Sallach, David L. (1974). "Class domination and ideological hegemony." *The Sociological Quarterly*. 15: 38–50.

Saltzstein, H.D. & T. Kasachkoff. (2004). "Haidt's moral intuitionist theory: A psychological and philosophical critique." *Review of General Psychology*. 8: 273–282.

Sampson, Steven L. (1987). "The Second Economy of the Soviet Union and Eastern Europe." *Annals of the American Academy of Political and Social Science*. 493: 120–136.

Samuels, David. (2004). "The Rap on Rap: The 'Black Music' that Isn't Either." In Murray Forman & Mark A. Neal *That's the Joint!: The Hip-Hop Studies Reader*. New York: Routledge.

Sankoh, F.P., X. Yan & A.M.H. Conteh. (2012). "A Situational Assessment of Socioeconomic Factors Affecting Solid Waste Generation and Composition in Freetown, Sierra Leone." *Journal of Environmental Protection*. 3, 7: 563–568.

Savage, Steve. (2003). "Psychology and law: a behavioural or a social science?" In David Carson and Ray Bull. *Handbook of psychology in legal contexts*. Chichester: Wiley. 645–658.

Schachter, S. (1964). "The interaction of cognitive and physiological detenninants of emotional state." In L Berkowitz (ed). *Advances in Experimental Social Psychology, Vol. 1*. New York: Academic Press. pp. 49–80.

Schnall, Simone, Jonathan Haidt, Gerald L. Clore & Alexander H. Jordan. (2008). "Disgust as Embodied Moral Judgment." *Personality and Social Psychology Bulletin*. 34, 8: 1096–1109.

Schulz, Gerhard. (1982). *Deutschland seit dem Ersten Weltkrieg 1918–1945*. (Germany since the First World War 1918–1945). Vandenhoeck & Ruprecht in Göttingen: Kleine Vandenhoeck-Reihe.

Sherif, M. (1935). "A study of some social factors in perception." *Archives of Psychology*. 27 (Whole No. 187).

Shultz, T.R., Wright, K. & Schleifer, M. (1986). "Assignment of moral responsibility and punishment." *Child Development*. 57: 177–184.

Shapiro, Adam R. (2013). *Trying Biology: The Scopes Trial, Textbooks, and the Antievolution Movement in American Schools*. Chicago: University of Chicago Press.

Shapiro, Fred R. (2000). "The Most-Cited Legal Scholars." *The Journal of Legal Studies*. 29, S1: 409–426.

Shelton, Dinah. (2005). *Encyclopedia of Genocide and Crimes against Humanity*. Farmington Hills, USA: Thomson Gale.

Sidanius, Jim, Levin, Shana & Pratto, Felicia. (1996). "Consensual social dominance orientation and its correlates within the hierarchical structure of American society." *International Journal of Intercultural Relations*. 20: 385 – 408.

Sidanius, J. & Pratto, F. (1993). "The inevitability of oppression and the dynamics of social dominance." In P. Sniderman & P. Tetlock (Eds.). *Prejudice, politics, and the American dilemma* (pp. 173–211). Palo Alto, CA: Stanford University Press.

Sidanius, J. & Pratto, F. (1999). *Social dominance: An intergroup theory of social hierarchy and oppression*. New York: Cambridge University Press.

Sidanius, J. & Pratto, F. (1999b). "'The more of "them" in prison, the better': Institutional terror, social control, and the dynamics of the criminal justice system." In Sidanius & Pratto (Eds.). *Social Dominance*. (pp. 202–224). New York: Oxford University Press.

Sidanius, J., F. Pratto, van Laar, C. & Levin, S. (2004). "Social dominance theory: Its agenda and method." *Political Psychology*. 25, 845–880.

Siegel, M. & Peterson, C.C. (1998). "Preschoolers' understanding of lies and innocent and negligent mistakes." *Developmental Psychology*. 34: 332–341.

Simon, Jose & Lauria, Carlos. (2007). "Mexican President Must Protect Freedom of Expression." *San Francisco Chronicle*. July 23, 2007.

Simon, Thomas W. (2007). *The Laws of Genocide: Prescriptions for a Just World*. Westport: Praeger Security International.

Singer, David. (1961). "The Level-of-Analysis Problem in International Relations World Politics." *The International System: Theoretical Essays*. 14, 1: 77–92.

Skogan, Wesley G. & Kathleen Frydl. (2004). *Fairness and Effectiveness in Policing: The Evidence*. Washington, DC: National Academy Press.

Skogan, Wesley G. & Tracey Meares. (2004). "Lawful policing." *The Annals of the American Academy of Political and Social Science*. 593: 66–83.

Skolnick, J.H. (1966). *Justice without trial: Law enforcement in democratic society*. New York: Wiley.

Sony. (1988). "Fuck Tha Police." In the album, *Straight Outta Compton*. Los Angeles: Sony/ATV Music Publishing LLC.

Soon, Chun Siong, Marcel Brass, Hans-Jochen Heinze & John-Dylan Haynes. 2008. "Unconscious determinants of free decisions in the human brain." *Nature Neuroscience*, 11: 543–545.

Sowell, Thomas. (2004). *Affirmative Action Around the World: An Empirical Study*. New Haven: Yale University Press.

Speidel, Joseph J., Cynthia C. Harper & Wayne C. Shields. (2008). "The potential of long-acting reversible contraception to decrease unintended pregnancy." *Contraception*. 78: 197–200.

Spiegelberg, Herbert. (1982). *The Phenomenological Movement. A historical introduction*. Kluwer Academic Publishing. The Hague.

Spillius, Alex. (2009). "Barack Obama fights presidential eligibility claims." *The Daily Telegraph*. London. March 2, 2009.

Staub, E. (1999). "The roots of evil: Social conditions, culture, personality and basic human needs." *Personality and Social Psychology Review*, 3(3), 179–192.

Stevens, H.B. (1949). *The Recovery of Culture*. New York: Harper and Brothers.

Stewart, Sherrel Wheeler. (2015). "Same-sex marriage begins in parts of Alabama, thwarted in others." Reuters. February 9, 2015 https://www.reuters.com/article/us-usa-gaymarriage-alabama/same-sex-marriage-begins-in-parts-of-alabama-thwarted-in-others-idUSKBN0LD1KX20150209.

Stimson, James A. (1975). "Belief systems: constraint, complexity, and the 1972 election." *American Journal of Political Science*. 19: 393–417.

Straubhaar, J.D., C. Heeter, B.S. Greenberg, L. Ferreira, R.H. Wicks & T.Y. Lau. (1992). "What makes news: Western, socialist, and Third-world newscasts compared in eight countries." In F. Korzenny & S. Ting-Toomey (Eds.). *Mass media effects across cultures*. (pp. 89–109). Newbury Park: Sage.

Streng, Franz. (1989). "Schuld ohne Freiheit?, der funktionale Schuldbegriff auf dem Prüfstand." (Guilt or innocence?, the functional conception of guilt on the stand for investigation) *Zeitschrift für die gesamte Strafrechtswissenschaft*. 101: 273.

Streng, Franz. (2007). "Schuldbegriff und Hirnforschung." (Concept of guilt and brain research) in: Festschrift für Günther Jakobs zum 70. Geburtstag am 26. Juli 2007, hrsg. v. Pawlik.

Stich, S.P. (1978). "Cognition and content in nonhuman species." *Behavioral and Brain Sciences*, 4: 604–605.

Stones, C.R. (2006). "Antigay prejudice among heterosexual males: Right-wing authoritarianism as a stronger predictor than social dominance orientation and heterosexual identity." *Social Behavior and Personality*. 34, 9: 1137–1150.

Sudworth, John. (2014). "The real costs of China's anti-corruption crackdown." *BBC News*. April 3, 2014.

Summers, C.H., G.L. Forster, W.J. Korzan, M.J. Watt, E.T. Larson, Ø. Øverli, E. Höglund, P.J. Ronan, T.R. Summers, K.J. Renner & N. Greenberg. (2005). "Dynamics and mechanics of social rank reversal." *Journal of Comparative Physiology*. 191 (3): 241–252.

Sypnowich, Christine, "Law and Ideology," *The Stanford Encyclopedia of Philosophy* (Fall 2010 Edition), Edward N. Zalta (ed.), URL = <http://plato.stanford.edu/archives/fall2010/entries/law-ideology/>.

Tajfel, H. (1978). *Differentiation between Social Groups: Studies in the Social Psychology of Intergroup Relations*. London: Academic Press.

Tajfel, H. (1978b). "Social categorization, social identity and social comparison." In H. Tajfel (ed.), *Differentiation between Social Groups: Studies in the Social Psychology of Intergroup Relations*. (pp. 61–76). London: Academic Press.

Talwar, V. & Lee, K. (2002). "Development of lying to conceal a transgression: Children's control of expressive behavior during verbal deception." *International Journal of Behavioral Development* 26: 436–444.

Talwar, Victoria & Lee, Kang. (2008). "Social and Cognitive Correlates of Children's Lying Behavior." *Child Development* 79, 4: 866–881.

Talwar, Victoria, Lee, Kang, Bala, Nicholas & Lindsay, R.C.L., (2006). "Adults' judgments of children's coached reports." *Law and human behavior*. 30, 5: 561–570.

Tamdgidi, M. (2002) "Ideology and Utopia in Mannheim: Towards the Sociology of Self-Knowledge." *Journal of Sociology of Self-Knowledge*. 1, 1: 120–139.

Teubner, Gunther. (1993). *Law as an Autopoietic System*. Oxford: Blackwell.

Teubner, Gunther, Richard Nobles & David Schiff. (2003). "The Autonomy of Law: An Introduction to Legal Autopoiesis." in Anne Barron, J. Penner, David Schiff & Richard Nobles. *Introduction to Jurisprudence and Legal Theory: Commentary and Materials*. London: Butterworths.

The Economist. (2016). "Youth unemployment in the Arab world." August 9th. https://www.economist.com/blogs/graphicdetail/2016/08/daily-chart-7.

Thornhill, Chris. (2008). "Towards a historical sociology of constitutional legitimacy." *Theoretical Sociology*. 37: 161–197.

Tomasky, Michael. (2011). "Birthers and the persistence of racial paranoia." *The Guardian*. London. April 27, 2011.

Tribe, L. & P. Gudridge. (2004). "The anti-emergency constitution." *Yale Law Journal*. 113(8): 1801–1870.

Tronchetti, Fabio. (2013). *Fundamentals of Space Law and Policy*. New York: Springer.

Tucker, Aviezer. (2009). *A Companion to the Philosophy of History and Historiography*. Wiley-Blackwell.

Tucker, Judith E. (1996). "Revisiting Reform: Women and the Ottoman Law of Family Rights, 1917." *The Arab Studies Journal*. 4, 3: 4–17.

Tyler, Tom, Robert Boeckmann, Heather Smith & Yuen Huo. (1997). *Social Justice in a Diverse Society*. Oxford, England: Westview Press.

Tyler, Tom. (2006a). "Psychological Perspectives on Legitimacy and Legitimation." *Annual Review of Psychology*. 57: 375–400.

Tyler, T.R. (2006b). *Why people obey the law: Procedural justice, legitimacy, and compliance*. Princeton: Princeton University Press.

Tyler, T.R. (2007). *Psychology and the Design of Legal Institutions*. Nijmegen, The Netherlands: Wolf.

Tyler, T.R. (2008). *Psychology and institutional design. Review of Law and Economics*. 4: Article 6.

Tyler, T.R. (2010). "Legitimacy in corrections: Policy implications." *Criminology and Public Policy*. 9, 1: 127–134.

Tyler, T.R. & E.A. Lind. (1992). "A relational model of authority in groups." *Advances in Experimental Social Psychology*. 25: 115–191.

Umseen, Bert & Anne M. Piehl. (2008). *Prison State: The Challenge of Mass Incarceration*. Cambridge: Cambridge University Press.

United Nations Development Programme, United Nations Environment Programme, World Bank, World Resources Institute. (2000). "A guide to world resources 2000–2001, People and ecosystems: the fraying web of life." Washington, D.C.: World Resources Institute.

United Nations Population Division. (2009). "World Population Prospects, the 2008 Revision." New York: United Nations.

Uvin, Peter. (1998). *Aiding Violence: The Development Enterprise in Rwanda*. West Hartford, USA: Kumarian Press.

Van der Toorn, Jojanneke, Tyler, Tom & Jost, John. (2011). "More than fair: Outcome dependence, system justification, and the perceived legitimacy of authority figures." *Journal of Experimental Social Psychology*. 47: 127–138.

Van der Toorn, J., Feinberg, M., Jost, J., Kay A., Tyler, T., Willer, R. & Wilmuth, C. (2014). "A sense of powerlessness fosters system justification: On the legitimation of authority, hierarchy, and government." *Political Psychology*.

Van Inwagen, P. (1996). "Why is there anything at all?" *Aristotelian Society Supplementary*. 70: 95–110.

Van Roermund, B. 1997. *Law, narrative and reality: An essay in intercepting politics*. Dordrecht: Kluwer Academic Publishers.

Van Roojen, Mark. (2016). "Moral Cognitivism vs. Non-Cognitivism." *The Stanford Encyclopedia of Philosophy*. Edward N. Zalta (ed.), URL = <https://plato.stanford.edu/archives/win2016/entries/moral-cognitivism/>.

Varela, Francisco J., Humberto R. Maturana & R. Uribe. (1974). "Autopoiesis: the organization of living systems, its characterization and a model." *Biosystems*. 5: 187–196.

Verenich, Vadim. (2003). "Legal System: Can one speak about secondary modeling system in law?" *Revue Internationale de Sémiotique Juridique*. 17: 77–100.

Villani, Susan & Nandita Joshi. (2003). "Television and Movies, Rock Music and Music Videos, and Computer and Video Games: Understanding and Preventing Learned Violence in the Information Age." In *Neurobiology of Aggression: Understanding and Preventing Violence*. Edited by Mark Mattson. Totowa, New Jersey: Humana Press.

Violanti, John M. (2004). "Letters to the Editor: Suicide among police officers." *Journal of American Psychiatry*. 161 (4): 766.

Violanti, John M., Michael E. Andrew, Anna Mnatsakanova, Tara A. Hartley, Desta Fekedulegn & Cecil M. Burchfiel. (2015). "Correlates of hopelessness in high suicide risk police occupation." *Police Practice and Research*. 17 (5): 408–419.

Violanti, J.M., L.C. Charles, T.A. Hartley, A. Mnatsakanova, M.E. Andrew, D. Fekedulegn, B. Vila & C.M. Burchfiel. (2008). "Shift-work and Suicide Ideation among Police Officers." *American Journal of Industrial Medicine*. 51: 758–768.

Violanti, J.M., J.E. Vena, J.R. Marshall & S. Petralia. (1996). "A comparative evaluation of police suicide rate validity." *Suicide and Life-Threatening Behavior*. 26: 79–85.

Vitousek, P.M., H.A. Mooney, J. Lubchenco & J.M. Melillo. (1997). "Human domination of earth's ecosystems." *Science*. 277: 494–499.

Vogel, Gretchen. (2012). "German Research Minister Faces Plagiarism Allegations." *ScienceInsider*. May, 2. http://news.sciencemag.org/2012/05/german-research-minister-faces-plagiarism-allegations.

Walder, Andrew, Bobai Li & Donald Treiman. (2000). "Politics and Life Chances in a State Socialist Regime." *American Sociological Review*. 65, 2: 191–209.

Waller, J. (2002). *Genocide and mass killing*. New York: Oxford University Press.

Walmsley, Roy. (2016). "World Prison Population List." 11th edition. World Prison Brief Online Data Base: Core Publications. http://www.prisonstudies.org/research-publications?shs_term_node_tid_depth=27

Walzer, Michael. (2006). *Just and Unjust Wars: A Moral Argument with Historical Illustrations*. New York: Basic Books.

Ward, I. (1998). *An Introduction to Critical Legal Theory*. Cavendish Publishing: London.

Wardell, Mark L. & Ellsworth R. Fuhrman. (1981). "Controversy and Ideological Hegemony in Sociological Theory." *The Sociological Quarterly*. 22, 4: 479–493.

Weber, Max. (1991/1904). *Schriften zur Wissenschaftslehre*. (Writings for the scientific teachings) Stuttgart: Reclam.

Webster, M.A., D. Kaping, Y. Mizokami & P. Duhamel. (2004). "Adaptation to natural face categories." *Nature*. 428: 557–561.

Wegner, D.M. & J.A. Bargh. (1998). "Control and automaticity in social life." In D. Gilbert, S. Fiske, & G. Lindzey (Eds.). *Handbook of social psychology*. (4th ed., pp. 446–496). Boston: McGraw-Hill.

Wegner, D.M. & T.P. Wheatley. (1999). "Why it feels as if we're doing things: Sources of the experience of will." *American Psychologist*. 54: 480–492.

Weitzer, R. (1996). "Racial discrimination in the criminal justice system: findings and problems in the literature." *Journal of Criminal Justice*. 24: 309–322.

Wellman, H.M., C. Larkey, S.C. Somerville. (1979). "Early development of moral criteria." *Child Development*. 50: 869–873.

Wendt, Simon. (2006). "The Roots of Black Power? Armed Resistance and the Radicalization of the Civil Rights Movement." in *The Black Power Movement: Rethinking the Civil Rights- Black Power Era*. Editor Penial E. Joseph. New York: Routledge.

Wilhite, D.A. & M.H. Glantz. (1985). "Understanding the drought phenomenon: The role of definitions." *Water International*. 10, 111–112.

Wilkinson, Dana. (2010). "Debt Collector Scam Reaches New Low: The Unicredit Bogus "Courtroom" Scam." *Bankruptcy Law Network*. November 2.

Williamson, Timothy. (2016). "Modal Science." *Canadian Journal of Philosophy*. 46, supplementary issue, and in MarkMcCullagh and Juhani Yli-Vakkuri (eds.). *Williamson on Modality*. London: Routledge.

Willock, Ian D. (1966). *The Origins and Development of the Jury in Scotland*. Edinburgh: Publications of the Stair Society.

Wimmer, H. & Perner, J. (1983). "Beliefs about beliefs: Representation and constraining function of wrong beliefs in young children's understanding of deception." *Cognition*. 13: 103–128.

Wordes, M. & T.S. Bynum. (1995). "Policing juveniles: Is there bias against youths of color." In: K.K. Leonard, C.E. Pope, W.H. Feyerherm (Eds.). *Minorities in Juvenile Justice*. Thousand Oaks: Sage Publication (pp. 47–65).

Yan, Kun. (2016). *Poverty Alleviation in China: A Theoretical and Empirical Study*. Heidelberg: Springer.

York, R., Rosa, E.A. & Dietz, T. (2003). "Footprints on the earth: the environmental consequences of modernity." *American Sociological Review*. 68: 279–300.

Young, A.W. & Leafhead, K.M. (1996). "Betwixt Life and Death: Case Studies of the Cotard Delusion." in *Method in Madness: Case studies in Cognitive Neuropsychiatry*. eds. P.W. Halligan and J.C. Marshall. Hove, Sussex: Psychology Press.

Young, Liane & Saxe, Rebecca. (2008). "The neural basis of belief encoding and integration in moral judgment." *Neuroimage*. 40, 4: 1912–1920.

Young, Liane & Saxe, Rebecca. (2009). "An fMRI Investigation of Spontaneous Mental State Inference for Moral Judgment." *Journal of Cognitive Neuroscience*. 21: 1396–1405.

Young, Liane, Scholz, Jonathan & Saxe, Rebecca. (2011). "Neural evidence for "intuitive prosecution": The use of mental state information for negative moral verdicts." *Social Neuroscience*. 6, 3: 302–315.

Yuill, N. (1984). "Young children's coordination of motive and outcome in judgements of satisfaction and morality." *British Journal of Developmental Psychology*. 2: 73–81.

Yuill, N. & Perner, J. (1988). "Intentionality and knowledge in children's judgments of actors responsibility and recipients emotional reaction." *Developmental Psychology*. 24: 358–365.

Yurdusev, Nuri. (1993). "Level of Analysis and Unit of Analysis: A Case for Distinction." *Millennium: Journal of International Studies*. 22, 1: 77–88.

Zabus, Chantel. (2008). *Fearful Symmetries: Essays and Testimonies Around Exicision and Circumcision*. Amsterdam: Rodopi.

Zadeh, Lotfi. (1978). "Fuzzy Sets as the Basis for a Theory of Possibility." *Fuzzy Sets and Systems* 1:3–28, 1978. (Reprinted in Fuzzy Sets and Systems 100 (Supplement): 9–34, 1999.)

Zedner, L. (2009). *Security*. London: Routledge.

Zeisel, H. (1971). "And then there were none: The diminunition of the Federal jury." *University of Chicago Law Review*. 38: 710–724.

Zelazo, P.D., Helwig, C.C. & Lau, A. (1996). "Intention, act, and outcome in behavioral prediction and moral judgment." *Child Development*. 67: 2478–2492.

Zillmann, Dolf. (1988). "Cognition-Excitation Interdependencies in Aggressive Behavior." *Aggressive Behavior*. 14, 1: 51–64.

Zimmermann, Reinhard. (2005). *The New German Law of Obligations: Historical and Comparative Perspectives*. Oxford, England: Oxford University Press.

Ziv, Margalit & Frye, Douglas. (2003). "The Relation between Desire and False Belief in Children's Theory of Mind: No Satisfaction?" *Developmental Psychology*, 39, 5: 859–876.

Zulasika, Joseba. (2009). *Terrorism: The Self-Fulfilling Prophecy*. Chicago: University of Chicago Press.

Index

www.ingramcontent.com/pod-product-compliance
Lightning Source LLC
LaVergne TN
LVHW011101300926
849160LV00008B/244